BANNED
PLAYS

BANNED PLAYS

CENSORSHIP HISTORIES OF
125 Stage Dramas

DAWN B. SOVA

Checkmark Books®
An imprint of Facts On File, Inc.

Banned Plays

Checkmark Books
An imprint of Facts On File, Inc.
132 West 31st Street
New York NY 10001

Library of Congress Cataloging-in-Publication Data
Sova, Dawn B.
Banned Plays : censorship histories of 125 stage dramas / Dawn B. Sova
p.cm.
Includes bibliographical references and index.
ISBN 0-8160-4018-4 (HC : alk. paper)—ISBN 0-8160-5070-8 (pbk. : alk. paper)
1. Theater—Censorship—History. 2. Drama—Censorship—History.   I. Title.

PN2042.S68 2003
792′.09—dc22   2003063113

Checkmark Books are available at special discounts when purchased in bulk quantities for businesses, associations, institutions, or sales promotions. Please call our Special Sales Department in New York at (212) 967-8800 or (800) 322-8755.

You can find Facts On File on the World Wide Web at http://www.factsonfile.com

Text design by Cathy Rincon
Cover design by Catherine Lau Hunt

Printed in the United States of America

MP Hermitage 10 9 8 7 6 5 4 3 2 1

This book is printed on acid-free paper.

This Book Is Dedicated to the Memory of a Man Who Always Refused to Allow Himself to Be Censored, My Father, Emil J. Sova

CONTENTS

Acknowledgments
ix

Introduction
xi

List of Entries
xv

BANNED PLAYS
1

Bibliography
329

Appendixes
I. Playwrights' Profiles
349

II. Reasons for Banning
375

III. 100 Additional Challenged,
Censored, or Banned Plays
378

Index
381

ACKNOWLEDGMENTS

I am profoundly grateful to the many people who made certain that this project would be completed and who urged me to continue when many obstacles appeared to stand in the way. So many cannot be named, but to them, as well as to the people listed below, I can only say "Thank you."

My sincere appreciation belongs to Bert Holtje, who began the project with me, and for over a decade wisely guided my writing projects as literary agent and friend. A grateful thank you to Gene Brissie, who became my literary agent mid-project and who had the difficult role of supporting and encouraging the completion of this work.

I appreciate the work of editors Anne Savarese, who initiated the project with me, and Jeff Soloway, who assumed guardianship of the book midstream and kept my writing going against all odds with his helpful and insightful suggestions and encouragement.

To I. Macarthur Nickles, director of the Garfield (New Jersey) Public Library, I can only say thank you once again for your help and that of your staff, including but not limited to Kathleen Zalenski, Patricia Gelinski, Karen Calendriello, and Linda Jackson, who found the obscure sources that the book required. The residents of my hometown, Garfield, New Jersey, are fortunate to have you.

Most significantly, I have to thank my son, Robert Gregor, and my mother, Violet Sova, for their patience with me as I often lost my way with the research and my patience with the details of daily life. We grieved together the death of my father, Emil J. Sova, which occurred soon after I began work on this book and we became stronger together. And, to my father, I dedicate the completion of this book.

In selecting entries for this volume, the author sought to represent within the reasonable space of a single book the many centuries and diverse countries in which censorship of plays has occurred. Many more plays could have been selected, and much more could have been written, because the number of censorship incidents is vast and the number of plays suppressed significant. Instead, those included are representative of the works and the incidents throughout 2,500 years of theater.

To aid both the scholarly researcher and the casual browser, entries are arranged alphabetically by title and include production dates, characters, plot summary, and censorship history. Each entry also includes a list of further readings for in-depth examination of the attempts to ban or censor the play. Works whose titles appear in small capital letters have their own entries in the volume. Appendixes contain brief biographies of the playwrights, categorizations of the profiled plays based on the reasons for which they were suppressed, and a list of 100 additional plays that have also been banned or censored.

INTRODUCTION

Drama is a powerful means of transmitting ideas, and one that has been censored from nearly the first organized performances in the Greek Golden Age around 500 B.C.E. Throughout history, changing political, social, and religious power structures have used drama as a propaganda tool, and these structures have also demanded the elimination or modification of plays that do not agree with their philosophies. A vast number of plays for which scripts are no longer available appear as entries in the records of official censors or receive brief mention in the accounts of long-dead playwrights or critics, thus suggesting that many works written for the stage were suppressed, then forgotten, once they were no longer topical or threatening. No one work can adequately identify the thousands that have been lost, but examination of the 125 plays in this volume, plays that have appeared from 411 B.C.E. to the present, provides a solid understanding of the many reasons why a wide selection of plays from diverse time periods have been challenged, censored, and banned.

The suppression of drama remains a disturbing reality in the 21st century, and one that is not dealt with often enough because many people mistakenly view stage censorship as an archaism belonging only to the past. Official government censors no longer exist in England, France, and the United States to determine which plays will be licensed for public performance, but organized groups remain effective in pressuring theaters and theater groups, both amateur and professional, to cancel planned performances of plays. Such power may be more dangerous than that wielded by governments in the past, because challenges in recent years have been based on the interests of one group having a specialized agenda against the many.

In 1999, performances of *WEST SIDE STORY* were canceled at a high school because Hispanic students protested that the play provides negative portrayals of Puerto Rican youth in the 1950s. In 2002, the Cincinnati Playhouse in the Park canceled scheduled performances of playwright Glyn O'Malley's work *Paradise*, an examination of the impact of war on Israeli and Palestinian youth, because Cincinnati Muslims protested that the play depicts a character based on Ayat al-Akhras, an 18-year-old girl who blew herself up in Jerusalem in March 2002, murdering three people. Censorship continues to occur on local and regional levels, and many incidents are not reported.

What constitutes grounds for a legitimate challenge to a play or even the reasons for such challenges are often difficult to define. Such plays as KISMET (1910), VENETIAN NIGHT (1912), and MAYA (1924), in which sexual activity does not occur on stage but remains in the minds of the audience, are condemned for the same reason—that of portraying "immoral conduct"—as OH! CALCUTTA! (1968), HAIR (1967), and ANGELS IN AMERICA (1994) in which nudity occurs and sexual activity is simulated.

Charges of "objectionable language and behavior" that have resulted in the censorship of plays on social grounds range from the uses of what is termed by censors obscene and blasphemous language, as in HAMLET (1601) and VICTOR, OR THE CHILDREN TAKE OVER (1964), to the discussion of taboo topics such as homosexuality, adultery, and abortion, as in THE BOYS IN THE BAND (1970), MARGARET FLEMING (1890), and STRANGE INTERLUDE (1928), or violence, as in SAVED (1963) and CAPEMAN (1998). A play by Oscar Wilde, THE IMPORTANCE OF BEING EARNEST (1895), was banned more because of the playwright's notoriety than objectionable content.

Challenges for religious reasons may be the result of the negative portrayal of one character, as in THE MERCHANT OF VENICE (1600), WITHIN THE GATES (1934), and THE DEPUTY (1963), or the presentation of the beliefs and activities of a specific religion in an unflattering light, as in SISTER MARY IGNATIUS EXPLAINS IT ALL FOR YOU (1979).

Political reasons for the censorship, suppression, and banning of plays have been equally diverse. In 1789, the English censor refused to grant a license for performance to ISLAND OF ST. MARGUERITE until the playwright removed lines that might be offensive to France. In 1907, after THE MIKADO had been licensed for performance for more than 20 years, the English censor revoked the license on grounds that the play contained "unsuspected dangers" and might offend England's Japanese allies. Plays have also been banned because they contain unfavorable portrayals of prominent individuals or politicians, as in TRIP TO CALAIS (1775) and THE PRESIDENT IS DEAD (1969), as well as for their antiwar views or criticisms of the government, as in WHAT PRICE GLORY? (1924) and THE THREE-PENNY OPERA (1969).

As with censorship in all areas—books, film, art, and other media—guidelines for objections have not always been clear, nor have the objections to one work remained consistent over time. For centuries, plays, and the reasons that groups seek to challenge, suppress, or ban them, have served as important indicators of the concerns, desires, passions, and obsessions of a society. What appears on stage and what raises objections often have less to do with merit than with present taste, as changes in political regimes, modified social values, different fashions in religious worship, and greater or lesser sexual permissiveness may condemn a play and playwright that were formerly lauded—or elevate those formerly viewed as politically, religiously, socially, or morally offensive.

LYSISTRATA provides an excellent example of such changing viewpoints over two and a half millennia. The play has been banned in some instances for being politically inflammatory and at other times for being obscene and sexually suggestive. In 411 B.C.E., the Greek government condemned the "political impropriety" of *Lysistrata;* the Nazis banned the play in 1942 during their occupation of Greece in fear that performances would encourage Greek nationalism; and in 1967, the Greek military regime banned the play along with a number of classic plays that contained antiwar themes or themes that emphasized freedom and independence. Although the sexual references and the situation of women refusing to engage in sexual activity until their men stop fighting wars did not bother the Greeks and Nazis, they were disturbing to English censors in 1910, as well as to reviewers in 1934, who agreed that "*Lysistrata* is far too gross for the English stage." In the United States in 1954, U.S. Post Office officials seized a rare illustrated copy of the book and charged that it was "obscene" material. In 1989, school board members in Lake City, Florida, gave in to demands by a religious group that charged *Lysistrata* promoted "women's lib" and pornography and removed the book from the curriculum, claiming the work was not appropriate for reading by high school students due to its "vulgarity and sexual explicitness."

Attempts continue by groups with specialized agendas to dictate what the majority will view, read, or enjoy, despite the repeal of censorship laws, such as the Theatres Act of 1737 in England and the Wales Padlock Law of 1927 in the United States. Force of opinion has replaced legal force.

LIST OF ENTRIES

Angels in America
Athalie
The Author
Le Barbier de Seville
The Beard
The Bedbug
The Beggar's Opera
The Best Little Whorehouse in
    Texas
The Boys in the Band
The Breaking Point
The Capeman
The Captive
Cat on a Hot Tin Roof
The Cenci
The Children's Hour
The Connection
Corpus Christi
The Council of Love
The Cradle Will Rock
The Crucible
Damaged Goods
La Dame Aux Camélias
The Deputy
Desire under the Elms
Early Morning
The Easiest Way
Edward and Eleanora
The Entertainer
Ethiopia
The First Step

A Game at Chesse
Ghosts
God of Vengeance
Gustavus Vasa
Hair
Hamlet
Hannele
The Happy Land
Henry IV, Part 2
Hernani
The Importance of Being Earnest
The Island of St. Marguerite
Jack Sheppard
Jack Straw
Jesus Christ Superstar
Killing No Murder
King Lear
Kismet
The Knack
Lips Together, Teeth Apart
Long Day's Journey into Night
Lysistrata
The Maid's Tragedy
The Man of the World
Marat/Sade
Margaret Fleming
The Marriage of Figaro
Marion de Lorme
The Martyrdom of Saint Sebastian
Mary Stuart
Maya

M. Butterfly
The Merchant of Venice
The Mikado
The Misanthrope
Miss Saigon
Monna Vanna
Mrs. Warren's Profession
The Normal Heart
Oedipus Rex
Oh! Calcutta!
One-Third of a Nation
The Parson's Wedding
Pasquin, a Dramatic Satire
A Patriot for Me
The Playboy of the Western World
The Pleasure Man
Polly
The President Is Dead
Press Cuttings
A Raisin in the Sun
The Respectful Prostitute
Revelry
The Revolution of Paris
Richard the Second
Roar, China!
Le Roi S'Amuse
La Ronde
Salomé
Sapho
Saved
The Second Maiden's Tragedy
Sex
The Shanghai Gesture

The Shewing Up of Blanco Posnet
Simon Called Peter
Sir Thomas More
Sister Mary Ignatius Explains It
    All for You
Sodom
Strange Interlude
The Tamer Tamed
Tartuffe
Tea and Sympathy
Thomas of Woodstock
The Three-Penny Opera
Tobacco Road
The Toilet
The Tragedy of King Richard the
    Second
Trio
Triple-A Plowed Under
Trip to Calais
The Vagina Monologues
Vectia
A Venetian Night
Victor, Or The Children Take Over
Victoria Regina
A View from the Bridge
Waiting for Lefty
Waste
The Weavers
West Side Story
What Price Glory?
Who's Afraid of Virginia Woolf?
Within the Gates
The Zoo Story

BANNED PLAYS

ANGELS IN AMERICA: MILLENNIUM APPROACHES

Author: Tony Kushner
Original date and place of production: May 1991, Eureka Theatre, San Francisco, California
Characters: The Angel, Belize, Roy M. Cohn, Louis Ironson, Hannah Porter Pitt, Harper Amity Pitt, Joseph Porter Pitt, Ethel Rosenberg, Prior Walter
Filmed versions: Made for television: *Angels in America* (2003)

SUMMARY

The first part of a two-part, seven-hour epic subtitled "Gay Fantasia on American Themes," *Angels in America: Millennium Approaches* is a highly complex play in which the locale moves from Salt Lake City, to Washington, D.C., to the Arctic Circle and Europe while actors play multiple roles and historical events overlap with events in the lives of the characters. Dead characters reappear, and comic and tragic events appear to be, at times, indistinguishable. The three acts are named: "Act I—Bad News October–November 1985"; "Act II—In Vitro December 1985–January 1986"; "Act III—Not-Yet-Conscious. Forward Dawning January 1986." The play, set in the conservative political climate of 1985, when Ronald Reagan was president of the United States, takes a satiric look at a range of social issues, such as the AIDS crisis, drug addiction, American politics, and racial, sexual, and religious bigotry.

Angels in America focuses on the lives of four homosexual men as a vehicle for examining the moral plight of society in the United States. Roy M. Cohn is a historical figure who played a major role in the "red scare" hearings conducted by Senator Joseph McCarthy in the 1950s, a witch hunt that targeted not only people believed to be members of the Communist Party but also people suspected of being homosexual. The ruthless and extremely powerful Cohn was also the prosecutor in the trial of Julius and Ethel Rosenberg; the couple was found guilty of treason, sentenced to death, and executed. The verdict in the case remains controversial. Cohn died of AIDS in 1986, at the age of 59.

The Roy Cohn of the play is an arbitrary and powerful man who uses the law as a weapon to tame what he views to be a dangerously chaotic world. Portrayed as fiercely hypocritical, Cohn is ruthless in prosecuting other homosexuals and excuses his actions as serving the public good, even as he acts on his own homosexual desires. He contends at one point in the play that he is not homosexual, rather "a heterosexual man . . . who fucks around with guys." Even as he is dying of AIDS, he insists that his affliction is liver cancer.

Joseph Porter Pitt, a Mormon and a young conservative lawyer who is a protégé of Cohn, has married a woman named Harper in an attempt to deny his homosexuality, which he believes does not fit the image of a Mormon or a political conservative. The loveless marriage between Joe and Harper has made them both miserable, and Harper's addiction to Valium leaves her much of the time in a hallucinatory state that the playwright makes both comic and sad. Joe struggles to maintain his heterosexual facade, but needs to be honest with himself and the world, so he leaves his wife and becomes the lover of Louis Ironson. Louis also has just left a relationship, exiting in a cowardly fashion when he could no longer face the AIDS-related illnesses of his lover Prior Walter, a drag queen with formidable ancestry. Both Joe and Louis exhibit feelings of self-hatred, and both are unable to forgive themselves for their dishonest actions toward their former lovers.

The play opens with the funeral of Louis's grandmother Sarah, followed by a scene in Roy Cohn's office. The audience watches Cohn bark orders and try to convince Joe Pitt to take a job in Washington, but Joe's sense of ethics and his worries about Harper make him refuse the offer. In scenes that follow, Prior reveals that the lesions on his body are signs of AIDS and that he is seriously ill, a conclusion that Louis finds hard to accept. Cohn also receives a diagnosis of AIDS from his doctor, but refuses to accept it, telling the doctor: "AIDS is what homosexuals have. I have liver cancer." When Prior is hospitalized, he has visions of visitations by two ancestors who died from plague, and they foreshadow the great role that Prior will have at the end of the play. Although Cohn tries to hide his illness, its severity is clear. When Joe visits Cohn at home to refuse the job offer, Cohn is wearing a bathrobe. He attempts several times to embrace Joe, who leaves just as Cohn doubles over in pain. Calls for the nurse are answered by the resurrected Ethel Rosenberg, who taunts Cohn, motivating him to tell her "I have forced my way into history. I ain't never gonna die." Moments later, the ambulance arrives to take him to die in the hospital.

While Prior sits alone and near death, Louis meets Joe by chance in the park. The two men kiss and plan to spend the night together. In the final scene, Prior is alone in his apartment, listening in fear to the sounds of something crashing down through the ceiling in a blaze of light and "triumphal music." As the building shudders and plaster and wire fall from the ceiling onto the floor around Prior's bed, the playwright's stage directions state, "in a shower of unearthly light, spreading great opalescent gray-silver wings, the Angel" greets him as "Prophet" and tells him that "the Great Work begins."

CENSORSHIP HISTORY

Angels in America: Millennium Approaches won the Pulitzer Prize for Drama for 1992–93, the New York Drama Critics Circle "Best Play, Regardless of Category" Award for 1992–93, and the Tony Award for Best Play in 1993, as well as the Bay Area Theater Critics Awards for Best Original Script and Best Direction in San Francisco area theater in 1992. These and other regional accolades were not sufficient to prevent various communities from attempts to stop the staging of the play by high school, college, and community theater groups. Although most efforts have resulted in quiet withdrawals of the play, at least one has erupted into violence and others have pitted threats of funding loss against principles.

In 1996 the Mecklenburg County (North Carolina) Commission tried to censor the Charlotte Repertory Theater production of *Angels in America* after members of the community expressed concern that the play dealt with homosexuality and undermined family values. Government officials in Mecklenburg County sought to censor the play, claiming that it violated the state's indecent exposure law because it contains a brief scene in which a nurse examines a naked man. To save the production, the theater director obtained a court order that allowed staging of the play and blocked government officials from making cuts in the content. Although the production took place, the Mecklenburg County Commission retaliated in April 1997 by cutting $2.5 million in funding to the Arts and Science Council, which annually financed $11 million in projects. The commission also took away the council's powers to make project funding decisions based on artistic merit and granted itself the power to provide money only to those performing arts projects that promote the "traditional American family value system." In the resolution, the commission vowed to deny money to any projects that "promote, advocate or endorse behaviors, life styles or values that seek to undermine and deviate from the value and societal role of the traditional American family."

In February 1999, Orthodox Christian protesters in Bucharest, Romania, temporarily blocked the staging of *Angels in America* by ripping down posters and issuing death threats to the owners and the staff of the Nottara Theater. When the theater attempted to stage the play a second time, Bucharest city officials posted uniformed police officers outside the theater and placed plainclothes officers inside with the aim of subduing any protesters who might try to disrupt the performance. The Young Orthodox Community, the principal group that opposed the play and that had long been among the leading opponents of gay civil rights reform in Romania, claimed its violent efforts were for the good of the country, and issued the following statement: "It's a shame and a lack of good sense to stage such evil plays, which fail to distinguish between right and wrong."

Students at Kilgore College, a tax-supported college in Kilgore, Texas, found themselves in the middle of battle over morality, censorship, and academic freedom in October 1999, when they sought to stage a production of *Angels in America*. Residents of Gregg County and local politicians protested the presentation of a production about gay characters and created an outcry against what they called a "vulgar play." Preachers at the mostly Baptist churches in the county condemned the play from their pulpits, and citizens circulated petitions to stop the production. Glenn D. Phillips, an attorney who lived in Kilgore, tried to limit the opening night audience by purchasing 150 of the 263 tickets. The college was undeterred and the box office staff, knowing the attorney's plan, resold the seats. After rumors circulated among townspeople that the male actors would be completely nude and would have sex on stage, college trustees approached college president William M. Holda and asked him to stop the production. Holda allowed the production to continue. Raymond Caldwell, the director, deleted some of the language considered offensive and cut a few of the more graphic sexual scenes from the play. When the playwright, Tony Kushner, heard of the controversy, he wrote a letter of encouragement to Holda and to the director, cast, and crew of the production in which he congratulated them for taking a "principled stand" and reminded them of the violence with which the production in Bucharest was met.

On opening night, protesters from Heritage Baptist Church stood in the street outside the Van Cliburn Auditorium, in which the play was staged, and heckled theatergoers while one of the protesters marched up and down the sidewalk waving an American flag. Some of the protesters carried signs that read "God Hates Fags" and contained a graphic illustration of two men having sex. Rocky Otwell, son of the minister of Heritage Baptist Church, told a reporter for *The Chronicle of Higher Education*, "This play is a kind of in-your-face to East Texas. This is the Bible Belt, and we're not going to put up with this." College officials moved forward with the production despite warnings from city and county politicians that doing so would mean a loss of $65,000 in funding to the college. In addition, after the performances, the McMillan Foundation, a local organization that funds educational and religious activities, told college officials that it would reassess its commitment of $600,000 to the college. Although the foundation did not, in the end, withdraw funding, the Gregg County commissioners carried out their threat and voted on October 28, 1999, two weeks after performances of *Angels in America*, to rescind the matching funds grant of $50,000. The protests gave the play free publicity and made it the most successful production that the theater had staged. Every performance was sold out. The success of the production mitigated the loss of the county funding.

In November 2000, teachers at the Paxon School for Advanced Studies in Jacksonville, Florida, were told by the school principal Jim Williams to cut the pages containing *Angels in America* from the *Bedford Introduction to Literature*, a college-level text that the private preparatory school had used for four years without incident. The play was not on any reading list, nor did teachers assign it, and the principal contended that he was not even aware that the textbook contained *Angels in America* until the mother of a ninth-grade student called him to raise objections about the play. Although the principal claimed to be "very sensitive to issues of censorship," he also justified the mutilation of the books because "some sections [of the play] are not appropriate for 14-year-olds." Williams specifically objected to the characters' use of profanity and the presence of the homosexual characters, of which a few have AIDS; "At some point adults have to draw the line," he said. His action had precedent: In 1997 the Duval County School Board had banned the play from all public classrooms after learning that it was being taught in the Douglas Anderson School of the Arts. Outraged parents had complained, and a committee composed of teachers, parents, and librarians concluded that the play was "not appropriate for the county's high school students" and recommended that the county school board ban the work from the classrooms. The play was removed from the required lists in the district.

FURTHER READING

American Civil Liberties Union. "ACLU Condemns North Carolina County for Censoring Arts Council Over Pulitzer Prize–Winning Play." ACLU Press Release, April 3, 1997.

Guernsey, Otis L., Jr., and Jeffrey Sweet, eds. *The Best Plays of 1992–1993*. New York: Limelight Editions, 1993.

———. *The Applause/Best Plays Theater Yearbook of 1991–1992*. New York: Applause, 1992.

Harris, Eugenia. "Theater Festival Loses County Funds after Texas College Stages Controversial Play." The Freedom Forum. November 12, 1999. Available online. URL: http://www.freedomforum.org.

Kushner, Tony. *Angels in America: Millenium Approaches*. New York: Theatre Communications Corporation, 1993.

———. "Tony Kushner's Letter about *Angels in America*." Correspondence between Tony Kushner and Dr. William Holda, Professor Raymond Caldwell and the cast and crew of *Angels in America*, October 14, 1999. Available online. URL: http://www.freedomforum.org. Posted November 12, 1999.

Mangan, Katherine S. "College Draws Hellfire for Staging Disputed Play." *The Chronicle of Higher Education* (October 29, 1999): A71–A72.

"Staging of Kushner Play in Romania Brings Protest." Associated Press, February 17, 1999.

Taylor, Phillip. "Student Assails School for Slicing Pulitzer-Winning Play from Textbook." The Freedom Forum Online, December 12, 2000. Available online. URL: http://www.freedomforum.org.

ATHALIE

Author: Jean Racine

Original date and place of production: 1716, Théâtre français, Paris, France

Characters: Abner, Athalie, Azariah, Hagar, Ishmael, Joad, Joash, Josabet, Mattan, Nabal, Salome

Filmed versions: None

SUMMARY

Jean Racine wrote *Athalie* in 1691 at the request of Madame Maintenon, who in 1684 had entered a secret marriage with King Louis XIV after the death of Queen Marie-Thérèse. Written in classical verse form and containing a chorus, the play is biblical in source and spirit and deals with the inner conflict of its main character. The play is based on the story of Athaliah, which appears in Kings 2 of the Old Testament, and it is set in the temple at Jerusalem. Athalie is queen of Judea, but she has made great efforts to destroy every vestige of Jewish worship and has decreed that her subjects worship the god Baal or suffer dire consequences. Although she believes that she has eradicated all members of the family of David, Joash, a grandson of David, remains. He was saved by the Jewish high priest Joad and his wife Josabet after followers of Athalie had plunged a dagger into his infant chest and left him to die. The high priest and his wife raised him secretly in the temple and plan to help David's last descendant to ascend the throne when he is of age, although the young boy has no knowledge of his true family. Although Athalie is unaware of Joash's parentage, she feels suspicious of him when she visits the temple after having a disturbing dream. As her suspicions grow, she tries to remove the boy from the temple, but she is unsuccessful in her efforts. When Joad and Josabet defy her, she threatens to lead her soldiers against them and to destroy the temple. This threat leads Joad to reveal Joash's parentage and to call together the other priests of the temple to prepare Joash to be anointed as king of Judea. Once others learn that Joash has been crowned, they abandon Athalie and eagerly pledge to defend Joash and Judaism. As Athalie returns with her troops to the temple, she sees Joash on the throne and orders her soldiers to attack his followers, but the troops turn against her and assassinate her. The play ends with a call for all of the people to pledge their allegiance to the new king and to "confirm / The covenant that Jacob made with God."

CENSORSHIP HISTORY

Athalie was banned from being professionally staged during the playwright's lifetime because of the extensive religious censorship of the period, and only after clerical intervention would Racine see the play performed in the subdued setting of a schoolroom, without sets or costumes. Religious censorship in France was strong in the late 17th century, and all passages and phrases quoted directly from the Bible as well as drama based directly on the Scriptures were prohibited on stage. France lifted this prohibition early in the 18th century, and *Athalie* was produced in 1716 in the Théâtre français, 17 years after Racine's death. In England, however, a similar prohibition against religious drama extended into the late 19th century. Although by the 19th century *Athalie* had attained the status of a classic in France, in March 1847 the play was refused a license for performance in England and banned from the English stage. John Mitchell Kemble, the Examiner of Plays, whose duty it was to read thoroughly any play 14 days before it was due to be performed and to recommend to the Lord Chamberlain Licenser of Theatres whether to grant the play a license, recommended that the play be suppressed because it violated the rule that prohibited the performance of plays based on subjects taken directly from the Scriptures.

FURTHER READING

Knapp, Bettina Leibowitz. *Jean Racine: Mythos and Renewal in Modern Theater.* Birmingham: University of Alabama Press, 1971.

Nelson, Robert James. *Corneille and Racine: Parallels and Contrasts.* Englewood, N.J.: Prentice-Hall, 1966.

Parkes, Adam. *Modernism and the Theater of Censorship.* New York: Oxford University Press, 1996.

Racine, Jean. *Athalie.* In *Six Plays by Corneille and Racine.* Edited and translated by Paul Landis. New York: Modern Library, 1931.

Stephens, John Russell. *The Censorship of English Drama, 1824–1901.* New York: Cambridge University Press, 1980.

Tilley, Arthur Augustus. *Three French Dramatists: Racine, Marivaux, Musset.* New York: Russell & Russell, 1967.

Tobin, Ronald W. *Jean Racine Revisited.* New York: Twayne Publishers, 1999.

THE AUTHOR

Author: Samuel Foote
Original date and place of production: February 5, 1757, Drury Lane Theatre, London, England
Characters: Arabella, Mr. Cadwallader, Mrs. Cadwallader, Cape
Filmed versions: None

SUMMARY

The Author is a slight play that would have little interest for contemporary readers if it were not for its role in the history of stage censorship. The story involves stock dramatic situations and characters, such as the plot of mistaken identity, the seemingly mismatched lovers, the mentally dense man of wealth, and the fluttering wife. Cape, the son of a man of great property and monetary wealth, lives in poverty as he tries to make a living as a writer. Arabella, the young and sweet daughter of the wealthy but ignorant and pretentious Mr. and Mrs. Cadwallader, meets Cape and the two fall instantly in love and secretly plan to marry. The Cadwalladers are horrified that their daughter will have anything to do with Cape and they try to prevent her from marrying a man whom they believe to be penniless. The author makes Mr. Cadwallader a subject of ridicule, with his foolish pride and his true ignorance. Possessing his own literary pretensions despite his lack of talent, he is disdainful of Cape's writing efforts. He predicts that Cape will fail as a writer and will ruin Arabella if she is allowed to marry him. In a comedic twist, Cape is revealed to be not a penniless hack writer but the son of a man of "capital Fortune," and Cadwallader immediately changes his opinion. Both Cadwalladers become champions of a union between Arabella and Cape, forgetting all of their former reservations, and the play ends on a happy note for all of the characters.

CENSORSHIP HISTORY

The Author is the first play to have been banned from the stage by the Lord Chamberlain Licenser of Theatres in England after it initially had received a license. The play is also the first production to be suppressed based on the complaint of an individual who claimed to be unjustly satirized in the work. Although the play enjoyed a long and popular run from its first performance at Drury Lane on February 5, 1757, and was revived the following season with an expectation of similar success, the final performance of the play took place on February 1, 1758. Mr. Apreece, a wealthy and eccentric Welshman who was well known in London at the time, approached William Cavendish, the Duke of Devonshire, who was then Lord Chamberlain, and demanded that the play be suppressed because it mocked and ridiculed him unjustly. Apreece had first approached David Garrick, manager of the Drury Lane Theatre, and attempted to persuade him to cancel future performances of the play, but Garrick refused. When Foote began advertising for the 1758–59 season, scheduled to begin on December 18, 1758, Apreece approached the Lord Chamberlain and persuaded him that Foote was mocking him in the character of Cadwallader, who was similar in appearance and behavior to Apreece in his corpulence, blank stare, awkward movements, loud and boisterous voice, and habit of moving his head constantly to his left shoulder with his mouth open. Apreece told Cavendish that he had become a public laughingstock, and that everywhere he went people would point at him and whisper the name of Mr. Cadwallader, then laugh.

The Lord Chamberlain told the theater company of the ban during the rehearsals for the December 18, 1758, opening. On May 14, 1759, actor and manager Tate Wilkinson defied the ban and presented a scene from *The Author* at the Drury Lane Theatre. News that the play had been illegally presented reached the Lord Chamberlain, who sent Wilkinson a letter that reprimanded him for "taking the liberty on Monday night to restore and act a scene from the Author, which had been prohibited." The letter stated that Mr. and Mrs. Apreece had been greatly offended by the play, and that the Lord Chamberlain expected that Wilkinson would not repeat the "rude infringement." In his memoirs, Wilkinson wrote that he complied with the ban because "high authority had laid its weighty commands, and I was obliged, though much against my will, to submit." The prohibition against the play continued in London until Apreece was dead, and the play was not again performed in its entirety until April 11, 1769.

FURTHER READING

Belden, Mary. *The Dramatic Work of Samuel Foote.* New Haven, Conn.: Yale University Press, 1929.

Connolly, L. W. *The Censorship of English Drama, 1737–1824.* San Marino, Calif.: Huntington Library, 1976.

Rosenfeld, Sybil. *Strolling Players and Dramas in the Provinces, 1660–1765.* Cambridge, England: Cambridge University Press, 1939.

Trefman, Simon. *Sam Foote, Comedian, 1727–1777.* New York: Oxford University Press, 1971.

LE BARBIER DE SEVILLE (THE BARBER OF SEVILLE)

Author: Pierre Augustin Caron de Beaumarchais
Original date and place of production: 1775, Paris, France
Characters: Ambrogio, Don Basilio, Berta, Count Almaviva, Dr. Bartolo, Figaro, Fiorello, Rosina
Filmed versions: *Le Barbier de Seville* (France, 1904, 1933, 1947); *Il Barbiere di Siviglia* (Italy, 1946, 1955, 1972); *The Barber of Seville* (U.S., 1944, 1984, 1994)

SUMMARY

Set in Seville, Spain, in the 17th century, *Le Barbier de Seville* has achieved fame as the basis of the opera by Gioacchino Rossini (1816). The plot includes a series of stock situations and characters, including love rivalry and a disguised suitor, but Beaumarchais's focus is on the cleverness of the servants in outsmarting their social superiors. Disguised as Lindoro, Count Almaviva, accompanied by his servant Fiorello, attempts to arrange a meeting with Rosina, the woman he wants to marry, whose guardian Dr. Bartolo has made secret plans to marry her the following day. As Lindoro/Almaviva waits beneath her window, he meets his former servant Figaro, now a barber, among whose clients is Dr. Bartolo. When Rosina appears at the window, she drops a letter to the street. As her jealous guardian runs out of the house to retrieve the letter, Lindoro/Almaviva picks it up and hides it. As Bartolo's barber, Figaro has access to the house and promises to help the lovesick Lindoro/Almaviva get inside.

The second act begins in Rosina's room, where Figaro enters to announce Lindoro's love for her. Figaro has given one servant a sleeping potion and another a sneezing potion, so chaos ensues when Bartolo enters the house and tries to question the servants Ambrogio and Berta about visitors. As Figaro hides, Rosina's music teacher Don Basilio tells Bartolo that Count Almaviva is in disguise in Seville and advises Bartolo to spread vicious rumors about him. As Figaro warns Rosina that Bartolo intends to marry her, Almaviva arrives at the house disguised as a soldier and orders Bartolo to give his soldiers lodging for the night. The trick lasts for a short while, but Bartolo grows increasingly suspicious and the act ends with Rosina praying for some peace of mind from her jealous guardian.

In the third act, after leaving the household as a soldier, Almaviva reenters in the disguise of Alonso, a music student meant to take the place of Basilio, whom he says is ill and has sent him. While Bartolo is busy watching Alonso with Rosina, Figaro steals the key to Rosina's window. The plan is almost upset because Basilio appears unexpectedly. For various reasons, everyone tries to convince Basilio that he is sick and should go home to rest, and the confused Basilio agrees and leaves. Figaro then distracts Bartolo by giving him a shave. He obstructs Bartolo's view of Rosina and Almaviva, who are discussing their plans for escape.

In the final act, Bartolo apprehends Rosina, who is waiting to elope with her lover, and tricks her into believing that Lindoro/Almaviva is unfaithful to her. She reveals the plans for the secret rendezvous and promises to marry Bartolo. After Bartolo leaves, Almaviva climbs a ladder into Rosina's room and reveals his true identity, causing the stunned Rosina to fall into his arms. Figaro enters to announce that the ladder has been removed, but the plan is saved when a notary and Don Basilio join them and Almaviva bribes the notary to perform a hurried ceremony, so that they are married by the time Bartolo returns.

CENSORSHIP HISTORY

The censorship of *Le Barbier de Seville* is intimately connected with similar censorship of Beaumarchais's later play, LE MARIAGE DE FIGARO. Although *Le Barbier de Seville* was written in 1773, King Louis XV condemned the play and refused to allow it to be performed until 1775, after Beaumarchais had edited the original significantly. The major objection to the play was that it too clearly portrayed a class-conscious sympathy in its depiction of the resourcefulness and cunning of the former servant and current Figaro, in contrast with the ridicule that the playwright rained down on the characters who represent the upper classes. Figaro is brash and resilient, but the aristocrats, such as Count Almaviva, and the professionals, such as Dr. Bartolo, are bumbling incompetents who require his assistance to achieve their aims. Moreover, Figaro does not feign respect for those who are socially his superiors, nor does he pretend to believe himself inferior. Such brashness in a servant was unacceptable to the monarchy in France, which feared that portraying such behavior on stage would endanger the entire social foundation of Europe. Although the play was presented at great risk in private performances in people's homes, Beaumarchais was not permitted to submit this play for public performance until he made extensive revisions in the portrayals of Figaro and other characters, and softened his criticisms of the upper classes. An edited and homogenized version of *Le Barbier de Seville* was finally allowed to be produced on a public stage in 1775.

FURTHER READING

Braun, Sidney D., ed. *Dictionary of French Literature*. New York: Philosophical Library, 1958.

Connolly, L. W. *The Censorship of English Drama, 1737–1824*. San Marino, Calif.: Huntington Library, 1976.

Green, Jonathan. *The Encyclopedia of Censorship*. New York: Facts On File, 1990.
Hemmings, Frederic William John. *Theatre and State in France, 1760–1905*. New York: Cambridge University Press, 1994.

THE BEARD

Author: Michael McClure
Original date and place of production: December 18, 1965, Actor's Workshop, San Francisco, California
Characters: Billy the Kid, Jean Harlow
Filmed versions: None

SUMMARY

The Beard is set on a stage described by the playwright as being "a blue-velvet dominated eternity" and contains two characters, the 1930s silver-screen sex symbol Jean Harlow and the 19th-century Wild West outlaw Billy the Kid (William Bonney), who tease and taunt each other with obscenities throughout the play. The action culminates in the two engaging in a sexual act. The characters are costumed to reflect clearly the people they represent, as the playwright's stage directions make clear: "Harlow's hair is in her traditional style. She wears a pale blue gown with plumed sleeves. Billy the Kid wears shirt, tight pants, and boots. Harlow has a purse." The stage is bare, except for two chairs and a table covered with furs. Both characters wear small beards of torn white tissue paper.

Throughout the play the two characters alternately attract and repel each other. Each throws out challenges that are meant to undermine the image that has become a part of the other's legend, suggesting that their real natures might have been significantly different. Throughout most of the play, Jean Harlow attempts to make Billy the Kid accept the image that she projected in real life, as the sex goddess whose sole aim is to be beautiful, yet she also challenges him by repeating the following statement many times: "Before you can pry secrets from me, you must find the real me! Which one will you pursue?" Billy the Kid makes a similar effort to maintain his own legendary image as the tough gunfighter who fears nothing.

What they both learn, and both tell each other repeatedly, is that each has been nothing more than a "bag of meat" living out illusions. Each attacks the other in ways that serve to tear apart the illusions of their physical lives, although both contend at the beginning that their lives are real. Jean Harlow must experience having Billy insult her appearance, her screen star clothes methodically torn from her, and her hair color insulted while the hair is mussed, after which Billy the Kid bites her on the toe and draws blood, all to earn the following assessment: "YOU'RE REAL NOW!" Billy the Kid suffers attacks on his masculinity as Jean Harlow mocks his long hair, telling him, "Maybe you'd like to be a chick!" She also tells him that he seems to want to be beautiful, as she is, and shouts, "You're crazier than Hell, you frozen eyed bastard!" As the play progresses, the sexual taunts become more graphic. Near the end of the play, the two characters appear to reverse their original roles, as Billy the Kid becomes the one to utter several times the following lines: "Before you can pry any secrets from me, you must first find the real me. Which one will you pursue?" He now states that he is beautiful, as she said of herself in the beginning of the play, and the two repeat many of the commands each gave earlier, but now with a loving, longing tone. As the play ends, the two grapple passionately, moving to the floor. Billy the Kid performs cunnilingus on the sexually ecstatic Jean Harlow, whose final words are 24 shouts of "STAR!" interspersed with "OH MY GOD" and "YOU'RE NEXT!"

CENSORSHIP HISTORY

In his foreword to the published play, Norman Mailer calls *The Beard* "a mysterious piece of work, for while its surface seems simple, repetitive and obscene" the action is "almost as if ghosts from two periods of the American past were speaking across decades to each other, and yet at the same time are . . . speaking to us of the nature of seduction, the nature of attraction, and, particularly, the nature of the perverse temper between a man and a woman." Mailer found spiritual meaning and inspiration in the work, but law enforcement officials did not. The play appeared four times before it was closed down by police, although restraints were placed on the performances from the first.

The first performance of the play was by the San Francisco Actor's Workshop, but McClure writes in the afterword to the published play that the management of the workshop made every effort to prevent any publicity about the play, to the extent of "forbidding the presence of newspaper reviewers." The director of the workshop was afraid that the play would permanently ruin the image of the institution. Despite the management's best efforts, a drama critic for the *San Francisco Chronicle* saw the play and wrote a review that hailed it as both "effectively upsetting" and "creatively stimulating." The second performance took place in the cavernous Fillmore Auditorium, where it was accompanied by a dazzling light show and rock music, and played to a capacity crowd. Despite this, producer Bill Graham canceled its run after one performance because he was apprehensive that the police would cancel his theater license due to the obscenity in the play.

The trouble began with the third and fourth performances, which took place at the Committee, a North Beach theater nightclub, where members of the San Francisco Police Department secretly recorded the play on audiotape. At the fifth performance, the police brought movie cameras, which they used during the end of the performance to tape the sexual act between Jean Harlow and Billy the Kid. Afterward, the police arrested the two actors and charged them with "obscenity," "conspiracy to commit a felony," and "lewd and dissolute conduct in a public place." McClure alerted the American Civil Liberties Union (ACLU), which provided representation at the next attempted performance in Berkeley, California. The performance was presented by Rare Angel Productions in front of 100 specially assembled "expert witnesses," including poet and owner of City Lights Bookstore Lawrence Ferlinghetti; Zen popularizer Alan Watts; members of the clergy; and academicians. Also present were photographers and tape-recording crews to photograph and record the seven members of the Berkeley Police Department and district attorney's office. The officials filmed and taped the performance despite demands from the ACLU and McClure that they refrain from doing so. Five days later, the Berkeley Police Department charged the management of Rare Angel Productions with "lewd and dissolute conduct in a public place." Marshall Krause of the ACLU took the case before the San Francisco Superior Court. After five months of litigation, the charges were dropped when the court decided that they were "inappropriate." After the decision in San Francisco, Berkeley withdrew its charges. The play was again produced in Berkeley in 1967 without incident.

In October 1969 the play opened at the Evergreen Theater in New York City. The production tried to recapture the feeling of the Fillmore Auditorium by preceding the play with a huge light show and placing closely stacked cages of doves and ferrets in the lobby, according to a review by the New York Theatre Wire, "to set off an adrenaline rush." The production won the *Village Voice* Obie (Off-Broadway) theater award for both of the actors.

FURTHER READING

Elsom, John. *Erotic Theatre.* New York: Taplinger Publishing Co., 1974.

"First Major Revival of 'The Beard' by Michael McClure." November 17, 1999. Available online. URL: http://www.nytheatre-wire.com/beard.htm.

Kreutz, Irving W. "The Music of Frustration: McClure's *The Beard.*" *Arts in Society* 4 (summer 1967): 197–201.

Laufe, Abe. *The Wicked Stage: A History of Theater Censorship and Harassment in the United States.* New York: Frederick Ungar, 1978.

McClure, Michael. *The Beard and VKTMS.* New York: Grove Press, 1985.

Nathan, John. "San Francisco Censorship—Michael McClure's *The Beard.*" *Evergreen Review* 11 (February 1967): 16–20.

Russo, Francine. "Theatre: A Little Chin Music." *Village Voice*, December 1–7, 1999: 23.

Stephenson, Gregory. "Notes on the Work of Michael McClure." Michael McClure Homepage. Available online. URL: http://www.thing.net/~grist/l&d/mcclure/mcclure.htm.

THE BEDBUG

Author: Vladimir Mayakovsky

Original date and place of production: 1929, Vsevolod Meyerhold Theatre, Moscow, Russia

Characters: Oleg Bayan, Zoya Beryozkina, the Mechanic, Ivan Prisypkin, Rosalie Pavlovna Renaissance
Filmed versions: None

SUMMARY

The Bedbug, which is divided into two parts set in 1929 and 1979, relates the experiences of Ivan Prisypkin, a Communist Party member who is about to marry. In the opening scene, he and his future mother-in-law, Rosalie Pavlovna Renaissance, the owner of a successful beauty parlor, shop in the huge State Department Store, where Prisypkin urges her to buy numerous unnecessary items. Her neighbor reassures Renaissance that such consumerism is the way of the up-and-coming working class, and she reluctantly agrees, if only to please Prisypkin, who brings into her family both his attractive proletarian pedigree and a union card. Renaissance's eccentric neighbor Bayan offers to arrange the wedding, and the described activities suit perfectly the Soviet consciousness that the author satirizes. Bayan plans for a red-lipped bride to arrive in a red carriage escorted by a red-faced bookkeeper to a hall filled with tables covered in red cloths and holding bottles with red seals. Prisypkin chastises Renaissance when she calls him "Comrade," warning her not to do so yet, because she will not be proletarian until after the wedding, when she marries him and is subsumed into his social class. As the wedding preparations continue, Prisypkin's mistress learns that he is marrying another woman and shoots herself, but survives. A youth and a mechanic mock Prisypkin, who practices how to dance properly, tries on new clothes, and takes lessons from Bayan in the proper way to scratch his back in public. They also find one of his new calling cards listing his name as "Pierre Skripkin" and laugh at the airs he has assumed. In response to their disapproval, Prisypkin tells them that he fought to "build the bridge to socialism," so he has the right to relax his standards a little. At the wedding, which takes place in the beauty parlor, Prisypkin is disappointed when the secretary of the factory committee sends regrets and misses the wedding because of a party committee meeting. The singing, dancing, and drinking at the wedding soon devolve into disorder. During a bout of pushing and shoving, an accountant pokes the bride with a fish, pushing her against the stove. Her veil catches fire and soon sets the entire room ablaze. Many of the guests perish as the beauty parlor is destroyed, and Prisypkin is left unaccounted for in the rubble- and water-filled structure.

The fifth scene moves 50 years into the future, to 1979. The Institute for Human Resurrection is debating whether to revive a human figure—Prisypkin—found frozen in a cellar in Tambov. The hands of the figure are calloused, which suggests that he was a worker, and those in favor of resurrection point out that every last worker is needed. The Epidemiological Office speaks against resurrection, noting that the figure might be infected with bacteria that once spread among people in the former Russia. The team that resurrects

Prisypkin is led by his former mistress Zoya, now an elderly and learned professor. Once revived, Prisypkin first thinks that he has simply gotten drunk and awakened in a jail, but he sees a calendar and thinks with horror that he owes 50 years of union dues and that he has 50 years of paperwork to catch up on. As he runs outside to scratch his back against a wall, a bedbug crawls off his back and escapes, despite his efforts to capture and kill it. Officials place Prisypkin in a cage, where to ease his transition he is allowed to partake of all the bad habits that are no longer common in 1979. His surroundings contain mounds of cigarette butts and empty liquor bottles, and the staff find his breath so debilitating that they install a ventilation system to protect themselves. Zoo employees also locate the bedbug, then proudly display it at the zoological gardens. In the final scene of the play, the bedbug and Prisypkin are displayed in the same cage, and the director of the zoo shares his conclusions with the audience that both are parasitical insects, different in size but identical in nature: The bedbug feeds off individual bodies, then falls under the bed, while the "bourgeoisies vulgaris" (Prisypkin) feeds off all humankind, then falls into the bed. The play ends as the zoo attendants drag Prisypkin away, then ventilate the stage to remove his foulness.

CENSORSHIP HISTORY

Mayakovsky exhibited his subversive nature long before *The Bedbug* was banned from performance. In 1908 he joined the Moscow committee of the Russian Social Democratic Party, the Bolshevik faction, and because of subversive activity against the government he was jailed for six months in 1909. In 1912 he joined other artists in writing the manifesto "A Slap in the Face of Public Taste," which attacked the long-revered literary giants such as Aleksandr Pushkin, Fyodor Dostoevsky, and Leo Tolstoy, advocating in their place Italian futurism, which called for a revolutionary attitude toward art and exalted speed, machinery, and war. In the decades that followed, Mayakovsky continued to resist the growing Soviet bureaucracy in both government and in the arts, and he exhibits in his satire *The Bedbug* how keenly he recognized that such resistance was useless. The play is a tirade against narrow-minded middle-class conventionality and it holds those in official positions up to ridicule. In the first half of the play, Prisypkin is cast in an unfavorable light as he seeks to enjoy the pleasures of being an individualist after having worked to achieve revolution, but the second half of the play creates an unflattering view of what Mayakovksy predicted would be the Soviet socialist society of the future. The individual is not permitted to exist unmolested, for his very existence poses a threat to society. The ending incorporates Mayakovsky's disillusionment with the revolution he had fought so hard to achieve and conveys his unhappiness with Russia in the 1920s and his belief that the bureaucrats, not the people, would have their way. The play anticipates the powerful campaign that the ruling bodies would undertake in the 1930s, after his death, to eliminate all political opponents and those whom the state decided were parasites working against the success of Soviet society. Although in the early 1920s Mayakovsky wrote propaganda in favor of the Soviet bureaucracy, his heart was not in it. As critic Aleksandr Voronsky wrote in his 1928 essay "On Artistic Truth,"

> Take Mayakovsky. Anyone who carefully examines the basic motifs of his works sees that this highly gifted poet is an extreme individualist, and that his true and genuine inner poetic core is found in such things as "Cloud in Trousers" or the poem "About that"; but that he stands on poetic stilts and does violence to himself when he writes pathetic and insincere poems about the human labour collective, about the development of capitalism in Russia (in his poem about Lenin), about the one hundred and fifty million, and so forth; the themes are superb, but completely alien to Mayakovsky. They are ideologically unconvincing in his works and thoroughly dishonest.

Mayakovsky's individualism made him a keen critic of any form of hypocrisy or self-serving bureaucracy, and he described the satirical drama written toward the end of his life as directed against growing "bureaucracy, narrowmindedness and indifference, and in favor of a broadening of horizons, inventiveness and enthusiasm." Such comments are similar to those of Leon Trotsky's own appeal in *Literature and Revolution* (in the chapter "Revolutionary and Socialist Art"), originally published by the Soviet government in 1924, for "a Soviet comedy of manners, one of laughter and indignation" and for satire and scathing criticism of [Soviet] "piggishness, vulgarity and knavery." In 1924 Trotsky and Joseph Stalin assumed power in the Soviet Union after the death of Vladimir Lenin, who had led the revolution and headed the first Soviet government. By 1927 Stalin ousted Trotsky from the Soviet power structure.

The 1929 premiere of *The Bedbug* brought together well-known and well-respected Soviet artists. The play was directed by Vsevolod Meyerhold, with scenery developed and built by the popular set designer Aleksandr Rodchenko and music created by the young and later renowned composer Dmitri Shostakovich. Despite the care in staging, the play became the object of hostile reactions from pro-Stalinist critics who complained that it contained "too few positive heroes" and portrayed "an unfavorable view of a future Soviet society." These criticisms were consistent with what had become a systematic campaign against all critical forms of art, which followed Stalin's adoption of measures to isolate the political opposition in Russia.

As the 1920s ended and the 1930s began, the Stalinist bureaucracy worked rapidly to stifle all independent and challenging art, seemingly with the full cooperation of many Russian critics. In January 1930 a seminar with the title "Do We Need Satire?" took place in Moscow, and the participants argued against the value of satirical work, which "must necessarily take an anti-Soviet form." They warned further that by employing satire "the class enemy can very easily disguise himself." This mode of thinking characterized the view taken toward *The Bedbug* and led the government to recommend in

1930 that Meyerhold refrain from further performances of the play, because they perceived it to contain an antisocialist tirade. In reality, the play is a powerful warning about the direction of Soviet society. The dire predictions made by Mayakovsky about the future became reality as Stalinist-influenced police terror continued to dominate both in Russia and the eastern satellite countries. The play was also banned from performance in East Germany; in October 1999 it was staged at the Maxim Gorki Theatre in east Berlin. Before the fall of the Berlin Wall, the theater had specialized in Russian and eastern European productions.

FURTHER READING

Brown, Edward James. *Mayakovsky: A Poet in the Revolution.* Princeton, N.J.: Princeton University Press, 1973.

Carlisle, Olga Andreyev. *Poets on Street Corners: Portraits of Fifteen Russian Poets.* New York: Random House, 1968.

Charters, Ann. *I Love: The True Story of Vladimir Mayakovsky and Lili Brik.* New York: Farrar, Straus & Giroux, 1979.

Marshall, Herbert. *Mayakovsky.* New York: Hill & Wang, 1965.

Mayakovsky, Vladimir. *The Bedbug and Selected Poetry.* Indianapolis: Indiana University Press, 1975.

Smeliansky, Anatoly. *The Russian Theatre after Stalin.* Translated from the Russian by Patrick Miles. New York: Cambridge University Press, 1999.

Voronsky, Aleksandr. *Art as a Cognition of Life, Selected Writings, 1911–1936.* Berlin: Mehring Books, 1998.

Worozylski, Wiktor. *The Life of Mayakovsky.* Translated from the Polish by Boleslaw Taborski. New York: Orion Press, 1970.

THE BEGGAR'S OPERA

Author: John Gay

Original date and place of production: January 29, 1728, John Rich's Theatre, Lincoln's Inn Fields, London, England

Characters: Beggar, Molly Brazen, Ben Budge, Mrs. Coaxer, Crook-fingered Jack, Jenny Diver, Wat Dreary, Filch, Lockit, Lucy Lockit, Captain Macheath, Mat of the Mint, Nimming Ned, Harry Paddington, Mr. Peachum, Mrs. Peachum, Polly Peachum, Player, Robin of Bagshot, Mrs. Slammekin, Sukey Tawdry, Diana Trapes, Dolly Trull, Jeremy Twitcher, Mrs. Vixen

Filmed versions: *Beggar's Opera* (U.K., 1953); *Beggar's Opera* (U.K., 1984); *Zebracka Opera* (Czechoslovakia, 1991)

SUMMARY

The Beggar's Opera satirizes both the Italian operas of John Gay's time, which many Londoners attended but few understood, and the corrupt political climate, to which most people turned a blind eye. Instead of the finely clothed aristocrats that appear in most early 18th-century operas, Gay's hero is a beggar who apologizes to his audience in the introduction, during which he converses with a character called simply Player: "I hope I may be forgiven that I have not made my opera throughout unnatural like those in vogue; for I have no recitative. Excepting this, as I have consented to have neither prologue nor epilogue, it must be allowed an opera in all its forms." The play then begins, and the principal characters make their appearances. Mr. Peachum, a receiver of stolen goods who also enjoys a substantial living from money paid by the authorities when he informs on his clients, and Mrs. Peachum, who uses his name but to whom he is not married, are the parents of the sweet and innocent Polly Peachum. In the opening scenes, the audience realizes how powerfully connected Peachum is as he reviews the work done by the many criminals whom he controls. When his assistant, Filch, arrives with a request for help from Black Moll, who is about to go to trial that afternoon, Peachum responds that he will find means to soften the evidence "as the wench is very active and industrious" and can continue to be of use to him once acquitted.

When Polly falls in love with the gallant highwayman Captain Macheath and marries him without her parents' consent, Mr. Peachum promises to make his daughter a widow soon by informing on the highwayman. He also rails against Polly's foolishness at marrying, asking her, "Do you think your mother and I should have lived comfortably so long together if ever we had been married?" Peachum's greater reason for wanting Macheath dead is that he is afraid that the highwayman will tell the authorities about his own business of receiving stolen goods. Playing upon Macheath's love of women, Peachum arranges for a constable to be present when the highwayman meets with a bevy of the ladies of the town for dancing and drinks.

Macheath is arrested for his crimes as a highwayman and sent to Newgate prison, where he is placed in chains by Lockit, the warden of Newgate. Lucy Lockit, the warden's daughter, was once seduced by Macheath; she berates him for having deceived her by marrying Polly, but he lies and charms Lucy into believing that Polly is lying and that he loves only Lucy. As he tries to persuade Lucy to help him to escape hanging for his crimes as a highwayman, Polly enters and the two women argue over whom Macheath really loves. After Peachum arrives and drags Polly home, the highwayman reassures Lucy that Polly means nothing to him, and Lucy steals the keys and frees him. Happy to be free, Macheath goes to a gambling hall, while Lockit and Peachum discuss how to recapture him. They are overjoyed when a woman of the town, Diana Trapes, gives them information of Macheath's whereabouts in exchange for payment.

When Macheath is returned to Newgate prison, Lucy and Polly beg their fathers to free him, but only after Lucy first tries to poison Polly's wine. Lockit and Peachum refuse, and Macheath stands trial and is sentenced to be hanged. As he waits in the Condemned Hold, members of his gang enter. They sing together, and Macheath implores them to "Bring those villains

[Lockit and Peachum] to the gallows before you." Lucy and Polly arrive to say their farewells, only to hear Macheath encourage them to travel to the West Indies, "where you'll have a fair chance of getting a husband apiece, or, by good luck, two or three, as you like best." As they protest, the jailer announces that four more women with a child apiece have arrived to say their farewells, but Macheath refuses to see them and prefers to head for the gallows.

As Macheath and the jailer exit, Beggar and Player take the stage and discuss how the opera should end, until they finally agree that it must be happy and Macheath must be spared. The highwayman is brought back to the stage, where he sings and confesses that he is legally married to Polly, and the play ends.

CENSORSHIP HISTORY

The wit and controversy contained in *The Beggar's Opera* made it a popular success at the outset. People flocked to 63 uninterrupted performances in the first season, after which it was renewed for a second season at Lincoln's Inn Theatre. The play was also performed extensively throughout England in traveling productions, as well as in Wales, Scotland, and Ireland. Alexander Pope wrote in 1742 in a footnote to his satire *The Dunciad* that "The fame of it was not confined to the author only, the ladies carried about with them the favourite songs of it in fans, and houses were furnished with it in screens. . . . Furthermore, it drove out of England for that season the Italian opera, which had carried all before it for ten years. . . . This remarkable period happened in the year 1728." Despite such early and continued popularity, the satire in the play and the creation of the likable Macheath, his gang, and their women followers—the "ladies of the town" in the cast list—were denounced as incentives to vice and immorality. The play has had a lasting influence on both drama and novels and Schultz relates that more than one critic has described *The Beggar's Opera* as "the first to make the English drama of rascality really popular," and, consequently, a clear danger to the morality of audiences. Henry Fielding's Tom Jones and Jonathan Wilde are similarly durable scoundrels and even so contemporary a hero as Han Solo of *Star Wars* has an illegal side to his character. Critics closer in time to its early performance, such as Samuel Johnson, appreciated the satiric and entertainment value of the play, although he also conceded that "at the same time I do not deny that it may have some influence, by making the character of a rogue familiar, and in some degree pleasing." The play was performed freely, without concern for licensing, until Prime Minister Robert Walpole gained the backing necessary to place restraints on the play under the guise of protecting society.

The subject matter and presentation of *The Beggar's Opera* have been identified as the catalysts in the early 18th century that led to Walpole's campaign to devise the drastic legislation of the Theatres Act of 1737, which both provided for the severe punishment of "rogues, vagabonds, sturdy beggars, and vagrants" and declared to be vagabonds all "common players of interludes," or actors in plays that had not been licensed by authorities. Once it was made law, Walpole promoted the application of the act because he was offended by the manner in which *The Beggar's Opera* launched an overt attack on the government and caricatured him as the warden Lockit. Members of the governing class claimed to have been offended by the pointed allusions to the corruption of society disguised in the actions of thieves and highwaymen. The act strengthened the laws against vagrancy, and declared that all actors in unlicensed plays on sites not approved by authority were vagrants or vagabonds and, thus, subject to severe punishment. Walpole used the act to stifle further performances of *The Beggar's Opera* and other plays that he and the governing class found offensive. The resulting law led to severe excising of speeches from the play by troupes seeking licenses to perform, or furtive performances by those who refused to cut scenes and were, thus, not granted licenses. In the early 19th century the play was frequently performed in Bath and other resort areas throughout England, but it was highly expurgated by individual theater managers who sought to preserve the high moral tone of the time.

FURTHER READING

Boswell, James. *Life of Johnson*. Vol. II. Edited by George Birkbeck Hill. Oxford, England: Oxford University Press, 1934.

Conolly, L. W. *The Censorship of English Drama, 1737–1824*. San Marino, Calif.: Huntington Library, 1976.

Fowell, Frank, and Frank Palmer. *Censorship in England*. London: F. Palmer, 1913. Reprint, New York: Benjamin Blom, 1969.

Kidson, Frank. *The Beggar's Opera: Its Predecessors and Successors*. Cambridge, England: Cambridge University Press, 1922.

Pope, Alexander. *The Dunciad*. Longman Annotated Texts. Edited by Valerie Rumbold. New York: Longman Publishing, 1999.

Schultz, William Eben. *Gay's 'Beggar's Opera': Its Content, History & Influence*. New York: Cambridge University Press, 1967.

Stephens, John Russell. *The Censorship of English Drama, 1824–1901*. New York: Cambridge University Press, 1980.

THE BEST LITTLE WHOREHOUSE IN TEXAS

Authors: Larry L. King and Peter Masterson

Original date and place of production: April 17, 1978, Entermedia Theater (Off-Broadway), New York, New York

Characters: Aggies Football Team, Amber, Chip Brenster, Sheriff Ed Earl Dodd, Farmer, Girls at Miss Mona's (Beatrice, Dawn, Curla, Eloise, Ginger, Linda Lou, Ruby Rae, Taddy Jo), Governor, Miss Wulla Jean, Jewel, Edsel Mackey, Doatsey May, Mayor Rufus Poindexter, Reporters, Rio

Grande Band Leader, C. J. Scruggs, Shy, Leroy Sliney, Mona Stangley, Senator Wingwoah

Filmed versions: *The Best Little Whorehouse in Texas* (1982)

SUMMARY

The Best Little Whorehouse in Texas is a musical based on the true life story of Edna Milton and the "Chicken Ranch," a brothel that was started in 1890 in LaGrange, Texas, and closed down by right-wing Christians in 1973. Larry L. King wrote a magazine article about the brothel for *Playboy* magazine in 1974 before collaborating with Peter Masterson on the script. The play begins with a country band singing about "the nicest little whorehouse you ever saw," and the song provides a history of the establishment. Currently run by Miss Mona Stangley, the Chicken Ranch is a no-nonsense place with rules, which the audience learns when Miss Mona interviews Shy and Amber, two young women looking for jobs. The girls must call their customers "guests," not "tricks" or "johns," and criminal records, drug use, kissing on the mouth, and orgies are not allowed. As Miss Mona tells the girls, her stern leadership has its advantages because they never have trouble with the law. But peaceful times are about to end: A crusading local television reporter named Melvin P. Thorpe seeks notoriety, so he stirs up a local church group to stage a public demonstration at the courthouse against the Chicken Ranch. The growing controversy worries Sheriff Ed Earl Dodd, a longtime friend and sometime lover to Miss Mona, and he tells her that Thorpe's actions can adversely affect both of them. Although she believes that the controversy will soon blow over, the situation becomes worse when Thorpe accuses Dodd of accepting bribes "to protect a notorious house of ill repute." Dodd stands up to Thorpe and threatens to run him out of town. Several leading citizens of the town are particularly concerned about Thorpe's campaign, because it is nearly time for the annual visit to the Chicken Ranch by the senior members of the Aggies college football team. The visit goes as planned, with Senator Wingwoah escorting the team and Dodd remaining on the premises to guarantee order. While Mona and Dodd sit together, they reminisce about 20 years before when she caught a bus from Amarillo headed for San Antonio, but made her fateful stop along the way.

As the sheriff falls asleep, Thorpe and his cohorts raid the brothel, and the newsman cavorts with his Melvin P. Thorpe singers (his cohorts who break into song) as the senator explains to the press that he "has no recollection of coming to the Chicken Ranch and must have been doped by 'Commonists.'" The governor arrives and is questioned about the fate of Miss Mona's establishment, but he deftly sidesteps the questions, claiming that he is "all for virtue" and knows Miss Mona only by name, so he will leave it to the local authorities to close the ranch. A crowd gathers at the ranch, but Miss Mona disperses them by firing a shotgun into the air, then sending her girls to their rooms to keep out of sight. Alone, Miss Mona recalls a week she spent in Galveston watching the inauguration of President Kennedy on television with Dodd, who must have been past 40 while she was barely 20. At the same time, annoyed by the publicity and pressure, the town fathers and the governor make Dodd realize that he will have to close down the Chicken Ranch. He thinks with sadness of Miss Mona, as he sings "A Good Old Girl," with whom he has "been some long, long miles together . . . she was never the clingin' kind. . . . Never talked no foolish talk. . . . Had no ties and held no rules. . . . There's lots of things I could have told her. . . . I suppose But what I would want to tell that good old girl She knows." The governor and citizens agree that the place must be closed, and Sheriff Dodd arrives at the Chicken Ranch to make certain that the girls leave as ordered. Even though Miss Mona is resigned to the closing, Dodd deplores such political expediency and bemoans that "It just got out of hand. It ate me up before I knowed it was hungry." In the final scene Miss Mona is headed for life on a farm, where she hopes that Sheriff Dodd will visit her. Before he leaves, she asks him where he was the day Kennedy was inaugurated, and he replies that he remembers the speech, but his memory of Kennedy's assassination is stronger, because that day he picked up three Mexican kids who had stolen a goat from an old man and were throwing themselves a barbecue. Although Miss Mona understands, she privately recalls their weekend together in Galveston, watching the inauguration on TV and the shine of the sun on the water in the Gulf. After Dodd leaves, Miss Mona ruminates while the band sings, once again, about the pleasing surroundings of the brothel.

CENSORSHIP HISTORY

Despite 1,576 performances on Broadway and many more in college venues, *The Best Little Whorehouse in Texas* has invited controversy throughout most of its history, mainly by religious groups. During the original run of the play, several New York City–area television stations refused to run advertisements for the play with its full title, so publicists had to sell the play to potential audiences without actually naming it. New York Transit Authority buses at first carried advertising placards that urged, "Have fun at the Whorehouse," but removed them due to pressure exerted on the city by the Catholic Archdiocese of New York. Instead, ads referred only to the house, leaving off "whore." In the late 1990s the word *whorehouse* stopped one college from staging the play, because the title sent what one administrator claimed was "the wrong message."

In 1997 students in the drama club at Wentworth Institute of Technology in Boston joined with students in the drama club at nearby Wheelock College to present a production. Casting for the play was already completed, show dates were scheduled, and rehearsals begun when Maureen C. Keefe, dean of students at Wentworth, informed the director of the production that the drama clubs would have to select another play, because the title was unacceptable and "would not be appropriate to mention in an alumni newsletter." In a newspaper interview, John Heinstadt, Wentworth vice president of business and finance, explained that the decision had been "a PR matter," designed to protect the "positive image" of the school, which was celebrating its 25th year of accepting female students. Wentworth officials also argued that "permitting a play with this title to be performed would increase sexual harassment on campus." (The choice of the play had been made by the drama club of Wheelock College, a school with a 90 percent female population at the time.) Wentworth College canceled the performance of *The Best Little Whorehouse in Texas* and temporarily suspended the Wentworth administration liaison to the drama club, whom the administration blamed for failing to seek what it termed "appropriate administrative review of the selection." To protest what it termed "a distressing censorship incident," the Boston Coalition for Freedom of Expression (BCFE) sent a letter on March 26, 1998, to Keefe in which director James D'Entremont wrote, "Wentworth appears not to be concerned about the impact on its alumni of imposing heavy-handed censorship on its students and faculty" and demanded that the college administration respond to the allegations of censorship. Wentworth did respond, but only reiterated that the decision to halt the play had been made because of its title. The students eventually launched a production of *Bound for Broadway* instead.

FURTHER READING

D'Entremont, James. Director, Boston Coalition for Freedom of Expression. *Letter to Maureen C. Keefe, Dean of Students, Wentworth Institute of Technology.* February 26, 1998.

Guernsey, Otis L., ed. *The Best Plays of 1977–1978.* New York: Dodd, Mead, 1978.

———. *The Best Plays of 1978–1979.* New York: Dodd, Mead, 1979.

———. *The Best Plays of 1981–1982.* New York: Dodd, Mead, 1979.

Silvergate, Harvey, and Gia Barresi. "Wentworth's Whorehouse." *The Boston Phoenix*, March 17, 1998. Available online. URL: http://www.shadowuniv.com/writings/980327phoenix-has-gb.html.

THE BOYS IN THE BAND

Author: Mart Crowley
Original date and place of production: April 14, 1968, Theatre Four (Off-Broadway), New York, New York
Characters: Alan, Bernard, Cowboy, Donald, Emory, Hank, Harold, Larry, Michael
Filmed versions: *The Boys in the Band* (1970)

SUMMARY

The Boys in the Band was written before the psychiatric community declassified homosexuality as a mental illness and while laws still existed to make frequenting a gay bar a crime. Divided into two acts, the play is set during one evening in the Manhattan apartment of Michael, who with the highly neurotic Donald, his lover, is giving a party for his friend Harold and has invited five gay friends and another man to celebrate the occasion. Michael begs his guests to "act straight" when his ostensibly straight former roommate Alan unexpectedly appears at the apartment. The characters represent the homosexual spectrum of the 1960s: Emory is a flamboyant queen; Harold, a Jewish pothead; Cowboy, a hustler provided as a one-night "gift" for the birthday boy; Bernard, a dapper African American; and Hank and Larry, straight in appearance, with none of the flamboyance of their friends. The group slings wisecracks, and characters refer to themselves in disparaging terms, as when Michael characterizes his intended guests as "six tired screaming fairy queens and one anxious queer." All fear aging; they have arranged the hustler as a gift for Harold because he will soon be too old to pick up young men based solely on his own physical attractiveness.

As the evening wears on, Michael reveals that he has been infatuated with Alan since college. Michael had dated the woman whom Alan married, and now Michael explains that he "butched it up quite a bit" in college and was "very large in the dating department," although he had numerous gay encounters under the guise of the "Christ-was-I-drunk-last-night-syndrome," a ploy used by many others to claim no memory of their sexual encounters. In pleading with his friends to "act straight," Michael protests that his request is not to protect himself but instead to protect Alan. Alan calls and in a tear-filled voice cancels his intended visit, but later appears unexpectedly at the apartment door and walks in as the friends are dancing. He is disconcerted by the scene, but accepts Michael's offer of a drink and attempts conversation with the other guests. Emory flounces around, trying to draw everyone's attention and making disparaging remarks about birthday boy Harold in his absence. Michael steers Alan upstairs where they can talk, but Alan apologizes for his earlier show of weakness in crying on the telephone after what seems to be a separation from his wife; he says he thinks Emory "seems like such a goddamn little pansy." When Alan and Michael rejoin the others, Harold's birthday gift arrives. The young man says he is early because he "wanted to get to the bars by midnight," and he sings the greeting to the wrong guest because Harold has not yet arrived. Alan strives to ignore Emory's exhibitionism and the increasing clues that Michael and his friends are gay by turning to the straight-seeming Hank, who has revealed that he has children and is in the midst of a divorce. Unaware that Hank and Larry are a couple, Alan invites Hank to visit his home in Washington, D.C., and to meet his family, while Emory mocks them both. Alan's anger finally explodes, and he shouts at Emory, "How'd you like to blow me?" to which Emory replies, "What's the matter with your *wife*, she got lockjaw?" This sets off a volley of abuse from Alan, who lashes out at Emory, punching him in the face and drawing blood before Hank pulls him away. The first act ends with Harold's arrival and Cowboy's singing of "Happy Birthday" as Michael stands at the bar, lost in thought.

As the second act begins, Alan observes the party from the couch, then suddenly runs upstairs to the bathroom to vomit. The others finish eating dinner and watch Harold open his gifts. Although all members of the group mock each other with sexual comments, Michael's comments take on a bitter tone. When Alan reappears and tries to leave, Michael tells him he has to stay and play a game, "The Affairs of the Heart." As Alan protests weakly, claiming to feel ill, and says he wants to leave, Michael tells the others that Alan really wants to stay, because if he wanted to leave "he'd have left a long time ago." The game requires that each man call on the telephone the one person he truly believes that he has loved. This makes several members of the group flinch, and Hank and Larry argue as Michael details the point system of the game: one point for making the call, two points if the person answers, two points if the caller identifies himself, and five points for saying "I love you" to the person called.

Alan urges Hank to leave with him, motivating Michael to mock Alan and Hank as "the he-men." As Alan repeats his suggestion, Michael reveals that Hank and Larry are lovers, to which a shocked Alan says to Hank, "But . . . but . . . you're married." The others mock Alan's naiveté and label as "quaint" his idea that "if a man is married, then he is automatically heterosexual." As Michael goads them, Bernard and Emory call men whom they have worshiped but not had relationships with, and Hank calls his answering service and leaves the message "I love you" for Larry. Alan listens in disbelief, and Hank says it is true that he loves Larry, for whom he left his wife. He explains how he realized that, despite marriage and children, he somehow knew that he had always been homosexual.

Michael continues to direct cutting remarks to the others, pushing each to make the call, until only Alan is left. He insists that Alan call the person he loves and suggests that the person might be another friend from college, Justin Stuart. Michael claims Justin had an affair with Alan, which Alan denies. Forcing the telephone into Alan's hand, Michael hands him an address book containing Justin's telephone number and watches as Alan dials, but he is surprised to hear that the voice on the telephone is Alan's wife, the person Alan truly loves. As Alan leaves, Harold tells Michael that what he has done this evening was out of self-hatred: "You're a homosexual and you don't want to be. But there is nothing you can do to change it. . . . Until the day you die."

CENSORSHIP HISTORY

The Boys in the Band opened to eager crowds, ran for 1,000 performances, and was made into a hit movie before seeming to disappear for nearly two decades in the United States. The success of the play, which paralleled the emerging gay liberation movement, helped drama that contained homosexual themes and characters to achieve freedom on stage, leading many to agree with *Washington Post* drama critic David Richards that at the time it was "the frankest, fiercest—not to mention funniest—picture of homosexuality ever put on an American stage." After the initial excitement had faded, the play experienced a reversal of fortune as detractors denounced it for portraying the homosexual characters in a negative manner, filled with self-loathing and locked in misery, capable only of bitterness and stinging remarks. Many members of the gay community found the negative portrayals distasteful and distorted. When *The Boys in the Band* was revived in San Francisco in 1990, a protester set up a stand outside the theater and provided theatergoers with tomatoes to pelt the actors with. Playwright Mart Crowley has characterized the self-deprecating humor in the play as "born out of low self-esteem, if you will; from a sense of what the time told you about yourself," a view that has led opponents of its staging to call the play "a homosexual period piece" that is no longer relevant.

Labeling *The Boys in the Band* a "gay-angst classic," theater reviewer Nelson Pressley of *The Washington Post* supported the March 2000 revival of the play at the American Century Theater in Washington, D.C., even though deeming it "an exercise in self-laceration, an artifact from the days before gay pride, thoroughly politically incorrect three decades later." He notes that the grim, even distorted portrayal of gay life in the play with its loveless misery remained "untouchable" in light of the fierce dramatic response to the AIDS crisis, which led to the need for lighter fare such as *La Cage aux Folles* and *Torch Song Trilogy* onstage.

Attempts to censor the play in Australia, however, came not from the gay community but from the vice squad, which labeled the language in the play "obscene." In July 1969 the actors John Krummell, John Norman, and Charles Little were prosecuted in the Melbourne Magistrates' Court with "using obscene language in a public place" as a result of their dialogue in performances of *The Boys in the Band* at the Playbox Theatre in Melbourne. Officers of the Melbourne Vice Squad cited the numerous times that the "f-word" and the "c-word" are spoken in the play. The court dismissed the charges on the grounds that they were "trifling," and the Melbourne Vice Squad then appealed to the Australian Supreme Court. In September 1969 Justice James Little reversed the decision on the grounds that the Australian Federal Parliament took a serious view of the offense and wrote, "In my opinion the offence of obscene language in a public place cannot be regarded as of a trivial or minor nature. . . . The most objectionable word was used by one actor more than once." This was the first time that actors in Australia had been prosecuted for obscenity; in the past, obscenity charges had focused on booksellers, theater and cinema managers, and printers. In this case, as footnote 110 in the 2001 Parliament of Victoria Law Reform Committee report on *The Review of the Theatres Act of 1958* states, although the actors were charged under obscenity laws for their role in the performance, "the play was allowed to continue with no actions being taken under the *Theatres Act*."

The case involving *The Boys in the Band* became an important step in ending Australia's rigid censorship laws, among the Western world's most archaic at the time, because many people were outraged by the prosecution and conviction of

Australian actors for simply saying their lines. On October 30, 1969, 150 actors and supporters marched from the Playbox to the Parliament House in a demonstration organized by Actors' Equity, and they carried a petition bearing 1,000 signatures. People in the streets applauded them, but Victoria chief secretary Sir Arthur Rylah, supporter of the vice squad and empowered by the Theatres Act to ban any theatrical production he deemed necessary, refused to speak with the leaders of the demonstration. Although the decision against the actors remained, observers of the time conclude that the case led to a serious effort by Australian intellectuals to break down the censorship regime. After Rylah retired in 1971, his successor, Dick Hamer, began a liberalization of censorship laws. Censorship was effectively ended soon after by the Whitlam government with Lionel Murphy as customs minister.

FURTHER READING

Barnes, Clive. "Theater Review: *The Boys in the Band.*" *The New York Times*, April 15, 1968, p. C1.

Clum, John M. *Acting Gay: Male Homosexuality in Modern Drama.* New York: Columbia University Press, 1992.

———, ed. *Staging Gay Lives: an Anthology of Contemporary Gay Theater.* Boulder, Colo.: Westview Press, 1995.

Costoupoulos, J. *Homosexuality on the New York Stage: Its Critical Reception, 1926 to 1968.* Doctoral dissertation, New York University, 1986.

Furtado, Ken, and Nancy Hellner. *Gay and Lesbian American Plays: An Annotated Bibliography.* Metuchen, N.J.: Scarecrow Press, 1993.

Hoffman, William M., ed. *Gay Plays: The First Collection.* New York: Avon Books, 1979.

Parliament of Victoria, Law Reform Committee. *Review of The Theatres Act 1958.* Report of No. 82 Session 1999–2001. Melbourne: Government Printer, May 2001.

Pressley, Nelson. "'Band' Still Plays On; The Gay-Angst Classic, Dated but Compelling." *The Washington Post*, March 28, 2000 p. C-05.

Richards, David. "Bringing Back 'The Boys'; Will N.Y. Warm to Crowley's Play." *The Washington Post*, June 16, 1996, p. G-01.

Shewey, Don, ed. *Out Front: Contemporary Gay and Lesbian Plays.* New York: Grove Press, 1988.

Weir, Greg. *Papers of Greg Weir—MS8915. Volume 1: Gay and Lesbian Issues Prior to 1974.* National Library of Australia. Available online. URL: http://www.nla.gov.au/ms/findaids/8915_1.html.

"The Wowsers' Last Stand." *OutRage*, June 1997. Available online. URL: http://www.adam-carr.net/boys.html.

THE BREAKING POINT

Author: Edward Garnett
Original date and place of production: 1907, private performance, London, England

Characters: Agatha, Collins, Miss Dorothea Elwood, Miss Grace Elwood, Professor James Elwood, Mr. Francis Mansell, Mary, Mr. Lewis Sherrington, Mrs. Alice Sherrington
Filmed versions: None

SUMMARY

The Breaking Point examines the tragic results suffered by a young woman who is manipulated by two strong-willed men, her father and her lover. Grace Elwood is 23 years old and the only daughter of Dr. James Elwood, a retired university professor. The two live in their home, Bewlands, with Dorothea Elwood, Elwood's 65-year-old sister, and a maid, Agatha. Living next door in Lutterton Lodge is Lewis Sherrington, 33, and a maid, Mary; Sherrington's wife, Alice, has left him. The drama opens at the Sherrington home as Lewis confides to his friend Mansell, a barrister, that he desperately wants a divorce. The Sherringtons, who "haven't one feeling in common," had been married for three years when Mrs. Sherrington ran off with her husband's friend Danby to live abroad. She has now reappeared and wants to reconcile, but Sherrington explains to Mansell that he must be free to marry: "There's a woman, a girl here. I love her to distraction, and she me. She's given herself to me—she's given me her future—her family know nothing. Do you see? And now it's *necessary* that she should come to me." Mansell questions if marriage is really necessary, and Sherrington admits uncertainty. Grace may be pregnant, but they will not know until after she consults a doctor. Sherrington describes Dr. Elwood as "one of those jealous old men who sacrifice their daughters to themselves" and tells Mansell that the only way he could get Grace away from her domineering father, who knows nothing of the affair, was to place her in a position where she has to choose between them. The barrister is shocked and tells Sherrington that what he has done is wrong. Sherrington has been meeting secretly with Grace for six months and he is "tortured." Her eyes now make him shudder because "she's strained to the breaking-point." Yet he insists that her father is the culprit, and "if *he* keeps me away from her, as he will, it'll kill her slowly."

As the two converse, Alice Sherrington arrives. Her lover, Danby, has died and she wants to return to Sherrington, but he offers her one-third of his money if she will divorce him and go away. She insists that she wants to reconcile, but he is so adamantly against the idea that she suggests he is involved with another woman, which he hotly denies. Alice leaves, promising to continue her efforts. Sherrington meets Grace the following evening and she tells him that the doctor is still not certain, but Sherrington insists that they run away before her father can separate them. Grace asks him not to hurry her, but Sherrington selfishly states that her father does not really love her and that staying is agonizing. The first act ends with Grace begging Sherrington to not force her to choose between him and her father.

In Act II, while Mansell pays a friendly call on the Elwoods and trades archaeological data with Dr. Elwood, Alice Sherrington arrives. She asks Dr. Elwood to persuade her husband to reconcile. When Elwood protests, Alice tells him: "people *are* talking about your daughter Grace and Lewis." After she leaves, Elwood confronts Grace. He tells her that the best course is for the Sherringtons to reconcile and for Grace to stop meeting with Lewis, but Grace refuses. When Mansell returns to Lutterton Lodge, he recommends that Sherrington meet with Elwood and "tell him everything," if he values Grace: "She can't bear any more. She's strained to the breaking-point." Mansell tells Sherrington to speak with Elwood so Grace will not have to choose between them, and Sherrington agrees. When Grace appears moments later, she begs Sherrington to wait until she is certain that she is pregnant, but he insists that they have to think about their child because to him "it *is* certain." She promises to wait in his study until he returns, but she becomes giddy and dazed and wanders out into the night soon after he leaves.

Act III begins as Sherrington forces a meeting with Elwood, telling him that Grace and he "are on terms of the greatest possible intimacy." Elwood seems unable to grasp what he hears and asks Sherrington to explain what he means, calling him a "libertine" when Sherrington states, "She may . . . have a child." Elwood becomes incensed and calls for his gardener to prepare the cart so that he can bring Grace back from Lutterton Lodge, as Sherrington pleads with him to at least appear to be reconciled to set her mind at ease and calm her. Elwood argues that he will never allow Sherrington to marry his daughter nor to even speak with her again. As the two men argue, Collins the gardener taps at the window and tells the men that Grace has fallen into the river and died.

CENSORSHIP HISTORY

The Breaking Point was rejected for licensing by the British stage censors because the drama deals with the possible pregnancy of an unmarried woman who has been the lover of a married man. Although the subject matter is not out of the ordinary, the play is important because of the way in which the author dealt with the rejection and because the author was already making his mark in the publishing world when he wrote the play. He would later gain greater renown as an editor at London publishing house Jonathan Cape for his work with Joseph Conrad, Leo Tolstoy, D. H. Lawrence, and other literary giants. The official banning of the play from London stages did not prevent large numbers of people from becoming familiar with the play through private performances and by reading the published version. Still, the action drew attention for several reasons. Rather than put his play aside, Garnett published it with Duckworth the same year, complete with a preface that fiercely denounces the censor and with an openly condemnatory letter to the examiner of plays, George Alexander Redford, Esq. In addition, 71 members of the London literary world, including George Bernard Shaw, J. M. Barrie,

Arthur Pinero, and Joseph Conrad, signed and sent a letter to Britain's theatrical censor to protest the banning and to condemn "an office autocratic in procedure, opposed to the spirit of the Constitution, contrary to justice and common sense." Such actions were startling to British censors because many British playwrights and theater managers in the late 19th and early 20th century submissively followed the procedure outlined by Colonel Sir Douglas Dawson, comptroller of the Lord Chamberlain's department:

> Let the author submit his play through the manager within a reasonable time; if any alterations appear necessary to the Censor, the manager can, if he and the author choose, smooth over the difficulties privately with the Examiner beforehand; or, failing this, it may be arranged when submitted to the Lord Chamberlain and Comptroller, in which case the play is assured production; or, if the negotiations are futile, it is refused and no one need be any wiser.

In essence, playwrights and theater managers were expected to submit plays before planning performances and to accept decisions stoically, grateful that the decisions were made privately and without publicity. The usual practice was that the Lord Chamberlain's office would suggest to a manager about to produce an objectionable play that he had better not apply for a license. Most managers and playwrights complied in order to avoid embarrassment and entanglement with the government, and the examiner of plays was absolved of any need to exert powers to censor.

Edward Garnett, however, was not so amiable when he learned that Frederic Harrison, the manager of the Haymarket Theatre in London where the play was to debut in 1907, had been refused a license for performance. He wrote to Redford and asked the reason for the veto. He received the following reply, which fails to mention any specific criticism and suggests that Garnett ask the theater manager.

> 5th July 1907
>
> Dear Sir,—I trust you will absolve me from any discourtesy if I point out that my official relations are only concerned with the managers of theatres. It is always painful to me to decline to recommend a licence, and in this case I hoped to avoid any possible appearance of censure on anyone by suggesting privately to Mr. Harrison the desirability of withdrawing this piece. I cannot suppose that he has any doubt as to the reason.—I am, dear sir, yours faithfully,
>
> G. A. R.

In Garnett's openly printed response to the censor, which he also included in the publication of the play, he challenged the censor's right to keep his play from being performed and questioned the motives of the censor in refusing to speak directly with the playwright.

> . . . you are simply trying to ensure silent acquiescence in your verdict. In how many cases you find this device successful I cannot say; but with me it has not

succeeded. . . . Is it possible you really imagine that any intelligent person feels the slightest stigma in your disapproval, or would be at the smallest pains to conceal from the world the fact of having incurred it?

Garnett charged that the censors were not attacking the play as immoral; the play was banned, he claimed, because it was too tragic and did "not give our middle-class public pleasure." After writing that the office and the manner in which Redford exercised his office were "out-of-date and ridiculous," Garnett asked, once again, the reason for the censor "declining to recommend a licence" for the play. In the appendix preceding the published play, in lieu of a censor, Garnett called for the formation of a Society for the Defence of Intellectual Drama, consisting of "a score of our leading critics and others, with a General Council consisting of as many literary men and lovers of the drama . . . whose verdict on any piece of intellectual drama suppressed by the Censor would carry great weight with the press and thoughtful people." Although such a society did not come into being, the outcry against the banning of both *The Breaking Point* and Harley Granville-Barker's *WASTE* in 1907 led Parliament to establish the Joint Select Committee on Censorship in 1909. The proceedings, which contained the testimony of 49 literary luminaries, among them William S. Gilbert, Arthur Pinero, G. K. Chesterton, Henry James, and George Bernard Shaw, sought to clarify the role of the censor and to create standards for theater managers and playwrights. The committee concluded in a 500,000-word report that submission of plays for review and licensing would be optional, but that theater managers would have to accept the risk of prosecution for plays that the director of public prosecutions or the attorney general found indecent or guilty of graver offenses. The report also recommended that the censor would be expected to license for performance all plays that were not judged:

1) to be indecent;
2) to contain offensive personalities;
3) to represent on stage in an invidious manner a living person or a person recently dead;
4) to do violence to the sentiment of religious reverence;
5) to be calculated to conduce to crime or vice;
6) to be calculated to impair friendly relations with any foreign power;
7) to be calculated to cause a breach of the peace.

Any play determined by the courts to violate the standards would be banned and would not be reassessed for 10 years. The report also recommended that the Lord Chamberlain be given the sole responsibility for granting licenses.

The Joint Select Committee on Censorship (1909) engaged in extensive debate and made sweeping recommendations, but no actual changes in English censorship practices occurred because the government failed to implement the suggestions contained in the report. Thus, *The Breaking Point* was instrumental in initiating protest against censorship, but the system under which Garnett's play was censored remained intact until 1968.

FURTHER READING

Conrad, Joseph. *Letters from Conrad, 1895 to 1924.* Edited with an Introduction and Notes by Edward Garnett. London: Nonesuch Press, 1928.

Elsom, John. *Erotic Theatre.* New York: Taplinger Publishing Co., 1974.

Fowell, Frank, and Frank Palmer. *Censorship in England.* London: F. Palmer, 1913. Reprint, New York: Benjamin Bloom, 1969.

Garnett, Edward. *The Breaking Point: A Censured Play with Preface and a Letter to the Censor.* London: Duckworth & Co., 1907.

———. "The Censorship of Public Opinion." *Fortnightly Review* 86 (July 1909): 137–148.

Godden, Gertrude M. *The Stage Censor, an Historical Sketch: 1544–1907.* London: Sampson Low, Marston, 1908.

Jefferson, George. *Edward Garnett: A Life in Literature.* London: Jonathan Cape, 1982.

THE CAPEMAN

Authors: Paul Simon and Derek Walcott
Original date and place of production: January 29, 1998, Marquis Theater, New York, New York
Characters: Aurea Agron, Esmeralda Agron, Salvador Agron, Carlos Apache, Bernadette, Cookie, Frenchy Cordero, Babu Cruz, Doo Wop Group, Reverend Gonzalez, Tony Hernandez, Mrs. Krzesinski, Lazarus, Santero, Angel Soto, Wahzinak, Warden, Yolanda, Mrs. Young
Filmed versions: None

SUMMARY

The Capeman is a musical based on the life of Salvador (Salvi) Agron, who, as a 16-year-old member of a gang named the Vampires, was sentenced to death in New York City in 1959 after knifing to death two teenagers whom he had mistaken for rival gang members. Reporters gave him the nickname "the Capeman," because on the night of the murders he wore a black-and-red cape that he later said had made him feel like the king of the vampires. Agron was the youngest person in New York state history to be sentenced to die in the electric chair. After all the publicity surrounding the case, the execution did not happen, because Eleanor Roosevelt and others sympathetic to Agron's age and difficult life convinced then-governor Nelson Rockefeller to commute the sentence in 1962. The musical begins 20 years after Agron's conviction, in 1979, just after he has been released from prison. Shown standing on a street corner, Agron views with amazement the Puerto Rican Day parade, the gaiety and color of which contrast so sharply with the images of his past in which he and his friends lived without status on the margins of society. He visits the site of the murders and holds above his head a "book of remembrance" that bears witness to all that he has been through and sets the scene for an extended flashback to his past. The scene shifts to Mayagüez, Puerto Rico, where in the early 1950s the boy Salvador, his sister Aurea, mother, Esmeralda, and father, Gumersindo, live. When Agron's father leaves, his mother takes her children to a convent for care, but the nuns are harsh to them and tie the little boy down on an anthill when he wets his pants, so his mother removes her children by force. Afterward she consults the santero, a thrower of shells who sees into the future, to find out what will become of her children. A vision of St. Lazarus rising from the dead appears to Esmeralda and speaks to her, telling her that a red-and-black cape, an umbrella, a knife, and murder will be her son's fate if they leave the island, but eventually her child will find a life-restoring rainfall.

The scene switches to New York City in 1959, with sounds of street singing in the background. The teenage Agron is interested in making Bernadette his girlfriend, but local tough Tony Hernandez, nicknamed the Umbrellaman, goads him to join a neighborhood gang, the Vampires, or risk getting hurt. Agron resists until he is cornered one night and beaten badly by a gang of Italian-American youths. When he returns home, Reverend Gonzalez, his stepfather, also beats him to keep him in line. Bereft of support, Agron joins what he now considers his "real" family, the Vampires, and moves into their poolhall home. He shoplifts, picking up a cape among other items. After Hernandez's brother is beaten by rival gang members, the Vampires set out for revenge. At a playground, the gang surrounds and pins down two teenagers, later found to be innocent bystanders with no gang connections, as Agron knifes them to death. The stage fills with sirens and an angry crowd, as the Capeman escapes to the rooftops. When he is arrested a few days later, as the spirit of Lazarus stands in the background, he shouts at reporters the same words used by the real-life Agron, "I don't care if I fry. My mother can watch me burn." After a brief trial scene, the convicted Agron and Hernandez are led away in shackles. Act I ends in 1962, as Aurea reads in a newspaper that the governor has commuted Agron's death sentence.

Act II, which opens with Esmeralda praying that Agron will keep his Bible near him and endure the years ahead, deals mainly with the years that Agron spent in various prisons, from 1963 to 1976. He is shown teaching himself to read and write properly and studying the Bible. He begins to write the story of his life. When he is transferred to the Fishkill (New York) penitentiary, he receives a letter from an Arizona woman named Wahzinak, who has read about him in the prison paper, and he is inspired to apply to take college courses outside the prison. His record as an inmate is spotless, so he expects to be paroled at the age of 32. Five months before he is due to be paroled, Agron escapes from prison by going to the bus station rather than to his college courses when the prison bus drops him off. Onboard a Trailways bus en route to Tucson, he sits next to a haggard-looking Lazarus, who is toting a backpack. Wandering across the desert the next morning, Agron has a vision in which he sees images of his childhood and of the murders, yet protests his innocence. Lazarus demands that he confess his guilt and reminds him of the arrogance that he showed when arrested. Agron turns himself in to the authorities, and three years are added to his prison time.

The scene returns to the 1979 Puerto Rican Day parade. Agron tries to enjoy the welcome-home party afterward but cannot. He goes home to Esmeralda, the two cry, and he confesses to her, telling her, "I alone must bear the blame for the madness that was done. I and I alone." He then shows her the manuscript that contains his life story, and she tells him, "It is repentance that makes good from evil."

CENSORSHIP HISTORY

The production of *The Capeman* ran from January 29 through March 28, 1998, marked by demonstrations and protests staged by relatives of the two boys Agron killed and by the group Parents of Murdered Children. As well, the play also faced public relations problems motivated by Broadway professionals who were upset by rock musician Paul Simon's audacity at staging an original theater production. Writing for *American Theatre* magazine, James Oseland expressed a feeling similar to that of others who later defended the play. He approached the show with discomfort ("I had been informed by everyone who should know—a very trusted friend had seen it, every review I had read—that the show was one of the worst to hit the Broadway boards in years," he said) but he stayed for the complete performance and "forgot all the venomous hype and was seduced."

Those who demonstrated against the musical were not won over. The protests began with the first preview of the play on December 1, 1997. Carrying signs bearing such statements as "Our Loss is Simon's Gain," relatives of Agron's victims demonstrated quietly in front of the Marriott Marquis Theater. Kim Erker, the cousin of one of Agron's victims, Robert Young, demanded that her cousin's murder should not be entertainment. She told an Associated Press reporter, "There's a million stories in New York City, why pick this one? You don't do a murder musical to jumpstart your career. Would Paul Simon do this if his son was murdered?" The following day, the cable network E! reported, "It's believed, though, that the protests have only just begun. The PR wars, for one, ignited last week, when an appearance by members of *The Capeman* at the star-crossed Macy's Thanksgiving Day Parade drew criticism from victims' families." On opening night, Donna Krzesinski, the sister of the second of Agron's victims, Tony Krzesinski, joined Kim Erker and dozens of others to protest what they called an exploitation of their tragedy. Erker stopped celebrities attending the premiere and urged them to boycott the play, which they politely refused to do. New York City members of the Cincinnati-based group Parents of Murdered Children (POMC) organized their own demonstration of about 60 people marching in protest. In November 1998 the Murder Is Not Entertainment (MINE) arm of the POMC online newsletter reported that "POMC protested this play portraying the life of a murderer, and after one [sic] month, the play was closed down."

The play was also said to have been driven off the stage by the negative reviews written by many leading theater reviewers, whose words exacerbated the technical difficulties that plagued *The Capeman* and its first-time producer, Paul Simon. As Otis Guernsey Jr. wrote in *The Plays of 1997–1998*, "To be fair, the press had their knives out long before the first preview. Simon, one of pop music's most bankable commodities, made the mistake of telling interviewers he wanted to do the show his way and not fall into the glitz and fakery that, for better or worse, make most Broadway musicals go. . . . What the press saw was a pop star who had never done a musical before thumbing his nose at a tight community of legends who put their reputations on the line every opening night." The press highlighted failings in the show that might have been excused in a producer who paid more homage to Broadway, overshadowing the ingenuity of the sets, the vibrance of the salsa music, and the freshness of Simon's approach to staging the musical. For the most part, those critics who defended the musical admitted that it was a failure, but they agreed that reports labeling the play an unmitigated disaster were untrue and due largely to Simon's shunning of the theater establishment. Margaret Spillane, in a theater review for *The Progressive*, wrote that "the New York showbiz press corps" worked to "crush" the musical because they feared the prospect of dealing with the difficult material of the story itself: The causes of violent crime among poor teenagers, the relationships between criminals and their victims' survivors, the practice of putting adolescents on death row, and the now-forgotten goals of rehabilitation at a time when politicians label such people as "superpredators."

FURTHER READING

Brantley, Ben. "The Lure of Gang Violence to a Latin Beat." *The New York Times*, January 30, 1998, p. E1.

Gonzalez, David. "As New Musical Opens, So Do Old Wounds; Families of Murder Victims Protest Paul Simon's Tale of a Killer." *The New York Times*, January 31, 1998, p. A13.

Guernsey, Otis, Jr., ed. *The Best Plays of 1997–1998*. New York: Limelight Editions, 1998.

Jacoby, Richard. *Conversations with the Capeman: The Untold Story of Salvador Agron*. New York: Painted Leaf Press, 2000.

McQueen, Anjetta. "Protest at *Capeman* Premiere." *The Washington Post*, January 30, 1998, p. D05.

"Murder Is Not Entertainment (MINE)." Available online. URL: http://www.pomc.com/mine.cfm.

Oseland, James. "Defending *The Capeman*." *American Theatre* (April 1998): 31.

Rabinowitz, Dorothy. "Audience Verdict on *Capeman:* Gallows at Last." *The Wall Street Journal*, March 27, 1998, p. W11.

Ryan, Joal. "Paul Simon's *Capeman* over Troubled Waters." E! Online News. December 2, 1997. Available online. URL: http://www.eonline.com/News/Items/Pf/0,1,2169,00.html.

Span, Paula. "The Sound of Violence; Paul Simon's *Capeman* Roils Troubled Waters of the Past." *The Washington Post*, January 4, 1998, p. G01.

Spillane, Margaret. "*The Capeman:* Theatre Review." *The Progressive* (June 1998): 36–37.

Zoglin, Richard. "Seeking Salvation for *The Capeman.*" *Time*, February 2, 1998, pp. 70–72.

THE CAPTIVE

Author: Edouard Bourdet

Original date and place of production: 1926, Thêâtre Fémina, Paris, France (as *La Prisonnière)*, September 26, 1929, Empire Theatre, New York, New York

Characters: Madame D'Aiguines, Monsieur Georges D'Aiguines, François Meillant, Gisèle de Montcel, Irène de Montcel, Jacques Virieu

Filmed versions: None

SUMMARY

The Captive, translated from Edouard Bourdet's French drama *La Prisonnière* and adapted for the Broadway stage by Arthur Hornblow Jr., was the first major stage production in the United States to contain a lesbian theme. The play opens with the heroine, Irène de Montcel, in discussion with her father, who wants to learn why his formerly amiable daughter now refuses to leave Paris and accompany him on a trip to Rome. Suspecting that she is under someone's malevolent influence, he has planned the trip to take his daughter away from what he sees to be her downfall if she stays. To calm his fears, Irène lies: She tells Monsieur de Montcel that she has fallen in love with Jacques Virieu and that she cannot bear to be apart from him. Therefore, she wants to stay in Paris in order to remain near her love. Jacques knows that Irène does not love him, but he does love her. To protect her, he pretends that what she tells her father is the truth while he tries to think of a way to capture her love from the man whom he believes that she really loves, and with whom he believes that she is having an affair, Monsieur Georges Aiguines. When Jacques confronts his supposed rival with these suspicions, he is stunned to learn that the love affair is actually between Irène and Madame Aiguines. A shaken Jacques tells Irène that he knows all about her "unnatural passion" and illicit affair, and the distraught young woman pleads with him to help her to overcome her desires. They decide to marry and to avoid all contact with Madame Aiguines. After they return from the honeymoon, Jacques seems to grow distant and to exhibit increasing discontent with the marriage. His emotional remoteness leaves Irène feeling abandoned and makes her vulnerable to the advances of Madame Aiguines. The affair begins again, but Irène fears the social disapproval of such an "unnatural desire" and eventually leaves Madame Aiguines. In the final act, the women end their relationship by exchanging a bunch of violets meant to symbolize the purity and poignancy of their love.

CENSORSHIP HISTORY

The Captive ran for 160 performances at the Empire Theatre before the New York City district attorney's office yielded to the pressure exerted by censorship advocates and closed the play on February 27, 1927. The production starred Helen Menken, then-wife of actor Humphrey Bogart, as Irène, and Basil Rathbone, later famous for his Shakespearean stage roles and for playing Sherlock Holmes in numerous films. When the play was closed, both were arrested, along with the rest of the cast, and charged with offending public morals. Rathbone later told interviewers that *The Captive* was "a great play" that "addressed an issue important to society" and that it was "something people needed to know about." The day after the police raided the play, the management of the Empire Theatre agreed to close the show and to dismiss the actors and producers associated with *The Captive*. The production director, Gilbert Miller, tried to gain support for a legal challenge from the Famous Players-Lasky Motion Picture Company, which had a controlling interest in all of the plays that he produced. Unwilling to risk negative publicity, the company refused Miller's request and demanded that the play remain closed. Later that year, as a response to agitation that had occurred for censorship of *The Captive* and two other plays, SEX and *The Virgin Man*, as well as concern that Mae West was currently directing out-of-town pre-Broadway tryouts for her play *Drag*, New York State passed the Wales Padlock Law, named for Senator B. Roger Wales, who sponsored the bill in the state legislature. Through the bill, New York officials gained the authority to arrest and prosecute producers and actors involved in "an immoral drama," defined by the legislature when it amended the public obscenity code to include a ban on any play "depicting or dealing with the subject of sex degeneracy, or sex perversion." The law also placed pressure on theater owners, forcing them to act as censors in their own establishments, for it specified that if the producers were convicted, the theater in which the play had been performed would be padlocked for a year. The New York City book publisher Horace Liveright acquired production rights to the play after its initial suppression, and appealed to the court for an injunction to prevent the play from being closed again if he produced it. The request was denied, and the play was kept from the stage until the repeal of the Wales Padlock Law in 1967.

J. Brooks Atkinson, theater critic for *The New York Times*, reviewed *The Captive* on September 30, 1926, and reported that many men viewed with horror the "twisted relationship" of the woman-to-woman love in the play, adding that it was perceived as a "warped infatuation" that was "loathsome and doomed." He praised Bourdet's handling of the topic, writing that less sensitivity in the playwright would have produced a work that would "degenerate into commercial exploitation of a revolting theme."

The fear with which middle-class Americans viewed the subject matter of *The Captive* showed in another, less expected, result, as the actions of the female characters at the end of the play dealt the violet industry a serious blow. In the final act, the characters end their relationship by exchanging a bunch of violets. In Paris, lesbian groups in the audience showed solidarity by pinning violets to their lapels and belts, but in America, this treatment of forbidden sexual issues was greeted with hesitance. When the New York police shut down the theater for scandalous behavior, the often-seen, innocent violets that had been carried by debutantes and various First Ladies, as well as by female celebrities seeking to display their innocence, suddenly lost favor. As *Harper's Bazaar* wrote in "The Story of Violets" in November 1934, "Way back in the violet county last year they were still cursing this play as the knell of the violet industry."

Repercussions of the banning were to be felt in later decades. Playwright Lillian Hellman revealed in an interview published in 1989 that producers felt apprehensive about her 1934 play THE CHILDREN'S HOUR.

> The play has nothing to do with lesbianism, of course; it's just one of the side issues. It's just the charge of the girl. But Mr. Shumlin, the producer, was very worried; everybody was very worried, because a play called *The Captive*, a French play, had played in New York a few years before and had been closed up by the police department. So we took every precaution.

FURTHER READING

Albert, Timothy Dow. "Sweetest Smelling Baby in New Orleans." *Conversations with Lillian Hellman*. Jackson, Mississippi: University Press of Mississippi, 1986.

"The American Theatre and the Censors." *Life*, May 2, 1937, p. A170.

Jessen, Marcia. "The Life of Basil Rathbone." Available online. URL: http://www.basilrathbone.net/biography. 2003.

Beredjiklian, Norma. "The Violets of Dutchess County." *The Violet Gazette* (Autumn 2000): V1-4, P3.

Bourdet, Edouard. *The Captive*. Translated from the French by Arthur Hornblow, Jr., with an introduction by J. Brooks Atkinson. New York: Brentano's, 1926.

Chauncey, George. *Gay New York*. New York: Basic Books, 1994.

Eggert, Andrew. "Captivating *The Captive*." *Off-off Broadway Reviews*. Available online. URL: http://www.oobr.com/top/volFour/twelve/captive.html.

Katz, Jonathan. *Gay/Lesbian Almanac*. New York: Harper & Row, 1983.

Laufe, Abe. *The Wicked Stage: A History of Theater Censorship and Harassment in the United States*. New York: Frederick Ungar, 1978.

Ricketts, Wendell. "Lesbians and Gay Men on Stage: A Necessarily Incomplete History." In *Out in All Directions: The Almanac of Lesbian and Gay America*. Edited by L. Witt, S. Thomas, and E. Marcus. New York: Warner Books, 1995.

Summers, Claude J. *The Gay and Lesbian Literary Heritage.* New York: Henry Holt, 1995.

Taylor, Leslie A. "Veritable Hotheads: Lesbian Scandals in the United States," *American Studies* (May 1998): 287–295.

CAT ON A HOT TIN ROOF

Author: Tennessee Williams

Original date and place of production: March 24, 1955, Morosco Theatre, New York, New York

Characters: Doctor Baugh, Big Daddy Pollitt, Big Mama Pollitt, Brick Pollitt, Children, Dixie Pollitt, Gooper (sometimes called Brother Man) Pollitt, Lacey, Mae (sometimes called Sister Woman) Pollitt, Margaret (Maggie) Pollitt, Sokey, Reverend Tooker

Filmed versions: *Cat on a Hot Tin Roof* (1958); *Cat on a Hot Tin Roof* (1976, U.K., made for television); *Cat on a Hot Tin Roof* (1985, U.S., made for television)

SUMMARY

Cat on a Hot Tin Roof is a play in three acts set in the 1950s with action occurring mainly in one room of a plantation home situated on "the biggest estate in the [Mississippi] Delta." Brothers Brick and Gooper have brought their families to the estate to celebrate the 65th birthday of their father, Big Daddy, who has been ill but believes that he is getting better. Only his sons and their wives know that Big Daddy is dying of cancer, and they have not told Big Mama. The childless couple, Brick and Maggie, are goaded frequently by Gooper and Mae, whose five unruly children run all over the house. The first act opens with Maggie rushing into her bedroom to change clothes, because "one of those no-neck monsters hit me with a hot buttered biscuit." As Maggie complains about Brick's five obnoxious nephews and nieces, Brick provides only perfunctory remarks from offstage before he appears to the audience, a handsome and charming man, former football star and sports announcer who has retreated into a haze of alcohol. He is drinking, and he is wearing a cast and walking with the aid of a crutch, having broken his ankle. The first act is mainly a monologue spoken by the beautiful but nervous Maggie, who complains about the children, speaks about Big Daddy's cancer, and suggests that Gooper and Mae have produced children simply to ensure that they will inherit the estate. The irony is that Maggie truly loves Big Daddy for his honesty in dealing with people, and he loves her vivacity. Big Daddy also favors Brick over Gooper, but he knows that Brick's drinking, irresponsible nature, and childless marriage would make it hard to justify leaving Brick control of the estate. Unable to decide, Big Daddy has not made out a will.

Maggie's monologue grows in intensity until she reaches the subject that Brick has made taboo: his late friend Skipper, also a football hero, whose friendship with Brick threatened Maggie's married contentment. Long ago, Maggie had confronted Skipper and charged him with having "unnatural feelings" for Brick. One night, she drank extensively with Skipper, then gave him the chance to prove that he was heterosexual by offering to sleep with him, but he refused. From that point, Skipper's life had disintegrated into drug and alcohol abuse until he died. Embittered by his friend's death, Brick accuses Maggie of "dirtying" his friendship, "the one great true thing" in his life.

One of the nieces barges into the room and taunts Brick and Maggie for having no children, which makes Maggie beg Brick to make love with her and to conceive a child, because she is in her fertile time of the month. Angered by her demand, Brick shouts at her, "How in hell on earth do you imagine— that you're going to have a child by a man that can't stand you?" Maggie responds, "That's a problem that I will have to work out."

In the second act, Big Daddy enters with the family. Big and coarse, he is a one-time farmer who worked on the plantation for years and inherited it from its former owners, Jack Straw and Peter Ochello, two lifelong bachelors who were openly homosexual. Big Daddy's respect for his former employers and his experiences traveling the country as a hobo have given him a tolerance for all kinds of behavior. Disgusted by the scheming of Gooper and Mae, he tries to talk with Brick, who continues to drink until Big Daddy pulls away his crutch and demands to know why Brick drinks. Although Brick ignores his questions, Big Daddy continues to probe. He says he knows that Brick's drinking began with Skipper's death. Brick angrily accuses Big Daddy of thinking "Skipper and me were a pair of dirty old men? . . . fucking sissies? Queer?" Brick then protests that their friendship was "a pure an' true thing an' that's not normal" in a mendacious world. He reveals that Skipper had telephoned him long distance just before his death and confessed drunkenly to his feelings, and that Brick had hung up on him. Big Daddy tells Brick that the disgust he feels "is disgust with yourself," to which Brick replies, "It is Skipper's truth," only to hear Big Daddy chastise him and tell him, "His truth, okay! But you wouldn't face it with him!" Brick becomes incensed and reveals that Big Daddy is dying from cancer, "You told *me!* I told *you!*" Big Daddy turns on his heel and walks out, muttering and cursing "all lying dying liars."

In the third act the family tells Big Mama about the cancer diagnosis. Gooper and Mae try to convince her to sign legal papers that would place trusteeship for the estate into their hands, but she surprises them with her vehement refusal to discuss it. Ignoring Gooper and Mae, Big Mama tells Brick and Maggie that Big Daddy would be very proud if "you gave him a child of yours." As Brick remains silent, Maggie boldly looks at her mother-in-law and announces that she and Brick are going to have a child. As Big Mama rushes joyfully to tell Big Daddy, Mae screams that Maggie is lying; she has eavesdropped on their arguments and knows that Brick has rejected Maggie's sexual advances. When Maggie and Brick return to their room, she thanks him for supporting her lie and tells him that they will make the lie come true tonight. She has taken all of Brick's liquor bottles out of the room and she throws his crutch out of reach, promising that after they make love, they will get drunk together in that room, "this place that death has come into." As Brick submits to her wishes, she gently holds him, cradling him in her arms. She tells Brick how greatly she loves him, to which he replies, "Wouldn't it be funny if that was true?"

The play as Williams originally wrote it ended with that line, but Elia Kazan, director of the stage production, convinced the playwright to rewrite the ending to bring Big Daddy back on stage. Thus, in the alternate ending that is most often used in staging the play, the family gathers in the living room to give Big Daddy his birthday presents. Big Mama praises the cashmere robe that Brick has given, and Maggie kneels before Big Daddy's chair to tell him that her birthday present is the news that "A child is coming, sired by Brick, and out of Maggie the Cat!" In the face of Mae's protests, Big Daddy touches Maggie and says, "This girl has life in her body. That's no lie." Brick supports Maggie's assertion and, when they return to their bedroom, even expresses his admiration for her when he sees her take his liquor and crutch out of reach. As she turns out the light, she tells him that she will return life and love to him. The play ends as she gently touches his cheek and states, "I'm determined to do it—and nothing's more determined than a cat on a tin roof—is there? Is there, baby?"

CENSORSHIP HISTORY

Cat on a Hot Tin Roof won both the Pulitzer Prize and the Drama Critics' Circle Award for the 1954–55 season, and ran for 694 performances on Broadway, but performances of the play have ignited controversy in the United States and in England. Longtime theater critic John Gassner wrote in 1960 that he had little to say about *Cat on a Hot Tin Roof* "except to acknowledge that its vivid characterizing power makes most playwrights look like anemic pygmies . . . [but] if Williams had anything of consequence to say in his family drama he did not manage to get it across." Gould described the play as "blatant with vulgarity," yet approved that it "blares out in praise of the vim and vigor of a healthy sex life." *Cat on a Hot Tin Roof* contained subject matter and language that were risqué for the conservative 1950s, and the dialogue is decidedly frank as the characters discuss homosexuality, greed, and sexual desire. When the play was awarded the Pulitzer Prize, many members of the theater establishment expressed shock and recalled the controversy that had emerged in 1925 when Hamlin Garland, the senior member of the Pulitzer Prize committee, had refused to recommend *WHAT PRICE GLORY?* because of its earthy language, despite the support of two Pulitzer jurors. He pressured them to vote instead for Sidney Howard's *They Knew What They Wanted*. Although the Pulitzer Prize committee accepted the language of *Cat on a Hot Tin Roof*, critics were less tolerant, and several suggested that the story could easily be told and the realism maintained without the rough dialogue. In a review for the *New York Daily News*, critic John Chapman condemned Williams's dialogue and wrote, "the considerable amount of dirty talk in it was mere boyish bravado and rather pointless." The language in the play led to difficulties with the authorities in New York City two weeks after the play opened. Edward T. McCaffrey, commissioner of licenses, received complaints from numerous individuals but took specific action only after the Children's Aid Society lodged a complaint with his office that the children in the cast were being exposed to "vulgar language" and "unhealthy suggestions" in the play. The commissioner attended the play, then conferred backstage with directors to determine the impact of the language on the child cast members. McCaffrey identified specific passages that he and the Children's Aid Society had found to contain objectionable language, and the directors assured him that the children remained in their dressing rooms while the identified dialogue was spoken on stage.

Although McCaffrey was assured that the children were protected, he demanded that directors cut one off-color joke from the play, claiming that it was gratuitous and added nothing to the action. The directors complied. The joke, which appears in Act III after Brick and Big Daddy have completed their intense discussion regarding Skipper, serves to further underscore Big Daddy's earthy nature. As he tells the joke, he uses Brick as his straight man, asking him at intervals, "Ain't that a nice way to put it, Brick?" and "Ain't I tellin' this story in decent language, Brick?" to which Brick replies at one point, "Yes, sir, too fuckin' decent!" The joke concerns a young married couple who take their son to the zoo on a Sunday to look at the animals. They see "this ole bull elephant" who is caged next to a female elephant in heat, and the bull "had somethin' else on his mind which was bigger'n peanuts." The joke describes the manner in which the bull, which "still had a couple of fornications left in him," begins to butt his head against the cage and "there was a conspicuous change in his *profile*—very *conspicuous!*" When the little boy asks his parents about the elephant's physiological change, "His mama said, 'Oh, that's—nothin'!—His papa said, 'She's just spoiled!'" McCaffrey also asked that Brick's use of slang regarding homosexuality be edited out, changes with which the directors also complied.

The play ran into greater difficulty with censors in London the following year, because public discussion of the subject of homosexuality was still largely unacceptable, especially on stage. The Lord Chamberlain, still in control of the licensing of plays for performance on the public stage, refused to grant *Cat on a Hot Tin Roof* a license for performance, so the producers staged the play at club theaters, among them the Comedy Theatre in Piccadilly Circus in London, which opened in 1881 specializing in comic opera but became a private club in the 1950s to avoid the prevailing tendency toward censorship. Such clubs provided private performances for members only.

FURTHER READING

Bloom, Harold, ed. *Tennessee Williams: Modern Critical Views.* New York: Chelsea House, 1987.

Gassner, John. *Theatre at the Crossroads: Plays and Playwrights of the Mid-Century American Stage*. New York: Holt, Rinehart and Winston, 1960.

Gould, Jean. *Modern American Playwrights*. New York: Dodd, Mead, 1966.

Laufe, Abe. *The Wicked Stage: A History of Theater Censorship and Harassment in the United States*. New York: Frederick Ungar Publishing Co., 1978.

Williams, Tennessee. *Cat on a Hot Tin Roof*. New York: New Directions Publishing, 1975.

THE CENCI

Author: Percy Bysshe Shelley

Original date and place of production: May 7, 1886, Shelley Society (private), Grand Theatre, Islington, England

Characters: Andrea, Cardinal Camillo, Beatrice Cenci, Bernardo Cenci, Count Francesco Cenci, Giacomo Cenci, Lucretia Cenci, Marzio, Olimpio, Orsino, Savella

Filmed versions: None

SUMMARY

The Cenci, a drama in verse set in Rome in 1599, is based upon events concerning the powerful Cenci family. Completed in 1819 and dedicated to Shelley's fellow writer Leigh Hunt, Esq., the drama begins with a preface in which the playwright relates that the source of the play is a manuscript given to him while he traveled in Italy, "which was copied from the archives of the Cenci Palace at Rome, and contains a detailed account of the horrors which ended in the extinction of one of the noblest and richest families of that city, during the Pontificate of Clement VIII, in the year 1599." Shelley sets the action of the play mainly in Rome, but Act IV moves to Castle Petrella in the Apulian Apennines. The play opens in the Palace Cenci, where Count Francesco Cenci and Cardinal Camillo discuss the price that Cenci will pay for Camillo to intercede with Pope Clement so that a murder Cenci committed will be covered up. While the pope has said of Cenci, "you / Bought perilous impunity with your gold," he has also indicated that the matter will be absolved if Cenci turns over a choice of property to the pope's nephew, who has already had architects out to survey the land. As Camillo speaks to Cenci of their long association, he reveals Cenci's brutish nature: Cenci has moved from "dark and fiery youth" to "desperate and remorseless manhood." The cardinal also asks Cenci why he has secluded his wife Lucretia and "barred from all society" his daughter Beatrice, a question to which Cenci responds with a threat. Once Camillo leaves, Cenci thinks in anger of his sons, whom the pope has ordered him to provide for, and whom he hopes will meet with fatal accidents as they travel from Rome to Salamanca—to spare him further expenses for them. The scene ends with Cenci's prayer, "God, send some quick death upon them!"

Beatrice then appears and speaks with the priest Orsino, her former lover, and begs him to petition the pope to release him from his vows and to rescue her. Although Orsino promises her that he will, he actually intends to maintain his place in the church and take advantage of her dependence on him to benefit from the Cenci fortune, viewing her as "a friendless girl/Who clings to me, as her only hope."

The castle soon buzzes with activity as Cenci calls his servants to prepare a joyous feast and to invite guests to celebrate with him, for God has answered his prayers. As the guests assemble, he hands Beatrice a letter and demands that she read it to Lucretia, then gloats to his guests: "My disobedient and rebellious sons/Are dead." Both have been killed in accidents that same day, one crushed by a falling church ceiling and the other stabbed in a case of mistaken identity. The incredulous guests show sympathy for Beatrice, who begs them to stay for her sake and that of Lucretia, but everyone leaves. Act I ends with Cenci drinking wine and planning a foray into his daughter's bedroom after midnight.

Act II opens with Beatrice's hopes destroyed by the return of her unopened petition to the pope, and she becomes unnerved, although Lucretia reminds Beatrice that she has been the strength for them all, "our refuge and defence," and must continue so. Orsino never submitted the petition to the pope, knowing that it would make Beatrice depend more upon him.

The opening scene of Act III portrays a traumatized Beatrice, who is staggering and speaking incoherently. After pouring out her torment to Lucretia and Orsino, she vows to murder her father. Seeing an opportunity to place the women in his debt, Orsino offers to contact "two dull, fierce outlaws" to carry out the plan. Beatrice's remaining brothers, Giacomo—who was cheated out of his wife's dowry and land by Cenci—and Bernardo, agree. The murder is planned for the following day when Cenci will transport Lucretia and Beatrice to the even more secluded Castle Petrella. The murder attempt is unsuccessful, however, and when Lucretia pleads with Cenci to leave Beatrice alone, he tells her that he hopes Beatrice becomes pregnant many times over so that she will be continuously tormented by images of herself surrounding her. Lucretia drugs his wine so he falls asleep before he can visit Beatrice. Olimpio and Marzio, two palace servants who have been wronged by Cenci, have agreed to assassinate him, but when they find him asleep, they demur because he looks so old and frail. After they return to Beatrice and she taunts them, the servants return and strangle Cenci, then receive their rewards of gold pieces. As the murderers leave, Savella, a legal envoy from Pope Clement, appears with a warrant for the execution of Cenci. After discovering the body, Savella's men find the murderers still lurking on the grounds and carrying bags of gold coins. He tells all present that they will have to appear in Rome to face a court, and Lucretia breaks down but Beatrice remains strong.

In Act V Marzio confesses to the murder after he is tortured on the rack, but he recants his confession when he faces Beatrice in the courtroom. The judge is not satisfied with Marzio's decision to shoulder the guilt and orders more time on the rack, but Marzio dies without saying anything more. Left without a perpetrator, the judge orders torture for Beatrice, Lucretia, Giacomo, and Bernardo. Orsino has fled in disguise. The drama ends with the remaining Cenci family preparing for their execution, for Pope Clement has refused to view the case with leniency because he does not want to encourage further acts of parricide.

CENSORSHIP HISTORY

Completed and dedicated to Shelley's fellow writer Leigh Hunt, Esq., in 1819, *The Cenci* was denied a license for performance for more than a century in England because of its allusions to father-daughter incest, despite the playwright's great efforts to keep the word *incest* out of the play. In his dedication to Hunt, Shelley recognizes the volatile nature of the topic and writes, "*The Cenci* deals, if ever so meticulously, with incest." Ironically, it was legally permissible to publish the play, and the published text of *The Cenci* was so well-received by the public that it became the only one of Shelley's works to go into a second printing during his lifetime. Thomas Love Peacock wrote an anonymous introduction to the play and tried to obtain permission for its performance, but the London censors refused to issue *The Cenci* a license. Approached to consider the play, Thomas Harris, manager of Covent Garden, claimed to be so "morally outraged" by the subject matter of the play that he refused to show it to the actress Eliza O'Neill, whom Shelley had hoped would play the part of Beatrice Cenci.

The play was banned from performance for more than 60 years before another attempt at public performance was made, although several theater managers considered an attempt in the intervening years. In 1847 William Charles Macready read through the play but decided against taking the risk, writing in his diary: "Looked through *The Cenci* as a matter of form. The *idea* of acting such a monstrous crime, beautiful as the work is!" In 1886, after the Examiner of Plays in London, Edward Pigott, refused to permit a public performance of the play, Dr. F. J. Furnivall, a Shakespearean scholar and bibliographer, became chairman of the newly formed Shelley Society, which had as one of its goals a professional performance of *The Cenci* at a London theater. The Examiner of Plays, in refusing the license, wrote that he recognized that the play was "a literary masterpiece . . . [but] all the genius in the world cannot make a play of which incest is the central theme, proper to be licensed for public representation." The Shelley Society decided that a private performance for its members alone was its only option. The society secured use of the Grand Theatre in Islington for one matinee performance on May 7, 1886. Attendees included literary luminaries Robert Browning, James Russell Lowell, and George Meredith, as well as others who had joined the Shelley Society for the sole purpose of seeing the play performed. Days before the performance, Furnivall and the theater manager were asked to appear before the

Examiner of Plays and warned that the performance was to remain "strictly private" and that "on no account" were they to distribute any publicity. In a report of the meeting, Pigott wrote, "it is enough to remark that all the genius of the greatest poets that have ever lived cannot make incest a subject fit for representation in a Christian country." The press attacked the Shelley Society, and reviews were filled with condemnations of the play, which critics felt was based on an act that was too horrible and revolting to talk about. The theater reviewer Austin Brereton wrote in *The Theatre* that *The Cenci* was "the most repulsive play that has been produced this century."

In 1892 the British House of Commons Select Committee on Theatres and Places of Entertainment published a report that detailed its proceedings in investigating whether to continue the present system of censorship. The drama critic William Archer testified that the present system of censorship of plays should be revised because it failed to eliminate the indecent at the same time that it suppressed the serious dramatic work; he provided *The Cenci* as an example. He argued that the public should be the only judge of the worth of a play and that any proven indecency should be a matter of police action. The proceedings concluded, instead, not only that the censorship of plays worked well but also that it should be extended to music hall performances and other forms of public entertainment. *The Cenci* was not performed on a public stage in England until 1922, when Dame Sybil Thorndyke starred as the ill-fated Beatrice, and in the United States until May 19, 1926, in a New York City production at the Lenox Hill Theatre.

FURTHER READING

Behrendt, Stephen C. "Beatrice Cenci and the Tragic Myth of History." In *History and Myth: Essays on English Romantic Literature.* Edited by Stephen C. Behrendt. Detroit, Mich.: Wayne State University Press, 1990.

Brereton, Austin. *"The Cenci." The Theatre* 7 (May 1886): 530.

Curran, Stuart. *Shelley's Cenci: Scorpions Ringed with Fire.* Princeton, N.J.: Princeton University Press, 1970.

Elsom, John. *Erotic Theatre.* New York: Taplinger Publishing Co., 1974.

Fowell, Frank, and Frank Palmer. *Censorship in England.* New York: Benjamin Blom, 1913. Reprinted by Burt Franklin, 1969.

Gassner, John. *Theatre at the Crossroads.* New York: Holt, Rinehart and Winston, 1960.

Great Britain. Parliament. House of Commons. Select Committee on Theatres and Places of Entertainment. *Report Together with the Proceedings of the Committee, Minutes of Evidence, Appendix, and Index.* London: H. M. Stat. Off., 1892 (Report 240, 1892, vol. 8).

Parkes, Adam. *Modernism and the Theatre of Censorship.* New York: Oxford University Press, 1996.

Shelley, Percy Bysshe. *The Cenci.* In *Nineteenth-Century British Drama: An Anthology of Representative Plays.* Edited by Leonard R. N. Ashley. Glenview, Ill.: Scott, Foresman and Company, 1967.

———. *The Letters of Percy Bysshe Shelley.* Vol. 2. Edited by Frederick L. Jones. Oxford, England: Clarendon Press, 1964.

Simpson, Michael. *Closet Performances: Political Exhibition and Prohibition in the Dramas of Byron and Shelley.* Stanford, Calif.: Stanford University Press, 1998.
Stephens, John Russell. *The Censorship of English Drama, 1824–1901.* New York: Cambridge University Press, 1980.

THE CHILDREN'S HOUR

Author: Lillian Hellman
Original date and place of production: November 20, 1934, Maxine Elliott Theater, New York, New York
Characters: Agatha, Helen Burton, Catherine, Doctor Joseph Cardin, Martha Dobie, Lois Fisher, Mrs. Lily Mortar, Evelyn Munn, Peggy Rogers, Mrs. Amelia Tilford, Mary Tilford, Rosalie Wells, Karen Wright
Filmed versions: *The Children's Hour* (1961); *These Three* (1936)

SUMMARY

Lillian Hellman's first play, *The Children's Hour,* is based upon an actual incident that occurred in Scotland in 1809, in which two unmarried, middle-aged women who ran a school for girls were accused of being lesbians by one of their students, whose grandmother brought charges against them. The two women spent more than a decade suing for libel and trying to undo the damage that the accusations created in their lives, but they lost their school and all of their money. Hellman became aware of the story in 1932 when the writer Dashiell Hammett gave her a copy of *Bad Companion,* an account of the case by William Roughead published in 1931, and suggested that she would be more successful in teaching herself how to write a play if she used a story that had foundation in fact. This was her first play. *The Children's Hour* relates the story of two female private school teachers in the 1930s whose lives are ruined when a malicious student spreads the lie that they are lesbians. A probing psychological study, the play contains no suggestive scenes or language, nor does it present any sexual political agenda. Instead, the theme focuses on the destructive effects of a community's cruelty, suspicion, and lack of compassion. The plot deals primarily with the results of the hysteria that the lies generate among the parents of other girls at the school who are frightened that their children are being taught by lesbians.

Single and in their late 20s the teachers, Martha Dobie and Karen Wright, share a home from necessity. They have also become close friends after teaching together for several years, but their relationship is not exclusive and Karen is engaged to Dr. Cardin, whom she plans to marry. The closeness of the women provides fuel for gossip when a student, disgruntled with Karen for chastising her for poor academic performance, spreads the rumors. The girl's family complains to the headmistress of the school and the two women are first ostracized, then forced into court, where Mrs. Tilford, the girl's mother, accuses them of having "sinful sexual knowledge of each other."Martha hopes that her aunt, the actress Lily Mortar, will testify for her, but Mortar ignores the pleading telegrams and returns to speak with Martha only after the trial is over. The one stalwart in both Karen and Martha's life is Dr. Cardin, who continues to love Karen and who sells his practice with the aim of taking both women away from the hurtful gossip, but even he must ask Karen directly if she and Martha have ever been lovers. Even though she denies it, she feels that she can no longer go through with the marriage. She asks him to leave, and to consider whether he really wants to marry her after all the gossip. Shocked by Karen's action, Martha tries to reassure her that Cardin will return, but Karen only wants to leave town. During their ordeal, Martha began to question much about her life, including her true feelings for Karen, leading to her realization that she not only is sexually attracted to Karen but also is in love with her. When Martha believes that Cardin has left for good, she confesses her love. Karen rebuffs her, asserting that she feels only compassion for her friend and respect for her fine qualities. Unable to withstand the social disapproval of the community, and finding her love for Karen hopeless, Martha shoots and kills herself. A short time later, Mrs. Tilford, mother of the accuser, appears to tell Karen that she knows now that the students lied. Mrs. Tilford has made arrangements for a public apology and a payment of damages to the two women. The play ends with Karen standing alone at the window and waving farewell to Mrs. Tilford.

CENSORSHIP HISTORY

In interviews given nearly five decades after *The Children's Hour* debuted, Hellman protested that "the play has nothing to do with lesbianism, of course; it's just one of the side issues. . . . I really don't think people who saw it ever thought of it as a lesbian play." Instead, she said, the play was about a lie: "This is not a play about lesbianism, but about a lie. The bigger the lie the better, as always." Those who sought to repress the play, however, considered lesbianism the main theme and faulted the playwright for her failure to include a moral judgment against it. The play opened in New York City in 1934 and ran for 64 weeks with substantial box office success, which prompted the producer, Herman Shumlin, to take the production to other cities and new audiences. Boston authorities told him that the play was not acceptable under the local community standards strictly enforced by the local Watch and Ward Society and that the play could not be presented in Boston. Shumlin sued the city of Boston and named Mayor Mansfield as the primary defendant in his $250,000 damage suit. In a hearing held in 1936 with Judge George E. Sweeney presiding, Mansfield admitted that he had not read the play nor seen a performance, but he claimed to understand "from hearsay" that it was "about lesbianism." Judge Sweeney defended Mansfield. He asserted that the mayor had simply acted on information that established the play as dealing with an "unfit" topic and, as such, that the mayor was upholding community standards.

In defense of the play, Shumlin produced favorable reviews of the New York City production and sworn affidavits from literary figures Herbert Bayard Swope, George S. Kaufman, Gilbert Seldes, Dorothy Parker, and Carl Van Doren, who attested to its cultural significance. The judge ruled that Shumlin had no basis for the damage suit, because Mansfield had pointed out that the play was "unfit" but had not banned it outright: Theater owners were still free to allow the production on their premises, even though the Watch and Ward Society and community opinion were firmly behind the mayor. Shumlin withdrew the production rather than fight the established political structure, which had been victorious in most earlier efforts to ban books and other plays.

The play was also rebuffed by Chicago authorities, who used the power granted to them under a municipal censorship ordinance passed in 1907 to withhold a permit for performance of the play. The law, which would later be used to ban hundreds of films, required that all entertainment be reviewed by a board of censors and receive a permit from the Chicago Police Department. Plays containing subject matter that was "objectionable," that portrayed "unlawful scenes," or that had the tendency to "outrage public morals" were not granted permits.

The Children's Hour, which ran for 691 performances in New York City, was strongly considered for the Pulitzer Prize for the 1934–35 season, but the Pulitzer committee avoided controversy and gave the award instead to *The Old Maid*, written by Zoe Akins. William Lyon Phelps, one of the judges on the Pulitzer committee, refused to attend a performance of *The Children's Hour.* After the drama award was announced, supporters of *The Children's Hour* accused committee members of acting as censors by rejecting the play for its subject matter. The Pulitzer committee defended its decision by explaining that the play was ineligible for the award because it was based on a court trial and therefore was not an original drama. In response, supporters protested that the choice of the Pulitzer committee should also have been considered ineligible, because Akins's *The Old Maid* was based on a novel by Edith Wharton. Members of the New York Drama Critics Circle, incensed by the decision, voted in 1935 to begin awarding their own prizes to notable dramas.

Will Hays, head of the Motion Picture Producers and Distributors Association (MPPDA), placed the play on the banned list for filmmakers as soon as it was produced, because it violated sections of the code to which studio- and theater-owning members of the MPPDA had promised to adhere. The Production Code Administration (PCA) required that "the sanctity of the institution of marriage and home shall be upheld" and stated further that "sexual perversion or any inference of it is forbidden." Hellman wrote the screenplay for *These Three* (1936), the first movie based on her play, and her version for the screen met the requirement set by studio head Samuel Goldwyn that she eliminate the lesbian issue in favor of a plot that dealt with a heterosexual love triangle. The playwright acquiesced because she had maintained from the outset that her play was about the destructive power of lies on people's lives, not about lesbian love. Despite the extensive change, the PCA forbade any mention in the publicity that the film was based on Hellman's play nor could the title of the play be used in the publicity for the film. In his work *The Celluloid Closet*, Russo quotes from a review of the film *These Three* that appeared in *Variety*, which stated "it is verboten to ballyhoo the original source."

FURTHER READING

Albert, Jan. "Sweetest Smelling Baby in New Orleans." *Conversations with Lillian Hellman*. Edited by Jackson Bryer. Jackson: University Press of Mississippi, 1986.

Gould, Jean. *Modern American Playwrights*. New York: Dodd, Mead, 1966.

Katz, Jonathan. *Gay/Lesbian Almanac*. New York: Harper & Row, 1983.

Labadie, Donald. "Movies: 'The Innocents' and 'The Children's Hour.'" *Lillian Hellman: Plays, Films, Memoirs*. Edited by Mark W. Estrin. Boston: G. K. Hall, 1989.

Laufe, Abe. *The Wicked Stage: A History of Theater Censorship and Harassment in the United States*. New York: Frederick Ungar, 1978.

"Mayor Admits Condemning Play without Seeing or Reading It." *Boston Evening Transcript*, January 29, 1936, pp. 1, 14.

Mikva, Abner J. "Chicago: Citadel of Censorship." *Focus/Midwest* 2 (March/April 1963): 16–17.

Morgenstern, Joseph. "New Children's Hour—Grim Power of Gossip." *Lillian Hellman: Plays, Films, Memoirs*. Edited by Mark W. Estrin. Boston: G. K. Hall, 1989.

Nugent, Frank. "Lillian Hellman's *These Three*." *The New York Times*, March 9, 1936, p. 22.

Russo, Vito. *The Celluloid Closet*. Rev. ed. New York: HarperCollins, 1987.

Turk, Ruth. *Lillian Hellman: Rebel Playwright*. Minneapolis: Lerner Publications Company, 1995.

Weiss, Andrea. *Vampires and Violets: Lesbians in the Cinema*. New York: Penguin, 1993.

THE CONNECTION

Author: Jack Gelber
Original date and place of production: July 15, 1959, The Living Theatre, New York, New York
Characters: Cowboy, Jim Dunn, Ernie, Harry, Jaybird, Leach, Sam, Sister Salvation, Solly, Musicians, Photographers
Filmed versions: *The Connection* (1961)

SUMMARY

The Connection is a starkly unsentimental drama in two acts that frankly portrays drug addiction. The play uses obscene language, character improvisations, and the background of a jazz combo to present the concept of a drama in which real addicts play characters in a film about drug addiction. In performances, characters panhandled in the audience to create a surreal blur between reality and fantasy. The play is framed by the character of Jim Dunn, portrayed as a novice filmmaker who is allowed to film the addicts as they buy their drugs; in return, he pays for their fix. Near the beginning of the play, a man named Harry appears at the door, suitcase in hand. He looks around, opens the suitcase, and takes out a record player that he plugs in. He puts on a record containing the music of Charlie Parker as the others watch and listen in silence. When the record ends, he packs up everything and leaves. The first act portrays the group of addicts waiting for the mysterious Cowboy, their "connection," to arrive at Leach's apartment with a delivery of heroin for their fix. As they mark time, they discuss the addictions of everyday people in the "straight" world, as Sam states, "the people who work every day, the people who worry so much about the next dollar, the new coat, the chlorophyll addicts, the aspirin addicts, the vitamin addicts, those people are hooked worse than me. Worse than me. Hooked." Solly reminds him that the "straight" may well be hooked, but "You happen to have a vice that is illegal."

The connection—and the junkies' fix—arrives in the beginning of the second act. Cowboy also brings Sister Salvation, a uniformed member of the Salvation Army, to the apartment as a cover in case the police arrive, and promises her a cup of orange pekoe tea. The addicts go one by one into the bathroom to shoot heroin. When they return, Sister Salvation makes her pitch to save them. She is completely oblivious to their heroin use, which the audience can see taking place in the bathroom. After entering the bathroom and finding empty wine bottles, Sister Salvation rants against the sins of drinking and tells the men, "Be not among the winebibbers. . . . For the drunkard and glutton shall come to poverty." Solly asks her who invented her uniform, but she brushes the question aside as she continues to preach. When it seems evident that she knows little about the context of her preaching, Solly gives her a thumbnail history of the uniform and origins of the Salvation Army. As she intones "you are not alone" several times, Cowboy leads her to the door and shows her out. Everyone begins to experience euphoria as the heroin takes effect, and some of the characters enter the audience while others go behind the scenes. Leach, however, has used heroin so often and in such quantity that he is unable to experience a high. He continues to take increments of the heroin while he tells the others, "I'm not high . . . I'm not high at all," until he finally overdoses and nearly dies. As Cowboy, Solly, and Jaybird watch over Leach and wait for him to come around, Dunn enters from the audience, panic-stricken that "the fuzz [police] are coming. . . . We're going to get busted." As the four discuss the nature of drug addiction, they hear a knock at the door. Harry enters, once again, and goes through the same ritual with the Charlie Parker record as the play ends.

CENSORSHIP HISTORY

The Connection shocked audiences and critics when it was first performed on July 15, 1959, at the Living Theatre, an enterprise started by theater producers Julian Beck and Judith Malina in 1946 in a former New York City department store. Theater reviews were generally unfavorable at first, and author Ruby Cohn reports that a review in the *New York Times* dismissed *The Connection* as nothing more than "a farrago of dirt, smalltime philosophy, empty talk and extended runs of cool music." Theater critic Judith Crist, writing for the *Herald Tribune*, described the play as "utterly tasteless" and denounced it as having no merit. Jim O'Connor, critic for the *Journal-American*, bemoaned the future of the American stage after having seen the "disgusting, depressing play." Writing for the *Village Voice*, the critic Jerry Tallmer contradicted the critics for the daily papers and described *The Connection* as a jazz play that is "extremely theatrical" and explores the "deep detumescence and utter hopelessness" of heroin addicts. In a letter to the editor of the *Village Voice* dated August 12, 1959, American author Norman Mailer supported the play, calling it "dangerous, true, artful and alive." Three weeks later, on September 2, 1959, a letter from the poet Allen Ginsberg also appeared in the *Village Voice* attacking the negative comments of the daily critics and supporting the play as a "miracle of local consciousness." Ginsberg convinced British theater critic Kenneth Tynan to see the play. As Tynan writes in his preface to the first publication of the play by Grove Press, "it had received a fairly thorough bludgeoning from the daily press" in the few months before gathering so loyal a cult of followers that, six months later, "there are few Broadway figures who would admit, with anything like pride, that they had not seen the play. . . . It has become a cultural must."

Once such celebrated playwrights as Lillian Hellman and Tennessee Williams expressed their enthusiasm for *The Connection*, and numerous celebrities, including then-UN secretary-general Dag Hammarskjold, and many in the entertainment business attended performances, the calls to close the play stopped. As the play continued, to an eventual 722 performances Off-Broadway, respected critics such as John Gassner might still consider it an "unclassified oddment," but they would also admit that the play was a "mesmeric drama." *The Connection* won the 1959–60 Obie (Off-Broadway) Award for "Best New Play" and "Best All-Around Production" and led the way to theater of the 1960s, by introducing in one production group improvisation, overindulgence in drugs, racial commingling, and audience infiltration. It was the first play to break through the "fourth wall" that separated the actors from the audience.

At the time of its initial performances, the hyperrealistic view of *The Connection*, complete with its hazy jazz score, street language, and graphic depictions of needles penetrating characters' arms, outraged the public and brought national attention to the Living Theatre. Individual complaints to New York City bureaucrats resulted in visits by law enforcement officials, but the failure to organize by those who challenged the play weakened the complaints of individuals. Nonetheless, hints of unsavory behavior behind the scenes fueled calls for the play to be shut down, as leaks revealed that most of the musicians were available and willing to take the very low wages paid for playing in the show because their own legal problems with heroin had made them unable to obtain cabaret licenses. As Beck and Malina have recalled in interviews, "musicians sometimes passed out during performances or disappeared during rehearsals because of drugs." While such behavior placed their theater license at risk, as a violation of public safety, Beck and Malina also accepted the drug ambience as a positive factor in relation to *The Connection* because it "helped foster a sense of family and community not conventionally associated with drugs." Larry Rivers, a painter who later acted in several productions at the Living Theatre and who became friends with many members of the cast of *The Connection*, reports in his autobiography that a number of the cast members experimented with heroin both offstage during the run of the play and onstage: "There was real heroin in the capsules handed out to the anxious actors waiting onstage, some of whom shot up in front of the audience." The actors provided actual, realistic reactions to the drug.

When the play was made into a film in 1961, its subject matter raised no formal objections, but its dialogue raised concerns among members of the New York State Board of Regents, which refused to grant the distributor of the film a license to exhibit the film in the state. The board claimed that the film contained obscenity and objected, in particular, to the repetition of the word *shit*, used as a slang term for heroin. The distributors appealed the decision before the appellate division of the state supreme court, which reversed the decision in *Connection Company v. Regents of the University of the State of New York*, 230 N.Y.S. 2d 103 (1962). For a full account, read Sova's *Forbidden Films*. In rendering a decision, the court acknowledged that the term is used "as a definite expression of the language of the narcotic" and that it may be "vulgar" but was not obscene.

FURTHER READING

Biner, Pierre. *The Living Theatre*. New York: Horizon Press, 1972.

Cohn, Ruby. *New American Dramatists, 1960–1990*. New York: St. Martin's Press, 1991.

Crist, Judith. "Theatre Reviews: *The Connection*." *Herald Tribune*, July 16, 1959.

Gassner, John. *Theatre at the Crossroads*. New York: Holt, Rinehart and Winston, 1960.

Gelber, Jack. *The Connection*. New York: Grove Press, 1960.

Gould, Jean. *Modern American Playwrights*. New York: Dodd, Mead, 1966.

Marwick, Arthur. "Experimental Theatre in the 1960s." *History Today*, October 1, 1994.

O'Connor, Jim. "*The Connection*." *Journal-American*, July 16, 1959.

Rivers, Larry. *What Did I Do?* New York: HarperCollins, 1992.

Roose-Evans, James. *Experimental Theatre from Stanislavsky to Today*. New York: Universe Books, 1970.

Sova, Dawn B. *Forbidden Films: Censorship Histories of 125 Motion Pictures*. New York: Facts On File, 2001.

Tynan, Kenneth. Preface to *The Connection: A Play by Jack Gelber*. New York: Grove Press, 1960.

Tytell, John. *The Living Theatre: Art, Exile, and Outrage*. New York: Grove Press, 1995.

CORPUS CHRISTI

Author: Terrence McNally
Original date and place of production: September 22, 1998, Manhattan
  Theatre Club, New York, New York
Characters: Andrew, Bartholomew, James, James the Less, John, Joshua,
  Judas Iscariot, Matthew, Peter, Philip, Simon, Thaddeus, Thomas
Filmed versions: None

SUMMARY

Corpus Christi is a version of the gospels of Jesus and his followers trans-
planted to the 1950s and the city of Corpus Christi, Texas, the town in which
playwright Terrence McNally grew up gay and Roman Catholic. Rather than
simply retelling the gospels, McNally continuously reminds the audience that
what appears on stage is not reality but the playwright's perceptions. The play
uses male cast members without costume changes to portray female characters as wailing and shrieking men in invisible drag. The playwright also fills
the play with contradictions that place actions and people related to the historical Christ in close proximity to the expected trappings of life in 20th-
century Texas. The whole effect of such seeming confusion is that the audience is encouraged to recognize the ambiguous nature of what appears on the
stage. Joshua/Jesus is born in a rundown hotel in Corpus Christi to Mary, a
virgin, and her husband Joseph, a carpenter. Addressed as "Son of God" from
the outset, he performs miracles, such as healing the sick and raising someone
from the dead, actions that make him suspect in the eyes of the townspeople.
Although the play makes clear at the outset that the Bible before the coming
of Joshua consists only of the Old Testament, the evidence of the existence of
Jesus Christ is everywhere, from the name of the city (*corpus Christi* means
"body of Christ" in Latin) to the characters' swearing "Jesus Christ." The
contradictions are compounded by the unexplained presence of Roman cen-
turions in 20th-century Texas and the existence of Pontius Pilate High
School, which Joshua attends.

   The play opens with a group of young men arriving on stage carrying
backpacks, from which they take brightly colored slacks that they change into
before undergoing a simple baptism. Having been transformed into the 12
apostles, they head for Corpus Christi, Texas, where they find Joshua and
move through McNally's version of a number of New Testament stories.
Nearly all the apostles have 20th-century professions: John is a writer; James,
a teacher; Peter, a fish seller; Andrew, a masseur; Philip, a hustler;
Bartholomew, a doctor and James's lover; Judas Iscariot, a restaurateur;
Matthew, a lawyer; Thomas, an actor; James the Less, an architect; Simon, a
singer and Thaddeus, a hairdresser.

   The focus in the first act is upon Joshua's self-discovery. On prom night,
he and his date attempt sex, but he is not sexually aroused. He has his first
sexual experience that night with Judas Iscariot. Unlike the New Testament

Jesus, Joshua is impatient and not open to passive acceptance. He shouts "Shut up, women" angrily at the "women," who wail as he raises Lazarus from the dead, and answers "I must have been in a very good mood that day," to a disciple who questions his use of physical force against a centurion and asks if he did not caution everyone to "turn the other cheek." While the play-wright does portray Joshua as teaching his 12 apostles to share their goods among themselves and with the poor, in the manner of the historical Jesus, he changes other New Testament stories. Rather than including the incident of Jesus offending the Pharisees by expelling the moneylenders from the temple, McNally has his Joshua conduct a male-male wedding to offend the priests. Joshua does perform some of the actions of the historical Jesus: He prays at Gethsemane, experiences a Last Supper, suffers being scourged, and is cruci-fied. In contrast, however, his Last Supper courts laughter by freezing the cast to resemble the Da Vinci painting, he is not crowned king of the Jews but "king of the Queers," and he is crucified because he is homosexual—the vic-tim of a gay hate crime. The play ends with the statement, "If we have offended you, so be it. He belongs to us as well as you."

CENSORSHIP HISTORY

Controversy has followed *Corpus Christi* from the first attempt to present the play on May 21, 1998, at the Manhattan Theatre Club (MTC) in New York City. On May 1, 1998, the *New York Post* carried an article about the upcom-ing play and asserted that the performance includes a scene in which "a Jesus-like figure has sex with his apostles." The distorted report angered several ultraconservative religious groups, but the most vocal and vehement in protesting was the Catholic League for Religious and Civil Rights (CLRC). William Donohue, president of the 350,000-member group, stated that his group found the play "insulting to Christians" and that they would "wage a war that no one will forget" in the effort to stop the production. Donohue and the CLRC wrote letters to numerous public officials and demanded "an immediate halt on public monies that support the Manhattan Theatre Club." The CLRC also built a coalition of Catholic, Protestant, Jewish, Muslim, and Italian groups who objected to the play and placed pressure on backers. Another group that identified itself only as the National Security Movement of America made telephone calls to the theater management and voiced threats against the "Jew guilty homosexual Terrence McNally," promising that because of him they would "exterminate every member of the theater and burn the place to the ground." The threats and demands undermined the confidence of one of the corporate sponsors, Trans World Airlines, which withdrew its financial support. The MTC announced on May 21, 1998, that the production was being canceled "because of security problems that have arisen around the production of the play and related concerns."

Many theater people criticized the decision loudly and called the action censorship. Within days of the cancellation, representatives of the National

Coalition against Censorship (NCAC), National Campaign for Freedom of Expression, New Yorkers for Free Expression, PEN American Center, People for the American Way, and Visual AIDS, as well as playwrights Edward Albee, Christopher Durang, William Hoffman, David Henry Hwang, Tony Kushner, Arthur Miller, Stephen Sondheim, and Wendy Wasserstein and author Judy Blume drafted, signed, and sent a letter to the MTC urging that it not cave in to the "censorship terrorists." South African playwright Athol Fugard withdrew from the MTC lineup his play *The Captain's Tiger* to protest the ban. In withdrawing his play, Fugard wrote, "In yielding to the blackmail and threats of the Catholic League, the theater management has compromised one of the basic freedoms of democracy, Freedom of Speech and they have done it by censoring themselves and collaborating in the attempt to silence Mr. McNally."

The theater management reconsidered and reversed the decision on May 28, 1998, during which announcement the theater's artistic director, Lynne Meadow, told a reporter for the *New York Times*, "We were outraged by a subsequent outcry which accused us of censorship. In our 25-year history, we have never censored a play or turned down a play because of content." When the play was produced in September 1998, tickets were sold out, but fear created by the earlier threats meant that the crowds had to pass through police barricades and metal detectors as they entered the theater. Guards were directed to inspect the floor under each seat before every performance, because of the bomb threats.

The British premiere of *Corpus Christi*, at the Bedlam Theatre, a converted church in Edinburgh, Scotland, on August 9, 1999, was greeted with protests similar to those experienced by the MTC. After the proposed staging of the play was announced in the media, the theater and actors received hate mail and threats of violence and death, as did Stephen Henry, the 26-year-old director of the play. On opening night, the theater hired extra security guards and the actors were escorted and watched carefully during the performance to forestall any attempts to harm them or to disrupt the production. The play provoked contrasting responses from the Scottish clergy. When the planned performances of the play were announced, the Reverend David Murray of the Free Church of Scotland denounced it as being "highly offensive" and called for its banning. In contrast, Right Reverend Richard Holloway, the bishop of Scotland, defended the play, saying that it fit into the tradition of retelling biblical stories in modern contexts.

When the play moved to London, Terrence McNally also became the object of a fatwa decree, and a price was placed on his head to be collected by anyone who would assassinate him as a religious act. Sheik Omar Bakri Mohammed, a 38-year-old Syrian who headed Al-Muhajiroun ("the Emigrant"), a London-based Islamic fundamentalist group with ties to Osama bin Laden and other terrorists, issued the decree. Although McNally is not Muslim, Mohammed convened a *shari'ah* (a court of Muslim law) with other Muslim clerics, who reasoned that Islam considers Jesus to be a messenger of God and the Qur'an instructs believers that "Whoever insults a messenger of God must be killed." The playwright, they decided, had blasphemed a prophet of God by portraying him as gay.

In March 2001, students of Florida Atlantic University staged performances of *Corpus Christi*. Complaints from individuals about the use of state money to fund the production led to threats by state lawmakers that they would cut funding to the university. State senator Debby Sanderson defended the move by lawmakers and stated, "For anyone who's Christian, it's very offensive."

The attempt by students at Indiana University-Purdue University in Fort Wayne (IPFW) to stage the play in August 2001 led to the filing of a preliminary injunction on July 5, 2001, against the university, brought by 32 individuals, including 21 legislators, and led by former Indiana Republican gubernatorial candidate John Price. The lawsuit alleges that using public funds for plays containing such content as that found in *Corpus Christi* violates the mandate of the U.S. Constitution that the government remain neutral in matters of religion, neither favoring nor disfavoring it. Lawyers for the group called the play "a full-blown, unmitigated attack on Christianity and its founders." The university defended the rights of students to present the play and characterized the matter as one involving academic freedom and the guarantee to exercise the right to free speech, no matter that others might be offended. The attorney for IPFW, Anthony Benton, also made clear in his response to the lawsuit that allowing the students to stage the play should not be construed as indicating university support for the content in the play. The Indiana Civil Liberties Union represented the student director of the play, Jonathan Gilbert. District Judge William C. Lee, who heard the case on July 17, 2001, denied the request for a preliminary injunction and refused to stop the play, writing in his decision that stopping the play would infringe on the free-speech rights of students. Opponents of the play appealed the decision in the Seventh Circuit Court of Appeals, which upheld the decision of the lower court by a vote of 2 to 1.

FURTHER READING

"Censoring Terrence McNally." Editorial. *New York Times*, May 28, 1998.

Chavez, Linda. "Free Speech Invoked to Justify Filth." *The Abilene Reporter-News*, October 7, 1998.

Dan Linnemeier, et al. v. Indiana University-Purdue University Fort Wayne, et al. Case No. 1:01-CV-0266. United States District Court, Northern District of Indiana, Fort Wayne Division.

Eck, Linda. "*Corpus Christi*—Terrence McNally." *Bad Subjects: Political Education for Everyday Life*. August 18, 2001. Available online. URL: http://eserver.org/bs/reviews/2001-8-18-4.45PM.html.

Foster, Paul. "Forbidden Theater." *Arts4All Newsletter* II, no. 14 (summer 2000). Available online. URL: http://www.arts4all.com/newsletter/issue14/foster14.html.

Smith, Anthony Burke. "Catholic Controversy I: Jesus Off Broadway." *Religion in the News* 1, no. 2 (fall 1998): 7.

Sumi, Glenn. "The Full McNally: After Four Tonys and Death Threats, Author Faces the Music." *NOW Online Magazine* 20, no. 39 (May 31–June 6, 2001). Available online. URL: http://www.thefullmonty.com/tour/press_now_05_31_01.htm.

"Terrence McNally's *Corpus Christi* under Attack in Indiana." *NCAC Resources Online,* July 24, 2001. URL: http://www.ncac.org/issues/corpuschristi.html.

"Theater Company Stands Up to Catholic League: Will Proceed with Play Featuring Gay 'Jesus' Figure." *American Atheist Website,* May 30, 1998. Available online. URL: http://www.atheists.org/flash.line/play.htm.

THE COUNCIL OF LOVE: A CELESTIAL TRAGEDY IN FIVE ACTS

Author: Oskar Panizza

Original date and place of production: June 1, 1967, Experiment am Lichtenwerd, Vienna, Austria

Characters: God the Father, Jesus Christ, The Virgin Mary, The Devil, The Woman, A Cherub, First Angel, Second Angel, Third Angel, Figures from Hell (Agrippina, Rodrigo Borgia, Helen of Troy, Heloise, Phryne, Salome); Children of the Pope (Cesare Borgia, Don Gioffre Borgia, Don Giovanni Borgia, Donna Lucrezia Borgia, Giovanni Borgia, Girolama Borgia, Isabella Borgia, Laura Borgia, Pier Luigi Borgia); Mistresses of the Pope (Alessandro Farnese, Julia Farnese, Adriana Mila, Donna Sancia, Vanozza); Nephews of the Pope (Collerando Borgia, Francesco Borgia, Luigi Pietro Borgia, Rodrigo Borgia); Confidants of the Pope (Burcard, Pietro Caranza, Giovanni Vera Da Ercilla, Remolina Da Ilerda, Giovanni Lopez, Juan Marades, three noblemen, a priest); Colombina, a courtesan; Pulcinello; assorted heavenly figures and courtiers

Filmed versions: *Das Liebenkonzil* (1981, Austria)

SUMMARY

The Council of Love is set in spring 1495, which Panizza identifies at the beginning of the play as the "date of the first outbreak of syphilis recorded in history." The setting varies among several locations, from Heaven and Hell to the court of Pope Alexander VI. Although the play has a cast of hundreds, the main characters are God, the Virgin Mary, Jesus Christ, the Devil, and the Woman. The opening scene is set in heaven, where a messenger arrives to tell God of the horrible occurrences in the city of Naples, which "is given over to the most ignoble vices." The messenger reports that lust-crazed women are running bare-breasted through the streets, making the men burn with "animal passion." This news of humanity running out of control alarms the inhabitants of heaven, and it enrages God the Father who, growing weak and senile, rages that he will destroy humans. His son, Jesus, a dull, whining, and sniveling fanatic who is asthmatic as well as physically tired of the role of savior, agrees: "We shall wipe them out." Only the Virgin Mary, portrayed as more human than divine, understands that even the current behavior of humans who "mingle like animals with ruthless scorn for the limits and restrictions set to the desires of the flesh" must be tolerated because "they are most filthy, that's all." In response to the intention of God the Father and Christ "to rub them out, filthy creatures . . . to have a nice clean Earth again . . . with animals in the forests," Mary reminds him, "if we are to have animals, we must have men." She also questions who will create humankind if all humans are obliterated.

Act Two reveals the terrible corruption of humans as it focuses on the court of Pope Alexander VI, complete with the numerous mistresses, courtesans, philandering spouses, and stories of secret vices. The women surrounding the pope are clad in diaphanous dresses, and some are bare-breasted. When word comes that the king of France is marching on Rome, the pope calls his servants to "take our strongboxes and valuables." After viewing the actions of the pope, the inhabitants of Heaven are desperate for a way to punish humans for their behavior, and they turn to the Devil, "our dearest cousin, Our ally, Our dearly beloved brother," to devise a plan. Mary tells the Devil that they "need someone, something, an influence, a force, a person, a disease, some little thing that will put a stop to the lewdness of humanity . . . from a sexual point of view. . . . Something that will call a halt to the bestiality of all those males and females who seem to be quite unaware that contact and penetration are purely incidental and to be tolerated within the absolute limits of the needs of reproduction." The Devil outlines a plan, to which Mary heartily agrees, as long as humans "continue to have need of redemption." When the Devil objects, Mary asks about his health, his foot, and his children, and then she presses him again to make a plan that will permit redemption. In a long scene, the Devil contemplates what he can do to punish humans for their licentiousness. He decides that creating an infection that is transferred at the point of sexual contact is the perfect scheme. He must introduce this punishment in the most tempting guise and, following Mary's suggestion, decides to use a woman to carry out his plan. From Hell, he calls various women who have betrayed love and loyalty and selects Salome to be the mother of his scourge, who will be named Syphilis. In the final act, the lightly clothed and dazzlingly beautiful Syphilis is sent to the court of Pope Alexander VI, where she appears as High Mass is being celebrated and immediately gains the attention of the pope and every man in the court. The play ends as the pope leaves with Syphilis and the crowd runs wildly after them.

CENSORSHIP HISTORY

As a physician, writer, and member of the German Münchner Moderne movement that criticized society, Oskar Panizza sought to create a play that would offend the sensibilities of his time as a means of making a strong social commentary. In making a social statement, he did not expect that imbuing God the Father and His Heavenly Host with all-too-human attributes would lead to confiscation of the play by the authorities and his imprisonment on the charge of having committed "crimes against religion." The play would not enjoy even selected public readings until October 6, 1962, performed at Das Massengrass Klub. The first complete public reading of the play occurred on December 9, 1965, at the Rationaltheater, located on the campus of the University of Munich. The world premiere of the play took place in 1967 in Vienna, decades after its composition. Productions soon followed in Paris, at the Théâtre de Paris on February 7, 1969, and at the Criterion Theatre, London, on August 24, 1970. Since then, *The Council of Love* has been performed in more than 80 productions in Europe, the United States, and Mexico.

Despite such widespread production, the play remains controversial. In 1895, although Panizza's play already had been published in Switzerland, the court in Munich banned the play and sentenced Panizza to a year in prison for blasphemy. He presented his defense before the Royal Court of Munich on April 30, 1895, and quoted from various scholarly sources to support the characterization of Pope Alexander VI as debauched and abusing the power of his position. Accused of distorting the facts, Panizza argued that in depicting the sexual escapades of church officials, he actually "toned down the scene. . . . The real scene, as it comes down to us from history, would have been impossible even in a closet drama [closed performance]." The court did not agree, nor did they agree with his assertion that *The Council of Love* is merely a satire that, of necessity, "must make use of human prototypes," which was his explanation for using the court of Pope Alexander. To defend his contention that the content of his play is "a mere trifle," Panizza read to the court from "one of the most libertine poems ever to have been written," "La Guerre des Dieux" by the French poet Parny, which had been published freely in Munich. Panizza contended that his work was that of a "moralist," while that of Parny was "frivolous wantonness." In a final appeal, Panizza told the court that "if you treat a book published abroad, where it does not enter into a conflict with the laws, as if it were published in the homeland, you pervert the intention of the author and place him in jeopardy in a situation where he cannot hope to defend himself." The court denied Panizza's request to be acquitted, and he spent a year in prison. The play remained banned from performance in Germany until the mid-1960s.

When the play premiered at the Criterion Theatre in London in 1970, it was attacked by Lady Dowager Jane (Graham) Birdwood, a proponent of radical conservatism and the leader of a movement to ban "filth" on the BBC and onstage. She attempted to have the satirist John Bird tried for blasphemy for staging *The Council of Love*, but the solicitor-general, Sir Geoffrey Howe, refused her request.

The German-made film *Das Liebenkonzil* (1981), based on Panizza's play, became an issue in the case of *Otto-Preminger-Institut für audiovisuelle Mediengestaltung (OPI) v. Austria*, in which the European Court of Human Rights was asked in 1987 to make a determination about the right of theaters to show the film. In making a determination, the judge wrote that the court cannot disregard the fact that Roman Catholicism is the religion of the overwhelming majority of Tyroleans. Therefore, the court decided, in seizing the film, the Austrian authorities acted to ensure religious peace in that region and to prevent some people from experiencing attacks on their religious beliefs in an unwarranted and offensive manner. In addition, at the request of the Innsbruck diocese of the Roman Catholic Church, the public prosecutor instituted criminal proceedings against OPI's manager, Dietmar Zingl, on May 10, 1985. The charge was "disparaging religious doctrines," an act prohibited by section 188 of the penal code.

On May 12, 1985, after the film had been shown at a private session in the presence of a duty judge, the public prosecutor made an application for its seizure under section 36 of the Media Act. This application was granted by the Innsbruck Regional Court on the same day. As a result, the public showings announced by OPI, the first of which had been scheduled for the next day, could not take place. Those who arrived for the first showing were treated to a reading of the script and a discussion instead. As Zingl had returned the film to the distributor, the Czerny company in Vienna, it was seized at the latter's premises on June 11, 1985. An appeal by Zingl against the seizure order, filed with the Innsbruck Court of Appeal, was dismissed on July 30, 1985. The Court of Appeal considered that artistic freedom was necessarily limited by the rights of others to freedom of religion and by the duty of the state to safeguard a society based on order and tolerance. It further held that indignation was "justified" for the purposes of section 188 of the penal code only if the film's object was to offend the religious feelings of an average person with normal religious sensitivity. That condition was fulfilled in the instant case and forfeiture of the film could be ordered in principle, at least in "objective proceedings." The wholesale derision of religious feeling outweighed any interest the general public might have in information or the financial interests of persons wishing to show the film.

On October 24, 1985, the criminal prosecution against Zingl was discontinued and the case was pursued in the form of "objective proceedings" under section 33, paragraph 2, of the Media Act aimed at suppression of the film. On October 10, 1986, a trial took place before the Innsbruck Regional Court. The film was again shown in closed session; its contents were described in detail in the official record of the hearing. Zingl appears in the official record of the hearing as a witness. He stated that he had sent the film back to the distributor following the seizure order because he wanted nothing more to do with the matter. The judgment, which was delivered the same day, showed that Zingl was considered to be a "potentially liable interested party."

FURTHER READING

Brown, Peter D. G. *Oskar Panizza: His Life and Works.* New York: Peter Lang, 1983.
Elsom, John. *Erotic Theatre.* New York: Taplinger Publishing Co., 1974.

Otto-Preminger-Institut für audiovisuelle Mediengestaltung (OPI) v. Austria. The European Court of Human Rights, May 10, 1985.

Panizza, Oskar. *The Council of Love.* Translated from the German by Oreste F. Puccinai. Introduction by André Breton. New York: Viking Press, 1973.

Schwartz, Barthelemy. "From the Subversion of Society by Art, to the Subsidy of Art by Society." *Le Monde Libertaire.* July/August 1995. Translated by Kenneth Cox. Available online. URL: http://abirato.free.fr/1book/aem/gbsubv.htm.

Sinclair, Lister. "Déjà vu: AIDS in Historical Perspective. An interview with science writer Colman Jones." *IDEAS.* Two-part series on CBC Radio. January 9 and 10, 1996. Available online. URL: http://www.radio.cbc.ca/programs/ideas/Aids.

THE CRADLE WILL ROCK: A PLAY IN MUSIC

Author: Marc Blitzstein

Original date and place of production: June 16, 1937, Maxine Elliott Theater, New York, New York (proposed) but actually presented at the Venice Theater, Washington, D.C.

Characters: Bugs, Cop, Dauber, Dick, Editor Daily, Larry Foreman, Gent, Ella Hammer, Harry the Druggist, Junior Mister, Mr. Mister, Mrs. Mister, Sister Mister, Moll, Gus Polock, Sadie Polock, President Prexy, Professor Trixie, Reverend Salvation, Professor Scoot, Dr. Specialist, Steve, Yasha

Filmed versions: None

SUMMARY

Dedicated to "Bert Brecht" and subtitled "A Play in Music," *The Cradle Will Rock* is a sharply satiric play that portrays upheaval in a mill town during a labor disturbance. Blitzstein uses the stage to criticize strongly the brutality of capitalist forces in opposing a union drive in "Steeltown, U.S.A." The play opens as a likeable Steeltown streetwalker named Moll flirts with a potential client, the Gent, and haggles over the price she will charge the Gent for a few hours of fun. As they speak, a street police officer named Dick arrives on the scene, chases away Moll's customer, and flirts with her while he waits for a telephone call from headquarters to call him into action against a proposed mob at a labor union rally. When the call comes, Dick rushes to the scene and joins fellow police officers in arresting not union organizers but the Liberty Committee, a group of zealots encouraged by Steeltown industrialist Mr. Mister to oppose the tide of unionism and other radical ideas. The Liberty Committee is made up of stereotypes—the Reverend Salvation, Dr. Specialist, President Prexy, and Editor Daily—who are all guilty of crimes worse than Moll's streetwalking or the drunken vagrancy of Harry the Druggist. (Blitzstein originally planned to give his industrialist the name of J. P. Morgan and to provide the members of the Liberty Committee with other names of actual people, but he changed his mind in the

63

final writing to avoid greater controversy.) All have sold out and fallen under the control of Mr. Mister, who wields absolute power in Steeltown, because he controls the church, the university, the newspaper, and other community institutions. A burlesque of the local power structure, Mr. Mister has the ideal spouse in Mrs. Mister, who preens when described as a "prominent clubwoman" and takes pride in her doltish son and sex-obsessed daughter, both of whom are spoiled, vicious near-idiots lacking character. While in night court, Moll listens sympathetically as Harry relates his sad story of how he lost his thriving drugstore business and became a drunk. He tells her how Mr. Mister has corrupted the Liberty Committee by offering its members money and power in return for their support, and he reveals that he himself has been corrupted by Mr. Mister, resulting in his son's death and his own sorry state. As Moll and Harry commiserate, the police bring the union organizer Larry Foreman into court, and Mr. Mister tries without success to bribe him and to gain his loyalty. Foreman's resistance gives the others hope, which is heightened when shouts are heard offstage and word comes that other unions have joined in solidarity with the steelworkers. The Liberty Committee knows that the combined unions will be a source to reckon with and they leave Mr. Mister alone to deal with his newly strengthened opponent. The finale occurs to shouts and music offstage indicating that the union drive was successful, and Larry Foreman states in a threatening tone that "the cradle will rock and fall."

CENSORSHIP HISTORY

The Cradle Will Rock was one of the many plays that during the Great Depression sought support from the government-funded Federal Theater Project (FTP). The producers John Houseman and Orson Welles approached for financial assistance Hallie Flanagan, who oversaw the New York office of the FTP, and she agreed to seek funding after listening to Marc Blitzstein perform one of the songs from the play, which she characterized as "not a play set to music, nor music illustrated by actors, but music plus play equaling something new and better than either." Before she could authorize funds for Welles and Houseman, however, Flanagan sought approval of FTP headquarters, because the play was potentially controversial. The play was approved and the producers commissioned massive, complicated sets, a huge chorus, a full orchestra, and elaborate costumes to carry out their vision. While the play was in rehearsals, labor union strikes were turning ugly and violent throughout the United States, leading to great concern among government officials. The U.S. Supreme Court had declared unconstitutional the National Labor Relations Act, which protected the rights of workers to organize and bargain collectively, and labor organizers and union strikers faced bloody attacks in many of the nation's industrial cities.

In June 1937 Flanagan was told by FTP headquarters in Washington, D.C., to institute a 10 percent funding cut for all plays and to postpone until

July 1, 1937, the opening of "any new play, musical performance or art exhibition," which canceled the scheduled opening night of *The Cradle Will Rock* and convinced the producers and the playwright that their leftist social criticism was being singled out for persecution. On June 16, 1937, the day of the proposed first performance, a sold-out crowd gathered outside the Maxine Elliott Theatre, where they were met by padlocked doors and guards hired by the FTP to prevent the cast and producers from removing any of the sets, costumes, or props that had been paid for with government funds. As the actors provided the crowd with improvised entertainment, Welles and Houseman called all over New York City to find a theater. Stage manager Jeannie Rosenthal drove around the city in a truck carrying the production's rented piano. As the ticket holders waited outside the Maxine Elliott Theater, Welles finally located the vacant Venice Theater, a non-union-sanctioned theater whose owner offered its use. Although the orchestra refused to play in the new venue, the actors defied the rules of their union that they appear only in union-sanctioned productions and performed. The props, sets, and costumes remained locked in the original theater, but the producers presented the play on a bare set with Blitzstein playing accompaniment on the piano and the only theatrical lighting available, a portable spotlight. The play was performed for two weeks at the Venice Theater, then reopened on December 5, 1937, at the Windsor Theatre without costumes or props, which had been confiscated permanently by the Works Progress Administration, the parent of the FTP.

FURTHER READING

Blitzstein, Marc. *The Cradle Will Rock.* New York: Random House, 1938.
Herron, Ima Honaker. *The Small Town in American Drama.* Dallas, Tex.: Southern Methodist University Press, 1969.
Laufe, Abe. *The Wicked Stage: A History of Theater Censorship and Harassment in the United States.* New York: Frederick Ungar, 1978.
"Steel, Yellow Dogs, and the New Deal." Marc Blitzstein Website. Available online. URL: http://www.marcblitzstein.com/pages/cradle/pages/steel.htm.

THE CRUCIBLE

Author: Arthur Miller
Original date and place of production: January 22, 1953, Martin Beck Theatre, New York, New York
Characters: Ezekiel Cheever, Giles Corey, Deputy Governor Danforth, Sarah Good, Reverend John Hale, Judge Hathorne, Marshal Herrick, Hopkins, Mercy Lewis, Francis Nurse, Rebecca Nurse, Betty Parris, Reverend Samuel Parris, Elizabeth Proctor, John Proctor, Ann Putnam, Thomas Putnam, Tituba, Susanna Walcott, Mary Warren, John Willard, Abigail Williams

Filmed versions: *The Crucible* (1980, made for television, U.K.); *The Crucible* (1996, U.S.); *Les Sorcières de Salem* (1957, France)

SUMMARY

The Crucible functions in two contexts: as a historical play, it relates the Salem witch trials of late-17th-century New England, and as a parable for the United States of the 1950s, it deals with the devastating effects of anti-communist mass hysteria and public pressure on the lives of individuals. The play premiered in 1953 at the height of the political furor created by the McCarthy hearings and the House Un-American Activities Committee (HUAC), which persecuted suspected members of the Communist Party and other groups declared subversive by the U.S. government (or suspected by Senator McCarthy). Although Miller has revealed that he meant his depiction of events in Salem of 1692 to reflect the modern governmental witch-hunt that was happening as he wrote *The Crucible*, the carefully researched drama has implications for all societies and eras in which the ugly forces at work in the minds of supposedly intelligent human beings can destroy individuals.

The play opens with Salem's minister, Reverend Samuel Parris, praying at the bedside of his sick daughter whom he had come upon "dancing like a heathen in the forest" with his older niece, Abigail Williams, and other girls the night preceding. He has heard other people whispering about witchcraft, and urges Abigail to reveal if the girls have been led into "unnatural acts" by his Barbadian slave Tituba, which Abigail denies. Other families report that their daughters were also found dancing, and they place the blame on "bewitchment." After the girls are threatened with whipping, Abigail lies and tells Parris that the girls had "trafficked with spirits." She threatens the younger girls to support her assertion. Abigail also tries to induce John Proctor to resume their love affair, which occurred while she was a servant in his home but ended when his wife, Elizabeth, discovered his unfaithfulness. When Proctor rejects her, she becomes spiteful and plots to implicate his wife as a witch. As the accusations escalate, Tituba panics and, in a desperate attempt to save her own life, confesses to Reverend John Hale, a demonologist, that she is guilty of "conjuring." Abigail pretends to have a sudden epiphany and cries out the names of people she claims to have seen "with the Devil." Parris's sick daughter deliriously joins in the accusations, and the first act ends with the minister shouting a prayer of thanksgiving.

A trial begins in the second act, and all of the girls are called to give testimony. Mary Warren, the Proctors' new servant, is also called. To pass the time in court she sews a rag doll, which she brings home when she reports the convictions of numerous formerly respected people and reveals that an anonymous accuser has implicated Elizabeth. When the court clerk arrives to arrest Elizabeth, he also takes as evidence the rag doll, which has a needle in it. Abigail, who knows about the doll, later claims to have had a fit and pulled a needle out of her flesh after Elizabeth's "familiar spirit pushed it in." Proctor demands that Mary tell the truth, but the terrified girl tells him that Abigail will kill her and accuse him of "lechery." Proctor appears in court after convincing Mary to confess that the doll is hers and that Abigail has lied. He brings fraud charges against the court with the support of 91 people who have signed a statement supporting the character of Elizabeth and the other accused women. Desiring revenge, Abigail condemns Mary's admission and further condemns Elizabeth, leading Proctor to overcome his shame and to reveal his affair with Abigail. He tells the court, "She thinks to dance on my wife's grave . . . it is a whore's vengeance, and you must see it." The court sends for Elizabeth to corroborate his admission, but she does not know that he has revealed the adultery, so she lies to protect his good name. Hysterical with joy, Abigail pretends that she is being attacked by Mary, whom she claims to see in the shape of a large black bird. As Mary cries out for her to stop the accusations, Abigail and the other girls mimic her cries until Mary also becomes hysterical and accuses Proctor of being the "Devil's agent." Danforth orders Proctor arrested, and Hale, the demonologist, resigns in disgust.

The final act takes place immediately before the hanging of Proctor and the others accused, none of whom have confessed to witchcraft. Against Hale's urging to pardon them, Danforth presses forward, hoping to make Proctor confess. During a visit from Elizabeth, Proctor considers trading a lie for his life, because he wants to live for his children and the baby that Elizabeth now carries. As much as Elizabeth wants her husband to live, she urges him to do what his conscience and character require. He rips up his confession and resolves to die with dignity. The play ends as Hale pleads with Elizabeth to persuade Proctor to lie and save his life. The sound of a heightened drum roll signals Proctor's death.

CENSORSHIP HISTORY

Arthur Miller was among the first prominent figures to protest the abuses of McCarthyism when the reactionary forces of the HUAC began to label the voices of 1930s and 1940s social progress as radicals and persecute them as revolutionaries. Miller wrote *The Crucible* as the anticommunist hysteria accelerated into hearings, between 1952 and 1953. When the play opened, in January 1953, audiences and critics called it heavy-handed and lacking in the passion they had anticipated, so Miller withdrew it after a few performances. He added a new scene between Proctor and Abigail before attempting another opening night, in July 1953, at the same theater. For this production, Miller removed all scenery and used the stage curtain as a backdrop. The new version drew praise from critics and audiences, but the stark stage emphasized the tragic message of the play and alerted government officials to the scathing criticism it contained. The renowned theater critic John Gassner saw Miller's motivation to include "taking a public stand against authoritarian inquisitions and mass hysteria" and identifies him as "one of the very few writers of the period to speak out unequivocally for reason and justice." Although no attempts were made to ban the play from the American stage, an event that occurred in 1954 is believed by many in the theater to have been an act of retaliation against Miller for his implied criticism of the McCarthy hearings in *The Crucible*. In mid-1954 Miller applied to the U.S. State Department to renew his passport so that he could travel to Brussels to attend the Belgian premiere of the play, but he was refused, as his file reveals, "because of believed CP [Communist Party] support." Ruth Shipley, the head of the Passport Bureau of the State Department, denied the renewal, citing regulations that permitted the department to refuse passports to individuals who were believed to be supporting the communist movement. Two years later, Miller was called before the HUAC for questioning and threatened repeatedly with imprisonment for his refusal to answer questions.

The play has also stirred negative emotions in later years. In 1970 all of Arthur Miller's plays were banned by the Soviet Union, because of his efforts to free dissident writers. In 1982 parents of students attending Cumberland Valley High School in Harrisburg, Pennsylvania, demanded the removal of the book from the curriculum. They presented a complaint to the district school board asserting that the play was dangerous to the moral well-being of their children because it contains "sick words from the mouths of demon-possessed people. It should be wiped out of the schools or the school board should use them [the texts] to fuel the fire of hell." In 1987 another challenge to the play was raised by parents of students attending Pulaski County High School in Somerset, Kentucky. They protested that the work was "junk" that students should not be required to read. In both cases the school boards kept the play on the reading list, but students whose parents had protested were permitted to select others plays for their children to read.

FURTHER READING

"*The Crucible* Challenged in Pennsylvania." *Newsletter on Intellectual Freedom* (March 1983): 6–7.

"*The Crucible* Challenged in Kentucky." *Newsletter on Intellectual Freedom* (May 1987): 90.

Gassner, John. *Theatre at the Crossroads: Plays and Playwrights of the Mid-Century American Stage*. New York: Holt, Rinehart and Winston, 1960.

Gould, Jean. *Modern American Playwrights*. New York: Dodd, Mead, 1966.

Herron, Ima Honaker. *The Small Town in American Drama*. Dallas, Tex.: Southern Methodist University Press, 1969.

Martine, James J. *The Crucible: Politics, Property, and Pretense*. New York: Twayne Publishers, 1993.

Miller, Arthur. *The Crucible*. New York: Penguin Books, 1981.

Miller, Jordan Y. *American Dramatic Literature*. New York: McGraw-Hill Book Company, 1961.

Robins, Natalie. *Alien Ink: The FBI's War on Freedom of Expression*. New York: William Morrow, 1992.

DAMAGED GOODS (LES AVARIÉS)

Author: Eugene Brieux

Original date and place of production: 1902, Paris, France (private performance); March 14, 1913, at the Fulton Theater, New York, New York

Characters: Doctor, George Dupont, Mrs. Dupont, Girl, Henriette, Loches, Maid, Man, Medical Student, Nurse, Woman

Filmed versions: *Are You Fit to Marry?* (1937, U.S.); *Damaged Goods* (1914, U.S.); *Damaged Goods* (1919, U.K.)

SUMMARY

Created by the playwright as a "study of syphilis in its bearing on marriage," *Damaged Goods* is structured more like a debate and lecture than a dramatic work. The play opens with George Dupont, the "damaged goods" of the title, speaking with his doctor, who has just informed him that he has syphilis. Dupont, who is about to be married, breaks down and sobs uncontrollably, while protesting to his doctor that he only had one "lark" from which he became infected. In a soothing manner, the doctor assures him that modern science has the pharmaceutical tools at hand to cure him of the venereal disease, but that Dupont will have to postpone his wedding for three years to ensure a complete cure so that he does not pass the disease on to his bride and any children they might conceive. The headstrong young man seeks a second opinion from a quack who fools him into believing that a quick cure is available, and Dupont marries as planned. He and his wife soon have a child who begins to exhibit the signs of syphilitic infection, which Dupont's mother fails to recognize as she seeks to save the child by retaining a wet nurse. The horrified doctor, whom Mrs. Dupont calls to treat the child, warns Mrs. Dupont of the true diagnosis, and the nurse learns that she is in danger of infection. As the indignant nurse leaves the Dupont home, she shouts out what she has learned, and Henriette collapses. After reviving, Henriette is filled with disgust and hatred for Dupont, and shouts at him, "Don't touch me!" She and her father, a politician, demand that the doctor provide them with certification of Dupont's condition for her to use in obtaining a divorce, but the doctor refuses. He explains to them that many men expose themselves to the dangers of syphilis and argues for better health laws and education about syphilis.

The last part of the play is mainly a lecture about the need to deal openly with sex and venereal diseases, rather than continuing "in a gigantic conspiracy of silence." The doctor recommends that Dupont and his wife try to save their marriage, because science can cure him and the young couple may yet have healthy children. To illustrate his point, the doctor relates the case study of a young prostitute with syphilis who would have benefited from compassion and treatment. Having lectured Henriette and Loches on the need for society to provide health laws, and on the need for politicians to advocate legislation that would require anyone who marries to obtain a medical certificate, the doctor bids them farewell and tells Loches, "If you give a thought or two to what you have just learned when you sit in the Chamber [the legislature where, as a politician, Dupont will be creating law], we shall not have wasted our time."

CENSORSHIP HISTORY

Damaged Goods was banned by the Parisian authorities from performance in the Théâtre-Libre in Paris in 1901 after the owner, André Antoine, had produced several earlier plays by Brieux. Undeterred, Antoine and Brieux gave a public reading of the play later in the year, accompanied by their impassioned pleas that society acknowledge the dangers of syphilis and pass health laws to protect the innocent wives and children who could become infected by unscrupulous or unknowing husbands and fathers. The following year a producer in England offered the play for review to the examiner of plays, George Alexander Redford, who refused a license for the play to be performed, after which British authorities banned the play from production in England. In the United States, major Broadway producers also rejected the play, but Edward L. Bernays, coeditor of *The Medical Review of Reviews*, retained Richard Bennett to produce one matinee performance of the play as a clinical study on March 14, 1913, as the program stated, "under the auspices of *The Medical Review of Reviews* Sociological Fund." Clergy members in New York City spoke out strongly against the production, which took place at the Fulton Theater, and called upon public officials to ban further performances, but a second performance was staged on March 17, 1913, when city authorities failed to take any action against the first production. To avoid further risk of censorship, Bernays solicited subscriptions for *The Medical Review of Reviews* Sociological Fund. He organized all paid subscribers into a theater club, similar to those in England used to circumvent official censorship, and presented the play only to members of the club.

Although clergy members condemned the play for its handling of the taboo topic of venereal disease, physicians and scientists endorsed Brieux's goal of enlightening society about the devastating effects of syphilis and called for the play's continued performance. To ensure the official acceptance of future productions, Bennett arranged to present a special performance for members of the president's cabinet, members of the U.S. Senate and House of Representatives, members of the U.S. Supreme Court, representatives of the diplomatic corps, and other politically prominent individuals and groups. The performance took place at the National Theater, in Washington, D.C., on April 6, 1913, before a crowd of distinguished politicians and noted clergy. The audience endorsed the play in the belief that "the ultimate welfare of the community is dependent upon a higher standard of morality and clearer understanding of the laws of health," and urged Bennett to present the play in major cities throughout the United States.

By late April *Damaged Goods* had gained acceptance as a serious and important clinical study in America, and producers were allowed to open performances to the general public. In contrast, reaction to the play remained negative in England, although the prohibition of Brieux's plays in England in 1909 led to an appointment of a Select Committee of Parliament with the task of investigating censorship. The move was motivated by petitions signed by numerous English writers, including George Bernard Shaw, who wrote that the English system suppressed serious plays such as Brieux's "whilst allowing frivolous or even pornographic plays to pass unchallenged." In 1914, when the American producer George Baxter staged the play in a private theater club in London, editors of several major London newspapers refused to send their theater critics to review it. World War I changed views in England toward venereal disease as medical reports emerged that many soldiers became victims. By 1916 the British government had embraced the play as a vital educational drama and sent stage companies on tour to perform the play at British military installations.

FURTHER READING

Elsom, John. *Erotic Theatre*. New York: Taplinger Publishing Co., 1974.

Fowell, Frank, and Frank Palmer. *Censorship in England*. London: F. Palmer, 1913. Reprint, New York: Benjamin Blom, 1969.

Laufe, Abe. *The Wicked Stage: A History of Theater Censorship and Harassment in the United States*. New York: Frederick Ungar, 1978.

McCarthy, Desmond. "Literary Taboos." *Life and Letters* 1 (October 1928): 329–341.

Sinclair, Upton. *Damaged Goods: The Great Play "Les Avaries" of Eugene Brieux*. Available online. URL: http://ibiblio.org/gutenberg/titles/damaged_goods_the_g.html.

Shaw, G. Bernard. Preface to *Three Plays by Brieux, Member of the French Academy. English Versions by Mrs. Bernard Shaw, St. John Hankin, and John Pollock*. 2d ed. New York: Brentano's, 1911.

LA DAME AUX CAMÉLIAS

Author: Alexandre Dumas *fils* (the Younger)

Original date and place of production: February 2, 1852, Vaudeville Théâtre, Paris, France

Characters: Armand Duval, M. Duval, Prudence de Duvernoy, Marguerite Gautier, Joseph, Nanine, Nichette, Olympia de Taverney, Baron de Varville

Filmed versions: *Camille* (1909, Italy); *Camille* (1912, France); *Camille* (1915, U.S.); *Camille* (1917, U.S.); *Camille* (1921, U.S.); *Camille* (1927, U.S.); *Camille* (1937, U.S.); *Camille 2000* (1969, Italy); *Die Kameliadame* (1987, Germany); *Kameliadamen* (1907, Denmark); *La dame aux camélias* (1910, France)

SUMMARY

Based on Dumas's novel of the same name, *La dame aux camélias* relates the romantic story of courtesan Marguerite Gautier, who falls in love with the young Armand Duval. Unlike Marguerite's many other admirers, Armand is not wealthy, and he bankrupts himself while trying to produce gifts that can at least compete with those given by her least affluent suitors. Influenced for a time by her love for Armand, Marguerite vows to give up her life as a pampered courtesan and join her young lover in enjoying the simple pleasures of country life. Although she occasionally longs for her life of opulence, Marguerite finds happiness with Armand—until his father appears when the younger Duval is away from home on business. M. Duval begs, pleads, and bullies her into acknowledging that her past casts a shadow on his son's life and will harm his future, and he tells her to prove that she is sincere in her love by leaving his son. Concerned that M. Duval's concerns for his son's social and professional futures are valid, Marguerite agrees to leave the country and to return to Paris. To prevent Armand from following her, despite her desire to remain with him, she writes that she has been unhappy and felt isolated from her former life and friends, so she must leave him and return to Paris.

Although she resumes her former life and spends time with her former companions, Marguerite continues to love Armand, but her concern for his well-being keeps her from seeing him until she becomes ill with tuberculosis. As she nears death, she fears that her harsh words regarding their life in the country will prevent him from coming to her. Marguerite's wish to see Armand is granted after M. Duval has an attack of conscience and tells his son that he goaded the young woman into lying about her feelings. Armand is devastated by the news, but he rushes to Marguerite's bedside and arrives in time to hold and comfort her before she dies in his arms.

CENSORSHIP HISTORY

Dumas adapted *La dame aux camélias* as a play in 1852 from his 1848 novel of the same name, and the first performance of the play took place at the Vaudeville Théâtre in Paris in February 1852. The play became one of the most popular dramatic pieces in 19th-century France, but the English censors banned the play from performance for more than 20 years because of a perceived explicitness that the English found unacceptable. The play was submitted in English translation in 1853 under the title *Camille* for review by William Donne, the examiner of plays, and promptly rejected because of its theme of the "fallen" woman and its sympathetic treatment of a courtesan. Donne was supported in his decision by the critic George Henry Lewes, who railed against the play as being an "idealization of corruption" and "a hideous parody of passion." (His extended attack on the play appears hypocritical to later observers who know that by 1853 the married Lewes had begun a long-term affair with the novelist Mary Ann Evans, who wrote under the pseudonym of George Eliot.) In an editorial that appeared in the *London Examiner* in March 1853, Lewes condemned Dumas for tending "to confuse the moral sense, by exciting the sympathy of the audience" and proclaimed the moral superiority of the English.

Paris may delight in such pictures, but London, thank God! has still enough instinctive repulsion against pruriency not to tolerate them. I declare I know of few things in the way of fiction more utterly wrong, unwholesome, and immoral, than *Dame aux Camélias*. . . . I am not being prudish, nor easily alarmed by what are called "dangerous" subjects, but *this subject* I protest against with all my might;—a subject not only unfit to be brought before our sisters and our wives, but unfit to be brought before ourselves.

While the play remained banned from the English stage, *La Traviata*, Giuseppe Verdi's operatic version of the play, was licensed for performance at Her Majesty's Theatre in May 1856 and received hearty acclaim. Critics generally observed that Verdi had softened the details of the play and made the heroine "irresistibly pathetic," so that viewers are moved by her sorrows. The popularity of the Italian opera was so strong that the examiner of plays also approved an English-language version, *La Traviata; or, the Blighted One*, to be performed at the Surrey Theater in June 1856, although the similarities to Dumas's original play were stronger than Verdi's version. The difference in acceptance points up the degree of tolerance with which the authorities viewed 19th-century opera in contrast to drama. In 1866, when Donne was questioned about the differing standards that his office had applied in approving or refusing licenses for plays and operas, he wrote that "it makes a difference, for the words [in the opera] are then subsidiary to the music." In March 1859 the management of the St. James's Theatre in London submitted a manuscript of the play to the censors and requested a license for performance, but the request was refused once again. In his March 24, 1859, report justifying the refusal to license the play, Donne described the play as "a glorification of harlotry [which] in the last act . . . profanes the sanctity of death." He was strongly supported by the Lord Chamberlain, Lord De La Warr, and by the comptroller of the Lord Chamberlain's Office, Spencer Ponsonby, who wrote in his concurrence with the decision that the play should never have been licensed in any form, including operatic versions.

The play was first presented in the United States on December 9, 1853, at the Broadway Theatre in New York City, but with a censored script. The actress Jean Davenport knew that the puritanical nature of American audiences would make acceptance of the original version unlikely, despite its popularity in France, so she adapted the play and renamed it *Camille, or, the Fate of a Coquette*. Her alterations of the story led one critic to report that having been "divested of all the immoral, objectionable features," the play had become "an entertainment of virtuous instruction." Among other changes, the heroine is no longer a courtesan and her behavior is more subdued. Other performers and producers also created adaptations for the American stage, often making copious changes to the story line and the presentation of the character of Marguerite. By 1857, when the actress Matilda Heron daringly presented her adaptation of the play, *La Dame aux Camélias*, which was faithful to the Paris production that she had seen, reviewers praised it for exhibiting "startling realism in acting" and for being a "problem play of contemporary 'real life'"; the actors received standing ovations.

FURTHER READING

Braun, Sidney D. *Dictionary of French Literature*. New York: Philosophical Library, 1958.

Dumas, Alexandre. *Camille*. New York: Modern Library, 1925.

Elsom, John. *Erotic Theatre*. New York: Taplinger Publishing Co., 1974.

Fowell, Frank, and Frank Palmer. *Censorship in England*. London: F. Palmer, 1913. Reprint, New York: Benjamin Blom, 1913.

Stephens, John Russell. *The Censorship of English Drama, 1824–1901*. New York: Cambridge University Press, 1980.

THE DEPUTY

Author: Rolf Hochhuth

Original date and place of production: February 23, 1963, Freie Volksbuhne, Berlin, West Germany (under the German title, *Der Stellvertreter*)

Characters: The Abbot, the Apostolic Nuncio in Berlin, the Cardinal, Carlotta, the Doctor, Eichmann, Count Fontana, Father Riccardo Fontana, Dr. Fritsche, Kurt Gerstein (Obersturmfuhrer SS), Helga, Professor Hirt (Reichs University Strassburg), Brother Irenaeus, Jacobson, Katitzky, Dr. Littke, Luccani Sr., Dr. Lothar Luccani, Julia Luccani, Julia Luccani's children (boy, age 9; girl, age 5), Muller-Salle, Pope Pius XII, Regierungsrat Dr. Pryzilla, Baron Rutta (Reichs Armaments Cartel), Lieutenant von Rutta, Salzer, Colonel Serge, Signora Simonetta, Witzel

Filmed versions: None

SUMMARY

The Deputy, produced on stage under the titles of *Der Stellvertreter* in Germany and *The Representative* in England, is a highly controversial play that uses the technique of semidocumentary stage reportage—the use of numerous details and actual facts from life—in the effort to prove a theory. The play generated controversy for its subject matter—the role the papacy played in the Holocaust—and for the playwright's use of actual people, some of whom were still living when the play was published. To emphasize the historical importance of his theme and to identify the sources of his ideas to "the historical persons mentioned in the play, and those of their relations who are still living," the playwright provides a lengthy epilogue to the published version of the play, which he entitles "Sidelights on History." Hochhuth asserts that "as a stage play the work requires no commentary," and he acknowledges that the unusual nature of the addition does serve "to burden a drama with an historical appendix," yet he feels it necessary because the events portrayed are the result of artistic manipulation of time and do not follow the historical events in a step-by-step manner. Thus, he provides potential detractors with an overview of the sources, such as memoirs, biographies, letters, diaries, records of conversations, and minutes of court proceedings, that he used in constructing his view of the roles played by individuals and of their actions in relation to the Holocaust.

In this play, Hochhuth postulates that the slaughter of millions of Jews as the "final solution" of the Third Reich could have been prevented if Pope Pius XII had voiced open opposition to the actions of the Germans. Yet Hochhuth does not indict all representatives of the Catholic Church, for he dedicates the play to a priest who lost his life at Auschwitz, "Father Maximilian Kolbe/Inmate No. 16670 in Auschwitz," who died in the starvation bunker in August 1941, after volunteering to take the place of another prisoner who later survived the war because of Kolbe's action. The play is also dedicated to "Provost Lichtenberg of St. Hedwig's Cathedral, Berlin," who made frequent efforts to help Jews escape from the Nazis. In a note accompanying the list of characters, Hochhuth explains that the list is arranged in groups of two, three, or four "for recent history has taught us that in the age of universal military conscription it is not necessarily to anyone's credit or blame, or even a question of character, which uniform one wears or whether one stands on the side of the victims or the executioners." *The Deputy*, a verse play written in free, iambically accented form, contains five acts, each of which carries a title: Act One: "The Mission," Act Two: "The Bells of St. Peter's," Act Three: "The Visitation," Act Four: "*Il Gran Rifiuto*," and Act Five: "Auschwitz, or Where Are You, God?" Set in Berlin, Germany, Rome, Italy, and Oświęcim (Auschwitz), Poland, during 1942–44, the play runs seven hours in its original form. Hochhuth sought to dramatize the lack of response by the Catholic Church to the annihilation of Jews by Germany and the perceived failure of Pope Pius XII, whom Hochhuth characterizes as "God's Deputy."

The play opens as the young Jesuit priest Father Riccardo Fontana urges the Papal Nuncio in Berlin to take a stand against the actions of the Nazis. He is supported in his request by Gerstein, a resistance fighter who has been posing as a lieutenant in the SS and who has witnessed atrocities, but the Nuncio refuses and promises only to pray for the victims. Riccardo also fails in attempts to convince a cardinal in Rome and his wealthy father, Count Fontana, that the church should openly oppose Hitler's actions. Instead, the high dignitaries of the church and the count support a neutral position for the papacy, to avoid conflict with Germany and because "the Pope will not/expose himself to danger for the Jews." Riccardo and Gerstein work to save individual Jews, but the mounting Nazi threat makes them desperate. They contemplate seizing the Vatican radio transmitter to broadcast a call to all Catholics to openly resist the Nazi regime, and assassinating the pope "to save him from complete perdition." As the Nazis begin to arrest Italians, the cardinal and other high-ranking church officials assure Riccardo that the pope will now act. The hope is false; the pope is busy discussing with Count Fontana the financial holdings of the church. When Riccardo does speak to him, he refuses to protest the Nazi atrocities because "Hitler alone, dear Count, is now defending Europe" against the Russians. When Riccardo presses him to write a proclamation denouncing the Nazi murders of the Jews, the pope becomes enraged and refuses, because Hitler "would only be antagonized and outraged." He protests that the church has done what it could and "We are—God knows it—blameless of the blood/now being spilled." In protest, Riccardo attaches a yellow cloth Star of David to his cassock and promises that he will wear it until the pope consents to condemn Hitler. Riccardo allows himself to be deported to Auschwitz, where the final act takes place. After he is in the concentration camp for a while, Gerstein appears with faked orders for his release, but Riccardo has traded his cassock for the clothes of a Jewish prisoner, whom he insists should be saved in his place. The plan is destroyed when the Doctor appears and orders Gerstein imprisoned. In a fit of anger after watching the Doctor kill an inmate, Carlotta, while he watches, Riccardo physically attacks the Doctor and is shot by guards, who carry him to burn alive in the crematorium. The stage darkens slowly and the audience sees only the dead Carlotta as an unemotional voice reminds them, "The gas chambers continued to work for a full year more. In the summer of 1944 the so-called daily quota of exterminations reached its maximum. On November 26, 1944, Himmler ordered the crematorium to be blown up. Two months later the last prisoners in Auschwitz were freed by Russian soldiers."

CENSORSHIP HISTORY

The Deputy has stirred controversy for its contention that because of their refusal to openly condemn the actions of Hitler and the Nazis, Pope Pius XII and the Roman Catholic Church were to blame for the mass murders of Jews. The play has also become controversial because of charges that Hochhuth skewed the historical evidence and created a biased, inaccurate account of the role played by the pope and other high-ranking church officials during World War II. When the play was set to open in West Germany in February 1963, Catholic leaders there attempted to stop the production because they feared lay Catholics would object to the accusations leveled against Pope Pius XII and question the motives of Hochhuth, a Protestant, as anti-Catholic. Church leaders spoke with authorities in Berlin and argued that the presentation of the play outside of Germany might also stir up anti-German feelings: audiences in other countries might view Hochhuth's play as German propaganda to deflect some of the blame of his own nation. Officials refused to stop the production, and it went forward without major difficulty. In London, plans by the Royal Shakespeare Company to stage performances of *The Deputy*, adapted for the English stage and renamed *The Representative* by Jerome Rothenberg, were delayed for several weeks. Lord Cobbold, the Lord

Chamberlain, refused to license the play until he was assured that several demands would be met. He insisted that the management display a notice barring children under 16 from seeing the play, because it contained some material that was "inappropriate" for young people. He also ordered that the theater program include a rebuttal statement written by "an authoritative Roman Catholic" of their choice. The managers of the Royal Shakespeare Company chose to include a letter from then-cardinal Montini, who later became Pope Paul VI, and a letter written by the editor of the *Catholic Herald*, who asserted the facts of the play were incorrect and that it had achieved popularity in Germany only because it made Germans feel less guilty. The opening of the play in October 1963 at the Aldwych Theater was greeted with protests by various religious groups. Protesters marched in front of the theater with signs denouncing the play and defaced posters outside the theater. Actors who played the roles of Eichmann, the Doctor, and other nefarious German characters reported to police that they received death threats. None of these actions stopped the play.

Even greater resistance occurred when the American producer Billy Rose announced his intentions to bring the play to Broadway, under the title *The Deputy*. Newspapers and magazines predicted that the play would be met with vigorous protests, and Catholic publications openly attacked the play and its author. The associate editor of the Roman Catholic weekly *America*, the Reverend Robert A. Graham, wrote an editorial that denounced the play as "typical Nazi literature." *Our Sunday Visitor* claimed that the play was fiction and accused Hochhuth of having been a member of the Nazi youth movement. Rose had hired Herman Shumlin to stage the play, and after Rose decided not to produce the play because the controversy would make producing it difficult, Shumlin decided to both produce and to direct the play. As the first performance of the play in February 1964 approached, clergy members protested in letters to New York City officials, and their supporters wrote letters to Shumlin, who also reported receiving numerous threats against his life. When the play opened on February 26, 1964, members of the American Fascist organization picketed the theater wearing storm trooper uniforms and scared some audiences away. The play continued to draw controversy, and detractors who asserted that the play was simply fiction even tried to stop the awarding of a Tony to Shumlin for bringing the play to Broadway.

The play continues to anger people, who point to the praise heaped on Pope Pius XII by the *New York Times* in an editorial published on December 25, 1941, which stated, "The voice of Pius XII is a lonely voice in the silence and darkness enveloping Europe this Christmas. . . . He is the only ruler left on the Continent of Europe who dares to raise his voice at all." They question the change in perception that led the *New York Times* to write in another editorial, published on March 18, 1998, "A full exploration of Pope Pius's conduct is needed. . . . It now falls to John Paul and his successors to take the next step toward full acceptance of the Vatican's failure to stand squarely against the evil that swept across Europe." For some observers, the change in perception is not the result of newly discovered historical facts or documents, but the fault of *The Deputy*. As Kenneth L. Woodward wrote erroneously in *Newsweek* in 1998, "Most of these accusations can be traced to a single originating source: 'The Deputy,' Rolf Hochhuth's 1963 play that created an image of Pius as moral coward. That Golda Meir, later a prime minister of Israel, and leaders of Jewish communities in Hungary, Turkey, Italy, Romania and the United States thanked the pope for saving hundreds of thousands of Jews is now considered irrelevant. That he never specifically condemned the Shoah is all that seems to matter." Historical fact lends substantial support to Hochhuth's perspective.

FURTHER READING

Aronowitz, Alfred G. "The Play That Rocked Europe." *Saturday Evening Post*, February 29, 1964, pp. 38–39, 42–43.

Bentley, Eric, ed. *The Storm over* The Deputy. New York: Grove Press, 1964.

Bernauer, James, S.J. "An Ethic and Moral Formation That Are Repentant: Catholicism's Emerging Post-Shoah Tradition: The Case of the Jesuits." Presented at the Remembering for the Future 2000 Conference: The Holocaust in the Age of Genocide. Oxford and London, July 16–23, 2000.

Nichols, James H. "Critic's Corner: *The Deputy* and Christian Conscience." *Theology Today* 1 (April 1964): 111–113.

Schmidt, Dolores, and Earl R. Schmidt. *The Deputy Reader.* Chicago: Scott, Foresman, 1965.

Woodward, Kenneth L. "Blaming the Wartime Pope for Failing to Stop the Holocaust from the Vatican Is a Neat Bit of Revisionist History." *Newsweek*, March 30, 1998, p. 35.

DESIRE UNDER THE ELMS

Author: Eugene O'Neill

Original date and place of production: November 11, 1924, Greenwich Village Theater, New York, New York

Characters: Eben Cabot, Ephraim Cabot, Peter Cabot, Simeon Cabot, Abbie Putnam

Filmed versions: *Desire under the Elms* (1958, U.S.), *Ljubov pod Vjazumi Qali bazrobidan* (1928, USSR)

SUMMARY

Set in 1850 in New England, *Desire under the Elms* is a stark drama in three parts that presents themes of lust, greed, vengeance, murder, adultery, and incest. Considered by critics to be one of Eugene O'Neill's most powerful plays, the work incorporates Freudian psychology into a modernization of the classical Greek myths in creating Abbie who willfully murders her baby, and the affair of Abbie with her stepson Eban and violent denunciation of her aged husband Ephraim. The drama opens with 25-year-old Eben and half-brothers Simeon and Peter admiring a sunset as they complain about their abusive father, Ephraim, and talk about getting out from under his tyranny. Simeon and Peter, who want to leave the farm and try their luck out west, tease Eben for being the "dead spit an' image" of Ephraim, but he protests that he looks more like his late mother. He tells them that Ephraim married his mother and took her land, then worked her to death, so he believes that the farm is rightfully his. Their father has been away for two months, but they soon learn that he has married again and is on the way home with his new bride.

Disillusioned because they believe that Ephraim will leave everything to his new wife, Simeon and Peter decide to leave, but Eben will stay. After surreptitiously stealing the money hidden by his father, Eben promises to pay them each $600 of the stolen money if they will sign over their inheritance claims to him. They consent. Seventy-five-year-old Ephraim arrives with his 35-year-old wife, Abbie Putnam, a full-figured and sensual woman who takes possession of the home immediately. Peter and Simeon insult the newlyweds and then leave, but Eben senses an immediate physical attraction to her, even as he feels hate for her. Two months pass, and Ephraim tells Abbie that he is "gittin' ripe on the bough" but that he would leave his farm to her if she can produce a son, which she promises to do, leading him to fall to his knees in prayer. In the bedroom, he tells her how hard he has worked in his life, building the farm out of fields of stone, and that he has always been a lonely man. Abbie ignores him because her attention is drawn to the far wall, which separates Eben's bedroom from theirs. When Ephraim finds that Abbie is unresponsive, he storms out of the bedroom and runs to the barn "to sleep with the cows." A short while later, Abbie gives in to her desires and enters Eben's room, where she kisses him passionately and leads him into the parlor, which has been closed since his mother's death years ago. Abbie seduces Eben and persuades him that his mother's spirit demands revenge. Afterward, Eben feels compelled to shake Ephraim's hand, telling him, "Yew 'n' me is quits. . . . Maw kin rest now an' sleep content." He has gotten his revenge.

When Abbie gives birth to a son the following spring, Ephraim believes it is his child and celebrates, but the townspeople laugh behind his back about "the old skunk gittin' fooled." Ephraim later tells Eben that Abbie wanted to have a son so she could inherit the farm, leading Eben to feel that Abbie has used him. Eben threatens to kill Abbie and blames the baby for his sorrow, so he decides to leave. Abbie panics at the thought of losing him and hysterically decides to kill the baby to prove that she was not plotting to steal the land. She rushes to Eben at dawn to announce that she has shown how much she loves him by killing the baby, but he is horrified and goes for the sheriff. Ephraim is furious when he learns that the baby was Eben's, and although he looks forward to Abbie's execution, he tells her that he would never have turned her in, "no matter what ye did, if they was t'brile [boil] me alive!" He decides that the time has come for him to leave the hard and lonely life on the farm, but becomes resigned to staying when he finds that the money he had counted on has been stolen. Eben returns with the sheriff and decides that he is also at fault for the baby's death, so he must share Abbie's punishment. The lovers hold hands as they leave for jail, and they kiss as they admire the sunset. As the curtain falls, the sheriff looks at the farm enviously and states, "It's a jim-dandy farm, no denyin' it. Wished I owned it!"

CENSORSHIP HISTORY

Desire under the Elms has endured as one of O'Neill's most popular and successful plays, but the language and frank sexuality of the play have made it the target of censors in New York, Boston, Los Angeles, and London. The play was first performed by the Provincetown Players on November 11, 1924, at the Greenwich Village Theater. On February 20, 1925, O'Neill received a letter from his literary agent Richard J. Madden telling him that the New York City police were "going after" *Desire under the Elms.* O'Neill scoffed at the threat until he received a frantic cablegram from Madden the following day informing him that the play was "about to be indicted." The play was not being singled out by the authorities, but it was one of a number of plays that became part of a crusade to "clean up" the New York stage. Late in the preceding year, ineffectual efforts had been made to drive WHAT PRICE GLORY? from the stage, but the new crusade launched against *Desire under the Elms* appeared to be more virulent. The newest effort was sparked by the producer of another play, whose publicity campaign aimed at increasing box office receipts had backfired. Seeking to boost business by drawing media attention to his production *A Good Bad Woman*, William A. Brady created a publicity hoax in which his leading lady protested to the press that she was shocked and offended by some of her dialogue in the play. Brady's plan was to titillate the public; instead, he drew the attention of the New York City law enforcement authorities, who declared his play to be "irreclaimably vicious," and the production was ordered closed by District Attorney Joab H. Banton.

Banton had attempted earlier to close down O'Neill's *All God's Chillun* without success, but the new censorship crusade drew his attention to O'Neill's latest stage production. In the order issued to close the production, Banton wrote that the play was "too thoroughly bad to be purified by a blue pencil," and he threatened to seek an indictment from the grand jury against the theater managers and playwright unless the production shut down. The theater community immediately suggested the creation of a "citizens' play-jury" to review allegedly objectionable plays and to function outside of the judicial system. The plan, developed with the backing of Actors' Equity, the theater union, in the hope of avoiding official harassment, proposed a panel of several hundred people in the arts and various professions, including the clergy and educators, from which juries for each questionable play would be drawn. Although Banton at first rejected the plan, stating that too much time was needed to make the system function effectively, the overwhelming criticism by the press changed his mind. He finally agreed to relegate to the play-juries *Desire under the Elms* and other works challenged as immoral. On March 13, 1925, one month after Banton issued threats to close down the play, a play-jury acquitted *Desire under the Elms* of all charges. The play gained notoriety as a result of the threats and attracted many people who never would have thought to see it. As a result, the weekly box office gross increased from an average $12,000 to $16,000 within a few weeks. The higher grosses and increased audiences both pleased and upset O'Neill, who welcomed the higher profits but despaired that the "wrong audience" was going to his play. He complained to Madden that it now attracted "the low-minded, looking for smut, and they are highly disappointed or else laugh whenever they imagine double-meanings."

The play also ran into difficulty in Boston, where the Watch and Ward Society influenced law enforcement authorities to refuse the producers a license for performances of the play because of its hints at incest and the forthright sexuality of its characters. In England, the examiner of plays, George S. Street, refused to recommend the play for licensing because of "improprieties" in the relationship between Abbie and Eban and the "suggestive lewdness" of the characters' behavior. In Los Angeles in 1925, after receiving several complaints from individuals, police arrested the entire cast of the play and charged them with "performing in an obscene play" because one of the female cast members appeared on stage in a nightgown.

FURTHER READING

Berlin, Normand. *Eugene O'Neill*. New York: St. Martin's Press, 1982.

Bloom, Harold. *Eugene O'Neill*. New York: Chelsea House, 1987.

Carpenter, Charles. *Modern British, Irish, and American Drama: A Descriptive Chronology*. Unpublished manuscript in progress. Available online. URL: http://www.eoneill.com/essays/carpenter.htm.

Clark, Barrett Harper. *Eugene O'Neill: The Man and His Plays*. Rev. ed. New York: Dover Publications, 1947.

Gassner, John. *O'Neill: A Collection of Critical Essays*. Englewood Cliffs, N.J.: Prentice-Hall, 1964.

Laufe, Abe. *The Wicked Stage: A History of Theater Censorship and Harassment in the United States*. New York: Frederick Ungar, 1978.

"Let Freedom Ring." *Philadelphia City Paper.Net*. March 9–16, 2000. Available online. URL: http://www.citypaper.net/articles/030900/ae.theater.desire.shtml.

Miller, Jordan Y., and Winifred L. Frazer. *American Drama between the Wars*. Boston: Twayne Publishers, 1991.

O'Neill, Eugene. *The Complete Plays of Eugene O'Neill*. Edited by Travis Bogard. New York: Library of America, 1988.

Schafer, Yvonne. "Introduction: Early Actors and Directors." Introduction to *Performing O'Neill: Conversations with Actors and Directors*, edited by Yvonne Schafer. New York: Palgrave Publishing, 2000.

Sheaffer, Louis. *O'Neill: Son and Artist*. Boston: Little, Brown, 1973.

EARLY MORNING

Author: Edward Bond
Original date and place of production: March 31, 1968, Royal Court
   Theatre, London, England
Characters: Prince Albert, Prince Arthur, Disraeli, Doctor, Prince George,
   Gladstone, Private Griss, Corporal Jones, Joyce, Len, Lord Chamberlain,
   Lord Mennings, Ned, Florence Nightingale, Queen Victoria
Filmed versions: None

SUMMARY

Early Morning presents a surrealistic version of history in which such late 19th-
century English icons as Queen Victoria, Prince Albert, and the politicians
Gladstone and Disraeli are stripped of the myths with which history has surrounded them and reinterpreted in ways that demolish the legends of pious
morality and religion they represent. The play is difficult to understand in many
instances, and audiences complained of not being able to follow what was happening because it combines commonplace details of everyday existence with
Bond's grotesque fantasies about his characters. The playwright prefaces his play
with the statement, "The events of this play are true," then presents a play in
which he so obviously and deliberately distorts well-known and external historical facts as to make their satiric intent clear to anyone. Viewers are treated to a
Queen Victoria who gives birth to conjoined twins, Princes Arthur and George,
and engages in a lesbian affair with Florence Nightingale. As the queen carries
on her private affairs, her spouse, Prince Albert, is busy conspiring with Disraeli
to overthrow her, and the British government holds the nation in terror as the
sadistic and power-hungry Gladstone and Disreali sacrifice all sense of morality
in their efforts to eliminate each other and to advance politically. The play fails
to follow a traditional chronological pattern, and the bizarre intrigues contained
within it are interspersed with accounts of episodes of cannibalism, all of which
lead to a ludicrous trial over which Queen Victoria presides. Len and Joyce must
answer to charges of cannibalism, which they do in language that is so matter-of-
fact as to make the horrific act seem commonplace. Near the end of the play,
most of the main characters have been murdered, but they enjoy a resurrection
in Bond's version of a heaven in which people devour each other for eternity.

   The tone of the play is farcical throughout. Queen Victoria is presented as a
monstrous predator who stalks the stage and plots to preserve the supremacy of
her position while using Prince George as her stooge in seeking Prince Albert's
destruction. At the same time, Prince Albert and Disraeli try to involve the other
twin, Prince Arthur, in their machinations to give their efforts "the appearance
of legality." To preserve her line, Queen Victoria seeks a "normal marriage" for
Prince George, and chooses Florence Nightingale for his wife because she "is an
expert sanitarian. We believe that to be a branch of Eugenics." Their meeting is
a parody of romance, for George greets his bride-to-be by reading a prepared

note, "Dear Miss Nightingale, I welcome you to Windsor and hope you will be happy here." In response, Florence reads her note: "Thank you."

As Bond clearly intended, and critics perceived, the characters come across as "grotesque caricatures" and "bizarre lampoons," not as the real personages for whom they are named. The political situation takes a similarly ludicrous turn, as Prince Albert and Disraeli decide to make their move against Queen Victoria during a royal picnic in Windsor Park. They provide a pistol to Len, freed after his trial for cannibalism, and order him to shoot Queen Victoria when he sees Prince Albert propose a toast of loyalty to her, but the queen is prepared. She poisons her husband's drink in advance and, while he weakens due to the effects of the poison, she strangles him with his own garter sash. When Disraeli enters, expecting to find Victoria dead, she confronts him with Albert's rifle, and he runs to "fetch reinforcements." Violence follows as Gladstone leads a lynch mob composed of Joyce, Corporal Jones, and Private Griss, all of whom kick and abuse Len to "explain the legal situation" to him. Bond also deals with the historical rumors of a relationship between Queen Victoria and her Highland servant John Brown, but he portrays Florence Nightingale role-playing as Brown, required to wear a kilt and "do the accent." In response to Florence's protests, Queen Victoria commands her. "Try. If they knew you were a woman there'd be a scandal, but if they believe you're a man they'll think I'm just a normal lonely widow." As the queen's feelings intensify while those of Florence cool, Bond depicts Victoria running wildly after her lover, calling out, "I need you, Florrie! You'll be killed! You're all I live for. Again, again! Things seem to get better, and then suddenly I lose everything. Freddie don't leave me! I'll let you do all the amputations. Don't! Don't!"

In a later scene, after Prince Arthur confronts his father's ghost, he despairs that humanity's natural tendency toward violence can lead to only one logical conclusion: that a great traitor is needed who will kill both sides. He views his mother at one point and perceives her to be surrounded by hanging corpses, and she explains that "They were all called Albert. . . . I can't take chances." In a series of outlandish sequences, the main characters are murdered and enter a heaven in which mutual cannibalism is the norm. When Arthur protests and refuses to eat, although already "dead," he "dies" and triggers the conclusion of the play, which is a parody of the Last Supper. As everyone sits around Arthur's coffin, Queen Victoria tells them, "He told you not to eat each other. . . . But he knew he was asking something unnatural and impossible. Something quite, quite impossible. . . . So he died, to let you eat each other in peace." Prince Albert enters with a hamper and the group cheerfully eats the food placed on Arthur's coffin.

CENSORSHIP HISTORY

Early Morning holds the distinction of being the last play to be banned by the English censors. In November 1967 William Gaskill, director of the first version of the play performed at the Royal Court Theatre in London, submitted the play to the Lord Chamberlain, Baron Cobbold, and requested a license for performance. The censor found *Early Morning* unacceptable and banned the play in its entirety, refusing to license the play for any performances. In defiance Gaskill and Bond began to present the play in club performances, legal in England because the audience bought "memberships" in advance and performances were limited to those who were "members" in the private club. Such performances were common in England for plays that were unable to obtain licenses for public performance, but *Early Morning* was performed under the guise of a private club at the Royal Court Theatre in London. So controversial was the play that Methuen Publishers, who had brought out Bond's earlier plays, was too nervous about the possibility of censorship to publish this one, so Calder and Boyars published the play script. The play was prevented from having a second Sunday-night private performance because London authorities threatened police action. A theater reviewer for the *Daily Telegraph* reported that despite the bizarre nature of the events in the play, the Lord Chamberlain's Office took seriously Bond's allegations against the historical figures, which "drove the Censor up the wall. He considered that Mr. Bond had offered 'gross insults' to highly respected characters of recent history—Queen Victoria, Prince Albert, Gladstone, Disraeli, Florence Nightingale—and, as that was the kind of thing his office had been empowered to stop, he stopped it." The actual reasons for the banning were not articulated, despite the efforts of writers such as Richard Findlater, who published *Banned!* in 1967. As Findlater wrote in a 1982 letter to fellow writer Niloufer Harben, the office of the Lord Chamberlain "could not give the reason why this play was not licensed for public production." Most opponents to the censorship of *Early Morning* surmised that the Lord Chamberlain banned the play because the British government viewed it as subversive and a threat to the establishment.

Not everyone who was against censorship of the play had kind words for it, and many felt that the battle against government censorship might be better fought with another work. Irving Wardle, theater critic for the London *Times*, wrote that he regretted that "the Royal Court's just and necessary fight for theatrical free speech should be conducted on behalf of a piece as muddled and untalented as this." Harold Hobson, theater reviewer for the *Sunday Times*, complained about the play's lack of "artistic probability" and described it in his review as providing a "demonstration of total anarchy." The theater management and the playwright were fully prepared to take their fight to the courts after London police ordered the performances to cease, but the growing movement against censorship removed the need to do so. In September 1968 the Theatres Bill, which removed previous standards for the licensing of plays, became law, ending government censorship in England and pushing *Early Morning* onto the public stage by early 1969.

FURTHER READING

Darlington, W. A. "Has Mr. Bond Been Saved?" *The Daily Telegraph*, April 15, 1968, p. 19.

Harben, Nilhoufer. *Twentieth-Century English History Plays*. Totowa, N.J.: Barnes & Noble Books, 1988.

Hobson, Harold. *"Early Morning." The Sunday Times*. Reprinted in *The Critic* 1 (April 19, 1968): 9.

Logan, Brian. "Still Bolshie After All These Years." *The Guardian*, April 5, 2000.

Sutherland, John. *Offensive Literature: Decensorship in Britain, 1960–1982*. Totowa, N.J.: Barnes & Noble Books, 1982.

THE EASIEST WAY

Author: Eugene Walter
Original date and place of production: January 19, 1909, Belasco Theatre, New York, New York
Characters: Willard Brockton, Burgess, Cleo Desmond, Nellie De Vere, Jerry, John Madison, Laura Murdoch, Elfie St. Clair, Jim Weston
Filmed versions: *The Easiest Way* (1917); *The Easiest Way* (1931)

SUMMARY

Set in Colorado Springs and New York City in 1908, *The Easiest Way* is a play in four acts that relates the story of Laura Murdoch, a young and beautiful woman raised in poverty, who tries but fails to succeed as an actress on Broadway. Untrained for any type of work that would provide her with a substantial income, and unwilling to take menial jobs to support herself, she becomes the lavishly kept mistress of Willard Brockton, a wealthy and older Wall Street broker. Although she enjoys her life of luxury, Laura feels guilty and sporadically returns to acting to try to live an independent life. During one of these fits of conscience, she meets and falls in love with journalist John Madison, who is battling his own demons, which earlier involved him in the "fast life" of bootlegging and women. He accepts Laura's past, but he also expects that she will not revert to her life as Brockton's mistress but make her own way while he is chasing his own success. Madison promises to marry her when he is financially secure. Laura makes a sincere effort to support herself, but with her limited skills she soon becomes despondent and sinks into sordid poverty. Unable to pay the rent on her small room, she approaches Brockton for a loan. He offers to take her back; contrite, she returns to him and takes "the easiest way" of being his mistress. Months later, Madison returns and wants to marry Laura, having made his fortune. Brockton insists that Laura tell the young journalist that she has resumed her role as mistress. When she fails to do so, Brockton tells Madison the truth of Laura's "fall," then leaves her. Despite all of her efforts to justify her actions to Madison, he refuses to listen and also leaves her, saying "Laura, you're not immoral, you're just unmoral, kind o' all out of shape, and I'm afraid there isn't a particle of hope for you."

The hysterical young woman first contemplates shooting herself, then abruptly decides to dress up and go out. She calls to her maid, "Dress up my body and paint my face. I'm going to Rector's [a well-known restaurant where the wealthy after-theater crowd of the time gathered] to make a hit—and to hell with the rest!" As sounds of a hurdy-gurdy organ drift in from the street playing what was for the time a suggestive song, "Bon-Bon Buddie, My Chocolate Drop," Laura stumbles toward her bedroom. The final stage directions state that the tune is "peculiarly suggestive of the low life, the criminality and prostitution that constitute the night excitement of that section of New York city known as the Tenderloin" and it portrays for Laura "a panorama of the inevitable depravity that awaits her."

CENSORSHIP HISTORY

Eugene Walter has been praised and vilified for writing *The Easiest Way*. The scholarly *Cambridge History of English and American Literature* hails Walter's play as a "real creative contribution . . . a whole piece . . . which goes to the bone of realistic condition, cruel, ironic, relating to a morbid type of emotionalism." Social activist Emma Goldman wrote in 1911, "The only real drama America has produced so far is 'The Easiest Way' by Eugene Walter" and characterized the play as an indictment of "the cruel, senseless fatalism conditioned in Laura's sex" and the ills of society, "the fundamental current of our social fabric which drives us all, even stronger characters than Laura, into the easiest way—a way so very destructive of integrity, truth, and justice." The public and critics were less observant of the play's inherent social criticism. A theater critic for the *Evening World* reflected the opinions of reviewers for other New York City newspapers in writing that the debut of *The Easiest Way* offered "an evening of good acting and bad morals." Before agreeing to produce the play, David Belasco asked Walter to make changes in the script, which portrays Laura as a jaded and hardened former chorus girl, but the playwright refused. Belasco became the producer nonetheless, but he barred the playwright from rehearsals and created a set that would soften Laura's character in order to build audience sympathy for her. Belasco sought to portray her as an innocent girl caught up in an inevitable fate. He used numerous stuffed animals and dolls in her stage bedroom to suggest a childlike nature, and he chose her wardrobe with an eye to emphasizing innocence. The audiences in New York City accepted the play with little outcry. Although city officials received isolated complaints from indignant citizens about the content of the play and the failure of the playwright to "punish" Laura unequivocally at the end, the authorities did not interfere with performances.

Censorship was an issue elsewhere, when the play toured. In 1909 the Watch and Ward Society of Boston placed pressure on city officials when producers sought a license to perform the play, and *The Easiest Way* was banned. In Norfolk, Virginia, the city licensing board demanded that a segment of the play involving a kiss be cut.

One unusual effect of the play was its damage to the previously thriving business of Rector's, the restaurant to which Laura recklessly vows she will go "to make a hit." The restaurant had been the place to be seen after theater performances and had hosted such regulars as actress Lillian Russell and financier "Diamond" Jim Brady, but many of the same people who had enjoyed the festive atmosphere of Rector's shunned it after *The Easiest Way* appeared. As the Broadway historian Robert Ruise writes,

> The play, despite the furor, was a hit. The play was deadly to Rector's, though. The "Place to be Seen" after the theater suffered irreparable damage from the play. This forerunner of Sardi's, and the playground of the likes of "Diamond" Jim Brady and Lillian Russell, was shunned by the majority of same people who created its "bon soire" [sic] atmosphere. The conception of the "bottle and bird" dinners of Rector's after-theater crowd was changed forever. The Party-palace never recovered.

FURTHER READING

Danton, Charles. "Theater: *The Easiest Way*." *Evening World*, January 20, 1909, p. 9.
"Drama, 1860–1918: The Broadway School." *The Cambridge History of English and American Literature in 18 Volumes*. Vol. XVII, *Later National Literature, Part II*. London: Cambridge University Press, 1907–21.
Goldman, Emma. "The Social Significance of Modern Drama." *Anarchism and Other Essays*. 2d rev. ed. New York: Mother Earth Publishing Association, 1911, pp. 247–272.
———. *The Social Significance of the Modern Drama*. Boston: Gorham Press, 1914.
Ruise, Robert. "Broadway 101: The History of the Great White Way." Talkin' Broadway Proudly Presents. Available online. URL: http://www.talkinbroadway.com/bway101/2.html.

EDWARD AND ELEANORA

Author: James Thomson
Original date and place of production: March 18, 1775, Covent Garden, London, England
Characters: Prince Edward, Princess Eleanora, Earl of Gloster, King Henry III, Archbishop Theald
Filmed versions: None

SUMMARY

Edward and Eleanora is set in Palestine, where Edward, the son of King Henry III of England, is fighting a holy war against the Muslims (called the Mohammedans in the play). While he fights valiantly, he remains preoccupied with the domestic situation in England and worries that the nation is being overcome by evil and corruption. When Edward confides his concerns to the Earl of Gloster, his chief adviser, Gloster urges him to return to England and to tackle the domestic problems that have engulfed the nation:

"Exhausted, sunk; drain'd by ten thousand Arts/Of ministerial Rapine, endless Taxes . . . evil Counsellors . . . Are gather'd round the Throne." He also tells Edward that the king needs him, because "low corrupt insinuating Traitors" have him trapped in their snare. In the second act Gloster again urges Edward to return to England to save the nation, which is "Robb'd of our antient Spirit, sunk in Baseness/At home corrupted, and despis'd abroad." Gloster convinces Edward that his concerns are well founded and he makes plans to immediately depart Palestine for England, but he is stopped from doing so when an emissary from the Muslim enemy stabs him with a poisoned knife. As Eleanora strives to save her husband's life, the concern with corruption in England becomes of secondary importance to the effect of Edward's injury and accompanying debilitation on the direction of the war. Even the death of Henry III, his father, is secondary, although the incident provides the occasion for Edward to express his bitter feelings over the ways in which evil ministers and other corrupt advisers misled his father. The play ends with his resolution to return to England and to restore order.

CENSORSHIP HISTORY

James Thomson was best known for his poetry, particularly *The Seasons*, written during 1726–30, which William Wordsworth praised as the first work by a poet since the writings of John Milton to offer new images of "external nature." In 1738 Thomson's patron George Lyttelton introduced him to the Prince of Wales, who granted him an annual pension of £100, thus creating a connection that led to a closer scrutiny the following year of his tragedy *Edward and Eleanora*, which he dedicated to the Princess of Wales. The play was the second to be suppressed under the Licensing Act of 1737, following Henry Brooke's GUSTAVUS VASA. On February 23, 1739, Covent Garden manager John Rich sent the play to the office of William Chetwynd, the examiner of plays, who scrutinized the play and waited more than a month, until March 26, 1739, to send Rich word that his request for a license to perform the play was rejected. Three days later, on March 29, 1739, the London *Daily Post* reported in a brief note that the play had been refused a license for its "immoral or seditious" intentions. Thomson made no effort to overturn the ban and simply withdrew his play from consideration by Covent Garden. He knew that his loyalties to the throne were public information, and to deny the political implications of the play would have been impossible.

The British prime minister, Sir Robert Walpole, had been the chief advocate in the passage of the Licensing Act of 1737, which required that all plays be licensed before they could be performed on public stages. Many plays that were denied licenses after passage of the act were political satires that were viewed as overly critical of the government, a sin of which *Edward and Eleanora* was also guilty. In keeping with the ban on criticisms of the government, the censor marked in the licensing copy of the play that survives that two speeches were particularly offensive. The first appears at the opening of

Act IV, in which Archbishop Theald learns of the death of King Henry III: "Awful HEAVEN!/Great Ruler of the various Hearts of Man!/Since thou has rais'd me to conduct they Church,/Without the base Cabal too often practis'd." The censor placed pencil marks through the final two lines of the speech. The second speech crossed out by the censor is that spoken by Edward in Scene VIII of the same act, when he learns of his father's death:

> Is there a Curse on Human Kind so fell,
> So pestilent, at once, to Prince and People,
> As the base servile Vermin of a Court,
> Corrupt, corrupting Ministers and Favourites?
> How oft have such eat up the Widow's Morsel,
> The Peasant's Toil, the Merchant's far-sought Gain,
> And wanton'd in the Ruin of a Nation!

Walpole seems to have believed that the "Corrupting, corrupting Ministers" referred to him, and he viewed the numerous references throughout the play to the political condition of the nation to be direct criticisms of his influence. The play was set aside for 35 years and not performed nor even read, for even reading the play publicly without a license from the examiner of plays was a felony. In 1775 Thomas Hull "adapted" the play for performance at Covent Garden, and the first performance took place on March 18, 1775, 27 years after Thomson's death. The adaptations of the play consisted of nothing more than censorship, for Hull chose to omit what he describes in his preface to the 1775 edition of the play as the "exceptionable passages," those which had provoked the censor into denying the play a license in 1739.

FURTHER READING

Fowell, Frank, and Frank Palmer. *Censorship in England.* London: F. Palmer, 1913. Reprint, New York: Benjamin Blom, 1969.

Connolly, L. W. *The Censorship of English Drama, 1737–1824.* San Marino, Calif.: Huntington Library, 1976.

Thomson, James. *Edward and Eleanora: A Tragedy.* London: J. Bell & Etherington, 1775.

THE ENTERTAINER

Author: John Osborne

Original date and place of production: April 10, 1957, Royal Court Theatre, London, England

Characters: Graham Dodd, Archie Rice, Billy Rice, Frank Rice, Jean Rice, Phoebe Rice, William Rice

Filmed versions: *The Entertainer* (1960, U.K.); *The Entertainer* (1975, U.S., made for television)

SUMMARY

The Entertainer, set in a large coastal resort in England, relates the story of the bitter, cynical, and impoverished Rice family. The central character is Archie Rice, a cheap, low-talent music hall entertainer who belittles the people around him in an effort to disguise his own failures in life. The main scenery of the play is a music hall stage that contains the Rice apartment as an inset. Archie is an aging vaudeville comedian whose satiric songs, gags, and improvised remarks have lost their popularity and their audiences in a world in which rock and roll has replaced the English music hall tradition. Despite Archie's forced efforts to exhibit a mood of geniality and charm, he and his audience, to whom he directly addresses his jokes, are fully aware that he is a failure whose time to make a success of himself on stage has passed. His hair is gray, his clothes are shabby, his humor focuses on self-irony, and his appearance is that of a weary showman with a "washed-up, tatty show," although he plods along and greets the lack of audience response with his lament, "I 'ave a go, don't I? I do . . . I 'ave a go."

As the play alternates between vaudeville skits and scenes from Rice family life, the audience learns about the many disappointments among the other members of the Rice family. Phoebe, Archie's wife, once exulted in having won his love and become his wife, but she is now so resigned to his abuse and their dismal existence that she appears unshaken by his announced plans to leave her and for a woman as young as his daughter Jean. His once-famous father, Billy Rice, reminisces about his glory days on the stage and exudes a false bravado in comparing his successes with Archie's failures. In an attempt to revive Archie's dying career, he convinces his father to join the show, but the stress and excitement of his return to the music hall stage lead to Billy's death. Archie's two sons are lost to him, one jailed for refusing to enter the military and the other dying as a soldier in the British army against the Egyptian in the Suez crisis. Between satiric songs, the audience learns that Jean has broken her engagement to a straitlaced lawyer and thrown herself into teaching art to "Youth Club kids," children of poor parents with no interest in art. Archie has accepted financial support over the years from his brother William, a successful attorney, but when tax debts threaten to send Archie to prison, he refuses William's offer to help him immigrate to Canada and set himself up in business as a hotel keeper. Instead, Archie declines the offer, and declares that he prefers to go to prison: "Here we are, we're alone in the universe, there's no God, it just seems that it all began by something simple as sunlight striking on a piece of rock. And here we are. We've only got ourselves. Somehow, we've just got to make a go of it." As the despair of the Rice family increases, Archie continues to sing until the very end of the play.

CENSORSHIP HISTORY

The Entertainer was blocked by censors in both London and New York City, where changes in the play were required before authorities allowed performances. In England, Lord Cobbold, the Lord Chamberlain, required numerous changes to the dialogue before licensing the play for performance at the Royal Court Theatre. Dialogue containing "obscenities" and "vulgarities," such as Archie's frequent use of the term *bloody* and references to "arses," respectively, were excised. The Lord Chamberlain also objected to Archie's "earthy expressions" and blatant references to sexuality, as well as to his own sexual prowess, as he speaks of the young woman for whom he plans to leave his wife. Several lines in the play that mocked religious practices and lines from religious writings that Archie quotes satirically also were cut.

In New York City, the Department of the Commissioner of Licensing expressed no objections to the dialogue, but the department demanded the removal of a seminude actress striking a pose as "Britannia" throughout most of Archie's performance. In the part as conceived by Osborne, "Britannia" entered the stage wearing only a sheer strip of mesh across her breasts. She then dropped the mesh and remained bare-breasted for a lengthy scene. The New York City censors ordered that "Britannia" keep her breasts covered, but they allowed the covering to be mesh.

FURTHER READING

Carter, Alan. *John Osborne*. Edinburgh, Scotland: Oliver & Boyd, 1969.

Ferrar, Harold. *John Osborne*. New York: New York University Press, 1973.

Hayman, Ronald. *John Osborne*. New York: Frederick Ungar Publishing Co., 1972.

Laufe, Abe. *The Wicked Stage: A History of Theater Censorship and Harassment in the United States*. New York: Frederick Ungar Publishing Co., 1978.

Osborne, John. *A Better Class of Person*. New York: Dutton, 1981.

———. *The Entertainer*. New York: Criterion Books, 1958.

Trussler, Simon. *John Osborne*. Harlow, England: Longmans, 1969.

ETHIOPIA

Author: Arthur Arent

Original date and place of production: January 24, 1936, Biltmore Theatre, New York, New York

Characters: British Foreign Secretary Anthony Eden, British Foreign Minister Sir Samuel Hoare, French Premier Pierre Laval, Soviet Ambassador Maxim Litvinoff, Italian Dictator Benito Mussolini, Emperor of Ethiopia Haile Selassie

Filmed versions: None

SUMMARY

Ethiopia was an hour-long show created by Arthur Arent for the Federal Theatre Project (FTP) as the first "Living Newspaper." Italian dictator Benito Mussolini had just invaded Ethiopia, and the play took the form of an outspoken documentary that questioned why the world's democracies had not put a stop to the brutal invasion. The topic was timely, because fascism threatened Europe and many Americans had spoken out against its dangers.

The play was structured in the format that all of the Living Newspaper plays would follow. It consisted of speeches, newspaper accounts, statements from public records, and material from broadcasts regarding events related to the invasion of Ethiopia, artfully juxtaposed to make a statement with the aid of voiceover techniques and large projection screens. Characters in the play were given the names of actual foreign leaders in 1936. The exact words of Mussolini, British foreign minister Sir Samuel Hoare, British foreign secretary Anthony Eden, French premier Pierre Laval, and Soviet ambassador Maxim Litvinoff were used. Further, the play was dynamic, because it would end differently each night according to the news from the war front in Ethiopia.

CENSORSHIP HISTORY

Ethiopia was presented in a dress rehearsal for the press on January 24, 1936, after all performances of the play were banned by order of the U.S. government. The play was an indictment of the West for its failure in assisting Ethiopia during the Italian invasion and takeover. When Washington got wind of the subject matter, it rejected a request by director Elmer Rice, also a playwright, to use the actual radio message delivered by President Franklin D. Roosevelt commenting on the reason behind the inaction. Washington immediately ordered that no current ministers or heads of state could be represented in the FTP plays, a policy that was eventually modified to allow for actual quotes, but still no depictions of real heads of state were allowed. The U.S. government was afraid that the play might have a negative effect on American foreign relations.

Steven Early, secretary to President Roosevelt, refused to read a script of the play. Instead, he insisted to Jacob Baker, who was administering the arts projects under the Works Progress Administration (WPA) supervision, that any play dealing with foreign relations was "dangerous" and that the impersonation of foreign dignitaries was "particularly dangerous." Hallie Flanagan, head of the FTP, appealed to First Lady Eleanor Roosevelt to speak with her husband, which she did but without significant benefit. In a telephone conversation, the First Lady told Flanagan that she had discussed the matter with the president and he felt that the production could open "if no foreign statesman was represented in person." Baker reiterated the directive in a memo: "No issue of the Living Newspaper shall contain any representation of the head of a foreign state unless such representation shall have been approved in advance by the Department of State."

The censorship caused many to wonder if the promise by WPA head Harry Hopkins of an uncensored theater was possible. Enraged, director Rice asked if Washington would ever permit any plays other than "pap for babies and octogenarians" to go on the Federal Theatre boards. Rice hoped that because of his prestige as a playwright Washington would be influenced by his stand against censorship, but the government accepted his resignation. As a final gesture of defiance, Rice invited employees, friends, and members of the press to the final dress rehearsal at the Biltmore Theatre. After the play ended, he spoke to the cheering crowd about the ban: "In short, we are confronted here not only with evidence of the growth of fascism which has always used censorship as one of its most effective weapons, but with the resolute determination of a political machine to re-elect its own underlings at all costs."

FURTHER READING

"Double Jeopardy: New Federal Theatre Project." *Time*, March 2, 1936, p. 59.
"Federal Theatre Project." Library of Congress. Available online. URL: http://memory. loc.gov/ammem/fedtp/ftbrwn02.html.
O'Conner, John, and Lorraine Brown, eds. *Free, Adult, and Uncensored: The Living History of the Federal Theatre Project.* Washington, D.C.: New Republic Books, 1978.
Prouty, Chris. "Ethiopia: A Dramatic Country." *Ethiopian Review Online.* Available online. URL: http://www.ethiopianreview.homestead.com/Article_ChrisProuty Jun91.html.
Whitman, Willson. *Bread and Circuses: A Study of Federal Theatre.* New York: Oxford University Press, 1937.

THE FIRST STEP

Author: William Heinemann
Original date and place of production: None recorded
Characters: Annie Ames, Lizzie Ames, Mrs. Courtree, Frank Donovan, Jack Durwen
Filmed versions: None

SUMMARY

The First Step, published in 1895, focuses on two characters, aspiring playwright Frank Donovan and his mistress Annie, who are living together in London as husband and wife. The young woman and her sister have been raised in a strict Nonconformist household in which even attending the theater is a forbidden entertainment. Although Annie has pangs of conscience for the way that she is living, she loves Donovan and rationalizes that they are as devoted to each other as any couple who have a marriage license. When the naive Lizzie visits Annie, she meets Frank's friend Jack Durwen, who takes her to a theater performance without a chaperone. Donovan owes Durwen a substantial amount of money. Donovan spends the evening with Mrs. Courtree, an actress who has paid him to write a play showcasing her talent, and he leaves Annie alone in their apartment as she waits for Lizzie to return. Durwen and Lizzie have still not returned when Donovan arrives home drunk at four o'clock in the morning. As he downplays Annie's fears for her sister's safety and jokingly suggests that Lizzie and Durwen have probably sought shelter from the rain in Durwen's rooms, Annie realizes that Donovan has arranged for Durwen to be alone with the innocent Lizzie. In horror, she accuses Donovan of selling her sister to have his debt to Durwen canceled: "You have sold her to him for his gold—you have bartered her away as if she had been your chattel." Annie realizes at the end that she is partly to blame for her sister's downfall and blames herself for what has happened to Lizzie.

CENSORSHIP HISTORY

The living arrangement of the central characters in *The First Step* was enough to doom the play in London in 1895. Examiner of Plays Edward Pigott refused to license the play when William Heinemann submitted it for approval. As George Bernard Shaw wrote in *Our Theatres in the Nineties*, "This fact [living together without marriage] alone must have been sufficient reason for the censor to ban the play, since it offended against Mr. Pigott's rule-of-thumb for determining whether a play is 'moral' or not."

At the time that Heinemann submitted the play, the Independent Theatre Society had already committed itself to staging it. When news of the official refusal to license the play was released, however, the theater withdrew from the agreement because no theater manager was willing to risk his reputation by staging an unlicensed play. Defenders of the play, such as M. Filon, who in 1897 published *History of the English Stage*, from which theater historians Fowell and Palmer quote, wrote that the English censor condemned the play because "the piece might have made it known to Londoners that there are couples in their great city whom the registrar has not united, and whom the clergyman has not blessed. . . . The censorship thought to spare them this revelation."

Others were more blunt in their condemnation of the censors. In *History of English Literature*, Edward Engel wrote that "There is nothing in it [*The First Step*] that could be objectionable to grown up people, and if a 'purpose' can be found in it—otherwise than that of its art—it is most assuredly a profoundly moral one . . . the English Censor is guilty of injustices and stupidities equal to those committed by Censors in other countries." Writing more than a decade later, Fowell and Palmer decried the continued banishment of the play and observed that Heinemann presented a moral lesson in the play but that his crime lay in "the fatal error of not preaching . . . to be popular in this country you must preach." The defense of the play did nothing to change the decision of the censors, and *The First Step* was permanently barred from the English stage: no amount of rewriting could change the central relationship in the play without making it an entirely different work. Although the movement in England against censorship from 1960 to 1982 would have permitted the presentation of the play after more than six decades, no note was taken of *The First Step*, nor was interest expressed in producing it. The play no longer had relevance for audiences.

FURTHER READING

Archer, William. *The Theatrical 'World' of 1895*. London: Walter Scott Publishing, 1896.
Fowell, Frank, and Frank Palmer. *Censorship in England*. London: F. Palmer, 1913. Reprint, New York: Benjamin Blom, 1969.
Heinemann, William. *The First Step: A Dramatic Moment*. London: John Lane/The Bodley Head, 1895.
Shaw, George Bernard. *Our Theatre in the Nineties*. London: Constable & Co., 1932.
Stephens, John Russell. *The Censorship of English Drama, 1824–1901*. New York: Cambridge University Press, 1980.

A GAME AT CHESSE

Author: Thomas Middleton
Original date and place of production: August 6, 1624, Globe Theatre, London, England
Characters: Black Bishop, Black Duke, Black King, Black Knight, Black Pawns, Black Queen, Black Queen's Pawn, Fat Bishop, Fat Bishop's Pawn, White Bishop, White Duke, White King, White Knight, White Pawns, White Queen, White Queen's Pawn
Filmed versions: None

SUMMARY

A Game at Chesse, a transparent political allegory that reflects contemporary popular views of the relationship between England and Spain, places political figures as chess pieces in what a contemporary of Middleton called "a great Catholic chess game." The play, which ridicules the Spanish monarchy and the Spanish ambassador to England and savagely satirizes the Roman Catholic Church, builds to a final scene in which Middleton consigns all of Spain to hell. In the play, Middleton uses the character of the White King to represent King James I of England and the Black King to represent King Philip IV of Spain. The literary sources of the play are among many of the pamphlets of the time that poured out anti-Spanish and anti-Catholic propaganda, many of which painted a lurid picture of the Roman Catholic Church, charging it with carrying out a campaign for worldwide domination with the aid of Spanish diplomacy.

The main historical source of the play is an incident that occurred in 1623, in which Prince Charles of England and the duke of Buckingham made a hurried visit to Madrid to negotiate a marriage between the prince and the Infanta Maria. The negotiations fell through and Charles returned to England still unmarried, much to the relief of the English, who had feared that the true goal of the marriage would be to convert their Protestant future king to Roman Catholicism. In the play, Middleton represents the frustrated end of the negotiations as a "checkmate by discovery" by the White Knight, representing Prince Charles, and the White Duke, representing the duke of Buckingham.

The play also launches a satirical attack on the Spanish ambassador to England until 1622, the count of Gondomar, who is represented in *A Game at Chesse* as the Black Knight. Audiences easily recognized the character as one of Spain's skilled diplomats, not only because of personal peculiarities of speech and action, but also because the players managed to obtain the litter, or "chair of ease," in which he was carried around when in England. As Middleton's contemporary John Chamberlain wrote, "they counterfeited his person to the life." The Black Knight is the supreme gamester and dominates every scene, urging the other players to keep the game running for the sport, rather than to seek an end through victory. When the Black King plots against the White Queen, hoping for victory, the Black Knight cautions him: "You're too hot, sir,/If she were took, the game would be ours quickly." An equally large portion of the play is devoted to caricaturing as the Fat Bishop, Marco Antonio de Dominis, the former archbishop of Spalatro, a well-respected theologian who had received preferments from King James I after deserting the Church of Rome and joining the Church of England. De Dominis later returned to Rome when conditions in Italy became more advantageous to him. In both cases, Middleton mocks cruelly their physical defects. In the play, the Black and the White contrast not only in color but in movement as well. Disunity predominates in the Black House, where the men seem unable to cooperate, and they spend much of their time in conflict. Differences in strategy spark disagreement between the Black Knight and the Black King: the Black Knight seeks revenge and launches an attack against the Fat Bishop, the Black Knight's Pawn is jeered by his fellow pawns when he tries to correct a blunder, and the Black Bishop's Pawn willfully ignores his duty to the Black King. In contrast, the white pieces are models of cooperation. Aided by the White King, the White Bishop rescues the White Queen, and the Bishop's Pawn joins with the White Knight and the White Duke to save the White Queen's Pawn. In the final scene, the white side wins and the mate is described as "the noblest mate of all," because it is the result of perfect coordination among all of the white pieces.

CENSORSHIP HISTORY

A Game at Chesse holds the distinction of being the first long-run play in English theatrical history, but it has not been performed publicly since August 16, 1624. In comparison to the habit of the day, in which a different play appeared each day, this one run for nine days. The play was presented to the London censor Sir Henry Herbert and licensed for performance on June 12,

1624, although the subject matter was obviously dangerous, which has led historians to surmise that the censor received approval from people in high places before licensing the play. Because the play advocates aggression against Spain, historians have suggested that Prince Charles and the duke of Buckingham, portrayed as the aggressive White Knight and the White Duke of *A Game at Chesse*, may have secretly supported the play and plotted its result in the two months that elapsed between the issuing of the license and the first performance.

In contrast to the usual procedure in English theaters of the time of presenting a different play each day, this play opened at the Globe Theatre and began performances by the King's Men players on August 6, 1624. *A Game at Chesse* ran for nine days straight, excluding Sunday, until the London authorities suppressed the production. The huge audiences—the smallest was 3,000—made the play a financial success, but it was shut down due to strenuous protests by the Spanish ambassador, Don Carlos Coloma, against what he termed "the insolence of the players," and the threat of igniting an international incident. The players were so certain of official interference that, after the first two performances attracted large audiences, they raised the price of admission to make as much money as possible in the short time they believed they had left. The unusual presentation of successive performances was carefully timed to begin when King James had left London, but after nine days of performances, the Privy Council ordered the Globe Theatre closed and issued a warrant for Middleton's arrest. In a letter to the Privy Council on August 12, 1624, after Ambassador Coloma had registered his complaints, the king's secretary Conway wrote the following:

> His Majesty hath received informacion from the Spanish Ambassador, of a very scandalous Comedie acted publickly by the King's Players, wherein they take the boldnes, and presumption in a rude, and dishonorable fashion, to represent on the Stage the persons of his Majesty, the King of Spaine, the Conde of Gondomar, the Bishop of Spalato & c. His Majesty remembers well there was a commandment and restraint given against the representing of anie modern Christian kings in those Stage-plays, and wonders much both at the boldnes nowe taken by that companie, and alsoe that it hath been permitted to bee so acted.

On August 18, 1624, the King's Men and Middleton were arraigned before the Privy Council and charged with violating the law that forbade the representation of any modern Christian king on the stage. Although the playwright named his monarchs the White King and the Black King, their true identity was hard to deny. After consultation with King James, the Lord Chamberlain wrote to the Privy Council and instructed members "to take such course with the actors as might give best satisfaction to the Spanish Ambassador" and recommended that their course of action also strive to "preserve the honour of the King of Spain and his ministers." Ambassador Coloma protested in a letter written on September 20, 1624, to the duke of Olivares that the play had been attended by "all the nobility still in London" and complained that it falsely displayed "the cruelty of Spain and the treachery of Spaniards." He wrote, "I have given the King of England this choice between punishing this roguery and sending me my papers, because every good reason and conjecture require that he should choose the first alternative, and it seemed to me that if he chose the second, he would find his actions condemned, not only by God, but also by the world." The Privy Council ordered that the play was to be "antiquated and silenced." King James banned the play on the pretext of disapproving of his impersonation on stage rather than for its anti-Spanish propaganda, for many of his subjects agreed with Middleton's portrayal of the Spaniards. The play was published in 1625, soon after the death of King James and the eruption of open hostilities between England and Spain.

FURTHER READING

Bald, R. "A New Manuscript of Middleton's *Game at Chesse*." *Modern Language Review* 25 (1930): 474–478.
———. "An Early Version of Middleton's *Game at Chesse*." *Modern Language Review* 38 (1943): 177–180.
Chamberlain, John. *The Letters of John Chamberlain*. Edited by N. E. McClure. Philadelphia: Lippincott & Co., 1939.
Clare, Janet. *"Art Made Tongue-Tied by Authority": Elizabeth and Jacobean Dramatic Censorship*. New York: Manchester University Press, 1990.
Harper, J. W. Introduction to *A Game of Chess*. Edited by J. W. Harper. New York: Hill and Wang, 1967.
Middleton, Thomas. *A Game at Chesse*. Edited by R. C. Bald. Cambridge, England: Cambridge University Press, 1929.
Moore, John Robert. "The Contemporary Significance of Middleton's *Game at Chesse*." *PMLA* 50 (1935): 764–765.
Wilson, Edward M., and Olga Turner. "The Spanish Protest Against *A Game at Chesse*." *Modern Language Review* 44 (1949): 476–482.

GHOSTS

Author: Henrik Ibsen

Original date and place of production: May 20, 1882, Aurora Turner Hall, Chicago, Illinois

Characters: Mrs. Helen Alving, Osvald Alving, Jacob Engstrand, Regine Engstrand, Pastor Manders

Filmed versions: *Ghosts* (1915; reissued in 1919 as *The Curse*); *Henrik Ibsen's Ghosts* (1997)

SUMMARY

Ghosts is a social drama that explores the devastating effects suffered by a family whose existence is based on a foundation of lies. The widowed Mrs. Alving had once left her husband because of his philandering but returned to him after being pressured by the self-righteous Parson Manders to remain married despite Captain Alving's continued unfaithfulness. Through dialogue, the audience learns that the captain had an affair with the housemaid, who became pregnant and gave up the child to be raised by local carpenter Jacob Engstrand, who is paid for his trouble. Although Mrs. Alving realized her marriage was a sham, she worked hard to protect her son Osvald from knowing the extent of his father's scandalous behavior, and, to do so, she sent him away to school in Paris at the age of seven. When Osvald returns after several years away, his father has died and he is kept ignorant of his father's past. To further wrap her husband's memory in respectability, Mrs. Alving builds an orphanage in his memory, a respectable-appearing monument that she believes will modify public opinion about her husband and eliminate any scandal that might be associated with the family name. As the orphanage is being built, Osvald begins an affair with one of the young women in town, Regine Engstrand, but he does not know that she is his half-sister, the daughter Captain Alving fathered with the housemaid years before. Osvald begins to show signs that he is suffering from inherited syphilis, and he has several episodes that signify that he is in the last stages of that disease. Before Mrs. Alving can tell Osvald of his relationship to Regine, the orphanage burns down. As Osvald's attacks increase in severity and he approaches madness, Regine discovers that they are related and leaves him. The play ends with Osvald begging to die, as Mrs. Alving recognizes that they cannot escape the ghosts of the past.

CENSORSHIP HISTORY

The world premiere of *Ghosts*, presented in Chicago by a Norwegian touring company, raised a local stir but no efforts toward censorship. Its German debut, performed before an invited audience in Augsburg on April 14, 1886, sparked a violent controversy that became even more heated at its first public German performance at the Freie Buhne in 1890 because of its subjects of venereal disease and adultery. In England the play was banned from performance because it failed to show due respect for the institution of marriage and it dealt with the taboo topic of venereal disease.

Edward F. S. Pigott, the Examiner of Plays in England, refused to license the play and stated unequivocally his objection to all of Ibsen's works:

> All I can say is this. I have studied Ibsen's plays pretty carefully, and all the characters in Ibsen's plays appear to me morally deranged. All the heroines are dissatisfied spinsters who look on marriage as a monopoly, or dissatisfied married women in a chronic state of rebellion against not only the conditions which nature has imposed on their sex, but against all the duties and obligations of mothers and wives; and, as for the men, they are all rascals or imbeciles.

His successor, George Alexander Redford, who became Examiner of Plays in 1895, was similarly hostile to the play: "Ibsen's Ghosts was refused by

Mr. Pigott, and will never be licensed." The play was rejected by the censor, who called it "blasphemous" because Mrs. Alving lives in a sham marriage and "revoltingly suggestive" for its references to the secret life of Captain Alving that produced an illegitimate daughter and the venereal disease his legitimate son inherits. Despite the lack of an official license to perform the play, J. T. Grein sought a theater in which his Independent Theatre Society, formed in 1891 as a permanent version of the private theater club the Shelley Society, could present a performance. (The Shelley Society had existed for each play, not as an enduring organization.) Grein sought to avoid the limitations on modern drama that traditional theater managers and official censorship imposed, but most theaters were fearful of governmental reprisals. Kate Santley, manager of the Royal Theatre, gave permission for one performance of the play, on March 13, 1891, but she soon had misgivings about her decision and feared that she would lose her valuable theater license. Santley wrote to the Office of the Lord Chamberlain to receive a statement of its official view of the play and was reassured that it would not interfere with the one performance, as long as it remained completely private. Public interest in the play was so intense that Grein was besieged with 3,000 applications for tickets. The newspapers covered the impending event far in advance and speculated about whether the large audience would still qualify the performance as "private." Numerous members of the press attended the performance, and newspaper reviews the next day fanned the controversy as reviewers called the play "a hideous nightmare," "a morbid and sickening dissection of corrupt humanity," and "a putrid drama the details of which cannot appear with any propriety in any column save those of a medical journal." The outcry by the reviewers confirmed for the censors that they were acting in the interest of public opinion in refusing the play a license. Grein, however, continued to receive a large demand for tickets, which he hoped to satisfy by arranging another performance at the Royal Theatre, but Santley was too frightened of losing her license and refused to once again sublease the theater. No other theater would take the risk, which led Grein to give up the effort. The Independent Stage Society resolved to present only plays that were sanctioned officially. The ban was lifted during World War I, when the British Board of Film Censors permitted the showing of the U.S.-made film Ghosts to troops, because, along with other films on the topic of venereal disease, it provided good education for the forces.

FURTHER READING

Brustein, Robert. *The Theatre of Revolt.* Boston: Little, Brown, 1964.

Elsom, John. *Erotic Theatre.* New York: Taplinger Publishing Co., 1974.

Fowell, Frank, and Frank Palmer. *Censorship in England.* London: F. Palmer, 1913. Reprint, New York: Benjamin Blom, 1969.

Gassner, John. *Theatre at the Crossroads: Plays and Playwrights of the Mid-Century American Stage.* New York: Holt, Rinehart, and Winston, 1960.

MacCarthy, Desmond. "Literary Taboos." *Life and Letters* 1 (October 1928): 329–341.

Meyer, Hans Georg. *Henrik Ibsen.* Translated by Helen Sebba. New York: Frederick Ungar Publishing Co., 1972.

Shaw, George Bernard, Gilbert Murray, et al. *The Censorship of Plays in the Office of the Lord Chamberlain: The Case for Abolition.* Letchworth, England: Arden Press, 1908.

Stephens, John Russell. *The Censorship of English Drama, 1824–1901.* New York: Cambridge University Press, 1980.

GOD OF VENGEANCE (*GOT FUN NEKOMEH*)

Author: Sholem Asch
Original date and place of production: 1907, Kammerspiele Theater, Berlin, Germany; December 1922, Provincetown Theater, New York, New York
Characters: Reb Aron, Basha, Rivkele Chapchovich, Sore Chapchovich, Yankel (Yekel) Chapchovich, Reb Elye, Hindle, Manke, Reyzl, Shloyme, the Stranger, a Woman
Filmed versions: *Bog Mesti* (1912, Russia)

SUMMARY

Sholem Asch's *God of Vengeance*, a popular play written in 1906 and produced in the following year in Yiddish theaters in Europe and the United States, is a hard and realistic portrayal of urban life at the beginning of the 20th century. Yankel Chapchovich, the vulgar and tough owner of a basement brothel, is married to Sore, a former prostitute. He cherishes the illusion that he can preserve his daughter Rivkele's chastity even as the family lives above the brothel and remains involved in its day-to-day operations. As the play opens, Yankel and his wife make clear to the audience that they have no illusions about themselves or their way of life, but that their daughter is wholesome and pure and admired because of her virtue. "Let the whole town know it. What I am, I am. . . . What she [his wife Sore] is, she is. It's all true, all of it. But they better not whisper against my child. If they do, I'll crack their skulls with this bottle." Sore justifies the dichotomy between their personal and business lives, reminding him, "You're in business. Everybody is in business." Yankel, however, feels the need for reinforcement despite his seemingly confident division between the personal and business, as between kosher and nonkosher food: "My home must be kept separate, do you hear, the way kosher food is kept separate from forbidden food." To this end, he arranges to purchase a Torah scroll to put into Rivkele's room, to help her retain her innocence as she waits for her impending marriage. He is too late. As her mother speaks from another room offstage and tells her daughter about the husband-to-be that a marriage broker has found, Rivkele embraces Manke, a young prostitute who works in the brothel, and the two kiss passionately. While her parents remain oblivious to her secret life, Rivkele sneaks into the brothel to meet her lover, and the pimp boyfriend of another of Yankel's prostitutes soon persuades her to run away and to become a prostitute in a rival brothel. When her father discovers that Rivkele is missing, he drags her mother around the room by her hair and frantically demands to know where Rivkele has gone. After Yankel and Sore discover Rivkele's whereabouts, the marriage broker assures them that no real harm has been done: "God helps. Troubles pass. The main thing is: nobody knows . . . you make believe nothing happened." Having prayed in front of the Torah scroll, Yankel cannot accept such continued hypocrisy. He believes that the tragedy has occurred because of his own deceptive life. As he agonizes over what has happened, Sore pays off the procurer and brings her daughter home.

Yankel confronts Rivkele and asks, "'Are you still a chaste Jewish girl?'" In defiance, she answers that she does not know, then asks her father about his life with Sore. True to her word, the matchmaker brings the originally chosen groom-to-be, a young rabbinical student, to meet Rivkele. Yankel, however, will not allow the deception. In front of the young man and his father, Yankel humiliates both his wife and his daughter, then sends Rivkele to the basement to become a prostitute. As the matchmaker leaves, he thrusts the Torah scroll at her, shouting that she take it: "I don't need it anymore!"

CENSORSHIP HISTORY

God of Vengeance is the first play to present a lesbian scene on the American stage and also is the first to be successfully convicted on the grounds of obscenity. The play remains one of the most popular and most frequently revived Yiddish plays, and recent productions have included one staged in November 1999 at Show World, a former strip club at 42nd Street and 8th Avenue in New York City, and a May 2000 production at Yale University. The play was produced in Europe and in Yiddish theaters in the United States for 17 years without complaints or efforts to censor it, but its first production in English resulted in the lodging of obscenity charges against the play and banning of the production. The lesbian relationship in the play, portrayed through passionate embraces and kissing, shocked, titillated, and entertained audiences, but complaints to close the play also came from prominent Jewish religious leaders who feared that the play would result in anti-Semitic attacks. The first English-language version of *God of Vengeance* opened on December 19, 1922, at the Provincetown Playhouse in New York City's Greenwich Village, and played to large audiences for 11 weeks without drawing serious complaints. Assured of success, the backers moved the play to the Apollo Theater on Broadway, where on March 6, 1923, the day after the play opened, vice squad officers from the New York City Police Department closed the production and arrested the theater owner and 12 cast members. Fifteen days later they were charged by a grand jury with presenting an "obscene, immoral and impure theatrical production." The objections came from two different quarters. Led by Rabbi Joseph Silverman, who headed the prestigious Temple Emanuel, members of the German Jewish community of

New York claimed that the play libeled the Jewish faith in showing the sexual immorality of an otherwise observant Jewish family. In contrast, the efforts by non-Jewish religious groups and the New York Society for the Suppression of Vice focused solely on the lesbian relationship and signs of physical affection. In the complaint filed by the society, which resulted in the indictment of the show's producer and cast, the Society for the Suppression of Vice stated that the play "tend(ed) to the corruption of the morals of the youth."

When the judge found against the play, it was the first time American performers were found guilty of presenting immoral public entertainment. Harry Weinberger, a libertarian attorney who had defended the alleged anarchists Emma Goldman and Jacob Abrams, was the play's manager. After taking the case before the Appellate Division, which upheld the verdict in June 1924, Weinberger, with the assistance of Theodore Schroeder, who had founded the Free Speech League in 1902, asked the American Civil Liberties Union (ACLU) to aid them in taking the case before the court of appeals to overturn the convictions of the theater manager and the cast. The ACLU refused the request. In explanation, Roger Baldwin, then head of the ACLU, wrote to Weinberger and Schroeder: "The issue in the case is not primarily one of freedom of opinion—it is one of censorship on the ground of morality . . . [which] has been accepted for several centuries." Despite the rejection, Weinberger and Schroeder took the case before the court of appeals, where they argued successfully for the verdict to be overturned. The court of appeals did not take a stand on the issue of the play's morality. Instead it overturned the convictions of the theater manager and cast members on purely technical grounds regarding the manner of their arrests.

FURTHER READING

Asch, Sholem. "God of Vengeance." In *The Great Jewish Plays.* Translated and edited by Joseph C. Landis. New York: Horizon Press, 1972.

Friedman, Andrea. *Prurient Interests: Gender, Democracy, and Obscenity in New York City, 1909–1945.* New York: Columbia University Press, 2000.

Rabban, David M. *Free Speech in Its Forgotten Years.* Cambridge, England: Cambridge University Press, 1997.

"Student Drama Centers on Play Once Charged with Being Obscene." *Yale University Bulletin* 28 (May 5, 2000): 33.

Talcott, Alexander. "GTU Professor to Discuss Asch's *Vengeance of God* [sic]." *Dartmouth Review.* Available online. URL: http://www.dartreview.com/issues/10.29.01/asch.html.

GUSTAVUS VASA

Author: Henry Brooke
Original date and place of production: 1777, Southwark Theatre, London, England

Characters: Cristiern, King of Denmark and Norway; Gustavus, King of Sweden; Trollis, Vice-Regent of Denmark and Norway
Filmed versions: None

SUMMARY

Gustavus Vasa is a politically charged account of the efforts of Swedish patriots to defend themselves against invasion by troops from Denmark and Norway, but this is a historical facade used by the playwright, Henry Brooke, to criticize the political conditions in England in 1739. Gustavus, king of Sweden, is a noble and courageous leader who leads his people in a patriotic struggle against oppression. The invading Norwegian and Danish troops are led nominally by their king, Cristiern, but the true power lies in Cristiern's chief minister and vice-regent, Trollis, who is scheming, vicious, and corrupt. In his prologue to the play, Brooke hinted at the political implications of his work by informing audiences that his play presents "a state distress'd . . . oppress'd," in which "Her peers, her prelates, fell corruption sway'd:/Their rights, for power, th' ambitious, weakly, sold, the wealthy, poorly, for superfluous gold." He bemoans the fact that "Truth, Justice, Honour, fled th' infected shore,/For Freedom, sacred Freedom—was no more." Readers of the play readily identified the "state distress'd" to be the plight of England under the domination of Prime Minister Robert Walpole and to associate with him the irresponsible and inhumane use of power, the tyrannical domination of population, and the cruel exploitation that Trollis practices in the play. His behavior contrasts strongly with that of Gustavus, who is a strong and compassionate leader. After a series of diplomatic and battlefield exchanges, the Swedish, under the wise leadership of Gustavus, are saved from the onslaught led by Trollis, to make Brooke's point that oppression must be overcome.

CENSORSHIP HISTORY

English prime minister Robert Walpole was the primary force behind the creation and passage of the Licensing Act of 1737, which required that all plays receive the approval of authorities and a license to be performed on a public stage. *Gustavus Vasa* has the distinction of being the first play in the history of drama to be refused a license under the Licensing Act. Henry Brooke sent his play to the examiner of plays, William Chetwynd, on February 24, 1739. Three weeks later, on March 16, 1739, he received an official notice from the Lord Chamberlain, the duke of Grafton, that banned *Gustavus Vasa* from being performed anywhere in England. The examiner gave Brooke no reason for the rejection, aside from declaring "there was a good deal of liberty in it." In response to the ban, Brooke arranged immediately for the private publication of his play as *Gustavus Vasa: or, the Deliverer of His Country: a Tragedy: As It Was to Have Been Acted at the Theatre Royal in Drury*

Lane and sold copies by subscription at five shillings apiece. In a preface to the text, Brooke assumed a tone of innocence and expressed disbelief that his intention could have been misunderstood by the censors. He claimed that he published the play not for financial gain but to show that "*Patriotism, or the Love of Country*, is the great and single *Moral* which I had in view thro' this Play," as well as to show that he was innocent "of pernicious Influence in the Commonwealth." He also protested that if anyone "among Hundreds who have perused the Manuscript, observed but a single Line that might inadvertently tend to Sedition or Immorality, I wou'd now be the last to publish it." Many supporters bought the play simply to help the author, including such subscribers as Lord Chesterfield, who bought 10 copies, and Samuel Johnson, who also bought 10. Brooke eventually earned nearly £1,000 from sales of the play. Johnson voiced his disagreement with the censors in a sharply satiric essay entitled *Complete Vindication of the Licensers of the Stage from the Malicious and Scandalous Aspersions of Mr. Brooke*, published in 1739, in which he assailed the decision while pretending to support it. Johnson wrote that the prologue to *Gustavus Vasa*

> is filled with such insinuations, as no friend of our excellent government can read without indignation and abhorrence, and cannot but be owned to be a proper introduction to such scenes, as seem designed to kindle in the audience a flame of opposition, patriotism, publick spirit, and independency; that spirit which we have so long endeavoured to suppress, and which cannot be revived without the entire subversion of all our schemes.

The essay also urged the government to extend the powers of the Licensing Act to make reading an unlicensed play illegal, in order that "The Licenser having his authority thus extended will in time enjoy the title and the salary without the trouble of exercising his power, and the nation will rest at length in Ignorance and Peace."

FURTHER READING

Brooke, Henry. *Gustavus Vasa; a Tragedy in Five Acts. Now Performed by the Old American Company at the Theatre in Southwark*. Philadelphia: Printed and sold by Enoch Story, 1778.

Conolly, L. W. *The Censorship of English Drama, 1737–1824*. San Marino, Calif.: Huntington Library, 1976.

Fowell, Frank, and Frank Palmer. *Censorship in England*. London: F. Palmer, 1913. Reprint, New York: Benjamin Blom, 1969.

Johnson, Samuel. "A Compleat Vindication of the Licensers of the Stage, from the Malicious and Scandalous Aspersions of Mr. Brooke, Author of *Gustavus Vasa*, with a Proposal for Making the Officer of Licenser More Extensive and Effective." In *Complete Works*. Edited by Arthur Murphy. New York: Harper Publishing, 1873, pp. 539–544.

Wright, Herbert. "Henry Brooke's *Gustavus Vasa*," *Modern Language Review* 14 (April 1919): 173–182.

HAIR: THE AMERICAN TRIBAL LOVE-ROCK MUSICAL

Authors: Gerome Ragni and James Rado
Original date and place of production: October 29, 1967, Joseph Papp's
   New York Shakespeare Festival Public Theater, New York, New York
Characters: Berger, Claude, Coolidge, Crissy, Father, Franklyn, General
   Grant, Hud, Jeannie, Abraham Lincoln, Mother, Scarlet, Sheila, Woof
Filmed versions: *Hair*, 1979

SUMMARY

Hair, a self-proclaimed "psychedelic tribal love-rock musical," is a virtually
plotless musical production that protests the strictures of established society
and U.S. involvement in the Vietnam War. It promotes, instead, a mildly
anarchistic, marijuana-smoking community in which love and peace will
reign, if given the chance by the system. Beginning with the "dawning of the
Age of Aquarius," the play presents a series of brief vignettes containing the
Tribe, characters clothed in the stereotypical "hippie" uniform of the late
1960s—long hair, beads, bells, long skirts or bell-bottom pants, and sandals—
espousing peace, protest, and love. Songs such as "Age of Aquarius,"
"Hashish," "I Believe in Love," "Good Morning Star Shine," "Easy to Be
Hard," "Walking in Space," "White Boys," "What a Piece of Work Is Man,"
and others, connect the scenes and provide the music for seemingly unchore-
ographed dancing by members of the tribe/cast.

   The plot centers on Claude, a hippie who lives in Flatbush (Brooklyn),
New York. Bored with his identity, Claude affects an English accent and pretends to be newly arrived from Manchester, England. Soon after, he moves
into an apartment in the East Village in New York City with his close friend
Berger and Berger's girlfriend Sheila, a politically active New York University student who is "spreading the groovy revolution." The three form a
ménage a trois, a fact made clear to the audience in an effort to shock, as is
the use throughout the play of words formerly forbidden on the stage, such
as "fuck," "cunnilingus," and other sexually charged words. The East Village
stage scene is filled with flower children, peace-loving hippies who wander
through scenes wearing flowers, giving each other the peace sign and
expressing contempt for society and, particularly, for the involvement of the
United States in the Vietnam War and for the limited opportunities of
minorities, exemplified in such songs as "I'm Black," "Colored Spade,"
"Dead End," and "Can't Do."

   Claude receives a draft notice in the mail and reports to the draft board
for a physical. After he passes the physical, he joins the others in plotting ways
to free him from service in Vietnam. At one point, Claude professes to have
burned his draft card, but the Tribe learns that it was his library card. After a
pseudo-orgy, a "be-in" for the benefit of tourists to the East Village in which

some cast members appeared in the nude, the members of the Tribe sing "Hare Krishna" and appear to become high on love, life, and marijuana, while Claude begins to burn his draft card but changes his mind.

The second act occurs after Claude is inducted into the army. The stage fills with images of George Washington at war with a group of Native Americans, and they are joined by Abraham Lincoln, Ulysses S. Grant, Calvin Coolidge, Scarlett O'Hara, Buddhist monks, and Catholic nuns, all of whom are engaged in war. The scene segues into singing about the ugliness of the war against the Vietcong. When the stage clears, the Tribe hovers on one side, banging on pots and chanting antiwar slogans, and Claude disappears for a time. He reappears to the audience wearing a U.S. Army uniform, but the Tribe cannot see him. The play ends with Claude lying alone at the center of the stage, with a cross made by his friend Berger lying on his chest.

CENSORSHIP HISTORY

Hair shocked audiences of the late 1960s with its references to drugs, religion, sex, and politics, and its undertones of homosexuality, as well as with the nudity of cast members at the end of the first act. The play ran for 49 performances at the New York Shakespeare Festival Public Theater, from October 29, 1967, through December 10, 1967, then ran for 45 performances at the Cheetah, a New York City nightclub with arena-type seating, all without complaints about the language and nudity of the play. Producer Michael Butler then took *Hair* to Broadway, where it opened on April 29, 1968, once again without any official interference. Although newspaper theater critics condemned the play for its "irreverence" and "vulgarity," as well as for its nudity, they reserved the greater part of their disapproval for what many viewed as amateurish and repetitive scenes and unintelligible lyrics. By the end of the season, in a poll taken by *Variety*, the majority of New York City drama critics had voted to name *Hair* composer Galt MacDermot best composer of the season and Gerome Ragni and James Rado as best lyricists. The play ran for 1,750 performances on Broadway, placing it among the top 30 longest-running plays.

Although the reception from New York City audiences was warm, touring companies of the play ran into difficulties in numerous other U.S. cities. The U.S. Army banned the play from military theaters. In 1969 Frank Kinsman, the field programming director for the army, defended the banning of *Hair* and "similarly offensive productions" as being unfit for military theaters by stating that it was "good judgment to avoid presenting productions that could cause trouble." In the Indiana cities of Indianapolis, South Bend, and Evansville, language in the play was modified and the nudity was eliminated before stage productions were permitted, and the same censorship occurred in St. Paul, Minnesota, and San Antonio, Texas. In Los Angeles, the production of *Hair* triggered a police crackdown on what officials termed "the growing fad of nude dancers." A city ordinance was enacted to authorize officers to arrest cast members, but the police were not empowered to close down productions, so performances continued.

The most extensive efforts to ban the musical occurred in Chattanooga, Tennessee, and resulted in a case argued before the U.S. Supreme Court in *Southeastern Promotions, Ltd. v. Conrad* (420 U.S. 546 [1975]). On October 29, 1971, Southeastern Promotions, Ltd., a New York corporation that promoted and presented theatrical productions, applied to the city of Chattanooga, Tennessee, to use the Tivoli Theatre, a privately owned theater under long-term lease to the city, for six days of performances of *Hair*. At that point, the play had already run for three years on Broadway and appeared via road companies in more than 140 cities across the United States. The city turned the review of the request over to the directors of the Chattanooga Municipal Auditorium, a municipal theater. After reviewing the application, the directors voted to reject the request, although no conflicting engagements were scheduled at the Tivoli and none of the directors had either seen the play or read the script. Instead, the directors reported that they understood "from outside reports" that the musical contained "nudity and obscenity on stage." The city informed Southeastern Promotions that the production would not be "in the best interest of the community," but it did not specify reasons for the rejection.

On November 1, 1971, Southeastern petitioned the U.S. District Court for the Eastern District of Tennessee for an injunction, alleging that the actions of the city abridged the First Amendment rights of the petitioner. In a hearing on November 4, 1971, the directors who had reviewed and rejected the request by Southeastern explained that it would, "as a board, allow those productions which are clean and healthful and culturally uplifting, or words to that effect. They are quoted in the original dedication booklet of the Memorial Auditorium." The court denied the promotion company preliminary relief and concluded that the "petitioner failed to show that it would be irreparably harmed pending a final judgment since scheduling was purely a matter of financial loss or gain and was compensable." In three days of hearings that began on April 3, 1971, the district court presented the issue of obscenity to an advisory jury, which used the full script and libretto, as well as production notes, stage instructions, a recording of the musical numbers, a souvenir program, and the testimony of seven witnesses who had seen the production in other cities. The jury concluded that the group nudity and simulated sex in the production would violate city ordinances and state statutes that made public nudity and obscene acts criminal offenses. The court determined that such conduct could not be considered either speech or symbolic speech and, being pure conduct, was not entitled to First Amendment protection, so it denied the injunction.

The promotion company appealed the ruling to the U.S. Court of Appeals for the Sixth Circuit, which by a divided vote affirmed the decision of the district court in *Southwestern Promotions, Ltd. v. Conrad et al.* Certiorari to the U.S. Court of Appeals for the Sixth Circuit, relying primarily on the reasoning of the lower court. Once again, the judges of the appeals court had not seen the musical performed. Southeastern took the case before the U.S.

Supreme Court, which in a 5-4 decision reversed the ruling of the lower court and determined that the directors in Chattanooga, Tennessee, had based their decision on a system of prior restraint "lacking in constitutionally required minimal procedural safeguards. . . . Respondents' action here is indistinguishable in its censoring effect from the official actions consistently identified as prior restraints in a long line of this Court's decisions."

FURTHER READING

Elsom, John. *Erotic Theatre*. New York: Taplinger Publishing Co., 1974.
Green, Jonathan. *The Encyclopedia of Censorship*. New York: Facts On File, 1990.
Hamilton, Neil A. *The ABC-CLIO Companion to the 1960s Counterculture in America*. Santa Barbara, Calif.: ABC-CLIO, 1997.
Laufe, Abe. *The Wicked Stage: A History of Theater Censorship and Harassment in the United States*. New York: Frederick Ungar, 1978.
Rose, Lloyd. "At Studio, Just a Touch of Gray in *Hair*; the Tribal Love-Rock Musical Still Has Plenty of Bang." *The Wall Street Journal*, July 29, 1997, p. E01.
Southeastern Promotions, Ltd. v. Conrad, 420 U.S. 546 (1975).
Southeastern Promotions, Ltd. v. Conrad et al. Certiorari to the U.S. Court of Appeals for the Sixth Circuit. No. 73-1004.

HAMLET

Author: William Shakespeare
Original date and place of production: July 1602, Globe Theatre, London, England
Characters: Bernardo, Claudius, Fortinbras, Gertrude, Ghost of Hamlet's father, Guildenstern, Hamlet, Horatio, Laertes, Marcellus, Ophelia, Polonius, Rosencrantz
Filmed versions: Feature films: *Amleto* (1910, 1914, 1917, Italy); *Gamlet* (1964, 1989, 1990, USSR); *Hamile* (1964, Ghana); *Hamles* (1960, Poland); *Hamlet* (1964, 1990, 1996, 2000, U.S.); (1973, Canada); (1910, 1921, Denmark); (1900, 1907, 1909, 1910, France); (1910, 1912, 1913, 1948, 1969, 1976, 1987, 1992, 1996, U.K.); (1958, Yugoslavia); *Hamlet liikemaailmassa* (1987, Finland); *Hamlet: Prince of Denmark* (1989, India); *Io Hamlet* (1952, Italy); *Khoon Ka Khoon* (1935, India); *Un Amleto di Meno* (1973, Italy). Made for television: *Hamlet* (1990, 2000, U.S.); (1974, Australia); (1988, France); (1992, Netherlands); (1955, 1984, Sweden); (1947, 1953, 1959, 1970, 1972, 1980, U.K.); (1960, West Germany). *Hamlet at Elsinore* (1964, U.K.).

SUMMARY

The most frequently filmed of Shakespeare's plays, the five-act tragedy of *Hamlet* is known in whole or in part by people in many nations. The play opens with guards standing watch on the battlements of Castle Elsinore in Denmark, fearful of an impending invasion led by Prince Fortinbras of Norway, who seeks to avenge his father's death and to retake land stolen by Denmark under forces led by the late King Hamlet. The guards have seen the ghost of King Hamlet wandering the battlements, and they hesitantly inform his son, Prince Hamlet, of what they have seen. Young Hamlet seeks out his father's ghost and learns that his father's brother Claudius had poisoned the king and then married Queen Gertrude. The ghost demands that Hamlet avenge his murder so that his soul may be at peace, but he warns his son not to harm Gertrude, who married Claudius only months after the murder, and to, instead, "leave her to heav'n." The shocked prince broods about the act of revenge, moodily wandering around the castle, verbally abusing his uncle and mother, and rejecting the affectionate overtures of Ophelia, his former girlfriend, who is the daughter of Polonius, lord chamberlain of Claudius.

Hamlet hires a wandering troupe of actors to perform a play that shows a king being murdered by his brother in an attempt to shock Claudius into confessing, then tries to kill Claudius himself, but he is unable to commit murder. When Hamlet confronts his mother in her chamber with news of the crime, he believes that Claudius is eavesdropping behind a tapestry. He drives a sword through the tapestry, only to find that he has killed Polonius. Made apprehensive by Hamlet's behavior, Claudius orders Hamlet to go to England. Hamlet's childhood friends Rosencrantz and Guildenstern accompany him and unwittingly carry orders to the English king that Hamlet be executed upon arrival. While Hamlet is gone, Ophelia becomes insane after learning of her father's murder, and her brother Laertes vows to kill Hamlet to avenge both his father's death and his sister's insanity and eventual suicide. Hamlet returns to Elsinore after pirates attack the ship and prevent completion of the journey. Using the pretense of engaging Hamlet and Laertes in a friendly fencing match, Claudius plans Hamlet's death and both dips Laertes's dagger in poison and prepares a goblet with poison. The plan goes awry when both Laertes and Hamlet are wounded with the dagger, after which Gertrude accidentally drinks the poison. Hamlet kills Claudius, then dies as Prince Fortinbras of Norway arrives to claim the throne, leaving only Hamlet's close friend Horatio alive among the major characters to tell the story.

CENSORSHIP HISTORY

Hamlet has been censored in both performed and written version for a range of reasons, from the effort to prevent giving insult to either the monarchy or to religion, to the desire to eliminate perceived profanity and obscenity. Manuscript copies of the 1605 quarto of the play containing playhouse annotations by Shakespeare show lines omitted from the second scene of the second act, in which Hamlet tells his friends Rosencrantz and Guildenstern that Denmark is a prison. By this time, King James ruled England joined with his consort, the Danish-born Queen Anne. Literary historian Janet Clare writes that these lines "no doubt might have invited imputations of an affront to the Queen." During the reign of Charles X in France, censors refused permission for performances to plays that presented the monarchy or members of the clergy on stage, arguing that such display would strip these groups of their dignity, even when the characters were depicted as carrying out their duties in highly commendable ways, such as a priest performing a wedding ceremony. In 1827, when a company of London actors presented a series of plays by Shakespeare at the Odeon Theatre in Paris, the censors demanded modifications in the dialogue to eliminate Ophelia's admonishment to her brother Laertes to refrain from acting like "some ungracious pastors who practice not what they preach," because such criticism of the clergy was considered too volatile to permit on stage. Scenes that dealt with the tensions existing between different social classes and the privileges accorded to some but not all were also banned from the stage, so the discussion in *Hamlet* between the gravediggers about the way that burials of suicides were handled differently according to class was also excised.

Dr. Thomas Bowdler, whose name has given a term for the expurgation of books, was the first to censor on a grand scale the written works of Shakespeare. In 1807 Bowdler published the first edition of *Family Shakespeare*, containing versions of the play from which his sister Harriet had helped to remove perceived profanity and obscenity, as well as what the Bowdler family considered indecencies that detracted from the "genius" of Shakespeare. Bowdler wrote that nothing "can afford an excuse for profaneness or obscenity; and if these could be obliterated, the transcendent genius of the poet would undoubtedly shine with more unclouded luster." To increase the "luster" of Shakespeare, Harriet Bowdler cut out large chunks of dialogue from *Hamlet* that she and Thomas believed were too indecent for families to read, and in some cases she substituted her own words or lines for the original. Readers of Bowdler's version of the play were denied Shakespeare's references to Gertrude's "incestuous sheets," as well as numerous suggestions of her sexual relationship with Claudius and Hamlet's taunting of Ophelia regarding the steadfastness of women. Other expurgators followed Bowdler. In 1880 J. M. D. Meiklejohn, professor of the theory, history, and practice of education at the University of St. Andrews in Scotland, produced a severely censored edition of *Hamlet* but failed to acknowledge the cuts in the preface to the play. Instead, Meiklejohn writes that "The text has been as carefully and as thoroughly annotated as any Greek or Latin classic" and tells readers that a careful study of Shakespeare's work will "have the effect of bringing back into the too pale and formal English of modern times a large number of pithy and vigourous phrases." Author Noel Perrin assesses the changes made by Meiklejohn and writes that "Professor Meiklejohn has quietly eliminated four or five hundred of the pithiest and most vigorous." In 1909 the publication of the play as part of the New Hudson Shakespeare series omitted all but the first four lines of the "Saint Valentine" song that Ophelia sings after becoming insane, fearing that the remaining lines were too "bawdy" to be read by high school and college students, and the editors gave readers no indication that more text should have followed the four lines.

FURTHER READING

Bailey, Helen Phelps. *Hamlet in France: From Voltaire to Laforgue.* Geneva: Droz Publishing, 1964.
Bowdler, Thomas. *The Family Shakespeare.* London: J. Hatchard, 1807.
Clare, Janet. *"Art Made Tongue-Tied by Authority": Elizabethan and Jacobean Dramatic Censorship.* New York: Manchester University Press, 1990.
Hemmkins, Frederic William John. *Theatre and State in France, 1760–1905.* New York: Cambridge University Press, 1994.
Perrin, Noel. *Dr. Bowdler's Legacy: A History of Expurgated Books in England and America.* Boston: David R. Godine, 1992.
Shakespeare, William. *Hamlet.* New Folger Library Series. New York: Washington Square Press, 1992.

HANNELE: A DREAM POEM IN TWO ACTS

Author: Gerhart Hauptmann
Original date and place of production: 1893, Berlin, Germany
Characters: Berger, Gottwald, Hanke, Hannele, Hedwig, Pleschke, Schmidt, Seidel, Sister Martha, Tulpe, Dr. Wachler
Filmed versions: None

SUMMARY

Translated variously as *The Assumption of Hannele* and *Hannele's Journey to Heaven*, the play is a poetic fantasy in two acts and expresses a naturalistic viewpoint regarding the cruelties suffered by Hannele Mattern, a physically abused young girl whose last hours are spent in a poorhouse on a stormy winter night. Written in both prose and verse, the play first reveals the terror experienced by Hannele, who has unsuccessfully attempted to drown herself in the almost-frozen town pond. Her body is covered with bruises, and she is delirious yet aware enough to express fear that her abusive stepfather will come for her, as she whimpers, "I'm afraid. . . . I'm so afraid that my father will come." The townspeople have seen her stepfather in a continually drunken state and whisper that he often sends her out into the night to get money for his liquor, never asking how she comes by the money. As the schoolmaster, Gottwald, the deaconess, Sister Martha, the magistrate, Berger, and the doctor, Wachler, try to comfort Hannele and allay her fears, she refuses to take the medicine because she wants to die. As Hannele's delirium increases, she sees apparitions, first of her stepfather, then of her mother, then Christ, all followed by the strains of heavenly music and a gathering of angels who promise Hannele that she will enjoy peace in paradise. In the second act, Hannele fantasizes that she has met the angel of death and her mother, then envisions herself dead. A village tailor brings her a bridal gown and tiny glass slippers, and she sees herself lying dead in a crystal coffin, admired by all the women of the town. When her drunken stepfather appears, a Christlike stranger who looks like Gottwald repulses him. The stranger raises Hannele from the dead and then holds and comforts her while angels appear and sing a chorus. The scene ends abruptly, and the setting returns to the poorhouse, where the doctor has just completed examining Hannele and pronounces her dead.

CENSORSHIP HISTORY

Hannele did not motivate any complaints when it debuted in Germany in 1893, but nearly a decade later English censors debated whether to allow the English version of the play to be performed. When the London Examiner of Plays, Edward F. S. Pigott, granted the play a license for a performance in German at St. George's Hall, a German-language theater, the censor required that the character of the Christlike stranger not resemble conventional pictures of Christ. When producers approached Pigott to license the same play for performance in English at the Afternoon Theatre in London, the censor wrote in response, ". . . it does not follow that a play licensed in German would be licensed in English. I should say that it would be the most difficult to translate and adapt for the English stage and would appeal only to the highly cultured." As the examiner delayed making a decision, representatives from religious journals and the Salvation Army professed outspoken support for the play. Although Pigott was reluctant to license the English version, four years after the original request he yielded to public pressure and agreed to allow the license for the German version of the play to serve as the license for the English version, as long as the producers would meet his requirement that the Christlike stranger in the play be "clean-shaven." The examiner made the demand to avoid offending "religious susceptibilities."

FURTHER READING

Fowell, Frank, and Frank Palmer. *Censorship in England.* London: F. Palmer, 1913. Reprint, New York: Benjamin Blom, 1969.

Gousie, Laurent. *Gerhart Hauptmann: A Transitional Period, 1892–1898, Naturalism to Realism.* Berlin: Fribourg, 1970.

Hauptmann, Gerhart. *The Weavers, Hannele, The Beaver Coat.* Translated by Horst Frenz and Miles Waggoner. New York: Holt, Rinehart and Winston, 1951.

Holl, Karl. *Gerhart Hauptmann: His Life and His Work, 1862–1912.* Chicago: A. C. McClurg & Co., 1914.

Klemm, Frederick Alvin. *The Death Problem in the Life and Works of Gerhart Hauptmann.* Philadelphia: Lippincott & Co., 1939.

Weisart, Joan. *The Dream in Gerhart Hauptmann.* New York: King's Crown Press, 1949.

THE HAPPY LAND

Authors: F. Tomlin (pseudonym for William S. Gilbert) and Gilbert á Beckett
Original date and place of production: March 3, 1873, Royal Court Theatre, London, England

Characters: Female Fairies (Darine, Leila, Locrine, Selene, Zayda); Male Fairies (Ethais, Lutin, Phyllon); Moral Counterparts (Right Honorable Mr. A., Right Honorable Mr. G., Right Honorable Mr. L.)
Filmed versions: None

SUMMARY

The Happy Land is a play in two parts that first appeared with the subtitle *"A Burlesque Version of 'The Wicked World,'"* a play also written by William S. Gilbert that was running concurrently at another London theater. Critics remarked upon the similarity in structure of the two plays, because in both happiness in Fairyland is endangered by the introduction of a human element ("mortal love" in *The Wicked World* and "popular government" in *The Happy Land*), and because a long speech extolling "popular government" in *The Happy Land* reflects the same tone and structure as a similar speech regarding "mortal love" in *The Wicked World*. Despite these similarities, *The Happy Land* is less a parody than it is a vehicle to satirize the English system of government and, specifically, three influential leaders of the time: Prime Minister William Ewart Gladstone (as Right Honorable Mr. G.), Chancellor of the Exchequer Robert Lowe (as Right Honorable Mr. L.), and Commissioner for Public Works A. S. Ayrton (as Right Honorable Mr. A.).

In "Part First," a group of female fairies in a brightly colored Fairyland, located on a cloud over the Earth, sit and look down on the mortal world, watching especially as three male fairies interact with the mortals, "expressing their detestation of the wickedness of the world in a Parisian quadrille." As they leave, the three male fairies, Ethais, Phyllon, and Lutin, appear and praise highly the merits of Victorian civilization, which they believe contrasts strongly with the dull and predictable Fairyland. When other fairies appear and clamor to visit the "wonderful, wicked world" below, the three original adventurers refuse to allow them to do so. Instead, they appeal to their fairy rulers to bring three men up to Fairyland. While the fairies discuss the possible visitors, fairy queen Selene explains that their visitors will be Englishmen, because England is superior to all nations and is blessed with "A Popular Government," which she extols in a lengthy speech. The three mortals who are brought to Fairyland, Mr. A., Mr. G., and Mr. L., bear striking resemblances to the three most famous politicians of the period, and their songs provide sharp satirical criticism of Ayrton, Gladstone, and Lowe, as they sing of themselves: "Oh, we are three most popular men! . . . We want to know who'll turn us out!" After looking around, the three decide to change Fairyland for the better by introducing "popular government." They divide the fairy population into two factions, Government and Opposition, then drive away those who belong to the Opposition. They next select fairies to fill ministerial positions, using what they say is "established practice" to give posts to those who are least fit to hold them.

Part First ends with the government chosen, as the three mortal visitors sing a finale. Part Second opens to a dull and gray-colored Fairyland in which Leila and other members of the Opposition fairy party plot revolution against the penny-pinching of the government that has turned their opulent Fairyland shabby. The government is in chaos, the Chinese are marching on the capital of Fairyland, the Emperor of Gozo has torn up his nation's treaty with Fairyland, the House of Peers is found singing the Marseillaise, the French national anthem, and the Fairyland navy has run aground. When the ill-prepared and incompetent Fairyland leaders seek to resign and apologize to their constituents, the Right Honorable Mr. G. cautions them that the situation is never so bad that a politician should admit wrong or consider resigning, but the Fairyland leaders reject this advice and the concept of "popular government." The three mortals are returned to Earth, and Fairyland returns to normal for a time, but Ethais, Phyllon, and Lutin soon appear with news that the fairy king has plans to create for his people a "popular government," an announcement to which the fairy citizens react with horror. The play ends with the fairies bitterly singing a parody of "Rule Britannia."

CENSORSHIP HISTORY

The Happy Land presented licensing authorities with a rigorous test of their authority in censoring plays containing political satire, and William S. Gilbert appears to have conceived the play largely with the goal of seeing how far he could push the public censors before they would ban his work. In February 1873 Gilbert submitted the play to William Donne, the Examiner of Plays, and received readily a license for performance because it contained what Donne termed in his letter of approval only "legitimate general satire." By the first performance on March 3, 1873, Gilbert had translated the general satire into specific and pointed criticisms of the English government and of three of the most powerful contemporary politicians. The characters were costumed and made up to resemble the sketches of these politicians appearing in *Vanity Fair* and other publications of the day, and a change in dialogue and actions openly lampooned their public policies.

Although audiences laughed uproariously during the play, Edward, Prince of Wales, who was also in the audience, viewed the play as direct attack on the government, which was officially headed by his mother, Queen Victoria. Angered, he alerted Lord Sydney, the Lord Chamberlain, of the subversive material in the play, which the Lord Chamberlain saw for himself when he attended a performance on March 5, 1873. Early the next morning, the Lord Chamberlain withdrew the play's license for performance. Marie Litton, manager of the Court Theatre, assured the censors that only the original text of the play would be used in further performances and that the makeup and costumes of the three mortals would be changed to prevent any imitation of the three English politicians, but the cast did not learn of her concessions until after the evening performance began. The Lord Chamberlain viewed the performance as a defiance of his directive and called Litton to meet with his representative Spencer Ponsby at St. James's Palace early on March 7, 1873. Official documents of the meeting record that Litton admitted that the whole episode had been staged by Tomline [Gilbert] and á Beckett as a way to test the censors. She showed Ponsby the original text passed by Donne and the prompt copy of the play used for performances, which included 18 pages of additions and deviations from the original. Litton convinced the censors that only the officially licensed version of the play would be performed, and the examiner of plays allowed *The Happy Land* to resume performances on March 10, 1873. Although the theater complied with the censor's demand, the authors and Litton published the version of the play that had been banned and placed in capital letters all of the text that the censors had excised, prefacing the work with the following note:

> This book contains the EXACT TEXT of the piece as played on the occasion of the Lord Chamberlain's official visit to the Court Theatre, on 5th March, 1873. Those who will take the trouble to compare the original text with the expurgated version, as played nightly at the Court Theatre, will be in a position to appreciate the value of the Lord Chamberlain's alterations.
>
> THE AUTHORS

FURTHER READING

Fowell, Frank, and Frank Palmer. *Censorship in England.* London: F. Palmer, 1913. Reprint, New York: Benjamin Blom, 1969.

Lawrence, Elwood P. "*The Happy Land:* W. S. Gilbert as Political Satirist." *Victorian Studies* 43 (December 1971): 162–183.

Plumb, Philip. "Gilbert and the Censors: the *Happy Land* Conspiracy." *W. S. Gilbert Society Journal* 1 (1994): 238–240.

Rees, Terence. "*The Happy Land:* Its True and Remarkable History." *W. S. Gilbert Society Journal* 1 (1994): 228–237.

Righton, Edward. "A Suppressed Burlesque—*The Happy Land.*" *The Theatre* (August 1, 1896): 63–66.

Stephens, John Russell. *Censorship of English Drama, 1824–1901.* New York: Cambridge University Press, 1980.

Tomline, F., and Gilbert á Beckett. *The Happy Land: A Burlesque of 'The Wicked World.'"* Available online. URL: http://math.boisestate.edu/gas/other_gilbert/hland.txt.

HENRY IV, PART 2

Author: William Shakespeare

Original date and place of production: 1598, London, England

Characters: Bardolph, Doll Tear-Sheet, Earl of Northumberland, Earl of Warwick, Earl of Westmoreland, Falstaff, Gower, Harcourt, Henry, Prince of Wales, Hostess Quickly, Justice Shallow, King Henry IV, Lady Percy, Lord Bardolph, Lord Chief Justice, Lord Hastings, Morton, Poins,

Prince Humphrey of Gloucester, Prince John of Lancaster, Archbishop
Scroop of York
Filmed versions: *Henry IV, Part 2* (1979, U.K., made for television)

SUMMARY

Henry IV, Part 2 continues the rebellion against King Henry IV of England
that Shakespeare had begun in Part 1 of the play. Three years have passed
since the actions in Part 1, in which the fiery Harry Hotspur, rebel leader and
the son of the earl of Northumberland, was defeated at Shrewsbury, and a
new insurrection threatens the throne. Plotters led by Archbishop Scroop of
York expect the support of Northumberland, but he yields to the pleas of his
son's still-grieving widow, Lady Percy, to preserve his safety, and he retreats
to Scotland. While new efforts toward war are under way, the comic Sir John
Falstaff, crude companion to Henry's dissolute eldest son, Prince Hal,
carouses in London with friends Bardolph and Pistol. The three engage in
sexual antics with prostitutes Doll Tear-Sheet and Hostess Quickly, while a
disguised Prince Hal and his chief attendant Poins spy on them and surprise
them. As the new rebellion spreads, Falstaff is called upon to recruit soldiers
and must travel to Gloucester, but he first visits his old friend Justice Shallow
at Inns of Court. Exploiting the nostalgia the justice feels for their past
friendship, the unscrupulous Falstaff eats and drinks extravagantly at Shallow's expense and borrows a large sum of money with no intent of repayment.
At the same time, Prince John of Lancaster, the younger brother of Prince
Hal, succeeds in quelling the rebellion by tricking the rebels and capturing
the leaders without a fight. The princes return to London to find Henry IV
near death. Prince Hal realizes the need to be a good ruler and promises his
father that he will end his carousing. As Henry V, he orders Falstaff to leave
him alone and demands that Falstaff change his behavior as well.

CENSORSHIP HISTORY

Henry IV, Part 2 was the object of censorship from its first presentation, and
scholars have identified many passages that are radically different or were
excised from the folio text after submission in 1597 to Edmund Tilney, Master
of Revels in England, for they do not appear in the published quarto version in
1600. The original name of Shakespeare's loud, gluttonous, crude knight Sir
John Falstaff was Sir John Oldcastle, but descendants of a knight of the same
name petitioned the throne so vigorously against the use of the name that
Queen Elizabeth I intervened. She ordered Shakespeare to change the name,
although she later expressed a fondness for the character and professed to have
enjoyed his exploits throughout the plays. Passages that detail the grievances
and strategies of the rebel leaders, which are largely concerned with the cause
of the insurgents, appear in the folio but not in the quarto version. Lines spoken by the rebels are cut in Act I, Scenes 1 and 3, to downplay the serious

nature of their grievances and to diminish the role of Scroop and his approval of their cause. In particular, the quarto omits most of Morton's speech at the end of the first scene, which reports that Scroop's endorsement of the insurrection has energized the rebels: "This word 'rebellion'—it had froze them up,/As fish are in a pond. But now the Bishop/Turns insurrection to religion" (I, i, 208–209). The revised version also removes many of Scroop's lines that admonish the monarchy and express the abuses to the people that have justified their insurrection. The censors insisted that all signs of approval of the rebellion be removed, and they also sought to excise doubts expressed by nobles regarding the invulnerability of the English throne. As an example, in the folio versions, Lord Bardolph considers the progress of the rebellion and speaks with some concern about the strategies of the rebels, calling it "this great work-/Which is almost to pluck a Kingdom down" (I, iii, ll. 54–55). Two additional passages relating to the rebels appear in the folio but not in the quarto version. Critic Janet Clare suggests that the excised passages might have proved too dangerous to retain as they place "an heroic gloss upon an assault on the Crown." Both passages involve the rebel leader Hotspur and the failure of his father, Northumberland, to provide support after urging his son to "stiff-borne action." In the first passage, Morton admonishes Northumberland for the indecisive behavior that leads to Hotspur's death. In the second passage, Lady Percy, Hotspur's widow, charges that Northumberland deserted his son in a worthy cause.

In addition to stage censorship, the play was also subject to print censorship by the ecclesiastical censors before publication in 1600. Censors required the revision of lines that appeared to refer to Queen Elizabeth I and Lord Essex. The passages were restored in the folio text published in 1623. Although Shakespeare's use of language was of no concern to English censors, the infamous Dr. Bowdler and his family of expurgators were offended by the oaths used by characters in the play. Dr. Thomas Bowdler, whose name has given a term for the expurgation of books, was the first to censor on a grand scale the written works of Shakespeare. In 1807 he published the first edition of *Family Shakespeare*, containing versions of the play from which his sister Harriet had helped to remove perceived profanity and obscenity, as well as what the family considered indecencies that detracted from the "genius" of Shakespeare. Bowdler wrote that nothing "can afford an excuse for profaneness or obscenity; and if these could be obliterated, the transcendent genius of the poet would undoubtedly shine with more unclouded luster." Harriet Bowdler severely modified many of Falstaff's references to God and eliminated many of his more bawdy comments, and in some cases substituted her own words or lines for the original.

FURTHER READING

Clare, Janet. "Art Made Tongue-Tied by Authority": *Elizabethan and Jacobean Dramatic Censorship*. New York: Manchester University Press, 1990.

Fowell, Frank, and Frank Palmer. *Censorship in England.* London: F. Palmer, 1913. Reprint, New York: Benjamin Blom, 1969.

Greenblatt, Stephen. "Invisible Bullets." In *Shakespearean Negotiations: The Circulation of Social Energy in Renaissance England.* London: Oxford University Press, 1988.

Perrin, Noel. *Dr. Bowdler's Legacy: A History of Expurgated Books in England and America.* Boston: David R. Godine, 1992.

Williams, Gerald Walton. "The text of *2 Henry IV:* Facts and Problems." *Shakespeare Studies* 9 (1976): 173–182.

HERNANI

Author: Victor Hugo

Original date and place of production: February 25, 1830, Comédie-Française, Paris, France

Characters: Don Carlos, Don Francisco, Don Gil Tellez Giron, Don Juan de Haro, Don Matias, Don Ricardo, Don Sancho, Don Ruy Gomez de Silva, Don Garci Suarez, Dona Josefa Duarte, Dona Sol de Silva, Duke of Bavaria, Duke of Gotha, Duke of Lutzelburg, Hernani, Iaquez

Filmed versions: None

SUMMARY

Hernani, subtitled *ou l'Honneur Castillan*, is written in verse and set in 16th-century Spain. The play deals with the themes of love and honor and relates the romantic story of the beautiful young Dona Sol de Silva, in love with Hernani, a disinherited young nobleman who has become a bandit after losing his title and his lands. Two men considerably older than Dona Sol, Don Carlos, heir apparent to the Spanish throne, and Don Ruy Gomez de Silva, her elderly uncle and guardian, are also rival suitors of the young woman, who is disgusted by their advances. Hugo originally titled the work *Tres Para Una* (Three for One) to reflect these relationships but, as he rewrote the play to develop the character of Hernani, he changed the title to emphasize the plight of the young nobleman-turned-outlaw and his love. To protect the man she truly loves, Dona Sol feigns mild affection for the two older suitors, and she is especially charming to Don Carlos, who has aggressively pursued Hernani for conspiring against him and his government. In contrast, Don Ruy is at first an ally who spares Hernani from the wrath of King Carlos. In return for saving Hernani's life by hiding him from the king, Don Ruy demands that the younger man promise to take his own life should Don Ruy ever sound his hunting horn as a call to death, a demand to which Hernani agrees.

As Don Carlos becomes further involved in efforts to be named emperor of the Holy Roman Empire, he loses interest in persecuting Hernani, but jealousy and resentment build up in Don Ruy Gomez, who continues to desire marriage to Dona Sol. After Don Carlos becomes Emperor Charles V, he generously restores to Hernani both his title of nobility and the lands that were taken from him, and he gives his blessing to a proposed marriage between Hernani and Dona Sol. Still resentful, Don Ruy waits until the two young lovers are about to marry before making Hernani keep his promise to respond to the call of the hunting horn. Although Dona Sol pleads with her guardian to revoke the agreement, he insists that the bargain be kept. Hernani is a man of honor who recognizes that, despite his love for Dona Sol, he must obey the code of honor. At the end of the play, the two lovers poison each other to meet the requirements of Castilian honor, leaving a remorseful Don Ruy to stab himself to death. Giuseppe Verdi based his 1844 opera *Ernani* on Hugo's play.

CENSORSHIP HISTORY

Victor Hugo has been credited by critics as having routed neoclassic conservatism from the French stage with *Hernani* and with preparing the way for modern French drama. He announced early in 1827 that he intended to write a play that would do away with the neoclassic rigidities of the unities of time, place, and action, and he would challenge the rules of decorum that demanded the playwright keep comedy and tragedy apart and separate the ugly from the beautiful. His efforts to initiate this revolution began with *Hernani*, and its production resulted in what was widely known at the time as "the battle of Hernani," which included both censorship difficulties and the heated reactions of theatergoers who formed camps to both support and to denounce Hugo's play.

The French censors recognized the play's political volatility, and they were unanimous in declaring the play to be "rubbish." In their reports, the four unnamed censors stated that "The bandit treats the King like a brigand, the daughter of a Spanish grandee is a shameless hussy, etc." They also criticized the suggestive intimacy of certain lines. As a lesson to the writers and others connected with Comédie-Française who sought to replace neoclassic restraint with romanticism, the censors wrote that *Hernani* should be performed exactly as Hugo wrote it, so that "the public will learn how far the human mind can go when it is freed from every rule and every form of decency."

While the play was in rehearsal in 1829, a group of playwrights headed by Casimir Bonjour petitioned the king without success to ban all romantic plays from Comédie-Française, while other playwrights produced parodies and epigrams that mocked Hugo's efforts. A group of artists and poets, including Théophile Gautier, Petrus Borel, and Gérard de Nerval, formed in support of Hugo to counteract the efforts of the classicists. Calling themselves the Hernanistes, they planned to join *claqueurs*—paid supporters—in the audience to prevent *Hernani* from being booed off the stage. On February 15, 1830, the crowd that gathered to see the play had filled the streets by one in the afternoon, and accounts of the period noted the costume-like apparel of the crowd of playgoing supporters who, as Hugo biographer Graham Robb reports, "looked as though it was about to go and sit for Velazquez—long hair, beards, clothes several centuries old." Antiromantic forces hoped to start a riot, and theater employees were positioned on the roof to use waste from the theater kitchens to pelt the people standing in line. Police ordered the auditorium entrance locked by three in the afternoon to allow no one else to enter, hoping to provoke a riot that would display the romantic supporters in a negative light, but they brought food and drink with them to pass the time. As the play was performed, the supporters of romanticism cheered and stamped their feet at various lines, drowning out the booing by their neoclassic opponents, and Pendell relates that several people were punched in the face as arguments erupted over several lines.

The battles between the two literary factions continued throughout the 39 performances of the play, and the continued arguments drowned out many of the lines onstage. As Gaudon writes, in March 1830 Hugo took an accounting of the audience reactions and noted them in a newly printed copy of the play. Writing in the margins, he observed the following: "laughter" (109 times), "hissing" (30), "sniggering" (9), "noise" (5), "stirring in the audience" (2), one "laugh in anticipation" and one "noise—nothing can be heard" next to the emperor's speech on the populace, that "mirror which seldom shows a King in a flattering light." Throughout the run of the play, police were stationed in the theater and made arrests during many of the performances, while as Pendell reports, the conservative press in Paris openly suggested that the vehement supporters of the play "reeked of lunacy and devil worship." A few weeks before the July Revolution, which sent France's Charles X into exile, Hugo returned home and found a bullet hole in his window and a letter stating, "If you don't withdraw your filthy play, we'll do you in."

To many critics, the chaos that occurred among members of the audiences for *Hernani* served as a symbol or even a cause of the revolution and threat to the monarchy that occurred in July 1830. Charles X dissolved the Parlement and abolished freedom of the press on July 25, 1830, which sparked a general strike on July 26, 1830. This was followed by a bloody three-day revolution known as Les Trois Glorieuses, July 27–29, 1830, which Robb describes as "a victory for the generation which had cheered at the first night of *Hernani*." Notre-Dame was captured by the rebellious crowds, which included large numbers of students, intellectuals, artists, and authors.

The subversive rhetoric of the play was more obvious to English audiences, who actually heard only modifications of many of the lines intended to soften the criticism of Don Carlos and of monarchy in general. Lord Francis Leveson-Gower, who translated *Hernani* in 1831, appended a prologue to the play as much to appease the British monarchy, members of which attended a performance on one occasion, as the literary spectators. In the prologue, he begged the audience to be indulgent of Hugo's "liberal muse":

> Against the unities our Muse has made
> Full in their front a perfect barricade;
> Whence with a dagger, and a poison bottle
> She sticks Voltaire, and pelts at Aristotle!

FURTHER READING

Gassner, John, ed. *A Treasury of the Theatre.* Vol. 1. *World Drama from Aeschylus to Ostrovsky.* New York: Simon and Schuster, 1967.

Gaudon, J. *Victor Hugo et la Théatre. Stratégie et Dramaturgie.* Paris: Suger, 1985.

Lesclide, Richard. *Propos de Table de Victor Hugo.* Paris: Dentu, 1885.

Pendell, William D. *Victor Hugo's Acted Dramas and the Contemporary Press.* Baltimore: Johns Hopkins University Press, 1947.

Robb, Graham. *Victor Hugo: A Biography.* New York: W. W. Norton, 1997.

THE IMPORTANCE OF BEING EARNEST

Author: Oscar Wilde

Original date and place of production: February 14, 1895, St. James Theatre, London, England

Characters: Lady Bracknell, Cecily Cardew, Reverend Canon Chasuble, Hon. Gwendolen Fairfax, Lane, Merriman, Algernon Moncrieff, Miss Prism, John Worthing

Filmed versions: *The Importance of Being Earnest* (1952, U.K.); *The Importance of Being Earnest* (2002, U.S.)

SUMMARY

The Importance of Being Earnest, subtitled "a trivial comedy for serious people," is a witty and literate drawing-room comedy that satirizes Victorian manners. The three-act play, set in an English country house and in London, contains a contrived plot that moves from one absurdity to another without exhibiting any attempt at achieving credibility with the audience. The play opens with a visit by Jack Worthing to the London home of his playboy friend Algernon Moncrieff. Known to Moncrieff as "Ernest," Worthing confesses his love for Moncrieff's cousin Gwendolen, the daughter of Lady Bracknell, and wants to marry her. As the two men talk, Moncrieff opens Worthing's cigarette case and finds it inscribed from "Little Cecily" to "Uncle Jack," and learns that Worthing uses an assumed name when in London, "Ernest in town and Jack in the country," where he is the guardian of a young woman named Cecily Cardew. To escape country life, Worthing pretends that he must care for his ailing brother Ernest in London, then assumes that name when in the city. Moncrieff admits that he leads a similarly double life, telling family that he must visit an out-of-town invalid friend named Bunbury whenever he desires to escape. He defends his practice of "Bunburying" as a commonplace among men of his social set. When Gwendolen arrives with her formidable mother, Moncrieff steers Lady Bracknell out of the room to leave Worthing and Gwendolen alone. The young woman confesses that she has always wanted to love someone named Ernest, and she refuses to give a thought to any other name such as Jack, telling him, "It does not thrill. It produces absolutely no vibrations." The two become engaged, and when Lady Bracknell returns to interrogate Worthing, she finds him acceptable because he admits to knowing nothing: "I do not approve of anything that tampers with natural ignorance." Before bestowing her approval, however, Lady Bracknell insists that "Ernest" must have at least one suitable parent, but he is at a disadvantage because as an infant he was found in a handbag in Victoria Station. The admission prompts Lady Bracknell to tell him that the situation displays "a contempt for the ordinary decencies of family life." She then sweeps out of the room. Gwendolen vows to love "Ernest" eternally and asks for his address, which Moncrieff notes because he is intrigued by the thought of meeting Cecily.

The second act, which takes place at Worthing's country home, opens with a discussion between Cecily and her governess, Miss Prism, about Worthing's presumably debauched and wicked brother Ernest, whom he visits frequently in London. Worthing appears and seeks to end the charade by announcing that Ernest has died, to which Miss Prism responds, "What a lesson for him! I trust he will profit by it!" Feigning grief, Worthing also asks the Reverend Chasuble to christen him as "Ernest" later in the day, but the appearance of Moncrieff pretending to be "Ernest" ruins his plans. Worthing insists that Moncrieff leave, but Cecily is intrigued by him and confesses that she has always been fascinated by the wickedness that she has heard about "Ernest." She has also always hoped to marry a man named Ernest and has created a fantasy relationship, complete with love letters and a diary that detail her engagement to an imaginary Ernest. In love with the name, Cecily also rebuffs Moncrieff's questions about whether she could love someone by any other name, such as Algernon, so Moncrieff also seeks to have the minister rechristen him. When Gwendolen arrives and the two women engage in conversation, they learn that they are both engaged to "Ernest." After moments of indignation, the women demand explanations from Moncrieff and Worthing, who assure them that both men will be named Ernest by the end of the day. Lady Bracknell appears and, after learning that Cecily is very wealthy, gives approval to a marriage with Moncrieff, but continues to refuse her blessing to Worthing and Gwendolen. Upon hearing the name of Miss Prism, she reveals that her household had once employed her—"a female of repellent aspect, remotely connected with education"—but fired her after Miss Prism lost Lady Bracknell's infant nephew, Algernon Moncrieff's older brother, while carrying him in a handbag. The baby grew up to be Jack Worthing. Now that his parentage has been established, Worthing is free to marry Gwendolen and learns that he has really been telling the truth about his name all along. The couples embrace and the plays ends as Worthing concludes, "I've now realized for the first time in my life the vital Importance of Being Earnest."

CENSORSHIP HISTORY

The premiere of *The Importance of Being Earnest*, at the St. James Theatre in London on February 14, 1895, was greeted enthusiastically by most critics of the day. Wilde was exceedingly confident that the play would receive a positive reception and told a friend the day before the premiere, "The play *is* a success.

The only question is whether the audience will be a success." In the weeks following, as the play drew enthusiastic crowds to the St. James Theatre, Wilde became embroiled in a court battle that placed both his literary work and his personal life on trial, and which resulted in the abrupt closing of the highly successful production. For several years in the early 1890s, although married and the father of two children, Wilde had engaged in a series of intimate relationships with young men, some as young as 16. During court trials, he defended these "intimacies" as being "spiritual" and "intellectual," calling them the "affection of an elder for a younger man as there was between David and Jonathan, such as Plato made the very basis of his philosophy, and such as you find in the sonnets of Michaelangelo and Shakespeare."

Because Wilde was relatively discreet and, for the most part, selected as companions young men of lower-class background, his sexual and literary flamboyance were tolerated for a time, but a relationship with Lord Alfred Douglas, the son of John Sholto Douglas, marquess of Queensberry, put an end to his social and literary reputations and resulted in his early death after two difficult years in prison. An emotionally volatile man, Queensberry had badgered his son for months regarding the social implications of his relationship with Wilde and tried without success to end it. Queensberry tried to attend the opening of *The Importance of Being Earnest* to make a public statement against Wilde for "literary obscenity" without implicating his son, but Wilde learned of this possibility in advance and ticket sellers were instructed to refuse to sell Queensberry a ticket for any performance. Police were on hand on opening night with specific instructions to refuse admittance to anyone without a ticket, and they turned Queensberry away but he returned a short time later with baskets of vegetables to take into the gallery and pelt the stage with, but he was again sent away.

Four days after the play opened, Queensberry went to Wilde's club, the Albemarle, and left his calling card on which he had written: "Oscar Wilde—posing as a sodomite." Wilde chose to put the charge into the public forum and sued Queensberry for having "published a false and malicious libel." The libel trial, which took place on April 3–5, 1895, contained testimony that used Wilde's literature as evidence for Queensberry's charges that Wilde had "certain tendencies" and ended with an acquittal for the defendant and arrest for Wilde, who would face two criminal trials in which the implications of his writings and veiled references in letters to Lord Alfred Douglas were used to condemn him. After the verdict in the libel trial, in which Queensberry was acquitted of the libel charges, and the arrest of the playwright on the charge of "gross indecency," Wilde's play *An Ideal Husband* was withdrawn from production at the Haymarket Theatre in London and his name was removed from all advertisements connected with the highly successful *The Importance of Being Earnest.*

A criminal trial began on April 26, 1895, in which Wilde, labeled by newspapers as the "High Priest of the Decadents" and an "obscene impostor," was accused of a series of "unnatural sexual practices," supported by testimony that attacked his writing, as well. His accusers charged that Wilde's "intellectual debauchery" functioned as a cover for his flagrant immorality and "unspeakable crimes."

Wilde was on trial as much for having violated the social and literary decorum of the period as for his choice of sexual partners. Critics dissected his work, and the currently popular *The Importance of Being Earnest* and Wilde's novel *The Picture of Dorian Gray* were treated most severely. As Parkes observes, a great deal was made over Wilde's subversion of the term *earnestness*, a quality highly valued in 19th-century England, denoting "the moral integrity and fidelity to truth at the heart of the British ideal of manhood." Critics of the time attacked the play as a metaphor for Wilde's moral delinquency, seeing parallels and messages throughout. They pointed out that the characters lead double lives, take mysterious leaves of absence from their seemingly respectable family surroundings, and feel a need to hide their activities spent away from their usual social milieu. Worthing's imaginary and disreputable brother, Ernest, and Moncrieff's imaginary invalid friend, Bunbury, became suspect as metaphors for homoerotic adventuring. W. H. Auden observed in an assessment of the play that the trials illuminated the homoerotic undertones of *The Importance of Being Earnest*, noting that "it was difficult to ignore Wilde's homosexuality when reading the play: now one always knows what Algernon means when he says he is going Bunburying." Wilde was found guilty of "committing acts of gross indecency" and sentenced to two years of hard labor in Reading Gaol. He died two years after his release. Withdrawn from the stage in May 1895, *The Importance of Being Earnest* would remain banned from the stage for more than a decade, because no producer dared to revive the play. Once revived, the play had a successful season in 1909–10, and John Gielgud's 1939 London production and 1947 New York productions were also highly successful.

FURTHER READING

Auden, W. H. *Forewords and Afterwords.* Selected by Edward Mendelson. New York: Random House, 1973.

Craft, Christopher. "Alias Bunbury: Desire and Termination in *The Importance of Being Earnest.*" *Representations* 31 (summer 1990): 19–46.

Gassner, John, ed. *A Treasury of the Theatre.* Vol. 3. *Oscar Wilde to Eugene Ionesco.* Rev. ed. New York: Simon and Schuster, 1977.

Green, William. "Oscar Wilde and the Bunburys." *Modern Drama* 21, no. 1 (1978): 70.

Hyde, H. Montgomery. *The Trials of Oscar Wilde.* New York: Dover Publications, 1973.

Katz, Jonathan. *Gay/Lesbian Almanac.* New York: Harper & Row, 1983.

Parkes, Adam. *Modernism and the Theater of Censorship.* New York: Oxford University Press, 1996.

THE ISLAND OF ST. MARGUERITE

Author: John St. John, librettist; Thomas Shaw, composer
Original date and place of production: November 1789, Drury Lane Theatre, London, England

Characters: Carline, M. du St.-Mars, M. du Junca, "The Mask," townspeople
Filmed versions: None

SUMMARY

The Island of St. Marguerite is an opera whose plot is filled with allusions to the fall of the Bastille on July 14, 1789, at the start of the French Revolution. The hero is the famous "Man in the Iron Mask," who was imprisoned on the island of St. Marguerite from 1687 through his death in 1704. The opera openly reminds the public of the atrocities suffered by prisoners who were imprisoned on the island and draws frequent parallels to the inhuman treatment that French prisoners had received at the Bastille. Most critics agree with the assessment by L. W. Conolly that the work is little more than "an indifferent opera which would not win its author great literary fame, but was sure to attract attention on account of its topicality," a feature that led Charles Kemble, manager of the Covent Garden theater, to sign the production for his stage. The hero of the play is the mysterious but real "Man in the Iron Mask," referred to in the play as "the Mask" or "Mask," whose identity was established upon his death as having been an Italian named Marchioli but who was rumored to be the exiled twin brother of King Louis XIV of France, although no proof of that relationship was ever established. The play depicts the prison as set near a town that prisoner commandant M. du St.-Mars views as being filled with "general confusion" and with people who represent a constant threat "to attack my Castle." Conditions in the prison are generally brutal, and the place is dark, crowded, and filthy, but the commandant defends his treatment of the masked prisoner and contends that "This Mask, has all the Luxuries of Life." The townspeople sympathize with the prisoners and, toward the end of the opera, as the mob forms, prior to storming the prison to liberate the incarcerated men, they sing a rousing song that calls upon them to "assert your freedom/Vindicate the Rights of Men." The song also makes appeals to Justice and to Liberty, urging the men to sacrifice their lives to regain the freedoms they have lost. The opera ends with the commandant's final speech, presented in the "Dead March," and the stage direction for the mob to lead the commandant to his execution and to release "the Mask" and the other prisoners.

CENSORSHIP HISTORY

Charles Kemble, manager of the Drury Lane Theatre, hoped to benefit from the topicality of the opera, although all of his notes from the period indicate that he considered the work itself to be of only minor literary importance. In mid-October 1789, only three months after the storming of the Bastille, Kemble submitted the play to London censors with a request for a license to present it at the Drury Lane Theatre. The Examiner of Plays refused to grant a license for performance until Kemble removed lines that might prove offensive to France. In 1789 some quarters of the French monarchy still wielded power and the possibility remained that many of the French aristocrats living in temporary exile in England might eventually return to power. The English government did not want to choose sides too early by being presumptuous in criticizing the old political system in France or too quickly embrace the new order. As a result, the censors determined that all "free sentiments" would have to be excised from the opera, especially allusions to the fall of the Bastille and any signs of a crusading tone of social and political reform. The playwright was required also to remove all descriptions of the atrocities and inhumane treatment given to prisoners, most pointedly the following lines in which St.-Mars defends his treatment of "the Mask" and contrasts his treatment with that of the other prisoners: "This is Heaven, to what some Wretches Suffer in this Place—This Mask, has all the Luxuries of Life—others depriv'd of Light, and Air & Space to move their Weary Members turn & wreathe in Vain each harrass'd Sinew till convuls'd with Agonies too sharp to bear they gain a Temporary Torpor." The censors also demanded that St. John remove the three verses that constituted the mob's rally song calling for justice and liberty and that urge them to "Assert your Freedom." The substituted versions are significantly milder, and in the censored version of the play, military officers guarding the prison sing the first and last verses, while the weakened mob sings only a mild middle verse. The end of the opera was censored to remove all references to an execution or to the release of prisoners by the mob. In an advertisement attached to the printed censored text, dated November 20, 1789, Kemble wrote the following:

> The subject, however proper for the Stage, was not free from difficulties. The Author, as appears from his prologue, knows the value of liberty, and, consequently, could not withhold his applause from a people struggling for a free constitution: but delicacy required that even the appearance of any thing that might be construed into an insult to a foreign country should be avoided. To steer through those opposite extremes seems to have been the design throughout the piece; and when the pruning hand of authority proscribed certain passages, the Author submitted cheerfully, though in all probability more was lost in spirit, than gained in decency, by such corrections.

FURTHER READING

Blakey, Robert. *The History of Political Literature from the Earliest Times.* Vol. II. London: Richard Bentley, 1855.

Conolly, L. W. *The Censorship of Drama, 1737–1824.* San Marino, Calif.: Huntington Library, 1976.

Fowell, Frank, and Frank Palmer. *Censorship in England.* London: F. Palmer, 1913. Reprint, New York: Benjamin Blom, 1969.

JACK SHEPPARD

Author: William Harrison Ainsworth (novel on which all stage versions were based)
Original date and place of production: October 28, 1839, Adelphi Theatre, London, England
Characters: Edgeworth Bess, Blueskin, Poll Maggot, Abram Mendez, Jack Sheppard, Sir Rowland Trenchard, Jonathan Wild
Filmed versions: None

SUMMARY

The play *Jack Sheppard*, adapted by John Baldwin Buckstone from the novel written by William Harrison Ainsworth, became a great success when it was first presented at the Adelphi Theatre in London on October 28, 1839. The play was one of many adaptations based on Ainsworth's novel that glorified the life and the adventures of one of the most daring criminals in 18th-century England. The fast-moving plot is unashamedly sensational, as it relates the story of the former apprentice who finds that crime is more rewarding and enjoyable than working as a carpenter. As a young and naive apprentice, Jack Sheppard meets petty criminal Blueskin and two "women of the town," Edgeworth Bess and Poll Maggot, who teach him a range of illegal skills, from picking pockets and housebreaking to the daring art of highway robbery. Although he is apprehended repeatedly, Sheppard manages to escape his prisons, and even escapes from Newgate prison three different times. He is finally arrested and executed at Tyburn Tree, dying for his life of crime at the age of 22. The play intersperses moments of high drama among the straightforward details of Sheppard's career, and includes a dramatic rescue from the Thames River during a thunderstorm, a touching reunion with his mother while she is dying, and a heartrending scene on the scaffold when he is finally caught and executed. The audience is also treated to such spectacular scenes of horror as Jonathan Wild and Abram Mendez brutally murdering Sir Rowland Trenchard and the violent behavior of the angry mob attending Sheppard's execution as they burn down Jonathan Wild's house.

CENSORSHIP HISTORY

The stage version of *Jack Sheppard* was extremely popular, and audiences clamored for additional plays of the same sort, which quickly acquired the label of "Newgate drama," for their emphasis upon the daring lives of criminals. Although the London censors, presided over by the Lord Chamberlain, Lord De La Warr, suspected soon after the first performance of the play that greater control would have to be exerted over the crime dramas, they did not move to censor such plays until after the three-day trial of François Benjamin Courvoisier, a Swiss valet who was found guilty of stabbing his employer, Lord William Russell, with a carving knife and sentenced to be hanged. According to a report in *The Times* on June 25, 1840, while waiting for his sentence to be carried out, Courvoisier claimed that he had gained the idea for the crime after seeing a performance of the J. T. Haines version of the play. The licensing authorities decided that they would not license further adaptations of the story of Jack Sheppard's life and activities, and they would also work hard to limit the future staging of productions that had already received the sanction of the lord chamberlain. The censors' actions were also motivated by the large number of letters sent by parents and schoolmasters, which requested that the censors prevent the exhibition of *Jack Sheppard* and similar plays, because they had "such an ill effect on their sons and apprentices."

Despite the censors' efforts to discourage productions, minor theaters continued to present the play. In 1845 police discovered that the play was being performed at the City of London Theatre, and less affluent patrons were being lured to the production by the offer of manager Frederick Fox Cooper to admit two people for the price of one. The Lord Chamberlain's Office ordered Cooper to immediately end the practice, and Cooper claimed that the order ended his business, because he could not draw paying spectators in any other way. The first formal banning of the play occurred in 1848, when the Lord Chamberlain's Office issued a statement to all London theater managers to inform them that it would not sanction any further versions of the play. When *Jack Sheppard* returned to the London stage in 1852 at the Haymarket Theatre, the censors required that the production use the classic Buckstone adaptation, and the managers included in the playbill the following statement to remind audiences that this version of the play had received official sanction:

> This statement is rendered necessary by the numerous unlicensed imitations that have been acted under the same title, and in which scenes and situations have been presented to the Audience that, however harmless when followed by the context in reading the novel, were deemed unfit for delineation on that stage. In the present adaptation all objectionable passages are carefully expunged, and whilst every care is taken to illustrate the striking incidents of the Drama, the most scrupulous may rest assured that in "adorning the tale" the great end of Dramatic Representation—"to point a moral"—has not been forgotten.

When the Haymarket production was announced, managers from the Pavilion Theatre and the Bower Saloon hurriedly submitted applications to stage their own productions, but both were refused. In a letter to the manager of the Pavilion Theatre, the lord chamberlain wrote, "the Drama of Jack Sheppard having been licensed some years back for the Adelphi Theatre, his Lordship does not think it right to revoke a Licence granted by one of his Predecessors, but it is not his intention to grant any further licence for its performance." The only reason that the Buckstone version of the play was permitted to continue while others were refused was because it had already received official sanction in 1839, though it would not receive approval if submitted in 1852, and no further "Newgate dramas" received approval. In the spring of 1859 Examiner of Plays William Donne extended the ban on "Highway Pieces" to include even previously licensed plays, and *Jack Sheppard* disappeared as a play title, although versions of the play under such titles as *The Idle Apprentice* and *The Young Apprentice*, both having the same story lines, were acceptable as long as the names of Jack Sheppard and other highwaymen were not identified.

In 1868 the Examiner of Plays reiterated the ban on *Jack Sheppard* by refusing a license to *Jack Sheppard; or, Vice and the Punishment and Virtue and the Reward*, despite the contention of the theater manager that "the work is exempt from all obnoxious scenes, characters and brutal murders: the part of Jack Sheppard is stripped of the honours and heroics in which he has been surrounded by novelists and stands forth in his true light—in boyhood envious, vicious, and treacherous; in manhood vain and desperate, sinning but suffering mentally and physically." In 1873 a revival of theatrical interest in *Jack Sheppard* occurred, and in February of that year four different versions of the Jack Sheppard story were submitted for licensing, but the applications were rejected. Encouraged by the sudden renewed interest in the topic, Adelphi Theatre manager Benjamin Webster submitted an application to the examiner of plays to revive the Buckstone adaptation, which had been sanctioned in 1839 and permitted in 1852. The licenser refused to sanction the play under the original title and required that Webster remodel the play radically. As public interest diminished in highwaymen and crime as entertainment, licensing restrictions relaxed, and most revivals of *Jack Sheppard* in the 1880s and 1890s were poorly attended.

FURTHER READING

Bleackley, Horace. *Jack Sheppard . . . with an Epilogue on Jack Sheppard in Literature and Drama.* London: Bodley Head, 1933.

Fowell, Frank, and Frank Palmer. *Censorship in England.* London: F. Palmer, 1913. Reprint, New York: Benjamin Blom, 1969.

Stephens, John Russell. *The Censorship of English Drama, 1824–1901.* New York: Cambridge University Press, 1980.

Thackeray, William Makepeace. "Going to See a Man Hanged." *Fraser's Magazine* 22 (1840): 150–158.

JACK STRAW

Author: Anonymous
Original date and place of production: c. 1593, England
Characters: King Richard, Tom Miller, Nobs, Jack Straw
Filmed versions: None

SUMMARY

Referred to as both *The Life and Death of Jack Straw* and the more common *Jack Straw*, the English verse drama contains the following qualifier on the title page of its 1593 edition: "a notable Rebell in England." The drama relates the role played in the rebellion by Jack Straw, characterized in the play as the leader of the Kentish faction in the Peasants' Revolt in 1381, although historically he was a minor cleric in Kent and the rebellion leader was actually Walter (Wat) Tighler (variously Tyler) who was not a peasant but a local minor landholder with a grudge against the monarchy. The dissatisfaction among the peasants ensues because the king has demanded that all of his subjects pay a poll tax on each member of their family. When the collector of the king's tax appears at his home, Straw refuses to pay the poll tax for his daughter, claiming that she is underage and "therefore goes cleare." The argument escalates into a physical altercation in which Straw kills the tax collector, which serves as the opening action in a coming rebellion. The peasants unite in their cause to free themselves of the crushing burden of the king's taxes, yet some, such as Nobs, recognize that the gallows will probably be their fate, because they are bound to fail in their effort. The second act is fragmented and consists of a series of extremely brief episodes. Nobs steals a goose from fellow farmer Tom Miller; the rebels shout their plans to march to London and to make their cause heard, and the king arrives in an attempt to appease them but departs abruptly. The remainder of the play focuses on the discussions between the Queen Mother and King Richard, and explains in a relatively lengthy manner the hierarchical doctrine of the king and his counselors.

CENSORSHIP HISTORY

Critics contend that the censorship of *Jack Straw* occurred before the first edition of the play was published, and they base this assumption on the episodic nature of the sole edition of the play, printed in 1593. The edition provides a light treatment of the basis for the Peasants' Revolt and lacks any description of the brutal incidents, violence, and victimization that permeate contemporary factual accounts. The play is only 1,210 lines long, and there is only one printed version. As critic Janet Clare points out, "speculations about textual censorship can only remain as such." Still, comparisons with accounts in the *Holinshed Chronicles*, a history of England published in 1577 by Ralph Holinshed, exhibit that much detail regarding the oppression by the monarchy and the violence by the peasants appears to have been excised. Further, a disproportionate amount of attention is given to the expression of sentiments by the Queen Mother and the plan for clemency enacted by King Richard, while the supposed main focus of the play, the rebellion, is dealt with in considerably briefer scenes. As Clare notes, "In theatrical terms the rebellion, such as it is, plainly has more vitality than the lengthy expositions of hierarchical doctrine by the King and his councilors which comprise much of the rest of the drama." No record exists to show that the drama was performed in a formal theater;

nonetheless, the diverse references to the play in manuals listing plays of the period suggest that it was performed widely in provincial venues.

The drama purports to relate the story behind the Peasants' Revolt in 1381 in England, but the discussion of the rebels' cause at the beginning of the play is minimal and the dramatization of the rebellion itself is cursory, so it is reasonable to assume that material detailing the actions of the rebels and the disposition of their lives was deleted from the original playbook. The issues and motives related to the rebellion, as well as the means taken by the peasants to achieve change, are lightly sketched, and none of the murders of public officials or details of such attacks as that on the Tower of London and the beheading of officials appear. Further, in contrast to the benevolent resolution of the issue that appears in the play, history recounts that after King Richard met with the leaders and promised reforms and clemency, Wat Tighler was killed by the lord mayor of London. The now-subdued rebels were sent home with promises of amnesty, which was effectively revoked two weeks later when King Richard ordered most of them arrested and executed.

FURTHER READING

Clare, Janet. *"Art Made Tongue-Tied by Authority": Elizabeth and Jacobean Dramatic Censorship*. New York: Manchester University Press, 1990.

Fowell, Frank, and Frank Palmer. *Censorship in England*. London: F. Palmer, 1913. Reprint, New York: Benjamin Blom, 1969.

Halsall, Paul, ed. "King Richard and the Peasants' Revolt." The Internet Medieval Sourcebook. Fordham University Center for Medieval Studies. Available online. URL: http://www.fordham.edu/halsall/source/anon1381.html.

Hazlitt, W. Carew. *A Manual for Collector and Amateur of Old English Plays*. Burt Franklin Bibliography and Reference Series #106. 1892. Reprint, New York: Burt Franklin, 1966.

Muir, Kenneth, and F. P. Wilson. *The Malone Society Reprint of* Jack Straw. Oxford, England: Malone Society, 1957.

JESUS CHRIST SUPERSTAR

Author: Tim Rice (lyrics) and Andrew Lloyd Webber (music)

Original date and place of production: October 12, 1971, Mark Hellinger Theatre, New York, New York

Characters: Anna, Caiphas, Cured Lepers, Jesus of Nazareth, Judas Iscariot, King Herod, Mary Magdalene, Peter, Pontius Pilate, Priests, Reporters, Simon, Soul Girls

Filmed versions: *Jesus Christ Superstar* (1973, U.S.)

SUMMARY

Jesus Christ Superstar is a rock opera in 24 scenes, divided into two acts, the first presenting the events of the six days that led up to the Last Supper and the Crucifixion of Jesus Christ, and the second beginning with the Last Supper. The action and the dialogue are expressed mainly in musical numbers phrased in contemporary slang ("What's the Buzz?") and set to a rock or jazz beat. The seven days in the life of Jesus of Nazareth are seen through the eyes of his disciple, Judas Iscariot, who has become disillusioned with the movement. At the opening of the play, Judas appears to sincerely agonize over his perception that the followers of Jesus have become fanatical and unrealistic, hailing him as a god and twisting his words into monstrous prophecies. After all, in Judas's mind, Jesus is only a man—a man with certain inconsistencies, as evidenced by his relationship with Mary Magdalene. As the crowds in the street grow more and more out of control, the rift between Jesus and Judas grows. After watching Jesus lose control in the temple, lashing out at the moneylenders and merchants, then begging to be left alone when a crowd of cripples surrounds him, asking to be healed, Judas is more convinced than ever that the man from Nazareth is just that—a man, and nothing more. He grows to believe that Jesus has lost control of the mob and, as a result, has become dangerous and must be stopped. To achieve that end, Judas goes to the priests and gives them all the information they need to catch Jesus alone so that they can take him prisoner without risking violence by the mob. After leading the soldiers to the Garden of Gethsemane, however, and watching the events that unfold, Judas soon realizes that he has been tricked by God into being the instrument of Jesus' martyrdom. He becomes furious that the man from Nazareth will be remembered as a "superstar" and so he hangs himself. The events, although familiar from the New Testament of the Bible, take on a modern meaning as they are told in rock-and-roll and jazz contexts, often in colloquial language.

CENSORSHIP HISTORY

Jesus Christ Superstar was initially created by Rice and Webber as a concept rock album and released in 1969. As the album sales reached into the millions, the concept developed into a concert attraction, but Rice, Webber, and their backers were reluctant to attempt a full-scale stage production, because they feared, at first, that a religious backlash would doom the production to financial failure. The success of the concerts convinced Rice and Lloyd-Webber that they should take the production into theaters. The first formal performance of the stage musical *Jesus Christ Superstar* took place on October 12, 1971, at the Mark Hellinger Theatre in New York City. As the authors had feared, the opening of the musical was greeted by loud controversy, and theater critics and religious groups questioned the propriety of the musical and the extent to which it demythologized Jesus of Nazareth. Religious groups found the play irreverent and accused the writers of blasphemy in suggesting a sexual relationship between Mary Magdalene and Jesus. Theater critics were more disapproving of the lavish sets, which they thought too flamboyant for the simple biblical story. Although numerous newspaper articles, both pro and con, were written about the production, no true effort was made to stop the Broadway production, which ran for 711 performances. In an article for *America*, Moira Walsh expressed the prevailing attitude, which was to consider the musical "benign" and to excuse scriptural transgressions and the use of stereotypes: "The essence, it seems to me, is the attempt of two young agnostics, Tim Rice and Andrew Lloyd Webber, to express their bemused admiration for the life and teachings of Christ in terms that are comprehensible to them."

Jesus Christ Superstar was smuggled into the Union of Soviet Socialist Republics (USSR) soon after its initial production in the United States in 1971, and Soviet authorities banned it immediately after its production in Vilnius (Lithuania) in 1973. Their efforts had a galvanizing effect on Soviet musicians, and *Jesus Christ Superstar* became the inspiration for many rock groups and millions of fans despite its being banned, because rock groups who had not received permission to perform nor authorization of show content performed much of the score at their shows. Performances occurred in the USSR throughout the 1970s and, by the end of the decade, the signature theme song was adopted by the Soviet television news program *Vremya*, exhibiting that a popular, religious rock opera had exerted a more powerful influence that the dominating bureaucracy.

In the United States numerous productions of the musical have been stopped at the conceptual stages, thus avoiding actual banning of an existing production. In contrast, in Abilene, Texas, the Abilene Community Theater was strongly discouraged from mounting a production in the late 1990s, but went ahead with the production without incident. The group had momentary misgivings because of the controversy stirred up more than two decades earlier by an Abilene Jaycees–sponsored performance of the play, which excited a number of local protests. Ministers had angrily denounced the production from the pulpit and in letters to the *Abilene Reporter-News*. A consortium of ministers also placed a full-page advertisement in the newspaper before and on the day of the production stating, "A production it is. Christian it is not."

Jesus Christ Superstar has continued to provoke controversy. Some followers of Christian fundamentalists continue to view the play as blasphemous, as an incident that occurred in 2002 in Kellenberg Memorial High School, a Catholic high school in Uniondale, New York, exhibits. Stewart Ain reported in the *New York Times* that a student and member of the school choir named Megan Gaffey refused to sing a medley of songs from *Jesus Christ Superstar* because she believed them to be "irreverent" and claimed that one of the songs was not consistent with the teachings of the Roman Catholic high school, because the song "only speaks of Jesus's humanity; it does not mention his divinity." Her family, self-described evangelical Christians, supported her decision. The student was asked to leave the choir and learned on June 17, 2002, that the school had barred her from returning for her senior year of classes.

FURTHER READING

Ain, Stewart. "Doctrine Separates a Girl and Her School." *New York Times*, June 30, 2002, p. L1.

Forshey, Gerald E. *American Religious and Biblical Spectaculars*. Westport, Conn.: Praeger Publishing, 1992.

Richards, Stanley, ed. *Great Rock Musicals*. New York: Stein & Day, 1979.

Rudnick, Paul. "If Sex Has Lost Its Shock Value, How About God?" *New York Times*, December 6, 1998, sec. 2, p. 7.

Ryback, Timothy. *Rock around the Bloc: A History of Rock Music in Eastern Europe and the Soviet Union*. New York: Oxford University Press, 1990.

KILLING NO MURDER

Author: Theodore Hook
Original date and place of production: August 21, 1809, Little Theatre in the Haymarket, London, England
Characters: Apollo Belvi, Busk, Hepzibah
Filmed versions: None

SUMMARY

Killing No Murder is a farce in two acts that, as playwright Theodore Hook acknowledges in his preface to the printed version of the play, was written to ridicule Methodist preachers so that "the lash of ridicule might be well applied to their backs." The play mocks the self-proclaimed nature of their call to preaching that was carried on while they continued in their former occupations. As the preface states, Hook sought to expose them "without touching indelicately on the subject" and characterizes as absurd the "open and violent expressions of inspired tailors and illuminated cobblers." The main character of *Killing No Murder* is Apollo Belvi, described in the play as "a consummate coxcomb—a strange mix of boor and beau—[who] is in high practice as a cutter of capers." While at Swansea, Belvi becomes infatuated with Hepzibah, the daughter of a Methodist minister. To win her over, Belvi becomes a Methodist preacher, and relates how he did so: "So I preached and I preached—la, how I did preach!—till at last I preached myself plump into the heart of my young saint." The two become engaged and set a wedding date, but Hepzibah becomes pregnant by Belvi and gives birth to a son the day before the wedding, and the marriage is postponed.

CENSORSHIP HISTORY

Killing No Murder was supposed to open at the Little Theatre in the Haymarket on June 20, 1809, but the Examiner of Plays in London, John Larpent, waited until the night before to announce that the play would not receive a license for performance until alterations were made in the text. In his assessment of the play, Larpent wrote that it was an "indecent and shameful attack on a very religious and harmless set of people" and warned Hook that "Government did not wish the Methodists to be ridiculed." Hook protested, but after learning that Larpent was a rigid Methodist, he decided to make the alterations in his own manner. As Fowell and Palmer observe, "he altered the offending parts and in their place inserted speeches written purposely to ridicule Larpent himself, and as these speeches touched neither on politics nor religion, the Examiner was unable to expunge them."

At the same time that the censored version of the play appeared on stage, Hook also published the play and placed the expunged scenes into an appendix, so that readers would see clearly where alterations had been made to meet the demands of the censor. Hook was required to remove all mention of the Methodist religion and to refrain from identifying his main character as a "Methodist preacher." Hook replaced each instance in which a character's dialogue contained those terms with a phrase such as "what I must not mention" or "what must not be mentioned," then provided footnotes for the reader and explained, "In the piece originally 'Methodist Preacher' but altered by order of the Licenser." The published play was bought eagerly by playgoers who enjoyed both the ludicrous effect of the corrections in the written version and in the performance. In effect, the manner in which Hook handled the censor's demands made the efforts of the censorship futile. Larpent also expunged as "profane" the following two lines in the original play submitted for licensing that speak of "grey hairs": "Bring my grey hairs in sorrow to the grave" and "What! insult me in grey hairs." Despite the best efforts of the censor, Hook managed to make clear to his audience that the goal of *Killing No Murder* was, as he proclaimed in the preface to the printed revised version, to be successful at "turning into ridicule the ignorance, and impudence of the self-elected pastors who infest every part of the kingdom."

FURTHER READING

Conolly, L. W. *The Censorship of English Drama, 1737–1824.* San Marino, Calif.: Huntington Library, 1976.

Fowell, Frank, and Frank Palmer. *Censorship in England.* London: F. Palmer, 1913. Reprint, New York: Benjamin Blom, 1969.

Hook, Theodore Edward. *Killing No Murder, a Farce in Two Acts. As Performed with Great Applause at the Theatre Royal Haymarket. Together with a preface and his scene suppressed by order of the Lord Chamberlain.* London: Printed by W. Flint for Samuel Tipper, 1809.

KING LEAR

Author: William Shakespeare
Original date and place of production: December 1607, Whitehall, London, England

Characters: Cordelia, Curan, Duke of Albany, Duke of Burgundy, Duke of Cornwall, Earl of Gloucester, Earl of Kent, Edgar, Edmund, Fool, Gentleman, Goneril, King of France, Lear, Oswald, Regan
Filmed versions: *King Lear* (1971, U.K.); *King Lear* (1987, U.S.-Swiss)

SUMMARY

King Lear relates the story of a king of Britain who had three daughters: Goneril, wife of the duke of Albany; Regan, wife of the duke of Cornwall; and the unmarried Cordelia, who is courted by both the king of France and the duke of Burgundy, both of whom are present in King Lear's court when the play opens. The king, now aged 80, is worn out with age and the fatigues of government and determined to take no further part in state affairs, but to leave the management in younger hands and take time to prepare for death, which he believes will come soon. With this intent he calls his three daughters to him to learn firsthand which of them loves him best, so that he might divide his kingdom among them according to the extent each loves him and in such proportions as their affection for him seems to deserve. Goneril, the eldest, declares that she loves her father more than words can tell, then flatters him by stating that he is "dearer to her than the light of her own eyes." The king is delighted to hear this assurance of her love and, thinking that she is sincere, bestows upon her and her husband one-third of his ample kingdom. He then summons his second daughter and demands to hear what she has to say. Regan is as false as her sister and declares that what her sister had spoken came short of her love and that she finds all other joys dead in comparison with the pleasure she takes in the love of her dear father. Lear blesses himself in having such loving children, and, after the handsome assurances that Regan has made, bestows one-third of his kingdom upon her and her husband, equal in size to that which he has already given to Goneril.

He then turns to Cordelia, his youngest daughter, whom he calls his joy, and asks what she has to say, expecting that she will utter even more fervent expressions of love than her sisters, because she has always been his favorite. But Cordelia, disgusted with the flattery and falseness of her sisters, makes no other reply but that she loved his majesty according to her duty, neither more nor less. Lear is shocked by what seems to be the ingratitude of his favorite child, and he warns her to consider her words and to change her speech, or she will damage her fortunes. Cordelia then tells her father that he has given her breeding, and loved her; that she returned those duties as was most fit, and did obey him, love him, and honor him, but that she will not make such large speeches as her sisters had. The earl of Kent, one of Lear's favorite courtiers and captains, tries to defend Cordelia, but Lear will not listen. He divides the kingdom between Goneril and Regan and tells them that he will keep only 100 knights at arms and will live with his daughters by turns.

When the duke of Burgundy learns that Cordelia will have no share of the kingdom, he gives up his courtship, but the king of France is wiser, and states, "Thy dowerless daughter, King, is Queen of us—of ours, and our fair France." Cordelia becomes queen of France, and the earl of Kent is banished from the kingdom for having ventured to take her part. The king stays first with Goneril, who mistreats him and even begrudges the 100 knights that he had reserved for himself. She is harsh and undutiful to him, and even her servants refuse to obey his orders. An unhappy Lear leaves Goneril to live with Regan, but she displays even worse conduct, saying that 50 knights are too many to wait on him, and even five were too many, because her servants could wait on him. When Lear sees that what they really want is to drive him away, he leaves them on a wild and stormy night and wanders the heath half mad with misery, and with no companion but the poor Fool. Presently his servant, the disguised earl of Kent, meets him and persuades him to lie down in a wretched little hovel. At daybreak the earl hurries to the French court to tell Cordelia what has happened. Cordelia's husband gives her an army, and she finds Lear wandering about the fields, wearing a crown of nettles and weeds. She takes him back to the French court, where she feeds and clothes him. Goneril and Regan join their armies and capture Cordelia and Lear, whom they throw into prison. Goneril then poisons Regan and later takes her own life, after arranging that Cordelia be hanged in prison. When Goneril's husband, the duke of Albany, learns of the scheme, he sends messengers at once, but they are too late to save Cordelia. King Lear staggers into Albany's tent with Cordelia's body in his arms, then dies.

CENSORSHIP HISTORY

Critics have identified *King Lear* as one of the most topical of plays to be performed in the public theater in the early 17th century because of its oblique references to the union of England and Scotland and because of similarities in behavior between Shakespeare's King Lear and Britain's King James. Comparisons of the quarto (transcript of the play in performance) text with the folio (play for publication) text exhibit that Shakespeare made significant revisions to the quarto version, most to remove sociopolitical references, to create the folio and as Janet Clare has assessed, "we might expect it to incorporate the censorship of the Master of the Revels [censors]." Clare has methodically identified the changes between the two versions and asserts that the changes are more likely the result of "the censor's direct intervention, or for self-censorship as distinct merely from artistic revision." One lengthy satiric passage in the quarto text that occurs between the Fool and King Lear has been removed from the folio version. The satire is wide-ranging in their exchange, as Lear is labeled a "fool" for his actions and the Fool rails about abuses of power and goes beyond the boundaries of the "all-licensed" fool in his comments. The satire reflects actions identified with King James, who excited resentment with his practice of granting monopolies to favored courtiers and whose reputation at the time in England was as the "wisest fool in Christendom." In the quarto, in a passage late in the play, two characters, Edmund and Edgar, discuss the way in which the events of Lear's downfall and the warring between his daughters' armies fulfill recent predictions of "dissolutions of ancient amities, divisions in state, menaces and maledictions against King and nobles." This passage is absent from the folio, and Clare observes that the words "suggest matters more immediate than power struggles in pagan Britain." The relationship between the French and British forces is modified in the folio text and lines spoken by Goneril and the earl of Kent that refer to a French invasion of Britain are cut, while lines spoken by Albany that consider a British response to a French invasion are modified. In the folio version, lines spoken by the earl of Kent simply paint the French as aware of the internal dissension in England and offer "no more than an oblique suggestion that the French may profit from internal dissension."

In 1681 English playwright Nahun Tate rewrote portions of *King Lear*. He replaced Lear's line "Rumble thy belly full" with "Rumble thy fill." The expurgation was not made in the attempt to preserve modesty in regard to the word *belly*; instead, Tate believed that the original line was too inelegant to include in the dialogue of a king. He also disagreed with Shakespeare's original ending, in which the courageous and loyal Cordelia is hanged in prison, and wrote a happy ending in which a widowed Cordelia is rescued and marries one of her rescuers.

In 1788 the English censors banned *King Lear* from the stage, because the madness of Lear was too reflective of the insanity of the reigning monarch King George III. The play remained banned from the English stage until 1820.

In 1796 an expurgated version of *King Lear* was published under the claim that it was an early version written by Shakespeare. The reality was that William Henry Ireland, only 18 years old at the time, had copied by hand the entire play onto old paper, making expurgations as he saw fit and adding archaic spellings and phrasings to his changes. He then pretended to have discovered the old manuscript, which he presented to his father, a collector of plays and related materials. As Perrin writes, "His father was completely taken in, along with the Duke of Somerset, James Boswell [biographer of Dr. Samuel Johnson], and Bishop Burgess." The forgery was printed and praised by many literary figures of the time as having a "pure but elegant style." Shakespeare scholar Edmund Malone exposed the forgery, but Ireland maintained until his death that his forgery had actually elevated the reputation of Shakespeare. He wrote in his account of the experience:

> the world supposed that all the ribaldry [in Shakespeare's] other plays was not written by himself but foistered in by the players and printers; herein it cannot be said I injured the reputation of Shakespear, on the contrary, the world thought him a much more pure and even writer than before.

FURTHER READING

Clare, Janet. *Art Made Tongue-Tied by Authority: Elizabethan and Jacobean Dramatic Censorship*. New York: St. Martin's Press, 1990.

Ireland, William Henry. *Confessions of William Henry Ireland, Containing Particulars of His Fabrication of the Shakspeare* [sic] *Manuscripts*. Facsimile reprint. New York: Burt Franklin, 1909.

Patterson, Annabel. *Censorship and Interpretation: The Conditions of Writing and Reading in Early Modern England*. Madison: University of Wisconsin Press, 1991.

Perrin, Noel. *Dr. Bowdler's Legacy: A History of Expurgated Books in England and America*. Boston: David R. Godine, 1992.

KISMET

Author: Edward Knoblock

Original date and place of production: December 25, 1911, Knickerbocker Theatre, New York, New York

Characters: Bashassi, Beggars, Caliph Abdullah, Haji, Imam, Jawan, Mansur the Wazir, Marsinah

Filmed versions: *Kismet* (1920, 1931, 1944, 1955, U.S.); (1930, Germany)

SUMMARY

Kismet, set in Baghdad in the year 1361 (Islam 752), is an Arabian Nights fantasy covering 24 eventful hours in the life of Haji, a beggar. He is surrounded by a gallery of colorful characters. Jawan, the White Sheik, is Haji's longtime adversary, a former outlaw who is now repentant and who years before stole Haji's wife and killed his son. The villainous Mansur the Wazir, who desires Haji's daughter Marsinah and wants to add her to his harem, wants to keep Haji from interfering with his plans and threatens Haji into pledging to assassinate the caliph. Unaware that she is in danger, Marsinah has fallen in love with the caliph, the handsome and all-powerful ruler of Baghdad whom she mistakes for a simple gardener and who seems to reciprocate her love. The play opens with Haji awakening one morning on the stairs of a mosque. He is soon accused of theft and escapes punitive mutilation of his hand only by demonstrating his "magical powers" to the wicked wazir, with whom he agrees to prevent the marriage of the caliph, unaware that the intended bride is his own daughter, Marsinah. The wazir, who wants Marsinah for himself, plots to violate her sexually, dishonoring her so that she will have no choice but to become part of his harem. Haji discovers the perfidy of the wazir, but he is imprisoned for plotting against the caliph and placed in a dungeon from which he escapes, after which he rescues Marsinah from Mansur's harem, then drowns the wazir. The play ends with Haji deciding to make a pilgrimage to Mecca, then falling asleep on the steps of the same mosque where he awakened at the beginning of the play.

CENSORSHIP HISTORY

Kismet opened at the Knickerbocker Theatre on Broadway in New York City on December 25, 1911, and ran for 184 performances without incident. In late 1911 the play premiered in London to an enthusiastic crowd that included King George V and Queen Mary and ran for 245 well-attended performances. After seven months on stage, what Frank Fowell and Frank Palmer have described as "the most colossal stupidity which the censorship has perpetrated in recent years" occurred in regard to *Kismet*. The Office of the Lord Chamberlain, Lord Sandhurst, ordered the modification of a scene in the play in which a young girl clothed in a flesh-color bodysuit slips off her flowing white dress and plunges into a bathing pool. The scene took place toward the back of the stage under lighting that simulated diffused moonlight. As critics of the censorship pointed out, the girl was "carefully wrapped from head to foot in fleshings and was in the water the instant she was out of her drapery." The censors demanded that the girl must wear more clothing than the bodysuit when she jumps into the harem bathing pool. Because the play had already run for seven months, the act of censorship caught critics and theatergoers by surprise, but *Kismet* was one of several plays and music-hall performances targeted by religious conservatives who had earlier demanded that London officials remove George Bernard Shaw's MRS. WARREN'S PROFESSION from the stage. In response to the growing number of such incidents, more than 60 prominent literary figures, including J. M. Barrie, William Butler Yeats, Arthur Symons, and Joseph Conrad, wrote a petition to King George V to call attention "to the grave injury inflicted on the art of the drama, and the obstacles placed in the way of its further development, by the present administration of the functions of the Censorship of Plays under the Department of your Majesty's Lord Chamberlain." The letter reflected a growing discontent by the public as well with the heavy-handed role of the censors and, although more than 40 years would pass before the abolishment of official censorship, the signs of weakening were clear.

FURTHER READING

Bordman, Gerald. *American Operetta from* H.M.S. Pinafore *to* Sweeney Todd. New York: Oxford University Press, 1981.
Dietrich, Richard F. *British Drama, 1890 to 1950: A Critical History*. New York: Twayne Publishers, 1989.
Fowell, Frank, and Frank Palmer. *Censorship in England*. London: F. Palmer, 1913. Reprint, New York, 1969.

THE KNACK

Author: Ann Jellicoe
Original date and place of production: October 9, 1961, Arts Theatre, Cambridge, England

Characters: Colin, Nancy, Tolen, Tom
Filmed versions: *The Knack, and How to Get It* (1965, U.K.)

SUMMARY

The Knack, set in the early 1960s, focuses on three young men who are roommates in a rented house in Tottenham, North London. The three seek to turn the house into their "bachelor pad." Tom, a condescending and inhibited schoolteacher, and Colin, a reticent young man in whose name the house is rented, do all of the work while womanizer Tolen sits at the open window calling out to every passing female. Colin imagines a long line of young women in tight white sweaters on the stairwell waiting to get into Tolen's room and, jealous of Tolen's incredible success with the ladies, asks Tolen for advice on how to attract women. As Tolen describes his successes with women and hints at his techniques for seduction, a young woman fresh from the country, Nancy Jones, stops by the house and asks for directions. She is new in London and wants to rent a room at the YWCA. Tolen decides that she is the perfect subject to use in showing Colin his techniques of seduction. As Tolen begins using the tricks that have guaranteed his "knack" in seducing women, he calls out directions to Colin in asides, but Nancy is so frightened by his actions that she faints. Once revived, she believes that she has been raped and begins to scream. Although shaken by the dangerous turn the situation has taken, the three young men try to bluff their way out of it. As Nancy calms down and listens, Tolen suggests that being raped is Nancy's deepest sexual fantasy while Tom openly derides his opinion. As the two men argue, Colin claims that he raped her. Tolen denies Colin's claim and derides him: "You can't even catch her, Colin, can you? Never mind rape her. I think you are quite incapable of making a woman, Colin. . . . Look, I'll show you." He grabs Nancy and pulls her to him, but Colin threatens to kill him if he touches her and wins her affection immediately. At the end of the play, Colin realizes that his teacher in seduction actually subjugates women and forces them to submit to him.

CENSORSHIP HISTORY

Many early audiences of *The Knack* focused their attention on the sexual premises of the play. Critics such as Bamber Gascoigne of *Spectator* condemned the play for its "sexual callousness," and the critic for *Theatre Journal* characterized the play as being about "love, sex, and . . . power." Although the powers of the London censors were largely weakened by 1961, the laws regarding the licensing of plays for public performances remained in force, and the producers of the Arts Theatre production of *The Knack* were concerned that Ann Jellicoe's intention of social criticism would be overshadowed by the play's treatment of sex as a sport. Although the censors raised questions about the "cavalier fashion in which sex is treated," and the potential sexual violence against Nancy, the Office of the Lord Chamberlain, Lord Cobbold, granted the play a license for performance. Several conservative groups in London, however, notified the censors well in advance of the October 9, 1961, debut performance, asking that the Lord Chamberlain refuse to license the play. After these early efforts were rebuffed, no formal efforts were made in London to suppress the play, although performances of the play in theaters outside London were usually required to modify some of the dialogue to lessen the callousness of Tolen's sexually predatory behavior and what one critic characterized as the "erotic freebooting" of the men.

FURTHER READING

Elsom, John. *Erotic Theatre.* New York: Taplinger Publishing Co., 1974.

Gascoigne, Bamber. "With a Bare Bedstead." *Spectator* 208 (April 6, 1962): 445.

Jellicoe, Ann. *The Knack: A Comedy in Three Acts.* New York: Samuel French, 1962.

King, Kimball. *Twenty Modern British Playwrights: A Bibliography.* New York: Garland Publishing, 1977.

Klein, Kathleen G. "The Knack." *Theatre Journal* 36, no. 2 (May 1968): 273.

Peacock, D. Keith. *Radical Stages: Alternative History in Modern British Drama.* No. 43 in the Contributions in Drama and Theatre Studies. Westport, Conn.: Greenwood Press, 1991.

Rusinko, Susan. *British Drama, 1950 to the Present: A Critical History.* Boston: Twayne Publishers, 1989.

Snyder, Laura. "Learn to Play the Game: Learning and Teaching Strategies in Ann Jellicoe's *The Knack.*" *Modern Drama* 37, no. 3 (fall 1994): 451–458.

LIPS TOGETHER, TEETH APART

Author: Terrence McNally
Original date and place of production: June 25, 1991, Manhattan Theater Club, New York, New York
Characters: Chloe Haddock, John Haddock, Sally Truman, Sam Truman
Filmed versions: None

SUMMARY

Lips Together, Teeth Apart is a tragic and comedic drama about one Fourth of July weekend spent by two heterosexual married couples at the Fire Island beach house that Sally Truman, one of the wives, has inherited from her gay brother David, who has died of AIDS. The title is taken from the advice that a dentist has given to Sally's husband, Sam, to cure him of grinding his teeth while he sleeps. Sally and Sam have invited Sam's sister Chloe and her husband John Haddock to join them for the weekend, and all four characters exhibit uneasiness in the long-established gay resort, although the audience does not see any of the neighbors. The play opens with the arrival of the couples. Sally, a painter, has experienced several miscarriages and believes that she is currently pregnant, which leads her to wonder how she might react if she had a son who were gay. Sam is a quick-tempered building contractor who seems to take no interest in his wife's artistic talents. Chloe talks incessantly and presses the others to eat and to drink the many canapés, muffins, and other foods that she has prepared, as she denies that her husband John is suffering from inoperable cancer. John has had a sexual relationship with Sally in the recent past and hopes to continue the relationship in the time that he has left. The four spend a day and a night trying to avoid discussing what has brought them together, and the fact that David was gay, although Sam becomes obsessed with testing the pool for HIV. During the play, Sam is astonished to observe offstage two men having sex in nearby bushes, and comments, "I hear huffing and puffing and biting and licking and kissing and grunting and groaning, but I don't hear anyone say, 'I love you'"; after a brief interval, however, one of the men does speak those words. Sally watches another man strip off his bathing suit, wave goodbye to the house, then swim out to sea to drown himself; she berates herself because she mentally willed him to die. She later admits that she helped her brother to die. These and other revelations by the characters climax with John's confirmation at the end of the weekend that he is dying of cancer. As the play ends, the two couples stand together, watching the Fourth of July fireworks, each voicing his or her deepest fear. Suddenly, after all of the human-created fireworks, they spot a shooting star, which seems to give each hope for the future.

CENSORSHIP HISTORY

Lips Together, Teeth Apart was honored by the New York Society of Critics as one of the 10 best plays for the 1991–92 Broadway theater season, but this acclaim did not prevent its condemnation by censors in Cobb County, Georgia. In 1993 a couple attending a performance of the play at the Theatre in the Square were allegedly so shocked by the subject matter that they wrote a letter of protest to Gordon Wysong, the chairman of the Cobb County Commission, and expressed outrage that the play was supported, in part, by public funds. They called on him to lead the commission to stop the production. The effort was supported by state chapters of the Christian Coalition, a national organization led by Pat Robertson, and the American Family Association, led by Donald Wildmon, which alerted its membership and conducted letter-writing campaigns against the play. In the fight that followed, protesters recalled an earlier production of *M. BUTTERFLY* that had been presented without protest but was now added to the current objections. Although he did not read the script, attend a performance, or view a videotape of either play, Wysong labeled both "immoral, pro-homosexual, and anti-community and supportive of the 'gay lifestyle.'" He also worked with local fundamentalist televangelist Nelson Price to design two resolutions. The first, passed by the Cobb County Commission on the Arts, proposed to restrict public arts funding to only those programs that "advance and support strong community, family-oriented values." The second resolution, which passed by majority vote in August 1993, condemned homosexuality and stated that the county would not support any "lifestyles advocated by the gay community" as a means of protecting the "safety, health and welfare of the community" from what the resolution termed "increasing assaults" on its standards by gay men and lesbians.

Palmer Wells, founder and executive director of the Theatre in the Square, enlisted the aid of the American Civil Liberties Union (ACLU), which charged that the first resolution amounted to censorship. The local ACLU chapter threatened to sue the commission for selectively denying arts funding to projects if it passed. After finding that defending their original criteria for funding was legally impossible, the commission then voted to end all arts funding. This move deprived the Theatre in the Square of $40,000, which it formerly received from the Cobb County Commission to offset its annual budget of nearly $800,000. While the commissioners claimed that they were simply working to conserve the money of taxpayers, their argument quickly lost ground when the Theatre in the Square management briefly considered moving to a more liberal township, which would risk a loss of approximately $3.5 million in local business that the theater generated. The total arts funding expense to the taxpayers had been only $110,000, and this had included funding for school arts and other popular programs, in addition to funding for the theater. Rather than resulting in a victory for the conservative elements of the community, the resolutions instead served to mobilize the gay community, which created a political action group that organized several demonstrations in the town square. The decision in August 1993 to eliminate all arts funding also meant that the Cobb County Commission was sacrificing the opportunity to participate in an arts festival that was timed to coincide with the Summer 2000 Olympic Games, held in Atlanta.

FURTHER READING

Alexander, Andrew. "On Art and Sodomy." *Creative Loafing Online: Atlanta Arts and Entertainment.* Available online. URL: http://www.cln.com/archives/atlanta/ newsstand/101098/a_artsa.htm. Posted October 10, 1998.

Brustein, Robert. "*Lips Together, Teeth Apart* (Manhattan Theatre Club, New York City)." *The New Republic,* October 21, 1991, pp. 28–29.

Caldwell, Stephen R. "The NEA and 'Culture Wars.'" Speech delivered to Black Hills Unitarian-Universalist Fellowship, Rapid City, S.D., November 14, 1993.

Guernsey, Otis L., Jr., and Jeffrey Sweet. *The Applause/Best Plays Theater Yearbook of 1991–1992.* New York: Applause Publishing, 1992.

Kingston, Jeremy. "*Lips Together, Teeth Apart* (Orange Tree Theater, Richmond, England)." *The London Times,* November 1998, p. 38.

Loche, Dick. "*Lips Together, Teeth Apart* (Mark Taper Forum, Los Angeles, California)." *Los Angeles Magazine,* September 1993, pp. 186–188.

Schapiro, Mark. "Who's behind the Culture War: Contemporary Assaults on the Freedom of Expression." Available online. URL: http://www.publiceye.org/theocrat/ Schapiro.html. Downloaded on August 9, 2003.

LONG DAY'S JOURNEY INTO NIGHT

Author: Eugene O'Neill

Original date and place of production: February 2, 1956, Royal Dramatic Theatre, Stockholm, Sweden

Characters: Cathleen, Edmund Tyrone, James Tyrone, Jamie Tyrone, Mary Cavan Tyrone

Filmed versions: Feature film: *Long Day's Journey into Night* (1962, 2000, U.S.); (1996, Canada). Made for television: (1973, U.K.); (1987, U.S.)

SUMMARY

Long Day's Journey into Night, completed by Eugene O'Neill in 1941, is set in the summer of 1912. The play begins at 8:30 A.M., in a setting described as foggy day at a Connecticut summer home, and ends at approximately midnight on the same day. Composed largely of psychological revelation rather than physical action, the play is O'Neill's attempt "to face my dead at last . . . with deep pity and understanding and forgiveness for *all* four haunted Tyrones," as he wrote in the dedication to his wife Carlotta. The Tyrones in the play are modeled on the O'Neills—the playwright, his parents and siblings—with their difficulties and agonies intact. The characters reveal details of their lives through their verbal interactions onstage; little physical action occurs. James Tyrone Sr., a miserly actor living on his former glory, caused the morphine addiction of his wife, Mary, many years before by calling in an unqualified doctor when she was suffering physical pain after the birth of Edmund. Although she has attempted to stop taking the drug many times, she has recently returned to its use after having strong suspicions that the 23-year-old Edmund is suffering from tuberculosis, not the "summer cold" that her husband and sons call it. Edmund resents his father, who is preparing to send him to a state-run sanitarium instead of a private rest home for treatment, and he also struggles with guilt that his birth caused the illness that led to Mary's use of morphine. Jamie is deteriorating into frequent bouts of drunkenness and envies his younger brother's apparent literary talent. He brags of his forays to the local brothel. The play reflects the philosophy that Mary expresses as she moves in and out of her drug-induced stupor: "The past is the present, isn't it? . . . It's the future, too. We all try to lie out of that but life won't let us."

As the play progresses, the characters reveal that the difficulties suffered by this generation of Tyrones are rooted in the past. Edmund has attempted suicide before the play opens, and James's father died a suicide. Edmund is suffering from tuberculosis ("consumption"), a condition that killed Mary's father. The dramatic events mirror the events of O'Neill's family, and none of the characters is free of blame, for none of the characters has shown the strength to escape what seems to be his or her fate. All four characters, excluding Cathleen, the maid, retreat further into their illusions as the day progresses—the three men into drunkenness and Mary into her morphine haze—until Mary appears with her wedding gown in her arms. As Jamie mocks her as the "Mad Ophelia" and Edmund tries to penetrate her drugged state by telling her of his illness, the curtain falls as Mary says sadly, "Then in the spring something happened to me. Yes, I remember. I fell in love with James Tyrone and was so happy for a time."

CENSORSHIP HISTORY

Long Day's Journey into Night was completed in 1941, but O'Neill withheld publication or production of the play at the request of his son, Eugene O'Neill Jr., then a student at Yale University. The younger O'Neill asked that the play be kept from the public for 25 years because, as Laufe reports, it would not "be good for my social position at Yale," a request to which his father agreed without telling his then-wife Carlotta, to whom the play was dedicated. The playwright died in 1953 and, despite promises to her husband, Carlotta O'Neill requested that Random House publish the play. Publisher Bennett Cerf refused her request, choosing to honor O'Neill's original decision to keep the play from the public for 25 years after it was completed, but the widow then sold publication rights to Yale University Press. On November 29, 1945, O'Neill had hand-delivered a copy of the play to Cerf where, at the playwright's insistence, the envelope was fastened with sealing wax and placed in the publisher's vault. Biographer Louis Sheaffer writes that O'Neill dictated and signed the following statement and insisted that Cerf also sign it: "I am this day depositing with you, on condition that it not be opened by you until twenty-five years after my death, a sealed copy of an original play, which I have entitled *Long Day's Journey Into Night*." Cerf had written to O'Neill in 1951, a year after the suicide of Eugene O'Neill Jr., and sent him manuscripts, including the play that had been kept at the Random House offices. O'Neill had responded in writing to Cerf and made his intentions for the play clear: "No, I do not want *Long Day's Journey Into Night*. That, as you know, is to be published twenty-five years after my death—but never produced as a play." Despite Cerf's efforts, as O'Neill's executor and sole heir, Carlotta O'Neill had the legal right to do as she pleased with the play. When Karl Ragner Gierow, director of the Royal Dramatic Theatre in Stockholm, Sweden, learned of the impending publication, he contacted Carlotta O'Neill and, with the assistance of then-secretary general of the United Nations, Dag Hammarskjold, negotiated permission to stage the premiere performance of the play. Although O'Neill's widow claimed at first that she would agree only to publication of the play in the United States but not to performance, she later gave in to the pressure exerted by numerous producers in New York City who sought the rights to launch a stage production. The first U.S. performance took place on November 7, 1956, at the Circle in the Square, where it ran for 390 performances.

Long Day's Journey Into Night was honored by the New York Society of Critics as one of the 10 best plays for the 1956–57 Broadway theater season and won a posthumous Pulitzer Prize for the playwright, but such acclaim was insufficient to prevent Baylor University officials from banning it. In 1962 Abner McCall, the president of the Waco, Texas, university, ordered that the University Theatre cease performances of the play, which had been presented to audiences four times and drawn complaints for both the "dissipations" of the character and for "blasphemous dialogue." McCall, who asserted that the drama was "not in keeping with the University ideals," had been approached by a delegation of ministers to close the production after the first performance and had received complaints from audience members after each ensuing performance about the situations depicted and the language. Further, in written statements to McCall, protesters claimed that the play ridiculed the Christian religion. McCall stated that he banned the play because he believed that it was not "in good taste for a church-related university to produce." The university, affiliated with the Baptist General Convention of Texas, agreed to reconsider a production of the play if the dramatic group would agree to remove specific dialogue from the script, but the contract made with representatives of Carlotta O'Neill specified that the play must be performed intact, with no changes or cuts. The banning of the play created dissension within Baylor University. Paul Baker, chairman of the Drama Department, admitted to reporters that the play had "strong language," but he defended it as being "one of the greatest plays of its time." The local newspapers supported Baker and others who wanted to continue the production, but Baylor officials adamantly refused to reconsider. In protest Baker resigned his position at the university and was joined by 11 members of the drama department, who all resigned. Within days, Trinity College, a Presbyterian-based college located in San Antonio, Texas, announced the appointment of Paul Baker as head of their drama department and the hiring of several of the others who had resigned.

FURTHER READING

Black, Stephen A. *Eugene O'Neill: Beyond Mourning and Tragedy.* New Haven, Conn.: Yale University Press, 1999.
Brustein, Robert. *The Theater of Revolt.* Boston: Little, Brown, 1964.
Burrone, Laura. "Eugene O'Neill's *Long Day's Journey Into Night:* A Publishing Success Story." *Endpapers* (fall 1998).
Laufe, Abe. *The Wicked Stage: A History of Theater Censorship and Harassment in the United States.* New York: Frederick Ungar Publishing, 1978.
Sheaffer, Louis. *O'Neill: Son and Artist.* Boston: Little, Brown, 1973.

LYSISTRATA

Author: Aristophanes
Original date and place of production: 411 B.C.E.; Athens, Greece
Characters: Athenian Ambassadors, Athenian Commissioner, Chorus of

Old Men, Chorus of Women, Cinesias, Kalonike, Lampito, Lysistrata, Myrrhina, Spartan Ambassadors, Spartan Herald

Filmed versions: *Die Sendung der Lysistrate* (1961, West Germany); *Lysistrata* (1976, Belgium); *Lystenstyret* (1914, Denmark); *Triomphe der Liebe* (1947, Austria)

SUMMARY

Lysistrata, which deals with such archetypal themes as war and sexuality, is one of the oldest comedies still regularly performed in the theater. The main character, Lysistrata, is the first comic heroine in Greek plays. Her tactics of passive resistance enable the Athenian women and their Spartan counterparts to stop the Peloponnesian War, which took place from 431 to 404 B.C.E. Aristophanes wrote *Lysistrata* in 411 B.C.E., after the Peloponnesian War had raged for 20 years and showed little signs of abating. His comedy actually masks a serious intention to protest the continued war and to draw attention to the waste of human life.

The play opens as Lysistrata and Kalonike await the appearance of a large gathering of women called together by Lysistrata. As the two speak, Lysistrata exhibits her political concerns and asserts the need to end the slaughter and the long-term absences of their husbands at war. She says that the very limitations placed upon women's activities can be their weapons in stopping the war. After Kalonike asks what women could possibly do to stop a war when their training and activities have been largely limited to adorning themselves, Lysistrata replies that such adornment and physical desirability will work as their greatest strength in this effort. When the women arrive, they all agree with Lysistrata's complaint that their husbands have been away at war for far too long, and they want to stop the war, as well, but they do not agree with her plan that both Athenian and Spartan women should stop performing their traditional domestic duties and refrain from sexual contact with their husbands until the men on both sides of the conflict agree to sign a treaty of peace to end the war. Kalonike blurts out, "Don't ask me to give up *that!* Why, there's nothing like it!"

Eventually the women agree, but they are unable to find a suitable sacrifice to seal their oaths. After considering and discarding the ideas of sacrificing a goat or disemboweling a horse, they agree that sacrificing a full wineskin and swearing their oath with their hands upon a cup of the blood-red wine will suffice. The oath to which each woman swears includes detailed mention of the sexually related activities in which she will not participate if her husband "shall e'er approach me with his penis up." Even if forced into sexual activity, they pledge to "do it badly and not wiggle in response." To strengthen their position, Lysistrata also instructs the older women to take over the Acropolis, thereby taking control of the treasury and keeping the money out of the hands of the warmongers. When the Chorus of Old Men attempts to storm the Acropolis, the women holding it pummel them with rotted fruits and vegetables.

149

The men are at first amused by their wives' assertiveness, but after a week passes both sexes begin to miss their sexual interactions. Several of the women make up excuses to return home, claiming that they must comb their wool or strip their flax. One woman places a large iron kettle under her clothing and claims that she must return home for she is about to give birth, but Lysistrata reminds her that she showed no signs of pregnancy only days earlier. Representing the husbands, Cinesias approaches his wife, Myrrhina, and promises that he will "think about" voting for peace but begs her to first "lie down with me once more." To bring Cinesias to a high state of arousal and frustration, Myrrhina pretends to yield to his desires but delays by leaving him numerous times to obtain articles such as pillows or quilts for his comfort. When he can stand the delay no longer, she walks away. Immediately after, Spartan men arrive to negotiate with the Athenian men, and the dialogue contains several clear references to the physical arousal of the men that shows in the protrusion under their cloaks and which is confirmed by one Spartan, who says the men "are all erect as well." The men want their wives back so much they consent to a treaty between the two cities. The play ends with the husbands and wives of both sides singing happily together of the way in which the goddess Aphrodite has provided a peaceful end to the war.

CENSORSHIP HISTORY

In *Lysistrata*, Aristophanes created a play that contains material that has provoked the ire of censors in different time periods. In the playwright's time the political implications of the play drew greater negative attention than the sexual situations and innuendo. Author Jeffrey Henderson writes that Aristophanes had no compunction about using his plays to criticize politicians and their actions. Despite the support of audiences, Aristophanes was brought to court for the "political impropriety" of his plays by Kleon, a politician who did not agree with the playwright's viewpoint regarding the government and whom he had mocked in his earlier play *The Wasps* (423 B.C.E.). Public opinion weighed heavily and Aristophanes escaped serious punishment. In 1910 the London Little Theatre earned the approval of the censors and presented a severely bowdlerized version of *Lysistrata*, prompting a somewhat mixed review by an anonymous reviewer in the publication *Athenaeum*, who praised the adapter "[who] has not retained any of the licentiousness of Aristophanes's text . . . [yet] keeps in view the sexual basis of the comedy . . . if the truth may be told, the piece as modified proves a rather tame and schoolgirlish affair."

Two decades later, would-be producers of the play continued to avoid the original text of the play in favor of more acceptable adaptations. In the 1934 introduction to his version of *Lysistrata*, which had been presented to large audiences in both England and the United States, Seldes writes that most contemporary reviewers were consistent in their opinion of the original play written by Aristophanes that "*Lysistrata* is far too gross for the English stage." The published version of Aristophanes' *Lysistrata* was one of many works, including Boccaccio's *Decameron*, Defoe's *Moll Flanders*, and Fielding's *The History of Tom Jones*, banned from being brought into the United States until 1930 under the Comstock Act of 1873, which also forbade the selling of birth control devices and the right to choose abortion. Officially known as the Federal Anti-Obscenity Act, this law banned the mailing of "lewd," "indecent," "filthy," or "obscene" materials.

In 1942, when Greece was under Nazi occupation, performances of all classic Greek plays, including comedies such as *Lysistrata*, were banned. In the United States in 1954, U.S. Post Office officials ordered the seizure of a rare illustrated copy of *Lysistrata* mailed from Fanfrolic Press in England to Harry A. Levinson, a bookseller in Beverly Hills, California, and charged that mailing the material violated the Comstock Act. The bookseller appealed to the American Civil Liberties Union, which asked famed First Amendment attorney Edward De Grazia to take the case to court in 1955. De Grazia charged that Postmaster General Arthur Summerfield "had no respect for the literature of the ages and that the court should remove him and his office from the business of literary censorship." The petition sought to have the federal court declare the Comstock Act unconstitutional and to abolish the practice of allowing postal officials to "supervise the sexual contents of literature and art sent through the mails." De Grazia argued that "even if *Lysistrata* were obscene, its social and cultural importance entitled it to constitutional protection." Faced with this challenge, the Post Office relented and released the illustrated copy of *Lysistrata* before the court had time to act.

In 1967 the play was banned in Greece by the military regime, which banned a number of classic plays that contained antiwar themes or themes that emphasized freedom and independence. In 1989 *Lysistrata* was central to a textbook controversy in Lake City, Florida, in which school board members acceded to the demands of a minister named Fritz Fountain and his followers to ban the high school humanities textbook because two selections—*Lysistrata* and Chaucer's "The Miller's Tale"—promote, in Fountain's opinion, "women's lib" and pornography. Opponents challenged the ban but lost in *Virgil v. School Board of Columbia County*, 862 F.2d 1517 when the Eleventh Circuit Court upheld the right of the school board to remove the textbook based "upon a concern related to a legitimate educational objective." The board defended the decision, claiming the works were not appropriate for reading by high school students "due to their vulgarity and sexual explicitness."

FURTHER READING

Aristophanes. *Lysistrata*. Translated by Donald Sutherland. New York: Harper & Row, 1961.

Backes, Anthony. "Aristophanes Would Laugh." *English Journal* (March 1999): 43–46.

De Grazia, Edward. "Allen Ginsberg, Norman Mailer, Barney Rosset: Their Struggles against Censorship Recalled." *Cardozo Life* (fall 1998). Available online. URL: http://www.grazian-archive.com/quiddity/Ginsberg/Ginsberg_.html.

Henderson, Jeffrey. "Aristophanes." In *Ancient Greek Authors*. Detroit, Mich.: Gale Research Publishers, 1997.

Loth, David. *The Erotic in Literature*. New York: Dorset Press, 1961.

"*Lysistrata.*" *Athenaeum* 4329 (October 15, 1910): 465–466.

Seldes, Gilbert. "Introduction." *Lysistrata*. New York: Limited Editions Club, 1934.

Virgil v. School Board of Columbia County, Fla., 862 F.2d 1517 (11th Cir. 1989).

THE MAID'S TRAGEDY

Authors: Francis Beaumont and John Fletcher
Original date and place of production: 1610, London, England
Characters: Amintor, Antiphilia, Aspatia, Calianax, Cleon, Diagoras, Dilphilus, Evadne, Lysippus, Melantius, Olympias
Filmed versions: None

SUMMARY

The Maid's Tragedy, a revenge written in verse, is generally acknowledged by critics to be the most powerful play to emerge from the collaboration of Beaumont and Fletcher. A drama of strong passions, the play appeals to a broad range of audiences with its elements of blood, lust, jealousy, greed, and romance, although the plot is relatively simple. Amintor, a nobleman, is betrothed to Aspatia, but the king makes him end the betrothal and arranges a marriage for him with Evadne. Faced with no alternative Amintor agrees, but he learns on his wedding night that Evadne has been the king's unwilling mistress and that the marriage has been arranged as a means of concealing the affair, which the king expects to continue.

As Evadne's lady-in-waiting Dula jokes with her about the wedding night ahead, playfully debating whether or not Evadne will reach morning with her maidenhead intact, Evadne becomes filled with remorse. She considers the shame that her affair with the king and continued betrayal will bring to her husband Amintor and brothers Melantius, a military officer who has fought valiantly in the king's service and been wounded, and Diphilus, who remained out of the fray at the king's request. She vows to correct the situation. She decides her only choice is to kill the king. She approaches the guard at the king's door and asks for the key, a request that is readily granted by the guard who leers as he refers to her previous entrances into the king's chambers. When Evadne enters the bedroom, she finds the king sleeping peacefully and decides that she must wake him up and chastise him for what he has done to her before killing him. In a lengthy soliloquy, she reveals her anguish in having lost her "virgin self" to the king and vows to "lay his sins before him." To prevent him from fighting her off, Evadne ties his arms to the bedposts with scarves. When the king awakens, he contemplates her eagerly, telling her that he had been dreaming of her, and tells her to climb into bed with him. He calls her his "queen of love" and asks "Let us be caught together, that the gods/May see, and envy our embraces." Evadne cautions him to cool his ardor, telling him, "You are too hot, and I have brought you physic/To temper your high veins." That "physic" is his death, which she accomplishes with a dagger. She then appears to Amintor, who recoils in horror, telling her, ". . . and to augment my woe/You now are present, stained with a king's blood/Violently shed."

As the play ends, Lysippus, the king's brother, expresses the ambiguous manner in which the playwrights present regicide in the play, both recommending that a ruler must deal fairly with his subjects and that would-be assassins of a monarch will be severely punished: "May this a fair example be to me/To rule with temper, for on lustful kings/Unlooked-for sudden deaths from God are sent;/But curs'd is he that is their instrument."

CENSORSHIP HISTORY

Early censors of *The Maid's Tragedy* were unconcerned with the sexual innuendo of the dialogues between Evadne's brothers or her maid Dula's references to the wedding night, but they drew the line at regicide. Although the play is cautious and evasive in presenting Evadne's intentions, and the ending is indefinite enough to allow the interpretation that the king's wooing will lead her to sex rather than murder, the moral and political implications of the act of killing a monarch were too strong for censors to ignore. Written in 1610 and first produced in 1611, the play was presented in censored form for nearly a decade before the original text of the play was published. The first printing of the play, in 1619, reproduced the approved stage version, but the printing in 1622 of a "newly perused, augmented, and inlarged" version contains 80 additional lines that had been excised after the censors had declared them to be offensive. Amintor's threat to the king's life and vow that he will not be satisfied unless he is sent the king's "limbs through all the land/To show how nobly I have freed myself" is absent, as are all other references to the murder of a king.

With the restoration of the monarchy to the throne of England and the reopening of the theaters in 1660, the subject of regicide in drama became even more forbidden, and both the censored and the restored versions of *The Maid's Tragedy* were banned from the stage by order of Charles II of England. As playwright Colley Cibber observed, "the killing of the king in the Play, while the tragicall Death of King Charles I was then so fresh in People's memory, was an Object too horribly impious for a Public Entertainment." In 1685 Edmund Waller rewrote the ending of the play; his version spares the life of the king and allows Evadne to retrieve her lost honor in the eyes of her family and her husband. This version was presented to the royal court in 1690 and became the only performed version for nearly a century.

FURTHER READING

Clare, Janet. *"Art Made Tongue-Tied by Authority": Elizabethan and Jacobean Dramatic Censorship.* New York: St. Martin's Press, 1990.

Craik, T. W. The Maid's Tragedy *by Beaumont and Fletcher.* New York: St. Martin's Press, 1999.

Fisk, Deborah Payne. *The Cambridge Companion to English Restoration Theatre.* New York: Cambridge University Press, 2000.

Fowell, Frank, and Frank Palmer. *Censorship in England.* London: F. Palmer, 1913. Reprint, New York: Benjamin Blom, 1969.

Giddons, E. E. "Calianax's Challenge in *The Maid's Tragedy.*" *Notes and Queries* 44, no. 4 (December 1997): 523.

THE MAN OF THE WORLD

Author: Charles Macklin

Original date and place of production: May 10, 1781, Covent Garden Theatre, London, England

Characters: Constantia, Lord Lambercourt, Egerton Mac-Sycophant, Sir Pertinax Mac-Sycophant, Lady Rodolpha

Filmed versions: None

SUMMARY

The Man of the World is a satire of politicians, whom Macklin embodies in the Scottish politician Sir Pertinax Mac-Sycophant, who has used his talent for being pliable to rise to prominence as a member of Parliament from his humble beginnings as a "beggarly clerk in Sawney Gordon's compting house." The buffoonish Mac-Sycophant aspires to acquire control of three parliamentary boroughs. As a means of accomplishing this goal, he arranges a marriage between his son Egerton and Lady Rodolpha, the daughter of another equally servile politician, Lord Lambercourt, whose only concern is that he receive a substantial amount of cash for agreeing to the marriage. Mac-Sycophant and Lambercourt rush the two young people through a one-day courtship, with the wedding ceremony planned for the day after Lady Rodolpha and Egerton first meet. Because Egerton is speechless in their first encounter, Lady Rodolpha takes control of the situation and, speaking in a broad Scottish brogue, makes the first advances. Within minutes, they become allies, as both admit to having affections for other people, and they plot to circumvent their self-serving fathers. Encouraged by Lady Rodolpha, Egerton secretly marries his father's ward Constantia, whom he has loved for years, while she waits for the opportunity to marry her sweetheart who, unknown to everyone but Egerton, is his younger brother. When Mac-Sycophant learns of Egerton's elopement, he immediately proposes a marriage between his younger son and Lady Rodolpha, who eagerly agrees to the marriage. Unconcerned with his daughter's feelings, Lord Lambercourt blesses the union by stating that he doesn't "care a pinch of snuff if she concorporates with the Cham of Tartary," as long as he receives the money that Mac-Sycophant promised. The play ends with everyone gaining what they wanted.

CENSORSHIP HISTORY

In the preface to *The Man of the World*, Macklin claimed that he wrote the play "to explode the reciprocal national prejudices that equally soured and disgraced the minds of both English and Scots men." The English censors and Lord Chamberlain Francis Seymour Conway, marquis of Hertford, viewed the play in a different light. Potential producers had to submit it three times for a license before a stage performance was allowed, although the play had already been produced in Dublin, Ireland, in 1766 under the title of *The True-Born Scotchman*. Fowell and Palmer note that the resulting three versions of the play are "in three different states of moderation, in the latest the severity of the satire having been sufficiently softened to satisfy the scruples of Lord Hertford." The first submission for a license was made on August 2, 1770, by Samuel Foote who had hoped to produce it in his Little Theatre in London. Nine years later, after Macklin had rewritten dialogue, Covent Garden manager Thomas Harris sent a revised version of the play to the lord chamberlain on December 4, 1779, who, once again, refused to grant a license for performance. More than a year later, in the spring of 1781, after Macklin had made further revisions in the dialogue, the manager of Covent Garden submitted to the censors still another version of the play. This final version was granted a license, and the play was finally performed at Covent Garden on May 10, 1781, nearly 11 years after the first attempt to obtain a license.

The objections of the censors were purely political, and the licensers rejected *The Man of the World* because of its open satire of political officials. Although Macklin contended in a letter to the lord chamberlain that his play "satirizes both public and private venality, and reprobates inordinate passions and tyrannical conduct in a parent," the government censors viewed the work as subversively presenting its representatives in a bad light. Macklin modified many of the politically controversial speeches to appease the censors, but he retained the portrayals of the two politician fathers.

FURTHER READING

Conolly, L. W. *The Censorship of English Drama, 1737–1824.* San Marino, Calif.: Huntington Library, 1976.

Fowell, Frank, and Frank Palmer. *Censorship in England.* London: F. Palmer, 1913. Reprint, New York: Benjamin Blom, 1969.

Kinservik, Matt. "New Light on the Censorship of Macklin's *The Man of the World.*" *Huntington Library Quarterly* 66 (1992): 43–66.

Macmillan, Dougald. "The Censorship in the Case of Macklin's *The Man of the World.*" *Huntington Library Bulletin* 10 (October 1936): 79–101.

MARAT/SADE

Author: Peter Weiss
Original date and place of production: April 29, 1964, Schillertheater, Berlin, Germany
Characters: Charlotte Corday, Madame Coulmier, Mademoiselle Coulmier, Monsieur Coulmier, Cucurucu, Simonne Evrard, Kokol, Lavoissier, Jean Paul Marat, Poloch, Rossignol, Jacques Roux, Marquis de Sade, Voltaire
Filmed versions: *Marat/Sade* (1966, U.K.)

SUMMARY

Marat/Sade is a drama in two parts with a rarely used full title, *The Persecution and Assassination of Jean-Paul Marat as Performed by the Inmates of the Asylum of Charenton under the Direction of the Marquis de Sade*. Set in the communal bath hall of the Charenton asylum in France, the drama takes place on July 13, 1808, a time of strong nationalism in France and a period of prosperity and global conquest. The premise is that of a play within a play written about Marat and set in 1793, four years into the French Revolution, by the marquis de Sade, who also directs the play. He argues about revolution with Marat while the inmate-actors writhe and scream hysterically on stage or sprawl in apathetic poses. As a representative of the Theatre of Cruelty movement promulgated by Antonin Artaud, the play features blaring music, spattering blood, and a wide range of acts of violence, including whipping. The play opens as the inmates, many of whom are political prisoners, file in and take their places, as do the director of the asylum, Monsieur Coulmier, his wife, and his daughter. Seated in a bathtub to soothe his painful skin disease, Marat is joined on stage by his mistress-nurse Simonne Evrard, the somnambulist Charlotte Corday, the erotomaniac Duperret, and the violent, anarchistic priest Roux, who is confined in a straitjacket, as well as a chorus of inmates who represent the populace of France and whose songs punctuate the ongoing debate. Marat defends revolutionary action at all costs, as the Coulmier family protest such sentiments with the goal of keeping the inmates calm. As Marat espouses patriotism and revolt, de Sade reacts with scorn and charges that the revolution resulted only in a "withering of the individual man/and a slow merging into uniformity." He then invites Charlotte Corday to "beat me/while I talk to you about the Revolution." As Corday whips de Sade, she speaks out against Marat's bloody approach and threatens to kill him, but de Sade asks her to wait. As Marat's bloody past is detailed by inmates, Voltaire and Lavoisier appear and ridicule his theories, but Roux defends him and the chorus of inmates calls loudly for revolution as the first part ends.

When the second part begins, Marat pretends to be addressing the French National Assembly, and he accuses the leaders of the French Revolution of corruption and treason. Concerned about the increasing agitation of the now-screaming inmates, the asylum director objects to the speech while de Sade draws the entranced Corday closer to Marat. He points out that Corday has a dagger in her hand and suggests that ". . . she carries a knife/to intensify the love-play" then asks "And what's the point of a revolution/without general copulation?" Corday slowly approaches Marat and caresses him gently before plunging the dagger into him. As Marat dies, the unruliness of the inmates increases, and they march and shout for "Napoleon . . . Nation . . . Revolution . . . Copulation," overcoming the asylum attendants and lunging toward the foot of the stage. The attendants retaliate with violence, and de Sade stands on his chair and laughs at the spectacle while the curtain falls slowly.

CENSORSHIP HISTORY

The debut of *Marat/Sade* in 1964 produced a censorship history that is significantly shorter than it might have been had the play been performed only five years earlier. The original Berlin performance was a wordy creation punctuated by multiple and simultaneous "happenings" across the stage, but no efforts were made to modify either the action or the dialogue. In England, however, the drama came close to being refused a license for performance by the Office of the Lord Chamberlain, Lord David Cobbold. Director Peter Brook, who had expected difficulty in gaining a license, described the theatrical experience of *Marat/Sade* as follows: "Starting with its title, everything about this play is designed to crack the spectator on the jaw, then douse him with ice-cold water, then force him to assess intelligently what has happened to him, then give him a kick in the balls, then bring him back to his senses again." When the script was reviewed by the censors, objections arose against the manner in which the play fused sexual anarchy, political protest, agitational theater, and cruelty. Lines such as that spoken by the marquis de Sade in the moment before Corday stabs Marat, "And what's the point of a revolution/without general copulation?" were heavily debated but permitted in the end. After some inmates' violence was decreased, and some of the sexual cruelty was diminished, the censors granted a license for performance to the still largely intact play. Despite the seven theatrical awards that the play won in four years, not all critics were enamored of the work. John Sutherland states that Brook was asked by a critic for the *Times Literary Supplement* if he had not observed "that books about concentration camps . . . turn up in shops dealing with near-pornography," thus suggesting that the play's surface appearance of social criticism and aim to change masked only a lewd and salacious true intention. The play served as a breakthrough production for the London stage.

In 1970 *Marat/Sade* existed in Russian translation and had circulated widely in the Soviet Union in a minuscule edition, but director Yuri Lyubimov could not obtain permission from the state censors to perform it. The theme of revolution and the violent behavior of the inmates as they struggle to escape the asylum while they chant about revolution were too strongly propagandic for the communist authorities. In 1982 Lyubimov's theater was taken away from him and, stripped of citizenship, he was sent into involuntary exile. He returned to Russia in 1988 but did not try to stage *Marat/Sade* until 2000, when he rewrote the play into the form of a good-natured sendup of the system, including a sly mockery of leaders Boris Yeltsin and Vladimir Putin. The production was permitted to proceed without interference, but it was significantly different from Weiss's original. Lyubimov changed the title to *Marat and Marquis de Sade* and turned the writhing and screaming of the asylum inmates into an array of frequently hilarious and satirical Russian cabaret and circus acts.

FURTHER READING

Laufe, Abe. *The Wicked Stage: A History of Theater Censorship and Harassment in the United States.* New York: Frederick Ungar Publishing Co., 1978.
Sutherland, John. *Offensive Literature: Decensorship in Britain, 1960–1982.* Totowa, N.J.: Barnes and Noble Books, 1982.
Tytell, John. *The Living Theatre.* New York: Grove Press, 1995.

MARGARET FLEMING

Author: James A. Herne
Original date and place of production: July 4, 1890, Lynn, Massachusetts
Characters: Maria Bindley, Mrs. Burton, Lucy Fleming, Margaret Fleming, Philip Fleming, Joe Fletcher, Dr. Larkin, Lena Schmidt
Filmed versions: None

SUMMARY

Margaret Fleming is a drama in the tradition of the Ibsenite "problem plays," which dealt with contemporary social issues. Set in the New England mill town of Canton, Massachusetts, in 1890, the play in four acts was first produced in 1890 and published in 1930. The play deals frankly with adultery, presenting the subject and the reactions of the characters in a realistic manner that avoids the excessive melodramatic elements and the use of euphemism that characterized many other attempts at representing social issues onstage in America of the time.

The drama focuses on the marriage of Margaret and Philip Fleming, parents of a daughter nearly one year old, but it also explores the pressing problems of poverty and progress. Major themes include the production problems experienced by the superintendent of the Fleming Mill; the growing dishonesty of Joe Fletcher, a once-trusted foreman; the efforts of Maria and Joe Bindley to keep their small shop; and the fate of poor immigrant girls like Lena Schmidt who labored in the mills. Philip is a member of a prominent

Canton family and the successful owner of Fleming Mill, and Margaret is his devoted wife whose genteel existence has sheltered and protected her from life's realities. When Margaret accidentally learns that Philip has been unfaithful to her, she develops a quiet courage that sustains her as she seeks to learn the details about Philip's affair with Lena Schmidt, a German immigrant and the sister of their child's nursemaid, Maria Bindley. Margaret, who remains weak since the birth of her daughter a year before, consults Dr. Larkin, who cautions her to relax because she is developing glaucoma and too much stress may result in her loss of eyesight. In Act III, despite this concern, when Maria tells her that Lena is dying and wishes to see Margaret, she goes to the cottage owned by Mrs. Burton. Lena has already died, but she has left a letter that names Philip as the baby's father. Her fears confirmed, Margaret's sight grows dimmer, but the wailing baby draws her attention. As a remorseful Philip rushes into the cottage, the nearly blind Margaret gropes her way to the sofa with Lena's baby in her arms as she tries to comfort it. As the playwright directs, "Then scarcely conscious of what she is doing, suddenly with an impatient swift movement she unbuttons her dress to give nourishment to the child, when the picture fades away into darkness."

Herne wrote two endings to the play. In the original version, five years pass between the end of Act III and the beginning of Act IV, as the action moves to Boston Common and a small shop at the North End. After learning that Lena's son has died, Maria kidnaps the Flemings' daughter Lucy as revenge. In their search for Lucy, the Flemings go to a police station, where Margaret renounces Philip, tells him that she can never forgive him, and sends him away, leaving her standing alone on stage as the curtain closes.

In the second version of Act IV, which was most frequently used in performances, Margaret faces a sightless life with a calm and dignified demeanor. Philip returns to their home in Canton after an unsuccessful suicide attempt. Although Margaret greets him courteously, she is also restrained in her behavior and tells him that she forgives his infidelity but hints that she can never again be his wife. She advises him to resume his activity with the mill and, when he agrees to do so, "a serene joy illuminates her face." Although she has intimated that they cannot resume their old marital relationship, she reassures him that "The past is dead. We must face the living future." The second version of Act IV ends with Philip going out into the garden to see both his child with Margaret and the child he fathered with Lena. Audiences found the second ending more favorable because it offered a possibility that the couple might be reconciled when enough time had passed.

CENSORSHIP HISTORY

The wealth of realistic detail in this serious dramatization of a controversial problem of social conduct was a major obstacle to the production of *Margaret Fleming*. The three privately subsidized tryout performances in Lynn, Massachusetts, were roundly criticized by reviewers as being too shocking, because Herne treated Philip sympathetically and failed to provide strong condemnation of his behavior. When Herne tried to secure a playhouse for performances in Boston and New York City, he was refused at first. After several prominent American writers, including Hamlin Garland, Mary E. Wilkins, and William Dean Howells, publicly praised the drama for its realism and importance, Herne was able to rent a small venue, Chickering Hall in Boston, for a two-week run beginning on May 4, 1891. Writing of the premiere performance, Hamlin Garland described *Margaret Fleming* as "one of the most radical plays from a native author ever performed in America." Although the Boston production received limited critical approval and the enthusiasm of intellectuals who were familiar with the concept of the problem play, most of the reviewers and audiences found the ideas in *Margaret Fleming* to be too daring. Herne suspended performances after the two-week run, then revived the play in October 1891, again at Chickering Hall, but the play received the same criticism as earlier, as did the New York production, a December 1891 matinee in Palmer's Theatre. Despite Herne's rewriting of Act IV to provide a hopeful rather than bitter ending, revivals of the play in 1894, 1907, and 1915 were still criticized by reviewers for its frank handling of a controversial topic, and Herne failed to make the play acceptable to audiences.

FURTHER READING

Herne, James A. "Margaret Fleming." In *Representative American Plays*. 7th ed. Edited by Arthur Hobson Quinn. New York: Appleton-Century-Crofts, 1953.

Herne, Julie A. Introduction to *Shore Acres and Other Plays*. Edited by Mrs. James A. Herne. New York: Samuel French, 1928.

Quinn, Arthur Hobson. *A History of the American Drama from the Civil War to the Present*. New York: Crofts, 1943.

Timberlake, Craig. "Herne—The First Collaborator." In *The Life and Work of David Belasco: The Bishop of Broadway*. New York: Library Publishers, 1954.

Waggoner, H. H. "The Growth of a Realist: James A. Herne." *New England Quarterly* 15 (March 1942): 62–73.

THE MARRIAGE OF FIGARO (LE MARIAGE DE FIGARO)

Author: Pierre-Augustin Caron de Beaumarchais

Original date and place of production: April 27, 1784, Comédie-Française, Paris, France

Characters: Antonio, Bartholo, Bazile, Cherubino, Count Almaviva, Countess Almaviva, Don Guzman Brid'oison, Fanchette, Figaro, Governor of Andulacia, Gripe-Soleil, Suzanne, Marceline, Pedrille

Filmed versions: *Die Hochzeit des Figaro* (1967, Germany); *Figaros Hochzeit* (1945, Germany); *Le Mariage de Figaro* (1959, France)

SUMMARY

Originally titled *La folle journée, ou Le marriage de Figaro, The Marriage of Figaro* has entertained both as a drama and as the basis for the opera *Le Mariage de Figaro*, with a libretto by Lorenzo da Ponte and music by Wolfgang Amadeus Mozart, which was first presented in Vienna, Austria, on May 1, 1786. Although a comic farce that elicits uproarious laughter from audiences, the play also provides sharp social criticism. The plot centers on Figaro, the clever and cunning valet of Count Almaviva, governor of Andalucia. Figaro is about to marry Suzanne, the maid of the count's wife, Countess Almaviva, and much is made of the count's recent abolition of droit du seigneur, his feudal right to sexually possess the women on his estate at least once before they marry. Suzanne is especially attractive, and Count Almaviva considers reviving the ancient custom because of his overwhelming desire for her. While Suzanne and Figaro remain concerned about their master's intentions, Figaro faces another detriment to his happiness as he strives to avoid being forced into an unwelcome marriage with Marceline, the count's housekeeper. Figaro has long owed her a financial debt that he appears still unable to repay, and Marceline attempts to make him marry her, promising that she will then forgive the debt entirely. Faced with the difficulties of his twin predicaments, Figaro enlists the aid of Countess Almaviva, who is upset with her husband's past philandering and his unhealthy interest in Suzanne. The countess tells Figaro that she will help him to outmaneuver both the court that will try Marceline's case against him and the count. The drama takes a turn for the ridiculous as several of the characters don disguises in attempts to trick each other, and Figaro's chances of success appear to diminish until the remarkable discovery that he is not an orphan as he had been raised to believe. Figaro learns that he is Marceline's cousin, and his natural father appears to pay all debts, leaving him free to marry Suzanne. His second problem is solved when the countess surprises Count Almaviva, attempting to seduce the reticent Suzanne. The infuriated countess insists that he forgo his pleasure. The play ends happily with the marriage of Figaro to Suzanne.

CENSORSHIP HISTORY

The egalitarian views with which Beaumarchais infused *Le Mariage de Figaro* and its clear attack on the aristocracy made it the target of censors in both France and Austria. Beaumarchais completed the play in 1778, the same year that France formally acknowledged the independence of the 13 American colonies and sent them military aid. Despite official diplomatic approval of egalitarianism across the ocean, King Louis XVI did not approve of egalitarianism closer to home. He refused to allow performances of *Figaro* because of what he deemed to be the improper manner in which Beaumarchais had portrayed the central character, as a lower-class citizen who is permitted to treat his class superiors with disrespect. The king was concerned that to allow performances of the play would be to endanger the European social structure since the play made fun of the overprivileged upper classes and placed emphasis on the crooked legal procedures of the time and the repression of the lower classes. Although King Louis XVI refused to allow public perform-ances of *Figaro*, private shows were presented in Paris and other cities, and one of the first productions took place at the private theater of the duc de Fronsac. After six years, during which the royal censors had overseen the removal of numerous lines that were perceived as too brazenly critical of the aristocracy, King Louis XVI finally relented and allowed the first public per-formance on April 27, 1784. The already growing political tensions in France were made more volatile, as playgoers and rabble-rousers rioted in the streets of Paris following the first public performance. Writing in 1803, Madame de Hausset, lady's maid to Madame du Pompadour, observed that the play was "replete with indecorous and slanderous allusions to the Royal Family," and she blamed the play for much of the ill will directed by the commoners toward the queen. In short, Beaumarchais's production of *Le marriage de Figaro*, "spread the prejudices against the Queen through the whole kingdom and every rank of France." The play became very popular among audiences and was soon translated into German, but King Joseph II of Austria feared that the drama would create public unrest and demanded that censors refuse the play a license for public performance. In an order issued on January 31, 1785, the king issued a public memorandum that prohibited a German ver-sion of the play from appearing in Vienna.

FURTHER READING

Conolly, L. W. *The Censorship of English Drama, 1737–1824*. San Marino, Calif.: Huntington Library, 1976.

Hemmings, Frederic William John. *Theatre and State in France, 1760–1905*. New York: Cambridge University Press, 1994.

Kennedy, Emmet. "Taste and Revolution." *Canadian Journal of History/Annales canadi-ennes d'histoire* 32 (December/Decembre 1997): 375–392.

Widmer, David, ed. The Project Gutenberg Etext Memoirs of Louis XV./XVI, v5. Being Secret Memoirs of Madame du Hausset, Lady's Maid to Madame de Pom-padour, http://www.gutenberg.config.com/etext03/cm43b10.txt. Official Release Date: March 2003 [Etext #3880].

MARION DE LORME

Author: Victor Hugo

Original date and place of production: July 14, 1829, Théâtre français, Paris, France

Characters: M. de Bellegarde, Didier, Le Comte de Gassé, Constable de Champagne, L'espion Laffémas, Marion de Lorme, King Louis XIII, Le Marquis de Nangis, Le Capitaine Quartenier, Cardinal Richelieu, Le Chevalier de Rochebaron, Dame Rose, Gaspar de Saverny, Scaramouche

Filmed versions: *Marion de Lorme* (1919, France); *Marion Delorme* (1967, France, made for television)

SUMMARY

Originally entitled *Un Duel sous Richelieu*, *Marion de Lorme* is a verse play in five acts set in France during the era of King Louis XIII, which lasted from 1610 to 1643. The plot centers on Marion de Lorme, a young courtesan and noblewoman who enjoys her many noble lovers and a life of opulence until she falls in love with the poor, orphaned commoner Didier. A high-minded and chaste young man, Didier presents a significant contrast to the popular and lively courtesan. Cast as a Byronic figure, costumed all in black and surrounded with an air of gloom, he is a political dissident whose subversive actions against the French monarchy have attracted the ominous interest of Cardinal Richelieu. Marion finds Didier's moral strength and virtuous dedication refreshing and she is deeply in love with him. She rejects one noble lover after another as she regains her moral sense, but this move toward a moral salvation will ironically destroy her happiness. Dominating the actions of the characters as he dominated the political atmosphere of the time, Cardinal Richelieu plots to destroy Didier's growing influence among the poor in order to protect the absolute monarchy that he has constructed so carefully. When he learns of the affair between Marion and Didier, he determines to manipulate their relationship in order to destroy Didier. Several of Marion's former lovers bear grudges because of their loss of her favors, and Richelieu urges the most jealous of her past suitors, de Gassé, to seek revenge. Although Richelieu has declared dueling illegal, at his instigation de Gassé provokes Didier to engage in a duel. Before either man can kill the other, Richelieu has both men arrested and sentenced to death. Frantic to save Didier, Marion approaches the constable de Champagne and agrees to submit to his sexual advances if Didier's life will be spared. Despite her sacrifice, Didier is executed.

CENSORSHIP HISTORY

The censorship of *Marion de Lorme* motivated what Hugo biographer Graham Robb has called a "lunatic hero-worshipping fringe" that led fashionably rebellious students in France of the 1830s to consider as essential among their possessions "a skull, a rapier, anything Eastern, and a well-thumbed copy of *Marion de Lorme*." Didier became an antiestablishment role model whose disillusionment with society and black clothing were highly attractive to the younger French generation. Hugo first gave a reading of the play at the home of Baron Taylor on July 10, 1829, to an audience that included many of his literary friends, among them Honoré de Balzac, Alfred de Vigny, Prosper Mérimée, Alfred de Musset, Alexandre Dumas *pére*, Charles Augustin Sainte-Beuve, Emile Deschamps, and Antoni

Deschamps. The play was received with enthusiasm and ecstatic outbursts for Hugo's genius. Four days later, *Marion de Lorme* was performed before the reading committee at the Théatre français, where the audience of both renowned literary men and a scattering of noblemen accepted the play with rapturous applause. The reading committee submitted the play to the government censors, who were not as approving. They refused to license the play for public performance. The censors were not concerned with the morality of the central character, but they were offended by Hugo's portrayal in Act IV of King Louis XIII, ancestor of the reigning king of France, Charles X, as weak and pusillanimous and willing to abnegate his monarchal responsibilities in favor of hunting and other pleasures. Hugo had researched the era and reign of Louis XIII and was convinced that his portrayal was historically accurate, so he decided to challenge the censors. Although the French prime minister, vicomte de Martignac, had approved the censor's ruling, he agreed to meet with Hugo and arranged for Hugo to meet with Charles X.

At an audience with the king at the Palace of Saint-Cloud on August 7, 1829, for which Hugo dressed in all of the regalia of his hereditary barony, the writer brought with him a copy of Act IV on expensive vellum, which Charles X agreed to read after reassuring Hugo that he admired his work. A week later, the king offered his verdict, which upheld the prohibition against performances of *Marion de Lorme*. To soften the refusal, and because Hugo had always been loyal in his writings, Charles X offered Hugo a yearly pension of 4,000 francs and a post on the Council of State, which the writer refused publicly. In a dignified letter written on August 14, 1829, to the comte de la Bourdonnaye, minister of the interior, Hugo thanked the king for his "signal graciousness" and assured all that "nothing hostile to the throne could ever be within my intentions," as he also made note of his noble ancestors, his royalist odes, his father's lost fortune, his numerous dependents, and that he lived on his income as a writer. He also refused the patronizing attempt to win him over.

The letter was soon summarized and publicized in every newspaper in the city, providing the young generation straining under the monarchy with a new hero in Victor Hugo. As the newspaper *Le Constitutionnel* wrote, "The youth of France is not as corruptible as Ministers would hope." After Charles X was deposed in July 1830, in the Revolution of 1830, the ban on *Marion de Lorme* was lifted and the play was produced publicly at the Théatre français in August 1831.

FURTHER READING

Hugo, Victor. *Correspondance*. 4 vols. Edited by C. Caubray. Paris: Imprimerie Nationale, 1947–52.

Maurois, André. *Olympio: The Life of Victor Hugo*. Translated by Gerard Hopkins. New York: Harper & Brothers, 1956.

Robb, Graham. *Victor Hugo*. New York: W. W. Norton & Company, 1997.

THE MARTYRDOM OF SAINT SEBASTIAN

Author: Gabriele D'Annunzio
Original date and place of production: May 22, 1911, Théâtre du Chatelet, Paris, France
Characters: Chorus, Dancers, Diocleciano, Narrator, Sebastian
Filmed versions: *Le Martyre de Saint-Sebastien* (1984, West Germany, made for television)

SUMMARY

The Martyrdom of Saint Sebastian (*Le Martyre de Saint-Sébastien*) is a mystery musical drama about the martyrs and saints, written in verse and based on the life of St. Sebastian, a young and handsome member of the Praetorian Guards who, Roman Catholic Church history relates, was sentenced to be executed by his own archers because of his Christian sympathies. While writing the play, D'Annunzio approached first Roger Ducasse, then Henry Fèvrier to compose the incidental music for the play, but both turned him down. D'Annunzio later approached Claude Debussy, who agreed to compose the music but only after the playwright entered into a contract that exempted the composer from any financial liability for the play and stipulated that the play could never be performed without his music. The performance of the complete musical drama takes five hours. Because of its length, the play is rarely staged, but concerts are performed using either the four symphonic fragments without voices or the complete incidental music connected only by brief narrative links.

D'Annunzio divides the work into five "mansions," the medieval synonym for acts. After a prelude typifying the Christian soul, the curtain rises to reveal two Christian maidens chained to pillars. Sebastian, chief of the archers, appears and dances over a bed of burning coals to reassure them of some greater force at work. After singing a hymn in praise of martyrdom and the exaltation of the faith and fortitude of martyrs, Sebastian shoots an arrow into the sky. The arrow does not return to the ground, which the crowd accepts as proof of his holiness, a realization that is ecstatically proclaimed by both the chorus and the orchestra. The act closes with a vision of heaven and its angels singing hallelujahs. The second act reveals the "Magic Chamber" where the magicians and astrologers perform their mystic arts. Sebastian breaks down the door, and, as he enters, the music swells to symbolize the advent of Christianity, and the song of the unseen Madonna, borrowed from medieval Italian music, is heard. The third act opens at the Roman Court and discloses Emperor Diocleciano receiving Sebastian, questioning him about the new faith, and trying to induce him to abandon it. A hymn to Apollo follows, and this is succeeded by the symbolizing of Christ's march to Calvary, which is assigned almost entirely to the instruments. The fourth act is mainly devoted to the martyrdom of Sebastian. The emperor's military aides first attempt to smother him, but he is saved by his archers. The emperor next commands his men to bind Sebastian to a tree in Apollo's grove, where his archers are forced to shoot their arrows at him. As his body is removed, the arrows disappear from it and are found in the tree. The gates of heaven open and the martyr enters. The last act, which pictures paradise, contains no spoken words, leaving the orchestra and some antiphonal choruses to produce the desired effect.

CENSORSHIP HISTORY

The Martyrdom of Saint Sebastian grew out of D'Annunzio's long-standing ambition to write a mystery play based on the life of St. Sebastian, a third-century Roman martyr who has traditionally been depicted by church artists as a beautiful, androgynous nude youth, replete with homoerotic overtones. Although church history does not elaborate on the personal feelings that the emperor may have had for Sebastian, as depicted in D'Annunzio's play these feelings are of an erotic nature. Despite his fascination with the martyrdom, the playwright claimed that he was not moved to write the play until he attended a performance of Diaghilev's ballet *Cleopatre* and saw the bare legs of Ida Rubinstein as she danced the lead role. Watching the Russian dancer's slim body, long legs, and slender neck glide gracefully across the stage, D'Annunzio realized that she was the incarnation of his vision for St. Sebastian. The two became lovers, and Rubinstein appeared as Sebastian when the musical drama was performed on May 22, 1911. News of the impending production shocked critics less for its homoerotic overtones than for the casting of a woman in the lead role of a male Roman soldier and later saint. The Roman Catholic hierarchy denounced the production and, shortly before the first production, the Vatican placed all of D'Annunzio's works on the Index of Forbidden Books. The archbishop of Paris issued a statement forbidding all Catholics from attending performances of the drama, telling them that the play was "blasphemous." The church's opposition to the play resulted, in part, from the magic, mysticism, and sexuality that D'Annunzio added to the legend of the martyr, enhanced by the sumptuous costumes and sets created by Léon Bakst. Other unannounced objections to the staging of the play may have also influenced the ban, and contemporary critics suggest that the Vatican viewed as sacrilegious D'Annunzio's casting of a Jewish female in the role of a male Christian martyr. The drama remained on the Index of Forbidden Books until 1966, when the Vatican ceased publication of the index.

FURTHER READING

Antongini, Tom. *D'Annunzio.* Boston: Little, Brown, 1938.

Bruno, Giuliana. *Streetwalking on a Ruined Map: Cultural Theory and the City Films of Elvira Notari.* Princeton: Princeton University Press, 1993.

Cox, David. "Le Martyre de Saint Sébastien," compact disc, London Symphony Chorus and Orchestra, conducted by Michael Tilson Thomas, 1991. Publishers: Éditions Durand S.A. Paris.

Rhodes, Anthony. *The Poet as Superman: A Life of Gabriele D'Annunzio.* London: Weidenfeld and Nicolson, 1959.

Spackman, Barbara. *Decadent Geneaologies: The Rhetoric of Sickness from Baudelaire to D'Annunzio.* Ithaca, N.Y.: Cornell University Press, 1989.

Valesio, Paolo. *Gabriele D'Annunzio: The Dark Flame.* Translated by Marilyn Migiel. New Haven: Yale University Press, 1992.

MARY STUART

Author: James Haynes

Original date and place of production: January 22, 1840, Drury Lane Theatre, London, England

Characters: Earl of Darnley; Elizabeth; Mary, Queen of Scots; David Rizzio; Ruthven

Filmed versions: None

SUMMARY

James Haynes's *Mary Stuart* is a verse play in five acts that portrays Mary Queen of Scots as a victim, neatly cast in the Victorian ideal of womanhood as a soft and yielding individual whose interests are domestic and who feels displaced from her sphere and unable to contend with hostile forces in the public realm. Unlike most versions of the historical events, this drama lessens the responsibility of Queen Elizabeth I in the tragedy that Mary suffers and, instead, attributes the evil machinations at court to the Scottish nobleman Ruthven. Trapped in an unhappy second marriage to Lord Darnley, whose drinking and brutish nature make Mary's life miserable, she reaches out to David Rizzio, who had been brought from Italy to court as a musician but was soon selected to be the queen's personal secretary. Mary soon forms an obvious attachment to Rizzo, and he becomes her favorite, an occurrence that does not go unnoticed by the court nobles and Darnley. Haynes refrains from imbuing the relationship with sexual overtones and, instead, casts the relationship into a virtuous light in which Rizzio serves as "a guardian saint" to Mary, despite the historical evidence that the two were sexually involved. Although Rizzio does seem to love Mary and she seems to return his love, the characters do not exhibit their feelings openly, choosing instead to bow to the higher influences that rule both of their lives. In one of the play's more passionate speeches, Rizzio vows, "Whate'er thou art/That in mysterious thralldom hold'st my soul;/I'm thine." Haynes creates a Mary Stuart who is clearly conscious of her unpopularity as a monarch and fearful of those who are plotting against her. She tells Rizzio, "Here is an envious malice in the stars,/That will not let me smile, but I must weep for it." Lord Darnley becomes jealous of Rizzio's relationship with Mary and incites loyal nobles led by Ruthven, a dying Scots nobleman whose life is given new purpose when he leads the conspiracy to rid his native country of "foreign reptiles" such as David Rizzio, who surround and counsel the queen. In a highly dramatic scene, the determined Ruthven, wearing full armor, bursts into Mary's private quarters, where he surprises her and Rizzio. Although she is the queen, Mary makes only a feeble effort to rebuff Ruthven's intrusion as she trembles and attempts to shield Rizzio from Ruthven's sword. Although Rizzio is murdered because of his attachment to the queen, she is sure that she has acted "light, not guiltily," and that the murder is "hell's device/to plunge it's [sic] victim into hopeless crime," meaning a situation in which retribution is called for.

CENSORSHIP HISTORY

W. J. Hammond, the new manager of the Drury Lane Theatre, eagerly accepted *Mary Stuart* for performance, seeing the play as an opportunity to reintroduce legitimate drama to the venue and to revive the theater's fading glory. Prominent actor William Charles Macready read the play and eagerly accepted the role of Ruthven. Within a week the play was submitted to the censors and granted a license for performance by John Mitchell Kemble, the Examiner of Plays. When rehearsals began, Macready flew into a rage when he found that the censor had removed "some important passages . . . that destroy its power and interest." The day after the censored manuscript was returned, Macready received a letter from Kemble that directed him by "command of the Lord Chamberlain to omit certain other passages, which had not been erased in the copy which Mr. Hammond had returned to his office." The motive behind all of the excisions was political expediency. The unusual measure of further censoring an already licensed manuscript that had not been performed signaled grave political concerns and hinted at the involvement of the monarchy. The production was scheduled to take place during the period in which preparations were being made for the marriage between Queen Victoria and Prince Albert of Saxe-Coburg-Gotha. The union had already been heavily criticized by many of Victoria's subjects, who were fearful that the British Crown would be too heavily influenced by what Stephens labels "malign foreign domination," similar to the feelings that Ruthven holds toward Rizzio. The first performance of the play took place on the same day that Albert was to voice a request for naturalization before the House of Commons, so the line excised by the censors, "Is there no corner free from these foreign reptiles?" might easily have been taken to be a criticism of Albert and his extensive German retinue.

Despite the excision of numerous lines in the effort to avoid a parallel between Albert and Rizzio, audiences made a connection. The theater reviewer for the *Literary Gazette* wrote on January 25, 1840, that "a few lines which the audience chose to apply politically to present affairs ought to be omitted, as they are not essential to the piece, and can only tend to uproar and confusion." The most flagrant example is the line spoken by Ruthven in referring to Rizzio: "I hate aliens, as all our noble forefathers have," to which audiences responded with hisses and applause. Although the line was most likely cut during one of the two reviews by the censors, entries in Macready's *Diaries* suggest that he may have conveniently forgotten to omit several of the officially prohibited passages.

The censor also cut 12 lines of a speech early in the play because they suggest a threatened rebellion led by Ruthven, and the censors feared that leaving them in for performance would have signaled official approval of the sentiments expressed.

> Throughout the track
> I've measured in my journey, discontent
> Was everywhere—the storm-cloud fills the sky:—
> From every pulpit loud anathems
> Are thundered at the Queen:—her enmity
> To the true worship shakes the crown upon
> Her head: nor is her love of foreigners
> Forgotten, nor her deadly hatred of
> The banished lords: in short, some dire explosion
> Is ripening fast; we must direct it, or
> Be swept away by't.

Despite the patriotic fervor expressed in these lines, the dedication to over-throwing the established order could not be permitted, so the lines were removed.

FURTHER READING

Downer, Alan S. *The Eminent Tragedian: William Charles Macready.* Cambridge, Mass.: Harvard University Press, 1966.

Haynes, James. *Mary Stuart: An Historical Tragedy, Now Performing at the Theatre Royal, Drury Lane.* 3rd ed. London: n.p., 1840.

Kavanagh, Peter. *The Irish Theatre.* Tralee, Ireland: The Kerryman, 1946.

Rafroidi, Patrick. *Irish Literature in English: The Romantic Period, 1789–1850.* Vol. 2. Gerrards Cross, England: Colin Smythe, 1980.

Stephens, John Russell. *The Censorship of English Drama, 1824–1901.* New York: Cambridge University Press, 1980.

Tönnies, Merle. "The Representation of Mary Stuart in Nineteenth-Century British Drama: A Comparative Analysis of Conflicting Images." *Erfurt Electronic Studies in English* 3 (1999). Available online. URL: http://webdoc.gwdg.de/edoc/ia/eese/artic99/toennies/3_99.html.

Toynbee, William, ed. *The Diaries of William Charles Macready, 1833–1851.* London: Chapman and Hall, 1912.

MAYA

Author: Simon Gantillon

Original date and place of production: May 2, 1924, Studio des Champs-Elysées, Paris, France; February 21, 1928, Comedic Theatre (later the Mercury), New York, New York

Characters: Bella, eight unnamed prostitutes, 13 unnamed men
Filmed versions: *Maya* (1949, France)

SUMMARY

Set in a licensed brothel in Marseilles, *Maya* is the story of Bella, a prostitute whose sole purpose in life is to act out the sexual fantasies of her clients. She is, as she states, "the plastic matter of man's desire; the caterpillar whose future wings are coloured by every man with hues of his longing." The play consists of a series of loosely connected scenes, each focused on the desires of a specific client. Audiences learn very little about the character, because the focus is not on Bella herself but upon what or who she becomes for each of her clients. Each man demands that she play a different role. For the miner, she is the nurturer who consoles him for his backbreaking labor, while another client asks her to wear a fancy nightgown and play the role of a marchesa. She represents a long-lost love for a quartermaster, and still another asks her to play the virtuous acquaintance. As Bella plays her many roles, she daydreams of her youth and, in a sentimental moment, advises a young girl to enjoy love while she can. In the final scene, an East Indian client waiting for Bella is shown telling three other men about the illusion of Maya, the Mother of Desire, who is all things to all men. Throughout the play, Bella has undergone a transformation to become the supreme illusion, nothing but a reflection of the desires of the men who visit her. She is the possession of others, a provider of dreams and nothing more.

CENSORSHIP HISTORY

Maya has the distinction of being the first play presented in New York City to be affected by the Wales Padlock Law. The law, passed in 1927 after citizens' groups called for the censorship of public entertainment, gave New York officials the authority to arrest and prosecute producers and actors believed to be associated with "drama depicting or dealing with the subject of sex." The law threatened theater owners as well, because it specified that if the producers were convicted, the theater in which the play had been presented would be padlocked and effectively out of business for a year. The law was suggested by Manhattan district attorney Joab H. Banton and Brooklyn district attorney Charles H. Dodd, but it was named after Senator B. Roger Wales, who sponsored the bill in the legislature. *Maya* was first performed in Paris, on May 2, 1924, and the play excited no controversy and little interest, because France had a tradition of plays set in brothels in which men visited prostitutes, enacted their sexual fantasies, and then left and resumed their normal lives. As critic John Elsom observes, the play "was considered superficial for the fantasies described were neither related to society nor to the Pirandellian assumption of roles, which became so important a feature of French drama in the 1930s." While the French were unimpressed, the English were shocked by the subject matter and the censors refused to license the play until the late 1950s. The New York production, based on a script translated by Ernest Boyd, opened on February 21, 1928, at the Comedic Theatre (later the Mercury Theatre) and ran for 15 performances. District Attorney Banton soon received protests about the drama from citizens' groups that claimed his office was turning a blind eye to corruption in the theater and threatened to launch a crusade for censorship similar to one against the movies only a few years before. Banton sent an assistant district attorney to review the play and, acting on the suggestions contained in the resulting report, ordered the play closed after the 15 performance. The producers refused to protest the closing and did not file an appeal, because they feared that the Comedic Theatre would be padlocked and their business shut down for a year. In 1954 a revival of *Maya* was presented at the Theatre de Lys on Christopher Street in New York City, and the play was allowed to run without protest.

FURTHER READING

Elsom, John. *Erotic Theatre.* New York: Taplinger Publishing Co., 1974.
Laufe, Abe. *The Wicked Stage: A History of Theater Censorship and Harassment in the United States.* New York: Frederick Ungar Publishing Co., 1978.
Witt, S. Thomas, and E. Marcus, editors. "Lesbians and Gay Men on Stage: A Necessarily Incomplete History." *Out in All Directions: The Almanac of Lesbian and Gay America.* New York: Warner Books, 1995.

M. BUTTERFLY

Author: David Henry Hwang
Original date and place of production: March 20, 1988, Eugene O'Neill Theater, New York, New York
Characters: Comrade Chin, René Gallimard, Helga, Kurogo, Song Liling, M. Toulon
Filmed versions: *M. Butterfly* (1993)

SUMMARY

Set in a Paris prison in 1988 and in Beijing and Paris for a flashback of the years from 1960 to 1986, *M. Butterfly* is a play in two parts. The story of a French diplomat involved in a sexual affair with a Peking opera singer who turns out to be both a spy and a man posing a woman was suggested by an actual event in the mid-1980s. The audience is not expected to be surprised by the revelation that Song Liling is a man, a fact assured by the inclusion of the following in theater programs for all performances:

A former French diplomat and a Chinese opera singer have been sentenced to six years in jail for spying for China after a two-day trial that traced a story of clandestine love and mistaken sexual identity . . . Mr. Bouriscot was accused of passing information to China after he fell in love with Mr. Shi, whom he believed for twenty years to be a woman. NY Times, May 11, 1986.

The play begins with French diplomat René Gallimard in his prison cell on the outskirts of Paris, where he stays throughout the course of the play and through the costume changes that allow for scenes recalling his affair and life with Song Liling. Gallimard tells the audience, "Alone in this cell, I sit night after night, watching our story play out in my head." Then, through costume and scene changes, the audience joins in the world that the visiting diplomat found exotic and mysterious. Entranced by his first sight of Song, during a performance at a diplomatic function, he falls immediately in love, forgets his wife and his responsibilities, and embarks on a mad passion that leads to scenes in which Song, remaining fully clothed, leads Gallimard into an erotic deception. He lovingly asks Song, "Are you my Butterfly?" to which Song has no answer except "Yes." The two carry on an intensely sexual affair, but Song communicates regularly with Comrade Chin to pass diplomatic secrets gained from Gallimard to the Chinese government. Gallimard claims at his trial to not have known that Song is a man, yet many clues might have alerted him during the lengthy affair. At one point, Song asks Comrade Chin, "Why, in the Peking Opera, are all women's roles played by men?" a fact of which diplomat Gallimard should have been aware. At the trial, Song explains the sexual relationship, stating, "he never saw me completely naked . . . I did all the work . . . I suppose he might have wondered why I was always on my stomach . . . it was my job to make him think I was a woman." There is a point at which Song fears the deception will be unmasked, so he claims to be pregnant and leaves for a period of false confinement in the country after which, with the cooperation of Comrade Chin, he returns with a Eurasian baby.

Gallimard moves in and out of his memories, and at the end of the play, when Song strips in front of him, he cries out, "You showed me your true self. When all I loved was the lie." Honor requires that Gallimard take his own life, but he does so in a highly ritualized manner. In the final scene of the play, he dresses himself as Butterfly, his perfect "lotus blossom," in white geisha makeup, a wig, and a kimono, showing his blindness to cultural differences, as well, in confusing the Japanese with his Chinese love. Before he plunges the knife into his body, he announces to the audience, "I have found her at last. In a prison on the outskirts of Paris. My name is René Gallimard—also known as Madame Butterfly."

CENSORSHIP HISTORY

M. Butterfly was honored by the New York Society of Critics as one of the 10 best plays of the 1987–88 Broadway season, and in 1993 it became one of two plays (the other was *LIPS TOGETHER, TEETH APART*) performed at

Cobb County, Georgia's Theatre in the Square that were condemned by local censors, resulting in a loss of arts funding. In 1993 a couple attending a performance of *Lips Together, Teeth Apart* were allegedly so shocked by the subject matter that they wrote a letter of protest to the chairman of the Cobb County Commission, Gordon Wysong. He recalled that another "homosexual play," *M. Butterfly*, had appeared there a short time before. He examined the county's arts policy and found that it specifically stated that arts organizations receiving public funds were granted "freedom of expression" and that the "government shall avoid the role of censors." He disagreed with this policy and drafted a "community standards resolution" to be added to the existing policy. The effort was supported by state chapters of the Christian Coalition, a national organization led by Pat Robertson, and the American Family Association, led by Donald Wildmon, which alerted their membership and conducted letter-writing campaigns against the play.

Wysong also worked with local fundamentalist televangelist Nelson Price to design two resolutions. The first resolution, passed by the Cobb County Commission on the Arts, proposed to restrict public arts funding to programs that "advance and support strong community, family-oriented values." The second resolution, which passed by majority vote in August 1993, condemned homosexuality and stated that the county would not support any "lifestyles advocated by the gay community" as a means of protecting the "safety, health and welfare of the community" from what the resolution termed "increasing assaults" on its standards by gays and lesbians.

Palmer Wells, founder and executive director of the Theatre in the Square, enlisted the aid of the American Civil Liberties Union, which charged that the first resolution amounted to censorship. The local ACLU chapter threatened to sue the commission for selectively denying arts funding to projects if the resolution passed. After finding that defending their original criteria for funding was legally impossible, the commission then voted to end all arts funding. This move deprived the Theatre in the Square of $40,000, which it had formerly received from the Cobb County Commission to offset its annual budget of nearly $800,000. While the commissioners claimed that they were simply working to conserve the money of taxpayers, their argument quickly lost ground when the Theatre in the Square management briefly considered moving to a more liberal township, which would risk a loss of approximately $3.5 million in local business that the theater generated. The total arts funding expense to the taxpayers had been only $110,000, and this had included funding for school arts and other popular programs, in addition to funding for the theater.

Instead of resulting in a victory for the conservative elements of the community, the resolution to first provide funding only to projects that the commission agreed supported "traditional family values" and then to withdraw all arts funding served to mobilize the gay community, which created a political action group that organized several demonstrations in the town square. The decision in August 1993 to eliminate all arts funding also meant that the Cobb County Commission sacrificed the opportunity to participate in an Atlanta arts festival timed to coincide with the Summer 2000 Olympic Games, held in Atlanta.

FURTHER READING

Achenbach, Joel. "A Report from the Front Line of the 'Culture War.'" *Washington Post*, September 26, 1993, p. G01.

Caldwell, Stephen R. "The NEA and 'Culture Wars.'" Delivered to Black Hills Unitarian-Universalist Fellowship, Rapid City, South Dakota, November 14, 1993.

Guernsey, Otis L., Jr., and Jeffrey Sweet. *The Best Plays of 1987–1988*. New York: Applause Publishing, 1992.

Remen, Kathryn. "The Theatre of Punishment: David Henry Hwang's *M. Butterfly* and Michael Foucault's *Discipline and Punish*." *Modern Drama* 37 (fall 1994): 391–397.

Schapiro, Mark. "Who's Behind the Culture War: Contemporary Assaults on the Freedom of Expression." The Public Eye. Available online. URL: http://www. publiceye.org/theocrat/Schapiro.html.

THE MERCHANT OF VENICE

Author: William Shakespeare
Original date and place of production: 1596, London, England
Characters: Antonio, Balthazar, Bassanio, Duke of Venice, Launcelot Gobbo, Old Gobbo, Gratiano, Jessica, Leonardo, Lorenzo, Nerissa, Portia, Prince of Morocco, Prince of Aragon, Salerio, Shylock, Solanio, Stefano, Tubal
Filmed versions: Feature films: *The Merchant of Venice* (1908, 1912, 1914, U.S.); (1916, U.K.); *Zalim Saudagar* (1941, India); *Le Marchand de Venise* (1952, France/Italy); *Te Tangata Whai Rawa O Weniti* (2002, New Zealand). Made for television: (1947, 1955, 1972, 1973, 1980, 2001, U.K.); (1976, 1996, Canada)

SUMMARY

The Merchant of Venice is a comedy in five acts set in Venice, Italy. Impoverished Venetian nobleman Bassanio hopes to woo the beautiful and wealthy heiress Portia, but he does not have the money needed to court her in style, so he asks his friend, a wealthy trader named Antonio, to lend him 3,000 ducats. Antonio has committed all of his capital to his business, but he views lending the money to Bassanio as an investment that will have great return, so he decides to borrow the money and, in turn, lend it to Bassanio. He approaches Shylock, the Jewish moneylender, who agrees to lend the sum if Antonio will sign a contract agreeing to make the repayment within a specified time period or forfeit a pound of his own flesh if he is late. Antonio signs the contract, receives the loan, and turns the money over to Bassanio, who wins Portia's heart and hand in a contest of wits devised by her late father. Bassanio's joy in winning Portia is cut short by news that Antonio lost his entire fortune when his fleet was destroyed at sea. Shylock takes the merchant to court and demands either his 3,000 ducats or the agreed-upon pound of flesh. Disguised as a lawyer, Portia argues Antonio's case before the duke of Venice, claiming that the contract with Shylock is invalid because it is essentially a conspiracy against the merchant's life. The judge agrees and sentences Shylock to death, but agrees to spare the moneylender's life if he will surrender half of his estate to the state and the other half to Antonio. After Shylock grudgingly agrees, Antonio tells Shylock that he will surrender his claim to half of the estate if the moneylender will convert to Christianity and reconcile with his daughter Jessica, whom he disinherited for marrying a Christian.

CENSORSHIP HISTORY

The portrayal of the character of Shylock in *The Merchant of Venice* has made the play the object of overt acts of suppression in high school classrooms in the United States since 1927, and, as Noel Perrin observes in *Dr. Bowdler's Legacy*, stage expurgations have been made as a matter of course in many productions. One of the earliest attempts to censor *The Merchant of Venice* occurred in England in 1701. Scholar Michael Dobson reports that censors objected to the play not due to its perceived anti-Semitism, but because it violated standards of sexual and national purity. In the revised version of the play, Antonio's attachment to Bassanio is downplayed as "foreign" sexual deviancy and replaced by the presentation of Shylock's attachment to money as a sexual perversion. The characters of Old Gobbo and Launcelot Gobbo are completely cut, because they resemble characters in French drama, considered improper stage presences in early 18th-century England. The most publicized stage expurgation of the play occurred in the 1970 production directed by Jonathan Miller and starring Sir Laurence Olivier. Miller sought to moderate the character of Shylock to make him sympathetic to audiences, but critics largely denounced the director's aims and asserted that the changes weakened the production.

The Merchant of Venice has been banned from many high schools because of the characterization of Shylock. In 1927 the Authors' League reported that the play had been removed from the curriculum in Los Angeles high schools and was "no longer permitted to be taught in the Los Angeles high schools because of pressures brought by Jewish groups." In 1931 the New York cities of Buffalo and Manchester removed *The Merchant of Venice* from high school curricula, due to protests from Jewish groups that it encouraged bigotry. In 1949 a group of Jewish parents in Brooklyn, New York, went to court claiming that the assignment of *The Merchant of Venice* to senior high school literature classes violated the rights of children to receive an education free of religious bias, and the court agreed and ruled in favor of the parents in *Rosenberg v. the Board of Education of the City of New York*, 196 Misc. 542, 92 N.Y. Supp. 2d 344. In

1980, Ockerbloom states, it was banned in Midland, Michigan, schools, also due to Shylock's depiction, and in 1986 the Kitchener-Waterloo, Ontario, board of education banned the play from ninth-grade classrooms until the Ontario Education Ministry or Human Rights Commission ruled a year later that the play was not anti-Semitic and could be returned to the classroom.

In 1988, in Suffern High School, in the Ramapo Central School District (Rockland County, New York), a substitute teacher complained that the BBC film of *The Merchant of Venice*, directed by Jonathan Miller, taught in conjunction with the written version of the play, was "harmful" to a high school audience. He sent a letter to three area rabbis, including with the letter a negative review of the film that appeared in the June 26, 1981, issue of *The Jewish Standard*. After being contacted by several Jewish groups, the superintendent of schools decided to remove the play from the English syllabus. Teachers at Suffern High School were forbidden to teach the play from 1988 through 1995, although many in the English department verbally protested the ban. In 1995 the school administration changed and the English department petitioned the new administration to reinstate teaching of *The Merchant of Venice*. The reinstatement did not result in returning the play to the classroom, however, because, as Robert Wilson, the English teacher whose substitute began the controversy, notes, no copies of the play were available. All copies of *The Merchant of Venice* had disappeared from the bookroom during its seven-year ban, and a tight school budget precluded the purchase of new textbooks.

FURTHER READING

Dobson, Michael. "Bowdler and Britannia: Shakespeare and the National Libido." *Shakespeare Survey* 46 (1994): 137–144.

Epstein, Norrie. *The Friendly Shakespeare.* New York: Viking, 1993.

Haight, Anne Lyon, and Chandler B. Grannis. *Banned Books: 387 B.C. to 1978 A.D.* New York: Bowker, 1978.

Ockerbloom, John Mark. "Banned Books On-Line." URL: http://onlinebooks.library open.edu/banned-books.html.

Perrin, Noel. *Dr. Bowdler's Legacy: A History of Expurgated Books in England and America.* Boston: David R. Godine, 1992.

Romain, Michael. *A Profile of Jonathan Miller.* London: Cambridge University Press, 1992.

Stechhan, H. O. "Censoring Shakespeare." *Authors' League Bulletin* 15, no. 1 (April 1927): 19.

Wilson, Robert J. "Censorship, Anti-Semitism, and *The Merchant of Venice.*" *English Journal* (February 1997): 43–45.

THE MIKADO

Authors: William S. Gilbert and Arthur Sullivan
Original date and place of production: March 14, 1885, Savoy Theatre, London, England

Characters: Go-To, Katisha, Ko-Ko, The Mikado of Japan, Nanki-Poo, Peep-Bo, Pish-Tush, Pitti-Sing, Pooh-Bah, Yum-Yum

Filmed versions: Feature films: *The Mikado, or the Town of Titipu* (1926, 1939, 1967, 1972, 1988, 1992, U.K.). Made for television: (1960, 1982, 1984, 1987, 1996, U.K.). Made for video: (2000, U.K.)

SUMMARY

The Mikado is a comic operetta in two acts with libretto written by William S. Gilbert and music by Arthur Sullivan. Set in the imaginary Japanese town of Titipu, the play contains a number of stock characters and situations: young lovers, interfering authority figures, corrupt government officials, mistaken identity, and the requisite happy, if illogical, ending. The play opens in the palace courtyard of Ko-Ko, a former tailor who has become Lord High Executioner through the political maneuvering of high-placed friends. Nanki-Poo, a handsome young minstrel who is really the son of the Mikado in disguise, arrives and seeks out Ko-Ko's ward, the lovely Yum-Yum. He meets Pooh-Bah, who holds all high positions in town aside from Lord High Executioner. After paying a fee for the information, he learns that Yum-Yum is going to marry Ko-Ko that very day. As they speak, Ko-Ko arrives to discuss the marriage arrangements with Pooh-Bah, followed soon after by Yum-Yum with her sisters and friends from school. In the general confusion that follows, Nanki-Poo manages to draw Yum-Yum aside to speak privately with her. He has fled from his father's court to escape marriage to Katisha, an elderly noblewoman who loves him and whom his father has ordered him to marry. Nanki-Poo and Yum-Yum leave together. Ko-Ko receives a letter from the Mikado chastising him that no executions have been reported in Titipu for more than a year and threatening that, unless someone is executed within a month, the Mikado will abolish the position of Lord High Executioner and Ko-Ko will return to being a mere tailor. As Ko-Ko ponders his predicament, he meets a despondent Nanki-Poo carrying a rope. When he learns that Nanki-Poo plans to commit suicide because Yum-Yum is marrying Ko-Ko, he offers the young man a deal in which he can marry Yum-Yum for a month if he will agree to be beheaded in public at the end of that month. Ko-Ko also agrees to provide sufficient funds to allow Nanki-Poo and Yum-Yum to live very well for that month. As the town rejoices, Katisha arrives and threatens to reveal the true identity of Nanki-Poo, but the singing townspeople drown out her words, leaving her to vow vengeance at the end of the act.

Act Two takes place in the garden of Ko-Ko's palace, where Yum-Yum prepares for her wedding and her friends remind her that she will be a widow within a month. Ko-Ko arrives with even worse news and tells Yum-Yum that the law states that the wife of a beheaded man must be buried alive, knowledge that leads Yum-Yum to reconsider her marriage plans. After several moments, the three decide that Pooh-Bah, the archbishop of Titipu, will perform the ceremony and the town will simply pretend to the Mikado that an

177

execution has been performed. The subterfuge works; after arriving in the company of Katisha, the Mikado expresses approval that an execution has taken place, but Katisha reads the name of Nanki-Poo on the death certificate and reveals the scheme to the Mikado, who casually states that Ko-Ko, Pitti-Sing, and Pooh-Bah will be executed after lunch. Once the Mikado and his party leave for lunch, Nanki-Poo suggests that Ko-Ko marry Katisha to solve the problem, a suggestion that horrifies the Lord High Executioner but to which he agrees. He meets with Katisha and begs her to marry him, finally winning her over by a lively singing of "Titwillow." When the Mikado arrives to witness the executions, Nanki-Poo appears. Although happy to see his son, the Mikado expresses displeasure with the elaborate lies, but Ko-Ko points out that "if the Mikado says let a thing be done, it is almost as good as done, practically, it is done." Unable to dispute Ko-Ko's reasoning, the Mikado declares that all is satisfactory, and the cast rejoices.

CENSORSHIP HISTORY

The Mikado was an immediate success in both England and the United States. Critic Gerald Bordman notes that the operetta was "rapturously received by American audiences," and in both nations it "was instantly recognized for the masterpiece it was." The popularity may have been due to the growing vogue for Orientalia in late-19th-century England as well as the fascination of London citizens with the growing company of recently arrived Japanese who had set up a village of their own within Knightsbridge. They had come with the approval of the Japanese emperor, who permitted his subjects to visit England to study Western civilization after Japan received the gift of a warship in 1857 from Queen Victoria. The operetta was heartily approved by the British monarch, and the first performance, on March 14, 1885, at the Savoy Theatre, took place before the duke and duchess of Edinburgh.

The Mikado had been performed to great accolades for more than 20 years when its license to perform was suddenly revoked in 1907. As England prepared for a state visit from the Japanese monarchy, Lord Chamberlain Earl Spencer expressed concern that *The Mikado* contained "unsuspected dangers" and might offend England's Japanese allies. Without communicating with anyone connected to the operetta, including the author, Spencer made a unilateral decision to prohibit all performances of the play for six weeks. Although government officials who sided with Spencer pointed to Japan's increasing power, journalists pointed out the irony of England's precautions, given the reports that music from *The Mikado* was being played by Japanese bands on the Japanese ships in the Medway River, which led to the busy Chatham docks in England, while the music was banned from stages in England. As W. G. Fitz-Gerald wrote in *Harper's Weekly*, "An amusing incident which would seem to heighten the absurdity of the entire affair occurred recently at Chatham, where the Japanese warship *Tsukuba* was lying. When Admiral Sir Gerard Noel, with the chief military and naval officers of the station, was entertained aboard the Japanese man-of-war, although these officers had issued imperative orders that their bands should not play any of the *Mikado* music, it was with selections from this very opera that the band of the Japanese ship regaled them." Despite the ban, Helen D'Oyly Carte, stage manager of the Savoy Theatre, went ahead with planned performances despite the irate protest of William S. Gilbert, who believed mistakenly that the ban had been requested by the Japanese government. She used this time to also undertake secret negotiations for the New York production. D'Oyly Carte wanted hers to be the first English company to stage the definitive version of *The Mikado* in the United States, so the members of the Savoy touring company were booked under assumed names on the train to Liverpool and told only that they were going on a provincial tour in England. A special tugboat was hired to transport them secretly to the ocean liner *Aurania*, which took them to New York and enabled D'Oyly Carte to fulfill her goal.

FURTHER READING

Bordman, Gerald. *American Operetta: From H.M.S. Pinafore to Sweeney Todd.* New York: Oxford University Press, 1981.
The Complete Plays of Gilbert and Sullivan, and including thirty-two photographs from recent performances by the D'Oyly Carte Company. Garden City, N.Y.: Garden City Publishing Co., 1938.
Fitz-Gerald, W. G. "Dramatic Censorship in England." *Harper's Weekly* 51 (January 5, 1907): 947.
Fowell, Frank, and Frank Palmer. *Censorship in England.* London: F. Palmer, 1913. Reprint, New York: Benjamin Blom, 1969.
Gilbert, W. S. *The Best Known Works of W. S. Gilbert, with the author's illustrations.* New York: World Publishing Company, 1932.

THE MISANTHROPE

Author: Molière (Jean-Baptiste Poquelin)
Original date and place of production: June 4, 1666, Théâtre français, Paris, France
Characters: Acaste, Alceste, Arsinoé, Basque, Célimène, Clitandre, Dubois, Eliante, A Guard, Oronte, Philinte
Filmed versions: Feature film: *Le Misanthrope* (1996, Canada). Made for television: (1994, France)

SUMMARY

The Misanthrope is largely the story of Alceste, who believes that the truth should be spoken, no matter what the consequences. He makes no concessions to ordinary courtesy and denounces the insincerity of contemporary society upon every possible occasion. His friend, Philinte, tries to make him see that honesty does not require him to offend and hurt people, and he points out that a few well-spoken words in the right place might go far toward bringing a favorable decision in the lawsuit Alceste has pending in the courts. Alceste rejects what he views as hypocrisy and tells Philinte that, if his suit cannot win through its own merits, he will renounce a society that sanctions such injustice and leave Paris to live the life of a hermit. When the young courtier, Oronte, begs him to give his opinion on some verses that Oronte has written, Alceste is rude. His harsh criticism makes an enemy of Oronte and brings the threat of a second lawsuit.

Despite his insistence upon honesty above all, Alceste has the misfortune to fall in love with Célimène, a young woman who has little regard for the truth. Her main interest is to surround herself with admirers, each of whom she says is her favorite. While Alceste attempts to persuade Célimène to openly acknowledge their engagement, Arsinoé, an acquaintance of Célimène's, under pretense of the frankness that Alceste admires, exposes Célimène's falseness. When her true nature is exposed, her other admirers abandon her, but not Alceste. Having lost his lawsuit, he asks Célimène to prove her love by sharing the hermit's existence to which he plans to retire. Although Célimène is willing to take Alceste's name in marriage in order to compensate him for doubting the sincerity of his regard, she is unwilling to leave her social life and friends in Paris and move with Alceste into the desert. This refusal awakens Alceste to Célimène's falseness. Éliante, Célimène's cousin, formerly in love with Alceste, turns to his friend Philinte when Alceste announces that he no longer has any interest in women after the disillusioning experience with Célimène. The play closes with the determined vow by Éliante and Philinte that they will change Alceste's outlook on life.

CENSORSHIP HISTORY

The Misanthrope was first performed on June 4, 1666, with the playwright in the role of Alceste. Critics have long associated Molière with the role and view the play as his most personal, because his 1662 marriage had become increasingly strained and biographers associate the embittering experience of his marriage with his strong attacks on women and hypocrisy in this comedy. Unlike *Tartuffe*, which was banned from the stage for several years during the playwright's lifetime, *The Misanthrope* enjoyed great success on stage for more than 100 years before this satire of human nature would become an issue for the censors. In the three months preceding the July 1794 revolution in France, government censors were active in demanding major modifications or rejecting for performance 151 plays, many formerly acceptable. As author Frederic Hemmings observes, "Alterations were made in the text of familiar classics, since the censors had to take into consideration 'revivals' as well as new plays." The censors judged classic plays in a new light, from a reactionary standpoint that required the dialogue and the characters to conform to the new ideals of the republic. Among the censors' objections were signs of "Charlatanism, ignorance and bad taste." As Kennedy quotes from the *Feuille du Salut Public*, the official newspaper of the Committee of Public Safety, the republic also wished to "proscribe pitilessly these meaningless dramas . . . these scandalous farces which outrage both good taste and moeurs." The Jacobin authorities ascribed their cause to a residuum of the old regime, which they recommended be purged. Before official censorship was organized on April 1, 1794, the police and Committee of Public Safety set about instituting the new standards: No more kings, dukes, marquis, counts, or lackeys would be permitted on stage. They would be replaced by nonsensical rhyming substitutes. All men were to be presented as equal, but there is no indication that the censors extended such egalitarian language to women characters. The police censors required revisions throughout *The Misanthrope* to eliminate any indication of social difference among characters. They demanded that all references to Dubois as the valet of Alceste be eliminated and required his identification, instead, as *l'homme le plus sot* (literally, "the man the more the fool").

FURTHER READING

Bentley, Eric, ed. *The Classic Theatre.* Vol. 4. *Six French Plays.* Garden City, N.Y.: Anchor Books, 1961.

Gassner, John, ed. *A Treasury of the Theatre.* Vol. 1. *World Drama from Aeschylus to Ostrovsky.* Rev. ed. New York: Simon and Schuster, 1967.

Kennedy, Emmet. "Taste and Revolution." *Canadian Journal of History/Annales canadiennes d'histoire* 32 (December 1997): 375–392.

Hemmings, Frederic William John. *Theatre and State in France, 1760–1905.* New York: Cambridge University Press, 1994.

Molière. *The Misanthrope, A Comedy.* Translated by Richard Wilbur. New York: Harcourt, Brace & World, 1955.

MISS SAIGON

Authors: Alain Boubil, Claude-Michel Schonberg, and Richard Maltby, Jr.

Original date and place of production: September 20, 1989, Theater Royal, London, England

Characters: Chris, the Engineer, Gigi, John, Kim, Mimi, Thuy, Yvette, Yvonne

Filmed versions: None

SUMMARY

Miss Saigon is a musical drama that transplants the story of Puccini's opera *Madame Butterfly* to Vietnam and explores the impact of war on one woman and her child. Chris, a U.S. marine serving in the last days of the U.S. presence in South Vietnam, is given one night with Kim, a prostitute, as a gift from a fellow marine. Kim is the new girl in a stable of prostitutes owned by a pimp named the Engineer. The night becomes the "most wonderful night" of Chris's life, and he falls in love. When Chris leaves money on the table, Kim refuses to take it, telling Chris that she has never done this before. To escape an arranged marriage, she had run to Saigon after her village burned and her parents were slaughtered. Chris asks Kim to live with him, and he buys her freedom from the Engineer. As Saigon becomes tumultuous, Chris and Kim share quarters and undergo a marriage ceremony, including a Vietnamese wedding chant. The wedding party is interrupted by Thuy, Kim's former betrothed, now a Vietcong soldier, who waves a gun and tries to take Kim away but fails. Although Chris and Kim vow to be together forever, they are separated in the chaos that accompanies the fall of Saigon and the resulting evacuation of American forces in 1975.

Three years later, in the United States, Chris is now married to Ellen, an American woman, when he learns through the efforts of a former military comrade now working to help the Vietnamese babies fathered by U.S. soldiers that Kim, whom Chris had believed was killed as Saigon fell, is still alive. He also learns that Kim has borne a son named Tam, and that she is supporting herself and their son by working as a bar girl in Bangkok.

Later, Thuy confronts Kim and tells her that he still wants her, but she clutches her son in her arms and tells Thuy that another love symbolized by Tam will forever have her heart. Thuy tries to kill Tam.

Tortured by guilt, Chris takes a trip to Bangkok with his wife, in the hope of fulfilling his responsibilities to Kim and Tam, but he fails to realize the depth of Kim's love for him. Kim feels betrayed when she meets Ellen. Both Chris and Ellen agree to support Kim and Tam financially, but they will not bring the mother and son to America despite Kim's pleading. In the final moments of the play, Kim dresses Tam in his best clothes and tells him how much she loves him, then goes behind the curtain. A gunshot is heard, and Kim's body falls from behind the curtain. She dies in Chris's arms, after saying, "The gods have guided you to your son."

CENSORSHIP HISTORY

Miss Saigon encountered no staging difficulties during its London run, but when the production was preparing for its April 11, 1991, Broadway debut, protests were raised by Asian-American and other theater workers who complained about the casting of Jonathan Pryce, a Caucasian, in a principal role as a Eurasian pimp. Channeling the complaint through the Committee on Racial Equality of Actors' Equity, a number of groups of Asian artists protested casting a Caucasian in what they believed should be an Asian role, and they cited the long history of such abuses on stage and in the movies. In an interview given to the *New York Times*, a representative of the Pan Asian Repertory Company stated, "In an ideal world, any artist can play any role for which he or she is suited. . . . Until that time arrives, artists of color must fight to retain access to the few roles which are culturally and racially specific to them." As authors Otis Guernsey and Jeffrey Sweet wrote, the issue was similar to the debate regarding white actors playing black roles: "If, as generally agreed, it is unacceptable for white actors to use blackface in playing black actors, then, they reasoned, it similarly should be unacceptable for whites to 'yellow up' and play Asian characters." After months of pressure from Asian groups and union members, Actors' Equity voted to bar Pryce from playing the role on Broadway, citing union rules that allow foreign actors to appear on the American stage only if they have been certified to have "star" status, or if they provide "unique services" that American actors cannot duplicate. (Pryce had won an Olivier Award for his work in the role in a London production.) The union contended that, despite his fame in England and his award, Pryce did not have "star" status. The issue of ethnic representation became even more heated, and in numerous magazine and newspaper interviews, actors, producers, and directors expressed indignation over what they called "trendy racism" and chastised what they saw as attempts by Actors' Equity to dictate casting decisions and "limit their artistic vision." Actors' Equity reversed the decision to bar Pryce after producer Cameron Mitchell threatened to withdraw the Broadway production and after 140 members of Actors' Equity petitioned the union to reconsider. The union relented and admitted that it had "applied an honest and moral principle [of equal employment opportunity] in an inappropriate manner."

FURTHER READING

Guernsey, Otis T., Jr., and Jeffrey Sweet, eds. *The Applause/Best Plays Theatre Yearbook of 1990–1991*. New York: Applause Theatre Book Publishers, 1991.

Gutmann, Staphanie, and Phil West. "Casting Call Still a Whisper." *Los Angeles Times*, August 16, 1990, p. F8.

Otis, Stuart. "The 'Miss Saigon' Mess." *Village Voice*, August 21, 1990, p. 87.

Rich, Frank. "Jonathan Pryce, 'Miss Saigon' and Equity's Decision." *New York Times*, August 10, 1990, p. C3.

Rothstein, Mervyn. "Equity Panel Head Criticizes 'Saigon' Producer." *New York Times*, August 16, 1990, p. C17.

———. "Equity Reverses 'Saigon' Vote and Welcomes English Star." *New York Times*, August 17, 1990, p. C3.

———. "Mackintosh and Equity Plan Meeting." *New York Times*, August 24, 1990, p. C3.

———. "Producer Demands a Free Hand to Cast 'Miss Saigon' Roles." *New York Times*, August 22, 1990, p. C11.

Sheehan, Henry. "When Asians Are Caucasians." *Boston Globe*, August 19, 1990, p. B30.

Will, George F. "The Trendy Racism of Actors' Equity." *Washington Post*, August 12, 1990, p. C7.

MONNA VANNA

Author: Maurice Maeterlinck
Original date and place of production: 1902, Théâtre de L'Oeuvre, Paris, France
Characters: Borso, Giovanna (Monna Vanna), Guido Colonna, Marco Colonna, Prinzivalle, Torello, Trivulzio, Vedio
Filmed versions: *Monna Vanna* (1922, Germany)

SUMMARY

Monna Vanna is a romantic play written in verse and set in Pisa, Italy, at the end of the 15th century. The play is highly symbolic and focuses on the moral and philosophical problems of the meanings of life, love, and honor, and the issue of sacrificing the individual for the good of society. The play opens as Pisa is besieged by the Florentines, commanded by Prinzivalle, who once loved Monna Vanna, the beautiful wife of the Pisan commander Guido of Colonna. Prinzivalle sends a message with Marco Colonna, father of the Pisan commander, promising to spare the city and its inhabitants if Guido will "send [his wife Vanna] in exchange, to give her up to Prinzivalle until tomorrow's dawn . . . for he will send her back when the first faint gray shows in the sky, only he exacts that, in sign of victory and submission, she shall come alone, and her cloak for all her covering . . ." Taking the demand of the Florentine commander as a mortal insult, Guido is ready to continue waging war unto the death of all his people rather than to face the dishonor of allowing another man to take possession of his wife, but Vanna does not hesitate. She weighs her life against that of the many starving children in Pisa, and determines to save them by meeting the demands of Prinzivalle, even if she must enter his camp "naked beneath her cloak." When the two meet, Prinzivalle tells her of his lifelong adoration of her, but he does not touch or harm her in any way, except to request "a kiss on the brow." Touched by his humanity and concerned for his safety as he is about to be deposed by a conspiracy of his Florentine followers, she convinces him to return with her to Pisa where she predicts he will be safe. When Guido confronts them, he refuses to believe Vanna's claims that Prinzivalle loves her and that is why he did not molest her or take advantage of her nakedness under the cloak, despite Marco's understanding and belief in her innocence. The infuriated Pisan commander orders Prinzivalle locked in the deepest of his dungeons until he can execute him. Seeing that she cannot change her husband's mind, Vanna changes her tactics. She hysterically confesses that she was taken advantage of and demands that she receive a key to the dungeon so that she can kill Prinzivalle herself. The play ends as Vanna plans to use the keys to the dungeon cell to free Prinzivalle and leave with him. In 1909 the play was transformed into the opera *Monna Vanna*, with music by Henri Fevrier.

CENSORSHIP HISTORY

Monna Vanna was banned in 1902 by the London Deputy Examiner of Plays, George Alexander Redford, who determined that because of the "immorality of the play," it was not "proper for the stage." The censors' objections centered on the directive issued by Prinzivalle that Monna Vanna go to his tent wearing nothing but her cloak. As authors Frank Fowell and Frank Palmer observed in 1913, "The idea of a heroine appearing in a cloak, under which she was nude, was more than the inflammatory English imagination could bear. . . . To what extent is an author expected to guard against the immorality of the audience's imagination?" Reaction against Redford's refusal to grant the play a license for public performance was strong. In an editorial in the *Athenaeum*, one writer stated, "It will grieve the lovers of all arts, but astonish no one accustomed to the ineptitudes of the Censor, to learn that the *Monna Vanna* of M. Maeterlinck has had to be confined to a private entertainment. . . . Once more the caprice of our Censor brings contempt upon us and makes us the laughing stock of Europe."

Unable to produce the play on a public stage in London, Philip Comyns-Carr arranged a private production at the Victoria Hall, Bayswater, in London on June 19, 1902. Critics attended the performance, and they and other members of the audience concluded that *Monna Vanna* was a very moral play, despite Redford's assessment. Immediately after the first private performance at the Victoria Hall, a letter of public protest entitled "Maeterlinck and the Censor" was sent to *The Times* and signed by well-known literary figures, including Thomas Hardy, George Meredith, and Charles Algernon Swinburne, defending the merits of the play. These opponents of Redford's decision wrote, "Whatever may be the individual estimate upon the merits of *Monna Vanna* as literature and drama, it requires the bat eyes of the Censor to be blind to its high-mindedness and the exquisite sense of feminine purity with which it is charged. . . . The interdict pronounced upon it is less of an affront to M. Maeterlinck than to English intelligence." In an inquiry held by the Joint Select Committee after the private performance, Redford defended his decision and claimed that "the whole tone of the work" was immoral. When Hugh Law of the Joint Select Committee asked Redford, "Is not the whole idea of the play that love is not only not identical with, but the enemy of lust? Do you call that immoral?" Redford replied, "I certainly do call the play immoral, from the point of view of the Examiner of Plays." As author John Elsom points out, "Mr. Redford therefore interpreted the taboo on physical nakedness also to mean scenes where physical nakedness was implied, where the plots suggested that true love could over-ride formal marriage and where the physical language was too explicit."

FURTHER READING

Elsom, John. *Erotic Theatre*. New York: Taplinger Publishing Co., 1974.
Fowell, Frank, and Frank Palmer. *Censorship in England*. London: F. Palmer, 1913. Reprint, New York: Benjamin Blom, 1969.

Goldman, Emma. *The Social Significance of the Modern Drama.* Boston: Richard G. Badger, 1914.

"Last of the Censors, The." *The New Age: A Weekly Review of Politics, Literature and Art* 5, no. 19 (September 2, 1909): 353.

Thomas, Edward. *Maurice Maeterlinck.* 2d ed. London: Methuen & Co., 1911.

MRS. WARREN'S PROFESSION

Author: George Bernard Shaw
Original date and place of production: January 1902, private performance, Stage Society, London, England
Characters: Sir George Crofts, Frank Gardner, Reverend Samuel Gardner, Praed, Mrs. Kitty Warren, Vivie Warren
Filmed versions: Made for television: *Mrs. Warren's Profession* (1972, U.K.); *Frau Warren's Gewerbe* (1960, West Germany)

SUMMARY

Mrs. Warren's Profession is a drama in four acts set in Surrey and London in which George Bernard Shaw explores society's hypocritical attitudes toward prostitution. The first act opens with the introduction of Vivie Warren, a 22-year-old woman who is enjoying a holiday in Surrey after completing her college education. Her mother, "a genial and fairly presentable old blackguard" whom she barely knows, as the young woman has spent most of her life in boarding schools, visits her in the company of the naive young artist Praed, who hints that Mrs. Warren has a dark secret, and the worldly Sir George Crofts, who becomes enamored with Vivie. The young woman rebuffs the attentions of George and Praed, because she has a romantic interest in Frank Gardner, a son of the pretentious Reverend Samuel Gardner, who warns his son about the dangers of women while hiding his own long-ago encounter with a barmaid, whom we later learn was the young Mrs. Warren.

In Act II, Mrs. Warren speaks with Vivie and admits that she does not know who Vivie's father is, and she explains her choice of prostitution as a career. Recalling the death of her eminently respectable half-sister from lead poisoning while working in a factory, Mrs. Warren states that her only alternative would also have been to work in a factory at starvation wages. Instead, she chose to use her good looks and youth to make money, which she saved and used to open her own "establishment," in which she provided jobs for young women under conditions better than those in a factory. As Mrs. Warren tells Vivie, "the only way for a woman to provide for herself decently is for her to be good to some man that can afford to be good to her." Although momentarily shocked to learn the source of the money that had provided her with a good education and luxuries, Vivie is impressed by her mother's determination and wants to become her friend, because she believes that her mother has left the profession.

In Act III, while Vivie and Frank embrace in the rectory garden, Crofts appears and proposes to her. He tells Vivie that he is her mother's partner in operating a chain of brothels, which shocks her because, unlike her mother who profited from prostitution out of necessity, Crofts simply views it as a profitable business. He reminds Vivie that she also has benefited from it: "If you're going to pick and choose your acquaintances on moral principles, you'd better clear out of this country, unless you want to cut yourself out of all decent society." After Vivie calls for Frank to join her, Crofts becomes angry and tells her that the Reverend Gardner is her father and that Frank is, therefore, her half-brother. Disgusted by the situation, Vivie leaves immediately for London.

In Act IV, which takes place a few days later, Frank and Praed appear at Vivie's office, each offering her their love, but she reveals her mother's profession and rejects them both. As the play closes, Vivie and Mrs. Warren have a final meeting in which Mrs. Warren tries to explain to Vivie that she must work, as does Vivie, but the younger woman rejects any explanation as hypocrisy: "I might have done as you did; but I should not have lived one life and believed in another. You are a conventional woman at heart." Vivie rejects her mother and breathes a sigh of relief as Mrs. Warren leaves.

CENSORSHIP HISTORY

George Bernard Shaw wrote *Mrs. Warren's Profession* in 1894 with the purpose of making a social statement, and he fully expected that the play would likely not be licensed for public performance by the censors. Shaw described the play to friends as "cold bloodedly appalling . . . but not in the least prurient," and declared, "I want to make an end, if I can, of the furtively lascivious Pharisaism of stage immorality, but a salutary dramatization of the reality." Aware that contemporary morality required that a woman such as Mrs. Warren would be expected to commit suicide at the end of the play, Shaw realized that allowing his character to live would condemn the play in the eyes of the censors, so he did not submit the play for official examination for several years after completing it. Instead he placed his hopes for a public performance with the Independent Theatre Society, which discussed the possibility with him for two years while trying to find a theater manager willing to risk staging the unlicensed and highly controversial play.

In 1898 Shaw sought to publish the collection *Plays Pleasant and Unpleasant*, which would include *Mrs. Warren's Profession*. In order to obtain the necessary protection for its publication, he was forced to apply for permission to produce a single copyright performance, which brought the play to the attention of the lord chamberlain, Edward Bootle-Wilbraham, earl of Latham. After the original 1894 text was rejected, Shaw suggested a drastic expurgation to the censors, including the removal of the entire second act, thus "leaving Mrs. Warren's profession unspecified." In response to Shaw's suggestion, the examiner of plays, George Alexander Redford, reminded Shaw of the author's job to submit "a licensable play," which Redford would read and "endeavour to forget that he ever read the original." Shaw complied, and the resulting innocuous three-act version was licensed for performance at Victoria Hall, Bayswater, in 1898. In January 1902 the full text of the play was presented by the Stage Society in a private London club, but the play was not licensed in England for public performance until 1926. In September 1907 the manager of the Midland Theatre in Manchester, England, submitted a copy of the play with the required fee to the examiner of plays. In response, Redford returned the fee and the play, with the following notation written on the manager's letter: "Surely you are aware that I have already refused to license this play.—G.A.R." Follow-up letters received no response.

The banning in England of *Mrs. Warren's Profession* provided a large market for the play in the United States, although audiences went to see the play for all the wrong reasons when it debuted at the Garrick Theatre on Broadway on October 23, 1905. The production closed after only one performance. New York critics denounced the drama as "an insult to decency" and likened it to "refuse in garbage cans." Anthony Comstock, the head of the Society for the Suppression of Vice, led a campaign against "this Irish smut-dealer," and warned that if one of Shaw's "filthy productions" were staged, his group would work to prosecute "to the fullest severity of the law." Before the first performance, Comstock and his followers besieged New York City officials, who ordered the police to stop the show after one performance and to arrest the producer, Arnold Daly, and leading lady, Mary Shaw, on the technical charge of disorderly conduct for presenting an "immoral drama" dealing with prostitution. The pair were released on bail and, eight months later, a jury acquitted them of all charges. As authors Frank Fowell and Frank Palmer write, the decision of the court stated that there was "nothing in the words themselves or in any particular phrase or expression which can be said to be indecent, and that the court was compelled to resort to the theme and motive of the play to find the indecency complained of." The decision of the court concludes that the playwright "has in this instance made vice less attractive than many other dramatists whose plays have escaped the censorious attention of the police. His attack on social evils is one which may result in effecting some reform." When the play opened on Broadway two years later, in 1907, no one protested.

FURTHER READING

Brustein, Robert. *The Theatre of Revolt: Studies in Ibsen, Strindberg, Chekhov, Shaw, Brecht, Pirandello, O'Neill and Genet.* Boston: Little, Brown and Company, 1964.

Elsom, John. *Erotic Theatre.* New York: Taplinger Publishing Co., 1974.

Fowell, Frank, and Frank Palmer. *Censorship in England.* London: F. Palmer, 1913. Reprint, New York: Benjamin Blom, 1969.

Laufe, Abe. *The Wicked Stage: A History of Theater Censorship and Harassment in the United States.* New York: Frederick Ungar Publishing Co., 1978.

Loth, David. *The Erotic in Literature.* New York: Dorset Press, 1994.

MacCarthy, Desmond. "Literary Taboos." *Life and Letters* 1 (October 1928): 329–341.

Parkes, Adam. *Modernism and the Theater of Censorship*. New York: Oxford University Press, 1996.

Schroeder, Theodore A. "Our Censorship of Literature." *Tomorrow* 4 (November 1908): 42–44.

Shaw, George Bernard. *The Author's Apology from Mrs. Warren's Profession*. New York: Brentano's, 1905.

———, Gilbert Murray, et al. *The Censorship of Plays in the Office of the Lord Chamberlain: The Case for Abolition*. Letchworth, England: Arden Press, 1908.

Stephens, John Russell. *The Censorship of English Drama, 1824–1901*. New York: Cambridge University Press, 1980.

THE NORMAL HEART

Author: Larry Kramer

Original date and place of production: April 21, 1985, Joseph Papp Public Theater/LuEsther Hall, New York, New York

Characters: Tommy Boatwright, Dr. Emma Brookner, David, Craig Donner, Examining Doctor, Hiram Keebler, Mickey Marcus, Bruce Niles, Felix Turner, Ben Weeks, Ned Weeks

Filmed versions: None

SUMMARY

The Normal Heart, a drama in two acts set in the New York gay community in 1981, focuses on the experiences of Ned Weeks, a promiscuous gay man who is driven to his first monogamous love affair and into acting for the good of society by the increased number of reported cases of AIDS in the gay community. Enraged as he watches the AIDS epidemic spreading among his friends while it is ignored by the community at large, Weeks joins with Dr. Emma Brookner, one of the first physicians to treat AIDS victims, to form a gay self-help group that quickly grows into an organization of significant influence. As Ned works to seek greater help from the gay community on all levels, he meets and falls in love with *New York Times* fashion correspondent Felix Turner. The two men create a stable personal relationship, but Ned soon alienates many members of both the straight and the gay communities, including fellow volunteers, with his extensive rage and his abrasive campaigning for those afflicted with AIDS. After he insists that if the gay community is to survive, members must follow the advice of Dr. Brookner and adopt a policy of temporary celibacy, Ned is no longer tolerated by the organization he founded and they eject him. Soon after, Ned learns that Felix has acquired AIDS, and the two seek to formalize their love before Felix dies. Grieving for his dying lover, Ned experiences his only relief when his brother Ben appears to attend a deathbed "marriage" between Ned and Felix, shortly before Felix dies.

CENSORSHIP HISTORY

The Normal Heart is one of the earliest plays to address AIDS directly and to confront it as a fact of gay life. First presented in 1985 at Joseph Papp's Public Theater in New York City, the play was hailed as a groundbreaking work and enjoyed a successful run of 294 performances. The reception was less warm at Southwest Missouri State University (SMSU) when a student theater group sought to produce the play in 1989. When the proposed production was announced, local citizens sought to force the university to cancel the production, which they alleged was obscene. The protesters took the controversy to the Missouri state legislature, the primary funding source of SMSU, where sympathetic legislators helped to form a group called Citizens Demanding Standards, Inc. (CDS). CDS undertook phone and letter-writing campaigns to pressure the state legislature to take punitive fiscal action against SMSU. Opponents of the play purchased newspaper advertisements that charged that the publicly funded production promoted a "homosexual, anti-family lifestyle." They held a rally that attracted approximately 1,200 demonstrators. An attorney representing SMSU argued that the First Amendment barred cancellation without substantial government interest, and asserted that the play was not obscene. Play opponents did not raise constitutional arguments, but suggested that freedom without commitment to moral order amounted to a "free-for-all." Some proponents of the production used the occasion to further AIDS education, while others labeled opponents of the play as bigots. An arson incident that destroyed the home of one of the organizers of the ad hoc student group People Acting with Compassion and Tolerance (PACT) while he attended the premiere of the play brought national attention to the controversy and accusations from both sides in the dispute. The controversy stirred so much antigay and anti-AIDS activity that the university formed a security committee, installed metal detectors, and positioned bomb-sniffing dogs in the theater lobby during the eight performances. Representatives of SMSU were successful in diverting attention away from the idea of public funding for allegedly immoral activities and toward the idea of free expression, while assuring the play's presentation. Many activists were pleased that AIDS awareness might have been heightened, although gay rights issues were overshadowed by the controversy.

FURTHER READING

Euben, Donna R. "The Play's the Thing." *AAUP Legal Watch*. Available online. URL: http://www.aaup.org/publications/Academe/01nd/01ndLW.htm

Munk, Erika. "Stage Left." *Village Voice*, November 14, 1989, p. 49.

"A Public University's Defense of Free Expression: The Issues and Events in the Staging of *The Normal Heart*." Paper presented at the 76th Annual Meeting of the Speech Communication Association, Chicago, Ill. November 1–4, 1990.

Roshan, Maer. "Larry Kramer: Queer Conscience." *New York*, April 6, 1998, pp. 144–147.

Rottmann, Larry. "The Battle of *The Normal Heart.*" *Academe*, July–August 1990, pp. 30–35.
Summers, Claude J. *The Gay and Lesbian Literary Heritage.* New York: Henry Holt, 1995.

OEDIPUS REX

Author: Sophocles
Original date and place of production: c. 425 B.C., Athens, Greece
Characters: Antigone, Chorus, Creon, Ismene, Oedipus, Polynices, Teiresias
Filmed versions: Feature films: *Oedipus Rex* (1909, Italy); (1911, U.K.); (1957, Canada). Made for television: (1984, U.K.); (1992, Japan); *Oedipus the King* (1967, 1984, U.K.); *King Oedipus* (1972, U.K.).

SUMMARY

Oedipus Rex (*Oedipus the King*) is one of three plays written by Sophocles based on the story of Oedipus found in the mythology of the ancient Greeks; the other two are *Antigone* and *Oedipus at Colonus.* The play opens 10 years after Oedipus first appeared in Thebes, where he was made king and married to Jocasta, the widow of the murdered former king Laius. Through references made in the dialogue, the audience learns of prophecies that had been made to Jocasta and Laius, as well as the manner in which Laius died. When the play opens, a pestilence is ravaging the population of Thebes, and Oedipus has sent Jocasta's brother Creon to the oracle at Delphi to learn why the gods have sent the plague. When Creon returns, he reveals that the oracle has foretold that the plague will remain upon Thebes until the murderer of Laius is identified and punished, leading Oedipus to curse the murderer and vow before all Thebes that he will avenge Laius. He summons the blind prophet Teiresias and demands that the soothsayer reveal all that he knows about the murder. When the prophet uses oblique references to identify Oedipus as the murderer, the king denounces Teiresias and accuses him of collaborating with Creon in an effort to usurp the throne. Jocasta seeks to save her brother, and she tries to convince Oedipus that the prophet is mistaken because many years earlier the oracle had predicted that Laius would be killed by his own son. She also provides Oedipus with information that he seems to hear for the first time, that Laius was murdered at the junction of three roads, leading Oedipus to recall that 10 years before, while on his way to Thebes, he had challenged and struck down a man at the point where three roads met. With growing horror, Oedipus realizes that he is the son of Laius and Jocasta and that he had actually murdered his father and married his mother, producing four children with her. Jocasta realizes the truth more quickly and commits suicide, while Oedipus gouges out his own eyes so that he might never again see the sunlight. Creon becomes king as Oedipus is exiled from Thebes.

CENSORSHIP HISTORY

Oedipus Rex was regarded for many years as impossible to present on the English stage, because the English censors found the theme of incest an unacceptable topic for the English audience. (See THE CENCI.) In the 1880s the respected English actor Sir Herbert Tree applied to the London Examiner of Plays, Edward Frederick Smyth Pigott, for a license to perform the tragedy on stage at his venue, His Majesty's Theatre, but Tree was refused without consideration as to whether a particular version of the play was being performed and without the suggestion to expurgate the play in any manner. The censors did not provide Tree with a reason for their refusal, but they did inform him that "the licence had been refused before, and it was no use submitting the play again." As authors Frank Fowell and Frank Palmer write, although public performances of *Oedipus Rex* were banned by the English censors, the written version of the play was assigned reading in many British public schools of the period and "its performance by undergraduates has not been known to produce objectionable or disastrous effects on the audience." The English ban remained in force until 1912, when the Theatre at Covent Garden sought permission to bring a highly popular German production of the tragedy to the London stages. The Max Reinhardt production acted by members of the Deutsches Schauspielhaus first appeared in Berlin and then went to Vienna in 1911 to perform *Oedipus Rex* in the Zirkus Busch. Reinhardt himself played the role of Teiresias. The Viennese papers were largely appreciative of the performance, and it was even given the honor of a parody in the Lustspielhaus on the Prater. When Reinhardt's production went to Covent Garden and was performed for private subscription and stayed for 26 performances, it provided an enormous stimulus for the performance of Greek drama in Great Britain and helped to end the ban on *Oedipus Rex* by the examiner of plays.

FURTHER READING

Baur, Eva Elise vom. "Max Reinhardt and His Famous Players." *The Theatre* 14 (1911): vi, 56–60.

Fowell, Frank, and Frank Palmer. *Censorship in England.* London: F. Palmer, 1913. Reprint, New York: Benjamin Blom, 1969.

Gregory, Lady Augusta Persse. "The Fight with the Castle." In *Our Irish Theatre: A Chapter in Autobiography.* New York: G. P. Putnam's Sons, 1913, pp. 140–168.

MacIntosh, Fiona. "Tragedy in Performance: Nineteenth- and Twentieth-Century Productions." In *The Cambridge Companion to Greek Tragedy.* Edited by P. E. Easterling. Cambridge: Cambridge University Press, 1997, pp. 284–323.

OH! CALCUTTA!

Author: Kenneth Tynan and others
Original date and place of production: June 16, 1969, Eden Theater, New York, New York

Characters: Revue performances
Filmed versions: *Oh! Calcutta!* (1972)

SUMMARY

Oh! Calcutta! is a series of musical numbers about sex and sexual mores separated into two acts. Most of the skits feature one or more performers standing nude or simulating sex on a fully lighted stage. The skits were written by Kenneth Tynan with contributions by Joe Orton, Samuel Beckett, John Lennon, Jules Pfeiffer, Leonard Melfi, and others who brought their unique perspectives to the musical revue. None of the sketches in the revue are identified with specific contributors, and the titles range from one thoughtful monologue entitled "Who: Whom," about the difference between women who are victims and those who passively submit to being victims and by their submission cooperate, through "Until She Screams," a sketch about a terrible yet seemingly conventional family in the Home Counties, near London. Several of the songs, such as "To His Mistress Going to Bed" and "One on One" are tritely sentimental, and the attempts at erotic sketches mechanically present repeated references to or simulations of fellatio, cunnilingus, sadomasochism, fetishism, masturbation, and groupies. As Elsom wrote, "we see sex through the eyes of a man's magazine on the stage," and even then, as *New York Times* theater critic Clive Barnes remarked, it is the sort of stuff "which gives pornography a bad name."

CENSORSHIP HISTORY

Hillard Elkins, the producer of *Oh! Calcutta!*, sought to avoid police action against the play and invited New York City officials to a preview performance, presumably to determine if the play would run into problems with the commissioner of licensing or with the police. In a preproduction statement, Elkins claimed that the revue "did not include the sex act," and the preview performance did not, so the production was granted permission to open Off-Broadway at the Eden Theater without interference from authorities. Actual performances of the play contained nude actors satirizing and simulating various sex acts, and the theater, with seating for 499, was filled to capacity by audiences paying $25 for seats in the first two rows and $15 for seats in the back, more than the cost of many Broadway tickets of the time. Critics failed to be shocked by the revue, although Clive Barnes wrote that *Oh! Calcutta!* "left nothing to the imagination." Despite generally negative critical reviews, the revue ran for two seasons Off-Broadway before moving to Broadway at the Belasco Theatre, to run for a total of 1,314 performances.

Attempts to censor the material did not occur until the revue was taken to England and began performances at the Roundhouse Theatre in Camden on July 27, 1970. Britain had abolished theater censorship in 1968, but mechanisms remained to ban a play from the public stage when public opinion was strong enough. The English critics were mixed in their views, and ranged from labeling the revue as nothing more than "sexual voyeurism" to lamenting that "*Oh! Calcutta!* is five years too late to be the great liberating sensation it was obviously meant to be. . . . What we are left with is a so-called erotic revue which is anti-erotic." The Roundhouse Theatre was supported by the Arts Council, and complaints were raised that the revue represented "state handouts for filth." After attending a preview of *Oh! Calcutta!* local politician Frank Smith asked the police to stop the revue. When they did not, he tried to convince British church leaders to attend a performance, but his efforts were rejected. In a formal response, the secretary of the archbishop of Canterbury replied that "it is unlikely that Dr. Ramsay will be going to *Oh! Calcutta!*" while Cardinal Heenan, the archbishop of Westminster, and others simply pleaded illness. On July 24, 1970, three days before the first official performance, the *Times* reported that the Department of Public Programs was "considering a complaint" against the production, under the 1968 Theatres Act, but the amorphous nature of the skits, which were visual, unscripted, and choreographic, would have made such action dependent upon police accounts and reactions to the onstage activity. In an ironic occurrence, on July 24, 1970, a bookseller at Dover was fined £150 for importing seven copies of the American book version of the play, and the copies were confiscated by police. Three days later, after a series of highly publicized previews, *Oh! Calcutta!* opened on July 27, with tickets selling for up to £50 each. The first-night audience was given a questionnaire to complete that asked them to declare whether or not they expected to be depraved by their experience. All answered in the negative. On August 1, 1970, the attorney-general, Sir Peter Rawlinson, announced that the government would not prosecute Tynan or the producers. The result was a moral backlash in England that led to a mobilization of church and government officials against pornography that would include the refusal of a license by London authorities in 1973 for the film version of *Oh! Calcutta!* to be shown, even while the play was currently in performance in the West End of London.

FURTHER READING

Elsom, John. *Erotic Theatre*. New York: Taplinger Publishing Co., 1974.
Laufe, Abe. *The Wicked Stage: A History of Theater Censorship and Harassment in the United States*. New York: Frederick Ungar Publishing Co., 1978.
Sutherland, John. *Offensive Literature: Decensorship in Britain, 1960–1982*. Totowa, N.J.: Barnes and Noble Books, 1983.

ONE-THIRD OF A NATION

Author: Arthur Arent
Original date and place of production: January 17, 1938, Adelphi Theatre, New York, New York
Characters: Senator Charles O. Andrews, Senator William E. Borah, the

Health Inspector, the Landlord, the Little Man, Little Man's wife, the Tenement House Inspector, Senator Robert F. Wagner
Filmed versions: *One-Third of a Nation* (1939)

SUMMARY

One-Third of a Nation begins with a fire in a bleak, rundown tenement, as a loudspeaker announces, "This might be 397 Madison Avenue, New York, or 245 Halsey Street, Brooklyn, or Jackson Avenue and 10th Street, Long Island City," all places where actual devastating fires had occurred. Organized like a newspaper account, the first act of the two-act play contains representatives named by their functions rather than individually named characters. Investigators from the fire department poke around the ruins, attempting to determine the cause of the fire, and the Tenement House Inspector complains, "If that building is a firetrap, then so is every old-law tenement in New York City." When officials confront the Landlord, he blames his failure to improve conditions in the tenement on the tenants, whom he claims do not pay him enough rent, and points out that his investment really is in the land on which the tenement stands: "You'll have to go back into history and blame whatever it was that made New York City real estate the soundest and most profitable speculation on the face of the earth."

The scene then shifts to the past, with the Landlord dressed in 18th-century clothing. He unrolls a grass mat, on which tenants join him at intervals, each paying a larger rent than the one previous and all crowding with him on the mat until no room is left. The Landlord then leaves the first mat and his tenants there to move to another property, stating that they will manage somehow because "a man's got to have a place to live," a line that is repeated throughout the play. The first act ends in 1854 with a cholera epidemic, which the New York City Health Inspector identifies as being caused by the "crowded and filthy state in which a great portion of our population lives." The Landlord responds to this criticism by stating that everyone would like to live "in a marble palace," but that is impossible, so "we take what God gives us and we're thankful." Confronted by his tenants, the Landlord points out the futility of their complaints and of their lives: "If you don't live here, where are you going to live? In the park? In the street? In another place that's no better than mine and maybe a hell of a lot worse? Because in case you're forgetting . . . you've got to have a place to live."

The second act returns to the spring of 1937 and presents a range of solutions to the tenement problem, before focusing specific attention on the U.S. Senate debate on the housing bill sponsored by Senator Robert F. Wagner of New York. The dialogue of most of the act is taken straight from the text of the *Congressional Record*. The loudspeaker introduces Senator William E. Borah of Idaho, who first asks Senator Wagner to explain "the causes of the slums" and to answer the question "Why do we have these awful degraded conditions?" Wagner blames the low incomes of people living in the slums for the conditions, but he is challenged by Senator Charles O. Andrews of Florida, who calls for a halt to immigration in order to prevent people from entering the United States and taking "advantage of our government in supplying them with homes." The play concludes that the only solution to the housing problem is for the federal government to create a program of clearance, building, loans, and code enforcement.

CENSORSHIP HISTORY

Originally named *Housing*, Arent's *One-Third of a Nation* was the most successful as well as the most controversial "Living Newspaper" production of the Federal Theatre Project (FTP), a government-subsidized movement created in 1935 under the Works Progress Administration (WPA) to employ professional theater workers and to provide the general public with access to inexpensive, quality theater while providing community services in developing regional and neighborhood theater and theatrical workshops. Like all drama in the Living Newspaper form, the play grew out of the economic and social upheaval of the Great Depression. These productions were designed to dramatize the socioeconomic conditions of the working class with the intent of arousing political consciousness and promoting social change. The plays were documentary theater that incorporated actual newspaper accounts, government testimonies, and other statements of public record into a specific format. The plot typically began in the present, to exhibit the immediacy of a problem rooted in the everyday experiences of the working class, then moved to the past to explore the causes of the problem before returning to the present to examine possible solutions. After various solutions are analyzed, one solution is selected, and the drama ends with a call for specific legislative, judicial, or other group action to rectify the existing situation.

The genesis of *One-Third of a Nation* was a pamphlet about housing published in 1935 by the Public Works Administration, which made headlines with its revelations that one-third of Americans had inadequate housing and its statement that the government had a responsibility to guarantee all citizens the right to adequate shelter. President Franklin Delano Roosevelt borrowed from the pamphlet for his second inaugural address, as he told onlookers that he saw "one-third of a nation ill-housed, ill-classed and ill-nourished." His words served as a catalyst to Hallie Flanagan, director of the FTP, who asked the Living Newspaper unit of the FTP to collect material about housing in the nation and the housing bill being drafted in 1936 by Senator Robert F. Wagner. Soon after the play opened, members of the U.S. Senate roundly questioned why the government was appropriating money to a function that undermined its efforts. Historian Jane Mathews notes that Senator Josiah W. Bailey of North Carolina denounced the play during a Senate session for making "us all actors on the stage forever" while failing to acknowledge the real work of the federal government. Senator Andrews, whose words against the provision of housing for the poor had been used verbatim from the *Congressional Record*, felt that the play had made him out to be a villain. Incensed, he contacted top Roosevelt aide Harry Hopkins, who had created and supported the FTP, demanding, "Who is responsible for this play, and what action, if any, has been taken by our department to have these particular scenes eliminated?" Andrews and other senators, including Senator Harry Byrd of Virginia and Senator Borah of Idaho, also demanded to receive a list of the names and addresses of every actor, writer, and producer connected with *One-Third of a Nation* and their weekly salaries, as well as other detailed financial information.

When Aubrey Williams, deputy administrator of the WPA, was called before the Senate Appropriations Committee in late February 1938, he was questioned extensively about the origin of the Living Newspaper plays and the authorization of their content. Senator Richard Russell of Georgia argued that "some very dangerous precedents" were being set by allowing productions such as *One-Third of a Nation*. Author Joanne Bentley relates that the Senate committee concluded that "when taxpayers' money was involved, plays should be 'very carefully censored' so as not to hold anyone up to ridicule." Hallie Flanagan states in *Arena*, her own account of the FTP, that Williams later confronted her and asked what she meant by "insulting senators," to which she replied that she had simply used material verbatim from the *Congressional Record*, which was in the public domain. She writes, "If senators and congressmen oppose an increase in appropriations for housing and say so in Congress, why should they object to being quoted?"

The play was also produced in other cities, including Detroit, Cincinnati, Philadelphia, Hartford, New Orleans, Seattle, Portland, and San Francisco, where officials also protested. In Seattle, to prevent an outcry against the play, producer Esther Porter Lane eliminated much of the controversy by mentioning no names in the production. In 1939 the Federal Theatre Project was defunded by Congress. Official statements claimed that the project had become "economically unnecessary" and "too controversial politically" to receive government support. The funding was officially removed by an act of Congress on June 20, 1939, and many supporters claimed that Senate dissatisfaction with *One-Third of a Nation* provided a major impetus for the move.

FURTHER READING

Bentley, Joanne. *Hallie Flanagan: A Life in the American Theatre.* New York: Alfred A. Knopf, 1988.

Buttitta, Tony. *Uncle Sam Presents: A Memoir of the Federal Theatre, 1935–1939.* Philadelphia: University of Pennsylvania Press, 1982.

Drake, Sylvia. "Stages Sentimental Trip Back to Federal Theater Years." *The Los Angeles Times,* July 12, 1989, p. 1.

Flanagan, Hallie. *Arena.* New York: Duell, Sloan and Pearce, 1940.

Laufe, Abe. *The Wicked Stage: A History of Theater Censorship and Harassment in the United States.* New York: Frederick Ungar Publishing Co., 1978.

Mathews, Jane DeHart. *The Federal Theatre, 1935–1939; Plays, Relief, and Politics.* Princeton, N.J.: Princeton University Press, 1967.

O'Connor, John, and Lorraine Brown, eds. *Free, Adult, Uncensored: The Living History of the Federal Theatre Project.* New York: Simon and Schuster, 1978.

THE PARSON'S WEDDING

Author: Thomas Killigrew

Original date and place of production: October 1664, Theatre Royal, London, England

Characters: Bawd, Captain, Cropp, Faithful, Lady Love-All, Lady Wild, Master Careless, Master Constant, Master Jolly, Master Sadd, Master Wild, Mistress Pleasant, Mistress Secret, Mistress Wanton, Parson

Filmed versions: None

SUMMARY

The Parson's Wedding is a bawdy comedy in five acts that satirizes the fashionable wits of London in the 1630s. Characters bear names that represent their personalities and behavior. Mistress Wanton and Master Careless dally with the affections of the opposite sex, and the widow Lady Love-all eagerly searches for a virile man to ease her loneliness, while Bawd, the maid to Mistress Wanton, speaks in bawdy language and her opposite, Faithful, is an errant honest woman to Lady Love-all. Master Jolly is a humorous gentleman and courtier, and Master Wild a nephew to the rich and somewhat youthful widow Lady Wild. As the men and women with more colorful names move from one sexual dalliance to another without apparent concern or harm to themselves, the serious-minded and monogamous, if dull spirited, Masters Constant and Sadd, suitors to Lady Wild and Mistress Pleasant, are cuckolded. The Captain is a leading wit who is filled with designs, one of them for Mistress Wanton, and he resents the interest shown in her by the Parson, himself a wit, but not as experienced as the Captain.

The play opens as the Captain rails against what he views as the Parson's hypocrisy. He has saved the Parson from preaching in the streets and arranged for a patronage to allow the Parson his own parish. Now the Captain learns that the Parson has been making sexual advances toward Mistress Wanton, against whom he had warned the Captain nightly, "Yet look back, and hunt not with good nature and the beauties of thy youth that false woman, but hear thy friend, that speaks from sad experience." Mistress Wanton laughingly tells the Captain that the Parson had even offered to marry her to enjoy her sexual favors, but the Captain surprises her by not joining in the ridicule. Instead he urges her to marry the Parson: "I conjure thee, take my counsel: marry him to afflict him." During the course of the play, as the Captain seeks to prove that the Parson is just as much of a scoundrel in regard to sexual affairs as any of the gentlemen, a series of plot devices such as misdirected letters and cases of mistaken identity are used. The Captain also devises plans to disrupt the complacency of Sadd and Constant by arranging for the abduction of the women they court, Lady Wild and Mistress Pleasant, and making them believe that the women have agreed to marry their abductors in what is supposed to be a sham wedding performed by the Parson.

When Sadd and Constant arrive and are confronted with the situation, they spend several minutes discussing having been cuckolded, and then are comforted by Careless, who advises them to "Ne'er think of marrying in this dull clime; wedlock's a trade you'll ne'er go through with. Wives draw bills upon sight, and 't will not be for your credit to protest 'em. Rather, follow counsel and marry à la Venetiano for a night . . . repenting in the morning and leave your woman and sin both i'th'bed."

Careless then has to deal with his own troubles, when the Parson reveals that he has tricked the men and, rather than a sham marriage, performed binding ceremonies. At once, Careless finds that other women near him "grow dangerously handsome, a thousand graces in each I never observed before. Now, just now, when I must not taste, I begin to long for some of their plums." Wanton, whose sham marriage to the Parson had been arranged by the Captain as a means of revenge, speaks freely at the end of the play, comforting Sadd, who bemoans his betrayal by the widow Lady Wild. Wanton questions, "Can any woman be pure or worth the serious sighing of a generous heart that has had above one hand laid upon her?" The sudden ardor of Sadd leads the widowed Lady Wild to question if she should reconsider him as a lover, which Wanton urges, stating, "try 'em both tonight and choose tomorrow." Her nephew adds his encouragement: "put him in your bed and fold him close in your arms, aunt." The play ends with the Captain dressed in the Parson's cloak in the hope of avoiding the elderly Lady Love-all, who has been trying to make him her lover. When confronted by the lecherous lady and her maid, he denies his identity but explains that deception has brought about three marriages and asks the audience, "Will you lend your hands to join them?"

CENSORSHIP HISTORY

The Parson's Wedding was produced in small private settings when it was first written in 1639, but with other drama it was put aside until after the Restoration. When Killigrew revived his play in public performance in 1664, at the Theatre Royal in Drury Lane, which he co-owned with William Davenant, he cast women in all the roles, which authors Frank Fowell and Frank Palmer state was "presumably on account of its indecency." All the roles were filled by women in the 1673 revival, as well. The play, with its numerous uses of the words "whore" and "bawds," blatant references to sexual activity, and advocacy of promiscuity, was considered daring and coarse by audiences of the day but witty enough to be acceptable on the stage. Ironically, when Charles II signed the royal grant on August 21, 1660, to provide Killigrew with the land on which to build the Theatre Royal in Drury Lane, the proclamation stated that the new theater would present material purged of anything that would be "offensive to all pious and well-disposed persons." Instead, the plays appeared to increase in coarseness, sexual references, and bawdy language. Samuel Pepys noted in his diary entry for October 1, 1664, that a friend named Luellin had recently attended the play in Drury Lane, and "He tells me what a bawdy loose play this *Parson's Wedding* is, that is acted by nothing but women in the King's house, and I am glad of it."

The passage of the Act of 1737 created the Office of the Examiner of Plays in England and ended the freedom enjoyed on stage by such plays as *The Parson's Wedding.* The new examiner, William Chetwynd, and his deputy assistant, Thomas Odell, reviewed hundreds of play scripts and exiled from the stage between 200 to 300, including Killigrew's *The Parson's Wedding.* In 1913 the language and plot premises of the play still had the ability to shock, as exhibited by the reluctance of Fowell and Palmer to quote from the play in their 1913 *Censorship in England:* "We had originally prepared one or two quotations to show what the Court Censor of 1660 regarded as fitting for public performance, but they have had to be excised from the later proofs as being much too coarse for inclusion."

FURTHER READING

Bowers, Fredson, ed. *Jacobean and Caroline Dramatists.* Detroit, Mich.: Gale Research, 1987.

Fowell, Frank, and Frank Palmer. *Censorship in England.* London: F. Palmer, 1913. Reprint, New York: Benjamin Blom, 1969.

Keast, William Rea. "Killigrew's Use of Donne in *The Parson's Wedding.*" *Modern Language Review* 45 (1950): 512–515.

Knowland, A. S., ed. *Six Caroline Plays.* New York: Oxford University Press, 1962.

Pepys, Samuel. *The Diary of Samuel Pepys M.A. F.R.S. Clerk of the Acts and Secretary to the Admiralty.* Transcribed from the shorthand manuscript in the Pepysian Library, Magdalene College, Cambridge, by Mynors Bright. With Lord Braybrooke's notes. Edited with additions by Henry B. Wheatley. London: G. Bell, 1893–99.

Robitaille, Marilyn. "Things Women Do: A Performance of *The Parson's Wedding* Revisited." A paper read at the annual South Central Society of Eighteenth Century Studies Conference, February 22, 2002.

PASQUIN, A DRAMATIC SATIRE ON THE TIMES

Author: Henry Fielding
Original date and place of production: March 5, 1736, Little Theatre in the Haymarket, London, England
Characters: Colonel Promise, Lord Place, Mr. Fustian, Mr. Trapwit, Pasquin, Queen of Common-Sense, Queen of Ignorance, Sir Henry Fox-Chace, Sneerwell, Squire Tankard
Filmed versions: None

SUMMARY

Pasquin, a Dramatic Satire on the Times is a powerful satire on contemporary corruption that took the form of two plays in early rehearsals, "The Election" and "The Death of Common-Sense." Backed by a producer named Pasquin, Trapwit and Fustian are presented as the authors of the play who, with the aid of the critic Sneerwell, direct the other characters in performing acts of bribery and other politically corrupt behavior. In "The Election," Fielding sought to ridicule the recently held elections of the members of Parliament and represented the candidates of both parties as bribing their voters. He names his court candidates Lord Place and Colonel Promise, suggesting that they have interests only in property and protecting their own concerns, without attention to keeping their word or their promises. His country candidates similarly reflect their main activities, as Sir Henry Fox-Chace and Squire Tankard show plainly that their chief interests are hunting and drinking rather than running the nation in an honest manner. They are as addicted to these activities as the court candidates are to gambling and seducing women. At the end of Act I, Scene I, Trapwit finds that the actors playing his characters are not realistic enough in their corruption, given the political circumstances of the day, and he coaches them as follows: "You Mr. that act my Lord, bribe a little more openly, if you please, or the audience will lose that joke, and it's one of the strongest in my whole play." As the play progresses, the characters become fully capable of engaging lustily in political corruption of every form.

The second play within *Pasquin*, "The Death of Common-Sense," is a comic allegory that ridicules the professions of law, medicine, and divinity, in which the Queen of Ignorance, surrounded by fiddlers, acrobats, singers, tumblers, and rope dancers, defeats the Queen of Common-Sense. This briefer and simpler play was received with less interest by audiences than "The Election."

CENSORSHIP HISTORY

Henry Fielding intended that his play would motivate political anger, and selected titles to ensure the attention of London's government officials. He could never have imagined that *Pasquin*, followed within months by another satire, *The Historical Register for 1736*, both of which ridiculed Prime Minister Robert Walpole, would result in legislation that would close theaters and result in censorship of the British stage for two centuries. *Pasquin* appeared soon after the close of elections for Parliament, and *Common-Sense* was the title of a political opposition newspaper to which Fielding often contributed that succeeded *Fog's Weekly Journal. Common-Sense* was published by George Lyttleton, Fielding's friend from Eton, and the earl of Chesterfield, an overt opponent of Prime Minister Walpole. The first issue of the publication proclaimed Fielding "an ingenious Dramatic Author" who was so dedicated to the concept of common sense that he had "dignified it with the title of Queen in the second half of his satirical play." The paper experienced harassment from political officials and was eventually forced out of business, but not before increasing the already unfavorable attitude of the government toward *Pasquin* and Fielding. In advance notices of the play placed in the *London Daily Post*, Fielding wrote that "Mr. Pasquin intending to lay about him with great Impartiality, hopes the Town will all attend and very civilly give their neighbours what [they] find belongs to them." A review published in the April 22, 1737, issue of the *Grub-Street Journal* observed, "Such qualifications in the Members, and the occasion and manner of returning them, must needs excite a proper regard and reverence for laws enacted by such Senators." As Fielding biographer Donald Thomas writes, *Pasquin* "exploited and magnified a public weariness of political parties and the cynicism that was widespread," which led to its immediate critical and financial success. In contrast, the conservative *Old Whig* recognized the danger that such popularized political satire might do to corrupt politicians and warned in the April 22, 1736, issue: "There are such strong Strokes in this *Satire*, that if it continues to be follow'd with the crowded Audiences it has now had for above 40 nights together; some Gentlemen will feel its Influence more effectually, and be more hurt in the Esteem of Mankind, than by a Thousand *Examinations*, tho' ever so well writ, to expose their *Schemes*."

Robert Walpole felt such political criticism personally and took steps to ban all such political satire from the English stage, an effort that culminated in the passage of the Act of 1737. The government served warning on Fielding through the publication of several proministerial articles, most pointedly "An Adventurer in Politicks," published in the *Daily Gazeteer* on May 7, 1737, in which Lord Hervey denounced him for undermining the reputation of the British government abroad and endangering its credibility in Europe by making it appear ridiculous on stage at home. The attack also suggested that politics should not be discussed upon the stage and was, instead, to be legitimately discussed only in periodicals and journals. Responding as Pasquin on May 21, 1737, Fielding wrote, "I do not believe foreign Ministers to be so weak, as to remain in an entire stupid Ignorance of what we are doing; nor do I think, if well considered, a more ridiculous Image can enter into the Mind of Man, than that of all the Ambassadors of *Europe* assembling at the *Hay Market* Play-house to learn the Character of our Ministry." He further wrote that ridicule serves as a laxative when a government has a sound constitution, but the "foul Distempers" of ministerial politics are "apt to give a terrible Shock, to work the poor Patient most immoderately; in the Course of which Working, it is ten to one but he beshits his Breeches." The response further inflamed Walpole, who was already working on the legislation that would impose censorship on the English stage for two centuries.

In late May 1737, as the parliamentary session was almost over and members of both houses prepared to disperse, Walpole's followers proposed new legislation to regulate the theater, so that it would become a criminal offense to charge admission for a play unless a copy had been submitted to the Lord

Chamberlain at least 14 days in advance and had been licensed for public performance. Although the government claimed that this was completely alien to the censorship imposed a century earlier by Oliver Cromwell and his followers, all unlicensed theaters were to be closed and only the Drury Lane and Covent Garden, which held royal grants, would remain. Still enraged by *Pasquin*, Walpole made the passage of the act a personal effort, and in speaking of the legislation, he emphasized its merits in preventing debauchery rather than acknowledge his anger toward it as a political satire. As Fowell and Palmer write, "The Act brought Fielding's work as a dramatist to a close, and, indeed, put an end to freedom of political reference on the stage."

FURTHER READING

Coley, W. B. "Henry Fielding and the Two Walpoles." *Philological Quarterly* 45 (1966): 166n.

Conolly, L. W. *The Censorship of English Drama, 1737–1824*. San Marino, Calif.: Huntington Library, 1976.

Fowell, Frank, and Frank Palmer. *Censorship in England*. London: F. Palmer, 1913. Reprint, New York: Benjamin Blom, 1969.

Hume, Robert D. *Henry Fielding and the London Theatre, 1728–1737*. Oxford, England: Clarendon Press, 1988.

Thomas, Donald. *Henry Fielding: A Life*. New York: St. Martin's Press, 1990.

A PATRIOT FOR ME

Author: John Osborne
Original date and place of production: June 30, 1965, Royal Court Theatre, London, England
Characters: Albrecht, Anna, Countess Sophia Delyanoff, Baron von Epp, Ferdy, Figaro, Lady Godiva, Mitzi Heigel, Hilda, Gen. Conrad von Hotzendorf, Second Lt. Viktor Jerzabek, Lt. Stefan Kovacs, Judge Advocate Jaroslav Kunz, Ludwig Max von Kupfer, Mischa Lipschutz, Lt. Col. Ludwig von Mohl, Col. Mischa Oblensky, Paul, Alfred Redl, Dr. Schoepfer, August Siczynski, Stanitsin, Steinbauer, Susanna-Lucia, Maximillian von Taussig, Tsarina
Filmed versions: None

SUMMARY

A Patriot for Me, set in the decaying Austro-Hungarian empire during the early 1900s, deals with the snobbery, racism, and sexual repression of the time and examines how these pressures affect Alfred Redl, a junior-level army officer. The play owes its title to Emperor Franz Joseph II who, upon being told that a man to whom he had been introduced was a "patriot," questioned, "Is he a patriot for me?" Dedicated to army life, Redl rises through the ranks because of his efficiency and dedication to duty as well as his fluency in languages. He is a model soldier, praised by his superiors as the "backbone of his country," as well as a "patriot" and "arch-spycatcher," of whom General von Hotzendorf states, "We can do with all the Redls we can get." For the first third of the play, Redl carouses with his fellow officers and engages in all of the sexual leisure activities with women expected of him by the other soldiers. He searches out and has sex with female prostitutes and suffers from syphilis acquired from one, and he even selects a countess as his mistress. All of these efforts are really meant to cover up what Redl will not admit even to himself, that he truly desires to be loved by and to make love to a man. Redl is an outsider on several fronts, and he must create a façade to hide his lower-class origins and his Jewish heritage, as well as his homosexuality. During his first sexual encounter with a man, a handsome young army private named Paul, a rapture-filled Redl questions himself, "Why didn't I do this before?" Only hours later, however, at the end of Act I, Paul betrays him, at first refusing to answer any questions about himself or his army unit, then by opening the door to four fellow soldiers who beat and kick Redl until he is covered with blood while Paul dresses and pockets Redl's gold cigarette case, cigar case, watch and chain, crucifix, and money. After propping up the bloody and limp Redl against the bed, Paul advises him, "Don't be too upset, love. You'll get used to it."

Act II begins with Redl in attendance at an opulent drag ball in Vienna where "respectable" men from the highest levels of society appear in drag, elaborately coiffed and costumed, as Marie Antoinette, Queen Alexandra, and other women from history parade past their admirers. The ball is hosted by the powerful Baron von Epp. Politicians, businessmen, and community leaders, all of whom condemn effeminate behavior in their daily world, debate and ridicule what the clergy, the medical establishment, and other social institutions say about their transvestite behavior. The guests represent the hierarchy in the outsiders' world of transvestites, from the lowly paid "bum boys," who hope that their charms will catch the attention of rich male patrons, to the discreet and rich drag queens who, Osborne wrote in the stage directions at the beginning of Act II, "remain in absolutely perfect taste." Attendees of the ball also include the men "who positively dislike women" and whose drag costumes are meant to ridicule women, as well as men "who don't even make that effort but wear, like Redl, full-dress uniform and decorations—or evening dress." To guide future directors, Osborne also cautioned: "Remember when they dance you don't find the male ones dancing only with the female ones, but possibly a hussar with a man in evening dress, or two men in evening dress together—or two shepherdesses together." Redl attends the ball with his protector Colonel von Mohl, and meets the Tsarina, a Russian spy who convinces him to betray his country and to become a double agent for the Russian secret service. Although Redl is paid well for his efforts, he cannot end his work as a double agent even when he experiences twinges of patriotic guilt because he is threatened with blackmail. He also enjoys the financial freedom that this new wealth provides.

As Redl grows increasingly cynical, he also is enabled to move about with greater ease in the highest circles of imperial society, becoming more corrupted by what he experiences and sees. He becomes cruel in his personal relationships, and exploits his young lovers without concern for their feelings or future. As Redl's financial status increases and he rises in rank to colonel, his personal world crumbles. The beautiful Countess Sophia, who is also working for the Russians, finds her love for him is not returned and she betrays him by seducing and marrying the handsome young officer Stefan Kovacs, whom Redl loves. Redl continues his decline, until the play ends with his necessary death.

CENSORSHIP HISTORY

Osborne's open treatment of homosexuality in *A Patriot for Me* and criticism of the hypocrisy of the English hierarchy as exhibited in the glitteringly opulent drag ball were more than the censors were willing to tolerate in 1965. Osborne first tried to stage the play in 1964 and submitted the script to the Office of the Lord Chamberlain, which refused to grant the play a license for public performance unless the playwright agreed to make extensive cuts in the dialogue and remove several scenes. He refused, so it was presented as a private club performance "for members only" at the Royal Court Theatre. The censors demanded that Osborne remove three scenes from the play that depicted homosexual behavior: Act I, Scene 1, which takes place in a hotel room after Redl has just had his first sexual experience with the young soldier Paul, in which both are naked; Act II, Scene 1, which depicts the annual drag ball for the ruling-class transvestites in Hapsburg Vienna, circa 1900; and Act III, Scene 5, in which Redl and his young lover Viktor, both naked, have a fight while lying in bed and then Redl viciously taunts Viktor, after which they embrace. Any appearance of Redl in bed with either a man or a woman was also to be removed, and the list of alterations issued by the lord chamberlain's office indicates that in Act I, Scene 4, depicting Redl and Hilda, "This scene is not to be played with the couple both in bed." Further, the stage directions for the scene were to be changed from "She moves over to the wall . . ." to "Presently, he turns away and sits on the bed." In Act III, Scene 1, the censors directed that "The two men must not be in bed together." The censors also demanded that Osborne omit all use of the words *clap* or *crabs* as slang terms for sexually transmitted diseases. Osborne was also directed to omit dialogue that suggests any physical intimacy between men, as in Act III, Scene 1, in which the censors suggested the change from "You'll never know that body like I know it" to "You've not even looked at him, you never will." In addition, the censors also found offensive such lines as "You were born with a silver sabre up your what-not" and "Tears of Christ."

Osborne was unwilling to make the changes required that would have allowed the Royal Court Theatre to obtain a license for public performance of the play, so the theater management withdrew the application for a license and created a "club theater" performance to circumvent the censors. The limited number of attendees to such performances, however, decreased the profit, and Wardle reports that, as a result, *A Patriot for Me* "made a loss of 16,500 pounds, in spite of being acclaimed as the best play of 1965."

FURTHER READING

Bas, Georges, and Victor Bourgy. *British Drama*. France: Longman, 1993.

Brown, John Russell. *Theatre Language: A Study of Arden, Osborne, Pinter and Wesker.* New York: Taplinger Publishing Co., 1973.

The English Stage Company at the Royal Court Theatre Correspondence, 1955–1959, ND. Harry Ransom Humanities Research Center at the University of Texas at Austin. Available online. URL: http://www.hrc.utexas.edu/research/fa/royal.court.html.

Jenkins, Gareth. "The Other Empire." *The Socialist Review* 191 (November 1995). Available online. URL: http://pubs.socialistreviewindex.org.uk/sr191/theatre.htm

Osborne, John. *A Better Class of Person: An Autobiography/John Osborne*. New York: Dutton, 1981.

———. *Four Plays by John Osborne*. New York: Dodd, Mead & Company, 1973.

Trussler, Simon. *John Osborne*. Harlow, England: Longmans, 1969.

Wardle, Irving. "Who's Afraid of the Lord Chamberlain?" *Peter Gill: Playwright, Theatre Director.* Available online. URL: http://dspace.dial.pipex.com/town/parade/abj76/PG/pieces/lord_chamberlain.shtml.

THE PLAYBOY OF THE WESTERN WORLD

Author: John Millington Synge

Original date and place of production: January 26, 1907, Abbey Theatre, Dublin, Ireland

Characters: Honor Blake, Susan Brady, Philly Cullen, Jimmy Farrell, Margaret Flaherty, Michael James Flaherty, Shawn Keogh, Christopher Mahon, Old Mahon, Pegeen Mike, Nelly, Widow Quin, Susan Tansey

Filmed versions: Feature film: *The Playboy of the Western World* (1966, Ireland). Made for television: (1946, 1983, U.K.)

SUMMARY

The Playboy of the Western World, a play in three acts, is set largely in a pub on the coast of County Mayo, Ireland, during the autumn. In Act I, Pegeen Mike, the pub owner's "wild-looking but fine" daughter, bemoans her boring life. When a frightened and exhausted young man, Christy Mahon, appears, throwing out mysterious hints that he wants very much to avoid the police, Pegeen is intrigued. She coaxes Christy to tell her what he is running from, and he confesses that he killed his father and ran away. Rather than condemn him, the inhabitants of the pub hail him as "a daring fellow" and Pegeen suggests that her father hire him as a potboy, to which her father agrees, saying

"Bravery's a treasure in a lonesome place, and a lad would kill his father, I'm thinking, would face a foxy divil with a pitchpike on the flags of hell." Pegeen becomes enamored of Christy, but she soon gains a rival in the form of the 30-year-old Widow Quin, which leads Christy to smugly conclude, "Two fine women fighting for the likes of me—till I'm thinking this night wasn't I a foolish fellow not to kill my father in the years gone by."

The following morning, girls from the village appear to gawk at Christy, and he impresses them by recounting his deeds until Pegeen angrily sends them away. The widow and Pegeen's fiancé arrive, offer him clothes, and beg him to leave, but Christy refuses. The widow proposes that Christy marry her instead, but Christy staggers back in terror as his father walks in the door, alive and with his head bandaged, asking if anyone has seen his pathetic weakling of a son, "a dirty, stuttering lout." The widow hides Christy and sends his father away, then laughs at Christy, telling him, "Well, you're the walking Playboy of the Western World, and that's the poor man you had divided to his breeches belt." Christy refuses her offer of marriage, but promises to pay her well when he becomes master of the pub, if she will keep his secret.

In Act III, Old Mahon returns to the pub while Christy competes triumphantly in village sports. The widow leads Old Mahon away when the crowd returns to the pub, where Christy proposes to Pegeen, as "the crowning prize I'm seeking now," and she accepts, marveling, "And to think it's me is talking sweetly, Christy Mahon, and I the fright of seven townlands for my biting tongue." As the crowd cheers, Old Mahon rushes into the room and begins to beat his son. The disillusioned crowd then jeers, while Christy chases his father with a spade and hits him over the head, knocking him out. The crowd is appalled, and after Pegeen throws a rope around him, they tie up Christy and get ready to turn him over to the police. As he writhes on the ground, Old Mahon crawls back and cuts his son free, then the two leave town. Before leaving, Christy thanks the town for changing his outlook and promises, "I'll go romancing through a romping lifetime from this hour to the dawning of the judgment day." As the Mahons leave, Pegeen laments, "Oh, my grief, I've lost him surely. I've lost the only Playboy of the Western World."

CENSORSHIP HISTORY

The strength of John Millington Synge's reputation among Dublin artistic and political circles and effective advance publicity produced a large opening night audience for *The Playboy of the Western World*. The opening of the play resulted in mixed reviews the following Monday, January 28, 1907. Some reviewers, such as H. S. D., of the *Evening Mail*, praised the brilliance of the comedy and the substance of the theme, but many more condemned Synge's portrayal of the Irish people. *The Freeman's Journal* printed a vehemently condemnatory review of the play and issued charges that would be repeated and endorsed by many later critics. Those who opposed the play called it a "slander against Ireland" and decried what they believed to be "its obscenity, its inauthenticity, and its inappropriateness to the Dublin stage." *The Freeman's Journal* claimed that the play was a "protracted libel upon Irish peasant men and, worse still, upon Irish peasant girlhood," and styled the comedy a "squalid, offensive production." Although the play is a comedy, critics found little humor in Synge's portrayal of the riotous behavior of the citizens of County Mayo and labeled the play a "hideous caricature," whose characters offered "the worst specimen of stage Irishmen." The play was scheduled to run for a week, but indignant critics and citizens called upon the management of the Abbey Theatre to withdraw it immediately, charging that it was "un-Irish." Synge was also roundly criticized for his use of the term *bloody* and "the indiscriminate use of the Holy Name on every possible occasion."

The audience at the second performance of the play, on Monday, January 28, 1907, showed their dissatisfaction by hissing, booing, and stamping their feet as the actors attempted to say their lines. People called out in Gaelic and beat on their seats with sticks, while some loudly sang "God Save Ireland" and others shouted "We won't have it." Partway through the first act, the performance ceased as the police were called. When they arrived, a dozen or more took up positions outside the orchestra pit, while constables were stationed outside the theater, but their presence failed to quiet the protesters, who continued their loud boos and hisses and drowned out the dialogue onstage. Throughout the remainder of the play, the audience shouted, sang, and stamped its feet, fully drowning out the actors while the police stood ready to deal with any physical efforts to halt the play, but none came. Synge sat through the first part of the play but refused the rioters' demands that he speak, pleading that he was ill with influenza. Despite efforts of the audience to intimidate him, Synge vowed at the end of the performance to complete the week-long run of the play and told a reporter for the *Irish Independent*, "There is nothing in it that we have reason to be ashamed of. We simply claim the liberty of Art to choose what subjects we think fit to put on." After the second performance, *The Freeman's Journal* renewed its attack and reminded readers that the hero of the play is "a foul-mouthed scoundrel and parricide" and the play a "very gross and wanton insult to the Irish people."

The third performance, on Tuesday, January 29, 1907, attended by Irish poet and playwright (and the managing director of the Abbey National Theatre) William Butler Yeats was produced under police protection. Before the play began, a group in the audience announced that it was made up of supporters of the play with the "determination to annihilate all opposition," which led to boos and hisses from audience members sitting in the pit. As some left their seats, intent upon a fight, the police filed in and dragged out those responsible for the disturbance. The performance began but was soon halted because the audience stomped its feet and shouted at dialogue to which it objected, and the disorder continued throughout the play.

A capacity audience gathered to attend the fourth performance of the play, on Wednesday, January 30, 1907, and the police presence was increased to cover every available point with a large contingent stationed at the stage door. Although the number of supporters had increased, and included many drunken students from Trinity College, so had the number of protesters. Representatives of one group of protesters stated before the performance began that they were there to "protest immorality on the Irish Stage, and would put down immorality in that theatre." During the production, the noise and disorder continued, as yells, boos, and hisses drowned out the dialogue, but the police ejected many of the interrupters. At the end of the performance, a prominent member of Sinn Fein spoke out against the play and was ejected by the police, who ordered the gallery cleared. The protest continued in the streets, as supporters and opponents of the play marched through the area, followed by large numbers of police to prevent serious disturbance from occurring.

The fifth performance of the play was accompanied by less disorder, although some booing and hissing occurred. When questioned by a reporter for the *Irish Independent*, Lady Gregory, cofounder of the Abbey National Theatre, denied that any significant modifications had been made in the dialogue, although she admitted that "a few adjectives have been taken out, as have been most of the invocations of the Holy Name, but curiously enough the words and phrases to which most objection has been raised have not been interfered with." The police remained inside and outside the theater for the sixth performance of the play, on Friday, February 1, 1907, but no major disturbance occurred. Following the performance, a small group conducted a peaceful demonstration against the play on Marlborough Street, across from the theater.

On February 2, 1907, in an editorial signed by editor Arthur Griffith, the weekly journal *Sinn Fein* revealed that it had rejected advertising from the Abbey Theatre as a protest against the play. When the play went on tour in England in June 1907, the English reviewers praised it, but trouble occurred at several performances, and even more violent protests occurred at performances on the American tour.

Over the years, objections ended and the original dialogue, once found offensive, was restored. In 1968 the Abbey Theatre Company had a special audience with the pope and presented him with a rare edition of the play, bound in white leather.

FURTHER READING

"The Abbey Theatre, *The Playboy of the Western World*." *The Freeman's Journal*, January 28, 1907, p. 10.

H. S. D. "A Dramatic Freak First Night at the Abbey Theatre—Paris Ideas and Parricides." *Evening Mail*, January 29, 1907, p. 7.

Kilroy, James. *The "Playboy" Riots*. Dublin, Ireland: Dolmen Press Limited, 1971.

"The People and the Parricide." *The Freeman's Journal*, January 29, 1907, p. 6.

"*Playboy:* A Fair Hearing Accorded." *Irish Independent,* February 1, 1907, p. 5.

"Police in a Play Howled Down—Extraordinary Scene in The Abbey Theatre Performed in Dumb Show All Over Disapproved Drama." *Irish Independent,* January 29, 1907, p. 5.

"Public Amusements: Abbey Theatre." *Irish Times,* January 28, 1907, p. 7.

THE PLEASURE MAN

Author: Mae West

Original date and place of production: September 17, 1928, Bronx Opera House, Bronx, New York

Characters: Mary Ann Arnold, Ted Arnold, Bridget, Paradise Dupont (aka "Bird of Paradise"), Mrs. Hetherington, Ripley Hetherington, Lizzie, Maggie, Steve McAllister, Edgar Morton, Fritz Otto, Herman Otto, Police Chief, Dolores Randall, Tom Randall, Stanley Smith, Rodney Terrill, Tillie, Toto

Filmed versions: *The Pleasure Man* (1932)

SUMMARY

The Pleasure Man is a play in three acts, with the first two acts set largely in a Midwest vaudeville theater and the third in the drawing room of the apartment of a wealthy former performer. The play opens with a scene in the vaudeville theater, showing the bare stage and the scrubwomen who have just cleaned the dressing rooms. Stagehands are shown moving scenery and trunks and the stage musicians are preparing to rehearse, as the theater manager arrives to review new acts for the current week. Through a series of brief rehearsal performances, the audience is introduced to the main acts: Edgar "It" Morton and his wife, female impersonator Bird of Paradise, and his four "manikins," also female impersonators; dancers Dolores and Tom Randall; dramatic actors Ripley Hetherington and his wife, and the lecherous headliner Rodney Terrill, the "pleasure man" of the title. Terrill flirts continuously with women and uses his charm and personality to make them fall desperately in love with him. He pursues Dolores Randall, whose husband warns her to have nothing to do with "the Pleasure Man." Steve McAllister, the theater manager, warns the women in his show to beware of Terrill, but the stage manager Stanley Smith secretly admires Terrill and tries without success to imitate his techniques with women.

The first act ends with rehearsal over and the show about to begin. The second act is set backstage, with four dressing rooms revealed in which dancers dress for their performance. Actors are shown being made up, girls in an upper dressing room discuss the affair between Terrill and Dolores, and female impersonators disrobe. Applause is heard offstage as acts end. As Terrill waits to go onstage, a worker tells him that a young woman wants to see him. The visitor is Mary Ann Arnold, a woman from the town, who announces that Terrill has made her pregnant and she wants him to keep his promise to marry her. While she pleads, he receives his signal to go on with his act and throws her roughly against the wall, making her faint and fall to the ground. Ted Arnold, Mary Ann's brother and an electrician with the theater, picks her up and places her in a rest room while other actors revive her. Paradise Dupont identifies strongly with Mary Ann, telling her, "You poor kid, you had an awful fall. Like happens to all us poor girls." When Terrill returns from the stage, he goes to Dolores Randall's dressing room, and while the two embrace, her husband walks in and the two men fight.

At the end of the second act, everyone in the cast is invited to a party at the home of the wealthy town resident and former vaudevillian Toto. The third act opens with noise, laughter, and dancing, and with town residents in evening clothes and the female impersonators in gowns. During the height of the party, an intoxicated Tom Randall appears, looking for his wife, who darts with Terrill into a side room. Randall leaves, threatening to kill Terrill. The party ends, and Terrill tries to convince Dolores to spend the night with him, but she refuses and leaves. After a few more drinks, Terrill staggers upstairs to sleep, and his host tells the butler to turn off the lights and retire. Dolores secretly returns and ascends to Terrill's room. Moments later, a loud scream awakens the household and Dolores cries out for help. After Toto sees what has happened to Terrill, he calls the police. During the questioning of all the party guests, the police chief reveals that Terrill died as the result of an operation. The police suspect Randall, but Ted Arnold confesses and tells them that he had not intended for Terrill to die. He had only "wanted to maim him so he would never be attractive to any other man's sister; so he wouldn't use any other woman for his filthy sport."

CENSORSHIP HISTORY

The Pleasure Man was performed during the week of September 17, 1928, without complaint and for a second week also without incident at the Boulevard Theatre in Jackson Heights, Queens, before opening at the Biltmore Theatre on Broadway on October 1, 1928. After the curtain fell the first night on Broadway, the police rounded up the whole cast and took them to jail. Mae West raised the bail to release everyone and to get them to the theater in time for the matinee performance the next day. Actors' Equity warned the performers not to appear in a second performance, but many ignored the warning. During the second act of the second performance, the New York City Police Department raided the theater once again and arrested the cast of 58 actors, all in full stage makeup and costume. Everyone associated with the production was taken to jail, where the actors were released, but Mae West and the producers were charged with presenting "an obscene, indecent, immoral and impure drama."

In an indictment handed down on October 5, 1928, the grand jury stated the play was so indecent and obscene that to do more than name the play in the document "would be offensive to this Court and improper to be spread upon the records thereof." The court charged in a second count that the play contained certain scenes and tableaux "depicting and dealing with the subject of sex degeneracy and sex perversion." In a third count, West and the cast were charged with "contriving and wickedly intending so far as in them lay, to debauch and corrupt the morals of youth and of other persons and to raise and create in their minds inordinate and lustful desires." The case did not go to court until March 17, 1930, by which time indictments against 34 cast members had been dropped, leaving 24 defendants, including West. Despite a spirited prosecution, the defendants were acquitted on April 3, 1930, after the jury was unable to come to a decision and the indictments were dismissed.

West had spent $60,000 for bail and court costs, and the play was not staged again. This was likely a wise move, because the critics were harsh in their reviews of the play, with the bulk of their negative remarks centering on the homosexual content of the play, viewed by some as an "abomination . . . prostitution of the rankest sort," and "an attempt to capitalize on filth and degeneracy." Jack Conway, a columnist for *Variety*, wrote, "It's the queerest show you've ever seen. All of the Queens are in it. . . . The party scene is the payoff. If you see those hussies being introduced to do their specialties, you'd pass out. . . . The host sang a couple of parodies, one going, 'When I go out I look for the moon.' Now I ask you. Another guest very appropriately sang, 'Banquets, Parties, and Balls' and I ask you again." The play remained off the New York stages for 73 years, until the Hourglass Group conducted a benefit public reading on March 17, 2003, at the Culture Project on Bleecker Street. The benefit was for the Actors' Fund Health Initiative.

FURTHER READING

Billington, Michael. *"The Pleasure Man." The Guardian*, February 7, 2000, p. 23.

Ferris, Lesley, ed. "I'm the Queen of the Bitches: Female Impersonation and Mae West's *Pleasure Man.*" *Crossing the Stage: Controversies on Cross Dressing*. New York: Cambridge University Press, 1993.

Kingston, Jeremy. "Come Up and See Me." *The Times*, February 7, 2001, p. 41.

Laufe, Abe. *The Wicked Stage: A History of Theater Censorship and Harassment in the United States*. New York: Frederick Ungar Publishing Co., 1978.

Schlissel, Lillian. "Mae West and the 'Queer Plays.'" *Women's History Review* 11 (January 2002). Available online. URL: http://www.triangle.co.uk/whr/content/pdfs/11/issue11_1.asp.

West, Mae. *Three Plays by Mae West: Sex, The Drag, The Pleasure Man*. Edited by Lillian Schlissel. New York: Routledge Kegan Paul, 1997.

POLLY

Author: John Gay
Original date and place of production: 1777, Little Theatre in the Haymarket, London, England

Characters: Capstan, Cawwawkee, Culverin, Cutlace, Jenny Diver, Mr. Ducat, Mrs. Ducat, Hacker, Laguerre, Morano (MacHeath), Pohetohee, Polly Peachum, Mrs. Trapes, Vanderbluff
Filmed versions: None

SUMMARY

Polly is a musical operetta written in 1729 by John Gay as a sequel to his extremely successful THE BEGGAR'S OPERA. The focus of the play is Polly Peachum, who in the earlier play married the highwayman Macheath against her father's wishes, then watched helplessly as her father framed Macheath and had him imprisoned. Although Macheath won temporary freedom by romancing the warden's daughter Lucy, he still loved Polly. *Polly* takes place some years later in the West Indies, where Polly has traveled to find Macheath, who has been transported with other prisoners to avoid hanging in England. Polly is hired to work as a maid on the plantation owned by the very wealthy Mr. Ducat, whom Mrs. Trapes counsels in the first scene to become more prodigal and profligate as the "fashion that is among all Ranks of people. . . . 'Tis genteel to be in debt. Your luxury should distinguish you from the vulgar. You cannot be too expensive in your pleasures." Mrs. Trapes preys upon Mr. Ducat's feelings of insecurity regarding his lowly birth despite his great wealth. She acts as a procuress, and she has acquired three new ladies to work in the house with the aim that one will earn her a hefty commission by becoming Ducat's mistress. When he seems put off by her suggestion, Mrs. Trapes urges him to "fling yourself into polite taste with a spirit," and he assures her that he will do so: "Sure, you cannot think me such a clown as to be really in love with my wife! We are not so ignorant here as you imagine; why, I married her in a reasonable way, only for her money."

After striking a bargain, Mrs. Trapes meets with the girl whom her servant has selected as the prettiest of the newcomers, Polly Peachum, whom she knows from London. She learns that Mr. Peachum was hanged seven months earlier for offenses committed because "he was in too much haste to be rich," and Mrs. Peachum's death occurred soon after. Freed from their watchful eyes, Polly has traveled to the West Indies to find Macheath, only to learn from Mrs. Trapes that a year and a half earlier Macheath had "robb'd his master, run away from the Plantation and turn'd pyrate." He has taken with him as companion and lover Jenny Diver, a prostitute whom Polly also knew from London. Mrs. Trapes advises Polly to put all thoughts of Macheath out of her head, because "he would disown you, for like an upstart he hates an old acquaintance," and to pass herself off as a widow of genteel background. After promising to look after Polly, Mrs. Trapes meets again with Ducat and demands 100 pistoles for Polly, whom she claims to have had "to inveigle away from her relations! she too herself was exceeding difficult. And I can assure you, to ruin a girl of severe education is no small addition to the pleasure of our fine gentlemen." Ducat agrees and meets with Polly, but she refuses to comply with his sexual advances. When he admonishes her as "an obstinate slut," and threatens "if you refuse play in the bed-chamber, you shall go work in the fields among the planters" she responds that her freedom may be lost but "you cannot rob me of my vertue and integrity." Despite Polly's protestations, Mrs. Ducat is misled into believing that Polly has designs on her husband, and she insults the young woman, stating that she hates "all strumpets, for they are smugglers in love, that ruin us fair traders in matrimony." Polly's sincerity and story of her unhappy marriage gradually overcome Mrs. Ducat's anger. As the plantation prepares its defense in anticipation of a raid by pirates, Mrs. Ducat agrees to help Polly escape in disguise to find Macheath.

Act II opens with Polly disguised as a man, wearing clothing supplied by Mrs. Ducat. When pirates Capstern, Hacker, Culverin, Laguerre, and Cutlace confront Polly, believing she is a young man, she professes her desire to join them and their leader, Morano, whom she does not recognize as her beloved Macheath because he has darkened his skin as part of the masquerade. The men believe Polly to be a rich plantation owner's son and they present her to their leader Morano/Macheath and Jenny, who has tried to convince him to rob his crew and to return in disguise to England. Jenny views the disguised Polly as another man to conquer, and she uses all of her charms and a few kisses to try to make Polly like her. Unwilling to reveal that she is a woman, Polly returns Jenny's kisses, leading her to state, "Consider, young man, if I have put myself in your power, you are in mine." When Polly refuses to take the familiarities further, Jenny leaves her and tells Morano/Macheath that she has suffered an attempt upon her virtue.

The action then moves to the results of the pirate raid upon the island, which has been defended by a coalition of the planters and Indians. The pirates return with a prisoner, "the Indian prince Cawwawkee," whom Morano orders his men to torture in order to learn where gold and silver are stored. Polly and Cawwawkee are imprisoned in a cottage, where they form a bond that leads Polly to suggest to several of the pirates that they might be rewarded handsomely if they were to free Cawwawkee. In the Indian Camp, the leader Pohetohee, Cawwawkee's father, speaks with Ducat and others and finds that the Europeans are unwilling to battle the pirates and blame their lack of spirit on "human infirmities." Pohetohee is grateful when the pirate deserters arrive with Cawwawkee and, based on his son's recommendation, appoints Polly—"this young man"—to accompany the prince into war. As the Indians engage in battle with Morano and his remaining men, Ducat and other plantation owners hang back, in the belief that only the common soldiers fight "but 'tis the officers that run away with the most fame as well as pay." The pirates are beaten back, and the still-disguised Polly captures Morano and places him under guard until Pohetohee arranges an execution. When she reveals that she is a woman, but also states that she is married, Cawwawkee becomes mournful. Jenny pleads for Morano's life, knowing that he has hidden treasure that will make her rich, and she reveals his true identity, which leads Polly to also plead for his life. When Ducat arrives to confirm that Macheath has been executed, Polly begins to wail in despair. Recognizing her, Ducat tries to take her back but is stopped by the Indians. The play ends with Cawwawkee's profession of love for Polly. He says he intends to make her his princess.

CENSORSHIP HISTORY

The success of *The Beggar's Opera* in 1728 inspired Gay to work on a sequel the following year. Although the Licensing Act would not be passed until 1737, the Lord Chamberlain, Charles Fitzroy, duke of Grafton, was already working with Prime Minister Robert Walpole to create what the government would view as a workable system of censorship. Persuaded by Walpole, who believed himself to be caricatured in the character of Ducat, King George II gave express instructions to Grafton to suppress *Polly* as the play was about to begin rehearsals. Gay writes in the preface to the printed version of the play, published by Jeffrey Walker in 1729, that before sending the play to the censors for review he had submitted it to "several Persons of the greatest distinction and veracity" and they had approved the content. On Saturday, December 7, 1728, Gay met with Grafton and asked "to have the honour of reading the Opera to his Grace," but the Lord Chamberlain told him to leave the play. Gay expected to receive a response by Monday, December 9, and he grumbles in the preface to the play, "I had it not till Thursday December 12, when I receiv'd from his Grace with his answer; that it was not allow'd to be acted, but commanded to be suprest. This was told me in general without any reasons assign'd, or any charge against me of my having given any particular offence." The playwright protested that he and his play were innocent of the charges of which others told him he had been accused: "I have been charged with writing immoralities; that it is fill'd with slander and calumny against particular great persons, and that Majesty itself is endeavour'd to be brought into ridicule and contempt." An indignant Gay writes that he could no longer bear to be so falsely accused and had decided to print the play, thus giving up "all present views of profit which might accrue from the Stage."

The suppression of *Polly* became a political issue after the play was printed, and members of the government and aristocracy took sides. As authors Frank Fowell and Frank Palmer report, the duchess of Marlborough paid £100 for a copy. The duchess of Queensberry, who had enlisted subscribers for the play within the palace, was so persistent in her defense of Gay and in attempting to convince King George II to cancel the order of the lord chamberlain that she was dismissed from court. Numerous other members of the court supported Gay. The ban against performances of the play made *Polly* famous and increased sales far beyond what Gay might have expected, while it also heated existing political controversies. In a letter to Jonathan Swift dated March 19, 1729, satirist John Arbuthnot observed,

THE PRESIDENT IS DEAD

The inoffensive John Gay is now become one of the obstructions to the peace of Europe, the terror of the ministers, the chief author of the *Craftsmen*, and all seditious pamphlets which have been published against the government. He has got several turned out of their places; the greatest ornament of the court banished from it for his sake; another great lady in danger of being chasseé [ousted] likewise; but seven or eight duchesses pushing forward like the ancient cirumcelliones [first monks to carry on a brisk traffic in spurious bones of martyrs] in the church, who shall suffer martyrdom on his account first. He is the darling of the city.

The play remained banned from the stage until George Colman presented an edited version for performance at the Little Theatre in the Haymarket in 1777.

FURTHER READING

Conolly, L. W. *The Censorship of English Drama, 1737–1824.* San Marino, Calif.: Huntington Library, 1976.
Fowell, Frank, and Frank Palmer. *Censorship in England.* London: F. Palmer, 1913. Reprint, New York: Benjamin Blom, 1969.
Fuller, John. "Cibber, *The Rehearsal at Goatham*, and the Suppression of *Polly*." *Review of English Studies* 13 (May 1962): 125–134.
Gay, John. *The Poetical Works of John Gay, Including* Polly, The Beggar's Opera, *and Selections from the Other Dramatic Work.* Edited by G. C. Faber. New York: Russell & Russell, 1969.

THE PRESIDENT IS DEAD

Author: Paul Shyre
Original date and place of production: None [written in 1969]
Characters: John Wilkes Booth, Abraham Lincoln, Mary Todd Lincoln, Dr. Samuel Mudd, John Parker, Edwin M. Stanton
Filmed versions: None

SUMMARY

The President Is Dead focuses on the assassination of President Abraham Lincoln and its aftermath. Shyre claimed to follow historical accounts in creating the plot. The play dramatizes the shooting of the president by John Wilkes Booth, as it occurred on April 14, 1865, at 10:15 P.M., then follows the efforts to keep Lincoln alive and the attempts to capture Booth. John Parker, Lincoln's bodyguard and a member of the Metropolitan Police Force, leaves his post and Booth sees his opportunity. He opens the door to the State Box, where Henry Rathbone and his wife Clara sat with the president and Mrs. Lincoln. The Rathbones were last-minute guests of the Lincolns at the performance; General Ulysses Grant had canceled. They watch in horror as Booth shoots Lincoln in the back of the head at close range. Booth struggles with Rathbone, stabs him in the arm, and jumps approximately 11 feet to the stage below, shouting "Sic Semper Tyrannis" ("As Always to Tyrants") as he hits the floor. Mrs. Lincoln screams, and Booth flashes his knife at the audience, making his way across the stage in front of the audience. Lincoln nears death, while the dialogue of Secretary of War Edwin Stanton with other characters suggests strongly that he had ordered Grant to refuse the theater invitation, that he had refused to release from duty the powerful Major Thomas T. Eckert after Lincoln asked for him as a bodyguard, and that he had issued orders for Booth to be killed rather than captured. Shyre's play also suggests that Vice President Andrew Johnson knew the conspirators were meeting at Surratt's Tavern to plot the assassination.

CENSORSHIP HISTORY

In 1969 Paul Shyre charged that the board of directors of the Ford's Theater Society, in Washington, D.C., had canceled plans to present performances of *The President Is Dead*, after they had made a commitment to opening the play in November 1969. In early August 1969 Shyre received a letter in which the president of the theater society board stated that it was withdrawing the offer to stage the drama because it "would be inappropriate for Ford's Theater." The playwright has said that the performances were banned because his play showed "a similarity between the assassination of President Lincoln and the murder of President Kennedy as well as the similarity to assassinations of other prominent people." Shyre also felt that the play had been rejected because his characterization of Edwin Stanton suggested that the secretary of war was "too much of a villain." F. C. Hewitt, president of the theater society, denied the charges of censorship and explained that, after initially accepting the play, the society had begun to question the historical accuracy of Shyre's portrayal of Stanton and his involvement in the assassination. Based upon a consensus of board opinion, Theodore Mann, the director of the theater, decided that the theater should not produce the play.

FURTHER READING

Harris, Richard Hough. *Modern Drama in America and England, 1950–1970: A Guide to Information Sources*. Detroit, Mich.: Gale Research, 1982.

Laufe, Abe. *The Wicked Stage: A History of Theater Censorship and Harassment in the United States*. New York: Frederick Ungar Publishing Co., 1978.

Szilassy, Zoltan. *American Theater of the 1960s*. Carbondale: Southern Illinois University Press, 1986.

PRESS CUTTINGS

Author: George Bernard Shaw
Original date and place of production: July 9, 1909, Royal Court Theatre, London, England

Characters: Prime Minister Balsquith, Mrs. Banger, Lady Corinthia Fan-
shawe, Mrs. Farrell, General Mitchener, The Orderly
Filmed versions: None

SUMMARY

Press Cuttings, subtitled "a topical sketch compiled from the editorial and correspondence columns of the daily papers," consists of one long act set in the
office of General Mitchener in the War Office. Women have surrounded the
government buildings, carrying placards and chanting repeatedly throughout
the play, "Votes for women!" As the general directs the orderly to secure the
building, a woman rushes into the building and horrifies the general by taking off her tailor-made skirt to reveal a pair of fashionable trousers. Mitchener demands that she stop, saying, "You must not undress in my presence. I
protest." He is shocked to see that the "woman" is really Prime Minister Balsquith, who has found that "the only way that the Prime Minister of England
can get from Downing Street to the War Office is by assuming this disguise;
shrieking 'Votes for women'; and chaining himself to your doorscraper." The
two discuss the recent attempt at imposing martial law on the suffragists by
"drawing a cordon round Westminster at a distance of two miles," a move
that Mitchener calls "a masterpiece of strategy." Balsquith informs him that
the women won't go, so the commander-in-chief, General Sandstone, has
ordered the soldiers to "Shoot them down." Mitchener also favors this plan,
stating, "Shoot a few, promptly and humanely; and there will be an end at
once of all resistance and of all the suffering that resistance entails." When
Balsquith protests, Mitchener blusters that the English government has
turned to the army to control the situation and that he is going to use "military methods." To Balsquith's protest that he depends upon votes to retain his
position, the general advises, "Have no next election," and to, instead, establish a magistry: "It answers perfectly in India. If anyone objects, shoot him
down." The two share stories about other prominent figures, and exhibit
through the stories the corruption of British society. Mitchener also plans to
face the protesting women and wants to do so in full dress uniform, but his
charwoman Mrs. Farrell, the mother of eight children, tells him he will have
to borrow a uniform from General Sandstone because Mitchener's are in the
waxworks in the Chamber of Glory.

They are joined by representatives of the Anti-Suffragette League, Mrs.
Banger, a physically powerful woman, and Lady Corinthia, a former music-
hall entertainer, who have arrived to inform the general that their group plans
to fight the suffragists and force them to comply with the recent government
demand that they move outside of a two-mile radius of Westminster. Even
though the government has seen the impractical side of the effort, members
of the Anti-Suffragette League have armed themselves with guns and swords
to begin the battle. When Mitchener reminds the women of the latest proclamation, under which "women are strictly forbidden to carry chains, padlocks,

tracts on the franchise, or weapons of any sort," Lady Corinthia threatens him with her revolver and Mrs. Banger tells him that her grandmother fought at Waterloo and that she "slew five Egyptians with my own hand at Kassassin, where I served as a trooper" while disguised as a man. Ridiculing the suffragists' fight for the vote, Mrs. Banger declares that what women really need is the right to military service and she intends to confront General Sandstone with that demand. As support for her request, she declares, "All the really strong men of history have been disguised women." Mitchener observes that female rulers "often show all the feminine weaknesses. Queen Elizabeth, for instance." Mrs. Banger counters, "Nobody who has studied the history of Queen Elizabeth can doubt for a moment that she was a disguised man." As they insult each other, Mitchener concludes that he much prefers the idea of giving women the vote to dealing with the Anti-Suffragettes, especially after Mrs. Banger flings into the air his orderly, whom Mitchener had directed to "put her out."

As Mrs. Banger searches for Sandstone, Lady Corinthia discourses with Mitchener, whom she annoys with her insistence that the country should be run by "lovely and accomplished women" with "artistic talent" who can wield "refining influence over the men." She denounces as "dowdies" most of English womanhood, including the suffragists, but Mitchener reminds her that "the average Englishwoman is a dowdy and never has half a chance of becoming anything else. . . . If we had to choose between pitching all the dowdies into the Thames and pitching all the lovely and accomplished women, the lovely ones would have to go." Lady Corinthia leaves in disgust, and the orderly appears to announce that Mrs. Banger has locked the door of General Sandstone's room "and she's sitting on his head until he signs a proclamation for women to serve in the army." Rather than throw her out, Sandstone has become enamored of her, finding at last his ideal mate, "the perfect soldierly woman." Mitchener calls for Mrs. Farrell and proposes to her, because she is "the only woman in the country whose practical ability and force of character can maintain her husband in competition with the husband of Mrs. Banger."

CENSORSHIP HISTORY

Shaw's success in outsmarting the English censors in producing his play THE SHEWING UP OF BLANCO POSNET led him to create *Press Cuttings*, which he knew deliberately violated the rule for plays licensed for public performance: "No offensive personalities, as representation of living persons to be permitted on the stage." At the beginning of May 1909, Shaw gave the one-act farce to Ben Iden Payne, manager of the Gaiety Theatre, who submitted the play to Examiner of Plays George Alexander Redford. The censor refused to license the original version and returned the play to allow the author "the opportunity of eliminating all personalities, expressed or implied." The censors believed that Shaw had named his army commander-in-chief General Mitchener as a caricature of the public figure General Horatio Herbert Kitchener, who was a viscount and commander of the British forces in India until 1909, when he was appointed to the position of field marshal. Shaw biographer Michael Holroyd writes that Shaw contended privately that he had intended no association between his general and the field marshal and had, instead, used as his model the duke of Cambridge, commander-in-chief of the British army and a brother of Queen Victoria. The censors also objected to the naming of the ridiculous Prime Minister Balsquith, believing that Shaw had combined the names of two prominent public figures, that of Conservative prime minister Arthur Balfour with that of Herbert Henry Asquith, leader of the Liberal opposition, to ridicule both. In response to the charge, Shaw replied that the figure of Balsquith was neither Balfour nor Asquith "and cannot in the course of nature be both."

Shaw was angered by the censor's decision because of its blatantly political bias. In 1904 the censors licensed without question his play *John Bull's Other Island*, which contained references to Liberal political figures, and he had expected that a play of the same kind in which, as Fowell and Palmer note, "the politicians ridiculed were on the other side," would also be licensed. After the examiner of plays refused a license for *Press Cuttings*, Shaw wrote in an editorial,

> The objection is clearly to my politics, and not to my personalities. The fact is that I have to ascertain what the Censor's politics are before I know whether the play will pass. If he is a Liberal, apparently I have to ridicule Conservatives, if I ridicule politicians at all, and *vice versa*. It is exceedingly difficult to find out sometimes what the mind of the Censor is or what his politics are.

With friends, Shaw created the Civic and Dramatic Guild and presented two private performances for members of the guild at the Royal Court Theatre, the first on July 9, 1909. Once Shaw had achieved his goal of evading the prohibition, he made alterations to the play that would satisfy the censors, renaming Mitchener and Balsquith as Bones and Johnson, names taken from the ringmaster and clown of the then-popular Christy Minstrels. Ben Iden Payne resubmitted the play to Redford, who approved a license for the play. The first public performance occurred at Payne's Gaiety Theatre in Manchester on August 17, 1909, where *Press Cuttings* played to a capacity audience.

FURTHER READING

Fowell, Frank, and Frank Palmer. *Censorship in England*. London: F. Palmer, 1913. Reprint, New York: Benjamin Blom, 1969.

Holroyd, Michael. *Bernard Shaw: A Biography*. Vol. 2. *The Pursuit of Power*. New York: Random House, 1989.

Shaw, George Bernard. *Press Cuttings: A Topical Sketch Compiled from the Editorial and Correspondence Columns of the Daily Papers. A Play*. London: Archibald Constable & Co., 1909.

A RAISIN IN THE SUN

Author: Lorraine Hansberry
Original date and place of production: March 11, 1959, Ethel Barrymore Theatre, New York, New York
Characters: Joseph Asagai, Bobo, Karl Lindner, George Murchison, Beneatha Younger, Lena Younger (Mama), Travis Younger, Walter Lee Younger
Filmed versions: *A Raisin in the Sun* (1961)

SUMMARY

In *A Raisin in the Sun*, Lorraine Hansberry creates a group portrait of the Youngers, a family composed of powerful individuals whose dreams and frustrations are typical of people of all races during the decade following World War II. The title is from the poem "A Dream Deferred" by Langston Hughes, which asks "What happens to a dream deferred? . . . Does it dry up like a raisin in the sun?" The characters in Hansberry's play have all had their dreams deferred. Lena, or Mama, the widowed mother; her daughter Beneatha, a medical student; Beneatha's brother Walter Lee, a struggling chauffeur; and Walter's wife, Ruth, and their young son live in a cramped apartment on Chicago's South Side, and they dream of better days. The family situation is brought to a crisis when Lena receives the first real money they have ever had, a $10,000 life insurance payment for her late husband, which provides the opportunity to buy a house of their own. Walter Lee struggles against the decision, but they buy a home in a white neighborhood and must then contend with the hostility of their new white neighbors who threaten their security and even their self-respect.

The characters embody ideals typical of most Americans of the period, yet they remain socially apart. Walter Lee typifies the upward-moving American male who honors ruthless capitalism and castigates African Americans in general for a lack of shrewdness in business. Although he denounces wealthy people who consider themselves superior, he is willing to use flattery to make the wealthy assist him, and he wants to give his son a better life. Ruth, Walter Lee's wife, behaves like a stereotypical housewife, while his sister Beneatha exhibits the frivolous values and behavior usually associated with immature and pampered American college students. Lena Younger is an embodiment of the traditionally affirmed American values of decency, Christianity, and hard work that are associated with the Puritan ethic.

Their values are indistinct from those of middle-class white families, yet Mr. Lindner, a white man, fails to recognize this as he tries to dissuade them from moving into Clybourne Park, a white community. In an ironic speech meant to convince the Youngers to change their minds, he recounts the attitudes of the whites in the neighborhood who are "hard working, honest people who don't really have much but those little homes and a dream of the kind of community they want to raise their children in." The Youngers do not seek to purchase the home in a white community as a means of achieving social integration; rather, Lena purchases the house because it is a wise investment in her effort to improve the lives of her children, especially because comparable houses in black neighborhoods cost more. Walter Lee supports this position when he affirms the Youngers' determination to enter the Clybourne Park community: "We don't want to make no trouble for nobody or fight no causes—but we will try to be good neighbors." Throughout the play, Walter Lee struggles to assert his manhood in the face of his economic dependence upon both his white employer and his mother. At the end of the play, Walter Lee is entrusted with the authority to affirm the family's determination to move from the ghetto, and he shows signs that he is ready to accept his mother's concept of manhood as the moral leader of the family.

CENSORSHIP HISTORY

The 1959 Broadway production of *A Raisin in the Sun*, which ran on Broadway for 530 performances, made theatrical history. At that time, most theater producers did not believe that a black Broadway audience existed, and they felt strongly that there was no commercial viability for a serious black play, nor would there be a significant "crossover" white audience for a play about African Americans. *A Raisin in the Sun* changed their thinking when it became an all-out commercial and critical success. Lorraine Hansberry, previously an unknown 29-year-old playwright, won the Best Play of the Year Award for 1959 from the New York Drama Critics Circle, becoming the first black author and only the fifth woman to do so. The play was produced without incident in major northern cities, but few cities in the South launched productions until the middle 1960s, although no overt reports of banning the play exist. The movie version of *A Raisin in the Sun* did experience censorship, particularly in regard to the bitterness expressed by Walter Lee toward white society. Several sections were trimmed from the 1961 film adaptation because censors found some material too provocative for white audiences.

The most rigorous efforts to ban *A Raisin in the Sun* have been directed toward the written rather than the performed versions of the play. The American Library Association Committee on Intellectual Freedom reports that in 1979, the Ogden (Utah) School District restricted circulation of the play in the school library to students with written permission from their parents and removed the book from the curriculum. An antipornography organization had openly criticized the teaching of the play, citing the references to abortion that appear briefly in the text. In Merrimack, New Hampshire, in 1956, the school board enacted Merrimack School Board Policy 6540, titled the "Prohibition of Alternate Lifestyle Instruction," which school board members explained stemmed from their wish "to keep from students any non-negative views about homosexuality." The policy was broadly applied to extend to works of literature written by gay people, those depicting gay characters or same-gender relationships, and those which discuss or depict gender ambiguity. *A Raisin in the Sun* was among works singled out by the policy, because the author has been gay-identified since her death. (Although married to Robert Nemiroff in 1953, Hansberry later had intimate relationships with women, as well. Around 1957, Hansberry joined the Daughters of Bilitis, the pioneering lesbian organization based in San Francisco, and began receiving their journal, *The Ladder.* Two lengthy letters were published in *The Ladder* in May and August of 1957 under the initials L.H.N. and L.N., respectively. Both are believed to have been written by Hansberry. The letters applauded the growing West Coast homophile movement and mused on butch-femme culture and the gaps between lesbians and gay men. The August letter asserted, "Homosexual persecution has at its roots not only social ignorance, but a philosophically active anti-feminist dogma.")

To overturn Policy 6540, a guidance counselor in the Merrimack district who was also a parent filed a complaint with the U.S. District Court in the District of New Hampshire to challenge the constitutionality of the policy under the First and Fourteenth Amendments to the U.S. Constitution. The complaint charged that "by voting for 6540, those Board members sought to deny students exposure to differing viewpoints with which the Board members disagree. In so doing, defendants sought to prescribe for the Merrimack schools what shall be the orthodox government-approved opinion in politics, religion, sexuality, and other matters of opinion." The school board revoked the policy in 1958, the following year.

FURTHER READING

Cheney, Anne. *Lorraine Hansberry.* New York: Twayne Publishers, 1984.

Hansberry, Lorraine. "A Raisin in the Sun." In *Four Contemporary Plays.* Edited by Bennett Cerf. New York: Vintage Books, 1961.

McKissack, Patricia C., and Frederick L. McKissack. *Young, Gifted, and Black.* New York: Holiday House, 1998.

"A Raisin in the Sun." Newsletter on Intellectual Freedom. American Library Association. May 1979, p. 49.

Trotts, Nancy Roberts. "Anti-Gay Policy Has Students Feeling Cheated, Teachers Fearing for Their Jobs." The Associated Press, March 3, 1996. The P.E.R.S.O.N. Project Homepage. Available online at URL: http://www.youth.org/loco/PERSONproject/Alerts/States/NewHampshire/policy.html.

Turner, Darwin T. "Visions of Love and Manliness in a Blackening World: Dramas of Life since 1953." *The Black Scholar* 25 (spring 1995): 2–9.

THE RESPECTFUL PROSTITUTE (*LA PUTAIN RESPECTUEUSE*)

Author: Jean-Paul Sartre
Original date and place of production: November 8, 1946, Théâtre Antoine, Paris, France

Characters: Fred, James, John, Lizzie, the Negro, the Senator
Filmed versions: *La Putain respectueuse* (1952, France)

SUMMARY

The Respectful Prostitute is a one-act play in two scenes that takes place in a furnished room somewhere in the American South. The play opens as Lizzie, a prostitute, has just opened the door to the Negro, who pleads with her to tell the white men who are hunting him that he has done nothing. He also pleads with her to hide him because the men will lynch him if they find him. As the scene unfolds, the audience learns that while traveling by train Lizzie had been harassed by four white men, one of them the nephew of U.S. senator Clarke, identified as "The Senator" in the play. Two African-American men were present in the train and, when a fight ensued, the senator's nephew Thomas shot and killed one of them while the other, who is now speaking with Lizzie, escaped. When the train stopped, the white men claimed that the two African Americans had tried to rape Lizzie and that Thomas was simply protecting her. The media attention is great, and the Clarke family has its status to protect, so they try to convince Lizzie to lie and to support their story. Confronted by the desperate and pleading man, Lizzie promises that she will tell the truth.

A short time later, Fred Clarke, the senator's son and cousin of the murderer, appears as a client for Lizzie's favors. The next morning, Fred offers Lizzie money both for their sex and to lie about the murder. He points out the status of his family, how much public good they have done, and their great value to the nation in regard to the future good they will do, in contrast to the Negro, who will contribute nothing. Lizzie staunchly resists his argument and refuses to sign a false statement, even when two police officers, John and James, arrive to coerce her. The Senator also appears. He is a slick politician whose words profess to support her honesty and sense of right, yet he plays upon her sympathy and speaks of the heartbreak that her decision will bring to his sister, the mother of the murderer. Touched by his rhetoric, Lizzie signs the false statement, but her conscience spurs her to recant immediately, although it is too late.

When the white men leave, the Negro reappears and begs her to hide him, which Lizzie attempts to do, but Fred appears. He is sexually attracted to her, even while her low status repulses him, and he is also proud that she has praised his lovemaking, asking repeatedly, "Is it true I gave you a thrill?" He discovers the Negro hiding in Lizzie's room, and chases him with a revolver, but his shots do not find their mark. When Fred returns to Lizzie, even though she resists, he tells her that she will become his mistress and that he will visit her three times weekly "after dark." In return, she will be well taken care of but have to submit entirely to his will: "You'll have nigger servants, and more money than you ever dreamed of; but you will have to put up with all my whims, and I'll have plenty!" As Lizzie agrees to the arrangement, Fred pats her cheek and declares, "Then everything is back to normal again."

CENSORSHIP HISTORY

Sartre wrote *The Respectful Prostitute* after his first trip to the United States in 1945, during which he observed the racial inequities in major cities. The trip was organized by the U.S. State Department, and Sartre was accompanied by a number of French journalists and writers. In an article published in *Le Figaro*, Sartre wrote of the African Americans that "they are third-class citizens" constituting "an essentially rural proletariat." He detailed in disapproval the extent to which segregation was practiced in the South, writing "These pariahs have absolutely no political rights." The incident that motivated the writing of *The Respectful Prostitute* occurred while the French visitors were traveling with an interpreter by Pullman railroad car from Baltimore to Philadelphia. As Sartre and his group, including Stéphane Pizella, who later wrote of the incident, sat in the dining car eating dinner, two black army officers who entered the car and asked the maître d' for a table were curtly refused, which disturbed the French group. Their American interpreter, aware of how the incident might be portrayed in Europe, approached the maître d' and asked discreetly that he reconsider the decision. As a concession, the officers were given a table at the back of the car and the maître d' drew a pink curtain between them and the rest of the diners.

The Respectful Prostitute was first performed in the United States at the Cort Theatre in New York City, from March 16, 1948, through December 18, 1948, on a double bill with Thornton Wilder's *The Happy Journey from Trenton to Camden*. Sartre's play was well received by critics and ran for 318 performances. When it then toured to major cities in 1949, Chicago authorities used the power granted to them under a municipal censorship ordinance passed in 1907 to withhold a permit for performance of the play. The law required that all entertainment be reviewed by a board of censors and receive a permit issued by the Chicago Police Department. Plays containing subject matter that was "objectionable," that portrayed "unlawful scenes," or that had the tendency to "outrage public morals," were not granted permits. The Chicago censors refused to issue a permit to *The Respectful Prostitute* mainly because it presented "a tract against racism in the States" and constituted a threat to the public peace. To bolster their position, the authorities referred to instances of "immorality" in the play. They note that the play portrays a prostitute who taunts one of her clients (Fred) by shouting, "That's what I call a good lay" and then demands that he look at her legs and breasts. Further instances in which Lizzie shouts "A fine bitch!" and Fred swears were also deemed too shocking for Chicago audiences. The censors did not offer producers the opportunity to modify the language for reconsideration, because the basic antiracism message, to which they primarily objected, would remain. Officials in Philadelphia also barred the play from performances, citing similar objections to "obscenity" and "immorality."

FURTHER READING

Cohen-Solal, Annie. *Sartre: A Life.* Translated by Anna Cancogni. New York: Pantheon Books, 1987.

Elsom, John. *Erotic Theatre.* New York: Taplinger Publishing Co., 1974.

Jack, Homer. *A Blue Pencil over Chicago: The Fine Art of Censorship.* Chicago: Chicago Division, American Civil Liberties Union, 1949.

Mikva, Abner J. "Chicago: Citadel of Censorship." *Focus/Midwest* 2 (March–April 1963): 10, 16–17.

Myers, Paul. "The Blue Hand of Censorship." *Theatre Time* 1 (summer 1949): 62–64.

Pizella, Stéphane. *Les Nuits Bout du Monde.* Paris: André Bonne, 1953.

Sartre, Jean-Paul. "Ce que j'ai appris du problème noir." *Le Figaro,* June 16, 1945, pp. 23–25.

REVELRY

Author: Maurine Dallas Watkins
Original date and place of production: September 12, 1927, Theatre Masque, New York, New York
Characters: Dan Lurcock, Charles Madrigal, Willis Markham, Jeff Sims
Filmed versions: None

SUMMARY

Revelry was adapted for the stage by Maurine Dallas Watkins from the novel of the same name written by Samuel Hopkins Adams following her highly successful 1926 Broadway production *Chicago.* The play, which the author professed was a fictional examination of a corrupt federal government, portrays a U.S. president who becomes deeply involved with graft and finds that the only way out is suicide. In reality, the play is a powerful attack on the administration of President Warren G. Harding and his "Ohio Gang."

The weak, easily corrupted president of *Revelry* is surrounded by a group of disreputable characters who have followed him from Ohio to the White House, where they engage in influence peddling. Markham, who relies on this group for his entertainment as well as advisement, meets regularly at the Crow's Nest to play poker, the name the play gives to the real house on Washington's H Street where Harding played poker with his cronies. Dan Lurcock, the corrupt right-hand man to whom Markham owes his rapid political success, is a thin disguise for Attorney General Harry Daugherty. In the play, Markham and Lurcock first meet in a hotel yard while both are having their shoes shined, as did Harding and Daugherty. The character of Jeff Sims, Lurcock's emotionally unstable friend, has the same characteristics and habit of showering bystanders with saliva as those of Daugherty intimate Jess Smith.

Markham becomes his party's nominee after Lurcock convinces party leaders that he is a "ductile personality." As president, Markham displays the same awe of intellectuals in his cabinet that Harding expressed, and he is a lazy, compliant politician who is easily manipulated by the cleverer Daugherty.

As corruption in the administration grows, congressional investigators increase the pressure on Markham and his men, who look for a scapegoat. They find one in Sims, who is found dead under suspicious circumstances that are hastily labeled "suicide," reflecting the similar real-life death of Jess Smith and its aftermath. Markham becomes increasingly worried by the possible humiliation of a scandal and, after accidentally swallowing a handful of bichloride-of-mercury tablets instead of a stomach pill, he decides to accept his potential death rather than chance the future by calling a doctor. His death is then covered up by a former Senate colleague, now an agent of the Justice Department in charge of the investigation.

CENSORSHIP HISTORY

The production of *Revelry* occurred at a time when the reputation of the late President Harding was already tainted with corruption, as the news media seemed to work tirelessly to link him securely to the Teapot Dome incident. Congressional hearings had already revealed the corruption of his secretary of the interior, Albert Fall, and the head of Veterans' Affairs, Charles Forbes. Although no evidence was found to directly link Harding to the scandals, the press judged him guilty by association. As historian Randolph Downes observes, the production of *Revelry* added to his disrepute and "made a shambles of his reputation." The play was taken to Philadelphia in 1927 for tryouts before opening on Broadway, but city officials sought to block the performances because it "presents the federal government and government agencies in a bad light" and "attributes acts of corruption to important political figures." Performances of the play were delayed while city leaders asked the Common Pleas Court to order a preliminary injunction that would block the production. They claimed that despite the assertions of the producers that the drama was a work of fiction, little doubt remained that the characters and subject matter of *Revelry* referred to the administration of the late President Harding. After hearing their request, Judge Robert H. Taulane refused to grant the injunction, and, although later than anticipated, the tryout of the play in Philadelphia was permitted. Although backers of *Revelry* had hoped that the attempted ban in Philadelphia would boost ticket sales for the Broadway production, they were disappointed. The play closed after 48 performances due to a lack of audience interest.

FURTHER READING

Downes, Randolph C. "The Harding Muckfest: Warren G. Harding—Chief Victim of the Muck-for-Muck's-Sake Writers and Readers." *Northwest Ohio Quarterly* 39, no. 3 (1967): 11–14.

Kiernan, Louise. "Murder She Wrote: Tribune Reporter Maurine Watkins Achieved Her Greatest Fame with *Chicago*, a Play Based on Two Sensational Local Crimes." *Chicago Tribune*, July 16, 1997, sec. 1, p. 5.

Laufe, Abe. *The Wicked Stage: A History of Theater Censorship and Harassment in the United States.* New York: Frederick Ungar Publishing Co., 1978.

Means, Gaston. *The Strange Death of President Harding, From the Diaries of Gaston B. Means.* New York: Elizabeth Ann Guild, 1930.

Mee, Charles L., Jr. *The Ohio Gang: The World of Warren G. Harding, An Historical Entertainment.* New York: Walker Evans Publishing, 1981.

THE REVOLUTION OF PARIS

Author: George Dibdin Pitt
Original date and place of production: None
Characters: Louis XIV, Cardinal Mazarin, Victor Roland
Filmed versions: None

SUMMARY

The Revolution of Paris, or The Patriot Deputy is a drama based loosely on the events of the Paris uprising of 1659 in which city workers with support of the Parisian middle class rebelled against the heavy taxes imposed by the government. In the play, the leader of the rebellion, Victor Roland, calls only for economic justice for the lower classes, not the downfall of the aristocracy. Instead of violence, Roland declares in Act I: "I would open the eyes of the King as well as those of the people for he is no true Patriarch that would deluge his natural land in Blood or seek to destroy its commerce & content by Anarchy & War." Despite Roland's moderate position, he is arrested by royal troops and the man who has betrayed him to the troops takes his place. His betrayer takes a much more violent stance and incites the mob to insurrection by crying out to them, "The hour is at hand—tear up the Pavement. Attack the Palace, Down with the Prison, up with the Tricolour. *A bas le Bourbon.*" The action then turns to the clash between the self-termed patriots and the government troops that seek to restore order. Because no complete manuscript of the play exists, the extent to which the characters wage major battles on stage has been lost to history.

CENSORSHIP HISTORY

The Revolution of Paris does not exist in complete manuscript, but the notes of the censors remain to document that the play was a victim of English preperformance censorship in 1848, a time when England was warily watching events of the contemporary uprisings in Paris. A popular uprising had begun in Paris on February 22, 1848, only weeks before the play was submitted to the censors, and the conservative regime of Prime Minister

Guizot had been overthrown while King Louis-Philippe had been forced to abdicate. Pitt asserted strongly that his play was based on the uprising in Paris in 1659, but the events depicted in the play mirrored too closely the turmoil of contemporary Paris, which, as John Russell Stephens observes, "was itself the terrifying image of what might take place in Britain." Samuel Lane, the manager of the Britannia Theatre, submitted the play to John Mitchell Kemble, the Examiner of Plays, in March 1848, with the subtitle *The Patriot Deputy* heavily scored out and with the following note intended to convince the censors that the play was irrelevant to the current situation in Paris:

> Notice / This piece does not in any way touch on the Present Crisis—except the Appointment of a *Provisional* Government. It is originally an Italian story— and the title given to it the most apposite to the leading Topic of the day; the *Monarch's Name* is never mentioned. . . . The title has been suggested, *since* the play has been wrote but as it will be seen—tis a *stage Revolution* not that of *Paris 1848*—and with the addition of some lines in the part of the Deputy—the Italian revolution of 1659 in Milan.

John Campbell, marquess of Breadalbane, the Lord Chamberlain, did not agree with the assertion that the play was politically innocuous. Kemble advised Lane to withdraw the play from examination. After Lane complied, the comptroller of the Lord Chamberlain's office sent him a note of appreciation and assured him that "such conduct on the part of those holding Licences from His Lordship, affords The Lord Chamberlain an additional Reason for contriving to encourage the Drama, with a due regard to the Interests of the Managers who uphold the respectability of their Establishments by good discretion and rightmindedness."

FURTHER READING

Blakey, Robert. *The History of Political Literature from the Earliest Times*. London: Richard Bentley, New Burlington Street, 1855. Reprint, Dubuque, Iowa: William C. Brown Reprint Library, 1934.

Stephens, John Russell. *The Censorship of English Drama, 1824–1901*. New York: Cambridge University Press, 1980.

RICHARD THE SECOND

Author: Richard Cumberland
Original date and place of production: None as originally written; April 4, 1792, Covent Garden, London, England (as *The Armorer*)
Characters: Jerry Furnace, Rosamund Furnace, King Richard II, Jack Straw, Wat Tyler
Filmed versions: None

SUMMARY

Richard the Second is a political opera that deals with the Peasants' Revolt led by Wat Tyler in 1381, but the subject of rebellion against the established government found opponents among English officials in 1792. At the beginning of the play, a peace-loving blacksmith named Jerry Furnace murders a tax collector to protect his daughter Rosamund after the government official has insulted her and tried to forcibly take her from her home. The tax collector made other enemies, even among the clergy, and a priest has told him that he is worth nothing "but to extort the filthy wages of Mammon, to whom thou art a hireling." Furnace's crime makes him sympathetic to the rebels led by Wat Tyler, whom he joins out of necessity, although the majority of the peasant rebels are foolish, violent, and unprincipled villains who have their own self-interest and not the greater cause at heart. Jack Straw, whom the rebels sing has "set us free from our Taxes & order & law," justifies the murders he has committed in the following way: "I can safely swear I never took off any head, that did not look like an Attorneys." When the cautious wife of a man preparing to join the rebels cautions him to be careful of what he says in order to avoid retaliation, he responds roughly, "Why we pay tax for our heads, don't we? Surely then we may sue our tongues at free cost." Cumberland provides sympathetic portrayals of King Richard II and his supporters, whom he depicts as being generous and courageous. Unlike the tax collector, who has abused his position, Cumberland's king exhibits remarkable courage in facing the rebels at the end of the play, and he is humane in his treatment of Furnace, whom he pardons for the murder of the tax collector.

CENSORSHIP HISTORY

Richard the Second was sent to the Office of the Examiner of Plays, John Larpent, on December 8, 1792. Larpent refused the play a license for public performance shortly after and suggested extensive rewriting to remove objectionable material. Despite Cumberland's unfavorable depictions of the rebels and generous portrayal of King Richard II, the willful murder of a government official, the tax collector, and the depiction of a popular uprising against the established government, as well as the presentation of people who are dissatisfied with their king, could not be allowed onstage. The political atmosphere in England in 1792 was particularly unstable as a French war was imminent, and the censors were especially sensitive to much of the dialogue, which appeared treasonous in the eyes of patriotic Englishmen. Cumberland made extensive changes in the play and resubmitted it for a license three months later under the name *The Armorer*. The greatly altered drama was granted a license for public performance and made its first of only three appearances at Covent Garden Theatre on April 4, 1792.

Although the play had been rewritten to the satisfaction of the Examiner of Plays, the excision of much of the original material substantially weakened the work and completely removed the political implications. The main plot regarding the rebellion is eliminated, and Wat Tyler is no longer a character in the play, nor is mention made of him. While Jerry Furnace, the "armorer" of the title, still commits a murder, the object of his violence is no longer a government tax collector, only a procurer who wishes to abduct Rosamund on the orders of his master, the earl of Suffolk. After committing murder, Furnace does not run to join the rebels, as he does in the original version. Instead, he stays to stand trial, and makes the patriotic statement "Let come what will, the laws of my Country, & the authority of my King shall neither be evaded, nor opposed by me." Although approved by the censors, the rewritten drama was rejected by the public, and the production closed after three nights.

FURTHER READING

Connolly, L. W. *The Censorship of English Drama, 1737–1824.* San Marino, Calif.: Huntington Library, 1976.

Green, Frederick Charles. *Literary Ideas in 18th Century France and England: A Critical Survey.* New York: Frederick Ungar Publishing Co., 1966.

Hampden, John. *Eighteenth Century Plays.* London: J. M. Dent & Sons, Ltd., 1928.

Moses, Montrose J., ed. *British Plays from the Restoration to 1820.* Boston: Little, Brown, 1929.

ROAR, CHINA!

Author: Sergei Tretyakov

Original date and place of production: January 23, 1926, Meyerhold Theatre, Moscow, Russia; October 27, 1930, Martin Beck Theatre, New York, New York

Characters: the American, Boy, the Chinaman, Lieutenant Cooper, the Englishwomen

Filmed versions: None

SUMMARY

Roar, China! is a satire that depicts a rebellion by the Chinese in reaction against the exploitation of the Chinese people by British imperialists and American capitalists. The original production took place at the Meyerhold Theatre in Moscow, Russia, on a stage that had 20 usable levels to allow for the creation of a wharf at the front of the stage with steps leading to a river at the rear. The production was viewed in Moscow by Hallie Flanagan, director of the Federal Theatre Project (FTP), a government-subsidized movement created in 1935 under the U.S. Works Progress Administration to employ professional theater workers and to provide the general public with access to inexpensive but good theater while providing community services in developing regional and neighborhood theater and theatrical workshops. In

Flanagan's words, during the production, "little boats with sails went up and down or rocked back and forth but they never pretended to be real boats in real China." Behind the boats, a very large ship was suggested by the presence of "wood and steel with real steps, girders and rigging." The play contrasts the rhythms of the coolies' lives with those of the Americans on the ship. As Flanagan observed, "The coolies' acting was pitched to the sound of the Chinese reed instruments, Chinese guns, or lap-lap of the water. The acting on ship was pitched to the sound of American jazz, played by the ship's orchestra, to which the passengers tangoed."

To the Americans and the British, the coolies are nonentities without names whom they treat as having no individuality, but the play emphasizes their uniqueness by clothing each in a distinct if similarly discolored blue shirt and giving each one different makeup. English sailors toss bales of goods to the coolies, who uncomplainingly stagger away with them as ordered. Leading them is the Chinaman, dressed in silk kimono and straw hat and carrying a fan with which he hits the coolies while he curses them to make them work faster. As the coolies struggle to unload the heavy cargo of the ship, an American dressed in casual but expensive clothes and a Panama hat appears. He carries a notebook and, after observing the coolies at work, he laughs, then tosses money at them, which some scramble after and others throw back at him.

The action moves from the wharf onto the ship where, in an extremely artificial atmosphere, two Englishwomen are shown flirting and dancing with the ship's officers, while others sit and drink at little round tables as jazz plays loudly in the background. The American enters the room and the American handshake and social manner with perceived peers are satirized. As they drink and talk, the group of English and Americans call for the Boy, who appears as a tragic clown, wearing the makeup of a clown in the commedia dell'arte, a white face under tumbled black hair, and wearing a white suit. He is suspicious of the group and appears to be frightened as he slowly comes down the stairs and looks first at one and then another. The Americans and the English alternately sneer and laugh at him, throwing things to him as to a dog, before sending him to fetch cigars.

The play changes in atmosphere when the British officer Lieutenant Cooper is killed by one of the Chinese, and the British threaten to destroy an entire town in retribution for that one death. The subservient behavior of the coolies is replaced by one of rebellion, suggesting the power of a waking China.

CENSORSHIP HISTORY

Roar, China! was first performed at the Meyerhold Theatre in Moscow on January 23, 1926. Four years later, on October 27, 1930, the play opened at the Martin Beck Theatre in New York City, presented by the Theatre Guild Acting Company, which included Lee Strasberg, Franchot Tone, and Luther Adler. Herbert Biberman, who would later be called to testify before the

House Un-American Activities Committee as the most devout communist among the infamous Hollywood Ten, was the first director for the production. Unlike the Moscow production, the Broadway stage did not contain 20 levels. Instead, as Meserve and Meserve recount, "an enormous British warship occupied the vast reaches of the Martin Beck stage." No efforts were made to suppress the play in New York. In Britain, Terence Gray, of the Cambridge Festival Theatre, was refused a license for public performance of the play in 1931. The office of the lord chamberlain viewed the anticolonial play as "offensive" to Britain's political interests and expressed the desire that the play would never be staged publicly in Britain. Before the play was banned, the lord chamberlain consulted the Home Office as well as the Foreign Office and the Admiralty to bolster his position. In a memo to the office of the lord chamberlain, the Admiralty suggested that the play was dangerous and it was "especially undesirable that young and inexperienced undergraduates should be subjected at their age to this kind of malicious Anti-British propaganda."

FURTHER READING

Bentley, Joanne. *Hallie Flanagan: A Life in the American Theatre.* New York: Alfred A. Knopf, 1988.

Flanagan, Hallie. *Arena.* New York: Duell, Sloan and Pearce, 1940.

Ley, Graham. *From Mimesis to Interculturalism: Readings of Theatrical Theory Before and After "Modernism."* Exeter, England: University of Exeter, 1999.

Meserve, W. J., and R. I. Meserve. "The State History of *Roar China!*: Documentary Drama as Propaganda." *Theatre Survey: The American Journal of Theatre History* 21 (1980): 1–13.

Nicholson, Steve. *British Theatre and the Red Peril.* Exeter, England: University of Exeter Press, 1999.

Roose-Evans, James. *Experimental Theatre from Stanislavsky to Today.* New York: Universe Books, 1970.

LE ROI S'AMUSE

Author: Victor Hugo
Original date and place of production: November 22, 1832, Comédie-Française, Paris, France
Characters: Dame Berade, Blanche, M. De Cossé, Mme de Cossé, King François I, M. de Latour-Landry, Maguelonne, M. de Pienne, M. de Saint-Vallier, Saltabadil, Triboulet
Filmed versions: None

SUMMARY

Hugo's verse drama tragedy *Le roi s'amuse* (*The King's Amusement*) is based on the life of King François I. In this play the king mistakenly dishonors the daughter of the physically deformed court jester Triboulet, believing her to be the fool's secret mistress, an action that results in a chain of tragic events. Triboulet is a bitter man who hates the king and the nobles because of their social positions and, as Hugo wrote in his preface to the printed version, "he hates ordinary men because they do not have humps on their backs." As the playwright concluded, because of Triboulet's "three-fold misery" of being deformed, unhealthy, and a court buffoon, he becomes evil. Much of his time is spent in creating dissension within the court, setting noble against noble, and taking every opportunity to set the nobles against the king. In venting his anger at one point, the jester shouts, "Your mothers prostituted themselves to lackeys!/You are bastards, one and all!" In a continuing effort to corrupt the king and to show others the depraved nature of the monarchy, Triboulet encourages the king to tyrannize his subjects and plays the role of sexual procurer, luring François to the homes of gentlemen with attractive wives and encouraging him to seduce them. He challenges the king to use his power to carry off one's sister or to dishonor another's daughter as the right of the king.

During a festival, which Triboulet ruins for all by his machinations, he is emphatically urging the king to carry away Madame de Cossé when Monsieur de Saint-Vallier intrudes and loudly denounces François for dishonoring his daughter, Diana de Poitiers. As the king remains silent, Triboulet jeers the grieving father and insults him, to which de Saint-Vallier responds by extending his hand and proclaiming a curse upon Triboulet. Hugo wrote in his preface, "It is from this scene that the whole play develops. The real subject of the drama is the *curse of M. de Saint-Vallier.*" Unknown to everyone, Triboulet is also a father, and his daughter, Blanche, is all that he has in the world. He has hidden her in a deserted part of the city to isolate her from the vice and the suffering that he creates for others in the king's court. Triboulet's greatest fear is that Blanche will fall victim to the same evil that he has spread. The curse uttered by the father of Diana de Poitiers is fulfilled when the king rapes Blanche, believing her to be a mistress that Triboulet has hidden. When Triboulet seeks revenge in an attempt to murder the king, he mistakenly kills his own child. As Triboulet is about to drop a sack into the river, which he believes to contain the body of François, he hears in his mind the words scratched on the window frame of Chambord by the historical King François I, "Women are often fickle. . . ." He thus realizes that truth and screams, "I have murdered my own child!"

CENSORSHIP HISTORY

Victor Hugo professed that he had based his play on the life of King François I (1494–1547), and to lend credence to the portrayal, he consulted original documents and researched the period thoroughly. Despite this effort, Hugo's political views soon overshadowed the play and his historical King François I became a thinly disguised King Louis-Philippe. The play was performed on November 22, 1832. In an unlucky coincidence for Hugo, only hours before the performance an attempt was made on the king's life, and rumors filled the theater that the king had been assassinated. The following morning, the stage manager of the Comédie-Française sent the playwright a letter informing him, "It is half-past ten, and I have just received the order to suspend the performance of *Le roi s'amuse*. It is M. Taylor who communicates this command from the Minister [who has] banned the play on his own authority." The ban was unexpected in 1832 because only two years earlier, after the 1830 Revolution, the government had proclaimed the Charter of Abolition of Censorship, which said in part, "The French have the right to publish. . . . Censorship must never be re-established." Hugo asserted that the theater was another form of publication and that censorship did not apply only to print. He concluded that by banning "on his own authority," the minister had deprived him of his rights to free expression.

Although the management of the Comédie-Française made limited efforts to reverse the order, they were unsuccessful. The government affirmed the ban, and the theater managers were afraid to complain further, fearful that their licenses would be revoked, so they complied. Hugo decided to sue the theater, because if censorship as a law no longer existed, then the theater did not have the right to ban his play. The case appeared before the Tribunal du Commerce on December 19, 1832, and a large crowd appeared to hear Hugo argue against the ban. For a half hour, he chastised the government for its "petty hypocrisy" and called it "a highwayman crouching in its forest of laws, picking off one freedom after another." He ended his speech by saying:

> Today, my freedom as a poet is taken by a censor; tomorrow, my freedom as a citizen will be taken by a policeman. Today, I am banished from the theatre; tomorrow, I shall be banished from the land. Today, I am gagged; tomorrow, I shall be deported. Today, a state of siege exists in literature; tomorrow, it will exist in the city.

A few days later, he asked the government to discontinue his government pension, thus transferring his allegiance as an artist from the king to the people, upon whom his future financial income would depend. The publicity resulting from the ban made the printed version of the play highly successful, and the play took on new life in productions in the United States under the title *The Fool's Revenge*, in which noted actor Edwin Booth often played. On November 22, 1882, exactly 50 years after the first Paris performance, the play returned to the Comédie-Française, where Hugo was in the audience surrounded by dignitaries.

In 1850 Giuseppe Verdi adapted *Le roi s'amuse* to create the opera *Rigoletto*, a version of the play that resulted from modifications made by Venetian censors. Early efforts to present the opera were thwarted by Venice officials who objected to the "immoral" subject of the story. Verdi directed his librettist Francesco Piave to take the libretto, first entitled *La Maledizione* [*The Curse*] to the manager of La Fenice, and to insist that the opera house accept it without change. The manager responded a few days later, writing that the

Office of Public Order had prohibited the opera, and the military governor of Venice had written that the work was "deplorable," "repugnant," and "obscene triviality," and warned La Fenice "not to insist further on this matter." Despite Verdi's outrage, Piave worked with the opera house manager to revise the story and produce a libretto of which the censors approved. On December 11, 1850, Piave gave Verdi a censored story, which contained a new title and setting, as well as the demotion of the king to the level of a duke, with the sex and other corrupt behaviors considerably decreased. In addition, Triboulet was no longer a hunchback nor ugly, and as a concession to the police, the sack in which he unknowingly drags his daughter's body to the river had been eliminated, thus making the climax of the play absurd. Verdi found the revisions unacceptable, and using the leverage that he had with La Fenice, for which each new season depended upon a new opera by Verdi, the managers scrambled to achieve a compromise, which they did on December 23, 1850. The sack was reinstated in the play, although the police requested the change of several names. By January 26, 1851, *Rigoletto* was complete and ready for performance.

FURTHER READING

Maurois, André. *Olympio.* New York: Harper & Row, 1956.

Pendell, William A. *Victor Hugo's Acted Dramas and the Contemporary Press.* Baltimore: Johns Hopkins University Press, 1947.

Porter, Laurence M. *Victor Hugo.* New York: Twayne Publishers, 1999.

Rigoletto and Le Roi S'Amuse. San Diego Opera Sourcebook. Available online. URL: http://www.sdopera.com/pages/education/edusourcebook/ArRigLeRoi.htm.

Robb, Graham. *Victor Hugo: A Biography.* New York: W. W. Norton, 1997.

LA RONDE

Author: Arthur Schnitzler

Original date and place of production: 1913, Budapest, Hungary

Characters: The Actress, the Count, the Girl of the Streets, the Husband, the Maid, the Poet, the Soldier, the Sweet Young Miss, the Young Gentleman, the Young Wife

Filmed versions: *La Ronde* (1950, France)

SUMMARY

The German title of Arthur Schnitzler's play is *Der Reigen* (the Round Dance), but it has become known best under the French title, *La Ronde*. The play portrays the manners and morals of Vienna in 1900, in which the sexual looseness of both men and women reduces all human relationships to physical pleasure. David Hare adapted it as *The Blue Room*, which appeared in London in 1998 and on Broadway in 1999.

Schnitzler structures his play as 10 dialogues that form a cycle in which superficial sexual encounters exhibit the absence of true love. The round dance begins with the Soldier and the Girl of the Streets engaged in a tryst in a secluded spot on the banks of the Danube. The two then separate, and the Soldier is next seen with a parlor Maid, on "a path leading from the Wurstelprater out into the dark avenues of trees." The next episode depicts the parlor Maid with her employer, a young Husband, who has called her into a room on the pretext of having her lower the blinds. After what is clearly a sexual tryst, the young Husband goes to his Wife who complains of the light in their room, so he takes her into an adjoining bedroom that is darker. Afterward, the two engage in conversation during which the Young Wife questions her Husband about his past experiences with women. The young Husband is then seen in the private room of a restaurant with the Sweet Young Miss. She moves on to a Poet, who rhapsodizes about her beauty in the candlelight, but she ignores his poetry and replies, "Ouch! You're dripping wax on me! Why can't you be more careful?" The Poet is next with the Actress, with whom he trades barbs, chiding her for missing a performance just to annoy him, while she professes, "I die for love of you, and you call it a whim?" After the Poet leaves, the Actress is joined by the Count, who tells her, "Happiness doesn't exist. . . . Love, for instance. It's the same with love. . . . Enjoyment . . . intoxication . . . there's nothing wrong with them. . . . And when it's over, it's over, that's all." The Actress coaxes the reluctant Count into bed, after which he falls into a deep sleep from which he awakens the next morning, lying next to the Girl of the Streets with whom the round dance had begun.

CENSORSHIP HISTORY

In 1900 Schnitzler paid for the printing of 200 copies of *Der Reigen* to distribute to his friends, but word of mouth soon made the work a sensation in literary circles. Schnitzler's publisher S. Fischer refused to publish the play, believing it was obscene, but a small publisher, Wiener Verlag, released a printing of 40,000 copies in 1903. Critics condemned the book as "a subversive and obscene work" and many newspapers would not review it, but the printing sold out. The authorities in Vienna refused to allow a public reading of the play, and in Germany copies were confiscated by police and banned from distribution.

Schnitzler refused for many years to allow the play to be performed. He did not hold a copyright on the play in Hungary, and the first public performance of the play appeared in Budapest in 1912, unauthorized by the playwright. As authors Haskell Block and Robert Shedd write, the performance was "tactless and offensive," and the police banned the play two days later.

The first authorized performance of the whole play occurred under the direction of Max Reinhardt at the Deutsches Theater in Berlin in December 1920. After hostile spectators threw stinkbombs in the theater, police were called in to quell the riot. The authorities ordered the actors arrested and further performances halted. In a sensational trial, the State Judicial Court banned the performance on grounds that it was "obscene" and violated "moral, religious, political, and artistic" standards of the theater. After Reinhardt and his supporters appealed the decision, the court relented on January 3, 1921, but the production was again blocked when a group of citizens launched a civil suit that charged the theater with being "a scandal, a sign of the deepest shame of our times."

Eric Bentley writes in the introduction to his translation of *La Ronde* that the Viennese premiere of *La Ronde*, which took place on February 1, 1921, at Kammerspiele in der Rothenturmstrasse became a rallying point for the "Christian vigilantes" in their crusade against "Jewish literature." *La Ronde* was denounced as "Jewish filth" and symptomatic of the "plague" that was threatening to contaminate Vienna. Supported by the Viennese Council of Bishops and the Church, the violent debate extended to City Hall and Parliament. The minister of the interior prohibited the performance as "unconstitutional" and opponents of the "bordello play" protested in demonstrations outside Vienna's city hall, but the play was presented. After the first performance, a crowd of 600 members of the Deutsche Volkspartei (German People's Party) stormed the theater, attacked the audience and actors, and destroyed the sets. The play was prohibited the next day for reasons of "public peace and security." The following day, the Viennese newspapers hailed the event as "A Triumph of Viennese Christian Youth." Schnitzler forbade further performances of the play for 50 years after becoming the target of vehement anti-Semitic attacks.

FURTHER READING

Block, Haskell M., and Robert G. Shedd. *Masters of Modern Drama*. New York: Random House, 1962.

Gay, Peter. *Schnitzler's Century: The Making of Middle Class Culture, 1815–1914*. New York: W. W. Norton, 2002.

Marcuse, Ludwig. *Obscene: The History of an Indignation*. London: MacGibbon & Key, 1965.

Schnitzler, Arthur. *La Ronde, Ten Dialogues*. Translated by Eric Bentley. New York: Samuel French, 1954.

Wolff, Janet. "The Culture of Separate Spheres: The Role of Culture in 19th Century Public and Private Life." In *The Culture of Capital: Art, Power and the 19th Century Middle Class*. Edited by Janet Wolff and John Seed. Manchester, England: Manchester University Press, 1988.

SALOMÉ

Author: Oscar Wilde
Original date and place of production: February 11, 1896, Théâtre de l'Oeuvre, Paris, France

Characters: Herod Antipas, Herodias, John the Baptist, Namaan, Narraboth, Salomé, Tigellinus

Filmed versions: Feature films: *Salomé, or the Dance of the Seven Veils* (1908, U.S.); *Salomé* (1923, U.S.); (1970, 1978, Spain); (1972, Italy); (1973, U.K.); (1986, 1990, France/Italy). Made for television: (1974, 1997, Germany); (1990, U.K./Germany)

SUMMARY

Salomé, subtitled "A Tragedy in One Act," was written in 1891 in French by Oscar Wilde and later translated into English in 1893 by Lord Alfred Douglas. Illustrated by Aubrey Beardsley in late 1893 and early 1894, the English publication bore the following dedication: "To My Friend Lord Alfred Bruce Douglas the Translator of My Play." The play was not performed until two years later to a private subscription audience as a means of circumventing the ban against *Salomé*. By then, Wilde was already incarcerated after an April 1895 criminal trial in which he was found guilty of "committing acts of gross indecency" and sentenced to two years of hard labor in Reading Gaol. (See THE IMPORTANCE OF BEING EARNEST for an account of the legal proceedings.) In 1905 Wilde's play was translated into German and became the libretto for Richard Strauss's opera *Salomé*.

The play dramatizes the biblical story of Salomé, daughter of Herodias and stepdaughter of Herod Antipas, the tetrarch of Judea and son of Herod the Great who had ordered the massacre of all infants when Jesus Christ was born. Herodias has married Herod after the murder of his half-brother, and the marriage is viewed as incest under Jewish law. John the Baptist has denounced the marriage and, at the insistence of Herodias, Herod has imprisoned him in a cistern, from which issue loud curses against Herodias and prophecies of the coming of Christ. Herod fears divine retribution and has spared the prophet's life, despite his wife's desire to have John the Baptist executed.

The play takes place on the night of a great feast, which Salomé leaves for a time to enjoy the night air, after being annoyed by Herod's lustful behavior. She hears the prophet cursing and convinces Narraboth, a young Syrian officer who is enamored of her, to bring John the Baptist before her. She tries to break through the prophet's unyielding and stern facade by caressing him sensually and begging him, "Let me kiss thy mouth . . . I will kiss thy mouth." John the Baptist rebuffs her and, instead, loudly denounces her, "Daughter of an incestuous mother, be thou accursed!"

When Salomé returns to the feast, Herod asks her to sit near him, and his attentions further upset Herodias, who is already angered by his refusal to execute John the Baptist. As the feast scene continues, the prophet's voice can be heard in the background, shouting, "Ah, the wanton! The harlot! Ah, the daughter of Babylon. . . . Let the people take stones and stone her." Feeling sad, Herod asks Salomé to dance for him. She refuses at first, with the approval of Herodias, then relents when Herod promises to give her anything she desires, "even unto half my kingdom." He offers his jewels and other valuables, but Salomé in collusion with Herodias insists on only one price: "I would that they presently bring me in a silver charger. . . . The head of John the Baptist." Filled with lust for his stepdaughter, Herod relents. After Salomé performs the very sensuous Dance of the Seven Veils, Herod sends the executioner to retrieve her reward. The audience sees the arm of the executioner extend from the cistern below, carrying a silver shield on which is placed the severed head of the prophet. As Herod hides his face, Herodias grins in triumph while guests at the feast fall to their knees in prayer. Undeterred by the gore, Salomé addresses the severed head, reminding it that she had been prevented earlier from kissing the prophet's mouth, "I will kiss it now. I will bite it with my teeth as one bites a ripe fruit." After watching her, Herod orders his soldiers, "Kill that woman!" The soldiers crush her to death with their shields.

CENSORSHIP HISTORY

The London stage success of *Lady Windermere's Fan* in 1891 made Wilde a highly popular literary and social figure. Richard Ellman writes in a 1988 biography of Wilde that Sarah Bernhardt approached the playwright at a party in 1892 and remarked that he should write a play for her. He responded that he had already done so, and sent her a copy of *Salomé*. Bernhardt decided to produce the play and to star as Salomé. Rehearsals began in June 1892, and after two weeks rumors reached Wilde that the Examiner of Plays, Edward Pigott, planned to ban the play because the play violated the censor's code that forbade the presentation onstage of characters from the Scriptures. In an interview with Robert Ross of the *Pall Mall Budget*, Wilde expressed his indignation that the play would be kept from the English stage and lashed out, "If the Censor refuses *Salomé*, I shall leave England to settle in France where I shall take out letters of naturalization. I will not consent to call myself a citizen of a country that shows such narrowness in artistic judgment. I am not English. I am Irish which is quite another thing." In an interview with *Le Gaulois*, Wilde stated that he did not like the English in general. "There is a great deal of hypocrisy in England. The typical Briton is Tartuffe, seated in his shop behind the counter."

As Wilde had anticipated, Pigott refused to license the play for public performance. In his report, the censor condemned the play as being both blasphemous and pornographic, as well as exhibiting the negative influence of the French decadent circles of fin-de-siècle Paris. In addition to citing the play's violation of the censors' rule against portraying biblical figures on the public stage, Pigott stressed as pornographic the "incestuous passion of Herod for his stepdaughter" and wrote of Salomé's kiss to the mouth of John the Baptist's severed head as being "a paroxysm of sexual despair." In summing up, he wrote, "This piece is written in French—half Biblical, half pornographic—by Oscar Wilde himself. Imagine the average British public's reception of it." Neither Wilde's enemies nor his friends felt sympathetic toward him, and among prominent theater critics, only George Bernard Shaw and William Archer defended Wilde and spoke out against the ban.

The American premiere of the Strauss opera *Salomé*, which used Wilde's original text as the libretto, evoked vehement criticism after the first performance on January 22, 1907, at the Metropolitan Opera House in New York City. Complaints to the board of directors contained objections to the plot and to the much-publicized Dance of the Seven Veils, and the board refused to allow a second performance. In 1909 Oscar Hammerstein successfully produced the opera at his Manhattan Opera House, and after other opera houses followed suit, the Met relented and made *Salomé* part of its repertoire.

In 1910, before the English Examiner of Plays would grant Strauss's opera a license for public performance, the producer Thomas Beecham had to make several changes in the libretto. Instead of John the Baptist, the character was called "The Prophet," and the scene showing the head on a platter was deleted.

Wilde's *Salomé* became the center of controversy in a 1918 trial, in which Canadian-American actress Maud Allan issued a libel suit against Noel Pemberton Billing, a member of Parliament. Allan was to star as Salomé in two privately presented performances in London, as the play was still banned from public performance. Pemberton Billing had learned of the planned performance and attacked the play and its cast in the February 16, 1918, issue of his magazine *Vigilante* in an article entitled "The Cult of the Clitoris." He alleged that the Germans, then at war with Britain, had a "Black Book" containing 47,000 names of men and women who were allegedly homosexuals.

> To be a member of Maud Allan's private performance in Oscar Wilde's *Salomé* one has to apply to a Miss Valetta of 9 Duke Street, Adelphi, W.C. If Scotland Yard were to seize the list of these members I have no doubt they would secure the names of several thousand of the first 47,000.

During the trial, Pemberton Billing described the play as being an exhibition that "directly ministers to sexual perverts, Sodomites, and Lesbians. . . . They have chosen, at a moment when our very national existence is at stake, to select the most depraved of the many depraved works of a man who suffered the extreme penalty at the hands of the law for practising of this unnatural vice, or one form of it." Pemberton attacked the play on the grounds of national security and, author Adam Parkes writes, "he invoked the higher morality of war quite explicitly, indicating that homosexuality was seen as a sign not only of Decadence but also of wartime dissent and subversion."

Among his witnesses, Pemberton Billing called various medical experts who offered views about the link between immoral literature and sexual perversion. None of them had seen the play, but all agreed that playing in it would pervert Maud Allan's character. The dramatic critics called as witnesses stated with confidence that the play was an evil and corrupting influence, although none had seen it performed.

The most notorious of Pemberton Billing's witnesses was Lord Alfred Douglas, Wilde's former lover, who had played a major role in sending Wilde to prison and, soon afterward, to his death. By then 48 years old, the man Wilde had called Bosie savagely attacked Wilde as a man and as a writer. He characterized Wilde as "the greatest force for evil that has appeared in Europe in the past 350 years" and criticized *Salomé* as "a most pernicious and abominable piece of work." He attacked the prosecution for its conduct of the case, and when the judge rebuked him for this, he attacked the judge for his conduct of this and previous trials, until the judge ordered him to leave.

For his closing address, Pemberton Billing offered a diatribe that focused on the link between *Salomé*, the Black Book, and England's inability to prevail on the western front. The suit was settled in Pemberton Billing's favor and he was acquitted of all charges. The private performances of *Salomé* took place as planned, but the play did not receive a license for public performance in England until 1931.

FURTHER READING

Ellman, Richard. *Oscar Wilde*. New York: Alfred A. Knopf, 1988.

Gagnier, Regenia. *Idylls of the Marketplace: Oscar Wilde and the Victorian Public*. Stanford, Calif.: Stanford University Press, 1986.

Hoare, Philip. *Oscar Wilde's Last Stand: Decadence, Conspiracy and the Most Outrageous Trial of the Century*. New York: Arcade Publishing, 1998.

Hynes, Samuel. *A War Imagined: The First World War and English Culture*. New York: Atheneum Press, 1991.

Laufe, Abe. *The Wicked Stage: A History of Theater Censorship and Harassment in the United States*. New York: Frederick Ungar Publishing Co., 1978.

Parkes, Adam. *Modernism and the Theater of Censorship*. New York: Oxford University Press, 1996.

Stephens, John Russell. *The Censorship of English Drama, 1824–1901*. New York: Cambridge University Press, 1980.

SAPHO

Author: Clyde Fitch
Original date and place of production: February 5, 1900, Wallack's Theatre, New York, New York
Characters: M. Anvers, Caoudal, Cesaire Gaussin, Dechelette, Dejoie, Divonne Gaussin, Alice Dore, Flamant, Francine, Jean Gaussin, Fannie Le Grand, Hettema, Madame Hettema, Margot, Tina de Monte, Toto
Filmed versions: *Sapho* (1917)

SUMMARY

Adapted by Clyde Fitch from Alphonse Daudet's novel *Sapho* (1884), the play relates the story of Fanny Legrand, the daughter of a coachman, whose early home is little more than a hovel in the slums of Paris. She begins her working life as a flower-seller on the streets of Paris, earning a few sous daily, which she is compelled to give toward the support of the family, but she becomes a famous and beautiful courtesan with many wealthy lovers. While selling her flowers in one of the big restaurants, she is seen by Caoudal, a famous sculptor, who recognizes her wonderful beauty and persuades her to pose for him. One of his sculptures for which Fanny poses is that of the ancient Greek poet Sapho, which soon becomes the topic of conversation for its beauty and provocative sensuality. Fanny becomes Caoudal's mistress, and she happily enjoys the luxury of his studio and the other beautiful things he can provide. Now called Sapho by the art world, she soon becomes the most talked-of and sought-after model in Paris, and the lover of other artists and poets.

Although she revels Caoudal's admiration, she is easily won when Dejoie, a poet, moved by her beauty, writes verses to her that make both himself and her still more famous. The poet is too old to hold the attention of the young girl, who craves young society and admiration, so when she meets Flamant, a handsome young engraver, she lightly tells Dejoie that he is "too old" and gains the friendship of the younger man. Not a wealthy man, Flamant is, at first, unable to gratify Fanny's expensive whims, but he very much loves the beautiful model and he is willing to commit a crime to keep her interest. He forges a name and obtains money under false pretenses. When his ruse is discovered, the police arrest him. As they lead him away to prison, Fanny calls out her undying love for him and promises to wait for his release. That same day, the courtesan receives an invitation to a masked ball to take place that very evening.

Fanny attends the ball dressed as Sapho. Surrounded by her many wealthy admirers, she meets a poor art student, Jean Gaussin, with whom she falls in love and who seems to know nothing about her past as a courtesan. It is a case of love at first sight on both sides. The two live together in a small cottage outside Paris and are very happy for a time, as Fanny enjoys the simple life with a man she loves. After a year together, they find their happiness disrupted when a party consisting of Caoudal and several other artists stops for dinner at an inn in the village and meets Jean. They welcome him to a drink and, assuming that he and Fanny have parted because Jean has little of material value to offer, they reminisce about the many hearts she has broken and the men she has driven to crime. They wonder where she is, and Caoudal suggests that she may be living with her father and with the child she had by the poet Dejoie. They also reveal that she is the model for the famed statue of Sapho, and that she is, in fact, the woman known widely by that name. Jean is shocked by her past life, and despite her pleading that she has finally found a decent life with him, he leaves her to return to his parents' home.

After enduring weeks away from her and living in abject misery, Jean returns to their cottage and begs her forgiveness. He promises that he will never mention her past and that he will always love her. Fanny soothes him and waits until he is asleep before she leaves. She knows that her past will always bother him and that he will raise issues whenever their relationship becomes strained.

CENSORSHIP HISTORY

Sapho holds the distinction of being the first play in the 20th century to be closed by the New York City police. The play opened at the Wallack Theatre on Broadway on February 5, 1900, and after 29 performances was closed down by police on March 5, 1900. The play had drawn the attention of the Society for the Suppression of Vice, led by Anthony Comstock, which had recently launched a new campaign against Broadway, viewed by the organization as "a bastion of subversive and morally corrupt works." The move against *Sapho* was strongly encouraged by Dr. Newell Hills, an outspoken and well-known minister who had deluged newspapers with letters and interviews regarding what he viewed as the "morally lax standards on display in Broadway plays."

Sapho was singled out because of the basic story line of a seductive woman with many lovers, as well as for three scenes that the crusading censors found especially offensive. The first offensive scene depicts Fanny begging Jean to seduce her, claiming that she loved him so much that she would shine his shoes and do any menial tasks if he would only stay with her. The second scene singled out by the censors was the masked ball that they characterized as a thinly disguised orgy. The scene that the censors found most offensive was an implied torrid offstage love scene, suggested by Jean sweeping Fanny into his arms and carrying her up a flight of stairs to her bedroom. Onstage, the curtain was lowered and the lights dimmed to suggest the passage of time, then raised as increased light exhibited that morning had arrived. Jean exits from Fanny's bedroom and hurries down the stairs.

Leading theater critics denounced the play in reviews, and newspaper magnate William Randolph Hearst wrote in a *New York Journal* editorial that *Sapho* was "an insult to decent women and girls." He urged, "We expect the police to forbid on the stage what they would forbid in streets and low resorts." After weeks of being pressured by the press and the Society for the Suppression of Vice, the New York City authorities ordered the police to close the show and to arrest producer and leading lady Olga Nethersole, on the charge that she had attempted "to corrupt public morals." Nethersole, her personal manager, the manager of Wallack's Theatre, and the male lead in the play, Hamilton Revelle, were given a magistrate's hearing, but her attorney demanded a jury trial.

Before the trial began, prominent writers of the time, such as Arthur Brisbane, Harriet Hubbard Ayers, and Samuel Untermeyer, joined with prominent anticensorship groups to protest the arrest. They circulated a petition that they sent to New York City officials. The trial began on April 3, 1900. On April 6, 1900, after the judge reminded the jury that they were "not the guardians of the morals of this community," the jury took 15 minutes to find Nethersole innocent of all charges. *Sapho* reopened on April 7, 1900, to even larger audiences than before, and continued for an additional 55 performances.

FURTHER READING

Goeringer, Conrad. "Their Name Was Legion." *American Atheist: A Journal of Atheist News and Thought.* February 18, 2001. Available online. URL: http://www.americanatheist.org/supplement/legion.html.

Houchin, John H. "Depraved Women and Wicked Plays: Olga Nethersole's Production of *Sapho.*" *The Journal of American Drama and Theatre* 6, no. 1 (winter 1994): 74–79.

Laufe, Abe. *The Wicked Stage: A History of Theater Censorship and Harassment in the United States.* New York: Frederick Ungar Publishing Co., 1978.

"Sapho Affair, The." *The American Experience: People & Events.* Available online. URL: http://pbs.org/wgbh/amex/1900/peopleevents/pande30.html.

SAVED

Author: Edward Bond
Original date and place of production: November 3, 1965, Royal Court Theatre, London, England
Characters: Barry, Colin, Fred, Harry, Len, Liz, Mary, Mike, Pam, Pete
Filmed versions: None

SUMMARY

Saved is a bleak play set among the working class in South London in the early 1960s. Composed of 13 scenes, the play recounts a series of events in the lives of a group of young men and women who are spiritually and morally, as well as materially, poor. Len meets Pam, who takes him to the house she shares with her parents, Mary and Harry, for what they both expect will be a one-night stand. Instead, Len begins to dream of a future with Pam and moves in with the troubled family. Mary and Harry have not spoken to each other in years and their daughter Pam is considered by the neighbors to be a "slag." As the even-tempered Len becomes increasingly assimilated into the family, Pam becomes bored and leaves him for his abusive friend Fred, while Len remains as a lodger. After Pam becomes pregnant, Fred and she separate, but Len remains in her parents' house and wants to help her despite Pam's outbursts of hysterical hatred. Fred refuses to acknowledge the baby, which Pam also resents, but she bears the child, nonetheless.

One day, Pam takes the infant in its baby carriage to the park, where she meets Fred, who is carousing with his friends. In a fit of anger, she thrusts the carriage at Fred and leaves. As Len watches, horrified, the other young men shove the baby carriage back and forth and spit into it, laughing loudly as the baby screams in terror. They pull the baby's ear and pinch it, then tear off the diapers and rub the baby's face in its own excrement. In a final moment of hysterical rage, the men stone the baby to death. Pam returns and wheels the carriage away without looking at her mangled child. Fred is sent to prison for the murder. When he leaves prison, Pam wants to resume their relationship, but he rejects her. In turn, Pam wants Len to leave her parents' house, where he is still a lodger, but he remains. He is pushed to his limit, however, when he is approached seductively by Mary, described by the playwright in stage directions as follows: "Fifty-three. Shortish. Round heavy shoulders. Big buttocks. Bulky breasts, lifeless but still high. Big thighs and little ankles. Curled grey hair that looks as if it is in a hair-net. Homely." Stunned into awareness by what he believes to be an affair between Len and his wife, Harry begins speaking to Mary. He and Len argue, then struggle with a knife, breaking up furniture as they do. Unable to cope with the situation, Len decides to leave but changes his mind when Harry asks him to stay. The last scene of the play consists of four minutes of complete silence, with Len, Pam, Mary, and Harry onstage. The only dialogue is the request, "Fetch us hammer," which no one does. Their moral inertia makes all four unable to move even to improve their circumstances, even in so small an act as fixing the furniture.

CENSORSHIP HISTORY

Saved has been given credit by writers such as John Sutherland for being "instrumental in finishing off the Lord Chamberlain." When the Royal Court Theatre accepted the play for production, the management expected to face difficulty with the central scene, in which the baby is stoned to death in the park. The text of the play was submitted to Lord Chamberlain Lord David Cobbold on June 24, 1965, and the office kept the play for five weeks before responding with changes that would have to be made for the play to be licensed for public performance. The censors required the removal of two complete scenes—the murder of the baby in the park and the attempted seduction of 24-year-old Len by 53-year-old Mary. The censors also demanded the removal of objectionable words and phrases, among them 12 "Christs," three "sods," and two "Get stuffed!"

Bond was willing, at first, to make all the required changes in order to have the play produced; yet in an article published in the autumn 1965 issue of *Censorship*, he pointedly questioned why novels are free of the interference that drama must endure. After playwright and theater manager William Gaskill persuaded Bond to keep the play intact, the management of the Royal Court Theatre decided to produce the play as a theater club production, attended only by members of the Royal Court English Stage Society, prompting the sale of 3,000 new memberships. Six months earlier, in June 1965, John Osborne's *A PATRIOT FOR ME* had evaded the censors in the same way.

The first club performance of *Saved* took place on November 3, 1965. Unknown to the Royal Court management, police officers were in the audience at various performances and, on January 1, 1966, the Office of the Lord Chamberlain prosecuted the directors of the theater for publicly presenting an unlicensed play. During the second hearing, on March 2, 1966, renowned English actor Laurence Olivier appeared in defense of the play, but the censors were not swayed. On April 1, 1966, the court found the defendants guilty but issued conditional discharges and ordered them to pay 50 guineas in costs. The punishment was mild, but the real consequence of the case was more disturbing because the case effectively ended use of the theater club presentation of plays that the lord chamberlain refused to license. Theater managers who persisted would face more punitive sentences. This decision sparked even greater efforts by legislators opposed to the Lord Chamberlain's censorship of the stage and led to public debate in both the House of Lords and the House of Commons. Legislators devised the Private Members' Bill for the abolition of the position of lord chamberlain and worked to complete the Theatres Bill, which would abolish official stage censorship. At the same time, the Royal Court Theatre chose to goad the censor by submitting the play *EARLY MORNING*, also by Bond, which was, as expected, banned entirely. The furor that followed led to the quick passage of the Theatres Bill, which became law in September 1968. In early 1969 the uncensored versions of *Saved* and *Early Morning* became part of the public repertory of the Royal Court Theatre.

FURTHER READING

Bond, Edward. "Censor in Mind." *Censorship* 4 (autumn 1965): 9–14.
———. *Saved.* New York: Hill and Wang, 1965.
Elsom, John. *Erotic Theatre.* New York: Taplinger Publishing Co., 1974.
Harben, Niloufer. *Twentieth-Century English History Plays.* Totowa, N.J.: Barnes & Noble Books, 1988.
Sutherland, John. *Offensive Literature: Decensorship in Britain, 1960–1982.* Totowa, N.J.: Barnes & Noble Books, 1982.
Urban, Ken. "*Saved.*" NYTheatre Archive. Available online. URL: http://www.nytheatre.com/nytheatre/arch_012.htm.

THE SECOND MAIDEN'S TRAGEDY

Author: Thomas Middleton
Original date and place of production: None
Characters: Anselmus, Bellarius, Govianus, Helvetius, the Lady, Leonella, Memphonius, the Tyrant, Votarius, the Wife
Filmed versions: None

SUMMARY

The Second Maiden's Tragedy is structured in five acts, each containing scenes that alternate between activities in the home of Govianus and those occurring in the home of his brother Anselmus. The play opens as the Tyrant, accompanied by nobles Memphonius, Sophonius, and Helvetius, enters the royal palace of King Govianus, whose throne he has just usurped. He soon becomes enamored of the Lady, whom Govianus loves and who is the daughter of Helvetius. Although her father pressures her to return the attentions of the Tyrant as a means of ensuring their safety and prosperity under the new ruler, the Lady vows to remain loyal to Govianus, the rightful king. Angered by her refusal to become his queen, the Tyrant attempts to force her to love him and, when his efforts fail, he imprisons her with Giovanus. After resisting repeated efforts by the Tyrant to make her submit to him, she begs Govianus to kill her, but he cannot because he loves her, so she stabs herself and dies.

In alternating scenes, the play focuses on Anselmus, who wonders if his wife really loves him and seeks to test her faithfulness by having his best friend, Voltarius, attempt to seduce her. Voltarius readily agrees to lay the trap for the Wife, but the two fall in love after their first tryst. To protect themselves from the wrath of Anselmus, they concoct a scheme to fool Anselmus. When they are within his hearing, the Wife will loudly rebuff the advances of Voltarius and to add realism she will also wave around a sword and press it lightly against his skin. Unknown to the lovers, the servant Bellarus suspects that Voltarius is having an affair with his lover Leonella, so he dips the sword in poison. Thus, when the Wife and Voltarius act out their strategy and she wields the sword to rebuff his advances, she accidentally breaks his skin. The poison enters Voltarius's body and he dies. As Govianus arrives to take shelter with Anselmus, Bellarus learns what he has done and takes his own life, as does the Wife.

Unable to aid the stricken household, Govianus returns to his home. While he has been gone, the Tyrant has removed the Lady from her sepulcher and placed her in his bedchamber as his queen. In a series of necrophiliac actions, which the ghost of the Lady relates to Govianus, the Tyrant attempts to bring her to life:

> I am now at court
> In his own private chamber. There he woos me
> And plies his suit to me with as serious pains
> As if the short flame of mortality
> Were lighted up again in my cold breast,
> Folds me within his arms and often sets
> A sinful kiss upon my senseless lip
> Weeps when he sees the paleness of my cheek,
> And will send privately for a hand of art
> That may dissemble life upon my face
> To please his lustful eye

Incensed, Govianus disguises himself as the man called to paint life onto the face of the dead young woman and infiltrates the court. He gives color to the dead woman's face and places strong poison on her lips, which the Tyrant kisses. As the Tyrant dies, Govianus reveals his true identity and reclaims his throne, to the joy of Memphonius and Helvetius, who had only pretended to support the Tyrant out of fear for their lives. As the play ends, Govianus prepares to return the Lady to her sepulcher, after declaring her to be his only queen, now the "queen of silence."

CENSORSHIP HISTORY

The play was first submitted for a license to the Master of Revels, censor Sir George Buc, in 1611 as an anonymous and untitled play. Because Buc determined that the play held notable similarities to THE MAID'S TRAGEDY, by Beaumont and Fletcher, he gave the play the title of *The Second Maiden's Tragedy* and on October 31, 1611, granted the play a license for performance on the condition that the requested changes and deletions be made: "The second Maydens tragedy (for it hath no name inscribed) may with the reformations bee acted publikely. 31 October 1611. G. Buc." The sole version of the manuscript in existence from that period is the one containing the marks of the censor, and no evidence appears that publication was intended until the play was entered in the Stationers' Register on September 9, 1653, as *The Maids Tragedie, 2d part*. According to author Janet Clare, neither copy of the manuscript exhibits signs that they are based upon performance.

Many of the censor's changes and deletions are oaths, such as "'Sheart," "Heart," "'Slife," "Life," and "By th' Mass" and other terms that Buc thought were too provocative. Buc also excised statements that are critical of the court and of the sexual mores of the time. He modified all unflattering references within individual lines to courtiers or nobles to remove criticism, and completely omitted the passage below spoken by Govianus because of its sustained attack on the nobles:

> I knew you one and twenty and a lord
> When your discretion sucked; it's come from nurse yet?
> You scorn to be a scholar; you were born better.
> You have good lands; that's the best grounds of learning.
> If you can construe but your doctor's bill,
> Pierce your wife's waiting women, and decline your tenants
> Till they're all beggars, with new fines and rackings,
> Y'are scholar enough, for a lady's son
> That's born to living.

The largest number of deletions and changes are made in the scenes regarding the Tyrant's desired sexual relationship with the Lady. The censor omits direct sexual connotation in Helvetius's attempts to convince the Lady to submit to the Tyrant and he omits Govianus's furious denunciation of

Helvetius as a pandering courtier, which follows. Buc excised all references to the sovereign's wantonness and the dissolute behavior of the court, with an eye toward appeasing the monarchy. All references in which Govianus contrasts the Lady's honor and virtue with the rampant promiscuity of other women are modified to remove all derogatory references to the court.

The censor had a difficult task in dealing with the justifiable murder of the tyrant, which remains subversive because he is the king and the censor could not condone regicide even if it is, as Clare characterizes the act, "the inevitable outcome of despotic government." Buc excised lines in which Govianus threatens to kill the Tyrant for not treating the Lady with respect, and he replaces the Tyrant's dying words, "Your King's poisoned," with "I am poisoned." Although Govianus, the legitimate ruler, murders the usurper, Buc felt duty bound to remove the passage in which Helvetius and other courtiers transfer their loyalties from the Tyrant to his murderer, albeit the rightful ruler. Overall, the censor's excisions and changes diminish the impact of subversive imagery and soften the lampoons of court life. The play was never published, and no evidence exists to show that it was ever performed.

FURTHER READING

Akrigg, G. P. V. *Jacobean Pageant or the Court of King James I.* Cambridge: Harvard University Press, 1962.

Clare, Janet. *"Art Made Tongue-Tied by Authority": Elizabethan and Jacobean Dramatic Censorship.* New York: Manchester University Press, 1990.

Fowell, Frank, and Frank Palmer. *Censorship in England.* London: F. Palmer, 1913. Reprint, New York: Benjamin Blom, 1969.

Lancashire, Anne, ed. *The Second Maiden's Tragedy.* Manchester, England: Manchester University Press, 1978.

SEX

Author: Jane Mast (pseudonym for Mae West)

Original date and place of production: April 26, 1926, Daly's 63rd Street Theatre, New York, New York

Characters: Agnes, Captain Carter, Condez, Curley, Dawson, Lieutenant Gregg, Flossie, Jenkins, Jones, Manly, Marie, Margy La Mond, Red, Clara Stanton, Jimmy Stanton, Robert Stanton, Rocky Waldron

Filmed versions: None

SUMMARY

Sex opens in an apartment in Montreal's red-light district, which prostitute Margy La Mont shares with her pimp, Rocky Waldron. After Rocky throws out Manly, whose job is to pick up the payoff money for the local police, he is confronted by Dawson, the corrupt police officer, who demands his weekly "commission." Margy refuses to pay up and Dawson leaves, but threatens them before he goes. Left alone, Rocky grumbles that Margy does not sew buttons on his shirt and that she has misplaced his collars, but she is unconcerned and tells him that she should have someone waiting on her. Rocky mocks her and asks, "Getting some fool ideas about bein' decent, eh?" and tells her that she can never leave the life of prostitution because people will always condemn her for her past. Besides, he needs her income. He tells her, "Stick to your trade, kid, you were made for it." He leaves for a date with a wealthy "society dame" whom he met at the Ritz, with one last warning to Margy that she belongs to him and he will kill her if she tries to leave him. After he is gone, Agnes, a younger prostitute, arrives with money that she wants Margy to hide for her. Agnes tells Margy she plans to leave her pimp, Curley, as soon as she has enough money to return home, but Margy cautions her that once her family learns of the way in which Agnes has made a living, they will reject her. "They won't let you go straight. They'll hold you up as an example." Margy suggests, instead, that she try to find a rich man who will take care of her, as Margy plans. In quick succession, three clients arrive at different times, and Margy tells each that she is "not entertaining company tonight." When Gregg, a navy lieutenant, arrives, Margy tells him to leave as well, but he gives her a bird-of-paradise feather as a gift and encourages her to tell him her troubles. He tells her that all the girls who are "following the fleet" are getting rich and promises to tell all of his friends about her, if she wants to set up her own prostitution business. Margy insists that she is "not entertaining," and Gregg amiably invites her out for a drink. While they are gone, Rocky brings wealthy older society woman Clara Stanton to the apartment "for a little thrill." He drugs her drink, then panics when she becomes incoherent and leaves her for Margy and Gregg to find when they return. Dawson arrives and threatens to take the three in for questioning, and Clara lies that Margy lured her to the apartment and stole her jewels. When Margy protests her innocence, Clara offers Dawson a bribe to protect her from publicity. As he leaves with her in his custody, he warns Margy that she had better leave town.

Act two takes place in Port-au-Prince, Trinidad, where Margy has followed the fleet. She is introduced to a young millionaire, Clara Stanton's son, Jimmy, who confesses that he had arranged for the introduction. He falls in love with Margy and asks her to marry him just before he is supposed to return to the United States. Margy cautions him that he does not really know her, but Jimmy insists that his family will love her, and he loves her. While Jimmy makes arrangements for their trip, Margy meets Agnes, who has followed her to Trinidad. She admits that Margy was right in telling her that her family would not let her live down her past, and she is now in ill health, as well. She urges Margy to take the chance at happiness, then leaves to walk on the beach and think. Gregg speaks with Margy and tells her that he is leaving the military and wants to marry her. They can go to Australia and start a new life. She refuses and tells him that she will marry Jimmy Stanton. She claims that he has made her see things in a different light: "Why ever since I've been old enough to know about Sex, I always looked as men as the hunters. They're filled with Sex. In the past few years I've been chattel to that Sex. . . . It's a clean, wonderful love I have for this boy."

Lieutenant Gregg accepts her decision. As Margy and Jimmy are about to leave, they hear a commotion and learn that someone has committed suicide. Jimmy tells Margy, "Nothing to worry us, dear. Just one of those poor wretches that follow the fleet."

In Act three, Margy has arrived in Connecticut to meet Jimmy's parents, and his mother, Clara, recognizes Margy from Montreal. Jimmy has also invited Lieutenant Gregg for the following day. When the men leave for a drink, Clara threatens to expose Margy's past, and Margy calls her bluff and threatens to seduce Jimmy that night. Clara becomes ill and goes to her room, while Margy carries out her threat. The next morning, Clara attempts to reason with Margy, reminding her that the past cannot stay hidden forever and that Jimmy will hate her when he learns the truth. Margy feels indecisive, then learns that Rocky has been blackmailing Clara and threatens to turn him in to the authorities in states where warrants are outstanding for his arrest. After Rocky leaves, Margy decides that she cannot marry Jimmy. She reminds him of their last night in Trinidad and of the woman who "threw herself into the bay . . . I was one of those women." When Clara asks if she is "going back to that life," Margy takes Gregg's hand and responds, "No, I'm going straight—to Australia."

CENSORSHIP HISTORY

Mae West challenged the rules of Broadway in writing a play containing a prostitute and a happy ending. As author Lillian Schlissel observes, "In *Sex*, Mae West broke with Broadway moralities and made sin a domestic product." She set the scenes not in the expected hotbed of immorality, the tropics, but in Montreal and Connecticut, with only the second act in Trinidad. Unlike the formulaic Broadway plays of the time, which required that a fallen woman suffer for her past and often die, West's Margy contentedly gives up her wealthy boyfriend for a retired navy lieutenant whom she loves passionately.

West actively courted controversy in the publicity for her plays. Posters advertising *Sex* contained a picture of West draped in a satin gown, with a cigarette hanging defiantly from the side of her mouth, as she strums a ukulele. In bold print, they blared: "WARNING: If you cannot stand excitement—see your doctor before visiting Mae West in *Sex*." The bottom of the posters carried the following teaser: "The story of a bad little girl who was good to the navy!" The play also contained a live band and musical numbers especially selected by West, so that sailors danced jigs with other sailors, or danced steamy tangos with women in the brothel, but she saved the most provocative for herself. West danced a new Charleston called "Sweet Man," which boasted lyrics about kisses that were as "hot as TNT, gasoline, and nitroglycerine." And she also danced her famous shimmy, in this play to a song named "Shake That Thing."

Audiences packed the theater and the show grossed $14,000 a week in its first month and $16,000 a week in its second, but theater critics of the major New York City newspapers and magazines expressed contempt for West's effort. Walter Winchell in the *Graphic* called it "a vulgar affair" and assured readers that the "stench was not the fault of the street cleaning department." Others characterized the play as "crude and inept" and "cheaply produced and ineptly acted." The *New York Herald Tribune* wrote the longest diatribe against the work, asserting that it was concerned with "a world of ruthless, evil-minded, foul-mouthed crooks, harlots, procurers and other degenerate members of that particular zone of society." While critics condemned the play, audiences filled the theater, making *Sex* the only play on Broadway to survive the summer of 1926 and to continue into the fall.

On February 9, 1927, while New York City mayor Jimmy Walker was out of town, Deputy Police Commissioner Joseph B. McKee ordered raids of THE CAPTIVE, *Sex*, and *The Virgin Man*, even though *Sex* had been running for almost a year to packed audiences. The acting mayor sent limousines for the other two playwrights but for Mae West he sent a Black Maria (police van) and crowded West and her entire cast into the van, then tumbled them out at the West 47th Street precinct in Hell's Kitchen. In night court, West played to the press by gathering her ermine close to her curves and telling them that unlike Menken's "lesbian play" *The Captive*, all the cast of *Sex* were "normal." After spending a night in the Jefferson Market Women's Prison, West provided bail—$100 for each of the six principals and $500 each for 16 other cast members named in the complaint.

The court offered to drop all charges against the play and the cast if West would shut down the play; she refused. Instead, her lawyer Jim Timony and manager C. W. Morganstern obtained a restraining order against police interference, which allowed the show to continue filling the theater seats until May 21, a week before the obscenity trial. A grand jury declared that West, Morganstern, Timony, 20 actors, and the theatre owner John Cort had prepared, advertised, and produced "an obscene, indecent, immoral and impure drama" that contributed to "the corruption of the morals of youth." The grand jury charged furthermore that the content of the play was "wicked, lewd, scandalous, bawdy, obscene, indecent, infamous, immoral and impure."

When the case went to trial on May 28, 1927, defense attorney Norman Schloss stated that the play had run for 339 performances in front of 325,000 patrons, including many members of the police department and their wives, as well as judges in the criminal courts and members of the district attorneys' staffs, and none had shown moral impairment. In response, District Attorney Joab Banton argued passionately that the play was obscene and called several detectives as witnesses who recited bawdy lines from the play, imitated the walks and gestures of the effeminate men on stage, and described in detail West's provocative physical actions. The newspapers carried every word and description of the testimony. *Variety* placed the jury under considerable pressure by publishing the names and addresses of every one of the jury members, all men. The jury took only an hour and a half to reach a guilty verdict. West and her attorney were given 10-day jail sentences and fined $500 each, but charges against the actors and the theater owner were dropped.

Resigned to her jail stay, West was driven in her limousine to the prison and carried armloads of white roses as she stepped out of the car and smiled for photographers. She later told reporters that during the eight days she spent on Welfare Island she dined with the warden and his wife and wore her silk underwear, not prison underthings. After her release, West gave an exclusive interview to *Liberty* magazine for a fee of $1,000, which she donated to establish the Mae West Memorial Library in the prison. George Eels and Stanley Musgrove write in their biography that West attended a charity luncheon given by the Women's National Democratic Club and the Penology Delinquency Division of the New York Federation of Women's Clubs, where she was honored for taking a stand for free speech. Although audience interest remained high, West withdrew *Sex* from Broadway and it remained unpublished and unperformed in New York City until the late 1990s.

FURTHER READING

Curry, Ramona. *Too Much of a Good Thing: Mae West as Cultural Icon.* Minneapolis: University of Minnesota Press, 1996.

Eels, George, and Stanley Musgrove. *Mae West: A Biography.* New York: William Morrow & Company, 1982.

Hamilton, Marybeth. *When I'm Bad, I'm Better: Mae West, Sex, and American Entertainment.* New York: HarperCollins, 1995.

Laufe, Abe. *The Wicked Stage: A History of Theater Censorship and Harassment in the United States.* New York: Frederick Ungar Publishing Co., 1978.

Schlissel, Lilian, ed. *Three Plays by Mae West: Sex, The Drag, The Pleasure.* New York: Routledge, 1997.

West, Mae. *Goodness Had Nothing to Do with It.* New York: Prentice Hall, 1959.

THE SHANGHAI GESTURE

Author: John Colton

Original date and place of production: February 1, 1926, Martin Beck Theatre, New York, New York

Characters: Amah, Lady Blessington, Sir John Blessington, Sir Guy Charteris, Lin Chi, Ex-Envoy Mandarin Koo Lot Foo, Mother Goddam, Caesar Hawkins, Ching Chang Mary, M. le Compte de Michot, Prince Oshima, Ni Pan, Poppy

Filmed versions: *The Shanghai Gesture* (1941)

SUMMARY

The Shanghai Gesture, a lurid tale of revenge set in a brothel in Shanghai, China, makes bitter statements about racial injustice and the chauvinistic treatment an Asian woman suffers at the hands of an Englishman. The action revolves around Mother Goddam, the proud owner of "the biggest bordello east of Suez," which offers clients gambling and opium, as well. Elegant and commanding, she has sworn to take revenge against Sir Guy Charteris, now Taipan of the British China Trading Company. Several decades earlier, he had seduced her and taken her inheritance, leaving her pregnant and alone. In a florid speech, she ferociously recounts the horrors she confronted after her English lover abandoned her. She has spent more than two decades waiting to avenge the wrong and mourning the daughter that she gave up. Now Shanghai's leading proponent of vice, she plots to enact her terrible revenge on the eve of the Chinese New Year. Industrialists such as Sir Guy Charteris hope to run her out of business and then claim her land, and the government likes his plan because his efforts will clean up Shanghai's notorious red-light district. Mother Goddam views the attempt with little concern: "Every so often Shanghai decides to clean itself like a swan in a muddy lake. . . . I shall not move and I certainly shall not close."

Mother Goddam's opulently decorated brothel contains rooms named the Little Room of the Great Cat, the Gallery of Laughing Dolls, and the Green Stairway of the Angry Dragon. Despite the elegance of the surroundings and the beauty of the women, the habitués of the establishment form a melancholy group. One night, Charteris's spoiled daughter Victoria, known as Poppy, stumbles upon Mother Goddam's establishment. When Mother Goddam learns her identity, she preys upon Poppy's weaknesses for gambling and opium. The young woman is soon laden with gambling debts, addicted to opium, and serving as a prostitute in the brothel. Mother Goddam plans to exact her revenge against Charteris on the eve of the Chinese New Year, at a lavish party attended by many of the most powerful citizens of Shanghai, including Sir John Blessington, Port Judge of Shanghai; M. Le Compte de Michot, "Number One" of the Bank of Europe-Asia; Ex-Envoy Mandarin Koo Lot Foo; and Charteris. In front of the assembled guests, Mother Goddam reveals her abandonment by Charteris and shows the degradation into which she has led Poppy. Shocked by what she has done, Charteris has his own surprise and tells the vengeful madam that Poppy is the daughter she gave up decades before, their child. The distraught Mother Goddam sees that she has destroyed Poppy's life and made her a hopeless drug addict; in despair, she strangles her daughter.

CENSORSHIP HISTORY

The Shanghai Gesture was one of a large number of plays featuring a sexual theme that were produced on Broadway in the 1920s. Similar to most such plays of the time, except those produced by Mae West, this one remained, as

Schlissel writes, "obedient to the unwritten rule that prescribed ruin for fallen women." The bordello in which the action occurs is suffocated by gloom and doom, and the play does not have a happy ending, as the offending character must suffer for her actions.

The Shanghai Gesture has been identified by *Playbill* as being one of the most sensational plays ever, yet the version that appeared in 1926 was considerably expurgated. Before the play was produced, the author agreed to self-censor the work and to remove instances of language, action, and innuendo that the crusading censors had already found offensive in other plays. Producer A. H. Woods realized that the Society for the Suppression of Vice was closely scrutinizing the plays that appeared on Broadway. Although the free publicity offered by notoriety could bring in large audiences, he knew that a court trial would be costly and legal proceedings would delay performances and result in lost revenue. Rather than risk his investment, he worked with playwright John Colton to make numerous modifications in the script to avoid direct references to the brothel setting or the profession of the heavily made up and seductively garbed women working in it. Dialogue that overtly spoke of sexual activity was toned down and replaced by euphemism and innuendo. They also decided against including the suspended cages containing scantily clad women that Mother Goddam uses to attract men to her establishment. In the effort to avoid charges of immorality, Woods and Colton also revised the means of Poppy's deterioration, placing a greater emphasis upon her addictions to gambling and opium than to her work as a prostitute.

Theatergoers were not put off by the modified script because they easily identified the setting and filled in areas that the playwright was forced to leave deliberately vague to avoid the censors. Fifteen years later, before the Hays Commission, the film industry censors rejected 32 versions of the screenplay before approving the final script for the filmed version of *The Shanghai Gesture*. Many of the changes made by Colton before the first stage performance were included. In addition, the name "Mother Goddam" was changed to "Mother Gin Sling," Charteris becomes the long-ago husband, not merely the lover who abandoned her and their child years before, and the setting is a gambling house, not a brothel.

FURTHER READING

Christianson, Richard. "*Shanghai Gesture* Retains Much of Its Power." *Chicago Tribune,* January 13, 1995, p. 18.

Colton, John. *The Shanghai Gesture.* Introduction by John D. Williams. New York: Boni and Liveright, 1926.

"Martin Beck Theatre." *Playbill* Theatre Information. Available online. URL: http://www.playbill.com/reference/theatre_info/2180.html.

Schlissel, Lillian. Introduction to *Three Plays by Mae West.* New York: Routledge, 1997.

Simonson, Robert. "Blowing Off the Dust, Breathing New Life." *The New York Times,* September 1, 2002, section 2, p. 3.

Wadler, Joyce. "The Play's His Thing, Even If You Never Heard of It." *The New York Times*, October 9, 2002, p. B2.

THE SHEWING UP OF BLANCO POSNET

Author: George Bernard Shaw
Original date and place of production: August 25, 1909, Abbey Theatre, Dublin, Ireland
Characters: Babsy, Elder Daniels, Emma, Feemy Evans, the Foreman, Hannah, Jessie, Strapper Kemp, Lottie, Blanco Posnet, the Sheriff, Waggoner Jo, the Woman
Filmed versions: None

SUMMARY

The Shewing Up of Blanco Posnet, a one-act play subtitled "A Sermon in Crude Melodrama," was described by Shaw as "a religious tract in dramatic form." Set vaguely in "a territory of the United States of America," the play relates the story of Blanco Posnet, who has been brought before a judge on charges of stealing the sheriff's horse from the barn of Elder Daniels. As Daniels explains, "It was the Sheriff's horse—the one he loaned to young Strapper. Strapper loaned it to me; and the thief stole it, thinking it was mine."

The townspeople are ready to believe the worst of Blanco, because he has taken every opportunity of showing his contempt for them. When Strapper, Sheriff Kemp's brother, tells him that Kemp "hangs horse-thieves," Blanco responds: "He's a rotten Sheriff. Oh a rotten Sheriff. If he did his first duty he'd hang himself. This is a rotten town. Your fathers came here on a false alarm of gold-digging; and when the gold didn't pan out, they lived by licking their young into habits of honest industry." His words taunt Daniels, who, unknown to the townspeople, is his brother who has turned from being a heavy drinker to selling liquor, because "what keeps America today the purest of nations is that when she's not working she's too drunk to hear the sound of the tempter." Daniels insists that no one will believe that the two are brothers and berates Posnet for being abstinent: "Oh, why didn't you drink like I used to? . . . It was drink that saved my character when I was a young man; and it was the want of it that spoiled yours." As Strapper goads him, Posnet insists that the hostile townspeople cannot hang him because they have found no witness who saw him ride away on the horse.

Daniels tries to wear Posnet down and make him confess, appealing even to God and promising salvation, but Posnet rejects the attempt, saying of God: "He's a sly one. He's a mean one. He lies low for you. He plays cat and mouse with you. . . . I gave Him the go-bye and did without Him all these years. But he caught me out at last."

Feemy Evans, the town prostitute, claims that she saw Posnet riding out of town on the horse early in the morning, but he denies it and says that a woman with a seriously ill child borrowed the horse to find a doctor. Waggoner Jo finds her with the horse, and the sheriff asks her why she took the horse from the stable to find a doctor when a doctor lives next to the stable. The woman reveals that she took the horse from a man riding past her while she sat holding her dying child. When he learns that the boy has died, Posnet cries out that the "little Judas kid" has betrayed him. The mother of the dead child staunchly asserts that she took the horse from "a bad man," and she challenges Feemy to say otherwise. Touched by the woman's loss of the child, Feemy reconsiders and claims that she has given false evidence just to hurt Posnet. The men hoot and shout that Posnet has been "shewed up" by a child.

As the play ends, Posnet preaches to the other men that he has "got the rotten feeling off me for one minute of my life; and I'll go through fire to get it off me again." He tries to find a decent husband for Feemy, who has shown herself to be a failure as a "bad woman," and he offers to buy a round of drinks for the men.

CENSORSHIP HISTORY

Shaw's play, written between February 16 and March 8, 1909, was commissioned by Herbert Beerbohm Tree for a matinee performance at His Majesty's Theatre in London as a benefit for a children's charity. The playwright claimed that he had written the part of Posnet especially to be played by Tree, who balked and asked that Shaw remove some of the unflattering references to God and to eliminate Posnet's insults to Feemy as a "slut" who has "had immoral relations with every man in this town." Tree was under consideration for knighthood, and he told Shaw that for him to "voice such words" would not be wise, but the playwright convinced him that he should have nothing to fear. As Holroyd writes, "If the Examiner of Plays passed the words, Tree would have obtained official blessing; and if he didn't the actor would never have to utter them."

Tree submitted the play to George Alexander Redford, the examiner of plays, who refused to grant a license for public performance to *The Shewing Up of Blanco Posnet* on the grounds that it was blasphemous. He suggested that if Shaw were willing to remove the passages in which Posnet rants against the unfairness of God and attacks Christian tenets, as well as change some of the language, the play might receive a license upon resubmission. Shaw was extremely pleased with the refusal and used the rejection as the basis for a series of letters to the *The London Times* that attacked the question of censorship in England. In the preface to the published play, Shaw recounts the case of the suppression of his work. Shortly after the rejection, Shaw appeared before the Joint Committee on Stage Plays (Censorship and Theatre Licencing) to recommend that censorship be abolished.

At the same time, he agreed to allow Lady Augusta Gregory and William Butler Yeats to produce the play at their Abbey Theatre in Dublin, Ireland.

Lady Gregory wrote to Shaw that she believed they could do the play well and that nothing would show "the hypocrisy of the British Censor more than a performance in Dublin where the audience is known to be so sensitive." When word of the planned production reached the under-secretary of the lord lieutenant of Ireland, Gregory and Yeats were summoned to meet at Dublin Castle with Viceroy Lord Aberdeen, who threatened to revoke the Abbey Theatre's license if they produced an uncensored version of *The Shewing Up of Blanco Posnet*. The two feared the loss of their theater, but they decided to challenge the threat by making the censorship part of the pattern of Anglo-Irish politics. They asserted that their theater license was being threatened "because English censorship is being extended to Ireland" and stated that "we must not, by accepting the English Censor's ruling, give away anything of the liberty of the Irish theatre of the future." Although they cared little for Shaw's politics, Sinn Fein and the Gaelic League added their support to the appeal made by Lady Gregory. In return for the license to produce the play, Gregory promised two small concessions: Shaw agreed to remove the word "immoral" in describing Feemy's relations with the men of the town and to remove the words "Dearly beloved brethren."

On the first night of the production, August 25, 1909, hundreds of people attended and most were surprised to find the play so innocuous. Shaw biographer Michael Holroyd writes that "some people questioned whether they had been victims of an Abbey hoax." Cheered by the reception of the Irish press and the Catholic Church, which approved of the play, Shaw decided to test the effect that such acceptance in Ireland would have on the English censors. He asked Annie Horniman, who held the lease on the Abbey and had applied to Dublin Castle for a license, to apply for a license to produce the play at her new theater in Manchester, the Gaiety. She submitted the Irish version of the play, which Redford noted retained all of the passages he had found objectionable in the earlier application for a license. He claimed that he had no ground on which to request Lord Chamberlain Earl Spencer to reconsider the decision, despite Shaw's contention that the performance in Dublin with the accompanying good reviews from the press and the clergy proved that the English censors had made an error. Shaw demanded that Redford resubmit the play to the lord chamberlain, which he did, and the play was again rejected. The result again delighted Shaw, who continued his attack on censorship and wrote in *The London Times* that "What the Censorship has actually done exceeds the utmost hopes of those who, like myself, have devoted themselves to its destruction." The play did not receive a license for public performance in England until 1921, 12 years after performance at the Abbey Theatre.

FURTHER READING

Fowell, Frank, and Frank Palmer. *Censorship in England*. London: F. Palmer, 1913. Reprint, New York: Benjamin Blom, 1969.

Holroyd, Michael. *Bernard Shaw: A Biography*. Vol. 2. *The Pursuit of Power*. New York: Random House, 1989.

Knowles, Dorothy. *The Censor, the Drama and the Film, 1900–1934.* London: Allen and Unwin, 1934.

Parkes, Adam. *Modernism and the Theater of Censorship.* New York: Oxford University Press, 1996.

Shaw, George Bernard. *The Doctor's Dilemma, Getting Married, and The Shewing Up of Blanco Posnet.* New York: Brentano's, 1911.

———. "Statement of the Evidence in Chief of George Bernard Shaw before the Joint Committee on Stage Plays (Censorship and Theatre Licensing)." In *The Doctor's Dilemma, Getting Married, and The Shewing Up of Blanco Posnet.* New York: Brentano's, 1911, pp. 345–380.

SIMON CALLED PETER

Authors: Jules Eckert Goodman and Edward Knoblock
Original date and place of production: November 10, 1924, Klaw Theatre, New York, New York
Characters: Reverend Peter Graham, Julie, Louise
Filmed versions: None

SUMMARY

Simon Called Peter, adapted by Jules Eckert Goodman and Edward Knoblock from the novel of the same name by Robert Keable, is the story of an Anglican chaplain serving in France during World War I. At first, Reverend Peter Graham tries to change what he views as the lax behavior of the servicemen and the women with whom they socialize. As the war continues, he finds that he becomes more accepting of their behavior and he suffers pangs of guilt that he has not succeeded in changing their behavior. Instead, he struggles continually to prevent himself from engaging in activities that he had disdained earlier. As his standards of personal behavior become lower, Graham begins to feel and to express greater compassion toward the other servicemen and toward the prostitutes, and he becomes a friend to one prostitute, Louise.

As the boundaries blur between what he once thought to be morally right and what he now thinks, he struggles to reconcile his duties with his growing sexual desires. Graham's self-esteem deteriorates and he becomes angry and disgusted with himself. In a moment of temptation, he begs Louise to have sex with him, despite his early sermonizing to the men to stay away from the prostitutes and his efforts at rehabilitating them. When she refuses because she knows that he will regret his actions later, he tells her, "And why not? You give to other men—why not to me, Louise? . . . I've a body like other men."

Graham's struggle to meet the spiritual needs of the servicemen increases. He meets and falls in love with Julie, with whom he becomes obsessed. They spend several passion-filled days in a London hotel, and neither expresses any guilt or hesitation for their unmarried state. At one point in expressing his love for Julie, Graham exclaims, "I believe I'd rather have you than—than God!" He tells her that their union is more solid than any that would be formalized by civil or religious ceremonies, for they are united by "the pure passion of human love, virginal, clean." Despite such professions, the two part because Graham feels that he has to give his first allegiance to the Anglican Church.

CENSORSHIP HISTORY

The 1921 novel by Keable from which the play was adapted by Goodman and Knoblock drew the attention of the Society for the Suppression of Vice in New York City, which picketed bookstores and tried unsuccessfully to have it banned. When the play was produced in 1924, members of the society led by president John Summer had already begun their crusade to eliminate all traces of sex, obscenity, blasphemy, and many other elements from the plays that appeared on Broadway. Their efforts would result in city officials creating a censorship law in 1927, the Wales Padlock Law, which gave city authorities the power to close down "theatres purveying immorality and smut."

Representatives of the society contacted producer William Brady when the play was in rehearsal in early 1924 to express their concern. They expected the play would contain much of the material that they had found objectionable in the novel, and they wanted to alert Brady that they planned to take action to keep "blasphemy and smut" off Broadway stages. Brady refused to offer them the opportunity to review the script and continued with the production. After the play opened, on November 10, 1924, lawyers representing the society asked a New York City court to issue an injunction against the play. The complaint charged that the play promoted immorality in depicting a clergyman who solicits sexual favors from a prostitute and who has a sexual relationship with a young woman in which neither shows remorse. The reformers were also shocked by a scene in which a woman opens her blouse in the effort to entice the clergyman.

The courts refused to issue an injunction to stop performances of the play, but the city agreed to undertake an investigation into the merits of the play and to determine whether it was immoral. The publicity generated by the efforts to ban the play brought out large audiences of curiosity seekers, and the play ran for 88 performances, ending right before the investigation was to begin.

FURTHER READING

Gelbert, Bruce Michael. "Look Again: Review & Miscellany." Available online. URL: htpp://tosos2.org/LookAgainEssay.htm.

Hewitt, Bernard. *Theatre U.S.A., 1668 to 1957*. New York: McGraw-Hill, 1959.

Laufe, Abe. *The Wicked Stage: A History of Theater Censorship and Harassment in the United States*. New York: Frederick Ungar Publishing Co., 1978.

SIR THOMAS MORE

Author: Anthony Munday
Original date and place of production: None
Characters: Bishop of Rochester, Sir Robert Cholmeley, Earl of Shrewsbury, Earl of Surrey, John Lincoln, Sir Thomas More, Sir Thomas Palmer, Doll Williamson
Filmed versions: None

SUMMARY

Sir Thomas More dramatizes an incident that took place while More served as sheriff of London, two decades before his opposition to Henry VIII's divorce from Catherine of Aragon and his subsequent refusal to swear that the king's authority superseded the pope's, which led to his execution in 1535. As the play opens, the English inhabitants of London are becoming increasingly hostile to the foreign individuals living in their midst, the French "straungers" whom they wish to eject from the city. From simmering resentment, the tension mounts until a rebellion is planned, led by the charismatic revolutionary John Lincoln. The English rebels blame the foreigners who have taken refuge in London for creating economic disadvantages for them, and they protest loudly against the rights and privileges assumed by the "straungers."

Lincoln, an articulate spokesperson, organizes a protest on May Day. He addresses the assembled group during the annual Spittle sermons in a speech that emphasizes the plight of the English citizens because the "aliens" now dominate the city economy.

> . . . wherfore, the premises considered, the redresse must be of the commons, knit and united to one parte. And as the hurt and damage greeveth all men, so must all men see to their willing power for remedie, and not suffer the sayde Aliens in their wealth, and the naturall borne men of this region to come to confusion.

While the riots gain momentum, several of the nobles meet and discuss how best to handle the insurrection. The earl of Shrewbury expresses sympathy for "the displeased commons of the Cittie" and the earl of Surrey vows that the "saucie Aliens" will be punished for their presumption of English rights. Sir Robert Cholmeley places blame for the unrest upon the king's advisers, who have kept him ignorant of the "base and dayly wrongs" his subjects have experienced.

In act four, Lincoln incites the mob to violence, and the mob sets fire to the homes of all known and suspected aliens. More arrives at the Guildhall and asks the rioters to remain calm and compassionate toward the foreigners, who will face dire hardship if they are forced to leave England. He argues vehemently for a return to order, and stresses that if the disorder continues, "men lyke ravenous fishes woold feed on one another." In act five, the final but incomplete act, the apprentices join the rebels to go "A Maying."

CENSORSHIP HISTORY

Sir Thomas More was submitted to the censor, Master of Revels Edmund Tilney (or Tyllney), in the early 1590s; the exact year is in dispute because the earliest extant manuscript is undated. The master of revels prevented its performance out of concern that scenes showing Londoners rioting might set a bad example. In 1559 Queen Elizabeth I had issued orders banning the presentation of plays that, in the opinion of government authorities, disparaged the established religion (the Church of England) or the government. In April 1593 the London city council members were directed by the king to discover the source of circulating tracts that contained bitter and hate-filled attacks on foreign inhabitants of the city. A month later, the Privy Council ordered searches of the houses of people suspected of posting threats of violence against the foreigners and demanding that they depart from the city. Suspects who, after cross-examination, refused to confess would be tortured in Bridewell prison. The authorities' desire to avoid fueling existing hostilities against foreign communities in London from which the government received considerable economic benefit was a strong reason for censorship of the play.

Among many changes that Tilney required was the removal of the insurrection scene in its entirety. He made his objections clear early in comments on the manuscript, which author Janet Clare writes is "the earliest extant manuscript to demonstrate state interference with secular drama." The censor wrote the following passage at the beginning of the play:

> Leave out ye insurrection wholy, and the Cause ther off, and begin with Sir Tho. Moore att ye mayors sessions, with a report afterwards off his good service don, being shrive off London, upon a meeting Agaynst ye Lumbardes, only by A short reportt, and nott otherwise, att your own perrilles.—E. Tyllney

In a scene following the beginning of the riot, the earls of Shrewsbury and Surrey discuss with Sir Robert Cholmeley the popular unrest in London. Tilney placed lines through the following phrases in Shrewsbury's speech that exhibit sympathy for the London rioters: "dangerous times," "frowning Vulgare brow," "distracted countenance of greefe," and "the displeased commons of the Cittie." In the margin, he wrote, "Mend this." The censor also placed a large cross over Cholmeley's criticism of the king's advisers. Further, he removed almost all references to "aliens" and "frenchmen" in the play and substituted "The Lumbards" as the object of hate. (The Lombards were merchants from the Italian republics of Genoa, Lucca, Florence, and Venice who, from the reign of Edward II (13th century), controlled the most profitable branches of English trade. With their greater wealth, they dominated native merchants and assisted the king with loans of money.) As Clare writes, no solid evidence exists to show that the play was ever produced or published.

FURTHER READING

Acheson, Arthur. *Shakespeare, Chapman and Sir Thomas More.* New York: AMS Press, 1994.

Clare, Janet. *"Art Made Tongue-Tied by Authority": Elizabethan and Jacobean Dramatic Censorship.* New York: Manchester University Press, 1990.

Metz, G. Harold. *Sources of Four Plays Ascribed to Shakespeare: The Reign of King Edward III, Sir Thomas More, The History of Cardenio, The Two Nobel Kinsmen.* St. Louis: University of Missouri, 1989.

Munday, Anthony. *Sir Thomas Tudor.* Tudor Facsimile Texts, Old English Plays Series Number 65. New York: AMS Press, 1974.

SISTER MARY IGNATIUS EXPLAINS IT ALL FOR YOU

Author: Christopher Durang

Original date and place of production: December 14, 1979, Ensemble Studio Theatre, New York, New York

Characters: Aloysius Benhelm, Sister Mary Ignatius, Philomena Restovitch, Gary Sullavan, Diane Symonds, Thomas

Filmed versions: Made for television: *Sister Mary Ignatius Explains It All For You* (2001)

SUMMARY

Christopher Durang's *Sister Mary Ignatius Explains It All For You* is a one-act play featuring a teaching nun whose devotion to her Catholic faith and to church dogma has become fanaticism. The play opens with Sister Mary Ignatius, dressed in the traditional nun's habit of flowing dark robe and wimple, providing her listeners with a description of the universe. She begins by identifying the planets and describing the universe in a vague manner, then identifies heaven, hell, and purgatory as being "outside the universe." Sister Mary describes each of these states in dogmatic rhetoric: "Heaven is where we live in eternal bliss with Our Lord Jesus Christ. . . . Hell is where we are eternally deprived of the presence of Our Lord Jesus Christ. . . . Purgatory is the middle area where we go to suffer if we have not been perfect in our lives." She presents further facts about purgatory in a manner that suggests scientific truth, and relates that time in purgatory may last "anywhere from 300 billion to 700 billion years."

From providing pseudoscientific instruction, Sister Mary plunges into a greatly compressed version of Catholic belief, explaining in minutes the concepts of limbo, original sin, the Immaculate Conception, and other beliefs in a manner that challenges her listeners to dare to disagree with what she presents as fact rather than faith. She calls upon Thomas, a small boy dressed in a parochial-school uniform, who is a student at Our Lady of Perpetual Sorrow School, where Sister Mary Ignatius teaches. The audience is informed that he is seven years old and "capable of choosing to commit sin or to not commit sin, and God will hold him responsible for whatever he does." He has achieved the age of majority in religious terms. Sister Mary asks a series of questions from the Catholic catechism in rapid succession, and Thomas responds to them by rote: "Who made you? . . . Why did God make you? . . . What is the sixth commandment? . . . What is the fourth commandment?"

As Thomas answers the catechism questions, Sister Mary interpolates information from her family's past among the answers and lectures the audience on the evils of using birth control, despite her mother's suffering in giving birth to 26 children, and despite the fact that her mother had to be institutionalized after she came to believe that her father was Satan. She details the sins of the worldly, then asks Thomas to provide a partial list of all those who are going to suffer in Hell, which he does: Christine Keeler, Roman Polanski, Zsa Zsa Gabor, the editors of *After Dark* magazine, Linda Lovelace, Georgina Spelvin, Big John Holmes, Brooke Shields, David Bowie, Mick Jagger, Patty Hearst, Betty Comden, Adolph Green. Sister Mary emphasizes that names are constantly being added to the list.

One-third of the way into the play, four students whom Sister Mary taught in 1959 enter, acting in the Christmas pageant that she required all of her parochial school classes to enact. It was written in 1948 by Mary Jane Mahoney, her "best student"—"in the 7th grade she didn't have her first period, she had a stigmata." As Sister Mary probes each of the four about their lives, she is shocked to learn that they hate her and blame her and her fanaticism for their misery. Gary and Diane, as Joseph and Mary, play out a bizarre version of the Nativity, complete with Philomena as Misty the camel and Aloysius as the narrator of a story that runs rapidly through all of the events of Christ's life related in the New Testament. After congratulating her former students for their presentation, Sister Mary asks them questions from the catechism. Through their answers, they reveal that they have all committed what Sister Mary views as mortal sins: Diane has had two abortions, Gary is homosexual, and Philomena has had a child outside of marriage. Only Aloysius has turned out well in the nun's eyes; although he admits that he is an alcoholic, beats his wife, and contemplates suicide, she brushes off these imperfections as "venial sins," for he is married, attends Mass, goes to confession and communion, and does not use birth control.

The four former students inform Sister Mary that they have never liked her because she is a bully, but she defends her actions as having prepared them for life. Diane says that she has appeared to shoot Sister Mary to death as repayment for lying to her. After being raped on the day that her mother died of cancer, being seduced and impregnated by her psychiatrist and experiencing other abuses, she has grown to hate Sister Mary "for making me once expect everything to be ordered and to make sense." As Diane aims her gun, the stage directions state, "Sister Mary whips out her own gun and shoots Diane dead." She then kills Gary and tells Philomena to leave, while she orders Thomas to keep the gun trained on Aloysius. As the play ends, an exhausted Sister Mary naps while Thomas continues to hold the gun and recites questions and answers from the catechism.

CENSORSHIP HISTORY

In autumn 1982 a small theater in St. Louis, the Theatre Project, announced its intention to present *Sister Mary Ignatius* in January 1983, in a rented space at the Mayfair Hotel. The St. Louis chapter of the Catholic League for Religious and Civil Rights read the script, then asked the Theatre Project to change its choice of the play, claiming *Sister Mary* was bigoted against Catholics. The Theatre Project refused, and the Catholic League approached the Mayfair Hotel, asking the management to cancel its arrangement with the Theatre Project. The Catholic League then brought the play to the attention of the St. Louis archbishop, John May, who wrote an editorial in a Catholic newsletter condemning the play as "a vile diatribe against all things Catholic." He urged St. Louis Catholics not to attend. A few days later, the Mayfair Hotel withdrew from its tentative agreement with the Theatre Project, citing "technical difficulties."

Two local universities offered their spaces to the Theatre Project; the privately funded Washington University and the publicly funded University of Missouri. Senator Edwin L. Dirck, the Democratic chairman of the Senate Appropriations Committee in the Missouri State Senate, supported the Catholic League in opposing the play. He called in Arnold B. Grobman, the chancellor of the University of Missouri, and asked him to defend allowing this "anti-Catholic" play to be performed on publicly funded property. Mr. Grobman responded he had allowed the Theatre Project to use space at the university in the past, and stated, "I don't tell them what plays to perform any more than I tell teachers what to teach or students what to read." He added that he did not find the play anti-Catholic, but rather a satire on parochial education. Senator Dirck told the newspapers that the chancellor had "offended every member of the committee" and threatened budgetary reprisals. The Theatre Project had in the past received a small grant from the Missouri State Arts Council amounting to about 3 percent of its budget. Senator Dirck called in Talbot McCarthy, the chairperson of the Missouri Arts Council, to defend her action in having given a grant to a theater performing "an anti-Catholic play." Dirck warned McCarthy that funding for the arts council was in jeopardy unless she took action against the Theatre Project; he wanted her to withdraw the grant, but McCarthy declined. She was quoted in the papers as being sorry she offended the Senate Committee, but said the council made its grant decisions based on the past performance of theater applicants, and that "our role is not to censor every work by the 500 groups we support."

The controversy was front-page news in St. Louis, and the city's two major newspapers traded editorials back and forth, one in favor of the play's right to be performed, the other against—all before the play opened. National media coverage followed, as Charles Kuralt, CBS News, *Sunday Morning, Entertainment Tonight,* and *The Phil Donahue Show* picked up the story. This publicity increased attendance at the box offices in New York and Los Angeles. The play opened in St. Louis and sold out for its entire run. According to *Variety,* it was the first production in the history of the Theatre Project to make a profit. In spring 1983 Senator Dirck followed through on his threat to Talbot McCarthy and sponsored an appropriations bill cutting funds to the arts council by $60,000. He was quoted as saying that it would be better to give the funds to something more wholesome, like county fairs. A rider was added to this bill, specifying that the Theatre Project in particular was never to be given a state arts grant again because it had presented the play. In a close vote, the Missouri senate defeated the proposed arts council budget cut; but it overwhelmingly approved (22-8) the ban on future grants to the Theatre Project.

The American Civil Liberties Union was prepared to initiate a lawsuit if the ban stood. However, in subcommittee conference, the ban was killed and was not a part of the final bill. In its place, the Missouri Senate Appropriations Committee wrote a letter of warning to the arts council to be more careful in the future to avoid funding any works that might cause offense.

Over the next several years, *Sister Mary Ignatius* caused controversy wherever it appeared, usually triggered by protests from the Catholic League for Religious and Civil Rights. The next major incident occurred in autumn 1983 in Boston, where the Catholic league tried to convince the management of the Charles Playhouse to cancel the play. The league threatened to boycott another play, *Shear Madness* at the same theater. The league approached the mayor of Boston, Raymond L. Flynn, and a few days before the play started previews, the mayor released a statement "repudiating the play and calling it 'blatantly and painfully anti-Catholic.'" The New England chapter of the Anti-Defamation League of B'nai B'rith joined forces with the Catholic League, and released a statement to the press calling the play "offensive, demeaning, and misrepresentative of the Catholic faith and of those who believe and practice it."

The protests intensified during the preview period, with large picket lines and daily statements in the press and on television. The protests weakened when leaders found that the play received no tax funding, thus precluding the tax money argument. The reviews were extremely favorable, and, more importantly for the protests, many of the reviewers, including Catholic ones, expressed their opinion that the play was not anti-Catholic; it was antiauthoritarian. A small picket line remained for most of the run, but the daily coverage on television and in the newspapers stopped, and the play was successful in Boston.

The Catholic League for Religious and Civil Rights initiated protests in other cities, as well. In Detroit a production of the play was canceled due to an organized letter-writing campaign. In Glen Ellyn, Illinois, a small college scheduled four performances of a student production after the drama department received petitions with 2,000 signatures each from two parishes, urging cancellation of the "bigotry." The protesting organizations intimated that a lawsuit regarding the misuse of public funds might follow. The college, scheduled to host a well-known playwright later in the year, felt it could not retreat on the principle of free speech, and refused to cancel. A student threatened to disrupt each performance, though he did not follow through, and the four performances occurred without incident. At its next meeting, the board of directors of the college was greeted by picketers holding large blow-up photos of each of the directors with the word *bigot* scrawled across the face, and the protest was photographed and published in the newspapers. The head of the drama department was told unofficially to avoid such controversy in the future.

An announced production of *Sister Mary* was canceled in Ponca City, Oklahoma, after a campaign that included anonymous phone calls warning prominent citizens that the proposed play might "destroy" the community, a letter-writing campaign to the theater, attempts to revoke the theater's lease, and ads in the newspaper advising "Catholics and all concerned Christians" to attend the theater's next board meeting. A local priest met with the theater management and expressed his concern over the perceived anti-Catholic conspiracy of the theater due to the proposed production of *Sister Mary Ignatius* and the previous production of *Man of La Mancha*, which he felt was also anti-Catholic, citing its reference to the Spanish Inquisition. The theater canceled the production.

FURTHER READING

"Costa Mesa to Look at *Sister Mary Ignatius* for Arts Grant Violations." *Los Angeles Times*, September 13, 1990, p. F9.

Durang, Christopher. *Christopher Durang Explains It All for You: Six Plays.* New York: Grove Weidenfeld, 1990.

———. *Sister Mary Ignatius Explains It All for You.* New York: Dramatists Play Service, 1999.

Fanelli, Sean A. "Drawing Lines at Nassau Community College." *Academe*, July/August 1990, pp. 24–27.

Goldstein, Richard. "Defending 'The Devil's Work.'" *Village Voice*, June 14, 1983, p. 37.

"Sister Mary Ignatius Isn't Happy." *Los Angeles Times*, September 13, 1990, p. B6.

SODOM

Author: John Wilmot, Earl of Rochester

Original date and place of production: c. 1678, private performance at the court of Charles I

Characters: King Bolloxinion, Borastus, Buggeranthos, Clytoris, Cunticula, Queen Cuntigratia, Dr. Flux, Fuckadilla, Pine, Prince Pockenello, Prince Pricket, Princess Swivia, Twely
Filmed versions: None

SUMMARY

John Wilmot's *Sodom*, subtitled *Or the Quintessence of Debauchery*, is a five-act play written in heroic couplets that was intended as a satire of the corruption and the vice of King Charles II of England and his court. The play opens with King Bolloxinion explaining that, unlike other monarchs who "keep their subjects less in awe than fear" and are "slaves to crowns," his "Nation shall be free" and his sole concerns are to eat and to copulate. He has become bored with heterosexual activity and declares that, from this point forward, sodomy shall become the rule of the land and heterosexuality will be viewed as abnormal. He abandons Queen Cuntigratia and selects Pockenello as his new mate, an offer that is graciously accepted.

In the second act, the stage appears as a pastoral garden filled with naked men and women posing as statues. In the middle stands a group of women who lament the king's rule and who express their feelings of abandonment as the result of this "proselyte to Pagafuck" (Wilmot's term for homosexual activity). They make plans for revenge, then engage in mutual masturbation and other sexual acts, as the statues come to life and join them.

In act three, Prince Pricket and Princess Swivia compare genitals, and Pricket declares that Swivia's vagina is "The strangest Creature that I ever saw." What follows is an explicit scene of incest in which the princess seduces her brother, the prince. In this act and the one that follows, the women eagerly seduce any man who is willing, regardless of differences in social rank. The queen overcomes the reluctance of General Buggeranthos, who has been charged with supervising and enforcing the king's rule of sodomy, and maids of honor recklessly seduce tradesmen.

In act five, as Bolloxinion stands in a grove of trees pruned in the shape of penises, Dr. Flux rushes in and informs him that the nation of Sodom is suffering from an epidemic of venereal disease. He also prophesies the end of procreation. The queen has died, Prince Pricket has syphilis, and Princess Swivia is insane, but Bolloxinion refuses to change the law. As the play ends, demons rise from the front of stage warning, "Fire doth descent/'Tis too late to amend." The ghost of the queen appears and promises to torment Bolloxinion in Hell, and the curtain falls as fire and brimstone appear in the distance.

CENSORSHIP HISTORY

This highly satiric and sexually graphic play was performed only once during Wilmot's lifetime, in a production for Charles II of England and his court a few years before the author's death. The play was not published until 1684, four years after Wilmot died, and because no English firm dared to publish the play, it appeared in Antwerp. Author David Loth writes that, rather than feel shocked by the content, "The audience, which . . . included women, amused itself by trying to identify the originals of the stage characters."

The play is filled with graphic language, direct references to the genitals of both sexes, and sexual behavior, and until the 20th century this work and others by Wilmot were, as critic Marius Reeves writes, "unprintable and were only really known to academics and scholars." The British Museum had a manuscript copy in its "secret collection," permitting access only to verified researchers until the early 1960s. As Norton writes, *Sodom* is "the first work in English literature ever to be censored by the government on the grounds of obscenity and pornography primarily because of its homosexual nature." Although court members may have been intrigued by the play, the sexually explicit farce offended the English censors as much for the sexual activity as for its attack upon an English monarch. In 1689 Joseph Streater and Benjamin Crayle were charged by the courts at the Guildhall Quarter Sessions with the selling of "librum flagitosum et impudicum" (obscene and lascivious books) when they tried to sell a copy of the play published in Antwerp. They were fined £20 and suffered the loss of their inventory. Writer Jonathan Green notes that in 1707, book dealer John Marshall was also prosecuted successfully for selling the play. *Sodom* was submitted for a license for public performance in 1727 and rejected summarily by Examiner of Plays Charles Fitzroy, duke of Grafton, who refused to consider this "scurrilous lampoon on the Court of Charles II."

To date, no public performances of the play in England have been recorded. In the United States in 1999, the Dysfunctional Theatre Company presented an updated version of *Sodom* at the St. Mark's Studio Theatre in New York City, as part of the third annual New York International Fringe Festival. For this production, the king and queen of Charles's court were transformed into the president and first lady of the United States in 1999 and, as theater reviewer David Roberts writes, "we see Monica [Lewinsky] appear quite often."

FURTHER READING

Green, Jonathan. *The Encyclopedia of Censorship*. New York: Facts On File, 1990.

Greene, Graham. *Lord Rochester's Monkey: Being the Life of John Wilmot, Second Earl of Rochester*. New York: Viking Press, 1974.

Loth, David. *The Erotic in Literature*. New York: Dorset Press, 1961.

Norton, Rictor. "The Gay Subculture in Early Eighteenth Century London." *Homosexuality in Eighteenth-Century England: A Sourcebook*. Available online. URL: http:// www.infopt.demon.co.uk/molly2.htm.

Pinto, Vivian de Sola. *The Restoration Court Poets*. London: Longmans, Green Publishing, 1965.

Reeves, Marcus. "Never Mind the Cods . . . an Interview with John Baker." Available online. URL: http://www.reevescorner.co.uk/words/never_mind_the_cods.htm. Downloaded on August 14, 2003.

Roberts, David. *"Sodom, or the Quintessence of Debauchery."* Theatre Reviews Limited. Available online. URL: http://www.theatrereviews.com/fringe1999/f99-sodom. htm.

Wilmot, John, Earl of Rochester. *Sodom, or The Quintessence of Debauchery.* Traveller's Companion series, no. 48. Paris: Olympia Press, 1957.

STRANGE INTERLUDE

Author: Eugene O'Neill

Original date and place of production: January 30, 1928, John Golden Theater, New York, New York

Characters: Madeline Arnold, Gordon Evans, Mrs. Amos Evans, Sam Evans, Nina Leeds, Professor Henry Leeds, Charles Marsden

Filmed versions: Feature Film: *Strange Interlude* (1932, U.S.). Made for television: (1987, U.K.)

SUMMARY

Strange Interlude, one of Eugene O'Neill's most experimental and most successful plays, uses such innovations as interior monologues, introspective asides, and a length of nearly six hours to perform the full nine acts of the play. O'Neill uses his characters to explore such themes as the individual's alienation from religion and disaffection with science. Performances of the entire play usually include a dinner intermission of one hour at the end of part I (act 5).

The play is largely the story of Nina Leeds, the daughter of Professor Henry Leeds. Her fiancé, Gordon Evans, a renowned athlete and war hero, has been killed in battle, and she resents her father for having prevented their marriage and deprived her of both sexual passion and the possibility of becoming pregnant with Gordon's child: "Gordon never possessed me! I'm still Gordon's silly virgin! . . . And now I'm lonely and not pregnant with anything at all, but—but loathing." She cries out her anguish to "dear old Charlie," a mother-fixated novelist who loves her but has not dared to give any indication. In grief, Nina decides that she will become a nurse at a military veterans' hospital as some way of making up for her loss, and her father reluctantly agrees to her decision.

Nina returns a year later for her father's funeral, and finds that she is still too bitter to grieve for him. Marsden is present, as are Gordon Evans's young brother Sam and Dr. Edmund Darrell, whom she met at the military hospital. All three men are in love with her, but Darrell subordinates his feelings to scientific objectivity. He tells Marsden that Nina has attempted to eliminate her grief by being promiscuous with the disabled soldiers and he says that her only salvation will be to marry Sam Evans, who will give her the "normal outlets" she needs. Nina confesses her promiscuous behavior to Marsden and asks him to punish her for her behavior; he assumes a paternal role and advises her to marry Evans.

After several months of marriage, Nina learns she is pregnant but receives a shock when she discusses the expected birth with Sam's mother. Mrs. Amos Evans tells her that the baby must not be born, because the Evans family contains congenital insanity, of which Sam is not aware. She counsels Nina to abort the baby and to become pregnant by a "healthy male," and states, "You've got to have a healthy baby—sometime—so's you can both be happy! It's your rightful duty!"

Nina undergoes an abortion and a few months later works with Marsden to write a biography of Gordon. Darrell appears and Nina tells him of the warning and the abortion, then berates him for putting her into the situation by urging the marriage. Professing that he is not emotionally interested in her, Darrell offers to serve as a disinterested "healthy male" to help Nina conceive. When Nina is pregnant once again, she and Darrell realize they love each other, but Darrell insists that she stay with her husband. He then leaves for Europe.

A year passes, and many changes have occurred. Marsden has aged visibly with the death of his mother, Darrell returns and professes undying love for Nina, whom he asks to leave with him. Nina refuses because she does not want to hurt Sam and separate him from their child, Gordon, even if Darrell is the biological father. She sits with the three men and her son, filled with happiness, and says in an aside: "My three men! . . . I feel their desires converge in me! . . . husband! . . . lover . . . father!"

Act seven opens on Gordon's 11th birthday. Marsden and Darrell have become wealthy by investing in Evans's business, although Darrell has become bitter over the years. Gordon loves Evans but hates Darrell and destroys his present after seeing the doctor kissing Nina.

The next act takes place 10 years later. Gordon is now engaged to Madeline Arnold, whom Nina hates. As the family watches 21-year-old Gordon row in a big navy race, Nina attempts to enlist Darrell's help to break up the engagement, but he refuses and tells her that he will never again meddle in the lives of others. Gordon wins the race and Evans rejoices, then falls dead of a stroke. Although Darrell grieves, Marsden is secretly exultant and says in an aside, "I will not have long to wait now!"

Months pass, and the final act opens a few months after Evans's death. After Darrell and Gordon have a violent fight and then make up, Nina gives her blessing to Gordon's marriage with Madeline. As his plane flies over them, Nina tells she is too old to do anything more than "to bleach in peace," and she rejects Darrell's offer of marriage. Instead, she agrees to marry Marsden, "dear old Charlie," to whom she says, "Yes, our lives are merely strange dark interludes in the electrical display of God the Father!"

CENSORSHIP HISTORY

O'Neill's *Strange Interlude* was the center of controversy in addition to being banned in Boston. The play opened on January 30, 1928, at the John Golden

Theater in New York, and the Society for the Suppression of Vice promptly sought to stop the production because it dealt openly with marital infidelity and abortion. As city officials considered the complaint, rumors arose that O'Neill was a likely candidate for his third Pulitzer Prize for the play, although no one acknowledged this openly. Despite pressure from the would-be censors, the play drew large audiences, ran on Broadway for two years, and grossed the largest ticket sales of any play to that point; in the same period, O'Neill was awarded the expected third Pulitzer Prize. After waiting a long while to take action, city officials simply let the issue die.

Not all critics believed that *Strange Interlude*'s Pulitzer Prize was justified. Some wrote unflattering reviews that focused on the length of the play or the immobility of the characters during their soliloquies, but most of the critics did endorse the Pulitzer selection. One of the most vocal dissenters among the critics was Alexander Woollcott, drama critic for the *New York World* and one of the most highly paid critics in the United States in the mid-1920s. Rather than hail O'Neill's work as innovative and worthy of the award, he called *Strange Interlude* the "*Abie's Irish Rose* of the pseudo-intelligentsia," a vituperative remark meant to imply that the play was filled with devices created to engage the emotions of a specific audience.

A year after the play opened, on May 27, 1929, a woman using the pseudonym Georges Lewys filed a suit in the New York courts claiming that O'Neill had plagiarized his play from her novel *The Temple of Pallas-Athenae*, which had been privately printed in 1924. She claimed that she had sent copies of the novel to both the Theater Guild, which produced the play, and to Horace Liveright (of O'Neill's publisher Boni & Liveright) several years before the play was produced. She sought an injunction to stop further performances of the play, already in its final month, as well as the sales of the written version. She also asked for damages of $1.25 million. The new publicity increased sales at the box office, and the Theater Guild kept the play running without interference from the court. Paramount Pictures, which had made an offer to buy the film rights to the play for $75,000, withdrew its offer and decided against making the film. The suit listed the following parallels between the two works:

- Both stories deal with the subject of selective paternity.
- Both stories have young heroines as the central character and both heroines marry young men.
- Both stories deal with hereditary insanity in the families of the young men.
- In both stories, the heroine asks a man not her husband to father her child, and in both stories the child is a boy.
- In both stories, the married heroine falls in love with the father of her child.
- In both stories, the boys grow up to be tall and athletic and fall in love with beautiful young women.

- In both stories, the mothers are jealous of their prospective daughters-in-law.
- In both stories, the healthy father is selected with a scientific attitude.

Lewys claimed that O'Neill had taken her material and "used it all wrong. He took a beautiful ideal and brought it so low that I was shocked and scandalized." The case went to trial on March 11, 1931, before Judge John W. Woolsey, who would later become famous for clearing James Joyce's novel *Ulysses* of obscenity charges. After a trial that lasted a week, Judge Woolsey ruled in O'Neill's favor and wrote in his decision that Lewys's suit was "wholly preposterous." He ordered her to pay O'Neill $7,500 for his expenses, $5,000 to the Theatre Guild, and $5,000 to Horace Liveright, although none of the defendants received any of the money: A year after the trial, Lewys filed for bankruptcy.

Months after O'Neill was named in the plagiarism suit, Mayor Nichols of Boston, under pressure from the Boston Watch and Ward Society, banned *Strange Interlude* on the grounds that it was "a plea for the murder of unborn children, a breeding ground for atheism and domestic infidelity, and a disgusting spectacle of immorality." Rather than fight the ban, the Theater Guild took advantage of the publicity and relocated the production to a site outside the city limits. The producers booked the play into a theater in Quincy, Massachusetts, where thousands bought tickets to the production.

FURTHER READING

Brustein, Robert. *The Theatre of Revolt*. Boston: Little, Brown, 1964.

"Eugene O'Neill's *Strange Interlude*." The File Room. URL: http://www.thefileroom. org/documents/dyn/DisplayCase.cfm/id/239.

Laufe, Abe. *The Wicked Stage: A History of Theater Censorship and Harassment in the United States*. New York: Frederick Ungar Publishing Co., 1978.

Schriftgiesser, Karl. "How Little Rollo Came to Rule the Mind of Boston; History of the Censorship of Plays and Books That Attracts the Attention of the Country." *Boston Transcript*, September 21, 1929, magazine section, pp. 1–2.

Sheaffer, Louis. *O'Neill: Son and Artist*. Boston: Little, Brown, 1973.

THE TAMER TAMED

Author: John Fletcher
Original date and place of production: 1611, London, England
Characters: Bianca, City Wives, Country Wives, Jaques, Livia, Maria, Moroso, Pedro, Petronius, Petruchio, Rowland, Sophocles, Tranio
Filmed versions: None

SUMMARY

The Tamer Tamed is a sequel to William Shakespeare's *The Taming of the Shrew*, which contains three characters from the original—Petruchio, Tranio, and Bianca—and references to the original, but it includes more burlesque and satire of the marriage relationship. The play portrays a battle of the sexes and turns the tables on Petruchio, who tamed his wife Kate in *The Taming of the Shrew* but who is tamed by his second wife, Maria.

Kate has died before the play opens, and Petruchio has just remarried, to Kate's cousin Maria, who resolves not to submit to the tyranny that Kate endured long after the first play ended. Maria joins a group of other women, including Kate's sister Bianca and her own sister Livia, who barricade themselves inside Maria's house. The women throw chamber pots at the men who gather with Petruchio for the traditional celebration on the first night of an Elizabethan marriage. Maria warns Petruchio that she will defy and tame him, just as he tamed her cousin Kate, and she is supported by a large contingent of city wives and country wives.

Petruchio and his male friends attempt to storm the women's fortress, but they are held at bay and can only shout threats across the barricades. The two groups finally achieve a truce and develop a peace treaty containing financial and personal advantages to Maria that society would not allow women for nearly 400 years.

Act three opens as Maria and Petruchio are living in apparent peace on his country estate, and Maria has dedicated herself to reading and to increasing her riding skills. The uneasy peace is disrupted when Maria refuses repeatedly to perform her "marital duties" and imposes further demands on Petruchio. To arouse his wife's pity, he feigns illness, but Maria is aware of the ruse and has Petruchio walled up in the house, claiming that he has the plague. Petruchio manages to escape in act four and finds a provocatively dressed Maria sitting and flirting with his friends. Disgusted by her behavior, Petruchio tells her that the marriage is over and he is leaving her to travel abroad. Maria surprises Petruchio by encouraging his departure and telling him that travel may turn him into a better human being.

By act five, Petruchio is ready to abandon all efforts at mastering Maria, but he makes one final attempt to secure her compassion. He pretends to die and is borne onstage in a coffin, which moves Maria to tears, not because of his death but by his "unmanly, wretched, foolish life." Unable to bear listening to the abuse, Petruchio sits upright, scaring Maria but also earning her respect. The two decide to give their marriage another chance. Inspired by Maria, Livia successfully outwits her father's plan to marry her off to the wealthy but unattractive, elderly Moroso. Instead she marries Rowland, the man she loves. While *The Tamer Tamed* does not question the conventional gender and power roles within the family, it does reveal that the ideal of the companionate marriage can be achieved only if both partners are willing to relinquish some authority.

CENSORSHIP HISTORY

At some point—possibly as late as 1641—the play was renamed *The Woman's Prize*, and given the subtitle *The Tamer Tam'd*. The play was finally published under the latter title in 1647 as a part of the First Folio and again in 1679 as part of the Second Folio of Fletcher's works. From that time on it would comprise one of 50-odd works in multivolume editions of "Beaumont and Fletcher."

The Tamer Tamed was performed without recorded incident when it was first written in 1611, but an attempted revival in October 1633 stirred up controversy. The Master of Revels, Sir Henry Herbert, the English censor, received the play from the King's Men theatrical company on October 18, 1633, and returned it the following Monday with numerous deletions and changes. Herbert wrote that he had "purg'd" the play "of oaths, prophaneness, and ribaldry." In a note attached to the returned script, Herbert warned:

> Purge their parts, as I have the booke. And I hope every hearer and player will think that I had done God good servise and the quality no wrong; who hath no greater enemies than oaths, prophaneness, and pulibque ribaldry, which for the future I do absolutely forbid to bee presented to mee in any play booke as you will answer it at your peril.

Most of the revisions eliminate or modify all phrases and words that might be construed as offensive to the church and the state. The antipatriarchal theme of the play offered a challenge to Herbert, who also eliminated or changed comparisons of the state of marriage to the political state and carefully modified any unflattering comparisons of the husband's role as head of the family to that of the king as head of state. Rather than approach *The Tamer Tamed* as a domestic comedy, he viewed it as a metaphor for the monarchy, and censored it with that parallel in mind.

FURTHER READING

Adams, J. Q. *Dramatic Records of Sir Henry Herbert.* New Haven, Conn.: Yale University Press, 1917.

Gross, Alex. "The Voice of the Dramaturg: Artist, Adaptor, or Scholar? Creating an Acting Version and an Annotated Edition of John Fletcher's *The Taming of the Tamer.*" A paper presented during the scholarly sessions of the Literary Managers and Dramaturgs of the Americas (LMDA) Conference in Atlanta, 1994.

Leech, Clifford. *The John Fletcher Plays.* London: Chatto & Windus, 1962.

Parrott, Thomas Marc, and Robert Hamilton Ball. *A Short View of Elizabethan Drama.* New York: Charles Scribner's Sons, 1943.

TARTUFFE

Author: Molière (Jean-Baptiste Poquelin)
Original date and place of production: 1669, Palais Royale, Paris, France
Characters: Cléante, Damis, Dorine, Elmire, Flipote, Laurent, Monsieur Loyal, Mariane, Orgon, Madame Pernelle, Tartuffe, Valère

Filmed versions: Feature films: *Tartuffe* (1926, Germany); *Le Tartuffe* (1984, France). Made for television: *Tartuffe* (1966, 1977, Sweden); (1971, U.K.); (1971, 1975, France); (1978, U.S.); *Tartuffe oder der Betrüger* (1969, West Germany); *Tartuffe, or the Imposter* (1983, U.K.); *Tartyuf* (1992, Russia)

SUMMARY

Tartuffe, a comedy in five acts that satirizes religious hypocrisy, is considered by critics to be the first perfect example of the *comédie de caractère*, the type of comedy that emphasizes universal psychological characteristics. Tartuffe, posing as a pious man of religion, ingratiates himself with the religious fanatic Orgon, who offers him hospitality and the deed to his house, as well as the promise of his daughter in marriage, despite the warnings of his family. Orgon's mother, Madame Pernelle, is also taken in by the impostor, and the two entrust Tartuffe with confidential matters and refuse to listen to the rest of the family, who suspect his true nature.

Damis, Orgon's son, warns that Tartuffe has made romantic overtures to his young stepmother, Elimire, but Orgon believes Tartuffe is innocent and orders his son to leave the house. Orgon is determined to believe only the best of Tartuffe, whom he views as a pious man of God. He is determined to marry his daughter Mariane to Tartuffe, despite her existing betrothal to and love for Valère. When Orgon's family members remain defiant, he chooses to spite them by writing a new will in which he leaves his estate to the impostor.

To expose the hypocrisy of Tartuffe, Elmire convinces Orgon to hide under a table while she meets with Tartuffe alone. As she expects, Tartuffe's basic human weakness is his sensual nature, which leads him to make romantic overtures to her. An enraged Orgon realizes that he has been fooled and throws the hypocrite out of his house, but Tartuffe reminds him whose house it is because Orgon had turned over the deed. Tartuffe claims both the house and all that Orgon holds as his own, and he also betrays Orgon to the government by handing over traitorous documents left in Orgon's safekeeping that he had entrusted to Tartuffe. With the aid of Laurent, Tartuffe's servant who has turned against his master, the king learns of Orgon's plight. After the king discovers Tartuffe's criminal past, he orders the impostor imprisoned for fraud and restores Orgon's house and fortune.

CENSORSHIP HISTORY

King Louis XIV appreciated art, society, good taste, and culture, and reserved a special place in his heart and court for Molière's extremely populist and sophisticated comedies and satires. A private presentation of the first three acts of *Tartuffe* at Versailles in 1664 sparked a controversy that rocked the foundation of the court and church. Accounts suggest that in the original version, Tartuffe was portrayed as a member of the clergy, which suggested some connection with the church. This was enough to scandalize the audience, for the use of ecclesiastical dress as a stage costume would have been shocking in France of the time. Powerful men tied to the Catholic Church were offended by the play, and the archbishop of Paris and the first president of Parliament opposed the production. Although an ardent supporter of Molière, the king feared offending religious zealots (who were becoming increasingly powerful) and promptly banned the play.

Molière, incensed, reacted to the censorship with equal zeal. Although he continued writing and performing, he never quelled his protests to the king— or failed to lobby him for support. When a nephew of Pope Alexander VII came to Fontainebleau as a papal envoy, Molière read the play to the delegation, which included influential churchmen, including a cardinal, none of whom expressed disapproval. He repeatedly read the play in front of influential people, hoping to gain support that the play was not subversive and that it was worthy of production.

In August 1667, while the king was in Flanders at the head of his army, Molière produced the second version of his play at the Palais-Royal, under the title *L'Imposteur* with a renamed central character, Panulphe. The next morning, the president of the Parliament of Paris (who was also a member of the Company of Holy Sacrament—a supposed target of the play) closed the theater. Within a week, the archbishop of Paris banned all public or private performances of the play, as well as readings or recitations under penalty of excommunication. In response, Molière sent a messenger with a petition to the king to lift the interdiction, which Louis promised to consider when he returned from war.

In February 1669, five years after its first performance, the king finally granted royal permission, and the third version of *Tartuffe* was presented for a public performance at the Palais-Royal. The opening night crowd was so large and raucous that many were nearly suffocated. The play continued with a hugely successful run of an unprecedented 44 performances.

The play enjoyed favor for more than a century, until the satire of human nature would become an issue for the censors in the months preceding the July 1794 revolution in France. Along with LE MISANTHROPE and 149 other plays, *Tartuffe* was subjected to revisions that would reflect the philosophy of the new French government.

FURTHER READING

Hemmings, Frederic William John. *Theatre and State in France, 1760–1905.* New York: Cambridge University Press, 1994.

Hubert, Judd David. *Molière & the Comedy of Intellect.* Berkeley: University of California Press, 1962.

Molière. *Tartuffe.* Translated and with an introduction by Robert W. Hartle. Indianapolis, Ind.: Bobbs-Merrill, 1965.

Tilley, Arthur Augustus. *Molière.* New York: Russell & Russell, 1968.

Turnell, Martin. *The Classical Moment: Studies in Corneille, Moliere and Racine.* New York: New Directions, 1963.

TEA AND SYMPATHY

Author: Robert Woodruff Anderson
Original date and place of production: September 30, 1953, Ethel Barry-more Theatre, New York, New York
Characters: Al, David Harris, Herbert Lee, Tom Lee, Paul, Phil, Ralph, Bill Reynolds, Laura Reynolds, Lilly Sears, Steve
Filmed versions: *Tea and Sympathy* (1956)

SUMMARY

Tea and Sympathy is a sentimental play in three acts set in a boys' boarding school in New England. The play contains stereotyped characterizations in dealing with the suspicion of homosexuality. Seventeen-year-old Tom Lee is accused by classmates of being homosexual after being seen on a beach near the school with faculty member Davis Harris, long suspected to be homosexual. This incident, combined with Tom's graceful way of walking, his refusal to wear a crew cut, his enjoyment of classical music, and his role in the school play as Lady Teazle, serve as "evidence" enough to brand him a "pervert."

Tom is a lonely adolescent whose mother is dead and whose father has placed him in one boarding school after another. Herbert Lee worries, "Why isn't my boy a regular fellow?" Tom's gruff and athletic housemaster, Bill Reynolds, questions the young man's lack of interest in sports and becomes his harshest judge and persecutor. Reynolds neglects his wife, Laura, and has made clear that her role in regard to the boys is peripheral, at most, although she is expected to offer tea and sympathy when need arises.

Laura attempts to convince Tom's roommate Al that it is too "easy to smear a person" and encourages him to stand up for Tom, but public opinion is too strong. Al fears being also labeled homosexual. A classmate taunts Tom to visit a prostitute to prove that he is heterosexual, but the experience is a failure because the woman's obviously coarse nature blocks his feelings of arousal.

He returns to the school and attempts suicide, because he feels that his failure with the prostitute "confirms" his "queerness." When Bill Reynolds rants about "this fairy," Laura becomes angry and points out that Bill's maliciousness toward Tom, his hypermasculine behavior, and his penchant for camping with boys may be masking his own repressed homosexuality: "You persecute him for the thing you fear most in yourself." She then goes to comfort Tom, having decided that she will leave her husband rather than continue to live a lie. As Laura consoles Tom and assures him that he is virile, she slowly unbuttons her blouse and she guides his hands gently as the curtain falls.

CENSORSHIP HISTORY

Tea and Sympathy opened on Broadway in 1953, at the height of the McCarthy trials when suspicion of being homosexual could result in social ostracism and the loss of a job. Anderson uses innuendo and suggestion to reveal to the audience the reasons for which Tom is persecuted and avoids direct reference or the use of overt terminology. Nonetheless, Broadway audiences were aware of the charges being directed against Tom, and they showed their acceptance of the play by keeping it running for 712 performances.

The play had a more difficult reception in England, where the Lord Chamberlain refused to grant a license for public performance because the play deals with a topic that is "inappropriate for the stage." The producers were forced to present the play in private clubs for several years, playing before audiences who were club members, if only for the one performance they attended. In 1957, after an appeal to the licensors, *Tea and Sympathy* was granted a license for public performance in England. The first public performance in England took place on April 25, 1957, at the Comedy Theatre, Haymarket, London.

FURTHER READING

Gassner, John. *Theatre at the Crossroads*. New York: Holt, Rinehart, Winston, 1960.

Gross, Alexander. "Inside the Sixties: What Really Happened on an International Scale." Available online. URL: http://language.home.sprynet.com/otherdex/sixties.htm#totop.

Loth, David. *The Erotic in Literature*. New York: Dorset Press, 1989.

Summers, Claude J., ed. *The Gay and Lesbian Literary Heritage*. New York: Henry Holt and Company, 1995.

THOMAS OF WOODSTOCK

Author: Anonymous

Original date and place of production: 1606, London, England

Characters: Anne of Bohemia, Queen of England; Cowtail, Crosby, Cynthia, Duchess of Gloucester, Duchess of Ireland, Earl of Arundel, Earl of Surrey, Edmund of Langley, Fleming, the Ghost of the Black Prince, the Ghost of King Edward III, John of Gaunt, Richard Exton, Simon Ignorance, Sheriff of Kent, Sheriff of Northumberland.

Filmed versions: None

SUMMARY

The title character of the play is Thomas of Woodstock, duke of Gloucester and lord protector of England, which meant he ruled the land until the appointed sovereign came of age. Thomas and his brothers, John of Gaunt (duke of Lancaster) and Edmund of Langley (duke of York), are gravely concerned for England's future because their young nephew, Richard, son of the late King Edward, has fallen under the influence of flatterers—Sir Henry Greene, Sir Edward Bagot, and Sir William Bushy. Richard already shows signs of being an unsuitable ruler, as he lives in luxury while squeezing his countrymen dry. The clash between the beloved, plainspoken Thomas and the hated, flamboyant Richard forms the crux of the play.

In addition to Thomas, Richard, Lancaster, York, and the flatterers, the play contains Anne of Bohemia, Richard's new bride and queen, who will soon be dead; Tresilian, a cunning lawyer, appointed by Richard to be chief justice of the land; Nimble, Tresilian's "devil"; the duchess of Gloucester, Thomas's wife and later his widow; and assorted townsfolk, messengers, and murderers.

Thomas is taken prisoner by Richard, then murdered in his cell to provide a foreshadowing of Richard's own fate in part two. Surprisingly, the playwright does not give Thomas a final lengthy speech. In his death scene, which takes place while he is writing a letter of reconciliation to Richard, Thomas calls upon heaven to help him achieve the right style and tone in the letter: "I will say nothing to excuse or clear myself,/for I have nothing done that needs excuse;/but tell him plain, though here I spend my blood./I wish his safety and all England's good."

As Thomas seeks the perfect words for his message, the two murderers consider the most effective means of attack. The first murderer orders: "Creep close to his back, ye rogue, be ready with the towel,/when I have knocked him down, to strangle him." The second murderer advises, "Do it quickly whilst his back is towards ye, ye damned villain;/if thou lettest him speak but a word, we shall not kill him." Thus, Thomas is murdered.

The text ends abruptly as Nimble betrays his master Tresilian to save his own skin when the tides turn against them.

CENSORSHIP HISTORY

It is believed that *Thomas of Woodstock* was subjected to censorship sometime after 1606, based on the deletion of oaths and the excision of profanity that appear in the marginal notes and penciled crosses on the censor's manuscript, probably an actual prompt book for a Jacobean production. The master of revels, Sir George Buc, also required the excision of Richard's claim to be "Superior Lord of Scotland" upon taking possession of the kingdom. As author Janet Clare observes, with James on the throne, "a reminder that Scottish kings had formerly paid homage to an English monarch, whilst satisfying the English sense of nationalism, would have been inapposite in the context of a Scottish occupant of the throne."

More important to the censors was the desire to eliminate the subversive language of the play, which is openly hostile to the king. In act two, Woodstock accuses Richard of neglecting his sovereign duty: "See here King Richard: whilst thou liv'st at ease/Lulling thyself in nice security,/Thy wronged kingdom's in a mutiny." The censor also marked for omission passages in which rebellion is suggested, the first of which occurs after Woodstock's murder and appears in act five in the soliloquy of Lapoole, who planned the murder: "The gentlemen and Commons of the realm/Missing the good old duke, their plain protector,/Break their allegiance to their sovereign lord/And all revolt upon the barons' side."

The censors also removed direct criticism of the king by Queen Anne, when she grieves in act two that misgovernment by her "wanton lord" has placed unfair burdens on the common people, as well as the response from the duchess of Gloucester that "England's not mutinous. . . . none dares rob him of his Kingly rule" even if he is "much misled by flatters" and "neglects, and throws his scepter carelessly." Additional lines that allude to the grievances of the common people due to the exorbitant taxation and political influence of flatterers were also excised, for they might have been viewed as criticisms of the current monarch.

The play's remaining text appears to be unfinished, but critics suggest that the ending was removed most likely because it showed the king being deposed. An ending used in some productions, also written anonymously, is sometimes used to close the play. In this ending, Richard sees the errors of his ways, banishes his flatterers, and is reinstated as king of England. When Richard kneels before Lancaster to be crowned, Lancaster, in disgust, simply hands the crown to his nephew to put it on himself without ceremony. Overall, most of the modifications required by the censors seem to be of material that might have been perceived as bearing a similarity to current affairs of state, or, as Clare writes, "as offering a dangerous precedent to disaffected subjects."

FURTHER READING

Clare, Janet. *"Art Made Tongue-Tied by Authority"*; *Elizabethan and Jacobean Dramatic Censorship*. New York: Manchester University Press, 1990.

Corbin, Peter, and Douglas Sedge, eds. *Thomas of Woodstock; or King Richard the Second, Part One*. New York: Manchester University Press, 2002.

THE THREE-PENNY OPERA

Author: Bertolt Brecht (book and lyrics); Kurt Weill (music)

Original date and place of production: August 31, 1928, Theater am Schiffbauerdamm, Berlin, Germany

Characters: Betty, Lucy Brown, Tiger Brown, Jenny Diver, Colly, Charles Filch, Jake, Reverend Kimball, Kitty, Mackie Messer/Mack the Knife, Matt, Nelly, Celia Peachum, Jonathan Peachum, Polly Peachum, Vixen

Filmed versions: *Die Dreigroschenoper* (1931, Germany); (1962, France/West Germany)

SUMMARY

Bertolt Brecht's *The Three-Penny Opera* (*Die Dreigroschenoper* in German) is based loosely on John Gay's 1728 *THE BEGGAR'S OPERA*, but unlike Gay's satire of the aristocracy, Brecht's work aims its satire at the middle class. The swashbuckling hero Macheath of the earlier play has become a common criminal and a product of his time, Polly is a coarse gun moll, and the thieves and prostitutes exhibit no charm. The play has enjoyed great popularity worldwide, and "The Ballad of Mack the Knife" became a popular song in the 1960s in the United States; in the 1980s the McDonald's corporation created the "Mac Tonight" character and used the song in its campaign to sell "Big Mac" hamburgers.

The setting is London's underworld at the time of Queen Victoria's coronation. The play opens at a street fair in Soho, where a company of beggars, thieves, and prostitutes are plying their trades. A street singer with a hurdy-gurdy sings about the exploits of the infamous Mack the Knife, detailing his crimes, which range from the robbery of cash boxes to slashing enemies with his knife to sexual violation of "the child-bride in her nightie." Mackie then appears and the action of the play begins.

The first act occurs largely near the docks, where Jonathan Peachum is a beggar king who outfits and taxes his crew of beggars and even turns them in to the authorities when a reward is offered. Surrounded by biblical exhortations, Peachum disciplines a potential beggar before providing him with a costume and setting him up in business. From his wife, he learns that his daughter Polly, that "heap of sensuality," is romantically involved with a well-dressed, handsome captain, whom he identifies as Mackie. As the Peachums search for their daughter, Mackie and Polly are married in a stable, surrounded by opulent carpets and other furnishings that the thieves have stolen for the occasion. Police Chief Tiger Brown, Mackie's friend and protector, attends and the two sing about their mutually profitable relationship. After the wedding, Polly visits her parents, who are angered by the wedding and promise to give Mackie up to the authorities.

In the second act, as Peachum plots with the police, Mackie explains his theories of business to Polly. He is an unmannerly, cynical, and toughened criminal who refers to himself as a businessman; he keeps books and praises efficiency and organization and claims that the only difference between a gangster and a businessman is that the gangster is "often a coward." Unlike Gay's dashing and romantic Macheath, Mackie is thoroughly middle class. He tells Polly that he expects to enter the banking profession, because thieves of his sort are being put out of business by legitimate businesses and banks:

> We artisans of the lower middle class who work with honest jimmies on the cash boxes of small shopkeepers, are being ruined by large concerns backed by the banks. What is a picklock to a bank share? What is the burgling of a bank to the founding of a bank? What is the murder of a man to the employment of a man?

When the authorities appear ready to capture him, Mackie makes Polly the new leader of his gang and the two part, with both promising to remain faithful. He is unable to resist stopping by a brothel to see his ex-girlfriend Jenny

Diver, a prostitute who betrays him to the police. Mackie is imprisoned but he escapes with the help of Lucy Brown, the police chief's daughter. Allowing his libido to overcome good sense, Mackie spends the night with another old girlfriend, Sukey Tawdrey, and he is recaptured. Peachum has convinced the police chief to capture Mackie by threatening to organize a massive demonstration of the beggars to disrupt the queen's coronation. As Mackie is led away, the chorus concludes, "Men live by foul misdeeds exclusively."

In the final act, Mackie tries desperately to raise bail money, but his gang members have all gone into legitimate banking and none are willing to help him. Lucy and Polly first argue, then agree to stand by him, and he sings a ballad that begs forgiveness from all humanity. As Mackie is being led to the gallows to be hanged, a messenger arrives to relate that, because of her coronation, the queen has pardoned Mackie, elevated him to nobility, and given him a lifetime pension.

CENSORSHIP HISTORY

Theater critic John Gassner has labeled *The Three-Penny Opera* as "probably the most 'subversive' play of the [twentieth] century exclusive of direct propaganda." The play was popular from the outset, and within the first year after the Berlin premiere, productions were launched in Italy, Poland, Hungary, France, Switzerland, and Russia. The rise of the Nazi government in Germany in the early 1930s brought an end to the production in that country. Rankled by its socialist message and attacks on governmental authority, as well as its relevance to the political and social climate, Hitler's Propaganda Office ordered performances to be interrupted by the police or forbidden outright, and they banned Brecht's books and plays. Brecht went into exile, first to Denmark and then to Finland, and did not return to Germany until 1949.

In the United States, Marc Blitzstein translated *The Three-Penny Opera* and produced it at the Theatre de Lys (now the Lucille Lortel Theatre), a former speakeasy in Greenwich Village, a neighborhood of New York City. Performances began on March 10, 1954, and ran until 1961. The play had to be adapted to meet the conservative standards of the Eisenhower era, because of stage censorship. Blitzstein's version of "The Ballad of Mack the Knife" omitted references to the "Ghastly fire in Soho," and later songs are softened and even changed to eliminate Brecht's abrasive and unsparing marxist vision of society. The use of the term *whores* is eliminated, and overt references to sexuality are made more circumspect throughout the play.

Laufe reports that in 1961, the John B. Kelly Playhouse in the Park in Philadelphia, Pennsylvania, canceled a production of *The Three-Penny Opera* on the recommendation of the mayor, H. J. Tate. Although Tate denied that he had acted as a censor for the playhouse, the Music Circus in Lambertville, New Jersey, where a production of the play was running, immediately used the cancellation as part of its advertising, hoping to entice audiences to a play that had been "banned in Philadelphia."

FURTHER READING

Brecht, Bertolt. *The Three-Penny Opera.* Translated by Desmond Vesey and Eric Bentley. In *From the Modern Repertoire.* Series One. Denver, Colo.: University of Denver Press, 1949.

Brustein, Robert. *The Theater of Revolt.* Boston: Little, Brown, 1964.

Gassner, John. *Theater at the Crossroads.* New York: Holt, Rinehart and Winston, 1960.

Gordon, Eric. *Mark the Music: The Life and Work of Marc Blitzstein.* New York: St. Martin's Press, 1989.

Laufe, Abe. *The Wicked Stage: A History of Theater Censorship and Harassment in the United States.* New York: Frederick Ungar Publishing Co., 1978.

TOBACCO ROAD

Author: Erskine Caldwell

Original date and place of production: December 4, 1933, Theatre Masque, New York City

Characters: Lov Bensey, Ada Lester, Dude Lester, Ellie May Lester, Grandma Lester, Jeeter Lester, George Payne, Henry Peabody, Sister Bessie Rice, Captain Tim

Filmed versions: *Tobacco Road* (1941)

SUMMARY

Tobacco Road was adapted for the stage by Jack Kirkland from Erskine Caldwell's provocative 1932 novel of the same name. Set in a squalid shack in the rural American South, the play relates the story of the impoverished Lester family. Jeeter, the family patriarch, a sharecropper, is a dirty, leering character who whines that the world and his family have let him down, but who makes no visible efforts to improve his life, while his long-suffering and chronically ill wife Ada yearns for a new dress in which to be buried. Three of their 15 children remain at home, but their lives appear just as hopeless as those of their parents. Sixteen-year-old Dude jeers at his parents and eventually runs over his mother with a car; 14-year-old Pearl has been sold to the 30-year-old neighbor Lov Bensey for seven dollars; 18-year-old Ellie May is unable to attract a man because of her harelip.

As the play begins, Pearl's husband Lov arrives and complains that Pearl refuses to speak to him or to sleep with him, but he rejects Jeeter's offer to speak to Pearl in trade for a bag of turnips. Lov flirts with Ellie May, who distracts him while Jeeter grabs the turnips and runs off. Soon after, a middle-aged evangelist appears, ostensibly to save the family, but she becomes distracted by Dude, whom she begins to touch. The act ends as Jeeter plots how he can obtain credit from the landowner to plant a large crop.

In the second act, the portly evangelist reappears and announces that God told her to "marry Dude first thing"; Dude is not interested until she promises to buy him a new car. Lov Bensey then attempts to locate Pearl, who has run away, but she appears as soon as Lov leaves. Jeeter insists that Pearl return to her husband, but Ada protects the girl and tells Jeeter that he has no say in the matter because he is not Pearl's biological father. The revelation does not make Jeeter angry, only curious, and the couple leave Pearl to talk and to steal some food. While they are gone, Lov returns and Ada beats him with a stick, but Jeeter is conciliatory and offers him Ellie May as a substitute. Despite Ellie May's wriggling with joy, Lov complains that she has an "ugly-looking face," which provokes her to beat her pretty sister Pearl. As this drama plays out, the evangelist returns with Dude and the new car and conducts her own marriage ceremony, after which she drags Dude into the house to consummate the marriage while the remaining family members peek in the window. They soon must rescue Dude from his overly amorous new mate, after which Jeeter sends him to the adjoining county to borrow money from one of his reliable sons.

Dude returns with news that his brother refuses to lend the family any money, and the evangelist refuses to allow Jeeter the use of her car to take firewood into town to sell. Lov appears and offers Jeeter salt pork and money to persuade Pearl to return to him, but Ada will not allow this even though her husband is willing. After Jeeter exhausts all of his options, he grasps Pearl and sends for Lov, eager to be paid for her. As Ada tries to save Pearl, Dude runs her over with the car in a seeming accident. Ada lies dying, and to distract Jeeter and to enable Pearl to run away, she bites his hand. The play ends with Ellie May happily leaving with Lov and Jeeter falling asleep in a chair on the porch, while a rotted shingle falls from the porch roof.

CENSORSHIP HISTORY

Tobacco Road was described by critics as both "repulsive" and "obscene" after its stage premiere on December 4, 1933, but the audiences kept the play running on Broadway for 3,182 performances.

In Chicago, Illinois, in 1935, Mayor Edward Kelley, responding to pressure from constituents, rescinded the license for the Blackstone Theater to continue to stage its production of *Tobacco Road*. No other theater dared to launch a production, for fear of reprisal from the mayor, and no other production of the play occurred in Chicago until 1972. The ban on *Tobacco Road* in 1935 resulted in Hallie Flanagan and the Federal Theatre Project abandoning plans for their production of Meyer Levin's *Model Tenement*, which dealt with housing problems that culminate in a rent strike. Highly placed administrators in the Chicago office of the Works Progress Administration (WPA) heard rumors that Mayor Kelly was upset about the subject matter of their upcoming play and, after his success in rescinding the license for *Tobacco Road*, decided to chance a ban.

In Canada in 1953, Vancouver and Victoria authorities ordered the removal of all copies of the novel *Tobacco Road* from newsstands. This occurred only weeks after the Vancouver City Prosecutor received complaints from a citizens group that the play *Tobacco Road*, in performance at the Everyman Theatre, was "obscene." The police closed the play and charged eight actors and other members of the theater management with indecency.

FURTHER READING

Birdsall, Peter. *Mind War: Book Censorship in English Canada*. Victoria, B.C.: CANLIT, 1978.

Bowman, Jim. "The Night Mayor Kelly Protected the Morale of Innocent Chicagoans." *Chicago Tribune Magazine*, May 2, 1983, p. 30.

Korges, James. *Erskine Caldwell*. Minneapolis: University of Minnesota Press, 1969.

Mikva, Abner J. "Chicago: Citadel of Censorship." *Focus/Midwest* 2 (March–April 1963): 10, 16–17.

"Tobacco Road." *The Vancouver Sun*, January 23, 1953, p. 3.

THE TOILET

Author: LeRoi Jones (Imamu Amiri Baraka)
Original date and place of production: December 1964, St. Mark's Playhouse, New York, New York
Characters: George Davis, Donald Farrell, Foots, Hines, Johnny Boy Holmes, Karolis, Knowles, Willie Love, Ora, Perry, Skippy
Filmed versions: None

SUMMARY

The Toilet is a one-act play that takes place in the filthy bathroom of an urban high school, and the stage set clearly shows urinals lining the wall and commodes in stalls with swinging doors. The play opens as African-American members of a gang dart in and out of the bathroom, reporting on their progress in cornering and capturing Karolis, a Puerto Rican student who has written a love letter to Ray Foots, the gang leader. The gang members subsequently force Karolis into the bathroom and beat him, while several members taunt him about his homosexual feelings. Ora, one of the gang members, tells Karolis several times, "I gotta nice fat sausage here for you."

Ray Foots arrives to fight Karolis and finds that the gang members have beaten him to near-unconsciousness. He asks the others how he can fight if Karolis is in that condition. Foots walks over to Karolis, trying not to show his concern to the others, and hesitates. As the gang members watch, Karolis rises up from the floor and says that he wants to fight Foots, despite the other boy's hesitance and desire to protect him from further abuse. When Foots refuses and says that the fight will be unfair, Karolis taunts him: "No. You have to fight me. I sent you a note, remember. The note saying I loved you. . . . The note saying you were beautiful. You remember that note, Ray? . . . The one that said I wanted to take you into my mouth."

The two boys fight, but Foots seems only half-hearted in his efforts. Karolis overpowers and chokes him. The other boys pull the two apart and drag Karolis to the ground while kicking and cursing him. They then help Foots to his feet and leave the bathroom. A short time later, Karolis revives and pulls himself to a sitting position; Foots quietly enters the bathroom and "quickly looks over his shoulder, then runs and kneels before the body, weeping and cradling the head in his arms."

CENSORSHIP HISTORY

The Toilet aroused indignation among critics and became the target of censorship efforts in New York City and Los Angeles. Typical of the reviews was that by Robert Brustein, writing for the *National Review*, who characterized the play as "inspired primarily by race hatred" and "designed for the acting out of sado-masochistic racial fantasies." Others protested the repeated use of obscenities in the play. Theater historian Abe Laufe writes, "Although the constant repetition of the words in *The Toilet* made them lose their shock value, the muddled filth and profanity angered many theater goers." Authorities seeking to ban the play focused on the language and did not raise the issue of violence or the homosexual advance.

In New York City Joseph DiCarlo, commissioner of licenses, received complaints calling upon his office to rescind the license for performance at St. Mark's Playhouse. The complaints focused on the "objectionable dialogue" and the "filthy content" of the play. DiCarlo had the power to revoke the license, but said that he would never do so merely on the charge of "objectionable dialogue." In responding to critics of his decision, the commissioner said that he had "no legal authority to censor." He also admitted that if he tried to close the play, the producers would appeal the decision; if he demanded excisions, the publicity would increase attendance.

In Los Angeles the police vice squad brought charges of obscenity against the play before it opened, and the authorities held up the production on grounds of "improper licensing" until the police commissioner decided to permit the play to open. Faced with the challenge from authorities, one theater canceled its booking, and two newspapers refused to accept advertisements for the play. The Authors League rose to the defense of *The Toilet* and challenged the decision of the newspapers, claiming that only advertisements containing obscenities could be refused. Although delayed, the play eventually was produced, because the case brought by the police did not stand up in court.

In 1984 parents of students attending Miami (Oklahoma) High School issued a complaint to the school superintendent requesting the removal of *Best American Plays: Sixth Series, 1963–1967* from the school library. They made their complaint because the anthology contained *The Toilet*, which they characterized as filled with "obscenities" and "filthy language." The request was rejected, but the book was placed for a time on a reserve shelf and students had to make specific requests for the book.

FURTHER READING

Baraka, Imamu Amiri. *The Baptism and The Toilet, by LeRoi Jones.* New York: Grove Press, 1967.
Brustein, Robert. *"The Toilet." National Review,* January 23, 1965, pp. 32–33.
Doyle, Robert. *Banned Books Resource Guide.* Chicago, Ill.: American Library Association, 1995.
Gould, Jean. *Modern American Playwrights.* New York: Dodd, Mead & Co., 1966.
Laufe, Abe. *The Wicked Stage: A History of Theater Censorship and Harassment in the United States.* New York: Frederick Ungar Publishing Co., 1978.

THE TRAGEDY OF KING RICHARD THE SECOND

Author: William Shakespeare
Original date and place of production: 1597, London, England
Characters: Abbot of Westminster, Bagot, Bishop of Carlisle, Harry Bolingbroke, Bushy, Duchess of Gloucester, Duke of Aumerle, Duke of Hereford, Duke of Lancaster, Duke of Norfolk, Duke of Surrey, Duke of York, Earl of Northumberland, Earl of Salisbury, Green, John of Gaunt, Lord Berkeley, Lord Fitzwater, Lord Marshal, Lord Ross, Lord Willoughby, Thomas Mowbray, Harry Percy, the Queen, King Richard II, Sir Piers Exton, Sir Stephen Scrope
Filmed versions: Made for television: *King Richard the Second* (1978, U.K.); *The Tragedy of King Richard the Second* (1970, U.K.)

SUMMARY

The Tragedy of King Richard the Second begins with a dispute between Bolingbroke and Thomas Mowbray. Richard wants John of Gaunt, Bolingbroke's father, to solve the matter, but Gaunt cannot and wants them to fight it out. Displeased, Richard takes control of the situation and, instead, banishes Mowbray for life and Bolingbroke for 10 years.

In the second act, Gaunt dies after insulting Richard, and the king claims his wealth to help finance his war with Ireland. Northumberland reveals that Bolingbroke is returning to England with an army to overtake Richard and promises that York, Willoughby, and he will support the king. The battle becomes fierce, and Richard's troops, commanded by the earl of Salisbury, disperse because they think Richard is dead.

As the third act begins, Bolingbroke executes Bushy and Green, who are both loyal to the king. Richard returns to England satisfied with his victory over the Irish, but he loses that zest when he learns that he has lost his troops, because Bolingbroke will surely defeat him. When Bolingbroke discovers that Richard is nearby in Berkeley Castle, he sends a messenger to ask the king to surrender, and Richard agrees.

The bishop of Carlisle reluctantly allows Bolingbroke to take over his castle, and Richard is summoned. After a dramatic exchange of words, Richard is sent to the Tower of London by Bolingbroke, who has become King Henry IV.

In the final act, Richard's loving and grief-stricken wife watches as he is taken to detention. The duke of Aumerle and others concoct a plot against Bolingbroke, but the duke of York learns about it, and supporters halt the plot. Although the duke of Aumerle is spared, the other rebels are not. Richard is killed by Sir Piers Exton, which the new king is not happy to hear, and he launches a crusade to ease his conscience.

CENSORSHIP HISTORY

The Tragedy of King Richard the Second became the object of censors soon after it was written. Authors Anne Haight and Chandler Grannis write that the original edition of the play contained a scene in which the king was deposed that so infuriated Queen Elizabeth I that she ordered the scene eliminated from all copies. Despite the royal order, late in 1597 the queen complained that the play in its entirety had been acted at least 40 times in the streets and in private venues "for the encouragement of disaffection."

Queen Elizabeth I had good reason to feel apprehensive about the scene in which King Richard II is deposed. Conspirators who supported Lord Essex planned a rebellion to overthrow the queen on February 8, 1601. Authors Frank Fowell and Frank Palmer write that, in the effort to encourage the common people to support the overthrow, the Essex conspirators bribed the actors at the Globe Theatre with an offer of two pounds each to play the expurgated scenes on February 7, 1601. The ploy did not work, but the scenes remained officially expurgated for two centuries.

FURTHER READING

Fowell, Frank, and Frank Palmer. *Censorship in England.* London: F. Palmer, 1913. Reprint, New York: Benjamin Blom, 1969.

Haight, Anne Lyon, and Chandler B. Grannis. *Banned Books 387 B.C. to 1978 A.D.* New York: R. R. Bowker Co., 1978.

Perrin, Noel. *Dr. Bowdler's Legacy.* Boston: David R. Godine, 1992.

TRIO

Authors: Dorothy and Howard Baker
Original date and place of production: December 29, 1944, Belasco Theatre, New York, New York

Characters: Janet Logan, Ray MacKenzie, Pauline Maury
Filmed versions: None

SUMMARY

Trio, adapted by Dorothy Dodds Baker and Howard Baker from Dorothy Baker's novel of the same name, deals with a lesbian relationship between college professor Dr. Pauline Maury and student Janet Logan, who idolizes the confident, assertive, and controlling woman. The two women live together in what appears at the outset of the play to be a relationship between a mentor and a young student. Ray MacKenzie, another student, feels a strong attraction toward Janet and wants to marry her, a plan to which she hesitantly agrees while she rebuffs all of MacKenzie's attempts at intimacy. He professes to understand that Janet is an intellectual disciple of the professor, as well as her confidante, but he protests that Pauline is taking advantage of Janet's good nature by asking her to type, research, and handle other details for the older woman. Janet asks him to be patient and promises that they will have more time together once the professor's "brilliant study of the French decadents" is published.

MacKenzie makes more frequent visits to the apartment the women share, and he begins to notice the "increasingly strange human relationships" and the personal intimacies that lie beneath the "academic amenities." He confronts Janet with his concerns and warns her that Pauline has begun to dominate the younger woman's life and even controls her mind. After professing his love, he asks Janet to leave the apartment and to find somewhere else to live or to marry him, because Pauline's "purposes are not life-giving." Janet protests that Pauline needs her and she wishes to stay with the glamorous older woman. Then she reveals that they are lovers. The revelation angers MacKenzie, who views Janet as the victim of the predatory college professor, and he vows to free Janet from "bondage" and from the "twisted currents of human behavior."

In the third act, MacKenzie discovers that Pauline's prizewinning study of the French decadents is plagiarized and tells Janet that her idol is a phony. He plans to reveal the truth to the literary world, unless Pauline releases Janet from her control. Unable to face blackmail, Pauline prepares to kill herself in a highly elaborate final scene. The play ends with the suggestion that Pauline will die a deserved death, while MacKenzie and Janet will live a long and happy life.

CENSORSHIP HISTORY

Trio was originally booked into the Shubert Theatre in New York City by producer Lee Sabinson, but theater owner Lee Shubert canceled the booking after the play ran into conflict with censors during Philadelphia tryouts. Philadelphia city officials had received complaints about the "unnatural relationship" between the college professor and her student, and they forced the production to close without allowing it to complete the run. Shubert was unwilling to challenge the Wales "Padlock" Law, passed in 1927, which forbade plays "depicting or dealing with the subject of sex degeneracy or sex perversion" on the stages of New York. He faced a loss of substantial income if the authorities were to close his theater for a year or more.

Sabinson tried without success to convince other theater owners to allow the production, but none were willing to take the risk. He then asked Paul Moss, New York commissioner of licenses, to review the play and to decide if *Trio* could be granted a license for performance, but Moss refused and told Sabinson that he issued the licenses but did not serve as censor. After extensive effort, Sabinson convinced the Belasco Theatre to grant a lease for the production.

The play opened on December 29, 1944, and immediately ignited controversy. Church groups in conjunction with the Society for the Suppression of Vice exerted pressure on public officials to have the play closed. In contrast, theater critics were largely supportive of the play. Lewis Nichols, theater reviewer for the *New York Times*, wrote, "*Trio* is not a censorable play. It is honest and it treats its subject with dignity and restraint." He also praised Sabinson's persistence in locating a theater in which to stage the play, and wrote, "It would not have been well for the theater had *Trio* been denied a hearing . . . because of fears over its subject-matter." Most of the complaints were lodged with Commissioner Moss, who notified the owners of the Belasco Theatre that they would have to evict the play if they expected to be granted a renewal of their theater license. Lee Sabinson appealed to the court to grant an injunction to block the order, but the judge upheld Moss's decision and the play closed on February 24, 1945, after 67 performances.

FURTHER READING

Baker, Dorothy Dodds. *Trio*. Boston: Houghton Mifflin Company, 1943.
Laufe, Abe. *The Wicked Stage: A History of Theater Censorship and Harassment in the United States*. New York: Frederick Ungar Publishing Co., 1978.
Nichols, Lewis. "Dorothy and Howard Baker's *Trio*." *The New York Times*, December 30, 1944, p. 13.

TRIP TO CALAIS

Author: Samuel Foote
Original date and place of production: None
Characters: Abbess, Kit Cable, Kit Codling, Hetty, Lady Kitty Crocodile, Dick Drugget, Gregory Gingham, Luke Lapelle, Miss Lydell, Minnikin, Jenny Minnikin, Mrs. Minnikin, O'Donnovan, Tromfort
Filmed versions: None

SUMMARY

Samuel Foote, author of *Trip to Calais*, was called by his contemporaries "the English Aristophanes" because he created characters based upon real people, unlike the stereotyped figures common to the sentimental comedy that was so popular at the time. In this play, Foote satirized Elizabeth Chudleigh, the duchess of Kingston, in the character of Kitty Crocodile.

The plot relates the efforts of Jenny Minnikin, daughter of a London pin-maker, to avoid marrying the man her parents have chosen for her, whom she does not love. After failing to convince them to change their minds, Jenny elopes to Calais with the man she loves. Her parents follow, so Jenny takes refuge in a convent, which her parents try unsuccessfully to make her leave. Minnikin and Mrs. Minnikin turn for advice to Lady Kitty Crocodile who is in deep mourning over the recent death of her husband.

Lady Kitty has traveled to France because "She couldn't bear to stay in England after the death of her husband, every thing there put her so much in mind of her loss. Why, if she met by accident with one of his boots, it always set her a-crying; indeed, the poor gentlewoman was a perfect Niobe." Lady Kitty's hypocrisy is soon revealed to the audience in her cruelty to her servants and her hypocrisy over her husband's death. Jealous of her maid of honor, Miss Lydell, Lady Kitty treats her kindly in public but cruelly in private. As one of her servants states, "There never was so ingenious, so refined a tormentor: The Fathers of the Inquisition themselves, would be proud to receive instructions from her." To impress visitors with her grief, Lady Kitty becomes "deck'd out in her dismals [mourning clothes]" and receives visitors in a special "Chamber of Tears."

Lady Kitty speaks with Jenny and advises her that the solution to the problem is to marry both men, her choice and her parents' choice as well. Jenny follows the advice and marries both men, then becomes a maid of honor to Lady Kitty, and the play ends.

CENSORSHIP HISTORY

In 1775, while Foote was completing *The Trip to Calais* and preparing it for production at the Haymarket Theatre, Elizabeth Chudleigh, duchess dowager of Kingston, was preparing to go on trial before the House of Lords for the crime of bigamy. She had married her second husband, the duke of Kingston, without informing him that she was still married to former naval officer Augustus John Hervey, with whom she had a child. Fearing that the presentation of the play, which satirized her in the character of the coarse and licentious Lady Kitty Crocodile, would have a damaging effect upon her forthcoming trial, the duchess offered Foote £1,600 to suppress the play. When he refused to do so, her friend Lord Mountstuart prevailed on the Lord Chamberlain, Lord Hertford, to forbid its production. The friends of the duchess, and among them her chaplain, Foster, declared falsely that Foote attempted to extort £2,000 from her. Several days before Foote submitted the play for licensing, the *Morning Post* reported that a reliable authority had revealed that "a certain new Comedy has been refused the Chamberlain's license, on account of the severity with which a certain Duchess is supposed to be treated herein." On July 21, 1775, the *Morning Chronicle* reported that "a certain dramatic piece shall not receive the Chamberlain's license, till every passage which is supposed to reflect upon her Grace [the duchess of Kingston], be totally expunged."

The play was refused a license, but Foote made plans for publication. The duchess wrote him an abusive letter published in the *Evening Post* on August 15, 1775, to which Foote replied, also in the *Evening Post*. In his response, Foote publicly apologized and denied the allegation that Kitty Crocodile was intended to portray the duchess, but he did so in such a way as to leave little doubt that it was indeed a caricature of her. He wrote that the duchess, after reading the play, "could not discern a single trait in the character of Lady Kitty Crocodile, that resembled herself." This made her furious; and she replied virulently against his impudence. He responded with scathing contempt, alluding to her bigamy: "Pray, madam, is not J——n the name of your female confidential secretary? and is not she generally cloathed in black petticoats made out of your weeds? 'So mourn'd the dame of Ephesus her love.'" This was a mocking reference to the duchess's male secretary, Reverend William Jackson, who would get his full revenge in the following year. The chamberlain, at the instigation of the duchess, refused to license the performance of *Calais*.

Foote rewrote the play and satirized Jackson as Dr. Viper in *The Capuchin*, which was presented on August 19, 1776. Angered by the portrayal, Jackson bribed one of Foote's former coachmen to bring charges of homosexual assault against Foote. Although Foote was acquitted of the charges in the Court of the King's Bench on December 9, 1776, the false charges and ensuing legal battle destroyed both his career and his health. He left the Haymarket Theatre and died in 1778.

FURTHER READING

Conolly, L. W. *The Censorship of English Drama, 1737–1824.* San Marino, Calif.: The Huntington Library, 1976.

Fowell, Frank, and Frank Palmer. *Censorship in England.* London: F. Palmer, 1913. Reprint, New York: Benjamin Blom, 1969.

Trussler, Simon. *The Cambridge Illustrated History of British Theatre.* New York: Cambridge University Press, 1994.

TRIPLE-A PLOWED UNDER

Authors: 70 news reporters under the supervision of Morris Watson and Howard Cushman; dramatized by 15 members, including Arthur Arent, of the Federal Theatre Project of the Works Progress Administration

Original date and place of production: March 14, 1936, Biltmore The-
atre, New York, New York
Characters: Earl Browder, Police Lieutenant, Narrator, Mrs. Sherwood,
Henry Wallace
Filmed versions: None

SUMMARY

Triple-A Plowed Under is a play about the history of American agriculture that
uses a series of rapidly presented pantomimes, radio broadcasts, and skits to
inform audiences how mortgages are foreclosed, farms auctioned, and crops
deliberately destroyed. The dramatization portrayed the devastating effects
of the drought, the organization of farmer-consumer cooperatives, and the
creation of the Agricultural Adjustment Administration (AAA) and the decla-
ration by the U.S. Supreme Court that the AAA was unconstitutional. It was
the first of the Living Newspaper series produced by the Federal Theatre
Project, after the suppression of ETHIOPIA.

The play contains many emotional scenes. In one, a woman goes to a
butcher shop to protest the high cost of meat and, as a meat truck passes, the
butcher tells her that the fault is not his but that of the meat processors. Frustrated with the high prices and her lack of options, the woman pours gasoline
on the meat in the shop.

In another scene, a woman enters a police station holding her child,
whom she has just murdered because he was hungry and she could not feed
him. The skit uses the actual words used by the woman who committed the
real crime. The audience is meant to sympathize with the woman, despite her
horrible action, as the police take her into custody.

Another, more volatile scene depicts farmers burning their wheat because
they are unable to sell it. As the fires blaze, a voice-over is heard on the loudspeaker stating, "Revolutions have been caused by less than this."

The play directly criticizes the members of the U.S. Supreme Court who
"plowed triple A under" by declaring it unconstitutional; they are made to
look foolish for destroying this mandate of President Franklin Delano Roosevelt. After the judges have their say, an actor playing a dignified and articulate Earl Browder, leader of the American Communist Party, speaks in support
of communism. The play ends with the government unable to offer a solution,
leaving a call for the unification of the farmers who produce the food and the
workers who buy it.

CENSORSHIP HISTORY

Triple-A Plowed Under was one of a series of Living Newspaper productions
of the Federal Theatre Project (FTP), a government-subsidized movement
created in 1935 under the U.S. Works Progress Administration to employ
professional theater workers and to provide the general public with access
to inexpensive but good theater while providing community services in

developing regional and neighborhood theater and theatrical workshops. Like the other dramas in this new theatrical form, the play grew out of the economic and social upheaval of the Great Depression. These productions were designed to dramatize the socioeconomic conditions of the working class with the intent of arousing political consciousness and promoting social change. The plays were documentary theater that incorporated actual newspaper accounts, government testimonies, and other statements of public record into a specific format. The plot typically began in the present to exhibit the immediacy of a problem rooted in the everyday experiences of the working class, then moved to the past to explore the causes of the problem before returning to the present to examine possible solutions. After various solutions were analyzed, one means of resolution was selected and the drama ended with a call for specific legislative, judicial, or other group action to rectify the existing situation by enforcing existing social legislation.

The play generated controversy from the inception of the idea. Bentley writes in her biography of FTP director Hallie Flanagan, "as rehearsals got under way, some of those participating in the production, in particular a group of older actors, complained that the set, which used ramps and projections, was strange and that the play had no plot. 'Who in New York cares about farmers and about wheat?' they demanded." Actors in the project who were members of the Federal Theatre Veterans' League called for suppression of the play. Flanagan convinced them to stay with the project by promising that there would be no more Living Newspapers if the public disliked this production.

Days before the first performance, at the Biltmore Theatre on March 14, 1936, in New York City, a veterans' group alerted city officials that they viewed the play as "unpatriotic" and planned a demonstration on opening night. Concerned about potential violence, city officials positioned extra police at the theater. At one point in the play, the loudspeaker announces, "January 6, 1935 . . . Supreme Court invalidates AAA in Hoosac Mills case," and the actor playing Earl Browder responds, "The Constitution of the United States does not give the Supreme Court the right to declare laws passed by the Congress unconstitutional." Hearing this, a veteran in the audience rose from his seat and began to sing "The Star-Spangled Banner." Police positioned at the rear of the theater had been cautioned to watch for signs of "communist activity," and they misunderstood the veteran's intentions, mistaking his singing for "communist agitation," and evicted him from the theater.

Despite the actors' misgivings that the play about farmers and crops would not interest sophisticated New York audiences, critics praised the play, which represented a new theatre technique. The play appeared without incident in Cleveland, Chicago, and Los Angeles. As Flanagan wrote in her account of the Federal Theatre Project, "Texas was a hard nut to crack and we failed to crack it." The Work Projects Administration director in the state feared "any new type of play," and wrote to Flanagan to reject the play. He recommended, "Such plays as are selected should be ones that are agreeable to Texans and will not cause unfavorable criticism. Has not *Triple-A Plowed Under* evoked such criticism?" Instead, the Texas project decided to do "old plays" such as those written by Shakespeare or already proved on Broadway that would avoid controversy.

FURTHER READING

Bentley, Joanne. *Hallie Flanagan: A Life in the American Theatre* New York: Alfred A. Knopf, 1988.
Federal Theatre Plays: Triple-A Plowed Under; Power; Spirochete: a History. Introduction by Hallie Flanagan. New York: Random House, 1938.
Flanagan, Hallie. *Arena: The History of the Federal Theatre.* New York: Benjamin Blom, 1965.
Garrett, G. "Federal Theatre for the Masses." *Saturday Evening Post,* August 1, 1936, pp. 23+.
Mathews, Jane DeHart. *The Federal Theatre, 1935–1939: Plays, Relief, and Politics.* Princeton, N.J.: Princeton University Press, 1967.
Roarty, Robert C. "The Federal Government's Wartime Food Play: It's Up to You." *Theatre History Studies* 19 (1999): 63–79.

THE VAGINA MONOLOGUES

Author: Eve Ensler
Original date and place of production: 1996, Contemporary Theatre, New York, New York; October 3, 1999, Westside Theatre, New York, New York
Characters: three or more performers speaking as hundreds of unnamed characters, ranging from a six-year-old girl to an elderly woman
Filmed versions: Made for television: *The Vagina Monologues* (2002)

SUMMARY

The Vagina Monologues originated as a solo monologue performed by playwright Eve Ensler and won an Obie Award for best Off-Broadway play in 1997. To gain material for the play, Ensler interviewed more than 200 women from diverse backgrounds in order to find out what they really thought about their sexuality and, more directly, their vaginas. From these interviews, Ensler created a work that combined a range of complex emotions with a variety of powerful characters and voices.

The 17 monologues that appeared in the initial version of the play are titled: Introduction; Hair; If Your Vagina Got Dressed, What Would It Wear?; If Your Vagina Could Talk, What Would It Say?; The Flood; The Vagina Workshop; Vagina Fact—Clitoris; Because He Liked to Look at It; Vagina Fact—Genital Mutilation; My Angry Vagina; My Vagina Was a Village; The Little Coochi Snorcher That Could; What Does Your Vagina Smell Like?; Reclaiming Cunt; I Asked a Six-Year-Old Girl; The Woman Who Loved to Make Vaginas Happy; I Was There in the Room. The performers have the monologues written on large index cards that they read and refer to. This is intentional, because playwright Eve Ensler felt that the cards were a reminder that the stories she was telling on stage were from real people.

The pieces are often funny and spontaneous, but at the same time they have important meanings behind them. Some of the monologues deal with rape, genital mutilation, and the Taliban, while others document such experiences as one vagina's anger over tampons and gynecological procedures. The play addresses a wide range of situations facing women all over the world, to create a sense of shared experiences among women of many different cultural backgrounds with the goal of bringing serious issues to the attention of the audience.

CENSORSHIP HISTORY

The Vagina Monologues has created controversy since its earliest performances. Although many objections have been raised to the fact that the play contains 136 uses of the word *vagina* and 16 moans of simulated sexual pleasure, the earliest dealt with the depiction of female-on-female rape in one of the monologues. The original version of the play included a monologue titled "The Little Coochi Snorcher That Could," which depicted an encounter between a 24-year-old woman and a 13-year-old girl in which the woman plies the girl with alcohol and then rapes her. Because the rape was portrayed in a positive light, with the child even calling it a "good rape," many audience members were enraged by what they considered to be the hypocrisy of the play. While the play denounced male violence against women, some viewers felt, it seemed to glorify female-on-female rape. When the play moved to the Westside Theater in 1999, Ensler omitted the offending monologue.

In February 2002, authorities in Kuala Lumpur shut down a production of the play after one performance, despite criticism that the move stifled women's right to freedom of expression. The permit for performance was withdrawn after the conservative Kedah Muslim Scholars Association filed a complaint of obscenity with the Kuala Lumpur City Hall against the producers of the play. After extensive protests and the submission of a formal petition from play organizers and women's groups, city officials relented and allowed the production to continue.

In February 2002 in Manila, students at Ateneo de Manila University tried to produce the play on their campus. After auditions were held and a cast was formed, the administration of the Jesuit-run university forbade the students to go ahead with the production. The vice president of the Loyola Schools of Ateneo, Anna Miren Gonzalez-Intal, wrote a memo to the students disapproving of the production "as an official activity of the Ateneo de Manila University" and stating that the students could stage the play as long as they "do so as individuals, in a venue of their choice outside the Ateneo." The memo was based on an evaluation of the play made by the chairperson of the theology department, who claimed in her appraisal that the repetition of the word *puki* (vagina) is "like a refrain, as *puki* is heard at every turn, grates on the psyche, until the metaphor is lost. What is left is the physical image of the vagina. . . . There is no need for vagina monologues." In an interview with *The Manila Times*, one of the students, Tebs Gomez, told a reporter "it was the word *vagina* and its Filipino counterpart—*puki*—that 'scandalized' the school administration, and made them decide to ban the play's production on campus."

In the United States several Catholic universities banned student productions of *The Vagina Monologues* from their campuses. In New York, officials at Iona College and the College of New Rochelle denied students permission to present performances in February 2002, but a commercial venue, the Fleetwood Stage company in New Rochelle, offered the students use of their theater. The College of New Rochelle drama group accepted the offer, but students of Iona turned it down and decided to present Henrik Ibsen's *A Doll's House* as a substitute production. Gonzaga University (Washington) banned production of the play from its campus in March 2002, but a campus women's group moved the production to a hotel ballroom. Bombarded by protests asserting that this was an issue of censorship and academic freedom, the university president, Father Robert Spitzer, responded that numerous conversations about the play were taking place in classrooms and students were receiving credit for attending the off-campus production. Officials at Loras College (Idaho) and Rivier College (New Hampshire) also refused students permission to hold performances of *The Vagina Monologues* on campus. Reverend David Tyson, president of the University of Portland, also a Catholic university, refused to allow the play and told students, "The play is offensive, questionable in its portrayal of violence, and not in keeping with the respect accorded the human body in this institution's religious tradition." At Xavier University (Ohio) on March 13, 2003, university president Michael Graham canceled three planned productions of the play after receiving complaints from alumni and donors who lobbied to have the play blocked. After a schoolwide meeting that exhibited extensive student and faculty support for the play, Graham agreed not to block the presentation of the play as part of one professor's class, which he felt "puts the play in a suitable environment of debate and discussion." Ironically, the three performances of the play took place at the Gallagher Student Center theater, as originally planned.

FURTHER READING

Araya, Alfred A., Jr. "Ateneo Bans *Vagina Monologues*." *The Manila Times*, March 2, 2002. Available online. URL: http://www.manilatimes.net/national/2002/mar/02/opinion/20020302opi5.html.

Coleman, Sarah. "Female Parts: *The Vagina Monologues* Goes Global." *World Press Online*, June 6, 2002. Available online. URL: http://www.worldpress.org/Americas/606.cfm.

"Colleges Ban 'VM.'" Cardinal Newman Society. Available online. URL: http:// www.cardinalnewmansociety.org/colleges_ban_vm.htm.

Eigelbach, Kevin. "Xavier: Professor Can Stage Play." *The Cincinnati Post*, March 13, 2002. Available online. URL: http://www.cincypost.com/2003/03/13/mono031303. html.

Ensler, Eve. *The Vagina Monologues.* Foreword by Gloria Steinem. New York: Villard Books, 2001.

Rowland, Kathy. "Thinking Outside the Box: A Brief History of Theatre Censorship in Malaysia." November 3, 2002. Available online. URL: http://www.kakiseni. com/articles/columns/MDE0NA.html.

VECTIA

Author: Marie C. Stopes
Original date and place of production: None
Characters: Heron, Vectia, William
Filmed versions: None

SUMMARY

Marie Stopes's play *Vectia* is a re-creation of her real-life marital situation, in which she claimed that her husband was impotent and insisted she had been so ignorant of sex that she remained unaware that marriage had not been consummated. In the play, Vectia is a "delightful English girl" who is married to William, "thin and ascetic-looking with pale, dun-coloured hair and face." Vectia wants very much to have a baby, and she is tormented by her inability to conceive a child with her husband.

Vectia hints at her distress to her neighbor Heron, described in Stopes's stage directions as "a well-groomed, virile, attractive man," who decides to educate her about physical intimacies in marriage. After he obligingly shows her a diagram of the sex organs of human physiology, Vectia realizes that William is impotent and they have never consummated their marriage. Although she is grateful to Heron for enlightening her, their relationship remains in the words of Vectia, "a pure and straightforward one" with no indication of an affair and "not the smallest hint of flirtation or love-making on either side."

CENSORSHIP HISTORY

Marie Stopes claimed in her preface to the play that *Vectia* told the truth about her marital situation with Ruggles Gates, and that she had been ignorant of "married love" until after she had read voraciously "every learned treatise and sexual theory and practice in English, French, and German (in the restricted access section of the British Museum known as 'the cupboard')." Although the marriage was annulled in 1916, Stopes did not complete her play and submit it to the office of the lord chamberlain for licensing until 1926. By then, she was already a well-known advocate for birth control in England and the author of *Married Love* (1918), which emphasized the woman's side of sex and pleaded for a better understanding by husbands of the physical and emotional side of the sex life of their wives.

The censors refused to grant the play a license for performance, unless the author would agree to make major modifications in the portrayal of the marital relationship and in the suggested relationship between Vectia and her neighbor. In a note to the producer, the censor required that fewer references would be made to William's "problem," and that the references that remained should less clearly signal a problem of sexual impotence. The censors also required that the relationship between Vectia and her neighbor Heron be portrayed more clearly as platonic, and that the nature of the physiological diagrams he shows her should be vague. Stopes put the play aside without making the revisions, and the play was never produced.

FURTHER READING

Rose, June. *Marie Stopes and the Sexual Situation.* London: Faber and Faber, 1992.
Stopes, Marie C. *A Banned Play and a Preface on the Censorship.* London: John Bale, Sons, & Danliesson, Ltd., 1926.

A VENETIAN NIGHT

Author: Karl Vollmoeller
Original date and place of production: 1911, Berlin, Germany
Characters: Anselmus Aselmeyer, Marchesina dei Bisognosi, Mestre Mangiabene, Offizier, Pipistrello
Filmed versions: *Eine Venetianische Nacht* (1914, Germany)

SUMMARY

A Venetian Night is a play in 12 episodes that relates the story of a bride married to a man she dislikes. On her wedding night at a hotel, she manages to evade her husband and rendezvous with her lover in her bedroom. The bride and lover are shown entering the bride's bedroom, then in a new episode a young stranger is shown dreaming what took place after the door closed. In his dream, the bride and her lover embrace each other and are immediately interrupted by the bridegroom. The lover and the bridegroom confront each other, and the lover is killed. As the dream continues, the young stranger becomes part of the action as he endeavors to help the bride by getting rid of the lover's body.

In the 12th and final episode of the play, the dream is over and the reality of the three lives returns. The lover is seen walking down the hallway of the hotel after leaving the bride's bedroom. Soon after, the bride leaves her room and, as she walks into the hallway, she is joined by her husband, who emerges from the adjoining room. The play ends with the suggestion that the couple are about to embark on a life of married deceit.

CENSORSHIP HISTORY

The London theater season eagerly awaited the opening on November 4, 1912, of *A Venetian Night,* produced by Max Reinhardt, who had already fascinated London with productions of *The Miracle, Sumurun,* and OEDIPUS REX. On November 3, 1912, a representative of the Lord Chamberlain's Office attended the final rehearsal, and the following afternoon Mr. Butt, the manager of the Palace Theatre, received a message stating that the play would not be granted a license for performance. The censors objected to the theme and the plot of the play, and expressed the belief that their objections were so serious that alterations to a scene or an incident would not be sufficient to make the play acceptable.

Max Reinhardt had powerful and influential friends, and he appealed to the German embassy, which sent telegrams to Berlin. Personal friends of high standing traveled to England to speak on behalf of the play in an attempt to reverse the decision. Reinhardt insisted that because of the magnitude of the production and the presence of influential Germans, Lord Sandhurst, the Lord Chamberlain, should himself inspect the play and make the decision for licensing. The review of the play was delayed, because the Lord Chamberlain was shooting in the country. When he returned to London, because of the agitation and the possibility of international friction, he agreed to intervene. After inspecting a rehearsal, he lifted the ban and approved a license for performance. As Frank Fowell and Frank Palmer write, "It may confidently be assumed, however, that in the hands of less important producers, the censorial ban would have been maintained."

FURTHER READING

Fowell, Frank, and Frank Palmer. *Censorship in England.* London: F. Palmer, 1913. Reprint, New York: Benjamin Blom, 1969.

Innes, C. D. *Modern German Drama: A Study in Form.* New York: Cambridge University Press, 1979.

Elfe, Wolfgang D., and James Hardin. *Twentieth-Century German Dramatists, 1889–1918.* Detroit: Gale Research, 1992.

VICTOR, OR THE CHILDREN TAKE OVER

Author: Roger Vitrac
Original date and place of production: 1928, Théâtre Alfred Jarry, Paris, France; August 5, 1964, Aldwych Theatre, London, England
Characters: Antoine Magneau, Esther Magneau, Therese Magneau, Ida Mortemart, Charles Paumelle, Emilie Paumelle, Victor Paumelle
Filmed versions: None

SUMMARY

Victor, Or the Children Take Over (*Victor, ou les enfants en pouvoir*) is a surrealistic, bitter drawing-room farce about the Paumelles, a middle-class family that contains a physically enormous and intellectually advanced nine-year-old boy named Victor. The boy and his playmate, six-year-old Esther, have discovered that his father and her mother have been having an adulterous affair. The action of the play takes place on Victor's ninth birthday. Already six feet tall, Victor also has extensive intellectual abilities that he uses to ridicule and exploit others. Before the adults arrive, he smashes one of his parents' expensive vases, then feigns innocence and later allows the blame to fall on Esther. Victor's parents, Charles and Emilie Paumelle, appear, accompanied by Esther's parents, Therese and Antoine Magneau, ready to celebrate Victor's birthday, but the guest of honor has other intentions.

In the second act, Victor confronts his father and Therese about their affair, and speaks a lengthy and somber soliloquy about the desolation of his life. The adults become deeply depressed by his speech and they sit inert and silent until Charles Paumelle calls out for a miracle. The miracle arrives in the person of the rich, elegant, and beautiful Ida Mortemart, who seems at first to be a shining star in what has become a somber get-together. As the audience soon learns, however, Ida is subject to frequent episodes of flatulence, which contrasts with her elegance and makes her as absurd and lost as the rest of the characters.

In the final act, the party has ended and Charles and Emilie argue loudly in their bedroom. Victor enters their room to learn what is happening. He soon seems to be overcome with a terrible weakness, then suffers a stroke and dies after proclaiming that he has discovered "the secret." The grieving parents then shoot themselves, but whether it is because their son has just died or because of the father's affair is left in doubt.

CENSORSHIP HISTORY

Victor first opened at the Théâtre Alfred Jarry in 1928, but the critics found its surrealistic dialogue and action difficult to understand and censors were opposed to the violence onstage, so the play closed after only three performances. In contrast, Jean Anouilh successfully produced *Victor* in 1962, and the play had a long run in Paris.

In 1964, during rehearsals of *Victor* at the Aldwych Theatre in London, a representative of the office of the lord chamberlain reviewed the play and recommended against granting the play a license for performance. Most of the censors' objections centered on the clearly identified adulterous relationship in the play. A suggestion was made to change the moral violation to something less sensational, and, similarly, more appropriate for a child to speak about. The censors also objected to the nine-year-old character's knowledge of an adulterous affair and his discussion of the affair with a six-year-old girl. Further, the censors also objected to the confrontation between Victor and his parents abour the affair, believing that a child of nine should not be speaking about such matters in so adult a manner. The deaths at the end also concerned the censors, who suggested that the ending of the play be rewritten to eliminate the onstage violence. The lord chamberlain insisted that the changes be made before a license for performance would be issued, but the Royal Shakespeare Company disagreed and lobbied the censors to change their decision. The play became a significant example of the weaknesses in the stage's antiquated form of censorship, and was instrumental in providing a case for the discussion of new, more democratic methods.

FURTHER READING

Levitt, Annette Shandler. *The Genes and Genders of Surrealism.* New York: St. Martin's Press, 1999.
Midgley, Robin. "*Victor*—Or The Chamberlain Takes Over." *Plays and Players* 11 (September 1964): 10.
Osborn, Tom. "Censor by Jury?" *Plays and Players* 11 (September 1964): 9.
Vaneigem, Raoul. *A Cavalier History of Surrealism.* Translated by Donald Nicholson-Smith. San Francisco: AK Press, 1999.

VICTORIA REGINA

Author: Laurence Housman
Original date and place of production: December 26, 1935, Broadhurst Theatre, New York, New York
Characters: Archbishop of Canterbury, John Brown, Benjamin Disraeli, Duchess of Kent, Duchess of Sutherland, Lady Grace, Lady Jane, Lady Muriel, Lord Conyngham, Lord Melbourne, Mr. Anson, Mr. Oakley, Mr. Richards, Prince Albert, Prince Ernest, Sir Arthur Bigge, Victoria
Filmed versions: *Victoria the Great* (1937, U.K.)

SUMMARY

Victoria Regina is a play in three acts that provides an intimate portrait of Queen Victoria from the first years of her reign through her diamond jubilee as queen. Set at various castles in England and Scotland during the years 1837 through 1897, the play depicts different phases of her life, starting at age 18 with her notification that the king is dead and that she will ascend the throne. The play deals with her courtship and marriage to Prince Albert, whom she marries despite the objections of her prime minister and other advisers who consider him "an ineligible prospect" and the objections of Albert's father who wants her to marry his other son, Prince Ernest. Act one ends on February 11, 1840, at dawn after the wedding, as Victoria delightedly watches Albert shave, "reveling in wifely submission."

The second focuses on the marriage of Victoria and Albert, and it begins with Albert defying Victoria's peremptory summons to appear, then taming her when she becomes furious. The act recounts their love and their heroism during an assassination attempt on Victoria in 1842 in which Albert risked death by using his body to shield Victoria from the assassin. The plot also presents scenes from the couple's domestic life, showing Victoria in a jealous rage and then apologizing and crying as she and Albert make up. The act ends with a severely ill Albert helping Victoria through an international crisis, then dying.

The third act opens in 1877 and depicts Victoria as a widow, first vacationing in the Scottish Highlands where she converses with a comical John Brown, engages in a serious political discussion with Prime Minister Disraeli, and then sits alone and cries for Albert. The second scene of the act moves ahead 20 years, to June 20, 1897, the celebration of the diamond jubilee at Buckingham Palace. Queen Victoria, seated in a wheelchair, is cheered by international royalty and her subjects. As she is wheeled away, triumphant in her popularity, she murmurs, "Albert! Ah! If only you could have been here!"

CENSORSHIP HISTORY

Laurence Housman, brother of poet A. E. Housman, adapted *Victoria Regina* from his Palace Plays, a series of plays written from 1930 to 1933 about the reign of Queen Victoria. He submitted the play to the London censors, but it was refused a license for performance on political grounds, because England continued to ban plays that portrayed personal lives of members of the royal family. The play was produced in the United States, opening on December 26, 1935, at the Broadhurst Theatre on Broadway in New York City, where it ran for 203 performances. Helen Hayes played the role of Victoria and Vincent Price was Albert.

Three years after his initial attempt, Housman once again submitted the play to the London censors for licensing, and this time he was successful. In 1937 England lifted its ban on plays portraying the royal family, and *Victoria Regina* was licensed for public performance on June 20, 1937, the centenary of Victoria's ascension to the throne. The London production was financially successful.

FURTHER READING

Housman, Laurence. "My Thirty Years' Fight with the Censors." *Living Age* 353 (November 1937): 264–265.
———. *Victoria Regina: A Dramatic Biography.* Illustrated by E. H. Shephard. London: Jonathan Cape, 1938.

A VIEW FROM THE BRIDGE

Author: Arthur Miller
Original date and place of production: September 24, 1956, Coronet Theatre, New York, New York

Characters: Alfieri, Beatrice Carbone, Eddie Carbone, Catherine, Mr. Lipari, Mrs. Lipari, Louis, Marco, Mike, Rodolpho

Filmed versions: *Uno Sguardo dal ponte* (1961, France/Italy, released in the United States in 1962 as *A View from the Bridge*)

SUMMARY

A View from the Bridge takes place on the Brooklyn, New York, waterfront, with most of the action occurring in the apartment of Eddie Carbone. The play is narrated by the lawyer Alfieri, who uses literary language and connects the events of the play to Greek tragedy. Eddie is a longshoreman of Italian descent who lives with his wife, Beatrice, and orphaned niece Catherine, an 18-year-old girl for whom Eddie has latent sexual desire.

Two of his wife's cousins, Marco and Rodolpho, are smuggled into the United States from Sicily to work on the New York docks, and they live in Eddie's apartment. Eddie welcomes them at first, and he gets along well with the older man, Marco, who is quiet and a hard worker. The younger man, Rodolpho, is an easygoing, strikingly handsome man with a warm sense of humor who always seems to be singing. He and Catherine soon fall in love and decide to marry, but Eddie objects fiercely to the match. As Eddie strives to repress his strong desire for Catherine, he mocks Rodolpho's lightheartedness, claims that Rodolpho wants to marry Catherine only to become an American citizen, and accuses him of homosexuality. Arriving home one evening half-drunk, Eddie orders Rodolpho out of the house. Catherine tries to leave as well. Eddie pulls her toward him and kisses her passionately. When Rodolpho pulls him away, Eddie then kisses him, as well, and tells Catherine, "You see? He ain't right."

Eddie finds that his protests have no effect on Catherine, so he reports the brothers to the immigration authorities, who arrive and arrest all of the "submarines" (illegal immigrants). After Marco denounces Eddie to the neighborhood, Eddie is shunned for turning in the men. He confronts Marco and demands that Marco retract his accusation, telling him, "I want my name." Eddie lunges at Marco with a knife, but the younger man twists his arm and presses the knife into Eddie, who dies in Beatrice's arms.

CENSORSHIP HISTORY

A View from the Bridge was first produced as a one-act classical tragedy paired with another one-act play by Miller, *A Memory of Two Mondays*. Miller expanded the play to two acts, enlarged the roles of the women, and enhanced the character of Eddie for presentation of the play in London. The play was then submitted to the office of the lord chamberlain to obtain a license for public performance. The censor returned the script, refusing to grant a license unless Miller rewrote portions of the script to eliminate the incestuous nature of Eddie's feelings toward Catherine and the passionate kiss he gives her while half-drunk. The censor also objected to Eddie's references to homosexuality and his taunts about Rodolpho's behavior. Special note was made of the passionate kiss that Eddie gives Rodolpho, and the censor suggested excision of this scene. Miller objected to the revisions, because they would change entirely the element of tragedy in the play, and the producers agreed. Although the censors refused to grant the play a license for public performance, it was quickly produced by subscription only at the Comedy Theatre in London.

In the United States, no efforts were made to repress the play, but the Federal Bureau of Investigation had an extensive file on Arthur Miller. Author Natalie Robins writes that records from 1960 characterize *A View from the Bridge* as "one of the greatest anti-American plays ever written in America in recent years" without elaboration. Although the play was not suppressed, Miller's alleged political undesirability required filming of the movie version in Italy and France.

FURTHER READING

Elsom, John. *Erotic Theatre*. New York: Taplinger, 1974.
Hall, Peter. "Sleaze Nation." *Guardian Unlimited*. October 2, 2002. Available online. URL: http://www.guardian.co.uk/freedom/story/0,2763,802897,00.html.
Moss, Leonard. *Arthur Miller*. Boston: Twayne Publishers, 1980.
Robins, Natalie. *Alien War: The FBI's War on Freedom of Expression*. New York: William Morrow, 1992.

WAITING FOR LEFTY

Author: Clifford Odets
Original date and place of production: January 5, 1935, Civic Repertory Company, New York, New York
Characters: Dr. Barnes, Dr. Benjamin, Clayton, Lefty Costello, Harry Fatt, Fayette, Florrie, Irv, Agate Keller, Edna Mitchell, Joe Mitchell, Reilly
Filmed versions: None

SUMMARY

Waiting for Lefty is a one-hour episodic drama rooted in the theater of agit-prop, which dealt with capitalist evils and propagandized for the benefits of communism. Made up of several vignettes separated by blackouts, the play takes place in a taxi union committee meeting room. Several taxi drivers sit in a semicircle, and off to one side stands a gunman. A union leader, Harry Fatt, tells the men that a strike is not a good idea. When a man in the crowd mocks this idea, Fatt calls him a "red" (communist) and says he is keeping an eye out for communists in the union. The crowd questions the whereabouts of Lefty, their elected chairman, and Fatt reminds them that their elected committee is already present. He lets Joe, one of the workers, speak. Joe asserts he is not a "red boy," and tells the crowd about his status as a wounded war veteran; he then criticizes the tendency of the union leaders to label as "red" any worker who expresses dissatisfaction and says his wife convinced him the previous week to strike for higher wages.

The scene fades to the first vignette, "Joe and Edna." The taxi drivers remain dimly visible onstage as Edna joins Joe in their home in a flashback scene. She tells him that their furniture, unpaid for, was repossessed, and they argue. She says his boss is "making suckers" out of the workers, and out of their families. Edna demands that Joe stand up to the union and encourages him to start a workers' union without the racketeers. Joe gets swept up in her passion and tells her he's going to find Lefty Costello. When Joe returns to the taxi drivers' meeting, his fellow workers tell him, "We gotta walk out!"

The second vignette is the "Lab Assistant Episode." Fayette, an industrialist, talks in his office to Miller, a lab assistant, to whom he is giving a raise for his loyalty; Fayette is also transferring Miller to a new laboratory the following day, where he will work under an important chemist, Dr. Brenner, to create poisonous gas for chemical warfare. Fayette tells him that the world is ready for war, and the United States needs to be ready. Miller becomes distraught, as he lost several relatives in the last war, including his brother. Fayette tells him he will also require a weekly confidential report on Dr. Brenner, but Miller refuses to spy. He is willing to lose his job, saying he would "Rather dig ditches first!" Outraged, Miller punches Fayette in the mouth.

In the third vignette, "The Young Hack and His Girl," Florence loves Sid, but her brother Irv and their mother disapprove of Sid since he makes little money as a taxi driver. She gives in and says she will talk to Sid. He arrives and laments their lowly status in life as "dogs," under the thumb of the powerful "big shot money men." He is upset that his brother, a college student, has joined the navy to fight foreigners who are, ultimately, just like himself. The scene ends as the despondent lovers collapse into each others' arms.

In the "Labor Spy Episode," Fatt tells the taxi drivers that they have not investigated the strike issue as he has and introduces Tom Clayton, who was in an unsuccessful strike in Philadelphia. Clayton says that his experience has taught him that Fatt is right. A man in the audience tries to shout him down, but Fatt tells his henchmen to "take care of him." The man runs up onstage and says that Clayton's real name is Clancy, and that he is a "company spy," as is his brother, who has been breaking up unions for years. Fatt tells Clayton to leave.

In the "Interne Episode," the elderly Dr. Barnes angrily tells Dr. Benjamin that he has been dismissed just before he is due to perform an important operation on a woman in the charity ward. His replacement is a senator's nephew who is "incompetent as hell." Barnes tells Benjamin that the hospital is closing the charity ward since it is rapidly losing money. Though Benjamin has seniority, he is losing his job because he is Jewish. The patient dies, and Benjamin throws down his surgical gloves and decides he has to work on America, and possibly get a job such as driving a taxi to allow him to keep working. He vows to fight, even to the death.

The final scene returns to the union hall, where union committee member Keller talks to the taxi drivers and proclaims that if "we're reds because we wanna strike, then we take over their salute too!" He makes a communist salute and tells them to "unite and fight!" then urges them not to wait for Lefty, who may never arrive. As he speaks, a man runs into the hall and says they have just found Lefty, shot dead. Keller yells to his fellow "WORKERS OF THE WORLD," and urges them to die to "make a new world," as he leads them in a chorus of "STRIKE, STRIKE, STRIKE!"

CENSORSHIP HISTORY

Waiting for Lefty opened on January 5, 1935, for a series of benefit performances at the Civic Repertory, but received little attention from the theater critics of major newspapers. Word of mouth soon made the play successful. The play moved to Broadway, opening on March 26, 1935, at the Longacre Theatre in New York City. As Harold Clurman writes, the opening-night audience welcomed the direct involvement with the actors in which cast members sat unobtrusively in the audience then ran up on stage at the appropriate moment: "A shock of delightful recognition struck the audience like a tidal wave . . . a kind of joyous fervor seemed to sweep the audience toward the stage. . . . Audience and actors had become one."

The play had no difficulties with the censors during the 144 performances of its first New York City run, but union propaganda and suggestion of communist sympathies resulted in local officials banning the play in Laguna Beach, California; Philadelphia, Pennsylvania; and Bridgeport, Connecticut. Abe Laufe writes that *Waiting for Lefty* opened in Boston, but after members of the Watch and Ward Society complained to city officials about the obscenity in the play, the city council ordered the play closed. The police arrested four members of the cast on charges of "using profanity in a public assembly," and the case was set for trial. Attorneys for the actors petitioned the court to delay the trial several weeks, during which the script was revised to delete the profanity. After city officials approved the revisions, the official ban was lifted and the play permitted to continue.

FURTHER READING

Brennan-Gibson, Margaret. *Clifford Odets, American Playwright: The Years from 1906 to 1940.* New York: Atheneum Press, 1981.

Clurman, Harold, ed. *Famous American Plays of the 1930s.* New York: Dell Publishing, 1959.

Laufe, Abe. *The Wicked Stage: A History of Theater Censorship and Harassment in the United States.* New York: Frederick Ungar Publishing Co., 1978.

Murray, Edward. *Clifford Odets: The Thirties and After.* New York: Frederick Ungar Publishing Co., 1968.

Weales, Gerald. *Clifford Odets: Playwright.* New York: Pegasus Publishing, 1971.

WASTE

Author: Harley Granville-Barker

Original date and place of production: November 24, 1907, Stage Society at the Imperial Theatre, London, England

Characters: Russell Blackborough, Lord Charles Cantelupe, Lady Davenport, Lucy Davenport, Edmunds, George Farrant, Mrs. Julia Farrant, Earl of Horsham, Walter Kent, Justin O'Connell, Mrs. Amy O'Connell, Simpson, Henry Trebell, Miss Frances Trebell, Gilbert Wedgecroft

Filmed versions: Made for television: *Waste* (1977, U.K.)

SUMMARY

Waste is a play in four acts set in the early 20th century in Hertfordshire and London and based loosely on actual politicians Sir Charles Dilke and Charles Stewart Parnell, whose careers were ruined by scandals of adultery. The play opens at a weekend house party in the home of Julia Farrant, wife of a ranking Tory. With the goal of bringing about a change in his political alliances, she has invited Henry Trebell, described as "hard-bitten, brainy, forty-five, and very sure of himself," who was elected as an Independent and has now aligned himself with the Liberal Party. He is expected to join the Conservatives, about to resume power, in return for a cabinet seat and support of his scheme to radically change the British system of education. The first scene functions to provide a political context, as the party guests discuss political events and social entanglements using the names of real and imagined politicians.

Trebell has drafted a bill that would dismantle the Church of England and reallocate its funds to a new educational system, replacing established religion with "a religion of knowledge." His high-minded and aloof behavior have set him apart from his colleagues. Amy O'Connell, who lives apart from her Catholic husband, a historian of the 13th century, because she refuses to bear the children that he demands and which he seeks to have by refusing to use birth control, flirts with Trebell. Ironically, she turns to the seemingly emotionless Trebell for love. When she becomes pregnant with his child, he is interested in having a child and horrified by her request for help in ending the pregnancy. Panicked, Amy seeks an abortion and dies afterward.

Justin O'Connell, Amy's husband, agrees to keep quiet that Trebell is the father of the child, but the affair damages the politician's reputation, nonetheless. Lord Horsham, soon to be prime minister, and his Tory shadow cabinet already dislike the uncompromising Trebell and his proposed education bill, and the affair provides an excuse to sever ties with both.

Trebell is devastated by the abortion and Amy's death, even though he acknowledges to himself that he never really cared for her. He defends himself to his colleagues after Amy's death: "Oh, cheer up. You know we're an adulterous and sterile generation. Why should you cry out at a proof now and then of what's always in the hearts of most of us?" Trebell spends a night waiting for Horsham's decision about his political future, and by morning, when the note arrives, he is resigned to the fate of an outcast. He commits suicide, after which his secretary cries in anguish at "the waste of a good man. Look at the work undone . . . think of it! Who is to do it! Oh . . . the waste . . . !"

CENSORSHIP HISTORY

Waste was supposed to be the centerpiece of the 1907 season at the Savoy Theatre in London, as part of a Barker-Vedrenne season, after Barker had enjoyed three years of success working with his business manager J. E. Vedrenne at the Royal Court Theatre in Sloane Square. The play was scheduled to open in November 1907, but the examiner of plays, George Alexander Redford, refused to grant the play a license for public performance. He wrote to Granville-Barker and demanded general alterations. After the playwright wrote Redford a letter asking for specific changes, Redford told him to "modify the extremely outspoken references to sexual relations." The censor also demanded the excision of all references to "a criminal operation" (the abortion). In his refusal, Granville-Barker wrote that he considered "sober plain speaking to be the only course" and considered that "innuendo would be indecent." The playwright also refused "to delegate my responsibility to him, in case the play was produced, by cutting out certain lines or certain things which he disapproved of."

The play remained banned from public performance; instead, two private performances were presented by the Stage Society at the Imperial Theatre. Norman McKinnel, who had rehearsed the lead, did not appear in the production, because his manager prevented him at the last moment from appearing in a banned play. Granville-Barker was forced to take the role. A. B. Walkley, theater critic for *The Times*, praised the work but supported Redford's decision: "The subject-matter of *Waste*, together with the sincere realism with which it is treated, makes it, in our judgment, wholly unfit for performance under ordinary conditions before a miscellaneous public of various ages, moods, and standards of intelligence." In a review appearing in the *Sunday Times*, J. T. Grein wrote that the play was too powerful and too dangerous to be released to the "unthinking and still imperfectly educated crowd."

Granville-Barker completely rewrote the play, and the published version appeared in 1927. The play was presented in its revised form on December 1, 1936, at the Westminster Theatre, directed by Granville-Barker and Michael MacOwan.

FURTHER READING

Craies, W. F. "Censorship of Stage Plays." *Journal of the Society of Comparative Legislation* 8 (1907): 196–202.

Elsom, John. *Erotic Theatre*. New York: Taplinger Publishing Co., 1974.

Fowell, Frank, and Frank Palmer. *Censorship in England*. London: F. Palmer, 1913. Reprint, New York: Benjamin Blom, 1969.

Godden, Gertrude M. *The Stage Censor, an Historical Sketch: 1544–1907. With 16 Illustrations from Photographs of Rare Prints, and Contemporary Portraits by Marie Léon.* London: Sampson Low, Marston, 1908.

Grein, J. T. "Harley Granville-Barker's *Waste*." *Sunday Times*, December 1, 1907, p. 4.

Kennedy, Dennis, ed. *Plays by Harley Granville-Barker: The Marrying of Ann Leete, The Voysey Inheritance, Waste*. New York: Cambridge University Press, 1987.

Walkley, A. B. *"Waste." The Times*, November 27, 1907, p. 8.

THE WEAVERS

Author: Gerhart Hauptmann

Original date and place of production: February 26, 1893, Freie Buhne Theatre Association, Berlin, Germany

Characters: Old Baumgart, Dreissiger, Mrs. Dreissiger, Heide, Old Hilse, Hornig, Moritz Jager, Johann, Mrs. Kittelhaus, Pastor Kittelhaus, Kutsche, Neumann, Pfeifer, Schmidt, Welzel, Anna Welzel, Mrs. Welzel, Wiegand, Old Wittig

Filmed versions: None

SUMMARY

The Weavers (Die Weber), subtitled "A Play of the Eighteen-Forties," is a naturalistic play in five acts that takes place in three Silesian towns at the foot of the Eulengebirge Mountains. The play was originally written in Silesian dialect, then rewritten by Hauptmann into High German. Based on an actual uprising among weavers in 1844, the play depicts the workers' hunger and oppression that lead to abortive riots. Rather than build this drama around a single hero, the playwright created a collective heroism in the weavers, as a succession of scenes chart the course of the weavers' uprising. Repetition of the weavers' song "Bloody Justice" serves as a leitmotif throughout the play.

The play opens at Dreissiger's textile plant, where emaciated workers wait to be paid for weaving they have completed at home. They are exploited by the arrogant staff, who lower the payments to those weavers who complain, and cheat further the starving but submissive workers. Dreissiger complains of the high cost of doing business and of the hard life of a factory owner; he exits hurriedly when individual weavers plead for his help.

The second act takes place at Old Baumgart's shack, where the destitute family has gathered with other weavers. Baumgart enters with a package containing their dog, which he has killed to provide his wife and children with food. As the weavers listen, Mortiz Jager, a former local weaver who is now a well-fed soldier who has money, tells them how the manufacturers live: "They don't hardly know what to do with their wealth and arrogance." As the group becomes angrier, Jager reads them lines from the song "Bloody Justice": "Here bloody justice thrives. . . . Men are slowly tortured. . . . A curse will be your payment." Stirred to rebellion, the weavers shout: "We won't take it no more, come what may!"

The third act takes place in a tavern to which Jager leads the weavers and treats them to drinks. A traveling salesman remarks that the government inspectors have found reports of local poverty greatly exaggerated, but the weavers describe some of the gruesome situations that the inspectors never see, as they are fearful of muddying their shoes. When a police officer prohibits the group from singing "Bloody Justice," the weavers become incensed and leave en masse, singing and heading to Dreissiger's house to demand a raise.

As the weavers head for the Dreissiger house, the factory owner is giving a party where a pastor chastises the family tutor for defending the weavers: "A keeper of souls must not concern himself with bellies." When the rioters reach the house, Jager is arrested and brought in by police. He defiantly refuses to "be a good Christian," and is taken to jail, but the weavers beat up the police and free Jager. Dreissiger and his family flee the house in fear for their lives, and the weavers arrive soon after, destroy the furnishings, and then threaten to wreck the factory and others where there are "steam-power looms."

In the final act, Old Hilse, a poor weaver, refuses to join the rioting, even when his daughter-in-law screams hysterically about those who have caused her children to die from starvation. Other weavers bring him food and objects they have taken from the factories, but Old Hilse accepts nothing and ridicules the men for dreaming that a better life is coming. He counsels them to instead look toward Judgment Day. His son and daughter-in-law join the front ranks of the fight, but Old Hilse sits at the window and weaves, muttering: "Not me! Not if ya all go bats. Here my Heavenly Father put me." Shots are heard, and Old Hilse falls to the ground. The play ends with his blind wife calling hysterically, "Father, say something; You're scaring me."

CENSORSHIP HISTORY

The Weavers was controversial from its inception, even though it is a historical play containing events that took place nearly 50 years before the play was written. Hauptmann completed the play near the end of 1891. In February 1892 he submitted the play to the Berlin Police Commission, which responded in March and banned all public performances of the work. During the next 10 months, the playwright rewrote the play from its original Silesian dialect into High German, eliminated obscenities spoken by Jager and the weavers, and removed one verse of "Bloody Justice"; he then submitted it once again to the Berlin Police Commission. The censors did not feel that the revisions were sufficient and banned the play from public performance once again, although S. Fischer in Berlin published both versions of the play in 1892. On February 26, 1893, the Freie Buhne Theater Association held a closed premiere of *The Weavers* in Berlin, and lawyers pressed their challenge to the ban on public performances while the closed performances continued throughout the first half of 1894.

The first public performance of *The Weavers* occurred on September 25, 1894, at the Deutsches Theater in Berlin; the German High Court agreed to allow the performance because the high admission prices of the theater would exclude the "common masses" who would be "most susceptible" to the influence of the drama. When the play was presented on October 1, 1894, at the Lobe-Theater in Breslau, the major city in Silesia, the police directed the theater manager to raise the price for the least expensive seats from 30 and 50 pfennig to 1 and 1.23 marks. Later that month, Kaiser Wilhelm canceled his theater box at the Deutsches Theater as a protest against what he labeled the "demoralizing tendency" of the play. He also expressed personal disapproval of the decision by the German High Court to allow public performances of the play, but he made no effort to reverse the decision.

FURTHER READING

Andrews, Wayne. *Siegfried's Curse: The German Journey from Nietzsche to Hesse.* New York: Atheneum, 1972.

Hauptmann, Gerhart Johann. *The Weavers, Hannele, The Beaver Coat.* Translated by Horst Frenz and Miles Waggoner. New York: Holt, Rinehart and Winston, 1962.

WEST SIDE STORY

Authors: Arthur Laurents (book); Leonard Bernstein (music); Stephen Sondheim (lyrics)
Original date and place of production: September 26, 1957, Winter Garden Theatre, New York, New York
Characters: Anita, Anybody's, Bernardo, Chino, Doc, Ice, Officer Krupke, Maria, Riff, Lieutenant Schrank, Tony
Filmed versions: *West Side Story* (1961)

SUMMARY

The idea for *West Side Story* was initiated in 1949 by New York director and choreographer Jerome Robbins, who wanted to produce a modern adaptation of *Romeo and Juliet*. He conceived of the project as titled *East Side Story* or *The Gang Way*, with the ill-fated romance occurring between a Jewish boy and an Irish Catholic girl on New York's Lower East Side. Robbins had asked the renowned composer Leonard Bernstein and writer Arthur Laurents to join him, but because of other commitments the project was put on hold. In 1954, after reading about the gang warfare between Puerto Ricans and Americans on New York's Upper West Side, Robbins revived the project, and the result was *West Side Story.*

In the prologue, two rival teenage gangs, the Jets (native-born Americans) and the Sharks (Puerto Rican immigrants) fight through dance movements over who will control the neighborhood. Accompanied by police whistles and taunting phrases, the prologue establishes the fierce rivalry between the two groups. Following a brief exchange with the ineffective police officers, Lieutenant Schrank and Officer Krupke, Riff, the leader of the Jets, devises a plan to gain control of the street. The members of the gang boast of their strength, restate their bond to one another, and declare their intention to protect their turf.

The first act takes place at a dance in a neighborhood gymnasium, where Riff has a difficult time convincing his best friend Tony to rejoin the Jets. Tony agrees out of a sense of loyalty to Riff, but expresses his unhappiness with his current life. He feels himself growing away from the gang and envisions a better future. Maria, the sister of the Sharks leader, Bernardo, also attends the dance. She has been in America only a short time and works with Anita, Bernardo's girlfriend, in a bridal shop. Maria sees this dance as the official beginning of her life in this country, and, like Tony, she is full of hope. Bernardo arrives with Chino, a quiet, intense member of the Sharks whom Maria's family has selected to be her future husband. Tony and Maria suddenly see one another, and, in a moment of romantic suspension, they dance together, oblivious of the tension around them. Bernardo interrupts the romantic idyll by roughly pulling Maria from Tony's arms and sending her home. Then Riff and Bernardo arrange a war council at the drugstore.

Doc, the owner of the drugstore, tries to convince the Jets not to have a rumble (an all-out fight) with the Sharks, but Riff and Bernardo set up the rumble for the next day and agree on weapons. Tony suggests a less dangerous fistfight. After the others leave, Tony dismisses Doc's fear with his conviction that nothing can go wrong because he is in love with Maria. The next day, Maria learns about the rumble from Anita at the bridal shop and begs Tony to stop the rumble; he promises her he will. They act out a mock marriage ceremony and swear that "even death can't part us now."

Tony tries to stop the rumble, in progress under a highway, but in the confusion of insults, pushing, and shoving, Bernardo stabs Riff, after which Tony stabs Bernardo. The sirens scream; everyone runs except Tony, who stands transfixed until Anybody's, a tomboy whose dream is to become a Jet, prods Tony to escape, just in time. The act ends with a stage empty except for the bodies of Riff and Bernardo.

The second act begins with Maria unaware of her brother's death, singing about how beautiful she feels. After Chino enters with the news that Tony has killed Bernardo, Maria prays and Tony enters through the window. He explains that he killed Bernardo in a moment of anger over Riff's death.

Maria forgives him, and they remain determined to be together. A dream sequence occurs in which Shark and Jet couples dance together in a surreal, peaceful, sunlit world; at the end of the dream, Tony and Maria are in her bed, in each other's arms. Anita arrives at Maria's apartment, and Tony escapes through the window, telling Maria to meet him at the drugstore so they can run away together. When Anita realizes Tony has been with Maria, she furiously berates Maria for making love to the boy who killed her brother. Maria explains her feelings, and Anita realizes Maria loves Tony as much as she loved Bernardo. She warns Maria that Chino plans to kill Tony and agrees to go to the drugstore to tell Tony to wait for her.

Anita is prevented from reaching Tony by the ethnic prejudice of the Jets. The gang's verbal taunting of Anita escalates into a threat of rape, but she is saved by Doc. In her fury and humiliation, Anita lies and tells the gang members that Chino has killed Maria. Doc tells Tony, who is hiding in his cellar, and he feels that his dreams for the future are dead because Maria is dead. He runs out to find Chino but sees Maria only seconds before Chino appears and kills him. As Maria kneels over Tony's body, the Jets and Sharks enter. Maria takes Chino's gun, but is unable to bring herself to fire it. The cycle of violence ends with her. Gradually, members of both gangs assemble on either side of Tony's body, while Maria kisses him gently. Members of both gangs form a procession and together carry Tony offstage. The lights fade.

CENSORSHIP HISTORY

West Side Story, which opened at the Winter Garden Theatre in New York City on September 26, 1957, was not well received by critics during its initial run. Critics declared that the violence and gang warfare were not appropriate subjects for musical theater, and reviews suggested that the play presented an overly harsh view of immigrant life in New York. Nonetheless, the play was included in the first list of musicals that the federal government considered to represent the United States at the 1958 World's Fair in Brussels. As Laufe writes, when the final selections were announced, *West Side Story* had been dropped and replaced by another Bernstein musical, *Wonderful Town*, based on the successful comedy *My Sister Eileen*. No official explanation was provided, but observers assumed that the government feared that the play, with its gang fights and violence, would give Europeans a distorted picture of American life.

In December 1999 a student production planned by the Amherst (Massachusetts) Regional High School was canceled by administrators after the school district received complaints from parents and students who said that the play demeans people of Puerto Rican descent. One parent was quoted in an article that appeared in the *Boston Globe* as saying, "The Latinos are basically put down in the play and are strongly stereotyped." Camille Sola, a 17-year-old student, gathered 158 signatures from fellow students on a petition to protest the choice of *West Side Story* as the school's annual spring dramatic production. Sola spoke out at a student forum and assailed Leonard Bernstein's 42-year-old musical for providing an "unflattering portrayal of Puerto Rican males," as well as its romanticization of gang fighting and its cavalier use of racial slurs.

In an interview in the *Boston Globe*, 81-year-old Arthur Laurents, who wrote the original Broadway stage production, dismissed students and parents who objected to the performance as "bigots" and declared that "It sounds like a few educators need to go back to school. Is it possible that anyone could have missed the point that badly?"

School principal Scott Goldman stressed that *West Side Story* was not banned but canceled. In an article published in the *Los Angeles Times*, he insisted, "This isn't about censorship. It's about sensitivity." Administrators replaced *West Side Story* with *Crazy for You*, producer Roger Horchow's 1990s rewrite of the 1930s musical *Girl Crazy* by George and Ira Gershwin.

FURTHER READING

Daly, Beth. "Protesters Enlist Free Speech Group over School Play." *Boston Globe*, December 1, 1999, p. B:3.

Laufe, Abe. *The Wicked Stage: A History of Theater Censorship and Harassment in the United States.* New York: Frederick Ungar Publishing Co., 1978.

McNamara, Eileen. "Writer's Point Lost on Amherst." *Boston Globe*, December 1, 1999, p. B:1.

Mehren, Elizabeth. "National Perspective: A New Drama Begins after Play Is Cancelled; High School Production of *West Side Story* Forces Debate on Racism and Ethnicity." *The Los Angeles Times*, December 7, 1999, p. 5.

Official West Side Story Website, The. URL: http://www.westsidestory.com.

Pennimen, Bruce. "When a School Decides There's No Place for *West Side Story*." *Amherst Online*, December 14, 1999. Available online. URL: http://www.csmonitor.com/durable/1999/12/14/fp18s1-csm.shtml.

"West Side Story cancellation sparks protest." http://cnn.com. Available online. URL: http://www.cnn.com/SHOWBIZ/News/9911/29/showbuzz.

"Wrong Side at Amherst High, The." *Boston Globe*, November 21, 1999, p. C:6.

WHAT PRICE GLORY?

Authors: Laurence Stallings and Maxwell Anderson

Original date and place of production: September 3, 1924, Plymouth Theatre, New York, New York

Characters: Brigadier General Cokeley, Captain Flagg, Charmaine de la Cognac, Corporal Gowdy, Corporal Kiper, Corporal Lipinsky, First Sergeant Quirt, Gunnery Sergeant Sockkel, Lieutenant Aldrich, Lieutenant Cunningham, Lieutenant Lundstrom, Lieutenant Moore, Lieutenant Schmidt, Monsieur Pete De La Cognac, Private Lewisohn, Private Mulcahy, Sergeant Ferguson

Filmed versions: *What Price Glory?* (1926, 1952)

SUMMARY

What Price Glory? is a play in three acts that takes place near and at the World War I battle front in France in 1918. The mixture of comedy, romance, and the naturalistic portrayal of war combined with earthy language shocked theater audiences, but the play's uniqueness made it highly successful.

The play opens in a French farmhouse converted into company headquarters, where Corporals Gowdy, Kiper, and Lipinski are discussing women. Captain Flagg prepares to travel to Paris, but he first consoles his girlfriend, Charmaine de la Cognac, daughter of the local innkeeper. Before he leaves, Sergeant Quirt, an old romantic rival, appears to help to train the new troops. Flagg places Quirt in command of the men, and warns him not to drink. While Flagg is gone, Quirt comforts the crying Charmaine, telling her "Well, baby, you better stick to me, and you'll have another papa." When Flagg returns, Charmaine's father insists that the Americans have corrupted *"ma fleur delicate"* (his delicate flower); he demands money and that someone marry her. In revenge, Flagg threatens to force Quirt to marry her, but the company is ordered into battle, so both men cheerfully say farewell to Charmaine. Still looking for someone to support her, Charmaine tries unsuccessfully to seduce an elderly sergeant.

In the second act, the horrors of war are blatantly shown in the suffering of the men. Flagg comforts one of the officers who has watched a German sniper bleed to death, "crying 'Kamerad! Kamerad!' just like a big crippled whippoorwill. What price glory now?" Quirt is slightly wounded, and gleefully tells Flagg that he can't wait to return to his "little skookum lady." Also anxious to earn leave promised as a reward for the capture of an enemy officer, Flagg hurriedly finds one and brings him in.

Quirt escapes from the hospital at the beginning of the third act and arrives at Charmaine's home, followed by Flagg. The two men drink and decide to settle their disagreement with a game of blackjack. The winner gets to shoot the loser just badly enough that he's hospitalized but not seriously hurt. "The man that wins gets a gun, and the man that loses gets a head start. Everybody wins, see? One gets the girl and the other gets the chance to stay in bed the rest of this war." Quirt loses and runs off to hide upstairs. Soon after, the company is ordered back to the front. Flagg hesitates but obeys, even if reluctantly: "There's something rotten about this profession of arms, some kind of damned religion connected with it that you can't shake." When Flagg leaves Charmaine, Quirt appears. After hearing the orders, he kisses Charmaine goodbye and leaves, calling: "What a lot of God damn fools it takes to make a war! Hey, Flagg, wait for baby!"

CENSORSHIP HISTORY

What Price Glory? shattered precedents with its frankness and its unromantic treatment of war. As authors Jordan Miller and Winifred Frazer write, "Its rousing depiction of cursing, hard-drinking, fornicating American fighting men permanently ended the long tradition of romanticizing war and glorifying its battles and its heroes." The play portrayed the filth, fear, heat, and suffering endured by soldiers; the characters used profanities that might have been milder than those used by actual soldiers in the trenches, but the earthy language was still shocking to New York audiences. Crusading reformers, especially members of the Society for the Suppression of Vice in New York City, raised an outcry against the play and complained to public officials that the language should be censored or the play banned from the stage. Despite repeated complaints, New York City officials refused to ask for any changes in the play.

Although not censored, the play was snubbed when the Pulitzer Prize committee dropped the drama from consideration. Two of the committee members, Jesse Lynch Williams and Clayton Hamilton, selected *What Price Glory?* to receive the Pulitzer Prize, but the senior member of the committee, Hamlin Garland, refused to recommend the play because he objected to the language. After repeated arguments over the merits of the play, the junior members of the committee agreed to support Garland's recommendation and to award the Pulitzer Prize to Sidney Howard's *They Knew What They Wanted.*

FURTHER READING

Gassner, John, ed. *A Treasury of the Theatre.* Vol. 3. New York: Simon & Schuster, 1966.

Gould, Jean. *Modern American Playwrights.* New York: Dodd, Mead & Co., 1966.

Miller, Jordan Y., and Winifred L. Frazer. *Drama Between the Wars: A Critical History.* Boston: Twayne Publishers, 1991.

WHO'S AFRAID OF VIRGINIA WOOLF?

Author: Edward Albee
Original date and place of production: October 10, 1962, Billy Rose Theatre, New York, New York
Characters: George, Honey, Martha, Nick
Filmed versions: *Who's Afraid of Virginia Woolf?* (1966)

SUMMARY

Who's Afraid of Virginia Woolf? takes place in the home of George and Martha in the fictitious New England college town of New Carthage. George, a 46-year-old associate professor of history, and his wife, Martha, the 52-year-old daughter of the college president, have returned from a faculty party where they have been drinking heavily. After they stumble around the living room, Martha announces that she has invited another married couple to join them for a drink, although the time is 2 A.M. As the two bicker, the young couple arrives. Nick, 30, is a good-looking, athletic new faculty member in the biology department, and his wife, Honey, 26, is a simpering, seemingly superficial person. George and Martha soon draw the younger couple into their psychological games. Martha reveals her disgust with George's lack of ambition and failure to exploit his advantage as the son-in-law of the university president, and George attacks her with his superior verbal skills. Nick attempts to remain detached from the bickering, but soon becomes caught up in the turmoil while Honey becomes too drunk to be aware of her surroundings. The verbal combat between George and Martha escalates when George learns that Martha has spoken to Honey about a forbidden topic, their son. As act one ends, Martha has figuratively twisted a knife in George's back by harping on his supposed failure as a man and as a teacher. The fight dissolves into a shouting match and Honey becomes physically ill as the result of the quarreling and too much alcohol.

Act two opens as George and Nick speak alone while Martha and Honey are out of the room. George tells the story of a young boy who killed his mother and then his father in an accident, a story that may or may not be autobiographical; Nick reveals that he married Honey when she thought she was pregnant, but that the pregnancy turned out to be a false alarm. Despite George's best efforts, his attempts to warn Nick about being "dragged down by the quicksand" of the college fall on deaf ears. When Martha and Honey return, the sexual attraction between Martha and Nick increases. They dance erotically with each other as Martha goads her husband by telling their guests of George's attempts to write a novel whose plot concerns a boy responsible for his parents' deaths. George physically attacks Martha and stops only when Nick intervenes. George then seeks his revenge on the guests. He tells a "fable" that mirrors Nick and Honey's early lives and her hysterical pregnancy, causing a humiliated Honey to run out of the room. The battle continues, and the first victory is Martha's, whose openly sexual advances to Nick fail to make George lose his temper. After she leads Nick to the kitchen, where George can hear them carousing, George decides on a final act of revenge that will change his and Martha's lives forever—he decides to tell her that their son is dead.

The third act begins with Martha alone, because Nick has been unable to perform sexually. When he returns to the scene, she expresses contempt for him and also reveals that George is the only man who has ever satisfied her. George appears at the front door, bearing flowers and announcing that there is one more game to play—"Bringing Up Baby." He first induces Martha to talk about their son in loving and idealized terms; then he announces the son's death. Martha furiously responds that George "cannot decide these things," which leads Nick to understand that their son is a creation of their imagination, a fantasy child created to help them to survive their failed lives. Nick and Honey leave, and George and Martha sit alone and holding each other, as George sings softly, "Who's afraid of Virginia Woolf?" to which Martha answers, "I am, George, I am."

CENSORSHIP HISTORY

Who's Afraid of Virginia Woolf? had the distinction of being banned in Boston in 1963. Richard Sinnott, the last official censor for the city of Boston, claimed in a *Boston Globe* interview appearing in 2002 that he rarely initiated censorship proceedings on his own. Instead, "cases were brought to me by the public, the police, or the district attorney's office, and then I investigated and made a call." In 1963 city officials received complaints from several Boston citizens that Edward Albee's play was "obscene" and "blasphemous"; Sinnott investigated and determined that "it was a case of blatant blasphemy, which was then, as it is now [2002], against the law." The censor met with Albee and the theater owner, and the playwright agreed to change the wording that Sinnott found objectionable. As Sinnott reported, "In one instance, he deleted the blasphemous use of 'Jesus Christ' and used 'Mary Magdalene' in its place." Albee made 11 additional excisions of such phrases as "My God," "damn," and "Dear God."

In Cheadle, England, the Cheadle Hulme Amateur Dramatic Society (CHADS) Theatre Company canceled plans to include *Who's Afraid of Virginia Woolf?* in its 1978–79 season after a member raised objections to the play on the grounds that it might harm the society. She noted that some members had not taken out season tickets on account of it.

Who's Afraid of Virginia Woolf? won the New York Drama Critics Circle Award for best play in the 1962–63 season. Two Pulitzer Prize drama committee members and two prominent theater critics of the time, John Gassner and John Mason Brown, nominated the play for a Pulitzer Prize, but the Pulitzer Prize advisory board refused to accept the jury's nomination. W. D. Maxwell, a member of the advisory board, simply announced, "I thought it was a filthy play." The two jurors who had nominated the play resigned in protest from the Pulitzer committee, and the Pulitzer advisory board decided not to award a prize for drama in 1963. Albee won the Pulitzer Prize for drama in 1967 for *A Delicate Balance* and in 1975 for *Seascape*.

FURTHER READING

Gould, Jean. *Modern American Playwrights.* New York: Dodd, Mead & Co., 1966.

Harris, Wendell V. "Morality, Absurdity, and Albee." In *Critical Essays on Edward Albee.* Edited by Philip C. Kolin and J. Madison Davis. Boston: G. K. Hall & Co., 1986, pp. 117–121.

Herron, Ima. *The Small Town in American Drama.* Dallas, Tex.: Southern Methodist University Press, 1969.

Mulvoy, Thomas F., Jr. "City Weekly." *Boston Globe,* December 15, 2002, p. 2.

Slater, Derek, and Alan Stock. *History of CHADS: The First Seventy-Five Years.* Compiled by Mary Bedford. Cheadle, England: Cheadle Hulme Amateur Dramatic Society, 1997.

WITHIN THE GATES

Author: Sean O'Casey

Original date and place of production: February 7, 1934, Royalty Theatre, London, England

Characters: The Atheist, the Bishop, the Bishop's Sister, the Dreamer, First Evangelist, First Nursemaid, a Gardener, a Guardsman, a Man Wearing a Bowler Hat, a Man Wearing a Straw Hat, a Man Wearing a Trilby Hat, the Man with the Stick, the Older Chair Attendant, the Policewoman, Second Evangelist, Second Nursemaid, a Young Salvation Army Officer, the Young Woman

Filmed versions: None

SUMMARY

Within the Gates is an expressionist parable in four scenes that span the four seasons, moving from a park on a spring morning to a summer noon, an autumn evening, and a winter night. The play is complex and filled with symbolic characters who dance, chant, sing, and interact according to stereotyped behavior related to their roles.

The play takes place within the gates of a park that resembles Hyde Park in London where the group of generally unnamed characters, each of whom represents a different aspect of life, is seen in a park setting that serves as a microcosm of life as a whole. The park symbolizes the ugliness of the modern world, yet its inherent beauty is also evident in Jannice, also known as "The Young Woman," who inspires the dreamer to write a song for her. Jannice wants desperately to be saved from her life as a prostitute, and she feels death is always imminent: "My heart is bad, and doctors say that death may seize me at any moment, and take me out of life." She has turned to prostitution after losing her job when she refused to allow the manager to see "how I looked with nothing on." But neither her family nor religion will help her. Her mother is a heavy drinker who grips Jannice roughly by the arm and holds her while demanding money: "I have you and I hold you till I get a little to help me on in life for a day or two!" When Jannice refuses, the Old Woman threatens to tear what few clothes her daughter has. Jannice's stepfather, the Atheist, rejects her request to live with him and warns her: "Live your own life. I'm not your father, so cut out the daddy business." The man she wants to marry, the Gardener, also sends her away, claiming "I'm too young to marry yet."

Religion also offers no solace. Jannice turns to the Bishop for assistance, but he tells her, "Oh, my child, I'm afraid I can help only those whom I know." His sister chastises him for speaking with the down and out and advises him, "A bishop should be in the midst of incense, in the sanctuary, safe away from the sour touch of common humanity." Their rejection of Jannice is ironic, for she is the Bishop's natural daughter. Jannice's mother hears the Bishop's voice and remembers, "Your voice has a strange echo in it. Behind that wizened face is hidden a look of the first young man who conquered me on a Sunday night. . . . I'm not much to look at now; but the man who first got the better of me's a big jack-a-dandy in the church." Rather than acknowledge his paternity, the Bishop speaks "roughly" and tells her, "Get away, get away, woman. . . . Get away, get away, I tell you!"

In the final scene, the Dreamer's affirmative and joyful poetic vision and the Bishop's rediscovered humility provide Jannice with her much-desired salvation. She dances with the Dreamer, who gives her courage and happiness, then she dies after receiving the blessing of the Bishop, who guides her hand in the sign of the cross. As music plays, the Dreamer looks down at her and tells her, "You fought the good fight, Jannice, and you kept the faith."

CENSORSHIP HISTORY

Within the Gates is highly original, controversial, and widely misunderstood. The play opened at the Royalty Theatre in London on February 7, 1934, then came to the United States where it opened on October 22, 1934, at the National Theatre in New York City with Lillian Gish in the lead. After 101 performances in New York City, producers of the play began a scheduled tour of 13 cities, beginning with Boston, Massachusetts. About the New York performances O'Casey wrote: "It was a beautiful production. . . . No voice, clerical or lay, was raised against its mood or its manner."

In Boston in 1935, Protestant and Roman Catholic religious groups led by Father Sullivan, S.J., representing the Boston College of Roman Catholic Organizations and head of the Legion of Decency, called upon Boston city officials to ban performances of the play. The complaint, composed by Father Sullivan, stated, "any religious affiliations would protest against the sympathetic portrayal of immorality, and all right-minded citizens, too, would protest against these things described in the play, and even more so the setting forth of the utter futility of religion as an effective force in meeting the problems of the world." O'Casey's reaction was to ask, "Do not the thoughts of this Jesuit themselves show how ineffective his part in religion is, anyhow, in meeting the problems of the world?"

In an article that appeared in the *Boston Post*, Rev. Terence Connelly, S.J., whom O'Casey sarcastically refers to in his autobiographies as the "noted dramatic critic," declared:

> The whole play is drenched in sex. The love song in the play is but a lyric of lust and a symbol of death. O'Casey has written on immoral subjects frequently in the past, but in art, as in life, the end does not justify the means. There are degenerates who delight in looking at raw human flesh, and in art there are those who demand life in the raw. But normal human beings swoon at the sight of human flesh exposed. They require the silken curtain of skin to tone down the sight, and give the human flesh the normal color that is the symbol of life.

Although O'Casey dismissed his critics as "Bum priests blathering," Boston mayor Mansfield and the city council banned the play from performance in Boston. The remaining 12 cities on the scheduled tour feared protests like those in Boston and banned the play as well. In response to the ban in Boston, students from Harvard University, Radcliffe College, Wellesley College, and Tufts University circulated petitions urging a reconsideration of the decision, which they presented to the mayor and the city council. The decision to ban the play stood, and hundreds of students from the four schools took special trains to New York City to see the play performed. In this assessment of the decision, O'Casey stated, "Wesleyan and Jesuit had joined hands to down the play. It seemed that even under a free democracy one had to be damned careful of what one said."

FURTHER READING

Atkinson, Brooks, ed. and introd. *The Sean O'Casey Reader: Plays, Autobiographies, Opinions.* New York: St. Martin's Press, 1968.

Bernstock, Bernard. *Paycocks and Others: Sean O'Casey's World.* Dublin: Gill and MacMillan, 1976.

Bloom, Harold, ed. and introd. *Sean O'Casey.* New York: Chelsea House Publishers, 1987.

Gassner, John. "The Prodigality of Sean O'Casey." In *The Theatre in Our Times.* Edited by John Gassner. New York: Crown Publishers, 1954, pp. 240–248.

O'Casey, Sean. *Within the Gates: A Play of Four Scenes, in a London Park.* London: Macmillan Publishing, 1933.

THE ZOO STORY

Author: Edward Albee

Original date and place of production: September 28, 1959, Schiller Theater Werkstatt, Berlin, Germany

Characters: Jerry, Peter

Filmed versions: Made for television: *Zoo Story* (1964, Sweden); (1968, France)

SUMMARY

The Zoo Story, an absurdist play subtitled "A Play in One Scene," takes place on a sunny Sunday afternoon in New York's Central Park and relates the encounter between Jerry, a "permanent transient" in his late 30s, and Peter, a "square" solid citizen in his middle 40s. Albee uses the dialogue between the two characters to explore his theme of people's failure to become involved with and to communicate with one another.

The play opens with Peter seated on one of two park benches on the set; he is reading. Jerry enters and, rather than sit on the empty bench, approaches Peter and initiates a conversation. He repeats several times that he has been to the zoo, until Peter responds, then states, "You'll read about it in the papers tomorrow, if you don't see it on your TV tonight." References to the zoo occur throughout the play, as Jerry manipulates Peter. By asking a series of blunt questions, Jerry learns that Peter is married, has two daughters but wanted a son, and works as a publishing company executive. His wife wants no more children and he does not want the cats and parakeets that his wife and daughters prefer to a dog. Jerry then reveals details of his own life. In contrast to the married Peter, who lives in a comfortable apartment in the East Seventies, an affluent New York City neighborhood, Jerry lives in a furnished room with only meager possessions. He recounts his sex life, which currently consists of frequent encounters with prostitutes: "I do love the little ladies; really, I love them. For about an hour." Jerry also tells Peter that his only relationship of duration, "for a week and a half," occurred when he was 15 and "I was a h-o-m-o-s-e-x-u-a-l. I mean, I was queer . . . queer, queer, queer. . . . But that was the jazz of a very special hotel, wasn't it?"

The differences between the two men's lives are exposed in the first third of the play. In the second third, their dialogue reveals how much alike they are beneath the surface. Jerry sits on the bench next to Peter and tells a long story about his struggles with his landlady's vicious dog, which he eventually poisoned; the poison did not kill the dog, but modified its behavior to allow Jerry free passage into and out of the rooming house. He also reveals why he visited the zoo: "I went to the zoo to find out more about the way people exist with animals, and the way animals exist with each other, and with people, too."

As the two talk, Jerry begins to push and poke Peter, insisting, "Move over!" As Peter acquiesces and moves repeatedly, Jerry becomes more insistent until Peter is pressed against the arm of the bench. When Peter protests, Jerry orders him to sit on the empty bench: "Get off this bench, Peter; I want it." The two men spar verbally for a time, but Jerry clicks open a knife, saying: "Very well, Peter, we'll battle for the bench, but we're not evenly matched." He takes out "an ugly-looking knife," causing Peter to shout, "YOU'RE GOING TO KILL ME!" In a surprise move, Jerry throws the knife on the ground and orders Peter to pick it up and fight, "You fight for your self-respect; you fight for that god-damned bench." Peter is goaded into picking up the knife, which he holds "with a firm arm, but far in front of him, not to attack, but to defend." After sighing heavily, Jerry rushes forward and impales himself on the knife; as he dies, he reminds Peter, "And now you know all about what happened at the zoo." He urges Peter to leave before anyone appears, and wipes fingerprints off the handle of the knife before dying.

CENSORSHIP HISTORY

The Zoo Story was Albee's first published play; as he writes in the preface to the first paperback publication in 1961, the play was "read and politely refused by a number of New York producers." After he sent the play to a friend, through a circuitous route the manuscript eventually landed in the hands of Stefani Hunzinger, who headed the drama department of S. Fischer Verlag, a large publishing house in Frankfurt, Germany. She sent it to a producer in Berlin, where the play was first performed at the Schiller Theater Werkstatt on September 28, 1959. Four months later *The Zoo Story* was produced Off-Broadway on January 14, 1960, at the Provincetown Playhouse in New York City.

Richard Kostelanetz argues that once "the critical veil" is lifted, *The Zoo Story* "describes an unsuccessful homosexual pass." Most critics have seen greater philosophical significance in the play, but the discussion of homosexuality resulted in an early clash with censors. In the first of a rather lengthy series of cases involving radio stations licensed by the Pacifica Foundation, the Federal Communications Commission (FCC) responded to complaints about several programs that aired on Pacifica-licensed stations in 1959 and 1963. These programs included a broadcast of *The Zoo Story*, a discussion of homosexual attitudes and problems, and readings of original works by several poets and authors. The complainants charged that these programs were offensive or "filthy" in nature. In a decision rendered in *In re Pacifica Foundation* 36 FCC at 147 (1964), in contrast to most of its later rulings, the FCC disagreed with the charges of indecency, deciding that most of the broadcasts served the needs and interests of the listening public and accepting without argument the licensee's judgment that the material was appropriate for its listening audience. In this case, the FCC appeared to define indecency primarily by the contemporary standards of the local community, although this definition of "community standards" was broadened in later decisions.

In 1969 the issue of community standards created difficulty for novelist Salman Rushdie, who was producing a televised version of *The Zoo Story* for a Pakistani television network. In describing his plan to poison the landlady's dog, Jerry describes his visit to the butcher shop to purchase ground meat into which he will insert the poison. Rushdie writes that the monologue states "'It was six perfectly good hamburgers with not enough pork in them to make them disgusting.' Because of the word 'pork,' the executive for the network ordered that the show be edited before it could be shown to the Pakistan public. Another line, which stated that God is a colored queen who wears a kimono and plucks his eyebrows, was also removed."

FURTHER READING

Albee, Edward. *The American Dream and The Zoo Story*. New York: New American Library, 1961.

Gayoso, Jay A. "The FCC's Regulation of Broadcast Indecency: A Broadlined Approach for Removing Immorality from the Airwaves." *University of Miami Law Review* 43 (March 1989): 871–919.

Kostelanetz, Richard. "The Art of Total No." *Contact* 4 (October/November 1963): 62–70.

Rushdie, Salman. "Casualties of Censorship." In *They Shoot Writers, Don't They?* Edited by George Theiner. London: Faber and Faber, 1984.

Way, Brian. "Albee and the Absurd: *The American Dream* and *The Zoo Story*." In *Critical Essays on Edward Albee*. Edited by Philip C. Kolin and J. Madison Davis. Boston, Mass.: G. K. Hall & Co., 1986.

BIBLIOGRAPHY

BOOKS

Acheson, Arthur. *Shakespeare, Chapman and Sir Thomas More*. New York: AMS Press, 1994.

Adams, J. Q. *Dramatic Records of Sir Henry Herbert*. New Haven, Conn.: Yale University Press, 1917.

Akrigg, G. P. V. *Jacobean Pageant or the Court of King James I*. Cambridge: Harvard University Press, 1962.

Albee, Edward. *The American Dream and the Zoo Story*. New York: New American Library, 1961.

Andrews, Wayne. *Siegfried's Curse: The German Journey from Nietzsche to Hesse*. New York: Atheneum, 1972.

Antongini, Tom. *D'Annunzio*. Boston: Little, Brown, 1938.

Archer, William. *The Theatrical 'World' of 1895*. London: Walter Scott Publishing, 1896.

Aristophanes. *Lysistrata*. Trans. Donald Sutherland. New York: Harper & Row, 1961.

Asch, Sholem. "God of Vengeance." In *The Great Jewish Plays*. Trans. and ed. Joseph C. Landis. New York: Horizon Press, 1972.

Atkinson, Brooks, ed. and introd. *The Sean O'Casey Reader: Plays, Autobiographies, Opinions*. New York: St. Martin's Press, 1968.

Auden, W. H. *Forewords and Afterwords*. Selected by Edward Mendelson. New York: Random House, 1973.

Bailey, Helen Phelps. *Hamlet in France: From Voltaire to Laforgue*. Geneva: Droz Publishing, 1964.

Baker, Dorothy Dodds. *Trio*. Boston: Houghton Mifflin Company, 1943.

Baraka, Imamu Amiri. *The Baptism and The Toilet*. New York: Grove Press, 1967.

Bas, Georges, and Victor Bourgy. *British Drama*. France: Longman, 1993.

Behrendt, Stephen C. "Beatrice Cenci and the Tragic Myth of History." In *History and Myth: Essays on English Romantic Literature*, ed. Stephen C. Behrendt. Detroit, Mich.: Wayne State University Press, 1990.

Belden, Mary. *The Dramatic Work of Samuel Foote*. New Haven, Conn.: Yale University Press, 1929.

Bentley, Eric, ed. *The Classic Theatre*. Vol. 4. *Six French Plays*. Garden City, N.Y.: Anchor Books, 1961.

———. *The Storm over the Deputy*. New York: Grove Press, 1964.

Bentley, Joanne. *Hallie Flanagan: A Life in the American Theatre*. New York: Alfred A. Knopf, 1988.

Berlin, Normand. *Eugene O'Neill*. New York: St. Martin's Press, 1982.

Bernstock, Bernard. *Paycocks and Others: Sean O'Casey's World*. Dublin: Gill and MacMillan, 1976.

Biner, Pierre. *The Living Theatre*. New York: Horizon Press, 1972.

Birdsall, Peter. *Mind War: Book Censorship in English Canada*. Victoria, B.C.: CANLIT, 1978.

Black, Stephen A. *Eugene O'Neill: Beyond Mourning and Tragedy*. New Haven, Conn.: Yale University Press, 1999.

Blakey, Robert. *The History of Political Literature from the Earliest Times.* London: Richard Bentley, New Burlington Street, 1855. Reprint, William C. Brown Reprint Library, 1934.

Bleackley, Horace. *Jack Sheppard . . . With an Epilogue on Jack Sheppard in Literature and Drama.* London: Bodley Head, 1933.

Blitzstein, Marc. *The Cradle Will Rock.* New York: Random House, 1938.

Block, Haskell M., and Robert G. Shedd. *Masters of Modern Drama.* New York: Random House, 1962.

Bloom, Harold, ed. and introd. *Sean O'Casey.* New York: Chelsea House Publishers, 1987.

———. *Eugene O'Neill.* New York: Chelsea House, 1987.

Bond, Edward. *Saved.* New York: Hill and Wang, 1965.

Bordman, Gerald. *American Operetta from* H.M.S. Pinafore *to* Sweeney Todd. New York: Oxford University Press, 1981.

Boswell, James. *Life of Johnson.* Vol. II. Ed. George Birkbeck Hill. Oxford, England: Oxford University Press, 1934.

Bourdet, Edouard. *The Captive.* Translated from the French by Arthur Hornblow, Jr., with an introduction by J. Brooks Atkinson. New York: Brentano's, 1926.

Bowdler, Thomas. *The Family Shakespeare.* London: J. Hatchard, 1807.

Bowers, Fredson, ed. *Jacobean and Caroline Dramatists.* Detroit, Mich.: Gale Research, 1987.

Braun, Sidney D. *Dictionary of French Literature.* New York: Philosophical Library, 1958.

Brecht, Bertolt. *The Three-Penny Opera.* Trans. Desmond Vesey and Eric Bentley. In *From the Modern Repertoire.* Series One. Denver, Colo.: The University of Denver Press, 1949.

Brennan-Gibson, Margaret. *Clifford Odets, American Playwright: The Years from 1906 to 1940.* New York: Atheneum Press, 1981.

Brooke, Henry. *Gustavus Vasa: A Tragedy in Five Acts. Now Performed by the Old American Company at the Theatre in Southwark.* Philadelphia: Enoch Story, 1778.

Brown, Edward James. *Mayakovsky: A Poet in the Revolution.* Princeton, N.J.: Princeton University Press, 1973.

Brown, John Russell. *Theatre Language: A Study of Arden, Osborne, Pinter and Wesker.* New York: Taplinger Publishing Co., 1973.

Bruno, Giuliana. *Streetwalking on a Ruined Map: Cultural Theory and the City Films of Elvira Notari.* Princeton, N.J.: Princeton University Press, 1993.

Brustein, Robert. *The Theatre of Revolt: Studies in Ibsen, Strindberg, Chekhov, Shaw, Brecht, Pirandello, O'Neill and Genet.* Boston: Little, Brown and Company, 1964.

Buttitta, Tony. *Uncle Sam Presents: A Memoir of the Federal Theatre, 1935–1939.* Philadelphia: University of Pennsylvania Press, 1982.

Carlisle, Olga Andreyev. *Poets on Street Corners: Portraits of Fifteen Russian Poets.* New York: Random House, 1968.

Carpenter, Charles. *Modern British, Irish, and American Drama: A Descriptive Chronology.* Unpublished manuscript in progress. URL: http://www.eoneill.com/essays/carpenter.htm.

Carter, Alan. *John Osborne.* Edinburgh, Scotland: Oliver & Boyd, 1969.

Chamberlain, John. *The Letters of John Chamberlain.* Ed. N. E. McClure. Philadelphia: Lippincott & Co., 1939.

Charters, Ann. *I Love: The True Story of Vladimir Mayakovsky and Lili Brik.* New York: Farrar, Straus & Giroux, 1979.

Chauncey, George. *Gay New York*. New York: Basic Books, 1994.

Cheney, Anne. *Lorraine Hansberry*. New York: Twayne Publishers, 1984.

Clare, Janet. *"Art Made Tongue-Tied by Authority": Elizabethan and Jacobean Dramatic Censorship*. New York: Manchester University Press, 1990.

Clark, Barrett Harper. *Eugene O'Neill: The Man and His Plays*. Rev. ed. New York: Dover Publications, 1947.

Clum, John M. *Acting Gay: Male Homosexuality in Modern Drama*. New York: Columbia University Press, 1992.

———, ed. *Staging Gay Lives: An Anthology of Contemporary Gay Theater*. Boulder, Colo.: Westview Press, 1995.

Clurman, Harold, ed. *Famous American Plays of the 1930s*. New York: Dell Publishing, 1959.

Cohen-Solal, Annie. *Sartre: A Life*. Trans. Anna Cancogni. New York: Pantheon Books, 1987.

Cohn, Ruby. *New American Dramatists, 1960–1990*. New York: St. Martin's Press, 1991.

Colton, John. *The Shanghai Gesture*. Introduction by John D. Williams. New York: Boni and Liveright, 1926.

The Complete Plays of Gilbert and Sullivan, and including thirty-two photographs from recent performances by the D'Oyly Carte Company. Garden City, N.Y.: Garden City Publishing Co., 1938.

Connolly, L. W. *The Censorship of English Drama, 1737–1824*. San Marino, Calif.: Huntington Library, 1976.

Conrad, Joseph. *Letters from Conrad, 1895 to 1924*. Edited with an Introduction and Notes by Edward Garnett. London: Nonesuch Press, 1928.

Corbin, Peter, and Douglas Sedge, eds. *Thomas of Woodstock; or King Richard the Second, Part One*. New York: Manchester University Press, 2002.

Costoupoulos, J. *Homosexuality on the New York Stage: Its Critical Reception, 1926 to 1968*. Doctoral dissertation, New York University, 1986.

Craik, T. W. *The Maid's Tragedy by Beaumont and Fletcher*. New York: Manchester University Press, 1999.

Curran, Stuart. *Shelley's Cenci: Scorpions Ringed with Fire*. Princeton, N.J.: Princeton University Press, 1970.

Curry, Ramona. *Too Much of a Good Thing: Mae West as Cultural Icon*. Minneapolis: University of Minnesota Press, 1996.

D'Entremont, James. Letter to Maureen C. Keefe, Dean of Students, Wentworth Institute of Technology. February 26, 1998.

Dietrich, Richard F. *British Drama, 1890 to 1950: A Critical History*. New York: Twayne Publishers, 1989.

Downer, Alan S. *The Eminent Tragedian: William Charles Macready*. Cambridge, Mass.: Harvard University Press, 1966.

Doyle, Robert. *Banned Books Resource Guide*. Chicago, Ill.: American Library Association, 1995.

"Drama, 1860–1918: The Broadway School." *The Cambridge History of English and American Literature in 18 volumes*. Vol. XVII: Later National Literature, Part II. London: Cambridge University Press, 1907–1921.

Dumas, Alexandre. *Camille*. New York: Modern Library, 1925.

Durang, Christopher. *Christopher Durang Explains It All for You: Six Plays*. New York: Grove Weidenfeld, 1990.

————. *Sister Mary Ignatius Explains It All for You.* New York: Dramatists' Play Service, 1999.

Eels, George, and Stanley Musgrove. *Mae West: A Biography.* New York: William Morrow, 1982.

Elfe, Wolfgang D., and James Hardin. *Twentieth-Century German Dramatists, 1889–1918.* Detroit, Mich.: Gale Research, 1992.

Ellman, Richard. *Oscar Wilde.* New York: Alfred A. Knopf, 1988.

Elsom, John. *Erotic Theatre.* New York: Taplinger Publishing Co., 1974.

Ensler, Eve. *The Vagina Monologues.* Foreword by Gloria Steinem. New York: Villard Books, 2001.

Epstein, Norrie. *The Friendly Shakespeare.* New York: Viking, 1993.

Ferrar, Harold. *John Osborne.* New York: New York University Press, 1973.

Findlater, Richard. Letter to Nilhoufer Harben. December 13, 1982. Reported in *Twentieth-Century English History Plays.* Totowa, N.J.: Barnes & Noble Books, 1988.

Fisk, Deborah Payne. *The Cambridge Companion to English Restoration Theatre.* New York: Cambridge University Press, 2000.

Flanagan, Hallie. *Arena.* New York: Duell, Sloan and Pearce, 1940.

Foote, Samuel. *Trip to Calais: A Comedy in Three Acts.* English Prose Drama. URL: http://library.stanford.edu/depts/hasrg/hds/epd-toc.html.

Forshey, Gerald E. *American Religious and Biblical Spectaculars.* Westport, Conn.: Praeger Publishing, 1992.

Fowell, Frank, and Frank Palmer. *Censorship in England.* London: F. Palmer, 1913. Reprint, New York: Benjamin Blom, 1969.

Friedman, Andrea. *Prurient Interests: Gender, Democracy, and Obscenity in New York City, 1909–1945.* New York: Columbia University Press, 2000.

Furtado, Ken, and Nancy Hellner. *Gay and Lesbian American Plays: An Annotated Bibliography.* Metuchen, N.J.: Scarecrow Press, 1993.

Gagnier, Regenia. *Idylls of the Marketplace: Oscar Wilde and the Victorian Public.* Stanford, Calif.: Stanford University Press, 1986.

Garnett, Edward. *The Breaking Point: A Censured Play with Preface and a Letter to the Censor.* London: Duckworth & Co., 1907.

Gassner, John, ed. *A Treasury of the Theatre.* Vol. 1. *World Drama from Aeschylus to Ostrovsky.* New York: Simon and Schuster, 1967.

————. *A Treasury of the Theatre.* Vol. 3. *Oscar Wilde to Eugene Ionesco.* Rev. ed. New York: Simon and Schuster, 1977.

————. *O'Neill: A Collection of Critical Essays.* Englewood Cliffs, N.J.: Prentice-Hall, 1964.

————. *Theatre at the Crossroads: Plays and Playwrights of the Mid-Century American Stage.* New York: Holt, Rinehart and Winston, 1960.

————. "The Prodigality of Sean O'Casey." In *The Theatre in Our Times.* Ed. John Gassner. New York: Crown Publishers, 1954, pp. 240–248.

Gaudon, J. *Victor Hugo et la Théatre. Stratégie et Dramaturgie.* Paris: Suger, 1985.

Gay, John. *The Poetical Works of John Gay, Including* Polly, The Beggar's Opera, *and Selections from the Other Dramatic Work.* Ed. G. C. Faber. New York: Russell & Russell, 1969.

Gay, Peter. *Schnitzler's Century: The Making of Middle Class Culture, 1815–1914.* New York: W. W. Norton, 2002.

Gelber, Jack. *The Connection.* New York: Grove Press, 1960.

Gelbert, Bruce Michael. *Look Again: Reviews & Miscellany.* http://tosos2.org/LookA-gainEssay.htm.

Gilbert, W. S. *The Best Known Works of W. S. Gilbert, with the author's illustrations.* New York: World Publishing Company, 1932.

Goldman, Emma. *The Social Significance of the Modern Drama.* Boston: Gorham Press, 1914.

Gordon, Eric. *Mark the Music: The Life and Work of Marc Blitzstein.* New York: St. Martin's Press, 1989.

Gould, Jean. *Modern American Playwrights.* New York: Dodd, Mead, & Co., 1966.

Gousie, Laurent. *Gerhart Hauptmann: A Transitional Period, 1892–1898, Naturalism to Realism.* Berlin: Fribourg, 1970.

Great Britain. Parliament. House of Commons. Select Committee on Theatres and Places of Entertainment. *Report Together with the Proceedings of the Committee, Minutes of Evidence, Appendix, and Index.* London: H. M. Stat. Off., 1892 (Report 240, 1892, vol. 8).

Green, Frederick Charles. *Literary Ideas in 18th-Century France and England: A Critical Survey.* New York: Frederick Ungar Publishing Co., 1966.

Green, Jonathan. *The Encyclopedia of Censorship.* New York: Facts On File, 1990.

Greenblatt, Stephen. "Invisible Bullets." In *Shakespearean Negotiations: The Circulation of Social Energy in Renaissance England.* London: Oxford University Press, 1988.

Greene, Graham. *Lord Rochester's Monkey: Being the Life of John Wilmot, Second Earl of Rochester.* New York: Viking Press, 1974.

Gregory, Lady Augusta Persse. "The Fight with the Castle." In *Our Irish Theatre: A Chapter in Autobiography.* New York: G. P. Putnam's Sons, 1913, pp. 140–168.

Guernsey, Otis L., ed. *The Best Plays of 1977–1978.* New York: Dodd, Mead & Company, 1978.

Guernsey, Otis L., Jr., ed. *The Best Plays of 1997–1998.* New York: Limelight Editions, 1998.

———. *The Best Plays of 1978–1979.* New York: Dodd, Mead & Company, 1979.

———. *The Best Plays of 1981–1982.* New York: Dodd, Mead & Company, 1982.

Guernsey, Jr., Otis L., and Jeffrey Sweet. *The Best Plays of 1987–1988.* New York: Applause Publishing, 1992.

———. *The Best Plays of 1992–1993.* New York: Limelight Editions, 1993.

———. *The Applause/Best Plays Theatre Yearbook of 1990–1991.* New York: Applause, 1991.

———. *The Applause/Best Plays Theatre Yearbook of 1991–1992.* New York: Applause, 1992.

Haight, Anne Lyon, and Chandler B. Grannis. *Banned Books 387 B.C. to 1978 A.D.* New York: R. R. Bowker, 1978.

Hamilton, Marybeth. *When I'm Bad, I'm Better. Mae West, Sex, and American Entertainment.* New York: HarperCollins, 1995.

Hamilton, Neil A. *The ABC-CLIO Companion to the 1960s Counterculture in America.* Santa Barbara, Calif.: ABC-CLIO, 1997.

Hampden, John. *Eighteenth-Century Plays.* London: J. M. Dent & Sons, Ltd., 1928.

Hansberry, Lorraine. "A Raisin in the Sun." In *Four Contemporary Plays.* Ed. Bennett Cerf. New York: Vintage Books, 1961.

Harben, Nilhoufer. *Twentieth-Century English History Plays.* Totowa, N.J.: Barnes & Noble Books, 1988.

Harris, Richard Hough. *Modern Drama in America and England, 1950–1970: A Guide to Information Sources.* Detroit, Mich.: Gale Research, 1982.

Harris, Wendell V. "Morality, Absurdity, and Albee." In *Critical Essays on Edward Albee.* Eds. Philip C. Kolin and J. Madison Davis. Boston: G. K. Hall & Co., 1986, pp. 117–121.

Hauptmann, Gerhart Johann. *The Weavers, Hannele, The Beaver Coat.* Trans. Horst Frenz and Miles Waggoner. New York: Holt, Rinehart and Winston, 1962.

Hayman, Ronald. *John Osborne.* New York: Frederick Ungar Publishing Co., 1972.

Hazlitt, W. Carew. *A Manual for Collector and Amateur of Old English Plays.* Burt Franklin Bibliography and Reference Series #106. New York: Burt Franklin, 1966.

Heinemann, William. *The First Step: A Dramatic Moment.* London: John Lane/The Bodley Head, 1895.

Hemmings, Frederic William John. *Theatre and State in France, 1760–1905.* New York: Cambridge University Press, 1994.

Herne, James A. "Margaret Fleming." In *Representative American Plays.* 7th ed. Ed. Arthur Hobson Quinn. New York: Appleton-Century-Crofts, 1953.

Herne, Julie A. "Introduction." In *Shore Acres and Other Plays.* Ed. Mrs. James A. Herne. New York: Samuel French, 1928.

Herron, Ima Honaker. *The Small Town in American Drama.* Dallas, Tex.: Southern Methodist University Press, 1969.

Hewitt, Bernard. *Theatre U.S.A., 1668 to 1957.* New York: McGraw-Hill, 1959

Hoare, Philip. *Oscar Wilde's Last Stand: Decadence, Conspiracy and the Most Outrageous Trial of the Century.* New York: Arcade Publishing, 1998.

Hoffman, William M., ed. *Gay Plays: The First Collection.* New York: Avon Books, 1979.

Holl, Karl. *Gerhart Hauptmann: His Life and His Work, 1862–1912.* Chicago: A. C. McClurg & Co., 1914.

Holroyd, Michael. *Bernard Shaw: A Biography.* Vol. 2. *The Pursuit of Power.* New York: Random House, 1989.

Hook, Theodore Edward. *Killing No Murder, a Farce in Two Acts. As Performed with Great Applause at the Theatre Royal Haymarket. Together with a preface and his scene suppressed by order of the Lord Chamberlain.* London: Printed by W. Flint for Samuel Tipper, 1809.

Hubert, Judd David. *Molière and the Comedy of Intellect.* Berkeley: University of California Press, 1962.

Hugo, Victor. *Correspondence.* 4 vols. Ed. C. Caubray. Paris: Imprimerie Nationale, 1947–1952.

Hume, Robert D. *Henry Fielding and the London Theatre, 1728–1737.* Oxford, England: Clarendon Press, 1988.

Hyde, H. Montgomery. *The Trials of Oscar Wilde.* New York: Dover Publications, 1973.

Hynes, Samuel. *A War Imagined: The First World War and English Culture.* New York: Atheneum Press, 1991.

Innes, C. D. *Modern German Drama: A Study in Form.* New York: Cambridge University Press, 1979.

Ireland, William Henry. *Confessions of William-Henry Ireland, Containing Particulars of His Fabrication of the Shakespeare* [sic] *Manuscripts.* Facsimile reprint. New York: Burt Franklin, 1909.

Jack, Homer. *A Blue Pencil over Chicago: The Fine Art of Censorship.* Chicago: American Civil Liberties Union, 1949.

Jacoby, Richard. *Conversations with the Capeman: The Untold Story of Salvador Agron.* New York: Painted Leaf Press, 2000.

Jefferson, George. *Edward Garnett, A Life in Literature.* London: Jonathan Cape, 1982.

Jellicoe, Ann. *The Knack: A Comedy in Three Acts.* New York: Samuel French, 1962.

Johnson, Samuel. "A Compleat Vindication of the Licensers of the Stage, from the Malicious and Scandalous Aspersions of Mr. Brooke, Author of *Gustavus Vasa*, with a Proposal for Making the Officer of Licenser More Extensive and Effective." *Complete Works.* Ed. Arthur Murphy. New York: Harper Publishing, 1873.

Jones, Frederick L., ed. *The Letters of Percy Bysshe Shelley.* Vol. 2. Oxford: Clarendon Press, 1964.

Katz, Jonathan. *Gay/Lesbian Almanac.* New York: Harper & Row Publishers, 1983.

Kavanagh, Peter. *The Irish Theatre.* Tralee: The Kerryman, 1946.

Kennedy, Dennis, ed. *Plays by Harley Granville Barker:* The Marrying of Ann Leete, The Voysey Inheritance, Waste. New York: Cambridge University Press, 1987.

Kidson, Frank. *The Beggar's Opera: Its Predecessors and Successors.* Cambridge, England: Cambridge University Press, 1922.

Kilroy, James. *The "Playboy" Riots.* Dublin, Ireland: Dolmen Press Limited, 1971.

King, Kimball. *Twenty Modern British Playwrights: A Bibliography.* New York: Garland Publishing, 1977.

Klemm, Frederick Alvin. *The Death Problem in the Life and Works of Gerhart Hauptmann.* Philadelphia: Lippincott & Co., 1939.

Knapp, Bettina Leibowitz. *Jean Racine: Mythos and Renewal in Modern Theater.* Birmingham: University of Alabama Press, 1971.

Knowland, A. S., ed. *Six Caroline Plays.* New York: Oxford University Press, 1962.

Knowles, Dorothy. *The Censor, the Drama and the Film, 1900–1934.* London: Allen and Unwin, 1934.

Korges, James. *Erskine Caldwell.* Minneapolis: University of Minnesota Press, 1969.

Kushner, Tony. *Angels in America: Millennium Approaches.* New York: Theatre Communications Corporation, 1993.

Labadie, Donald. "Movies: 'The Innocents' and 'The Children's Hour.'" *Lilian Hellman: Plays, Films, Memoirs.* Ed. Mark W. Estrin. Boston: G. K. Hall & Co., 1989.

Lancashire, Anne, ed. *The Second Maiden's Tragedy.* Manchester, England: Manchester University Press, 1978.

Laufe, Abe. *The Wicked Stage: A History of Theater Censorship and Harassment in the United States.* New York: Frederick Ungar Publishing Co., 1978.

Leech, Clifford. *The John Fletcher Plays.* London: Chatto & Windus, 1962.

Lesclide, Richard. *Propos de Table de Victor Hugo.* Paris: Dentu, 1885.

Levitt, Annette Shandler. *The Genes and Genders of Surrealism.* New York: St. Martin's Press, 1999.

Ley, Graham. *From Mimesis to Interculturalism: Readings of Theatrical Theory Before and After "Modernism."* Exeter, England: University of Exeter, 1999.

Loth, David. *The Erotic in Literature.* New York: Dorset Press, 1961.

MacIntosh, Fiona. "Tragedy in Performance: Nineteenth- and Twentieth-Century Productions." In *The Cambridge Companion to Greek Tragedy.* Ed. P. E. Easterling. Cambridge: Cambridge University Press, 1997, pp. 284–323.

Marcuse, Ludwig. *Obscene: The History of an Indignation.* London: MacGibbon & Key, 1965.

Marshall, Herbert. *Mayakovsky.* New York: Hill & Wang, 1965.

Martine, James J. *The Crucible: Politics, Property, and Pretense.* New York: Twayne Publishers, 1993.

Mathews, Jane DeHart. *The Federal Theatre, 1935–1939; Plays, Relief, and Politics.* Princeton, N.J.: Princeton University Press, 1967.

Maurois, André. *Olympio: The Life of Victor Hugo.* Trans. by Gerard Hopkins. New York: Harper & Brothers, 1956.

Mayakovsky, Vladimir. The Bedbug *and Selected Poetry.* Indianapolis: Indiana University Press, 1975.

McClure, Michael. *The Beard and VKTMS.* New York: Grove Press, 1985.

McKissack, Patricia C., and Frederick L. McKissack. *Young Gifted and Black.* New York: Holiday House, 1998.

Means, Gaston. *The Strange Death of President Harding, From the Diaries of Gaston B. Means.* New York: Elizabeth Ann Guild, 1930.

Mee, Charles L., Jr. *The Ohio Gang: The World of Warren G. Harding: An Historical Entertainment.* New York: Walker Evans Publishing, 1981.

Metz, G. Harold. *Sources of Four Plays Ascribed to Shakespeare:* The Reign of King Edward III, Sir Thomas More, The History of Cardenio, The Two Noble Kinsmen. St. Louis: University of Missouri, 1989.

Meyer, Hans Georg. *Henrik Ibsen.* Trans. Helen Sebba. New York: Frederick Ungar Publishing Co., 1972.

Middleton, Thomas. *A Game at Chesse.* Ed. R. C. Bald. Cambridge, England: Cambridge University Press, 1929.

Miller, Arthur. *The Crucible.* New York: Penguin Books, 1981.

Miller, Jordan Y. *American Dramatic Literature.* New York: McGraw-Hill, 1961.

Miller, Jordan Y., and Winifred L. Frazer. *American Drama between the Wars.* Boston: Twayne Publishers, 1991.

Molière. *Tartuffe.* Trans. and introd. by Robert W. Hartle. Indianapolis, Ind.: Bobbs-Merrill, 1965.

———. *The Misanthrope, A Comedy.* Trans. Richard Wilbur. New York: Harcourt, Brace & World, 1955.

Morgenstern, Joseph. "New Children's Hour—Grim Power of Gossip." *Lillian Hellman: Plays, Films, Memoirs.* Ed. Mark W. Estrin. Boston: G. K. Hall & Co., 1989.

Moses, Montrose J., ed. *British Plays from the Restoration to 1820.* Boston: Little, Brown and Company, 1929.

Moss, Leonard. *Arthur Miller.* Boston: Twayne Publishers, 1980.

Muir, Kenneth, and F. P. Wilson. *The Malone Society Reprint of Jack Straw.* Oxford, England: Malone Society, 1957.

Munday, Anthony. *Sir Thomas Tudor.* Tudor Facsimile Texts, Old English Plays Series Number 65. New York: AMS Press, 1974.

Murray, Edward. *Clifford Odets: The Thirties and After.* New York: Frederick Ungar Publishing Co., 1968.

Nelson, Robert James. *Corneille and Racine: Parallels and Contrasts.* Englewood, N.J.: Prentice-Hall, 1966.

Nicholson, Steve. *British Theatre and the Red Peril.* Exeter, England: University of Exeter Press, 1999.

O'Casey, Sean. *Within the Gates: A Play of Four Scenes, in a London Park.* London: Macmillan Publishing, 1933.

O'Conner, John, and Lorraine Brown, eds. *Free, Adult, and Uncensored: The Living History of the Federal Theatre Project.* Washington, D.C.: New Republic Books, 1978.

O'Neill, Eugene. *The Complete Plays of Eugene O'Neill.* Ed. Travis Bogard. New York: Library of America, 1988.

Osborne, John. *A Better Class of Person: An Autobiography/John Osborne.* New York: Dutton, 1981.

———. *Four Plays by John Osborne.* New York: Dodd, Mead & Company, 1973.

———. *The Entertainer.* New York: Criterion Books, 1958.

Panizza, Oskar. *The Council of Love.* Trans. Oreste F. Puccinai. Introd. André Breton. New York: Viking Press, 1973.

Parkes, Adam. *Modernism and the Theater of Censorship.* New York: Oxford University Press, 1996.

Parliament of Victoria Law Reform Committee. *Review of The Theatres Act 1958.* Report of No. 82 Session 1999–2001. Melbourne, Australia: Government Printer, May 2001.

Parrott, Thomas Marc, and Ball, Robert Hamilton. *A Short View of Elizabethan Drama.* New York: Charles Scribner's Sons, 1943.

Patterson, Annabel. *Censorship and Interpretation: The Conditions of Writing and Reading in Early Modern England.* Madison: University of Wisconsin Press, 1991.

Peacock, D. Keith. *Radical Stages: Alternative History in Modern British Drama.* No. 43 in the Contributions in Drama and Theatre Studies. Westport, Conn.: Greenwood Press, 1991.

Pendell, William A. *Victor Hugo's Acted Dramas and the Contemporary Press.* Baltimore, Md.: Johns Hopkins University Press, 1947.

Pepys, Samuel. *The Diary of Samuel Pepys M.A. F.R.S. Clerk of the Acts and Secretary to the Admiralty.* Transcribed from the shorthand manuscript in the Pepysian Library, Magdalene College, Cambridge, by Mynors Bright. With Lord Braybrooke's notes. Edited with additions by Henry B. Wheatley. London: G. Bell, 1893–99.

Perrin, Noel. *Dr. Bowdler's Legacy: A History of Expurgated Books in England and America.* Boston: David R. Godine, Publisher, 1992.

Pinto, Vivian de Sola. *The Restoration Court Poets.* London: Longmans, Green Publishing, 1965.

Pizella, Stéphane. *Les Nuits Bout du Monde.* Paris: André Bonne, 1953.

Pope, Alexander. *The Dunciad.* Longman Annotated Texts. Ed. Valerie Rumbold. New York: Longman Publishing, 1999.

Porter, Laurence M. *Victor Hugo.* New York: Twayne Publishers, 1999.

Quinn, Arthur Hobson. *A History of the American Drama from the Civil War to the Present.* New York: Crofts, 1943.

Rabban, David M. *Free Speech in Its Forgotten Years.* Cambridge: Cambridge University Press, 1997.

Racine, Jean. *Athalie.* In *Six Plays by Corneille and Racine.* Ed. and trans. by Paul Landis. New York: Modern Library, 1931.

Rafroidi, Patrick. *Irish Literature in English: The Romantic Period, 1789–1850.* Vol. 2. Atlantic Highlands, N.J.: Humanities Press, 1980.

Rhodes, Anthony. *The Poet as Superman: A Life of Gabriele D'Annunzio.* London: Weidenfeld and Nicolson, 1959.

Richards, Stanley, ed. *Great Rock Musicals.* New York: Stein and Day, 1979.

Rigoletto and Le Roi S'Amuse. San Diego Opera Sourcebook. http://www.sdopera.com/pages/education/edusourcebook/ArRigLeRoi.htm.

Ricketts, Wendell. "Lesbians and Gay Men on Stage: A Necessarily Incomplete History." In *Out in All Directions: The Almanac of Lesbian and Gay America.* Eds. L. Witt, S. Thomas, and E. Marcus. New York: Warner Books, 1995.

Rivers, Larry. *What Did I Do?* New York: HarperCollins, 1992.

Robb, Graham. *Victor Hugo.* New York: W. W. Norton, 1997.

Robins, Natalie. *Alien Ink: The FBI's War on Freedom of Expression.* New York: William Morrow, 1992.

Romain, Michael. *A Profile of Jonathan Miller.* London: Cambridge University Press, 1992.

Roose-Evans, James. *Experimental Theatre from Stanislavsky to Today.* New York: Universe Books, 1970.

Rose, June. *Marie Stopes and the Sexual Situation.* London: Faber and Faber, 1992.

Rosenfeld, Sybil. *Strolling Players and Dramas in the Provinces, 1660–1765.* Cambridge: Cambridge University Press, 1939.

Rushdie, Salman. "Casualties of Censorship." In *They Shoot Writers, Don't They?* Ed. George Theiner. London: Faber and Faber, 1984.

Rusinko, Susan. *British Drama, 1950 to the Present: A Critical History.* Boston: Twayne Publishers, 1989.

Russo, Vito. *The Celluloid Closet.* Rev. ed. New York: HarperCollins, 1987.

Ryback, Timothy. *Rock around the Bloc: A History of Rock Music in Eastern Europe and the Soviet Union.* New York: Oxford University Press, 1990.

Schafer, Yvonne, ed. "Introduction: Early Actors and Directors." *Performing O'Neill: Conversations with Actors and Directors.* New York: Palgrave Publishing, 2000.

Schnitzler, Arthur. *La Ronde, Ten Dialogues.* Trans. Eric Bentley. New York: Samuel French, 1954.

Schultz, William Eben. *Gay's 'Beggar's Opera': Its Content, History and Influence.* New York: Cambridge University Press, 1967.

Seldes, Gilbert. "Introduction." *Lysistrata.* New York: Limited Editions Club, 1934.

Shakespeare, William. *Hamlet.* New Folger Library Series. New York: Washington Square Press, 1992.

Shaw, George Bernard. "Preface." In *Three Plays by Brieux, Member of the French Academy. English Versions by Mrs. Bernard Shaw, St. John Hankin, and John Pollock.* 2d ed. New York: Brentano's, 1911.

———. *Our Theatre in the Nineties.* London: Constable & Co., Ltd., 1932.

———. *The Author's Apology from Mrs. Warren's Profession. By Bernard Shaw. With an Introduction by John Corbin, The Tyranny of Police and Press.* New York: Brentano's, 1905.

———. *The Doctor's Dilemma, Getting Married, and The Shewing Up of Blanco Posnet.* New York: Brentano's, 1911.

Shaw, George Bernard, et al. *The Censorship of Plays in the Office of the Lord Chamberlain: The Case for Abolition.* Letchworth, England: Arden Press, 1908.

Sheaffer, Louis. *O'Neill: Son and Artist.* Boston: Little, Brown and Company, 1973.

Shelly, Percy Bysshe. *The Cenci.* In *Nineteenth-Century British Drama: An Anthology of Representative Plays.* Ed. Leonard R. N. Ashley. Glenview, Ill.: Scott, Foresman and Company, 1967.

Shewey, Don, ed. *Out Front: Contemporary Gay and Lesbian Plays.* New York: Grove Press, 1988.

Simpson, Michael. *Closet Performances: Political Exhibition and Prohibition in the Dramas of Byron and Shelley.* Stanford, Calif.: Stanford University Press, 1998.

Slater, Derek, and Alan Stock. *History of Chads: The First Seventy-Five Years.* Compiled by Mary Bedford. Cheadle, England: Cheadle Hulme Amateur Dramatic Society, 1997.

Smeliansky, Anatoly. *The Russian Theatre after Stalin.* Trans. Patrick Miles. New York: Cambridge University Press, 1999.

Spackman, Barbara. *Decadent Geneaologies: The Rhetoric of Sickness from Baudelaire to D'Annunzio.* Ithaca, N.Y.: Cornell University Press, 1989.

Stephens, John Russell. *Censorship of English Drama, 1824–1901.* New York: Cambridge University Press, 1980.

Stopes, Marie C. *A Banned Play and a Preface on the Censorship.* London: John Bale, Sons, & Danliesson, Ltd., 1926.

Summers, Claude J. *The Gay and Lesbian Literary Heritage.* New York: Henry Holt, 1995.

Sutherland, John. *Offensive Literature: Decensorship in Britain, 1960–1982.* Totowa, N.J.: Barnes & Noble Books, 1982.

Szilassy, Zoltan. *American Theater of the 1960s.* Carbondale: Southern Illinois University Press, 1986.

Taylor, Leslie A. "Veritable Hotheads: Lesbian Scandals in the United States." Ed. Harold Bloom. *Tennessee Williams: Modern Critical Views.* New York: Chelsea House Publishers, 1987.

Thomas, Donald. *Henry Fielding: A Life.* New York: St. Martin's Press, 1990.

Thomas, Edward. *Maurice Maeterlinck.* 2d ed. London: Methuen & Co., 1911.

Thomson, James. *Edward and Eleanora: A Tragedy.* London: J. Bell & Etherington, 1775.

Tilley, Arthur Augustus. *Molière.* New York: Russell & Russell, 1968.

———. *Three French Dramatists: Racine, Marivaux, Musset.* New York: Russell & Russell, 1967.

Timberlake, Craig. "Herne—The First Collaborator." In *The Life and Work of David Belasco: The Bishop of Broadway.* New York: Library Publishers, 1954.

Tobin, Ronald W. *Jean Racine Revisited.* New York: Twayne Publishers, 1999.

Toynbee, William, ed. *The Diaries of William Charles Macready. 1833–1851.* London: Chapman and Hall, 1912.

Trefman, Simon. *Sam Foote, Comedian, 1727–1777.* New York: Oxford University Press, 1971.

Trussler, Simon. *John Osborne.* Harlow: Published for the British Council and the National Book League by Longmans, 1969.

———. *The Cambridge Illustrated History of British Theatre.* New York: Cambridge University Press, 1994.

Turk, Ruth. *Lillian Hellman: Rebel Playwright.* Minneapolis: Lerner Publications Company, 1995.

Turnell, Martin. *The Classical Moment: Studies in Corneille, Molière and Racine.* New York: New Directions, 1963.

Tynan, Kenneth. "Preface." *The Connection: A Play by Jack Gelber.* New York: Grove Press, 1960.

Tytell, John. *The Living Theatre: Art, Exile, and Outrage.* New York: Grove Press, 1995.

Valesio, Paolo. *Gabriele D'Annunzio: The Dark Flame.* Trans. Marilyn Migiel. New Haven, Conn.: Yale University Press, 1992.

Vaneigem, Raoul. *A Cavalier History of Surrealism.* Trans. Donald Nicholson-Smith. San Francisco: AK Press, 1999.

Voronsky, Aleksandr. *Art As a Cognition of Life, Selected Writings, 1911–1936.* Berlin: Mehring Books, 1998.

Way, Brian. "Albee and the Absurd: *The American Dream* and *The Zoo Story.*" In *Critical Essays on Edward Albee.* Ed. Philip C. Kolin and J. Madison Davis. Boston, Mass.: G. K. Hall & Co., 1986.

Weales, Gerald. *Clifford Odets: Playwright.* New York: Pegasus Publishing, 1971.

Weir, Greg. *Papers of Greg Weir—MS 8915.* Vol. 1: *Gay and Lesbian Issues Prior to 1974.* National Library of Australia. http://www.nla.gov.au/ms/findaids/8915_l.html.

Weisart, Joan. *The Dream in Gerhart Hauptmann.* New York: King's Crown Press, 1949.

Weiss, Andrea. *Vampires and Violets: Lesbians in the Cinema.* London: Jonathan Cape, 1992.

West, Mae. *Goodness Had Nothing to Do with It.* New York: Prentice-Hall, 1959.

———. *Three Plays by Mae West:* Sex, The Drag, The Pleasure Man. Ed. Lillian Schlissel. New York: Routledge Kegan Paul, 1997.

Whitman, Wilson. *Bread and Circuses: A Study of Federal Theatre.* New York: Oxford University Press, 1937.

Williams, Tennessee. *Cat on a Hot Tin Roof.* New York: New Directions Publishing, 1975.

Wilmot, John, Earl of Rochester. *Sodom, or The Quintessence of Debauchery.* Number 48 of the Traveller's Companion series. Paris: Olympia Press, 1957.

Wolff, Janet. "The Culture of Separate Spheres: The Role of Culture in 19th-Century Public and Private Life." *The Culture of Capital: Art, Power and the 19th-Century Middle Class.* Ed. Janet Wolff and John Seed. Manchester: Manchester University Press, 1988.

Worozylski, Wiktor. *The Life of Mayakovsky.* Trans. Boleslaw Taborski. New York: Orion Press, 1970.

Zeigler, Jerry. *The Arts in Crisis: The National Endowment for the Arts versus America.* New York: A Cappella Books, 1994.

ARTICLES

"Abbey Theatre, *The Playboy of the Western World,* The." *The Freeman's Journal* (January 28, 1907): 10.

Achenbach, Joel. "A Report from the Front Line of the 'Culture War.'" *The Washington Post,* September 26, 1993, p. G01.

Ain, Stewart. "Doctrine Separates a Girl and Her School." *New York Times,* June 30, 2002.

American Civil Liberties Union. "ACLU Condemns North Carolina County for Censoring Arts Council Over Pulitzer Prize-Winning Play." ACLU Press Release, April 3, 1997.

"American Theatre and the Censors, The." *Life,* May 1937, A170.

Araya, Alfred A., Jr. "Ateneo Bans *Vagina Monologues.*" *The Manila Times,* March 2, 2002. http://www.manilatimes.net/national/2002/mar/02/opinion20020302opi5.html.

Aronowitz, Alfred G. "The Play That Rocked Europe." *Saturday Evening Post,* February 29, 1964, pp. 38–39, 42–43.

Backes, Anthony. "Aristophanes Would Laugh." *English Journal* (March 1999): 43–46.

Bald, R. "A New Manuscript of Middleton's *Game at Chesse.*" *Modern Language Review* 25 (1930): 474–478.

Bald, R. "An Early Version of Middleton's *Game at Chesse.*" *Modern Language Review* 38 (1943): 177–180.

Barnes, Clive. "Theater Review: *The Boys in the Band.*" *The New York Times*, April 15, 1968.

Baur, Eva Elise vom. "Max Reinhardt and His Famous Players." *The Theatre* 14 (1911): vi, 56–60.

Beredjiklian, Norma. "The Violets of Dutchess County." *The Violet Gazette* (autumn 2002): V1–4, P3.

Berka, Walter. "Press Law in Austria." http://www.bild.net/pressAU.htm.

Bernauer, James, S. J. "An Ethic and Moral Formation That Are Repentant: Catholicism's Emerging Post-Shoah Tradition: The Case of the Jesuits." Presented at the Remembering for the Future 2000 Conference: The Holocaust in the Age of Genocide. Oxford and London, July 16–23, 2000.

Billington, Michael. "*The Pleasure Man.*" *The Guardian*, February 7, 2000, p. 23.

Bond, Edward. "Censor in Mind." *Censorship* 4 (autumn 1965): 9–14.

Bowman, Jim. "The Night Mayor Kelly Protected the Morale of Innocent Chicagoans." *Chicago Tribune Magazine*, May 2, 1983, p. 30.

Brantley, Ben. "The Lure of Gang Violence to a Latin Beat." *The New York Times*, January 30, 1998, p. E1.

Brereton, Austin. "*The Cenci.*" *The Theatre* VII (May 1886): 530.

Brustein, Robert. "*Lips Together, Teeth Apart* (Manhattan Theatre Club, New York City)." *The New Republic*, October 21, 1991, pp. 28–29.

———. "*The Toilet.*" *National Review*, January 23, 1965, pp. 32–33.

Burrone, Laura. "Eugene O'Neill's *Long Day's Journey into Night:* A Publishing Success Story." *Endpapers* (fall 1998).

Caldwell, Stephen R. "The NEA and 'Culture Wars.'" Speech delivered to Black Hills Unitarian-Universalist Fellowship, Rapid City, South Dakota. November 14, 1993.

"Censoring Terrence McNally." Editorial. *New York Times*, May 28, 1998.

Chapman, John. "Theater Review: *Cat on a Hot Tin Roof.*" *New York Daily News*, March 25, 1955.

Chavez, Linda. "Free Speech Invoked to Justify Filth." *The Abilene Reporter-News*, October 7, 1998.

Christianson, Richard. "*Shanghai Gesture* Retains Much of Its Power." *Chicago Tribune*, January 13, 1995, p. 18.

Coleman, Sarah. "Female Parts: *The Vagina Monologues* Goes Global." World Press Online (June 6, 2002). http://www.worldpress.org/Americas/606.cfm.

Coley, W. B. "Henry Fielding and the Two Walpoles." *Philological Quarterly* 45 (1966): 166n.

"Colleges, Ban 'VM.'" http://www.cardinalnewmansociety.org/colleges_ban_vm.htm.

"Costa Mesa to Look at *Sister Mary Ignatius* for Arts Grant Violations." *Los Angeles Times*, September 13, 1990, p. F9.

Craft, Christopher. "Alias Bunbury: Desire and Termination in *The Importance of Being Earnest.*" *Representations* 31 (summer 1990): 19–46.

Craies, W. F. "Censorship of Stage Plays." *Journal of the Society of Comparative Legislation* 8 (1907): 196–202.

Crist, Judith. "Theatre Reviews: *The Connection*." *New York Herald Tribune*, July 16, 1959.

Daly, Beth. "Protesters Enlist Free Speech Group over School Play." *Boston Globe*, December 1, 1999, p. B:3.

Dan Linnemeier, et al. v. Indiana University-Purdue University Fort Wayne, et al. Case No. 1 :01-CV-0266. United States District Court, Northern District of Indiana, Fort Wayne Division.

Danton, Charles. "Theater: *The Easiest Way*." *Evening World*, January 20, 1909.

Darlington, W. A. "Has Mr. Bond Been Saved?" *The Daily Telegraph*, April 15, 1968.

De Grazia, Edward. "Allen Ginsberg, Norman Mailer, Barney Rosset: Their Struggles Against Censorship Recalled." Cardozo Life (fall 1998). http:// www.grazian-archive.com/quiddity/Ginsberg/Ginsberg_html.

Dobson, Michael. "Bowdler and Britannia: Shakespeare and the National Libido." *Shakespeare Survey* 46 (1994): 137–144.

"Double Jeopardy: New Federal Theatre Project." *Time*, March 2, 1936, p. 59.

"Dowager Lady Birdwood, The." Obituary. *London Times*, June 29, 2000.

Downes, Randolph C. "The Harding Muckfest: Warren G. Harding—Chief Victim of the Muck-for-Muck's-Sake Writers and Readers." *Northwest Ohio Quarterly* 39, no. 3 (1967): 11–14.

Drake, Sylvia. "Stages Sentimental Trip Back to Federal Theater Years." *Los Angeles Times*, July 12, 1989, p. 1.

Eck, Linda. "*Corpus Christi*—Terrence McNally." *Bad Subjects: Political Education for Everyday Life*. August 18, 2001. http://eserver.org/bs/reviews/2001-8-18-4.45PM. html.

Eggert, Andrew. "Captivating *The Captive*." *Off-off Broadway Reviews*. http://www. oobr.com/top/volFour/twelve/captive.html.

Eigelbach, Kevin. "Xavier: Professor Can Stage Play." *Cincinnati Post*, March 13, 2002. http://www.cincypost.com/2003/03/13/mono031303.html.

"*English Stage Company at the Royal Court Theatre Correspondence, 1955–1959*." http://www.hrc.utexas.edu/research/fa/royal.court.html.

Euben, Donna R. "The Play's the Thing." *AAUP Legal Watch*. http://www.aaup. org/publications/Academe/01ndLW.htm.

"Eugene O'Neill's *Strange Interlude*." The File Room. http://www.thefileroom.org/ documents/dyn/DisplayCase.cfm/id/239.

Fanelli, Sean A. "Drawing Lines at Nassau Community College." *Academe* (July/August 1990): 24–27.

"Federal Theatre Project." Library of Congress. http://memory.loc.gov/ammem/fedtp/ ftbrwn02.html.

Ferris, Lesley, ed. "I'm the Queen of the Bitches: Female Impersonation and Mae West's *Pleasure Man*." *Crossing the Stage: Controversies on Cross Dressing*. New York: Cambridge University Press, 1993.

"First Major Revival of 'The Beard' by Michael McClure." November 17, 1999. http://www.nytheatre-wire.com/beard.htm.

Fitz-Gerald, W. G. "Dramatic Censorship in England." *Harper's Weekly*, January 5, 1907, p. 947.

Foster, Paul. "Forbidden Theater." *Arts4All Newsletter* (summer 2000). http://www. arts4all.com/newsletter/issue14/foster14.html.

Fuller, John. "Cibber, *The Rehearsal at Goatham*, and the Suppression of *Polly*." *Review of English Studies* 13 (May 1962): 125–134.

Gardner, Lyn. "Unholy Racket." *The Guardian*, August 11, 1999.

Garnett, Edward. "The Censorship of Public Opinion." *Fornightly Review* 86 (July 1909): 137–148.

Gascoigne, Bamber. "With a Bare Bedstead." *Spectator* 208 (April 6, 1962): 445.

"Gay Christ in Play Triggers Lawsuit." *The Record*, July 6, 2001.

"Gay Jesus May Star on B'Way." *New York Post*, May 1, 1998.

Gayoso, Jay A. "The FCC's Regulation of Broadcast Indecency: A Broadlined Approach for Removing Immorality from the Airwaves." *University of Miami Law Review* 43 (March 1989): 871–919.

Gibson, David. "The Gospel According to McNally." *The Record*, October 25, 1998.

Giddons, E. E. "Calinax's Challenge in *The Maid's Tragedy*." *Notes and Queries* 44, no. 4 (December 1997): 523.

Goeringer, Conrad. "Their Name Was Legion." *American Atheist: A Journal of Atheist News and Thought*. February 18, 2001. http://www.americanatheist.org/supplement/legion.html.

Goldstein, Richard. "Defending 'The Devil's Work.'" *Village Voice*, June 14, 1983, p. 37.

Gonzalez, David. "As New Musical Opens, So Do Old Wounds; Families of Murder Victims Protest Paul Simon's Tale of a Killer." *New York Times*, January 31, 1998, p. A13.

Green, William. "Oscar Wilde and the Bunburys." *Modern Drama* 21, no. 1 (1978): 70.

Grein, J. T. "Harley Granville-Barker's *Waste*." *Sunday Times*, December 1, 1907, p. 4.

Gross, Alex. "The Voice of the Dramaturg: Artist, Adaptor, or Scholar? Creating an Acting Version and an Annotated Edition of John Fletcher's *The Taming of the Tamer*." A paper presented during the scholarly sessions of the LMDA Conference in Atlanta, 1994.

Gross, Alexander. *Inside the Sixties: What Really Happened on an International Scale*. http://language.home.sprynet.com/otherdex/sixties.htm#totop.

Gutmann, Stephanie, and Phil West. "Casting Call Still a Whisper." *Los Angeles Times*, August 16, 1990, p. F8.

Hall, Peter. "Sleaze Nation." *Guardian Unlimited*. October 2, 2002. http://www.guardian.co.uk/arts/features/story/0,11710,802756,00.html.

Halsall, Paul, ed. "King Richard and the Peasants' Revolt." The Internet Medieval Sourcebook. Fordham University Center for Medieval Studies. http://www.fordham. edu/halsall/sbook.html.

Harris, Eugenia. "Theater Festival Loses County Funds after Texas College Stages Controversial Play." The Freedom Forum. November 12, 1999. http://www.freedomforum.org.

Hobson, Harold. "*Early Morning*." *The Sunday Times*. Reprinted in *The Critic* 1 (April 19, 1968): 9.

Houchin, John H. "Depraved Women and Wicked Plays: Olga Nethersole's Production of *Sapho*." *The Journal of American Drama and Theatre* 6, no. 1 (winter 1994): 74–79.

Housman, Laurence. "My Thirty Years' Fight with the Censors." *Living Age* 353 (November 1937): 264–265.

H. S. D. "A Dramatic Freak First Night at the Abbey Theatre—Paris Ideas and Parricides." *Evening Mail*, January 29, 1907, p. 7.

Jenkins, Gareth. "The Other Empire." *The Socialist Review* 191 (November 1995).

Keast, William Rea. "Killigrew's Use of Donne in *The Parson's Wedding*." *Modern Language Review* 45 (1950): 512–515.

Kennedy, Emmet. "Taste and Revolution." *Canadian Journal of History/Annales canadiennes d'histoire* 32 (December 1997): 375–392.

Kiernan, Louise. "Murder She Wrote: Tribune Reporter Maurine Watkins Achieved Her Greatest Fame with *Chicago*, a Play Based on Two Sensational Local Crimes." *Chicago Tribune*, July 16, 1997, sec. 1, p. 5.

Kingston, Jeremy. "Come Up and See Me." *The Times*, February 7, 2001, p. 41.

———. "*Lips Together, Teeth Apart* (Orange Tree Theater, Richmond, England)." *The London Times*, November 1998, p. 38.

Kinservik, Matt. "New Light on the Censorship of Macklin's *The Man of the World*." *Huntington Library Quarterly* 66 (1992): 43–66.

Klein, Kathleen G. "The Knack." *Theatre Journal* 36, no. 2 (May 1968): 273.

Kostelanetz, Richard. "The Art of Total No." *Contact* 4 (October/November 1963): 62–70.

Kreutz, Irving W. "The Music of Frustration: McClure's *The Beard*." *Arts in Society* 4 (summer 1967): 197–201.

Kushner, Tony. "Tony Kushner's Letter about *Angels in America*." Correspondence between Tony Kushner and Dr. William Holda, Professor Raymond Caldwell and the cast and crew of *Angels in America*, October 14, 1999. http://www.freedomforum. org, November 12, 1999.

"Last of the Censors, The." *The New Age: A weekly Review of Politics, Literature and Art.* 5, no. 19 (September 2, 1909): 353.

Lawrence, Elwood P. "*The Happy Land*: W. S. Gilbert as Political Satirist." *Victorian Studies* 43 (December 1971): 162–183.

"Let Freedom Ring." *Philadelphia City Paper.* March 9–16, 2000. http://www.citypaper. net/articles/030900/ae.theater.desire.shtml.

Loche, Dick. "*Lips Together, Teeth Apart* (Mark Taper Forum, Los Angeles, California)." *Los Angeles Magazine*, September 1993, pp. 186–188.

Logan, Brian. "Still Bolshie after All These Years." *The Guardian*, April 5, 2000.

"*Lysistrata.*" *Athenaeum.* No. 4329 (October 15, 1910): 465–466.

MacCarthy, Desmond. "Literary Taboos." *Life and Letters* 1 (October 1928): 329–341.

Macmillan, Dougald. "The Censorship in the Case of Macklin's *The Man of the World*." *Huntington Library Bulletin* 10 (October 1936): 79–101.

Mangan, Katherine S. "College Draws Hellfire for Staging Disputed Play." *The Chronicle of Higher Education* (October 29, 1999): A71–A72.

"Marianne in 'Horror' Stage Play Role." *Disc and Movie Echo*, March 30, 1968. http://pithuit.free.fr/FAITHFULL/THEATRE/ear.html.

Marwick, Arthur. "Experimental Theatre in the 1960s." *History Today*, October 1, 1994.

"Mayor Admits Condemning Play without Seeing or Reading It." *Boston Evening Transcript*, January 29, 1936, pp. 1, 14.

McCarthy, Desmond. "Literary Taboos." *Life and Letters* 1 (October 1928): 329–341.

McNamara, Eileen. "Writer's Point Lost on Amherst." *Boston Globe*, December 1, 1999, p. B:1.

McQueen, Anjetta. "Protest at *Capeman* Premiere." *Washington Post*, January 30, 1998, p. D05.

Mehren, Elizabeth. "National Perspective: A New Drama Begins after Play Is Cancelled; High School Production of *West Side Story* Forces Debate on Racism and Ethnicity." *Los Angeles Times*, December 7, 1999, p. 5.

Merserve, W. J., and R. I. Merserve. "The State History of *Roar China!*: Documentary Drama as Propaganda." *Theatre Survey: The American Journal of Theatre History* 21 (1980): 1–13.

Midgley, Robin. "*Victor*—Or The Chamberlain Takes Over." *Plays and Players* 11 (September 1964):10.

Mikva, Abner J. "Chicago: Citadel of Censorship." *Focus/Midwest* 2 (March–April 1963): 10, 16–17.

Miller, Phil. "Soap Villain to Star as Gay Judas." *The Scotsman*, June 30, 1999.

Moore, John Robert. "The Contemporary Significance of Middleton's *Game at Chesse.*" *PMLA* 50 (1935): 764–765.

Mulvoy, Thomas F., Jr. "City Weekly." *Boston Globe*, December 15, 2002, p. 2.

Munk, Erika. "Stage Left." *Village Voice*, November 14, 1989, p. 49.

Murder Is Not Entertainment (MINE). http://www.pomc.com/minealerts.cfm.

Myers, Paul. "The Blue Hand of Censorship." *Theatre Time* 1 (summer 1949): 62–64.

Nathan, John. "San Francisco Censorship—Michael McClure's *The Beard.*" *Evergreen Review* 11 (February 1967): 16–20.

Nichols, James H. "Critic's Corner: *The Deputy* and Christian Conscience." *Theology Today* 1 (April 1964): 111–113.

Nichols, Lewis. "Dorothy and Howard Baker's *Trio.*" *New York Times*, December 30, 1944, p. 13.

Norton, Rictor. "The Gay Subculture in Early Eighteenth-Century London." Homosexuality in Eighteenth-Century England: A Sourcebook. http://www.infopt.demon.co.uk/molly2.htm.

Nugent, Frank. "Lillian Hellman's *These Three.*" *The New York Times*, March 9, 1936, p. 22.

Ockerbloom, John Mark. "Banned Books On-Line." http://www-2.cs.cmu.edu/People/spok/banned-books.html. (March 19, 1999).

Official West Side Story Website, The. http://www.westsidestory.com.

Osborn, Tom. "Censor by Jury?" *Plays and Players* 11 (September 1964): 9.

Oseland, James. "Defending *The Capeman.*" *American Theatre* (April 1998): 31.

Otis, Stuart. "The 'Miss Saigon' Mess." *Village Voice*, August 21, 1990: 87.

Otto-Preminger-Institut für audiovisuelle Mediengestaltung (OPI) v. Austria. The European Court of Human Rights, May 10, 1985.

Pennimen, Bruce. "When a School Decides There's No Place for *West Side Story.*" Christian Science Monitor Electronic Edition. December 14, 1999. http://www.csmonitor.com/durable/1999/12/14/fp18sl-csm.shtml.

"People and the Parricide, The." *The Freeman's Journal* (January 29, 1907): 6.

"*Playboy*: A Fair Hearing Accorded." *Irish Independent* (February 1, 1907): 5.

Plumb, Philip. "Gilbert and the censors: The *Happy Land* Conspiracy." *W. S. Gilbert Society Journal* 1 (1994): 238–240.

"Police in a Play Howled Down—Extraordinary Scene in The Abbey Theatre Performed in Dumb Show All Over Disapproved Drama." *Irish Independent* (January 29, 1907): 5.

"Press Comments on the Play." Damaged Goods: The Great Play "Les Avaries" of Eugene Brieux. http://ibiblio.org/gutenberg/titles/damaged_goods_the_g.html.

Pressley, Nelson. "'Band' Still Plays On; The Gay-Angst Classic, Dated but Compelling." *Washington Post*, March 28, 2000, p. C-05.

Prouty, Chris. "Ethiopia: A Dramatic Country." *Ethiopian Review Online*. http://www.ethiopianreview.homestead.com/Article_ChrisProutyJun91.html.

"Public Amusements: Abbey Theatre." *Irish Times,* January 28, 1907, p. 7.

"Public University's Defense of Free Expression: The Issues and Events in the Staging of *The Normal Heart.*" Paper presented at the 76th Annual Meeting of the Speech Communication Association, Chicago, Ill. November 1–4, 1990.

Quinn, Michael L. "Uncertain Slovakia: Blaho, Uhlar, Stoka and Vres." *Theatre Survey* 36 (1995): 97–110.

Rabinowitz, Dorothy. "Audience Verdict on *Capeman:* Gallows at Last." *The Wall Street Journal,* March 27, 1998, p. W11.

"Raisin in the Sun, A." *Newsletter on Intellectual Freedom.* American Library Association (May 1979): 49.

Rees, Terence. "*The Happy Land:* Its True and Remarkable History." *W. S. Gilbert Society Journal* 1 (1994): 228–237.

Remen, Kathryn. "The Theatre of Punishment: David Henry Hwang's *M. Butterfly* and Michael Foucault's Discipline and Punish." *Modern Drama* 37 (fall 1994): 391–397.

Rich, Frank. "Jonathan Pryce, 'Miss Saigon' and Equity's Decision." *New York Times,* August 10, 1990, p. C3.

Richards, David. "Bringing Back 'The Boys'; Will N. Y. Warm to Crowley's Play?" *Washington Post,* June 16, 1996, p. G-01.

Righton, Edward. "A Suppressed Burlesque—*The Happy Land.*" *The Theatre* (August 1, 1896): 63–66.

Robitaille, Marilyn. "Things Women Do: A Performance of *The Parson's Wedding* Revisited." Paper read at the annual South Central Society of Eighteenth-Century Studies Conference, February 22, 2002.

Rose, Lloyd. "At Studio, Just a Touch of Gray in *Hair,* the Tribal Love-Rock Musical Still Has Plenty of Bang." *Wall Street Journal,* July 29, 1997, p. E01.

Roshman, Maer. "Larry Kramer: Queer Conscience." *New York,* April 6, 1998, pp. 144–147.

Rothstein, Mervyn. "Equity Panel Head Criticizes 'Saigon' Producer." *New York Times,* August 16, 1990, p. C17.

———. "Equity Reverses 'Saigon' Vote and Welcomes English Star." *New York Times,* August 17, 1990, p. C3.

———. "Mackintosh and Equity Plan Meeting." *New York Times,* August 24, 1990, p. C3.

———. "Producer Demands a Free Hand to Cast 'Miss Saigon' Roles." *New York Times,* August 22, 1990, p. C11.

Rottmann, Larry. "The Battle of *The Normal Heart.*" *Academe* (July–August 1990): 30–35.

Rowland, Kathy. "Thinking Outside the Box: A Brief History of Theatre Censorship in Malaysia." November 3, 2002. http://www.kakiseni.com/articles/columns/MDEONA.html.

Ruise, Robert. "Broadway 101: The History of the Great White Way." Talkin' Broadway Proudly Presents. http://www.talkinbroadway.com/bway101/2.html.

Russo, Francine. "Theatre: A Little Chin Music." *Village Voice,* December 1–7, 1999.

Ryan, Joal. "Paul Simon's *Capeman* over Troubled Waters." E! Online News. December 2, 1997. http://www.eonline.com/News/Items/0,1,2169,00.html.

"*Sapho* Affair, The." The American Experience: People & Events. http://pbs.org/wgbh/amex/1900/peopleevents/pande30.html.

Sartre, Jean-Paul. "Ce que j'ai appris du problème noir." *Le Figaro,* June 16, 1945, pp. 23–25.

Schapiro, Mark. "Who's behind the Culture War: Contemporary Assaults on the Freedom of Expression." http://www.publiceye.org/theocrat/Schapiro.html.

Schlissel, Lillian. "Mae West and the 'Queer Plays.'" *Women's History Review* 11 (January 2002). http://www.triangle.co.uk/whr/content/pdfs/11/issue11_1.asp#5.

Schriftgiesser, Karl. "How Little Rollo Came to Rule the Mind of Boston; History of the Censorship of Plays and Books That Attracts the Attention of the Country." *Boston Transcript*, September 21, 1929, Magazine Section, pp. 1–2.

Schroeder, Theodore A. "Our Censorship of Literature." *Tomorrow* 4 (November 1908): 42–44.

Schwartz, Barthelemy. "From the Subversion of Society by Art, to the Subsidy of Art by Society." *Le Monde Libertaire*. July/August 1995. Trans. Kenneth Cox. http://abirato.free.fr/1book/aem/gbsubv.htm.

Sheehan, Henry. "When Asians Are Caucasians." *Boston Globe*, August 19, 1990, p. B30.

Silvergate, Harvey, and Gia Barresi. "Wentworth's Whorehouse." *Boston Phoenix*, March 17, 1998. http://www.shadowuniv.com/writings/980327phoenix-has-gb.html.

Simonson, Robert. "Blowing Off the Dust, Breathing New Life." *New York Times*, September 1, 2002, section 2, p. 3.

Sinclair, Lister. "Déjà Vu: AIDS in Historical Perspective: An Interview with Science Writer Colman Jones." IDEAS. Two-part series on CBC Radio. January 9 and 10, 1996. http://www.radio.cbc.ca/programs/ideas/Aids/excerpt.html.

"Sister Mary Ignatius Isn't Happy." *Los Angeles Times*, September 13, 1990, p. B6.

Smith, Anthony Burke. "Catholic Controversy I: Jesus Off Broadway." *Religion in the News* 1 no. 2 (fall 1998).

Snyder, Laura. "Learn to Play the Game: Learning and Teaching Strategies in Ann Jellicoe's *The Knack*." *Modern Drama* 37, no. 3 (fall 1994): 451–458.

Span, Paula. "The Sound of Violence; Paul Simon's *Capeman* Roils Troubled Waters of the Past." *Washington Post*, January 4, 1998, p. G01.

Spillane, Margaret. "*The Capeman*: Theatre Review." *The Progressive* (June 1998): 36–37.

"Staging of Kushner Play in Romania Brings Protest." Associated Press. Wednesday, February 17, 1999.

Stechhan, H. O. "Censoring Shakespeare." *Authors' League Bulletin* 15, no. 1 (April 1927): 19.

"Steel, Yellow Dogs, and the New Deal." http://www.marcblitzstein.com/pages/cradle/pages/steel.htm.

Stephenson, Gregory. "Notes on the Work of Michael McClure." Michael McClure Homepage. http://www.thing.net/~grist/l&d/mcclure/mcclure.htm.

"Student Drama Centers on Play Once Charged with Being Obscence." *Yale University Bulletin* 28 (May 5, 2000).

Sumi, Glenn. "The Full McNally: After Four Tonys and Death Threats, Author Faces the Music." NOW Online Magazine 20, no. 39 (May 31–June 6, 2001). http://www.thefullmonty.com/tour/press_now_05_31_01.htm.

Talcott, Alexander. "GTU Professor to Discuss Asch's *Vengeance of God* [sic]." *Dartmouth Review*. http://www.dartreview.com/issues/10.29.01/asch.html.

Tallmer, Jerry. "Deep Freeze." *Village Voice*, July 29, 1959.

"Terrence McNally's *Corpus Christi* under Attack in Indiana." NCAC Resources Online, July 24, 2001. http://www.ncac.org/issues/corpuschristi.html.

Thackeray, William Makepeace. "Going to See a Man Hanged." *Fraser's Magazine* 22 (1840): 150–158.

"Theater Company Stands up to Catholic League: Will Proceed with Play Featuring Gay 'Jesus' Figure." American Atheist. May 30, 1998. http://www.atheists.org/flash.line/play.htm.

"Tobacco Road." *Vancouver Sun*, January 23, 1953, p. 3.

Tomline, F., and Gilbert A'Beckett. *"The Happy Land: A Burlesque of 'The Wicked World.'"* http://math.boisestate.edu/gas/other_gilbert/hland.txt.

Tonnies, Merle. "The Representation of Mary Stuart in Nineteenth-Century British Drama: A Comparative Analysis of Conflicting Images." *Erfurt Electronic Studies in English* 3 (1999). http://webdoc.gwdg.de/edoc/ia/eese/artic99/toennies/3_99.html.

Turner, Darwin T. "Visions of Love and Manliness in a Blackening World: Dramas of Life since 1953." *The Black Scholar* 25 (spring 1995): 2–9.

Urban, Ken. *"Saved." NYTheatre Archive.* http://www.nytheatre.com/nytheatre/arch_012.htm.

Virgil v. School Board of Columbia County, Fla., 862 F.2d 1517 (11th Cir. 1989).

Wadler, Joyce. "The Play's His Thing, Even If You Never Heard of It." *New York Times*, October 9, 2002, p. B2.

Waggoner, H. H. "The Growth of a Realist: James A. Herne." *New England Quarterly* 15 (March 1942): 62–73.

Walkley, A. B. *"Waste." The Times*, November 27, 1907, p. 8.

Wardle, Irving. "Who's Afraid of the Lord Chamberlain?" *Peter Gill: Playwright, Theatre Director.* http://dspace.dial.pipex.com/town/parade/abj76/PG/pieces/lord_chamberlain.shtml.

Weir, Greg. *Papers of Greg Weir—MS 8915. Volume 1: Gay and Lesbian Issues Prior to 1974.* National Library of Australia. http://www.nla.gov.au/ms/findaids/8915_1.html.

"West Side Story cancellation sparks protest." http://www.cnn.com/SHOWBIZ/News/9911/29/showbuzz.

Will, George F. "The Trendy Racism of Actors' Equity." *Washington Post*, August 12, 1990, p. C7.

Williams, Gerald Walton. "The Text of *2 Henry IV*: Facts and Problems." *Shakespeare Studies* 9 (1976): 173–182.

"William Shakespeare Is Bowdlerized." http://www.thefileroom.org/documents/dyn/DisplayCase.cfm/id/76.

Wilson, Edward M., and Olga Turner. "The Spanish Protest Against *A Game at Chesse.*" *Modern Language Review* 44 (1949): 476–482.

Wilson, Robert J. "Censorship, Anti-Semitism, and *The Merchant of Venice.*" *English Journal* (February 1997): 43–45.

Witt, S. Thomas, and E. Marcus, eds. "Lesbians and Gay Men on Stage: A Necessarily Incomplete History." *Out in All Directions: The Almanac of Lesbian and Gay America.* New York: Warner Books, 1995.

Woodward, Kenneth L. "Blaming the Wartime Pope for Failing to Stop the Holocaust from the Vatican Is a Neat Bit of Revisionist History." *Newsweek*, March 30, 1998.

"Wowsers' Last Stand, The." *OutRage*, June 1997. http://www.adam-carr.net/boys.html.

Wright, Herbert. "Henry Brooke's *Gustavus Vasa.*" *Modern Language Review* 14 (April 1919): 173–182.

"Wrong Side at Amherst High, The." *Boston Globe*, November 21, 1999, p. C:6.

Zoglin, Richard. "Seeking Salvation for *The Capeman.*" *Time*, February 2, 1998, p. 70–72.

APPENDIX I

PLAYWRIGHTS' PROFILES

AINSWORTH, WILLIAM HARRISON (1805–1882)

Ainsworth's many novels were highly popular and profitable in mid-19th-century England. He originated the concept of the "Newgate novels," adapted by many into often-censored "Newgate plays," which exalted the lives of highwaymen such as Dick Turpin and Jack Sheppard. Among his 39 novels, chiefly historical, the most successful were *Guy Fawkes* (1841) and *Jack Sheppard* (1839). *Jack Sheppard* was repeatedly adapted for the stage from 1839 to 1848, when the English censors banned all productions in an effort to suppress a rising crime rate in London.

ALBEE, EDWARD (1928–   )

An American playwright. Albee's early work was largely representative of the Theater of the Absurd, which explored the meaningless and incomprehensible nature of modern life. Albee's explorations of sexual fantasy, frustration, and domestic anguish in such plays as *THE ZOO STORY* (1959) and *WHO'S AFRAID OF VIRGINIA WOOLF?* (1962) are provocative; other Albee plays, including *A Delicate Balance* (1966), which received the Pulitzer Prize in 1966, and *Three Tall Women* (1991) have earned critical acclaim. He has been alternately criticized for subversively creating heterosexual characters within gay themes and for not exploring gay themes at all. Arguing against the notion that the heterosexual married couple in *Who's Afraid of Virginia Woolf?* was actually supposed to be a gay couple, Albee put a stop to an all-male production of the play in 1984.

ANDERSON, MAXWELL (1888–1959)

Born in Atlantic, Pennsylvania, he was a schoolteacher and journalist until 1924, when *WHAT PRICE GLORY?* (1924), written in collaboration with Laurence Stallings, was successfully produced. He was noted for a wide-ranging dramatic style in 30 produced plays and wrote several historical dramas in blank verse, including *Elizabeth the Queen* (1930), *Mary of Scotland* (1933), and *Anne of the Thousand Days* (1948). He also wrote the librettos for several musicals, including *The Knickerbocker Holiday* (1938) and *Lost in the Stars* (1949). Anderson was awarded the Pulitzer Prize in drama for *Both Your Houses* (1933); his verse play *Winterset* (1935), inspired by the 1920s Sacco-Vanzetti case, is considered a classic.

ANDERSON, ROBERT WOODRUFF (1917–   )

Born in New York City and a graduate of Harvard, he is best known for his plays *TEA AND SYMPATHY* (1953) and *I Never Sang for My Father* (1968), which explores the alienation between a father and son. His other major works include *The Eden Rose* (1949), *All Summer Long* (1953), *The Days Between* (1965), and *You Know I Can't Hear You When the Water's Running* (1967). He won the National Theater Conference Prize for *Come Marching Home* (1945). Anderson also wrote a number of film scripts, including *The Nun's Story* (1959) and *The Sand Pebbles* (1965), as well as those for his plays *Tea and Sympathy* and *I Never Sang for My Father.* Critics have praised his sensitive handling of the themes of alienation and loneliness in human relationships.

ARENT, ARTHUR (1904–1972)

Born in Jersey City, New Jersey, he wrote sketches and staged reviews for a resort in Green Mountains, New York, before joining the Living Newspaper Unit of the Federal Theatre Project (FTP). After FTP director Hallie Flanagan recruited him for the project, Arent supervised and edited and assisted in the writing of the scripts of the Living Newspaper productions ETHIOPIA (1936), TRIPLE-A PLOWED UNDER (1936), *1935* (1936), *Injunction Granted* (1936), *Power* (1938), and ONE-THIRD OF A NATION (1938). In 1938 he received a Guggenheim Fellowship and left the Living Newspaper Unit to travel to Europe. He intended to write an antiwar Living Newspaper, but conditions in Europe caused him to change his views; instead, he helped the French produce an enlistment film. He joined the Office of War Information when the United States entered World War II and wrote several documentaries for the war effort, including *Cowboy* (1943), and the documentary play (produced by Elia Kazan) *It's Up to You* (1943), which toured the country under the sponsorship of the Department of Agriculture. After the war he worked as a writer for the radio theater programs *Cavalcade of America, Theatre Guild of the Air, Hallmark Hall of Fame,* and *U.S. Steel Hour.* His novel, *The Laying-On of Hands,* was published in 1969.

ARISTOPHANES (448 B.C.–c. 388 B.C.)

A Greek comic playwright. Aristophanes' works of broad social satire ridicule public figures, institution, and even the gods. His highly imaginative plays also include the invention of completely new characters and situations as well as entire worlds, such as the poetic and improbable "Cloudcuckooland" in *The Birds* (414 B.C.), which uses a kingdom of birds and men to express topical satire. Among his most famous and controversial plays were *The Birds* and LYSISTRATA (411 B.C.), which contain numerous literary allusions and plays on words, charming lyrics, and soothing songs. His last works, *Ecclesiazusae* (392 B.C.) and *Plutus* (388 B.C.), were produced after the fall of Athens and are neither as biting nor as witty as his earlier works because many targets of his satires no longer existed. The majority of Aristophanes' plays are difficult, and, sometimes, impossible to translate, because of their intricate word play and topicality, but many of his comedic themes continue on in today's plays and movies.

ASCH, SHOLEM (1880–1957)

Born in Poland, the Yiddish novelist and playwright immigrated to Palestine in 1908, then to the United States in 1909, where he lived until moving to Israel in 1954. Although known primarily as a novelist for such works as *Three Cities* (1933), *The Nazarene* (1939), and *The Apostle* (1943), he achieved international fame as a playwright with the production of GOD OF VENGEANCE (1907). The play is characteristic of Asch's early work in its blend of the spiritual with erotic themes, which he included in many of his other 20 plays, among them *Winter* (1906), *The Sinner* (1910), and *Yiftakh's Tokhter* (1915). Asch's plays, like his novels, do not deal with only one religious faith; instead, his works explore the tensions that exist between traditional and emancipated Jews, Christians and Jews, the beliefs of the old against the beliefs of the young, and other conflicting positions.

BARAKA, IMAMU AMIRI (1934–)

Born LeRoi Jones in the industrial city of Newark, New Jersey, he attended Howard University in Washington, D.C., and served in the U.S. Air Force before settling in New York's Greenwich Village in the late 1950s, where he was a central figure of that bohemian scene. He became nationally prominent in 1964 with the New York production of his Obie Award-winning play, *Dutchman*. After the death of Malcolm X he became a Black Nationalist, moving first to Harlem and then back home to Newark. Many of his angriest plays, including THE TOILET (1964), were written in this period. In the mid-1970s, he became a Third World Marxist-Leninist. Baraka has continued to generate controversy. In 2002, he was appointed New Jersey poet laureate, but the state legislature attempted to fire him in late 2002 after Jewish leaders protested public readings of his poem "Somebody Blew Up America," which suggested that Jewish workers knew in advance about the September 11, 2001, attack on the World Trade Center and stayed out of work that day.

BAKER, DOROTHY DODDS (1907–1968)

A novelist and dramatist, she was born in 1907 in Missoula, Montana. In 1929 she graduated from the University of California at Los Angeles, where she met the poet Howard Baker. They married in Paris in 1930. Her first novel, *Young Man with a Horn* (1938), later made into a film by Kirk Douglas from her screenplay, won a Houghton Mifflin Literature Fellowship, and she received a Guggenheim Fellowship in 1942. Her next book was TRIO (1943), which she adapted into a play with her husband in 1944. The play opened in December 1944, causing an immediate controversy, and was closed the following February as a result of a campaign mounted against it by Protestant clergy. She returned to the novel form with *Our Gifted Son* (1948) and *Cassandra at the Wedding* (1962). In 1967, she again collaborated with her husband to produce the television play *Ninth Day* for *Playhouse 90*.

BAKER, HOWARD (1905–1990)

Poet, dramatist, and literary critic, he was born in Philadelphia in 1905. In 1928 he received his master's degree in English from Stanford University, where he served as coeditor of the literary magazine *Gyroscope* (1929–1930). After graduating from Stanford, Baker moved to Paris to pursue his studies at the Sorbonne. While living in France he met and was influenced by the writers Ernest Hemingway and Ford Madox Ford, who helped him to publish his first novel, *Orange Valley* (1931). After returning to the United States in 1931, he taught first at the University of California at Berkeley, then from 1937 to 1943 at Harvard University. In addition to collaborating on plays such as TRIO (1944) and *Ninth Day* (1967) with his wife, DOROTHY DODDS BAKER, he also wrote the poetry collections *Letter from the Country* (1941) and *Ode to the Sea* (1954).

BEAUMARCHAIS, PIERRE (1732–1799)

Born Pierre Augustin Caron, he worked as a courtier and watchmaker to Louis XV, before becoming one of the more recognized dramatists of the time. His most famous works include *LE BARBIER DE SEVILLE* (1775) and *LE MARIAGE DE FIGARO* (1784), comedies that depict the adventures and intrigues of one of literature's most scheming servants. Beaumarchais published other plays, among them *Eugénie* (1767) and *Les Deux Amis (The Two Friends)* (1770), as well as *Memoires* (1774). Although these dramas were not as popular as his comedies, they did bring Beaumarchais desired notoriety and minor fame in 18th-century French society. In 1787, Beaumarchais wrote the libretto for the opera *Tarare*.

BLITZSTEIN, MARC (1905–1964)

A composer, playwright, and pianist, his works were experimental, with a focus on formal techniques and proletarian themes, and he had a major influence on other composers who sought to blend classical and popular forms, especially Leonard Bernstein and Stephen Sondheim. Important Blitzstein works include his *Symphony: The Airborne* (1946), written while the composer was stationed in Great Britain during World War II and first performed in New York under conductor Leonard Bernstein; the opera *Regina* (1949), based on Lillian Hellmann's play *The Little Foxes*; a successful adaptation and translation of Weill and Brecht's *The Three-Penny Opera* (1952); and the opera *Juno* (1959), based on Sean O'Casey's play *Juno and the Paycock*. He is best known today for *THE CRADLE WILL ROCK* (1937), a politically charged work about unionism that reflects his belief in the doctrines of Kurt Weill, Bertolt Brecht, and Hanns Eisler, writers who worked to create a socially conscious, popular theater in Germany. The success and notoriety of *The Cradle Will Rock* made Blitzstein famous as a leading exponent of politically committed musical theater.

BOND, EDWARD (1934–)

Born in Holloway, north London, Bond is a marxist dramatist who uses both realism and epic theater to express his grim vision of society and human nature. His plays focus on the capacity of human beings to be brutal. The depiction of infanticide in *SAVED* (1965) and the graphic violence in both *Saved* and *EARLY MORNING* (1968) aroused controversy; the plays were banned in England. The incident caused such a public outcry against the banning of theater that censorship on the British stage soon ended. After the bans were lifted, Bond continued to write, using vivid visual images to communicate his characters' messages of disgust and abhorrence of society. Other Bond plays include *Lear* (1971), *Bingo* (1974), *Restoration* (1981), *Human Cannon* (1985), *War Plays* (1985), and *In the Company of Men* (1996).

BOUBIL, ALAIN (1941–)

Born in Tunis, Tunisia, Boubil began his collaboration with composer Claude Michel Schonberg with the rock opera *La Revolution Française* (1973), which was followed by an international sensation, their adaptation of Victor Hugo's *Les Miserables*, which premiered in Paris in 1980 and was then translated into English for performances in the United States in 1985, where it won the Tony Award for best musical in 1987 and numerous other theater and musical awards worldwide. The collaborators next reset the tragedy of *Madame Butterfly* into the Vietnam War for their musical *MISS SAIGON*, which was written in English and premiered in London in 1989, then reached Broadway in 1991, where it had a long run. It then toured to numerous cities. Their most recent effort, *Martin Guerre* (1996), has achieved mixed critical and financial success.

BOURDET, EDOUARD (1887–1945)

An administrator of the Comédie-Française from 1936 to 1940, the French playwright was popular in Paris and abroad for his light-hearted social satires and serious dramatic studies of social problems. In *Le Rubicon* (*The Rubicon*) (1910), champagne succeeds in curing a bride's shyness, while in *Les Fleurs de Pois* (*The Snobs*) (1932), Bourdet provides a light treatment of homosexuality. His serious treatment of lesbianism in the psychological study *La Prisonnière* (*THE CAPTIVE*) (1926), created controversy and the play was banned from Broadway. His later plays include *Vient de paraître* (*Best Seller*) (1927), a satire of writers and publishers, *Le sexe Faible* (*The Weaker Sex*) (1929), which satirizes the corruption of fashionable Parisian life, and *Le temps difficile* (*Hard Times*) (1934), a satire of middle-class venality.

BRECHT, BERTOLT (1898–1956)

Born in Augsburg, Germany, the poet, playwright, and theatrical reformer created drama that departed from the conventions of theatrical illusion and served as a social and ideological forum for leftist causes. His first play, *Baal*, was produced in 1922. He worked briefly for directors Max Reinhardt and Erwin Piscator; with composer Kurt Weill, he wrote the satirical and ballad opera *THE THREE-PENNY OPERA* (1928) and *The Rise and Fall of the Town of Mahagonny* (1929). He also wrote a series of what he called "exemplary plays," heavy-handed, didactic plays meant for performance in venues other than the traditional theater. He went into exile in 1933, traveling first to Scandinavia (1933–1941), then to the United States, where from 1941 to 1947 he did some writing for film. In Nazi Germany his books were burned and his citizenship was withdrawn, but between 1937 and 1941 he wrote most of his great plays: *Mother Courage and Her Children* (1949), *The Life of Galileo* (1943), *The Good Woman of Szechuan* (1953), *The Resistible Rise of Arturo Ui* (1965), and *The Caucasian Chalk Circle* (1948). Brecht left the United States in 1947 after being forced to testify before the House Un-American Activities Committee. He spent a year in Zurich, working mainly on *Antigone-Modell* (1948) and on his most important theoretical work, "A Little Organum for the Theatre." In 1949 Brecht went to Berlin and formed the Berliner Ensemble, which staged his plays. In 1955 in Moscow, he received a Stalin Peace Prize.

BRIEUX, EUGENE (1858–1932)

Born in Paris, the naturalist playwright's concern with contemporary social problems and social abuses attracted the attention of George Bernard Shaw who proclaimed him "the most important dramatist" of Europe and "incomparably the greatest writer France has produced since Molière." In 1911, Shaw wrote a praise-filled preface for *Three Plays by Brieux*, which contained *The Three Daughters of M. Dupont* (1894), *DAMAGED GOODS* (1902), and *Maternity* (1904), the last of which was translated by Mrs. Shaw. Most of Brieux's more than 30 plays are highly didactic and contain excessive sermonizing that prevented them from attracting large audiences. Although he is largely forgotten today, Brieux was highly respected in his time; he was made a Chevalier of the Legion of Honor and elected in 1910 to the French Academy.

BROOKE, HENRY (1703–1783)

A poet, playwright, and novelist, Brooke was born in Dublin and lived a few years in London, where he became a part of a literary circle that included Alexander Pope and other literary figures of the period. The group met on a regular basis for discussions of diverse subjects, especially politics and religion. Brooke usually focused on Irish topics, the most common of which was the repeal of anti-Catholic legislation, and this interest characterized his writing, as well. In 1735 he published one of his most famous poems, *Universal Beauty*, which critics believe was the inspiration behind Erasmus Darwin's *The Botanic Gardens*. Brooke published his most controversial play, GUSTAVUS VASA, or *The Patriot*, as it was known in Ireland, in 1739, and it was instantly banned. He subsequently continued to write and published the novels *Fool of Quality* (1765–1770) and *Juliet Grenville* (1774).

CALDWELL, ERSKINE (1903–1987)

An author and screenwriter born in the American South, he is best known for TOBACCO ROAD, his 1932 novel about the dark depression years in the South. The story was adapted into a popular, long-running play by Jack Kirkland in 1933. In 1941 producer Darryl F. Zanuck made a film version, but Caldwell disliked it because Zanuck insisted on adding a happy ending. Caldwell's novels *Tobacco Road* and *God's Little Acre* (1933) were two of the biggest-selling novels in the 1930s. In Hollywood, Caldwell frequently adapted his works to the screen as well as writing original scripts. As one of the first authors to be published in mass-market paperback editions, he is a key figure in the history of American publishing; by the late 1940s, Caldwell had sold more books than any writer in the nation's history.

COLTON, JOHN (1891–1946)

Born in Minnesota, he wrote titles for silent films, then Hollywood screenplays, many based on his plays. Among his screenplays are *Laughing Boy* (1934) and *Werewolf of London* (1935), as well as *The Shanghai Lady* (1929), based on his play *Drifting* (1923), and *The Shanghai Gesture* (1941), based on his 1926 play THE SHANGHAI GESTURE. He also served as miscellaneous crew on the film *The Wind* (1928) and as editor for the film *Telling the World* (1928).

CROWLEY, MART (1936–   )

Born in Vicksburg, Mississippi, he worked with several television studios in various positions and was secretary to actress Natalie Wood before becoming a playwright. He is known primarily for writing the landmark play THE BOYS IN THE BAND (1968), the first play to deal openly with male homosexual lifestyles; it was praised by critics who acknowledged him as a master of economical, pungent, and bitingly humorous dialogue. His second play, *Remote Asylum* (1970), was less autobiographical and not as successful, but his return to semiautobiography with *A Breeze from the Gulf* (1975) revived the power of his first play and earned a second place vote for the New York Drama Critics Circle Award. From 1979 to 1980 he served as a television executive script editor. In 1984 he wrote the play *Avec Schmaltz* for the Williamstown (Massachusetts) Theatre Festival. He has not written any plays since then, but in 1996 he produced the television movie adaptation of James Kirkwood's *There Must Be a Pony*.

CUMBERLAND, RICHARD (1732–1811)

This English dramatist was the great-grandson of the 17th-century philosopher of the same name. His family connections earned him a clerical position with the British board of trade, but he was more interested in the theater and wrote more than 40 plays, both tragedies and comedies. Although he was most successful with his sentimental comedies, the best of which are *The Brothers* (1769) and *The West Indian* (1771), he gained more fame for one of his tragedies, *Richard the Second* (1793), which was banned from the stage by the English censors. After he rewrote the play, removing the material that the censors had viewed as seditious, it was performed under the name *The Armorer*, but the play was not successful. He also wrote two seldom-read novels, *Arundel* (1789) and *Henry* (1795), and an autobiography (1806–07).

D'ANNUNZIO, GABRIELE (1863–1938)

A prolific writer, D'Annunzio was also an ardent Italian nationalist and supporter of the Fascist Party. His greatest talents seem to have been his portrayal of women and the passionate experience. Some of his better-known plays are *The Triumph of Death* (1894), *La Gioconda* (1899), and THE MARTYRDOM OF SAINT SEBASTIAN (1911). In his novels and plays, characters live decadent lifestyles, ignoring middle-class obligations and morality, instead, allowing their passions and desire for sensual pleasures to rule them. Their ability to enjoy such sensual pleasures and what D'Annunzio calls "perfect passion" makes them believe that they are beyond ordinary laws, and reflects the concept of the the Nietzschean Superman.

DUMAS, ALEXANDRE (1824–1895)

Identified as Dumas *fils*, or Dumas the younger, to distinguish him from his father, French novelist Alexandre Dumas (Dumas *père*), he was a playwright in 19th-century France. His plays are realistic and focus on the social and moral problems of upper-class French society. They deal frequently with adulterous affairs and financial scandals. His works include *LA DAME AUX CAMELIAS* (1852), *Le Demi-Monde* (*The Half-World*) (1855), and *La question d'argent* (*The Money Question*) (1857). As Dumas aged, he expressed his moral and ethical beliefs more forcefully, as in the play *Les Idées de mme Aubray* (*Madame Aubray's Ideas*) (1867), which is more disapproving of upper-class behavior than earlier plays.

DURANG, CHRISTOPHER (1949–)

After graduation from Harvard University, Durang began his career as a parodist, writing *The Idiots Karamazov* (1974) and *The Vietnamization Of New Jersey* (1976) before finding his trademark blend of satire and black comedy. Influenced by Eugene Ionesco and Tom Stoppard, among others, Durang takes on the issues of religion and family using wit and absurdity. His best-known works are the domestic comedies *The Marriage of Bette and Boo* (1987) and *Baby with the Bathwater* (1983) and the religious satire SISTER MARY IGNATIUS EXPLAINS IT ALL FOR YOU (1979). He has also acted in several films, including the role of Santa in *Life with Mikey* (1993).

ENSLER, EVE (1953–)

A playwright, activist, and screenwriter, she shocked audiences by using the word *vagina* 136 times during the course of her one-woman play THE VAGINA MONOLOGUES (1996). She has used the popularity of the play to create awareness about violence against women and girls and conceived the idea of the annual "V-Day" benefit event in 1998, for which *The Vagina Monologues* has become the focal point. The benefit takes place throughout the world on Valentine's Day, and readings of the play occur in conjunction with activities designed to remind participants of the violence that continues to traumatize women and girls. She has also written plays titled *Floating Rhoda and the Glue Man* (1995) and *Necessary Targets* (1996).

FIELDING, HENRY (1707–1754)

One of the most influential English playwrights and novelists of the 18th century, he began as a playwright, writing *Tom Thumb* (1730), *Rape Upon Rape* (1730), *The Golden Rump* (1735), *The Historical Register for 1736* (1737), and PASQUIN, A DRAMATICK SATIRE (1736), all satires and the last two particularly fierce political criticisms of the existing government. His works angered government officials, particularly Prime Minister Robert Walpole, who lobbied strenuously for the creation and passage of the Licensing Act of 1737, which required that all plays have a license to be performed on a public stage and which set out a range of stringent requirements, including rules that prevented the use of the stage for political satire. Once this act was passed, Fielding's career as a playwright ended, and he turned to the study of law, later becoming the first government magistrate to be supported by a state salary, rather than by bribes and fines. He continued to write, but his output was mainly novels, such as *Joseph Andrews* (1741) and *The History of Tom Jones* (1749), which contained satire of society and politics in a lighter vein.

FITCH, (WILLIAM) CLYDE (1865–1909)

Born in Elmira, New York, he began by writing plays based on historical figures: *Beau Brummel* (1890) and *Nathan Hale* (1898). He soon changed direction to write social comedies, which were highly popular with audiences despite their contrived endings. An extremely prolific and versatile playwright, he wrote more than 36 original plays, including melodramas, farces, social comedies, and historical dramas. Much of his best work reflects American social life of the period. Among his most notable plays are *Nathan Hale, The Climbers* (1901), *The Girl with the Green Eyes* (1902), *The Truth* (1907), and *The City* (1909). His works were popular both in the United States and in Europe. His play SAPHO (1900) was the first play of the 20th century to be closed by the New York City police.

FLETCHER, JOHN (1579–1625)

An English playwright, he wrote 16 plays on his own and 15 with Sir Francis Beaumont, a collaboration that began in approximately 1605. Works of which he was the sole playwright include the comedies *The Faithful Shepherdess* (c. 1608), THE TAMER TAMED (1611), *Women Pleased* (1620), *A Wife for a Month* (1624), and *Rule a Wife and Have a Wife* (1624). Works written in collaboration with Beaumont include *The Coxcomb* (1609), THE MAID'S TRAGEDY (1610), and *The Scornful Lady* (1615). After Beaumont died of plague, Fletcher worked a number of other collaborators to produce another dozen or so plays. His works are recognized as presenting important characterizations of late 16th- and early-17th-century English society.

FOOTE, SAMUEL (1721–1777)

An English actor and dramatist, Foote was a talented mimic who often acted in his own plays and who sometimes savagely caricatured his fellow actors and others who were well known in English society. One of Foote's most popular pieces was *The Minor* (1760), in which he mimicked the Methodists' customs and belief structure. Other works include *The Mayor Of Garratt* (1764), *The Maid of Bath* (1771), and *TRIP TO CALAIS* (1778), which was banned after Elizabeth Chudleigh, the duchess of Kingston, claimed that the play satirized her in the character of the coarse and licentious Lady Kitty Crocodile. Foote rewrote the play and viciously satirized her secretary, Reverend William Jackson, as Dr. Viper in *The Capuchin.* Angered by the portrayal, Jackson bribed one of Foote's former coachmen to bring charges of homosexual assault against Foote, but he was acquitted of the trumped-up charges.

GANTILLON, SIMON (1887–1961)

French screenwriter and dramatist, he wrote the dialogue for *Love around the House* (1946) and *Snares* (1939) and the screenplays for *Special Mission* (1945), *Rumors* (1946), and *Lured* (1947). His play *MAYA* (1924) has the distinction of being the first play banned in New York City under the regulations of the Wales Padlock Law. He wrote the screenplay for the 1949 movie based on the play.

GARNETT, EDWARD (1868–1937)

Literary critic, biographer, essayist, and playwright, he was famous for discovering and publicizing British writers such as Joseph Conrad, John Galsworthy, and D. H. Lawrence. He also published several novels, critical works, and plays, including his most popular and controversial piece *THE BREAKING POINT* (1907). Garnett's wife, Constance, was a distinguished translator who published the first Russian-to-English translations of many eastern European authors, such as Dostoevsky. Their son, David, also a writer, became famous for his romantic novels and love stories.

GAY, JOHN (1685–1732)

The English poet and playwright John Gay was best known for his sardonic and satirical portrayals of contemporary society. His plays gained him a reputation as being a morbid visionary and social critic, whose humor softened only slightly the grotesque and horrifying aspects of early 18th-century London. Although *London* (1719) showed an early tendency toward social satire, his most successful works were *THE BEGGAR'S OPERA* (1728) and its sequel, *POLLY* (1728). Both works mocked Sir Robert Walpole and the court of King George II, and they won Gay instant notoriety and popular fame. Gay was also close friends with Alexander Pope, and became a member of the infamous Scriblerus Club, whose members included Pope, Jonathan Swift, John Arbuthnot, and Thomas Parness. Gay dedicated his 1713 poem *Rural Sports* to Pope. *Fables*, published in 1738, contained a collection of 66 verse stories, 16 of which were published after his death in 1732.

GELBER, JACK (1932–)

This American playwright is often credited as one of the founders of the "New American Theater." His first play, THE CONNECTION (1959), was his most notorious and controversial, and it established his reputation as a writer of social protest. The play was unique to American theater of the time in its risqué subject matter and in its use of popular jazz throughout. Gelber's later plays, including *The Apple* (1961), *Square in the Eye* (1965), and *The Cuban Thing* (1968), were not as popular. While Gelber continued to write plays attacking contemporary society, he was never again able to achieve his first work's level of success or notoriety.

GILBERT, WILLIAM SCHWENCK (1836–1911)

Born in London in 1836, the son of a retired naval surgeon, he was trained as an artillery officer and was tutored in military science with hopes of participating in the Crimean War, but the war ended before he could join. After practicing law for several years, he contributed dramatic criticism and humorous verse to the popular British magazine *Fun*, accompanying some of his work with cartoons and sketches that were signed "Bab." Many of the characters in the later Gilbert and Sullivan operas were modeled after some of Gilbert's "Bab" characters. A collection of these, *Bab Ballads*, was published in 1869. In 1871 Gilbert began to collaborate with composer Arthur Sullivan, and their partnership continued for 25 years and produced 14 operas, including THE HAPPY LAND (1873) and THE MIKADO (1885). Gilbert was knighted by Edward VII in 1907 and died in 1911, at age 74, while attempting to save a drowning woman.

GOODMAN, JULES ECKERT (1877–1962)

Born in Peekskill, New York, he wrote 19 plays that appeared on Broadway from 1908 through 1937. Among his successes are *The Trap* (1915), *The Lawbreaker* (1922), and SIMON CALLED PETER (1924).

GRANVILLE-BARKER, HARLEY (1877–1946)

An English critic, producer, director, actor, and dramatist, he is more frequently remembered for his critical writing and for his years as a theater manager than as a dramatist. His *Prefaces to Shakespeare* (1927–1948) remain studies of major importance, and his role as theatrical director of the Royal Court Theatre from 1904 to 1907 is considered by theater historians to be a significant contribution to the development of English theater; the works of leading old and new playwrights such as Shaw and Ibsen were produced in that time. The position brought Granville-Barker to the national spotlight, and he was acclaimed as one of the brilliant young writer/directors of the age. He wrote nearly 20 plays from 1895 through 1928, including *A Miracle* (1907), *The Marrying of Ann Leete* (1902), and *The Voysey Inheritance* (1905). One of his earliest plays, WASTE (1907), was banned from being performed at the Savoy, where Granville-Barker (he added the hyphen to his name in 1917) experienced some of his greatest successes. Between 1910 and 1912, three of his productions, *The Madras House* (1910), *The Winter's Tale* (1912), and *Twelfth Night* (1912), appeared to rave reviews at the Savoy. After World War I, Granville-Barker retired from the theater, and became president of the new British Drama League; in 1927, he began a series of books that presented the theater from the point of view of the producer, rather than the author.

HANSBERRY, LORRAINE (1930–1965)

Born in Chicago to parents who were intellectuals and activists, she used the experience of her father's antisegregation case before the Illinois Supreme Court as a foundation for the events in *A RAISIN IN THE SUN* (1959), her best-known work. In 1950, she moved to New York and became an associate editor of Paul Robeson's *Freedom*, and met, among others, writer Langston Hughes, from whose poem "A Dream Deferred" she took the title, *A Raisin in the Sun*. In 1953 Hansberry married Robert Nemiroff, a songwriter. She waited on tables and worked as a cashier while writing her first play. She followed her success with *The Drinking Gourd* (1959) and *The Sign in Sidney Brustein's Window* (1964). After she died of cancer at the age of 34, her husband published a collection of her letters and other writings, from which he adapted the play *To Be Young, Gifted, and Black* (1969).

HAUPTMANN, GERHART (1862–1946)

German playwright, novelist, and poet, he is viewed by many critics as Germany's leading early modern playwright. Although he wrote 46 plays, his reputation rests on his early naturalist dramas written from 1892 through 1903, particularly his most famous and controversial play *THE WEAVERS* (1892). He won the Nobel Prize in 1912. He began his career as a playwright with the grimly naturalistic *Before Sunrise* (1889), but occasionally deviated, as he did in another of his controversial pieces, *HANNELE* (1893), which departed in several scenes from naturalistic ideas to focus, instead, on the colorful images and visions of a dying girl entering heaven. *The Weavers*, produced in the same year, returns to a strongly naturalistic theme. Many of his later plays, including *Drayman Henschel* (1898) and *Un Pippa Tanzt!* (1906), are more symbolic and lack the harsh characterizations of the earlier works. Hauptmann's later works include comedy and farce, as well as plays based upon legend or historical incidents.

HEINEMANN, WILLIAM (1863–1920)

Born in England, he founded a publishing house in London in 1890, and established its reputation with the works of Stevenson, Kipling, Wells, Galsworthy, Maugham, and Priestley, as well as with translations of major works from continental European authors. He was also the author of several plays of limited success, including *THE FIRST STEP* (1895) and *Summer Moths* (1898), both of which were refused licenses for performance in England.

HELLMAN, LILLIAN (1906–1984)

An American playwright known for interweaving social and psychological issues into the characters in her plays, she worked for a publisher, reviewed books for the *New York Herald Tribune*, and read scripts in Hollywood before taking a job in New York City as a play reader for a Broadway producer. After meeting writer Dashiell Hammett, who challenged her to write a play and gave her a book about an obscure Scottish lawsuit, she wrote her first play, *THE CHILDREN'S HOUR* (1934); it was one of her most controversial. Her later dramatic efforts were original plays and adaptations of older European works, including *Watch on the Rhine* (1941), *Another Part of the Forest* (1946), and *Toys in the Attic* (1960). During the late 1960s and early 1970s Hellman began to draw upon her life for material. In 1969 she published *An Unfinished Woman*, and then its follow-up, *Pentimento* (1973), both adaptations of her memoirs. These were published with *Scoundrel Time* (1976), a scathing personal account of the anti-communist McCarthy hearings of the 1950s, in a book entitled *Three* (1979).

HERNE, JAMES AHEARN (1839–1901)

Born in Cohoes, New York, Herne began as an actor, then turned to writing melodrama in collaboration with producer David Belasco. His later, more serious plays were strongly influenced by Henrik Ibsen, and were often praised more highly by literary critics than by audiences. Among his most important failures were *Drifting Apart* (1888) and MARGARET FLEMING (1890), a play that deals with the consequences of a husband's infidelity.

HOCHHUTH, ROLF (1931–)

A German dramatist, he achieved notoriety with the production of THE DEPUTY (1963), which contains a scathing denunciation of Pope Pius XII for failing to denounce the slaughter of the Jews in World War II. His next work was *The Soldiers* (1968), in which he criticizes the saturation bombing tactics of World War II and denounces Winston Churchill as a tragic leader whose loss of touch with his own humanity allowed him to commit atrocities. He also attacked crime and corruption in American politics in *Guerillas* (1970) and the military in *Lysistrata and NATO* (1974).

HOOK, THEODORE (1788–1841)

Founder of the brilliantly satirical newspaper *John Bull*, his satirical writings had a direct influence on British history of the 1820s, and he created a style of satire that remains relevant in the present. He was also known to instantly compose witty songs on any subject, and he perpetrated the Berners Street hoax, which astonished London. Offended by a Mrs. Tottenham, he exacted revenge by sending out hundreds of letters inviting people from all walks of society to visit her elegant home on various pretexts on the same day, then watched with friends as carriages belonging to the lord mayor of London, the duke of Gloucester, and many other notables struggled for space on the street. He was England's best-selling novelist immediately before Charles Dickens and is also believed to have been the inventor of the postcard, sending the first one to himself in 1840. His sole attempt at drama, KILLING NO MURDER (1809), was banned from the stage by the English censors.

HOUSMAN, LAURENCE (1865–1959)

A novelist and dramatist, he was the younger brother of poet A. E. Housman, whose success overshadowed his. Laurence Housman's first work was as a book illustrator with London publishers. Finding it difficult to make a living, he turned more and more to writing and published several volumes of poetry in the 1890s. The anonymously published novel *An Englishwoman's Love-Letters* (1900) was his first success. After that he turned to drama with *Bethlehem* (1902). Time and again he found himself at odds with the accepted standards of the day, which dictated that biblical characters and members of the Royal Family could not be depicted on the stage; therefore, many of his plays first appeared at private theater clubs before censorship restrictions were lifted. A prolific writer, with more than 100 published works, he covered a wide range of subjects and forms, including poetry, novels, plays, nonfiction, and stories for children, but he is probably best remembered now for his series of plays, *The Little Plays of St. Francis* (1922), and VICTORIA REGINA (1934).

HUGO, VICTOR (1802–1885)

A French poet and novelist, Hugo was also the leader of the French romantic movement, and his play HERNANI (1830) was one of the principal works of this literary revolution. After the Revolution of 1848 in France, Hugo became politically active as a defender of French liberty, and his actions led to his exile from 1851 to 1870, which he spent in Guernsey, England. His literary style in creating verse dramas for the stage introduced sonority, flexibility, and melody and provided a radical departure from the verse drama that had previously dominated the French stage. Among Hugo's important plays are *MARION DE LORME* (1829), *LE ROI S'AMUSE* (1832), and *Ruy Blas* (1838). Hugo's fame today is largely due to popularizations of his novels *Les Misérables* (1862) and *Notre Dame de Paris* (in English, *The Hunchback of Notre Dame*) (1831).

HWANG, DAVID HENRY (1957–)

Hwang was born in Los Angeles to an affluent family, and grew up to become the first playwright of Asian descent to win a Tony Award. Hwang became the principal spokesperson for Asian immigrants in the American theater; most of his plays deal with the clash between Eastern and Western value systems and the issue of racial stereotyping. His *M. BUTTERFLY* (1988), winner of the Tony Award and nominated for a Pulitzer Prize, was one of the most provocative plays in recent Broadway history. Among other plays by Hwang are *The Dance and the Railroad* (1981), *Rich Relations* (1986), and *Broken Promises* (1987).

IBSEN, HENRIK (1828–1906)

A Norwegian playwright whose "problem plays" focused on social reform, Ibsen helped to popularize realism in the theater. His early works, such as *The Warriors at Helgeland* (1862) and *Love's Comedy* (1862), were historical romantic dramas, but disillusionment with the Norwegian government led Ibsen to use his drama to make serious political and social statements. He wrote the lyrical dramas *Brand* (1866) and *Peer Gynt* (1867) to give voice to his political despondency. Afterward, he focused on writing plays that examined the relationship of the individual to his or her social environment and exposed the falsehoods and social conventions that repress the individual. Among these are *A Doll's House* (1879), GHOSTS (1881), *An Enemy of the People* (1882), and *Hedda Gabler* (1890).

JELLICOE, ANN (1927–)

An English director and playwright, Jellicoe wrote plays largely concerned with characters who are unable to analyze and articulate their emotions, fears, and insecurities. Jellicoe's method of seeking to excite the audience through visual action rather than through dialogue limited her popular success, and plays such as *The Sport of My Mad Mother* (1958) and *The Rising Generation* (1960) were not financially successful. She achieved a popular success with THE KNACK (1961), in part because she relaxed her method and created dialogue as well as action that produced a hilarious depiction of three men and a woman, all obsessed with sex. Jellicoe has also achieved prominence as a director, particularly for her adaptations of plays by Anton Chekhov and Henrik Ibsen.

KILLIGREW, THOMAS (1612–1683)

Often referred to by critics as Thomas Killigrew, the Elder, to distinguish him from his son Thomas Killigrew, the Younger, a gentleman of the king's bedchamber and the author of one play, *Chit Chat* (1719), he was a favorite companion of King Charles II of England and the owner of a theater in London. Between 1637 and 1642, he wrote several plays, including *The Princess* (c. 1637), *Claracilla* (c. 1636), and *The Prisoners* (c. 1635). His most popular play is THE PARSON'S WEDDING (written in 1639 but not produced until after the Restoration in 1664). It was described by contemporaries as extremely coarse and without humor, but it was a stage success.

KING, LARRY L. (1929–   )

The author of 13 books and seven stage dramas, as well as television documentaries, screenplays, short stories, and hundreds of magazines articles, he is a high-school dropout who became a Nieman Fellow at Harvard and a Communications Fellow at Duke and held an endowed chair at Princeton. He has also been awarded the Stanley Walker Journalism Award, the Helen Hayes and Molly Goldwater awards as a playwright, a television Emmy, nominations for a Broadway Tony, and a National Book Award. King began as a magazine journalist, writing for many of the best-known publications of the 1960s and 1970s. After publishing an article in *Playboy* about a brothel named the Chicken Ranch, King wrote the Broadway musical THE BEST LITTLE WHOREHOUSE IN TEXAS (1978). The success of the play allowed him the opportunity to step off what he had come to feel was the "magazine treadmill" and develop his talent in a different arena.

KNOBLOCK, EDWARD (1874–1945)

Born in New York City and educated at Harvard University, he settled in England where he lived most of his life. Biographers claim that Knoblock was involved in as many as 90 theater productions, of which 40 never made it to the stage, and that he was most successful as a silent collaborator who worked out other people's ideas, rather than his own. He collaborated with Arnold Bennett and J. B. Priestley, among others. Knoblock's major success was KISMET (1911), which made his reputation as a playwright and made him a wealthy man.

KRAMER, LARRY (1935–   )

The first creative artist and the first openly gay person to be honored by a Public Service Award from Common Cause, he is also a recipient of the Award in Literature from the American Academy of Arts and Letters. With five friends in 1981, he founded Gay Men's Health Crisis, still the world's largest provider of services to those with AIDS, and in 1987 he founded the AIDS advocacy and protest organization ACTUP. While living in London from 1961 to 1970, Kramer coproduced and cowrote the highly successful film *Here We Go 'Round the Mulberry Bush* (1967), then later produced and wrote the screenplay for the film of D. H. Lawrence's classic novel *Women in Love* (1969). THE NORMAL HEART (1985), Kramer's play about the early years of AIDS, holds the record for being the longest-running play at Joseph Papp's Public Theater in New York. He has written other controversial works, including *Just Say No, A Play about a Farce* (1988), Kramer's treatment of how sexual hypocrisy in high places (the Reagan administration) allowed AIDS to become a plague; it concerns a First Lady, her gay son, and the gay mayor of America's "largest northeastern city." His novel, *Faggots* (1978), continues to be one of the best selling of all gay novels.

KUSHNER, TONY (1956–)

The son of classical musicians, he was born in New York City and grew up in Lake Charles, Louisiana, where he felt very much the outsider as both a Jew and a homosexual, although he did not openly acknowledge the latter until he attended Columbia University. In 1988 Kushner began to write ANGELS IN AMERICA: MILLENNIUM APPROACHES, which won the Pulitzer Prize in drama and the Tony Award in 1993. The sequel to this play, *Angels in America: Perestroika*, won the Tony Award in 1994. The winning of successive Tony Awards was unprecedented in Broadway history. Kushner has told interviewers that his goal in writing for the stage is to fuse the political theater of Bertolt Brecht with the psychological tradition of Eugene O'Neill and Tennessee Williams to create what he calls a "theater of the fabulous."

MACKLIN, CHARLES (1699–1797)

An Irish actor and playwright, born Charles McLaughlin, he first appeared on the stage as Richmond in *Richard III*. In 1733 he began to act at the Drury Lane Theatre, where he stayed until 1748, aside from a short stint at the Haymarket Theatre in 1734. In 1753 Macklin left the theater to open a tavern near the theater at Covent Garden, but returned to acting shortly after the tavern failed. He was known for his quick temper; he killed a fellow actor over a wig in 1735 in the green room at Drury Lane, and he was constantly suing others over his various contracts and quarrels. In 1770, he wrote the highly successful MAN OF THE WORLD (1781); a subscription edition of the play gave him a steady income after he retired from the stage in 1787. His daughter, Mary Macklin (c. 1734–81), was a well-known actress.

MAETERLINCK, MAURICE (1862–1949)

Belgian dramatist, poet, and essayist, he has been ranked by critics as the most successful of the symbolist playwrights and one of the most important writers of the early 20th century, although he died in oblivion. His theories of drama, particularly regarding the importance of atmosphere and concept of stasis on stage, were exhibited in such now-forgotten plays as *The Blue Bird* (1909) and *The Death of Tingagiles* (1905). Maeterlinck's popular success came with MONNA VANNA (1902), a play in which he avoided his earlier reliance on atmosphere and heavy suggestive elements. In the more than 30 plays that followed, he abandoned his earlier use of interior monologue in favor of exterior monologue that was more easily understood by audiences.

MASTERSON, PETER (1934–)

Born in Texas, he went to New York City to start a career in the theater and made his stage debut in *Call Me by My Rightful Name* in 1961. He later worked in movies, theater, and television. Masterson was praised by critics for his role in the theater production of *The Trial of Lee Harvey Oswald* (1967) and in the television movie *A Question of Guilt* (1978), and he also played the role of one of the husbands in the film *The Stepford Wives* (1974). In 1978, he cowrote THE BEST LITTLE WHOREHOUSE IN TEXAS with fellow Texan Larry L. King. He also co-directed the production.

MAYAKOVSKY, VLADIMIR (1893–1930)

Born in Georgia (Russia), he was a staunch supporter of the Russian Revolution and was held up as a model of the revolutionary poet. He became a member of the Bolshevik Party while still a child and, at the age of 15, he was arrested for his political activities and spent nearly a year in solitary confinement, after which he emerged and joined a group of cubist and futurist artists. He published his "Cubo-Futurist" manifesto in 1912, in which he called for an unorthodox and surreal approach to artistic expression. Through his political activities, Mayakovsky soon became an official Bolshevik spokesman, and he was called upon to speak his verses to marching workers. In 1919 he was appointed the director of propaganda for the Soviet wire service, a position he held until 1922. He achieved popularity through such plays as *The Bath House* (1930) and THE BEDBUG (1929), as well as through the grandiose pageant play *Mystery-Bouffe* (1918).

MCCLURE, MICHAEL (1932–   )

Born in Kansas, he went to San Francisco in his early 20s and became part of the emerging Beat movement that grew out of the San Francisco poetry renaissance. He read with Beat poets Philip LaMantia, Allen Ginsberg, Gary Snyder, and Phil Whalen at the famous Six Gallery poetry reading in 1955, an event that took place in a small art gallery in a former auto repair shop. His first book of poetry, *Passages*, was published in 1956, and he later wrote the original words upon which Janis Joplin's song "Oh Lord, Won't You Buy Me a Mercedes Benz" was based. He also wrote several controversial plays, including THE BEARD (1965) and *Josephine, The Mouse Singer* (1978), which were major theater events of the 1960s and 1970s. In the early 1990s McClure began collaborating with Ray Manzarek, keyboardist with the 1960s rock group the Doors, on live poetry set to music.

MCNALLY, TERRENCE (1939–   )

Although his first play was produced when he was only 25, and such early plays as *Next* (1969) and *The Ritz* (1975) earned critical praise, McNally's first success did not come until 1987, when *Frankie and Johnny at the Claire de Lune* (1987) was adapted for film. In 1990 he won an Emmy Award for best writing in a miniseries or special for *Andre's Mother*. A year later, LIPS TOGETHER, TEETH APART (1991) appeared on stage. McNally also collaborated with Manuel Puig on the play *Kiss of the Spider Woman* (1992) and won the Tony Award for best book of a musical. McNally's other plays include *Love! Valour! Compassion!* (1994) and *Master Class* (1996), which won the 1996 Tony Award for best play. The mild complaints from some observers about gay themes in McNally's earlier plays became major controversy when he retold the story of Jesus Christ in CORPUS CHRISTI (1998), depicting Christ and his followers as homosexuals.

MIDDLETON, THOMAS (1580–1627)

Born in London, he was a prolific playwright and collaborator, as well as the writer of pageants and masques for official occasions in London. His early plays, such as *The*

Honest Whore (1604), *A Trick to Catch the Old One* (c. 1605), and *A Mad World, My Masters* (1606), are mostly comedies. In 1624, the production of his political satire *A GAME AT CHESSE* caused a furor, and Middleton and the actors of his play were called before the Privy Council. He remains known today largely through two of his plays that continue to be anthologized, *The Changeling* (written in 1622, published in 1653) and *Women Beware Women* (written in 1621, published in 1657).

MILLER, ARTHUR (1915–   )

Considered by critics to be one of America's foremost playwrights, he began his career by working with the Federal Theatre Program of the Work Projects Administration in 1938. He published *Focus* (1945), a novel about anti-Semitism, and nine plays before writing *All My Sons*, which won the 1947 Drama Critics' Circle Award for best play, and *Death of a Salesman* (1949), which established his reputation as a playwright. His social and political views came under fire during the investigations by the House Committee on Un-American Activities conducted by Senator Joseph McCarthy. Miller incorporated the moral problems of that period into his controversial plays *THE CRUCIBLE* (1953) and *A VIEW FROM THE BRIDGE* (1955). His plays deal largely with the struggles of the individual in relation to larger society.

MOLIÈRE (1622–1673)

Born Jean-Baptiste Poquelin, he began as an actor before writing 30 comedies that satirized French society. His plays depend upon conflicts for their humor: husbands versus wives, youth versus age, professional versus domestic life, the noble versus the peasant, and artifice versus reality. Although all of his plays were offensive to members of French society to varying degrees, *LE TARTUFFE* (1664) and *LE MISANTHROPE* (1666) created the greatest controversy during his lifetime.

O'CASEY, SEAN (1880–1964)

Born the last of 13 children of impoverished Dublin Protestants, he grew up in poverty and squalor in a series of tenement homes. Unable to attend school, he taught himself to read and write and became fascinated by the dramas of William Shakespeare. O'Casey's early drama was influenced by his radical politics. He was a member of the Irish Transport and General Workers' Unions and secretary of the nationalistic labor organization the Irish Citizen Army. The Abbey Theatre, founded by William Butler Yeats, produced his early plays, including *The Shadow of a Gunman* (1923) and *Juno and the Paycock* (1924), but his honest portrayal of Irish society caused the audience to howl in indignation when *The Plough and the Stars* (1926) was staged. After the Abbey Theatre rejected his play *The Silver Tassie* (1928), he left Ireland in disgust, to spend time in England and the United States. Although well-received in New York City, his 1934 play *WITHIN THE GATES* created controversy in Boston, where it was banned from production.

ODETS, CLIFFORD (1906–1963)

Born to a poor Jewish-American family, Odets began his career as an actor, sound-effects man, and radio announcer before taking roles in stock theater productions. He joined the Communist Party, but quit after eight months because it inhibited his ability to write plays. Nonetheless, the social ideals that led him to join permeate his plays. He joined the Theater Guild and later helped to found the Group Theatre, which featured drama about social problems and produced his first play, *WAITING FOR LEFTY* (1935). Later that year, the theater also produced his *Till the Day I Die* and *Paradise Lost*. After a commercial failure with *Night Music* (1940), Odets moved to Hollywood, where he spent the rest of his life as a screenwriter.

O'NEILL, EUGENE (1888–1953)

Born in Connecticut to Irish Catholic immigrant parents, he dramatized in his plays the intense love-hate relationships that existed among his mother, father, brothers, and himself. The most explicit such depiction occurs in *LONG DAY'S JOURNEY INTO NIGHT* (written in 1941 but not staged until 1956). O'Neill spent his early boyhood on tour with his father, actor James O'Neill. After less than a year at Princeton University, O'Neill went to sea as a sailor, then returned and was hospitalized with tuberculosis. While in a sanatorium, he began to write. His early plays, such as *Bound East for Cardiff* (1916) and *The Dreamy Kid* (1919), were produced by the Provincetown Players. After *Beyond the Horizon* was produced on Broadway in 1920, he became America's leading playwright. In the 14 years following, he wrote 21 plays, including *STRANGE INTERLUDE* (1928). In 1936 O'Neill became the first American to win the Nobel Prize.

OSBORNE, JOHN (1929–1994)

Born in London, he developed a concept of playwriting that would eventually change the face of British theater. After completing school, he became involved in the theater by taking a job as the tutor to a touring company of young actors. Osborne later served as actor-manager for a string of repertory companies before deciding to try his hand at playwriting. His first play, *Look Back in Anger*, was produced in 1957, and many critics consider it the turning point in postwar British theater, creating as it did the concept of the "Angry Young Men." In his next play, *THE ENTERTAINER* (1957), Osborne used three generations of a family of entertainers to symbolize the decline of England after the war. After this, however, the quality of Osborne's work became erratic. Although he produced a number of hits, including *Luther* (1961), a play about the leader of the Reformation, and *Inadmissible Evidence* (1965), the study of a frustrated solicitor at a law firm, he also produced a string of unimportant works. In 1965 he shocked audiences with a play containing the theme of homosexuality, *A PATRIOT FOR ME*. This followed other plays on the subject of British degeneration, but none made the impact of his early plays.

PANIZZA, OSKAR (1853–1921)

Panizza was born in Germany. His works have been largely ignored by students of German literature because many of his books were banned, confiscated, and destroyed during the 1890s under German censorship. Few attempts have been made to republish his works, and many are no longer available, because family members destroyed as many copies as they could purchase. Although Panizza wrote in the same period as the German naturalists, who sought to depict reality, no matter how ugly or vulgar, and although he was a medical doctor, his literary treatment of syphilis, excretory functions, vomiting, masturbation, and acute paranoia were considered to be in such bad taste that they were banned. Even more controversial were his savage attacks on religion, exhibited prominently in THE COUNCIL OF LOVE, which was written in 1895 and immediately banned, after which the author spent a year in prison. When he emerged, his mental health deteriorated rapidly and he was placed in an insane asylum, where he lived for the remaining 17 years of his life.

PITT, GEORGE DIBDIN (1799–1855)

The son of dramatist and songwriter Thomas Pitt Dibdin, who is thought to have written more than 2,000 songs and 200 operas and plays for the early 19th-century London theater, he changed his name around and became a playwright. Pitt specialized in horrific melodramas produced in theaters that 18th-century audiences referred to as "blood tubs," as they specialized in depicting gore and murder in performances that recreated on stage the sensational crimes of the period. Among George Dibdin Pitt's works are *The Monster of Eddystone: or, The Lighthouse Keeper* (1835), *Simon Lee: or, The Murder of the Five Fields Copse* (1839), and *Marianne, the Child of Charity: or, The Head of a Lawyer* (1844). In 1841, he wrote the sensational novel *Sweeney Todd, the Barber of Fleet Street: or, The String of Pearls*, which, he claimed in the preface, was "Founded on Fact." The following year, he adapted the novel into a melodrama first performed in the Britannia Theatre in London and then all over the country. His work REVOLUTION OF PARIS, OR THE PATRIOT DEPUTY (1848) was a departure from his usual writing, but the strong political criticism perceived by the English censors kept it from performance.

RACINE, JEAN (1639–1699)

Born in France, he was orphaned at an early age. After studying law, he became involved in the theater and was befriended by Molière, who produced several of his early plays but who became his enemy after Racine seduced and lured away the lead actress of Molière's troupe. Racine wrote a number of tragedies based on Roman and Greek themes. *Britannicus* (1669) chronicles the story of Agrippa, mother of the Roman emperor Nero; *Iphigenia in Aulis* (1674) is Racine's version of the events leading to the sacrifice of Iphigenia to appease the gods; Racine's masterpiece, *Phèdre* (1677), is based on Euripides' *Hippolytus*. In 1677, Racine retired from the theater to assume the position of royal historiographer, but Madame de Maintenon, consort of Louis XIV, convinced him to write two plays for the schoolgirls of St. Cyr, *Esther* (1689) and ATHALIE (1691). These were the last plays he wrote.

RADO, JAMES (1939–)

Born in Washington, D.C., he was an out-of-work actor when he wrote the musical HAIR (1967) with Gerome Ragni. A writer, lyricist, and performer, he performed in *Marathon '33* (1963) and *The Lion in Winter* (1966) before appearing in *Hair* in the role of Claude.

RAGNI, GEROME (1942–1991)

Born in Pittsburgh, he was a lyricist, writer, and performer before collaborating with James Rado to write the musical HAIR (1967). He appeared in *War* (1963), *Hamlet* (1964), *Hang Down Your Head and Die* (1964), and *Viet Rock* (1966). He collaborated with Galt McDermot on another musical, *Dude* (1972), which had only limited box office success.

RICE, TIM (1944–)

Born in Amersham, Buckinghamshire, England, he has gained world renown as a lyricist and is best known for his collaborations with Andrew Lloyd Webber. He was knighted by Queen Elizabeth II in 1994. Rice has written the lyrics to JESUS CHRIST SUPERSTAR (1971), Evita (1979), Joseph and the Amazing Technicolor Dreamcoat (1968), Chess (1988), Beauty and the Beast (1994), and numerous other musicals, but his first musical created the greatest controversy.

ST. JOHN, JOHN (UNKNOWN)

Librettist who was credited in the Drury Lane playbill as the Hon. John St. John. After THE ISLAND OF ST. MARGUERITE (1789) was rejected by the London censors, he reworked the material to placate the censors, and the play was staged in 1790 as The Man in the Iron Mask. He is not identified with other literary efforts.

SARTRE, JEAN-PAUL (1905–1980)

Born and educated in Paris, he was a philosopher, dramatist, novelist, and political journalist, as well as a leading exponent of existentialism. He was imprisoned by the Germans at the outbreak of World War II and, after his release, was active in the French Resistance. His antiauthoritarian play The Flies (1942) and the publication of his major philosophic work Being and Nothingness (1943) were the first important works of existentialism. His play No Exit (1946) was written the same year as THE RESPECTFUL PROSTITUTE; like all of his literary works, they contain an existential viewpoint. In 1964, Sartre rejected the Nobel Prize in literature because he felt that to accept such an award would compromise his integrity as a writer.

SCHNITZLER, ARTHUR (1862–1931)

Born in Austria, the playwright and novelist infused his works, such as The Fairy Tale (1891) and LA RONDE (1896), with the light-heartedness and charm of Vienna in the late 19th century. He was also a medical doctor who wrote medical reviews on such subjects as hypnotism and psychotherapy. Most of his more than 40 plays contain a clinical and ironic portrayal of sex, despite the surface romantic appearance. Although Schnitzler's works were popular in Austria and Germany before World War I, he became a target of anti-Semites and pro-Nazi supporters during the 1920s, and his works were banned until after World War II. Schnitzler never regained his earlier renown.

SCHONBERG, CLAUDE-MICHEL (1944–)

A French composer, author, and record producer, he worked with Alan Boubil to stage the first rock opera in France, La Revolution Francaise (1973). In 1978 he and Boubil wrote the musical Les Misérables, which was produced in Paris in 1980 and on Broadway in 1987. Schonberg won Tony Awards for the Broadway production for best score and book, and a Grammy for best original cast recording. In 1989 Schonberg and Boubil produced MISS SAIGON, which in December 1994 became the longest-running musical ever at the Theatre Royal, Drury Lane, eclipsing the 2,281-performance record set by My Fair Lady. A later joint project, Martin Guerre (1996), was less successful with audiences.

SHAKESPEARE, WILLIAM (1564–1616)

Little is known about Shakespeare's early theater career, but he was an important member of the Lord Chamberlain's Men acting troupe at their reformation in 1594. He helped to develop the group into London's leading theater company, and with it took up residence at the Globe Theatre in 1599. After James I ascended the throne, the company was renamed the King's Men in 1603. Shakespeare's early published works were long poems such as *Venus and Adonis* (1593) and *The Rape of Lucrece* (1593–94). Scripts of only half of his plays appeared during his lifetime. Among his early works are *Henry VI*, Parts One, Two and Three (c. 1589–92), *Richard III* (c. 1591–92), and such comedies as *The Taming of the Shrew* (1594) and *The Comedy of Errors* (1594). His most controversial plays appeared after he had become well established in the theater: THE TRAGEDY OF KING RICHARD II in 1595, HENRY IV, Part Two, in 1598, THE MERCHANT OF VENICE in 1596, HAMLET (1602), and KING LEAR in 1607. Although early challenges to Shakespeare's productions occurred largely due to their political content, later expurgators such as the infamous Thomas Bowdler protested what they found to be blasphemous, indecent, and obscene references and language in the plays. The last plays associated with Shakespeare appear to have been written in collaboration with dramatist John Fletcher.

SHAW, GEORGE BERNARD (1856–1950)

Born in Dublin, Ireland, the Anglo-Irish dramatist and critic wrote extensively in various fields. His drama criticism in the 1890s drew attention to the works of Henrik Ibsen, and he advocated a new drama in England that would focus on modern problems while he attacked the "bardolatry" that had elevated William Shakespeare to a position that Shaw felt was unwarranted. Shaw's plays, such as MRS. WARREN'S PROFESSION (1902), THE SHEWING UP OF BLANCO POSNET (1909), and many others, scandalized English society because he turned expectations around by showing seemingly virtuous women who are not virtuous, heroes who act unheroically, villains who are not completely villainous, and similar challenges to social comfort. Although Shaw's plays were often criticized for being too caustic and propagandistic, they enjoyed huge popularity with audiences. In 1925, Shaw was awarded the Nobel Prize.

SHELLEY, PERCY BYSSHE (1792–1822)

Born to a Member of Parliament who later become a baronet, Percy Shelley appeared to be destined for a political career before becoming enamored of the radical ideas of William Godwin and Thomas Paine that he read while at Oxford. He gave speeches and wrote early pamphlets condemning marriage, royalty, meat-eating, and religion, and later expressed his revolutionary philosophy in *Queen Mab* (1813). Aside from his notorious personal life, which included affairs, elopements, and multiple simultaneous sexual liaisons, he is best known as a romantic poet. Shelley was also a fervent essayist, writing *The Revolt of Islam* (1817), among other works. THE CENCI (1819) was written in Pisa, Italy, in his period of greatest creativity, during which he also published numerous poems and essays, including his famous "To a Skylark" and "The Cloud."

SHYRE, PAUL (1929–1989)

A producer, writer, director, and performer, Shyre was born in New York City and worked on Broadway for more than three decades. In 1956 he performed in and adapted the book for *Pictures in the Hallway*. He did the same in 1957 for *I Knocked at the Door*, which he also produced. In 1964 he directed *Fair Game for Lovers* and later that decade began a relationship with Ford's Theater Society, in Washington, D.C., which commissioned him to write a play about the assassination of President Abraham Lincoln. THE PRESIDENT IS DEAD (1969) was, however, suppressed by the society. Shyre continued to write, perform, and produce until his death; his last play was *Hizzoner* (1989), which began performances nine months before his death.

SIMON, PAUL (1941–)

Born in Newark, New Jersey, the songwriter and singer Paul Simon is best known for his popular music. He has earned 10 Grammy Awards and a Britannia Award for his song "Bridge over Troubled Water," recorded with singing partner Art Garfunkel. In 1998 he became a theatrical producer with THE CAPEMAN, a controversial play that angered parents of murder victims and led to charges that Simon was using a tragedy to revive a lagging musical career.

SOPHOCLES (c. 496–c. 406 B.C.)

This tragic dramatist of the Greek Golden Age is the most admired of the three great Greek tragedians, which also include Euripides and Aeschylus. Though he wrote more than 100 plays, his reputation rests on the few that have survived, seven tragedies and part of a satyr play. Among the seven tragedies, the best known are *Electra* (c. 409 B.C.) and the plays about Oedipus and his family: OEDIPUS REX (c. 425 B.C., sometimes referred to as *Oedipus Tyrranus* or *Oedipus the King*), *Oedipus at Colonus*, and *Antigone* (c. 442 B.C.). The themes of Sophocles' plays were well known to audiences of his time, who were more concerned with the relationship of the individual to the moral order in the plays than in the themes of incest, adultery, and murder that audiences in later centuries found offensive.

STOPES, MARIE (1880–1958)

A passionate feminist and crusader for birth control, she won a scholarship to University College in London, where she became Britain's youngest doctor of science. In her book *Married Love* (1918) she argued that marriage should be an equal partnership between husband and wife; U.S. courts declared the book obscene and promptly banned it. The next year, Stopes wrote a concise guide to contraception called *Wise Parenthood*, which upset the leaders of the Church of England, who believed it was wrong to advocate the use of birth control. In 1921 she founded the Society for Constructive Birth Control and opened the first of several birth control clinics in London. She also wrote novels and poetry, including *Love's Creation* (1928) and *Love Songs for Young Lovers* (1919). Her sole play, VECTIA (1926), was refused a license for performance in London. Rather than distort her message by removing material that the censors found objectionable, she withdrew it from consideration.

SULLIVAN, SIR ARTHUR (1842–1900)

An accomplished composer before beginning collaboration with W. S. Gilbert, he wrote successful music for several plays by William Shakespeare, among them *The Tempest*, *Macbeth*, and THE MERCHANT OF VENICE. He is also the author of the hymn "Onward, Christian Soldiers." In 1871 Sullivan began to collaborate with Gilbert, and their partnership continued for 25 years and produced 14 operas, including THE HAPPY LAND (1873) and THE MIKADO (1885). Sullivan attempted a serious opera in 1891, *Ivanhoe*, based on the novel by Sir Walter Scott, but the work was not a success.

SYNGE, JOHN MILLINGTON (1871–1909)

Born near Dublin, he is acclaimed by critics as the foremost dramatist of the Irish Renaissance. He began his writing career by translating the poetry of Stephen Mallarmé and other French symbolists into English, but turned to drama after meeting William Butler Yeats, who convinced him to write about the peasants of western Ireland. Most of Synge's plays reflect the speech patterns and lives of these people, including the stark and realistic *Riders to the Sea* (1904), *The Well of the Saints* (1905), PLAYBOY OF THE WESTERN WORLD (1907), *The Tinker's Wedding* (1909), and the unfinished *Deirdre of the Sorrows* (1910).

THOMSON, JAMES (1700–1748)

Born along the Scottish border and educated at Edinburgh University, he showed an early talent for poetry. After serving as a tutor to the son of the solicitor-general, Thomson began to publish poetry. His first poem, *The Seasons* (1726), remains one of his most frequently reprinted. Soon after, he began to write tragedies, such as *Agamemnon* (1738), EDWARD AND ELEANORA (1739), and the posthumously published *Tancrid and Sigismunda* (1745) and *Coriolanus* (1749). Romantic poets William Wordsworth and Samuel Taylor Coleridge praised Thomson for his ability to offer new images of nature.

TRETYAKOV, SERGEI (1892–1939)

The works of this Russian poet, literary critic, and playwright were among those purged in the Soviet Union in the 1930s. Tretyakov became interested in the Far East during the Bolshevik Revolution and later joined Vladimir Mayakovsky's group of futurist poets. During 1922 and 1923, he worked with Sergei Eisenstein writing adaptations at the Prolcult Theatre and produced several communist propaganda plays set in Germany. In 1924 he went to Peking, where he became literary professor at the National University and wrote his most famous play, ROAR, CHINA! (1926). During the 1930s, after returning to Russia, Tretyakov wrote film scripts.

TYNAN, KENNETH (1927–1980)

Born in England, he began his work life as a newspaper writer. His support for new playwrights, such as John Osborne, Arnold Wesker, Shelagh Delaney, Samuel Beckett, and others, played a leading role in shifting tastes in the theater from drawing-room comedies and verse dramas to a more naturalistic, working-class drama. He was a vigorous opponent of the Lord Chamberlain and his censors, and played a major role in the development of British theater as a moving force in the creation of the National Theatre in 1963, for which he served as director from 1963 to 1969. As one of the major contributors to the skits and sketches of the play *OH! CALCUTTA!* (1969), Tynan, challenged the censors and the stodgy theater that had long dominated England.

VITRAC, ROGER (1899–1952)

A French surrealist poet and playwright, he joined Franco-Romanian poet and playwright Tristan Tzara to found the artistic movement known as dadaism. After making plans with director and dramatist Antonin Artaud to produce avant-garde drama commercially, he was expelled from the dadaist inner circle and with Artaud founded the Théatre Alfred-Jarry in 1927. Their productions anticipated the Theater of the Absurd that would arise decades later. In 1928 Vitrac produced his most important play, *VICTOR, OR THE CHILDREN TAKE OVER*, a bitter drawing-room farce that deals with the banality of language and human relationships. His later plays were more conventional.

VOLLMOELLER, KARL GUSTAV (1878–1948)

A German symbolist poet and dramatist, he was a disciple of Austrian poet and dramatist Hugo von Hofmannsthal and Belgian poet and dramatist Maurice Maeterlinck. The romantic moods, bordering on decadence, of his early works reflect their influence. Although he became a successful writer in Germany, Vollmoeller's influence on Austrian theater was more pronounced. His plays, such as *VENETIAN NIGHT* (1911), relied more on spectacle than on dialogue, and his topics focused on the unusual, from a didactic portrayal of Casanova in *Der Deutsche Graf* (1906) to the first play ever written about an aviator, *Wieland* (1910).

WALCOTT, DEREK (1930–   )

Born on the island of Saint Lucia in the West Indies to an English father and African mother, this poet, dramatist, and essayist has been the recipient of numerous awards for his work in all three areas. He was awarded the 1992 Nobel Prize in literature, a MacArthur Foundation "genius" award, a Royal Society of Literature Award, and, in 1988, the Queen's Medal for Poetry. In addition, his play *Dream Monkey Mountain* won an Obie Award in 1971 for distinguished foreign play presented in an Off-Broadway venue. Although widely known as a poet, Walcott had already published 10 plays, including *The Last Carnival* (1969), *The Joy of Seville* (1978), *The Isle Is Full of Noises* (1982), and *The Odyssey: A Stage Version* (1992), when he collaborated with popular musician Paul Simon to write *THE CAPEMAN* (1998).

WALTER, EUGENE (1874–1941)

Walter began his writing career as a newspaper reporter in Cleveland, Ohio, and also worked as a public entertainment manager for minstrel shows and circuses, as well as for symphony orchestras and grand opera companies. He wrote more than 24 plays, including *The Undertow* (1906), *Paid in Full* (1907), *THE EASIEST WAY* (1908), and *Fine Feathers* (1911).

WEBBER, ANDREW LLOYD (1948–)

Born in London, the son of composer William Lloyd Webber and brother of Julian Lloyd Webber, a world-renowned cellist, he began writing music at an early age. In 1965 he met lyricist Tim Rice, who became his collaborator on his first musical-theater successes during the 1960s, 1970s, and 1980s. These included *Joseph and the Amazing Technicolor Dreamcoat* (1968), JESUS CHRIST SUPERSTAR (1971), and *Evita* (1979). After their collaboration ended, Webber worked with numerous different lyricists to produce *Cats* (1981), *Starlight Express* (1984), and *Whistle Down the Wind* (1998), among others. He was knighted in 1992, and in 1997 was named Lord Lloyd-Webber of Sydmonton.

WEISS, PETER (1916–1982)

A German-born novelist, playwright, and film producer, he began his career as a painter. Although his first play, *The Tower*, was produced in 1950, he did not consider himself to be principally a playwright until after the great success of MARAT/SADE (1964), for which Berlin critics hailed him as "the new Brecht." His next play, *The Investigation* (1965), focused on the Auschwitz trials in Frankfurt in 1963–65. Later plays, including *Vietnam Discourse* (1968), also focus on social and political themes.

WEST, MAE (1893–1980)

An American actress and author, she is often remembered as an exaggerated sex symbol whose characteristics were a swaggering walk, tough talk, and snappy one-liners. She also wrote most of the movies she starred in, as well as several Broadway shows that scandalized New York City officials, who closed them down and brought West even greater publicity for her other projects. She wrote SEX (1926) using the pseudonym "Jane Mast," but THE PLEASURE MAN (1928) appeared under her name. Her other plays include *Diamond Lil* (1928) and *Sextet* (1961).

WILDE, OSCAR (c. 1854–1900)

Wilde was an Irish-born playwright, novelist, and social figure. His notoriety as the defendant in an 1895 sodomy trial long overshadowed critical appraisals of his work. After graduation from Oxford University, he proclaimed himself to be an art critic, a "Professor of Aesthetics," and began to write and lecture on the necessity of producing "art for art's sake." His flamboyant behavior, clothing, and mannerisms, and his biting satire, soon drew public attention. Wilde published his first play, *Vera*, in 1880, but his most popular works were written in the three years preceding the trial: *Lady Windemere's Fan* (1892), *A Woman of No Importance* (1893), SALOMÉ (1893), and THE IMPORTANCE OF BEING EARNEST (1895). After being convicted on moral charges, Wilde spent two years in Reading Gaol, and died of syphilis in a cheap hotel in Paris a little more than two years after his release.

WILLIAMS, TENNESSEE (1911–1983)

Born in Mississippi, he spent much of his youth in St. Louis, Missouri, where his father was transferred in 1918. A prolific writer, Williams wrote 25 full-length plays and produced dozens of short plays and screenplays, two novels, a novella, 60 short stories, more than 100 poems, and an autobiography. He attended the University of Missouri, where he decided to become a playwright after seeing a production of Henrk Ibsen's GHOSTS. After his father demanded that he withdraw from school, he got a job at the International Shoe Company, where he worked with a man named Stanley Kowalski, whom he would later make a character in *A Streetcar Named Desire* (1947), for which he won a Pulitzer Prize in 1948. Often cited by critics as his best play, *The Glass Menagerie* (1944) was his first clearly autobiographical play, but many more would follow. Director Elia Kazan said of the playwright: "Everything in his life is in his plays, and everything in his plays is in his life." *The Glass Menagerie* won the New York Drama Critics' Circle Award for best play of the season in 1950. Williams's later plays also achieved popular success, among them CAT ON A HOT TIN ROOF (for which he earned a second Pulitzer Prize in 1955), *Orpheus Descending* (1957), and *Night of the Iguana* (1961), which won both a Drama Critics' Circle Award and a Tony Award. After the death from lung cancer in 1961 of his longtime love, Frank Merlo, the playwright went into a deep depression that lasted for 10 years, during which he battled addictions to prescription drugs. Williams was subsequently unable to resume his literary achievement.

WILMOT, JOHN, EARL OF ROCHESTER (1647–1680)

A leading member of the court wits who surrounded Charles I of England, Wilmot was also a lyric poet and satirist, as well as a predecessor of the neoclassic writers of early and mid-18th-century England with his social and literary verse satires. He is famous for his correspondence and discussions with a number of theologians, particularly the deist Charles Blount. He is also known for his biting satires and for writing more frankly about sex than perhaps any writer before the 20th century in such dramatizations as SODOM (1684).

APPENDIX II

REASONS FOR BANNING

The plays discussed in this book are listed below according to the charges or court decisions made in efforts to ban or to censor them. Several plays appear in two and even three categories because of the different grounds upon which they were censored; all are identified from the viewpoint of the censor and not based upon what audiences of the time or the present might see in the material. Plays banned, censored, and challenged for "sexual" reasons include those in which the appearance of the naked human body might have been suggested, as in *KISMET*, and those containing simulated sexual acts, as in *OH! CALCUTTA!* Plays banned, censored, and challenged for "social" reasons include those containing objectionable language, as well as the discussion of and inclusion of material regarding racism, abortion, birth control, adultery, homosexuality, prostitution, violence, and drug use. "Political" reasons for banning, censoring, and challenging plays include satire of politically powerful people, an unfavorable representation of an allied nation, portrayal of an inflammatory political incident, or a call for revolution. Plays banned, censored, and challenged for "religious" reasons include the mention in the play of food forbidden by the majority religion of a nation, as in *ZOO STORY*, the use of God's name in curses, the unflattering depiction of religious officials, and suggestions that the Roman Catholic Church and its officials are not infallible. In short, the reasons for which plays have been banned, censored, and challenged are diverse and often do not withstand scrutiny when judged in the cold light of reason, or years or centuries later, yet restrictions upon the performance and reading of such material have had major impact on literary, theater, and social history.

SEXUAL REASONS

Angels in America
The Beard
The Best Little Whorehouse in Texas
Corpus Christi
Desire under the Elms
The Entertainer
Hair
Kismet
The Knack
Lysistrata
Marat/Sade

Maya
Miss Saigon
Monna Vanna
Oh! Calcutta!
La Ronde
Salomé
Sapho
Second Maiden's Tragedy
Sex
The Shanghai Gesture
Simon Called Peter
Sodom
A Venetian Night

SOCIAL REASONS

Angels in America
Le Barbier de Seville
The Beard
The Best Little Whorehouse in Texas
The Boys in the Band
The Breaking Point
The Capeman
The Captive
Cat on a Hot Tin Roof
The Cenci
The Children's Hour
The Connection
Corpus Christi
Damaged Goods
La Dame Aux Camélias
Desire under the Elms
Early Morning
The Easiest Way
The Entertainer
The First Step
Ghosts
God of Vengeance
Hair
Hamlet
The Importance of Being Earnest
Jack Sheppard
Jack Straw
King Lear
La Ronde

Lips Together, Teeth Apart
Long Day's Journey into Night
Lysistrata
The Maid's Tragedy
The Man of the World
Marat/Sade
Margaret Fleming
Le Mariage de Figaro
Marion Delorme
Mary Stuart
M. Butterfly
The Merchant of Venice
The Mikado
The Misanthrope
Miss Saigon
Mrs. Warren's Profession
The Normal Heart
Oedipus Rex
One Third of a Nation
Pasquin, A Dramatic Satire
A Patriot for Me
The Pleasure Man
Polly
The President Is Dead
Press Cuttings
A Raisin in the Sun
The Respectful Prostitute
Revelry
The Revolution of Paris
Richard the Second
Roar, China!
Saved
The Second Maiden's Tragedy
The Shanghai Gesture
Strange Interlude
Tamer Tamed
Tea and Sympathy
Tobacco Road
The Toilet
Trio
The Vagina Monologues
Vectia
Victor, or the Children Take Over
A View from the Bridge
Waiting for Lefty

Waste
The Weavers
West Side Story
What Price Glory?
Who's Afraid of Virginia Woolf
Zoo Story

POLITICAL REASONS

Athalie
The Bedbug
The Beggar's Opera
The Cradle Will Rock
The Crucible
The Deputy
Edward and Eleanora
Ethiopia
A Game at Chesse
Gustavus Vasa
Hair
Hamlet
The Happy Land
Henry IV
Hernani
The Island of St. Marguerite
Thomas of Woodstock
The Three-Penny Opera
The Tragedy of King Richard II

Trip to Calais
Triple-A Plowed Under
Victoria Regina
The Weavers
What Price Glory?

RELIGIOUS REASONS

Corpus Christi
The Deputy
The Entertainer
Hannele
Henry IV
Jesus Christ, Superstar
Killing No Murder
Long Day's Journey into Night
The Martyrdom of Saint Sebastian
The Parson's Wedding
The Playboy of the Western World
The Shewing Up of Blanco Posnet
Simon Called Peter
Sir Thomas More
Sister Mary Ignatius Explains It All
 for You
The Tamer Tamed
Tartuffe
Within the Gates
Zoo Story

APPENDIX III

100 ADDITIONAL CHALLENGED, CENSORED, OR BANNED PLAYS

The following list of plays is extensive but not exhaustive, yet its length provides a clearer view of how broad the reach of the stage censor has been. In some cases, city authorities or local censorship groups demanded changes in dialogue or scenes before approving a play for performance, while in other cases performances of a play were banned entirely. Many of these plays are known to audiences only in their censored forms; readers of their early published versions may also have had access only to censored versions, but recent restorations of manuscripts have given drama fans the opportunity to know the original. A large number of plays may never be seen in their original form because the plays were banned from the stage when they were most topical, and the subject matter that made them interesting to audiences is no longer relevant. In other cases, sections that were excised have been lost. Whatever the case, these acts of censorship represent significant instances of freedom lost. The dates below indicate when a play was banned or censored.

Alasco (Sir Martin Shee, 1824)
Audience, The (Federico García Lorca, 1932)
Balance (Sarah Colvin, 2002)
Bent (Martin Sherman, 1979)
Bharatha Ratham (KP [Kunhirama Poduval], 1984)
Blood Knot (Athol Fugard, 1960)
Bon-Bons and Parades for Dolly (Dorothy Hewitt, 1974)
Brighton Beach Memoirs (Neil Simon, 1991)
Brimstone and Treacle (Dennis Potter, 1976)
Burghers of Calais, The (George Kaiser, 1938)
Calabar (Rui Guerra and Chico Buarque, 1968)
Call Me by My Rightful Name (Michael Shurtleff, 1962)
Ché (Lennox Raphael, 1969)
Comrade Mayor (Russell Heng Hiang, 2002)

Conspiracy and Tragedy of Charles Duke of Byron, The (John Chapman, 1608)
Czar, The (John O'Keefe, 1790)
Days of the Turbins, The (Mikhail Bulgakov, 1929)
Death of a Salesman, The (Arthur Miller, 1981)
Design for Living (Noel Coward, 1933)
Die Rauber (Frederich Schiller, 1793)
Doll's House, A (Henrik Ibsen, 1983)
Don Juan (Molière, 1665)
Drag, The (Mae West, 1927)
Eastward Ho (Ben Jonson, 1605)
Eater of Dreams (H. R. Lenormand, 1922)
Electra (William Shirley, 1763)
Entertaining Mr. Sloane (Joe Orton, 1965)
Fallen Angels (Noel Coward, 1925)
Family Change, The (Ivan Turgenev, 1845)
Faust (Johann Wolfgang von Goethe, 1808)
Fazio (Henry Milman, 1818)
Fences (August Wilson, 1993)
Florida Enchantment, A (Archibald Gunter, 1896)
Forest, The (Alexander Ostrovsky, 1870)
Freedom, Freedom (Millor Fernandes, 1965)
From Morn to Moonlight (George Kaiser, 1938)
Garden Party, The (Vaclav Havel, 1968)
Good, The (Chester Erskin, 1938)
Greater Tuna (Jaston Williams, Joe Sears, and Ed Howard, 1991)
Green Bay Tree, The (Mordaunt Shairp, 1933)
Hanging the President (Michelle Celeste, 1989)
Hedda Gabler (Henrik Ibsen, 1895)
Hero's Cradle, The (Dias Gomes, 1965)
Hour between Dog and Wolf, The (Daniela Fischerova, 1979)
Ideal Husband, An (Oscar Wilde, 1895)
Incubator (John Lyman and Roman Bohnen, 1932)
Incubus, The (Henry Brieux, 1910)
Jack the Giant Queller (Henry Brooke, 1749)
Juno and Ganymede (Delisle de Sales, 1770)
Kosciuzsko at Raclawice (Wladyslav Anezyc, 1870)
Let My People Come (Earl Wilson, Jr., 1976)
Lilac Lampshade (Plinio Marcos, 1978)
Lure, The (George Scarborough, 1913)
Macbird (Barbara Garson, 1967)
Marinseh's Song from beneath the Earth (Ratna Sarumpaet, 1997)
Master Harold and the Boys (Athol Fugard, 1982)
Merchant of Venice, The (William Shakespeare, 1987)
Minor, The (Samuel Foote, 1760)
Miracolo d'Amore (Martha Clarke, 1983)

Next Religion, The (Israel Zangwill, 1923)
No for an Answer (Marc Blitzstein, 1941)
Notre-Dame de Paris (Victor Hugo, 1834)
Occupations (Trevor Griffith, 1971)
Oscar Wilde (Leslie and Sewall Stokes, 1936)
Other Shore, The (Gao Zingjian, 1986)
Paméla (François de Neufchateau, 1793)
The Parisian Woman (Henry Becque, 1885)
Peer Gynt (Henrik Ibsen, 1875)
Philistines, The (Maxim Gorky, 1902)
Philotas (Samuel Daniel, 1605)
Presumed Miracle, or Cracovians and Highlanders (Stanislaw Boguslawski, 1794)
Rival Queens, The (Thomas Holcroft, 1752)
Roda Viva (Chico Buarque, 1968)
Sack of Miletos, The (Phrynichus, 494 b.c.)
Screens, The (Jean Genet, 1961)
Secret Woman, The (Eden Philpotts, 1912)
Secrets of the Harem, The (Max Goldberg, 1901)
Sejanus, His Fall (Ben Jonson, 1603)
Semi-Monde, The (Noel Coward, 1926)
Shakespeare's Dog (Leon Rooke, 1988)
Silver Tassie, The (Sean O'Casey, 1935)
Streetcar Named Desire, A (Tennessee Williams, 1954)
Sud (Julien Green, 1953)
Suicide, The (Nikolai Erdman, 1929)
Summer Moths (William Heinemann, 1898)
Tales from the Vienna Woods (Oden von Horvath, 1935)
Taste of Honey, A (Shelagh Delaney, 1958)
They Shall Not Die (John Wexley, 1934)
Three on a Gas Ring (David Osborn, 1959)
Virgin Man, The (William Francis Dugan, 1927)
Wedding Day, The (Henry Fielding, 1743)
Wernyhhora (Wlodzimierz Lewicki, 1894)
Whim, The (Lady Eglantine Wallace, 1795)
Wild Oats (John O'Keefe, 1791)
Witts (William D'Avenant, 1636)
Ye Bare and Ye Cubb (Philip Alex Bruce, 1665)
Yerma (Federico Garcia Lorca, 1936)
You Made Me a Communist (Thoppil Bhasi, 1952)
Young Woodley (John van Druten, 1925)
Zoya's Apartment (Mikhail Bulgakov, 1926)

INDEX

Note: **Boldface** page numbers indicate the primary discussion of a play.

A

AAA. *See* Agricultural
  Adjustment Administration
Abbey National Theatre,
  Dublin, Ireland 208–209,
  258–259
á Beckett, Gilbert, *The Happy
  Land* **113–116**
Abilene, Texas, censorship in
  134
abortion, discussion of
  in *Strange Interlude* 273
  in *Waste* 311
Abrams, Jacob 103
ACLU. *See* American Civil
  Liberties Union
Actors' Equity
  Miss Saigon and 182–183
  The Pleasure Man and
  211
Adams, Samuel Hopkins
  226
Adelphi Theatre, London,
  England 128, 130
Adler, Luther 232
adultery, depiction of
  in *Margaret Fleming* 158
  in *Strange Interlude* 273
agit-prop, theater of 307
Agricultural Adjustment
  Administration (AAA) 295
Agron, Salvador (Salvi) 33
AIDS crisis, portrayal of
  in *Angels in America* 2–3
  in *The Normal Heart* 189,
  190
Ain, Stewart 134
Ainsworth, William Harrison
  349
  Jack Sheppard **128–130**
Akhras, Ayat al- xi
Akins, Zoe, *The Old Maid* 50

Alasco 378
Albee, Edward 349
  A Delicate Balance 321
  Seascape 321
  stand against censorship
  57
  *Who's Afraid of Virginia
  Woolf* **319–321**
  The Zoo Story **324–327**
Albert, Prince
  in *Early Morning* 82–83
  marriage to Queen
  Victoria 168
  in *Victoria Regina*
  304–305
Aldwych Theater, London,
  England 77, 303
Alexander VI (pope) 60, 61
Alexander VII (pope) 278
Allan, Maud 241–242
All God's Chillun 80
American Century Theater,
  Washington, D.C. 27
American Civil Liberties
  Union (ACLU) 14, 103,
  145, 151, 173, 267
American Family Association
  144, 173
Amherst (Massachusetts)
  Regional High School
  316–317
Anderson, Maxwell 349
  What Price Glory? xii, 42,
  80, **317–319**
Anderson, Robert Woodruff
  349–350
  Tea and Sympathy
  279–280
Andrews, Charles O.
  196–197
Anezyc, Wladyslav, *Kosciuzsko
  at Raclawice* 379

*Angels in America: Millennium
  Approaches* xii, **2–6**
  censorship history of xii,
  3–6
  summary of 2–3
Anouilh, Jean 303
Anti-Defamation League of
  B'nai B'rith 267
anti-Semitism, charges of
  against *God of Vengeance*
  102–103
  against *The Merchant of
  Venice* 175–176
Antoine, André 70
Apollo Theater, New York
  City 102
Apreece, Mr. 9
Arbuthnot, John 215
Archer, William 47, 241
Arent, Arthur 350
  Ethiopia **91–93**
  One-Third of a Nation
  194–198
  Triple-A Plowed Under
  294–297
Aristophanes 350
  Lysistrata xii–xiii,
  148–152
  The Wasps 150
The Armorer 230
Artaud, Antonin 156
Arts Theatre, Cambridge,
  England 142
Asch, Sholem 350–351
  God of Vengeance
  101–103
Athalie **6–8**
  censorship history of 7
  summary of 6–7
Atkinson, J. Brooks 38–39
Auden, W. H. 125
Audience 378

audience infiltration 51, 53
Australia, censorship in
 of *The Boys in the Band*
 27–28
 of *La Ronde* 237, 238
Austria, censorship in
 of *The Council of Love*
 61–62
 of *Le Mariage de Figaro*
 161, 162
The Author **8–10**
 censorship history of 9
 summary of 8
Les Avariés. See Damaged Goods
Ayers, Harriet Hubbard 244
Ayrton, A. S. 114

B

Bailey, Josiah W. 196
Baker, Dorothy Dodds 351
 Trio **290–292**
Baker, Howard 351
 Trio **290–292**
Baker, Jacob 92
Baker, Paul 148
Bakst, Léon 166
Balance 378
Baldwin, Roger 103
Balzac, Honoré de 163
Banton, Joab H. 80–81, 170,
 253
Baraka, Imamu Amiri 351
 The Toilet **287–289**
*Le Barbier de Seville (The
 Barber of Seville)* **10–12**
 censorship history of 11
 summary of 10–11
Barnes, Clive 193
Barrie, J. M. 30, 141
Baxter, George 71
Bay Area Theater Critics
 Awards, for *Angels in
 America* 3
Baylor University, Texas 148
The Beard **12–14**
 censorship history of
 13–14
 summary of 12–13
Beardsley, Aubrey 239
Beaumarchais, Pierre
 Augustin Caron de 352
 Le Barbier de Seville
 10–12
 Le Mariage de Figaro 11,
 160–162

Beaumont, Francis, *The
 Maid's Tragedy* **152–154**,
 249
Beck, Julian 52, 54
Beckett, Samuel 193
Becque, Henry, *The Parisian
 Woman* 380
The Bedbug **14–18**
 censorship history of
 16–18
 summary of 15–16
Bedlam Theatre, Edinburgh,
 Scotland 57
Beecham, Thomas 241
The Beggar's Opera **18–21**,
 282
 censorship history of
 20–21
 summary of 18–20
Belasco, David 86
Belasco Theatre, New York
 City 193, 292
Bennett, Richard 70
Bent 378
Bentley, Eric 238
Bentley, Joanne 197
Benton, Anthony 58
Bernays, Edward L. 70
Bernhardt, Sarah 240
Bernstein, Leonard, *West Side
 Story* xi, **314–317**
*The Best Little Whorehouse in
 Texas* **21–24**
 censorship history of
 23–24
 summary of 22–23
Bharatha Ratham 378
Bhasi, Thoppil, *You Made Me
 a Communist* 380
Biberman, Herbert 232–233
Billy the Kid 12
Biltmore Theatre, New York
 City 93, 211–212, 296
bin Laden, Osama 57
Bird, John 61
Birdwood, Lady Dowager
 Jane (Graham) 61
Blackstone Theater,
 Chicago, Illinois 286
Blitzstein, Marc 352
 *The Cradle Will Rock: A
 Play in Music* **63–65**
 No for an Answer 380
 and *The Three-Penny
 Opera* 284

Block, Haskell 237
Blood Knot 378
The Blue Room 236
Blume, Judy 57
Bogart, Humphrey 38
Boguslawski, Stanislaw,
 Presumed Miracle 380
Bohnen, Roman, *Incubator*
 379
Bon-Bons and Parades for Dolly
 378
Bond, Edward 352
 Early Morning **82–85**,
 247
 Saved xii, **245–247**
Bonjour, Casimir 120
Bonney, William (Billy the
 Kid) 12
Booth, Edwin 235
Borah, William E. 195, 197
Bordman, Gerald 178
Borel, Petrus 120
Boston, Massachusetts,
 censorship in
 of *The Children's Hour* 49
 of *Desire under the Elms*
 81
 of *The Easiest Way* 86
 of *Within the Gates*
 323–324
 of *Margaret Fleming* 160
 of *Maya* 171
 of *Sister Mary Ignatius
 Explains It All for You*
 267
 of *Strange Interlude* 274
 of *Waiting for Lefty* 309
 of *Who's Afraid of Virginia
 Woolf* 321
Boston Coalition for
 Freedom of Expression
 (BCFE) 24
Boubil, Alain 352–353
 Miss Saigon **181–183**
Bourdet, Edouard 353
 The Captive **37–40**
Bowdler, Harriet 111, 118
Bowdler, Thomas 111, 118
Boyd, Ernest 171
The Boys in the Band xii,
 24–28
 censorship history of
 26–28
 summary of 24–26

Brady, "Diamond" Jim 87
Brady, William A. 80, 261
Breadalbane, John Campbell, marquess of 229
The Breaking Point **28–33**
  censorship history of 30–33
  summary of 29–30
Brecht, Bertolt 353
  The Three-Penny Opera xii, **282–285**
Brereton, Austin 47
Bridgeport, Connecticut, censorship in 309
Brieux, Eugene 353–354
  Damaged Goods **69–71**
Brieux, Henry, *The Incubus* 379
Brighton Beach Memoirs 378
Brimstone and Treacle 378
Brisbane, Arthur 244
Britain. *See* England; Scotland
Britannia Theatre, London, England 229
British Museum, secret collection of 270, 300
Broadhurst Theatre, New York City 305
Brook, Peter 157
Brooke, Henry 354
  Gustavus Vasa 88, **103–105**
  Jack the Giant Queller 379
Browder, Earl 295, 296
Brown, John Mason 321
Browning, Robert 46
Bruce, Philip Alex, *Ye Bare and Ye Cubb* 380
Brustein, Robert 288
Buarque, Chico
  Calabar 378
  Roda Viva 380
Buc, Sir George 249, 281
Buckingham, duke of 97
Buckstone, John Baldwin 128
Bulgakov, Mikhail
  The Days of the Turbins 379
  Zoya's Apartment 380
The Burghers of Calais 378
Butler, Michael 107
Byrd, Harry 197

C
La Cage aux Folles 27
Calabar 378
Caldwell, Erskine 354
  Tobacco Road **285–287**
Caldwell, Raymond 5
California, censorship in
  of *Desire under the Elms* 81
  of *Hair* 107–108
  of *The Merchant of Venice* 175
  of *The Toilet* 288–289
  of *Waiting for Lefty* 309
Call Me by My Rightful Name 378
Cambridge Festival Theatre, England 233
Camille, or, the Fate of a Coquette 73
Canada, censorship in
  of *The Merchant of Venice* 176
  of *Tobacco Road* 286–287
cannibalism, depiction of, in *Early Morning* 82–83
The Capeman xii, **33–37**
  censorship history of 35–36
  summary of 33–35
The Captain's Tiger 57
The Captive **37–40**
  censorship history of 38–39, 253
  summary of 37–38
The Capuchin 294, 357
Catherine of Aragon 262
Catholic Church
  censorship encouraged by
    of *Corpus Christi* 56
    of *The Council of Love* 61–62
    of *Within the Gates* 323–324
    of *The Martyrdom of Saint Sebastian* 166
    of *Sister Mary Ignatius Explains It All for You* 266–268
    of *Tartuffe* 277–278
    of *The Vagina Monologues* 299
  role in Holocaust 74–76
  satire of 95–96

Cat on a Hot Tin Roof **40–44**
  censorship history of 42–43
  summary of 40–42
Cavendish, William 9
Celeste, Michelle, *Hanging the President* 379
The Celluloid Closet (Russo) 51
The Cenci **44–48**
  censorship history of 46–47
  summary of 44–46
Cerf, Bennett 147
Chamberlain, John 96
Chapman, John 42
  The Conspiracy and Tragedy of Charles Duke of Byron 379
Charles I (king of England) 153
Charles II (king of England) 153, 199, 269
Charles X (king of France) 110–111, 121, 164
Charles, Prince 97
Charles Playhouse, Boston 267
Chattanooga, Tennessee, censorship in 108–109
Ché 378
Cheadle Hulme Amateur Dramatic Society (CHADS) Theatre Company 321
Cheetah, New York City 107
Chesterfield, Lord 105
Chesterton, G. K. 32
Chetwynd, William 88, 104, 200
Chicago 226
Chicago, Illinois, censorship in
  of *The Children's Hour* 50
  of *The Respectful Prostitute* 225
  of *Tobacco Road* 286
Children's Aid Society 43
The Children's Hour **48–51**
  censorship history of 39, 49–51
  summary of 48–49
Christian Coalition 144, 173
Cibber, Colley 153

Cincinnati, Ohio, censorship in xi
Circle in the Square, New York City 147
Citizens Demanding Standards, Inc. (CDS) 190
City of London Theatre, London, England 129
Clare, Janet 110, 118, 131, 138, 139, 263, 264, 281, 282
Clarke, Martha, *Miracolo d'Amore* 379
class issues, censorship on grounds of
of *Le Barbier de Seville* 11
of *Hamlet* 111
of *Le Mariage de Figaro* 161–162
Clurman, Harold 309
Cobb County, Georgia, censorship in 144–145, 173
Cobbold, David 76–77, 84, 91, 143, 157, 246
Cohn, Roy M. 2
Cohn, Ruby 53
College of New Rochelle 299
colleges and universities, censorship in
of *Angels in America* 4–5
of *The Best Little Whorehouse in Texas* 23–24
of *Corpus Christi* 58
of *Long Day's Journey into Night* 148
of *Sister Mary Ignatius Explains It All for You* 266–268, 268
of *The Vagina Monologues* 299
Colman, George 216
Coloma, Don Carlos 97–98
Colton, John 354
The Shanghai Gesture **254–257**
Colvin, Sarah, *Balance* 378
Comedic Theatre, New York City 171
comédie de caractère 277
Comédie-Française, Paris, France 120, 235
Comedy Theatre, London, England 43, 280, 307

Common-Sense (newspaper) 201–202
communism, support for
in *Triple-A Plowed Under* 295
in *Waiting for Lefty* 307–309
Comrade Mayor 378
Comstock, Anthony 188, 244
Comstock Act of 1873 (U.S.) 151
Comyns-Carr, Philip 185
The Connection **51–54**
censorship history of 52–54
summary of 51–52
Connection Company v. Regents of the University of the State of New York 54
Connelly, Terence 323
Conolly, L. W. 126
Conrad, Joseph 30, 31, 141
The Conspiracy and Tragedy of Charles Duke of Byron 379
Conway, Jack 212
Cooper, Frederick Fox 129
Corpus Christi **55–59**
censorship history of 56–58
summary of 55–56
Cort, John 253
Cort Theatre, New York City 225
The Council of Love: A Celestial Tragedy in Five Acts **59–63**
censorship history of 60–62
summary of 59–60
Court Theatre, London, England 115
Courvoisier, François Benjamin 128–129
Covent Garden, London, England 88, 89, 155, 192, 203, 230
Coward, Noel
Design for Living 379
Fallen Angels 379
The Semi-Monde 380
The Cradle Will Rock: A Play in Music **63–65**
censorship history of 64–65
summary of 63–64

Crayle, Benjamin 270
Crazy for You 317
crime, depiction of, censorship on grounds of 128–130
Crist, Judith 53
Cromwell, Oliver 203
Crowley, Mart 354–355
The Boys in the Band xii, **24–28**
The Crucible **65–68**
censorship history of 67–68
summary of 66–67
Cumberland, Richard 355
Richard the Second **229–231**
Cumberland Valley High School, Harrisburg, Pennsylvania 68
Cushman, Howard, *Triple-A Plowed Under* **294–297**
The Czar 379

D

Daly, Arnold 188
Damaged Goods **69–71**
censorship history of 70–71
summary of 69–70
La dame aux camélias **71–74**
censorship history of 72–74
summary of 71–72
Daniel, Samuel, *Philotas* 380
D'Annunzio, Gabriele 355
The Martyrdom of Saint Sebastian **165–167**
Daudet, Alphonse 243
Daugherty, Harry 226
D'Avenant, William 199
Witts 380
Davenport, Jean 73
Dawson, Sir Douglas 31
The Days of the Turbins 379
The Death of a Salesman 379
Debussy, Claude 165
De Grazia, Edward 151
Delaney, Shelagh, *A Taste of Honey* 380
De La Warr, Lord 73, 128
A Delicate Balance 321
D'Entremont, James 24

The Deputy **74–78**
  censorship history of xii,
    76–78
  summary of 74–76
Deschamps, Antoni 163–164
Deschamps, Emile 163
Design for Living 379
Desire under the Elms **78–81**
  censorship history of
    80–81
  summary of 78–80
Detroit, Michigan,
  censorship in 268
Deutsches Theater, Berlin,
  Germany 237, 314
Diaghilev, Sergey 166
DiCarlo, Joseph 288
Dilke, Sir Charles 310
Dirck, Edwin L. 266, 267
Disraeli, Benjamin 82–83
Dobson, Michael 175
Dodd, Charles H. 170
A Doll's House 379
Don Juan 379
Donne, William 72, 73, 115,
  130
Donohue, William 56
Dostoevsky, Fyodor 16
Douglas, Alfred 124, 239,
  242
Downes, Randolph 227
D'Oyly Carte, Helen 179
The Drag 38, 379
Drama Critics Circle awards.
  See New York Drama
  Critics Circle awards
*Die Dreigroschenoper. See The
  Three-Penny Opera*
drug addiction, depiction of,
  in *The Connection* 51–52
Drury Lane Theatre,
  London, England 9,
  126–127, 168, 203
Druten, John van, *Young
  Woodley* 380
Ducasse, Roger 165
Dugan, William Francis, *The
  Virgin Man* 380
Dumas, Alexandre (the
  Older) 163
Dumas, Alexandre (the
  Younger) 355
  La dame aux camélias
    71–74
The Dunciad (Pope) 20

Durang, Christopher 57,
  355
  *Sister Mary Ignatius
    Explains It All for You*
    xii, **264–268**
Dysfunctional Theatre
  Company 270

E

Early, Steven 92
Early Morning **82–85,** 247
  censorship history of
    83–84
  summary of 82–83
The Easiest Way **85–87**
  censorship history of
    86–87
  summary of 85–86
Eastward Ho 379
Eater of Dreams 379
Eden, Anthony 92
Eden Theatre, New York
  City 193
Edward, Prince of Wales
  115
Edward and Eleanora **87–89**
  censorship history of
    88–89
  summary of 87–88
Eels, George 254
Electra 379
Eliot, George 72
Elizabeth I (queen of
  England) 117, 118, 167,
  263, 290
Elkins, Hillard 193
Elsom, John 170, 185
Empire Theatre, New York
  City 38
Engel, Edward 94
England, censorship in
  of *Athalie* 7
  of *The Author* 9
  of *The Beggar's Opera*
    20–21
  of *The Breaking Point*
    30–33
  of *Cat on a Hot Tin Roof*
    43
  of *The Cenci* 46–47
  of *Corpus Christi* 57–58
  of *The Council of Love* 61
  of *Damaged Goods* 70, 71
  of *La dame aux camélias*
    72–73

of *The Deputy* 76–77
of *Desire under the Elms*
  81
of *Early Morning* 83–84
of *Edward and Eleanora*
  88–89
of *The Entertainer* 90–91
of *The First Step* 94–95
of *A Game at Chesse*
  97–98
of *Ghosts* 99–100
of *Gustavus Vasa* 104–105
of *Hamlet* 110, 111
of *Hannele* 113
The Happy Land 115–116
of *Henry IV, Part 2*
  117–118
of *Hernani* 121
of *The Importance of Being
  Earnest* 125
of *The Island of St.
  Marguerite* 127
of *Jack Sheppard* 128–130
of *Jack Straw* 131–132
Joint Select Committee
  on Censorship and 32
of *Killing No Murder*
  135–136
of *King Lear* 139
of *Kismet* 141
of *The Knack* 142–143
of *Lysistrata* 150–151
of *The Maid's Tragedy*
  153
of *The Man of the World*
  155
of *Marat/Sade* 157
of *Mary Stuart* 168–169
of *Maya* 170–171
of *The Merchant of Venice*
  175
of *The Mikado* 178
of *Monna Vanna* 185
of *Mrs. Warren's Profession*
  187–188
of *Oedipus Rex* 192
of *Oh! Calcutta!* 193–194
of *The Parson's Wedding*
  199–200
of *Pasquin, A Dramatic
  Satire on the Times*
  201–203
of *A Patriot for Me*
  205–206
of *Polly* 215–216

of *Press Cuttings* 219–220
of *The Revolution of Paris*
228–229
of *Richard the Second*
230–231
of *Roar, China!* 233
of *Salomé* 240–241,
241–242
of *Saved* 246–247
of *The Second Maiden's
Tragedy* 249–250
of *The Shewing Up of
Blanco Posnet* 258, 259
of *Sir Thomas More* 263
of *Sodom* 270
of *The Tamer Tamed* 276
of *Tea and Sympathy*
280
Theatres Act of 1737 and
xiii, 20–21, 88, 104,
202–203
Theatres Bill of 1968 and
84, 247
of *Thomas of Woodstock*
281–282
of *The Tragedy of King
Richard the Second* 290
of *Trip to Calais* 293–294
of *Vectia* 301
of *A Venetian Night* 302
of *Victor, or the Children
Take Over* 303–304
of *Victoria Regina* 305
of *A View from the Bridge*
306–307
of *Waste* 311
of *Who's Afraid of Virginia
Woolf* 321
Ensler, Eve 356
The Vagina Monologues
297–300
The Entertainer **89–91**
censorship history of
90–91
summary of 90
Entertaining Mr. Sloane 379
Erdman, Nikolai, *The Suicide*
380
Erker, Kim 35
Ernani 120
Erskin, Chester, *The Good*
379
Ethiopia **91–93**
censorship history of
92–93

summary of 91–92
European Court of Human
Rights 61–62
Evans, Mary Ann 72
Evergreen Theater, New
York City 14

F

Fall, Albert 227
Fallen Angels 379
The Family Change 379
Family Shakespeare (Bowdler
and Bowdler) 118
Famous Players–Lasky
Motion Picture Company
38
Faust 379
Fazio 379
Federal Communications
Commission (FCC) 326
Federal Theater Project
(FTP) 92
Arent, Arthur, and 350
and *The Cradle Will Rock*
64
defunding of 197
and *Ethiopia* 91, 92
and *One-Third of a Nation*
196
and *Triple-A Plowed Under*
295–296
Fences 379
Ferlinghetti, Lawrence 14
Fernandes, Millor, *Freedom,
Freedom* 379
Fèvrier, Henry 165
Fielding, Henry 20, 356
*Pasquin, A Dramatic
Satire on the Times*
200–203
The Wedding Day 380
Fillmore Auditorium, San
Francisco 13
Filon, M. 94
Findlater, Richard 84
The First Step **93–95**
censorship history of
94–95
summary of 93–94
Fischerova, Daniela, *The
Hour between Dog and Wolf*
379
Fitch, Clyde 356
Sapho **242–245**
Fitz-Gerald, W. G. 178

Flanagan, Hallie
and *The Cradle Will Rock*
64
and *Ethiopia* 92
and *Model Tenement* 286
and *One-Third of a Nation*
196, 197
on *Roar, China!* 231–232
and *Triple-A Plowed Under*
296
Fletcher, John 356–357
The Maid's Tragedy
152–154, 249
The Tamer Tamed
274–276
Florida, censorship in 5, 151
Florida Atlantic University
58
A Florida Enchantment 379
Flynn, Raymond L. 267
The Fool's Revenge 235
Foote, Samuel 357
The Author **8–10**
charges of homosexuality
against 294
and *The Man of the World*
155
The Minor 379
Trip to Calais xii, **292–294**
Forbes, Charles 227
Ford's Theater Society,
Washington, D. C. 217
The Forest 379
Fountain, Fritz 151
Fowell, Frank 141, 155, 185,
188, 192, 199, 200, 203,
215, 220, 290, 302
France, censorship in
of *Athalie* 7
of *Le Barbier de Seville* 11
Charter of Abolition of
Censorship 235
of *Hamlet* 110–111
of *Hernani* 120–121
July 1794 revolution and
180–181
July 1830 revolution and
121, 164
of *Le Mariage de Figaro*
161–162
of *Marion de Lorme* 164
of *The Misanthrope*
180–181
of *Le roi s'amuse* 234–235
of *Tartuffe* 277–278

Francois I (king of France) 233–234

Franz Joseph II (emperor of Austria-Hungary) 203

Freedom, Freedom 379

Freie Buhne Theater Association, Berlin, Germany 314

From Morn to Moonlight 379

FTP. *See* Federal Theater Project

Fugard, Athol
  Blood Knot 378
  The Captain's Tiger 57
  Master Harold and the Boys 379

Fulton Theater, New York City 70

funding withdrawal, as censorship mechanism
  for *Angels in America* 4, 5
  for *Corpus Christi* 58
  for *Lips Together, Teeth Apart* 145
  for *Sister Mary Ignatius Explains It All for You* 266

Furnivall, F. J. 46

G

Gaffey, Megan 134

Gaiety Theatre, Manchester, England 220

A Game at Chesse **95–98**
  censorship history of 96–98
  summary of 95–96

gang warfare, depiction of
  in *The Capeman* 33–35
  in *West Side Story* 314–316

Gantillon, Simon 357
  Maya **169–171**

García Lorca, Federico
  Audience 378
  Yerma 380

The Garden Party 379

Garland, Hamlin 42, 160, 319

Garnett, Edward 357
  The Breaking Point **28–33**

Garrick, David 9

Garrick Theatre, New York City 188

Garson, Barbara, *Macbird* 379

Gascoigne, Bamber 142

Gaskill, William 83, 246

Gassner, John 42, 53, 67, 284, 321

Gates, Ruggles 300

Gautier, Théophile 120

Gay, John 357
  The Beggar's Opera **18–21,** 282
  Polly **212–216**

Gelber, Jack 358
  The Connection **51–54**

Genet, Jean, *The Screens* 380

George II (king of Britain) 215

George III (king of Britain) 139

George V (king of Britain) 141

Georgia, censorship in
  of *Lips Together, Teeth Apart* 144–145
  of *M. Butterfly* 173

Germany, censorship in
  of *The Bedbug* 18
  of *The Council of Love* 60–61
  of *The Deputy* 76
  of *Ghosts* 99
  of *La Ronde* 237–238
  of *The Three-Penny Opera* 284
  of *The Weavers* 313–314

Gershwin, George and Ira 317

Ghosts **98–101**
  censorship history of 99–100
  summary of 98–99

Gielgud, John 125

Gierow, Karl Ragner 147

Gilbert, Jonathan 58

Gilbert, William S. 358
  The Happy Land **113–116**
  The Mikado xii, **176–179**
  stand against censorship 32
  The Wicked World 114

Ginsberg, Allen 53

Girl Crazy 317

Gish, Lillian 323

Gladstone, William Ewart 82–83, 114

Glen Ellyn, Illinois, censorship in 268

Globe Theatre, London, England 97, 290

God of Vengeance **101–103**
  censorship history of 102–103
  summary of 101–102

Goethe, Johann Wolfgang von, *Faust* 379

Goldberg, Max, *The Secrets of the Harem* 380

Goldman, Emma 86, 103

Goldman, Scott 317

Goldwyn, Samuel 50

Gomes, Dias, *The Hero's Cradle* 379

Gonzaga University, Washington 299

Gonzalez-Intal, Anna Miren 298

The Good 379

A Good Bad Woman 80

Goodman, Jules Eckert 358
  Simon Called Peter **260–261**

Gorky, Maxim, *The Philistines* 380

Got fun nekomeh. See God of Vengeance

Grafton, Charles Fitzroy, duke of 104, 215, 270

Graham, Bill 13

Graham, Michael 299

Graham, Robert A. 77

Grannis, Chandler 290

Granville-Barker, Harley 358
  Waste 32, **310–312**

Gray, Terence 233

Great Depression
  depiction of 64, 296
  theater during. *See* Federal Theater Project

Greater Tuna 379

Greece, censorship in 151

Green, Jonathan 270

Green, Julien, *Sud* 380

The Green Bay Tree 379

Greenwich Village Theater, New York City 80

Gregory, Lady Augusta 258–259

Grein, J. T. 100, 311

Griffith, Arthur 209

Griffith, Trevor, *Occupations* 380
Grobman, Arnold B. 266
Guernsey, Otis, Jr. 36
Guerra, Rui, *Calabar* 378
Gunter, Archibald, *A Florida Enchantment* 379
Gustavus Vasa **103–105**
   censorship history of 88, 104–105
   summary of 104

H

Haight, Anne 290
Haines, J. T. 129
Hair: The American Tribal Love-Rock Musical xii, **106–109**
   censorship history of 107–109
   summary of 106–107
Hamer, Dick 28
Hamilton, Clayton 319
Hamlet **109–112**
   censorship history of xii, 110–111
   summary of 109–110
Hammarskjold, Dag 53, 147
Hammerstein, Oscar 241
Hammett, Dashiell 48
Hammond, W. J. 168
Hanging the President 379
Hannele: A Dream Poem in Two Acts **112–113**
   censorship history of 113
   summary of 112–113
Hansberry, Lorraine 223, 359
   A Raisin in the Sun **221–223**
The Happy Journey from Trenton to Camden 225
The Happy Land **113–116**
   censorship history of 115–116
   summary of 114–115
Harben, Niloufer 84
Harding, Warren G. 226–227
Hardy, Thomas 185
Hare, David 236
Harlow, Jean 12
Harris, Thomas 46, 155
Harrison, Frederic 31

Hauptmann, Gerhart 359
   Hannele: A Dream Poem in Two Acts **112–113**
   The Weavers **312–314**
Hausset, Madame de 162
Havel, Vaclav, *The Garden Party* 379
Hayes, Helen 305
Haymarket Theatre, London, England 31, 129, 293, 294
Haynes, James, *Mary Stuart* **167–169**
Hays, Will 50
Hearst, William Randolph 244
Hedda Gabler 379
Heinemann, William 359
   The First Step **93–95**
   Summer Moths 380
Heinstadt, John 24
Hellman, Lillian 359–360
   The Children's Hour 39, **48–51**
   on *The Connection* 53
Hemmings, Frederic 180
Henderson, Jeffrey 150
Henry, Stephen 57
Henry III (king of England) 87
Henry IV, Part 2 **116–119**
   censorship history of 117–118
   summary of 117
Henry VIII (king of England) 262
Herbert, Sir Henry 96, 276
Hernani **119–122**
   censorship history of 120–121
   summary of 119–120
Herne, James A. 360
   Margaret Fleming xii, **158–160**
Heron, Matilda 73
The Hero's Cradle 379
Hertford, Francis Seymour Conway, marquis of 155, 293
Hervey, Augustus John 293
Hewitt, Dorothy, *Bon-Bons and Parades for Dolly* 378
Hewitt, F. C. 217
Hiang, Russell Heng, *Comrade Mayor* 378

Hills, Newell 244
His Majesty's Theatre, London, England 192, 258
Hoare, Sir Samuel 92
Hobson, Harold 84
Hochhuth, Rolf 360
   The Deputy xii, **74–78**
Hoffman, William 57
Holcroft, Thomas, *The Rival Queens* 380
Holda, William M. 5
Holinshed, Ralph 131
Holloway, Richard 57
Holocaust, discussion of, in *The Deputy* 74–76
Holroyd, Michael 220
homosexuality, censorship on grounds of
   of *Angels in America* 4
   of *The Captive* 38
   of *Cat on a Hot Tin Roof* 43
   of *Corpus Christi* 56
   of *The Importance of Being Earnest* 125
   of *M. Butterfly* 173
   of *The Martyrdom of Saint Sebastian* 166
   of *The Normal Heart* 190
   of *A Patriot for Me* 205–206
   of *Sodom* 270
   of *The Toilet* 288–289
   of *Trio* 291–292
   of *A View from the Bridge* 307
   of *The Zoo Story* 326
homosexuality, charges of
   against Foote, Samuel 294
   against Wilde, Oscar 124–125, 242
homosexuality, portrayal of
   in *Angels in America* 2–3
   in *The Boys in the Band* 24–26
   in *The Captive* 37–38
   in *Cat on a Hot Tin Roof* 41
   in *The Children's Hour* 48–49
   in *Corpus Christi* 55–56
   in *God of Vengeance* 102
   in *Lips Together, Teeth Apart* 144

in *The Normal Heart* 189
in *A Patriot for Me*
204–205
in *Tea and Sympathy* 279
in *The Toilet* 287–288
in *Trio* 291
Hook, Theodore 360
Killing No Murder
135–136
Hopkins, Harry 92, 197
Horchow, Roger 317
Hornblow, Arthur, Jr. 37
Horniman, Annie 259
Horvath, Oden von, *Tales
from the Vienna Woods* 380
*The Hour between Dog and
Wolf* 379
Hourglass Group 212
Houseman, John 64, 65
House Un-American
Activities Committee
(HUAC) 66, 67, 68
Housman, A. E. 305
Housman, Laurence
360–361
Victoria Regina **304–305**
Howard, Ed, *Greater Tuna*
379
Howard, Sidney, *They
Knew What They Wanted*
42, 319
Howe, Sir Geoffrey 61
Howells, William Dean 160
HUAC. *See* House Un-
American Activities
Committee
Hughes, Langston 221
Hugo, Victor 361
Hernani **119–122**
Marion de Lorme
162–164
Notre-Dame de Paris 380
Le roi s'amuse **233–236**
before Tribunal du
Commerce 235
Hull, Thomas 89
Hungary, censorship in, of
La Ronde 237
Hunt, Leigh 44, 46
Hunzinger, Stefani 326
Hwang, David Henry 57,
361
M. Butterfly 144,
171–174
Hyde, Anne 110

I
Ibsen, Henrik 361
A Doll's House 379
Ghosts **98–101**
Hedda Gabler 379
Peer Gynt 380
An Ideal Husband 124, 379
Imperial Theatre, London,
England 311
*The Importance of Being
Earnest* **122–125**
censorship history of xii,
123–125
summary of 122–123
incest, censorship against
depiction of
in *The Cenci* 46
in *Desire under the Elms*
81
in *Oedipus Rex* 192
in *A View from the Bridge*
306
Incubator 379
The Incubus 379
Independent Theatre
Society, England 94, 100,
187
Index of Forbidden Books
(Vatican) 166
Indiana, censorship in, of
Hair 107
Indiana University-Purdue
University in Fort Wayne
58
Iona College, New York 299
Ireland, censorship in
of *The Playboy of the
Western World* 207–209
of *The Shewing Up of
Blanco Posnet* 259
Ireland, William Henry 139
Islamic fundamentalists, on
Corpus Christi 57–58
The Island of St. Marguerite
125–127
censorship history of xii,
126–127
summary of 126
Italian futurism 16

J
Jack Sheppard **128–130**
censorship history of
128–130
summary of 128

Jackson, William 294
Jack Straw **130–132**
censorship history of
131–132
summary of 131
Jack the Giant Queller 379
James, Henry 32
James II (king of England)
97, 98, 110, 138–139
jazz play 53
Jellicoe, Ann 361–362
The Knack **141–143**
Jesus Christ Superstar
132–135
censorship history of
133–134
summary of 132–133
Jews, plays about 102. *See
also* anti-Semitism
John Bull's Other Island 220
Johnson, Samuel 20, 105
Jones, LeRoi. *See* Baraka,
Imamu Amiri
Jonson, Ben
Eastward Ho 379
Sejanus, His Fall 380
Joseph II (king of Austria)
162
Joseph Papp's Public
Theater, New York City
190
Joyce, James 274
Juno and Ganymede 379

K
Kaiser, George
The Burghers of Calais 378
From Morn to Moonlight
379
Kaufman, George S. 50
Kazan, Elia 42
Keable, Robert 260, 261
Keefe, Maureen C. 23
Kellenberg Memorial High
School, Uniondale, New
York 134
Kelley, Edward 286
Kemble, Charles 126–127
Kemble, John Mitchell 7,
168, 229
Kentucky, censorship in 68
Kilgore College, Texas 4–5
Killigrew, Thomas 362
The Parson's Wedding
198–200

Killing No Murder **135–136**
  censorship history of
    135–136
  summary of 135
King, Larry L. 362
  article for *Playboy*
    magazine 22
  *The Best Little Whorehouse
    in Texas* **21–24**
King Lear **136–140**
  censorship history of
    138–139
  summary of 137–138
*The King's Amusement. See Le
  roi s'amuse*
King's Men theatrical
  company, London,
  England 276
Kingston, Elizabeth
  Chudleigh, duchess of
  293–294
Kinsman, Frank 107
Kirkland, Jack 285
Kismet **140–141**
  censorship history of xii,
    141
  summary of 140
Kitchener, Horatio Herbert
  219–220
The Knack **141–143**
  censorship history of
    142–143
  summary of 142
Knickerbocker Theatre, New
  York City 141
Knoblock, Edward 362
  Kismet xii, **140–141**
  Simon Called Peter
    260–261
Kosciuzsko at Raclawice 379
Kostelanetz, Richard 326
KP (Kunhirama Poduval),
  Bharatha Ratham 378
Kramer, Larry 362–363
  The Normal Heart
    189–191
Krause, Marshall 14
Krummell, John 27
Krzesinski, Donna 35
Krzesinski, Tony 35
Kushner, Tony 363
  Angels in America xii,
    2–6
  on *Corpus Christi* 57

L

Lady Windermere's Fan 240
LaGrange, Texas, censorship
  in 22
Laguna Beach, California,
  censorship in 309
Lake City, Florida,
  censorship in 151
Lane, Esther Porter 197
Lane, Samuel 229
Larpent, John 135–136, 230
Lathom, Edward Bootle-
  Wilbraham, earl of 187
Laufe, Abe 288, 309
Laurents, Arthur, *West Side
  Story* xi, **314–317**
Laval, Pierre 92
Law, Hugh 185
Lawrence, D. H. 30
Lee, William C. 58
Lenin, Vladimir 17
Lennon, John 193
Lenormand, H. R., *Eater of
  Dreams* 379
Lenox Hill Theatre, New
  York City 47
lesbianism, theme of. *See also*
  homosexuality
    in *The Captive* 37–38
    in *The Children's Hour*
      48–49
    in *God of Vengeance* 102
    in *Trio* 291
Let My People Come 379
Leveson-Gower, Francis 121
Levin, Meyer, *Model
  Tenement* 286
Levinson, Harry A. 151
Lewes, George Henry
  72–73
Lewicki, Wlodzimierz,
  Wernyhhora 380
Lewys, Georges 273–274
Licensing Act of 1737
  (England). *See* Theatres
  Act of 1737
Das Liebenkonzil (film)
  61–62
Lilac Lampshade 379
Lips Together, Teeth Apart
  143–145
  censorship history of
    144–145, 173
  summary of 143–144
Little, Charles 27

Little Theatre in the
  Haymarket, London,
  England 135, 150, 155,
  216
Litton, Marie 115–116
Litvinoff, Maxim 92
Liveright, Horace 38, 273
Living Newspaper plays
  Ethiopia **91–93**
  One-Third of a Nation
    194–198
  Triple-A Plowed Under
    294–297
Living Theatre, New York
  City 52–54
Longacre Theatre, New
  York City 309
Long Day's Journey into Night
  146–148
  censorship history of
    147–148
  summary of 146–147
Loras College, Idaho 299
Los Angeles, censorship in
  of *Desire under the Elms*
    81
  of *Hair* 107–108
  of *The Merchant of Venice*
    175
  of *The Toilet* 288–289
Loth, David 270
Louis III (king of France)
  163, 164
Louis XIV (king of France)
  6, 126, 277
Louis XV (king of France)
  11
Louis XVI (king of France)
  161–162
Louis-Philippe (king of
  France) 229, 234
Lowe, Robert 114
Lowell, James Russell 46
The Lure 379
Lyman, John, *Incubator* 379
Lysistrata **148–152**
  censorship history of
    xii–xiii, 150–151
  summary of 149–150
Lyttleton, George 88, 201
Lyubimov, Yuri 157–158

M

Macbird 379
MacDermot, Galt 107

Macklin, Charles 363
The Man of the World
154–155
MacOwan, Michael 311
Macready, William Charles
46, 168, 169
Madame Butterfly (opera)
181. *See also M. Butterfly*
Madden, Richard J. 80, 81
Maeterlinck, Maurice 363
Monna Vanna **184–186**
The Maid's Tragedy **152–154**
censorship history of
153, 249
summary of 152–153
Maiklejohn, J. M. D. 111
Mailer, Norman
on *The Beard* 13
on *The Connection* 53
Maintenon, Madame 6
Malaysia, censorship in, of
The Vagina Monologues 298
Malina, Judith 52, 54
Malone, Edmund 139
Maltby, Richard, Jr., *Miss
Saigon* **181–183**
Manhattan Theatre Club
(MTC), New York City
56–57
Mann, Theodore 217
Man of La Mancha 268
The Man of the World
154–155
censorship history of
155
summary of 154–155
Marat/Sade **156–158**
censorship history of
157–158
summary of 156–157
Marcos, Plinio, *Lilac
Lampshade* 379
Margaret Fleming **158–160**
censorship history of xii,
159–160
summary of 158–159
Le Mariage de Figaro
160–162
censorship history of 11,
161–162
summary of 161
Marie-Thérèse (queen of
France) 6
*Marinseh's Song from beneath
the Earth* 379

Marion de Lorme **162–164**
censorship history of
163–164
summary of 163
Mark Hellinger Theatre,
New York City 133
Marquis Theater, New York
City 35
*The Marriage of Figaro. See Le
Mariage de Figaro*
Married Love (Stopes) 301
Marshall, John 270
Martin Beck Theatre, New
York City 232
*The Martyrdom of Saint
Sebastian* **165–167**
censorship history of 166
summary of 165–166
Mary (queen of Britain) 141
Mary Stuart **167–169**
censorship history of
168–169
summary of 167–168
Massachusetts, censorship in
of *The Children's Hour* 49
of *Desire under the Elms* 81
of *The Easiest Way* 86
of *Within the Gates*
323–324
of *Margaret Fleming* 160
of *Maya* 171
of *Sister Mary Ignatius
Explains it All for You*
267
of *Strange Interlude* 274
of *Waiting for Lefty* 309
of *West Side Story*
316–317
of *Who's Afraid of Virginia
Woolf* 321
Mast, Jane. *See* West, Mae
Master Harold and the Boys
379
Masterson, Peter 363–364
*The Best Little Whorehouse
in Texas* **21–24**
Mathews, Jane 196
Maxine Elliott Theatre, New
York City 65
Maxwell, W. D. 321
May, John 266
Maya **169–171**
censorship history of xii,
170–171
summary of 170

Mayakovsky, Vladimir 364
The Bedbug **14–18**
propaganda written by
17
subversive activities of 16
M. Butterfly **171–174**
censorship history of
144, 172–174
summary of 171–172
McCaffrey, Edward T. 43
McCall, Abner 148
McCarthy, Joseph 2
McCarthy, Talbot 266, 267
McCarthy hearings 66, 67,
279
McClure, Michael 364
The Beard **12–14**
McKee, Joseph B. 253
McKinnel, Norman 311
McMillan Foundation 5
McNally, Terrence 364
Corpus Christi **55–59**
fatwa decree on 57–58
Lips Together, Teeth Apart
143–145
Meadow, Lynne 57
Mecklenburg County, North
Carolina, censorship in 4
Meir, Golda 78
Melfi, Leonard 193
Menken, Helen 38
The Merchant of Venice
174–176
censorship history of xii,
175–176
summary of 174–175
Meredith, George 46, 185
Mérimée, Prosper 163
Merrimack, New
Hampshire, censorship in
222–223
Methodist preachers, ridicule
of 135
Metropolitan Opera House,
New York City 241
Meyerhold, Vsevolod 17
Meyerhold Theatre,
Moscow, Russia 231, 232
Miami (Oklahoma) High
School 288–289
Middleton, Thomas
364–365
A Game at Chesse **95–98**
*The Second Maiden's
Tragedy* **247–250**

The Mikado **176–179**
censorship history of xii,
178–179
summary of 177–178
Miller, Arthur 365
The Crucible **65–68**
The Death of a Salesman
379
FBI file on 307
A Memory of Two Mondays
306
stand against censorship
57
A View from the Bridge
305–307
Miller, Gilbert 38
Miller, Jonathan 175, 176
Milman, Henry, *Fazio* 379
Milton, Edna 22
Milton, John 88
Minnesota, censorship in, of
Hair 107
The Minor 379
The Miracle, Sumurun 302
Miracolo d'Amore 379
The Misanthrope **179–181**
censorship history of
180–181, 278
summary of 179–180
Missouri, censorship in
of *The Normal Heart* 190
of *Sister Mary Ignatius
Explains It All for You*
266–268
Miss Saigon **181–183**
censorship history of
182–183
summary of 181–182
Mitchell, Cameron 183
Model Tenement 286
Mohammed, Sheik Omar
Bakri 57
Molière (Jean-Baptiste
Poquelin) 365
Don Juan 379
The Misanthrope
179–181
in role of Alceste 180
Tartuffe 180, **276–278**
Monna Vanna **184–186**
censorship history of 185
summary of 184
More, Sir Thomas 262–263
Morganstern, C. W. 253
Moss, Paul 292

Motion Picture Producers
and Distributors
Association (MPPDA) 50
Mozart, Wolfgang Amadeus
161
Mrs. Warren's Profession
186–189
censorship history of
141, 187–188
summary of 186–187
Al-Muhajiroun 57
Munday, Anthony, *Sir
Thomas More* **262–264**
Murphy, Lionel 28
Murray, David 57
Musgrove, Stanley 254
Music Circus, Lambertville,
New Jersey 284
Musset, Alfred de 163
Mussolini, Benito 91, 92

N

National Coalition Against
Censorship (NCAC)
56–57
National Labor Relations
Act (U.S.) 64
National Theater,
Washington, D.C. 70
National Theatre, New York
City 323
Nemiroff, Robert 223
Nerval, Gérard de 120
Nethersole, Olga 244
Neufchateau, François de,
Paméla 380
New Hampshire, censorship
in
of *A Raisin in the Sun*
222–223
of *The Vagina Monologues*
299
New York City, censorship
in. *See also specific theaters*
of *The Captive* 38
of *Cat on a Hot Tin Roof*
43
of *Maya* 170
of *Sex* 253
of *Simon Called Peter* 261
New York Drama Critics
Circle awards 50
for *Angels in America* 3
for *Cat on a Hot Tin Roof*
42

for *A Raisin in the Sun*
222
for *Who's Afraid of
Virginia Woolf* 321
New York International
Fringe Festival 270
New York Society of Critics
147
on *M. Butterfly* 172
The Next Religion 380
Nichols, Lewis 292
Nightingale, Florence
82–83
Noel, Sir Gerard 178
No for an Answer 380
Norfolk, Virginia, censorship
in 86
The Normal Heart **189–191**
censorship history of
190
summary of 189
Norman, John 27
North Carolina, censorship
in, of *Angels in America* 4
Notre-Dame de Paris 380
nudity, censorship on
grounds of
of *The Entertainer* 91
of *Hair* 107
of *Monna Vanna* 185

O

Obie (Off-Broadway) Award
for *The Connection* 53
for *The Vagina Monologues*
297
obscenity, censorship on
grounds of xii
of *The Beard* 13
of *The Boys in the Band*
27
of *Cat on a Hot Tin Roof*
42–43
of *The Entertainer* 91
of *God of Vengeance*
102–103
of *The Pleasure Man*
211–212
of *The Respectful Prostitute*
225–226
of *La Ronde* 237–238
of *Sapho* 244
of *Sex* 253–254
of *The Shanghai Gesture*
256

of *Sodom* 270
of *The Toilet* 288–289
of *The Vagina Monologues*
298–299
of *Waiting for Lefty* 309
of *The Weavers* 313
of *Who's Afraid of Virginia
Woolf* 321
O'Casey, Sean 365
Within the Gates xii,
322–324
The Silver Tassie 380
Occupations 380
O'Connor, Jim 53
Odell, Thomas 200
Odets, Clifford 365–366
Waiting for Lefty
307–310
Oedipus Rex **191–192**
censorship history of
192, 302
summary of 191
Ogden, Utah, censorship in
222
Oh! Calcutta! **192–194**
censorship history of xii,
193–194
summary of 193
Ohio, censorship in
of *Paradise* xi
of *The Vagina Monologues*
299
O'Keefe, John
The Czar 379
Wild Oats 380
Oklahoma, censorship in
of *Sodom* 268
of *The Toilet* 288–289
The Old Maid 50
Olivier, Sir Laurence 175,
247
O'Malley, Glyn, *Paradise* xi
O'Neill, Carlotta 147
O'Neill, Eliza 46
O'Neill, Eugene 366
All God's Chillun 80
Desire under the Elms
78–81
*Long Day's Journey into
Night* **146–148**
plagiarism suit against
273–274
Strange Interlude xii,
271–274
O'Neill, Eugene, Jr. 147

One-Third of a Nation
194–198
censorship history of
196–197
summary of 195–196
Orton, Joe 193
Entertaining Mr. Sloane
379
Osborn, David, *Three on a
Gas Ring* 380
Osborne, John 366
The Entertainer **89–91**
A Patriot for Me
203–206, 247
Oscar Wilde 380
Oseland, James 35
Ostrovsky, Alexander, *The
Forest* 379
The Other Shore 380
Otwell, Rocky 5

P

Pacifica Foundation 326
Pakistan, censorship in, of
The Zoo Story 326
Palace Theatre, London,
England 302
Palais-Royal, Paris, France
278
Palmer, Frank 141, 155, 185,
188, 192, 199, 200, 203,
215, 220, 290, 302
Paméla 380
Panizza, Oskar 366–367
The Council of Love **59–63**
Paradise xi
Parents of Murdered
Children (POMC) 35–36
The Parisian Woman 380
Parker, Dorothy 50
Parnell, Charles Stewart 310
The Parson's Wedding
198–200
censorship history of
199–200
summary of 198–199
*Pasquin, A Dramatic Satire on
the Times* **200–203**
censorship history of
201–203
summary of 201
A Patriot for Me **203–206**
censorship history of
205–206, 247
summary of 203–205

Paul VI (pope) 77
Paxon School for Advanced
Studies, Jacksonville,
Florida 5
Payne, Ben Iden 219, 220
Peacock, Thomas Love 46
Peer Gynt 380
Peloponnesian War 149
Pemberton Billing, Noel
241–242
Pennsylvania, censorship in
of *The Crucible* 68
of *The Respectful Prostitute*
225–226
of *Revelry* 227
of *The Three-Penny Opera*
284
of *Trio* 291–292
of *Waiting for Lefty* 309
People Acting with
Compassion and Tolerance
(PACT) 190
Pepys, Samuel 200
Perrin, Noel 111, 175
Pfeiffer, Jules 193
Phelps, William Lyon 50
Philadelphia, Pennsylvania,
censorship in
of *The Respectful Prostitute*
225–226
of *Revelry* 227
of *The Three-Penny Opera*
284
of *Trio* 291–292
of *Waiting for Lefty* 309
Philippines, censorship in, of
The Vagina Monologues
298–299
The Philistines 380
Phillips, Glenn D. 4
Philotas 380
Philpotts, Eden, *The Secret
Woman* 380
Phrynichus, *The Sack of
Miletos* 380
Piave, Francesco 235
Pigott, Edward 46, 47, 94,
99, 113, 192, 240–241
Pinero, Arthur 31, 32
Pitt, George Dibdin 367
The Revolution of Paris
228–229
Pius XII (pope) 75–76, 77
Pizella, Stéphane 225

Playbox Theatre,
Melbourne, Australia 27
Playboy (magazine) 22
*The Playboy of the Western
World* **206–210**
censorship history of
207–209
summary of 206–207
Playhouse in the Park,
Cincinnati, Ohio xi
The Pleasure Man **210–212**
censorship history of
211–212
summary of 210–211
political reasons, censorship
for xii
of *Athalie* 7
of *The Bedbug* 16–18
of *The Beggar's Opera*
20–21
of *The Cradle Will Rock*
64–65
of *The Crucible* 67–68
of *The Deputy* 76–78
of *Early Morning* 84
of *Edward and Eleanora*
88–89
of *Ethiopia* 92–93
of *A Game at Chesse*
96–98
of *Gustavus Vasa* 104–105
of *Hamlet* 110–111
The Happy Land 115–116
of *Henry IV, Part 2*
117–118
of *Hernani* 120
of *The Island of St.
Marguerite* 127
of *Jack Straw* 131–132
of *King Lear* 138
of *Lysistrata* 150
of *The Maid's Tragedy* 153
of *The Man of the World*
155
of *Mary Stuart* 168–169
of *One-Third of a Nation*
196–197
of *Pasquin, A Dramatic
Satire on the Times*
201–203
of *The President is Dead*
217
of *Press Cuttings* 219–220
of *The Respectful Prostitute*
225–226

of *Revelry* 227
of *The Revolution of Paris*
228–229
of *Richard the Second*
230–231
of *Roar, China!* 233
of *Le roi s'amuse* 234–235
of *The Second Maiden's
Tragedy* 249–250
of *Sir Thomas More* 263
of *Sodom* 270
of *The Tamer Tamed* 276
of *Thomas of Woodstock*
281–282
of *The Three-Penny Opera*
284
of *The Tragedy of King
Richard the Second* 290
of *Triple-A Plowed Under*
295–297
of *Victoria Regina* 305
of *Waiting for Lefty* 309
of *The Weavers* 313–314
of *What Price Glory?*
318–319
Polly **212–216**
censorship history of
215–216
summary of 213–215
Pompadour, Madame du
162
Ponca City, Oklahoma,
censorship in 268
Ponsonby, Spencer 73
Ponte, Lorenzo da 161
Pope, Alexander, *The
Dunciad* 20
Potter, Dennis, *Brimstone and
Treacle* 378
The President Is Dead
216–217
censorship history of xii,
217
summary of 216–217
Press Cuttings **217–220**
censorship history of
219–220
summary of 218–219
Pressley, Nelson 27
Presumed Miracle 380
Price, John 58
Price, Nelson 144, 173
Price, Vincent 305
*La Prisonnière. See The
Captive*

Provincetown Playhouse,
New York City 102, 326
Pryce, Jonathan 182, 183
Puccini, Giacomo, *Madame
Butterfly* 181
Pulaski County High
School, Somerset,
Kentucky 68
Pulitzer Prize
for *Angels in America* 3
for *Cat on a Hot Tin Roof*
42
for *The Children's Hour,*
consideration of 50
for *Long Day's Journey
into Night* 148
for *Strange Interlude* 273
for *What Price Glory?,*
consideration of 319
for *Who's Afraid of
Virginia Woolf,*
consideration of 321
Pushkin, Aleksandr 16
*La Putain Respectueuse. See
The Respectful Prostitute*
Putin, Vladimir 158

Q

Queensberry, John Sholto
Douglas, marquess of 124

R

racial and ethnic issues,
censorship on grounds of
of *Miss Saigon* 182–183
of *A Raisin in the Sun*
222–223
of *The Respectful Prostitute*
225–226
of *The Toilet* 288
of *West Side Story*
316–317
Racine, Jean 367
Athalie **6–8**
radio programs, censorship
of 326
Rado, James 367
Hair xii, **106–109**
Ragni, Gerome 367
Hair xii, **106–109**
A Raisin in the Sun
221–223
censorship history of
222–223
summary of 221–222

Raphael, Lennox, *Ché* 378
Rare Angel Productions 14
Rathbone, Basil 38
Die Rauber 379
Rawlinson, Sir Peter 194
Rector's (restaurant) 86–87
Redford, George Alexander
30, 31, 70, 99, 187–188,
219, 220, 258, 259, 311
Red Scare 2, 66
Reeves, Marius 270
Der Reigen. See La Ronde
Reinhardt, Max 192, 237,
302
religious reasons, censorship
for xii
of *Angels in America* 4
of *Athalie* 7
of *Corpus Christi* 56–58
of *The Council of Love*
60–62
of *The Deputy* 77
of *Hamlet* 111
of *Jesus Christ Superstar*
133–134
of *Killing No Murder*
135–136
of *Kismet* 141
of *Lips Together, Teeth
Apart* 144
of *Long Day's Journey into
Night* 148
of *The Martyrdom of Saint
Sebastian* 166
of *The Parson's Wedding*
199–200
of *Salomé* 240
of *The Shewing Up of
Blanco Posnet* 258
of *Simon Called Peter* 261
of *Sister Mary Ignatius
Explains It All for You*
266–268
of *Tartuffe* 277–278
of *Who's Afraid of Virginia
Woolf* 321
of *Within the Gates*
323–324
*The Representative. See The
Deputy*
The Respectful Prostitute
223–226
censorship history of
225–226
summary of 224–225

Revelle, Hamilton 244
Revelry **226–228**
censorship history of 227
summary of 226–227
The Revolution of Paris
228–229
censorship history of
228–229
summary of 228
Rice, Elmer 92–93
Rice, Tim 368
Jesus Christ Superstar
132–135
Rich, John 88
Richard II (king of England)
131, 132, 230, 289–290
Richards, David 26
Richard the Second **229–231**
censorship history of
230–231
summary of 230
Richelieu, Cardinal 163
Rigoletto 235–236
The Rival Queens 380
Rivers, Larry 54
Rivier College, New
Hampshire 299
Rizzio, David 167
Roar, China! **231–233**
censorship history of
232–233
summary of 231–232
Robb, Graham 120, 121, 163
Robbins, Jerome 314–315
Roberts, David 270
Robertson, Pat 144, 173
Robins, Natalie 307
Rockefeller, Nelson 33
Roda Viva 380
Rodchenko, Aleksandr 17
Le roi s'amuse **233–236**
censorship history of
234–236
summary of 233–234
Roland, Victor 228
Romania, censorship in, of
Angels in America 4
romanticism 120–121
La Ronde **236–238**
censorship history of
237–238
summary of 236–237
Rooke, Leon, *Shakespeare's
Dog* 380
Roosevelt, Eleanor 33, 92

Roosevelt, Franklin D. 92,
196, 295
Rose, Billy 77
Rosenberg, Ethel 2
Rosenberg, Julius 2
*Rosenberg v. the Board of
Education of the City of New
York* 175
Rosenthal, Jeannie 65
Ross, Robert 240
Rossini, Gioacchino 10
Rothenberg, Jerome 76
Roughead, William 48
Roundhouse Theatre in
Camden, England 193–194
Royal Court Theatre,
London, England 83, 84,
91, 100, 205–206, 220,
246–247
Royal Dramatic Theatre,
Stockholm, Sweden 147
Royal Shakespeare Company
76, 77, 304
Royalty Theatre, London,
England 323
Rubinstein, Ida 166
Ruise, Robert 87
Rushdie, Salman 326
Russell, Lillian 87
Russell, Richard 197
Russell, William 129
Russo, Vito 51
Rylah, Sir Arthur 28

S

Sabinson, Lee 291, 292
The Sack of Miletos 380
Sainte-Beauve, Charles
Augustin 163
St. James's Theatre, London,
England 73, 123
St. John, John 368
The Island of St. Marguerite
xii, **125–127**
St. Mark's Studio Theatre,
New York City 270
St. Paul, Minnesota,
censorship in 107
Sales, Delisle de, *Juno and
Ganymede* 379
Salomé **238–242**
censorship history of
240–242
summary of 239–240
San Antonio, Texas,
censorship in 107

Sanderson, Debby 58
Sandhurst, Lord 141, 302
San Francisco Actor's
    Workshop 13
Santley, Kate 100
Sapho **242–245**
    censorship history of
        244–245
    summary of 243–244
Sartre, Jean-Paul 368
    The Respectful Prostitute
        223–226
    trip to U.S. 225
Sarumpaet, Ratna, *Marinseh's
    Song from beneath the Earth*
    379
Saved **245–247**
    censorship history of xii,
        246–247
    summary of 245–246
Savoy Theatre, London,
    England 178, 179, 311
Scarborough, George, *The
    Lure* 379
Schiller, Frederich, *Die
    Rauber* 379
Schiller Theater Werkstatt,
    Berlin, Germany 326
Schlissel, Lillian 252
Schloss, Norman 253
Schnitzler, Arthur 368
    La Ronde **236–238**
Schonberg, Claude-Michel
    368
    Miss Saigon **181–183**
schools, censorship in. *See
    also* colleges and
    universities
    of *Angels in America* 5–6
    of *The Crucible* 68
    of *Jesus Christ Superstar*
        134
    of *Lysistrata* 151
    of *The Merchant of Venice*
        175–176
    of *A Raisin in the Sun*
        222–223
    of *The Toilet* 288–289
    of *West Side Story*
        316–317
Schroeder, Theodore 103
Scotland, censorship in, of
    Corpus Christi 57–58
The Screens 380
Sears, Joe, *Greater Tuna* 379

Seascape 321
Seattle, Washington,
    censorship in 197
Sebastian, St. 166
The Second Maiden's Tragedy
    247–250
    censorship history of
        249–250
    summary of 248–249
The Secrets of the Harem 380
The Secret Woman 380
Sejanus, His Fall 380
Seldes, Gilbert 50
The Semi-Monde 380
Sex **250–254**
    censorship history of 38,
        252–254
    summary of 250–252
sexual reasons, censorship for
    xii
    of *Angels in America* 4
    of *The Beard* 13
    of *The Best Little
        Whorehouse in Texas*
        23–24
    of *Corpus Christi* 56
    of *Desire under the Elms*
        80–81
    of *The Easiest Way* 86
    of *The Entertainer* 91
    of *Within the Gates*
        323–324
    of *Hair* 107–108
    of *Kismet* 141
    of *The Knack* 142–143
    of *Lips Together, Teeth
        Apart* 144–145
    of *Lysistrata* 150
    of *Marat/Sade* 157–158
    of *Maya* 170–171
    of *Monna Vanna* 185
    of *Oh! Calcutta!* 193–194
    of *La Ronde* 237–238
    of *Salomé* 240–241
    of *The Second Maiden's
        Tragedy* 249–250
    of *Sex* 252–254
    of *The Shanghai Gesture*
        255–256
    of *Simon Called Peter* 261
    of *Sodom* 270
    of *A Venetian Night* 302
    in *A View from the Bridge*
        306–307
    of *Waste* 311

Shairp, Mordaunt, *The Green
    Bay Tree* 379
Shakespeare, William 369
    censorship of works of
        111, 118
    Hamlet xii, **109–112**
    Henry IV, Part 2
        116–119
    King Lear **136–140**
    The Merchant of Venice
        xii, **174–176**
    The Taming of the Shrew
        274
    *The Tragedy of King
        Richard the Second*
        289–290
Shakespeare Festival Public
    Theater, New York City
    107
Shakespeare's Dog 380
The Shanghai Gesture
    254–257
    censorship history of
        255–256
    summary of 255
Shaw, George Bernard 369
    John Bull's Other Island
        220
    Mrs. Warren's Profession
        141, **186–189**
    Press Cuttings **217–220**
    *The Shewing Up of Blanco
        Posnet* 219, **257–260**
    stand against censorship
        30, 32, 71, 94, 241, 258,
        259
Shaw, Mary 188
Shaw, Thomas, *The Island of
    St. Marguerite* xii,
    125–127
Sheaffer, Louis 147
Shear Madness 267
Shedd, Robert 237
Shee, Sir Martin, *Alasco* 378
Shelley, Percy Bysshe 369
    The Cenci **44–48**
Shelley Society 46–47
Sherman, Martin, *Bent* 378
*The Shewing Up of Blanco
    Posnet* **257–260**
    censorship history of
        219, 258–259
    summary of 257–258
Shipley, Ruth 68
Shirley, William, *Electra* 379

Shostakovich, Dmitri 17
Show World, New York City
102
Shubert, Lee 291, 292
Shubert Theatre, New York
City 291
Shumlin, Herman 49–50, 77
Shurtleff, Michael, *Call Me
by My Rightful Name* 378
Shyre, Paul 370
The President is Dead xii,
216–217
Silverman, Rabbi Joseph
102
Simon, Neil, *Brighton Beach
Memoirs* 378
Simon, Paul 370
and Broadway 36
The Capeman xii, **33–37**
Simon Called Peter **260–261**
censorship history of 261
summary of 260–261
Sinnott, Richard 321
Sir Thomas More **262–264**
censorship history of
263–264
summary of 262–263
*Sister Mary Ignatius Explains
It All for You* **264–268**
censorship history of xii,
266–268
summary of 264–266
Smith, Frank 194
Smith, Jess 226, 227
Society for the Suppression
of Vice 188, 244, 256, 261,
292, 319
Sodom **268–271**
censorship history of
269–270
summary of 269
Sola, Camille 316–317
Sondheim, Stephen 57
West Side Story xi,
314–317
Sophocles 370
Oedipus Rex **191–192**
*Southeastern Promotions, Ltd.
v. Conrad* 108–109
Southwest Missouri State
University (SMSU) 190
Soviet Union, censorship in
of Arthur Miller's plays
68
of *The Bedbug* 17–18

of *Jesus Christ Superstar*
134
of *Marat/Sade* 157–158
Soviet Union, satire of
15–16
Spencer, Earl 178, 259
Spillane, Margaret 36
Spitzer, Robert 299
Stalin, Joseph 17
Stallings, Laurence, *What
Price Glory?* xii, 42, 80,
317–319
Stanton, Edwin 217
Star Wars (film) 20
*Der Stellvertreter. See The
Deputy*
Stephens, John Russell 229
Stokes, Leslie, and Sewall
Stokes, *Oscar Wilde* 380
Stopes, Marie C. 370
Vectia **300–301**
Strange Interlude **271–274**
censorship history of xii,
272–274
summary of 271–272
Strasberg, Lee 232
Strauss, Richard, *Salomé*
239, 241
Streater, Joseph 270
Street, George S. 81
A Streetcar Named Desire 380
Sud 380
The Suicide 380
Sullivan, Sir Arthur 371
The Mikado xii, **176–179**
Sullivan, Father 323
Summer, John 261
Summerfield, Arthur 151
Summer Moths 380
Sutherland, John 157
Sweden, *Long Day's Journey
into Night* in 147
Sweeney, George E. 49
Swift, Jonathan 215
Swinburne, Charles
Algernon 185
Swope, Herbert Bayard 50
Sydney, Lord 115
Symons, Arthur 141
Synge, John Millington 371
*The Playboy of the Western
World* **206–210**
syphilis, discussion of
in *The Council of Love* 59,
60

in *Damaged Goods* 69–70
in *Ghosts* 99

T

Tales from the Vienna Woods
380
Tallmer, Jerry 53
The Tamer Tamed **274–276**
censorship history of
275–276
summary of 274–275
The Taming of the Shrew 274
Tartuffe **276–278**
censorship history of
180, 277–278
summary of 277
A Taste of Honey 380
Tate, H. J. 284
Tate, Nahun 139
Taulane, Robert H. 227
Tea and Sympathy **279–280**
censorship history of
279–280
summary of 279
Teapot Dome incident 227
The Temple of Pallas-Athenae
273
Texas, censorship in
of *Angels in America* 4–5
of *The Best Little
Whorehouse in Texas* 22
of *Hair* 107
of *Jesus Christ Superstar*
134
of *Long Day's Journey into
Night* 148
of *Triple-A Plowed Under*
296–297
Theater Guild 273, 274
Théâtre Alfred Jarry, Paris,
France 303
Theatre de Lys, New York
City 284
Théâtre français, Paris,
France 164
Theatre Guild Acting
Company 232
Theatre in the Square, Cobb
County, Georgia 144–145,
173
Théâtre-Libre, Paris, France
70
Theatre of Cruelty
movement 156

Theatre Royal, London, England 199–200
Theatres Act of 1958 (Australia) 27
Theatres Act of 1737 (England) xiii, 20–21, 88, 104, 202–203
Theatres Bill of 1968 (England) 84, 247
These Three (film) 50–51
They Knew What They Wanted 42, 319
They Shall Not Die 380
Thomas, Donald 202
Thomas of Woodstock **280–282**
  censorship history of 281–282
  summary of 280–281
Thomson, James 371
  Edward and Eleanora **87–89**
  poetry of 88
Thorndyke, Dame Sybil 47
Three on a Gas Ring 380
The Three-Penny Opera **282–285**
  censorship history of xii, 284
  summary of 282–284
Tighler (Tyler), Walter (Wat) 131, 132
Tilney, Edmund 117, 263
Tobacco Road **285–287**
  censorship history of 286–287
  summary of 285–286
The Toilet **287–289**
  censorship history of 288–289
  summary of 287–288
Tolstoy, Leo 16, 30
Tomlin, F. *See* Gilbert, William S.
Tone, Franchot 232
Tony Award, for *Angels in America* 3
Torch Song Trilogy 27
The Tragedy of King Richard the Second **289–290**
  censorship history of 290
  summary of 289–290
La Traviata 73
Tree, Sir Herbert 192, 258

Tretyakov, Sergei 371
  Roar, China! **231–233**
Trio **290–292**
  censorship history of 291–292
  summary of 291
Triple-A Plowed Under **294–297**
  censorship history of 295–297
  summary of 295
Trip to Calais **292–294**
  censorship history of xii, 293–294
  summary of 293
Trotsky, Leon 17
Turgenev, Ivan, *The Family Change* 379
Tyler (Tighler), Walter (Wat) 131, 132, 230
Tyllney, Edmund. *See* Tilney, Edmund
Tynan, Kenneth 53, 371–372
  Oh! Calcutta! xii, **192–194**
Tyson, David 299

U

Ulysses (Joyce) 274
United States, censorship in
  of *Angels in America* 4–6
  of *The Beard* 13–14
  of *The Best Little Whorehouse in Texas* 23–24
  of *The Boys in the Band* 26–27
  of *The Capeman* 35–36
  of *The Captive* 38–39
  of *Cat on a Hot Tin Roof* 42–43
  of *The Children's Hour* 49–50
  Comstock Act of 1873 and 151
  of *The Connection* 52–54
  of *Corpus Christi* 56–57
  of *The Cradle Will Rock* 65
  of *The Crucible* 68
  of *The Deputy* 77
  of *Desire under the Elms* 80–81
  of *The Easiest Way* 86

  of *The Entertainer* 90–91
  of *Ethiopia* 92–93
  of *Within the Gates* 323–324
  of *God of Vengeance* 102–103
  of *Hair* 107–109
  of *Jesus Christ Superstar* 133–134
  of *Lips Together, Teeth Apart* 144–145
  of *Long Day's Journey into Night* 148
  of *Lysistrata* 151
  of *Margaret Fleming* 159–160
  of *Maya* 170
  of *The Merchant of Venice* 175–176
  of *Miss Saigon* 182–183
  of *Mrs. Warren's Profession* 188
  of *The Normal Heart* 190
  of *One-Third of a Nation* 196–197
  of *The Pleasure Man* 211–212
  of *The President Is Dead* 217
  of *A Raisin in the Sun* 222–223
  of *The Respectful Prostitute* 225–226
  of *Revelry* 227
  of *Salomé* 241
  of *Sapho* 244–245
  of *Sex* 253–254
  of *The Shanghai Gesture* 256
  of *Simon Called Peter* 261
  of *Sister Mary Ignatius Explains It All for You* 266–268
  of *Strange Interlude* 272–274
  of *The Three-Penny Opera* 284
  of *Tobacco Road* 286
  of *The Toilet* 288–289
  of *Trio* 291–292
  of *Triple-A Plowed Under* 296–297
  of *The Vagina Monologues* 299
  of *Waiting for Lefty* 309

Wales Padlock Law of 1927 and xiii, 38, 170, 261, 292
of *West Side Story* 316–317
of *What Price Glory?* 319
of *Who's Afraid of Virginia Woolf* 321
of *The Zoo Story* 326
universities, censorship in. *See* colleges and universities
University of Missouri 266–268
University of Portland 299
Untermeyer, Samuel 244
Utah, censorship in 222

V

The Vagina Monologues **297–300**
censorship history of 298–299
summary of 297–298
Van Doren, Carl 50
Vatican, censorship by 166. *See also* Catholic Church
Vaudeville Théâtre, Paris, France 72
Vectia **300–301**
censorship history of 300–301
summary of 300
Vedrenne, J. E. 311
A Venetian Night **301–302**
censorship history of xii, 302
summary of 301–302
Venice Theater, New York City 65
Verdi, Giuseppe
Ernani 120
Rigoletto 235–236
La Traviata 73
Victor, or the Children Take Over **302–304**
censorship history of xii, 303–304
summary of 303
Victoria (queen of Britain) 115, 178
in *Early Morning* 82–83
marriage to Prince Albert 168
in *Victoria Regina* 304–305

Victoria Regina **304–305**
censorship history of 305
summary of 304–305
A View from the Bridge **305–307**
censorship history of 305–306
summary of 305
Vigny, Alfred de 163
violence, censorship on grounds of xii
of *The Capeman* 35–36
of *Saved* 246–247
of *West Side Story* 316
Virgil v. School Board of Columbia County 151
Virginia, censorship in, of *The Easiest Way* 86
The Virgin Man 38, 253, 380
Vitrac, Roger 372
Victor, or the Children Take Over xii, **302–304**
Vollmoeller, Karl Gustav 372
A Venetian Night xii, **301–302**
Voronsky, Aleksandr 17

W

Wagner, Robert F. 195–196
Waiting for Lefty **307–310**
censorship history of 309
summary of 307–309
Walcott, Derek 372
The Capeman xii, **33–37**
Wales, B. Roger 38, 170
Wales Padlock Law of 1927 (U.S.) xiii, 38, 170, 261, 292
Walker, Jeffrey 215
Walker, Jimmy 253
Walkley, A. B. 311
Wallace, Lady Eglantine, *The Whim* 380
Wallack Theatre, New York City 244
Waller, Edmund 153
Walpole, Sir Robert 20–21, 88, 89, 104, 201, 202–203, 215
Walsh, Moira 134
Walter, Eugene 372
The Easiest Way **85–87**
war, play about 318–319
Wardle, Irving 84

Washington State, censorship in
of *One-Third of a Nation* 197
of *The Vagina Monologues* 299
The Wasps 150
Wasserstein, Wendy 57
Waste **310–312**
censorship history of 32, 311
summary of 310–311
Watkins, Maurine Dallas, *Revelry* **226–228**
Watson, Morris, *Triple-A Plowed Under* **294–297**
Watts, Alan 14
The Weavers **312–314**
censorship history of 313–314
summary of 312–313
Webber, Andrew Lloyd 373
Jesus Christ Superstar **132–135**
Die Weber. See The Weavers
Webster, Benjamin 130
The Wedding Day 380
Weill, Kurt, *The Three-Penny Opera* xii, **282–285**
Weinberger, Harry 103
Weiss, Peter 373
Marat/Sade **156–158**
Welles, Orson 64, 65
Wells, Palmer 145, 173
Wentworth Institute of Technology, Boston 23–24
Wernyhhora 380
West, Mae 373
criminal trial of 253–254
The Drag 38, 379
The Pleasure Man **210–212**
Sex 38, **250–254**
Westminster Theatre, London, England 311
West Side Story **314–317**
censorship history of xi, 316–317
summary of 314–316
Wexley, John, *They Shall Not Die* 380
Wharton, Edith 50

What Price Glory? **317–319**
  censorship history of xii,
    42, 80, 318–319
  summary of 318
Wheelock College, Boston
  23–24
The Whim 380
Who's Afraid of Virginia Woolf
  319–321
  all-male production of
    349
  censorship history of
    321
  summary of 319–320
The Wicked World 114
Wilde, Jonathan 20
Wilde, Oscar xii, 373
  criminal trial and
    imprisonment of
    124–125, 242
  An Ideal Husband 124,
    379
  *The Importance of Being
    Earnest* **122–125**
  Lady Windermere's Fan
    240
  Salomé **238–242**
Wilder, Thornton, *The
  Happy Journey from Trenton
  to Camden* 225
Wildmon, Donald 144, 173
Wild Oats 380
Wilhelm, German Kaiser
  314
Wilkins, Mary E. 160
Wilkinson, Tate 9

Williams, Aubrey 197
Williams, Jaston, *Greater
  Tuna* 379
Williams, Jesse Lynch 319
Williams, Jim 5
Williams, Tennessee
  373–374
  Cat on a Hot Tin Roof
    40–44
  on *The Connection* 53
  A Streetcar Named Desire
    380
Wilmot, John, Earl of
  Rochester 374
  Sodom **268–271**
Wilson, August, *Fences* 379
Wilson, Earl, Jr., *Let My
  People Come* 379
Wilson, Robert 176
Winchell, Walter 253
Windsor Theater, New York
  City 65
Within the Gates xii,
  322–324
  censorship history of xii,
    323–324
  summary of 322–323
Witts 380
*The Woman's Prize. See The
  Tamer Tamed*
Wonderful Town 316
Woods, A. H. 256
Woodward, Kenneth L. 78
Woollcott, Alexander 273
Woolsey, John W. 274
Wordsworth, William 88

Works Progress
  Administration 65, 92,
  196, 295
World's Fair (1958) 316
World War I, play about
  318–319
Wysong, Gordon 144, 173

X

Xavier University, Ohio 299

Y

Yale University 102
Yeats, William Butler 141,
  208, 258–259
Ye Bare and Ye Cubb 380
Yeltsin, Boris 158
Yerma 380
Yiddish plays 102
You Made Me a Communist
  380
Young, Robert 35
Young Woodley 380

Z

Zangwill, Israel, *The Next
  Religion* 380
Zingjian, Gao, *The Other
  Shore* 380
Zingl, Dietmar 62
The Zoo Story **324–327**
  censorship history of
    325–326
  summary of 324–325
Zoya's Apartment 380